DANTE for the New Millennium

Fordham Series in Medieval Studies
H. Wayne Storey, Series Editor

1. Richard F. Gyug. ed., *Medieval Cultures in Contact.*

The Fordham Series in Medieval Studies (FSiMS) was founded to promote monographic studies, editions, and collections of essays devoted to a wide variety of medieval topics. The Series' primary interest is in methodological diversity and innovation in fields evermore under represented in Anglophone academic presses. Its fields of inquiry include material, textual and manuscript culture, the linguistic and literary cultures of the medieval world, historical studies based particularly on new or newly interpreted documentation, and editions of works that contribute to the reevaluation of historical and literary documentation.

DANTE for the New Millennium

Edited by

TEODOLINDA BAROLINI *and* H. WAYNE STOREY

FORDHAM UNIVERSITY PRESS
New York

Fordham Series in Medieval Studies, No. 2
ISSN 1542-6378

Library of Congress Cataloging-in-Publication Data

Dante for the new millennium / edited by Teodolinda Barolini and H. Wayne Storey.—1st ed.
p. cm.—(Fordham series in medieval studies, ISSN 1542-6378 ; no. 2)
Proceedings of "Dante2000," held at Columbia University on Apr. 7–9, 2000.
Includes bibliographical references and index.
ISBN 0-8232-2271-3 (alk. paper)—ISBN 0-8232-2272-1 (pbk. : alk. paper)
1. Dante Aligheri, 1265–1321—Criticism and interpretation—Congresses.
I. Barolini, Teodolinda, 1951– II. Storey, Wayne. III. Series.
PQ4390.D2815 2003
851'.1—dc21 2003012315

Printed in the United States of America
07 06 5 4 3 2
First edition

CONTENTS

Introduction ix
Teodolinda Barolini

Notes for an Introduction xix
H. Wayne Storey

Abbreviations xxv

I PHILOLOGIES

1. What Did the First Copies of the *Comedy* Look Like? 1
John Ahern

2. Early Editorial Forms of Dante's Lyrics 16
H. Wayne Storey

3. Material Philology, Conjectural Philology, Philology without Adjectives 44
Guglielmo Gorni

Philologies: Works Cited 56

II APPETITES

4. Beyond (Courtly) Dualism: Thinking about Gender in Dante's Lyrics 65
Teodolinda Barolini

5. Queering Nature, Queering Gender: Dante and Sodomy 90
Gary P. Cestaro

6. Does the Stilnovo Go to Heaven? 104
Lino Pertile

7. Love for Beatrice: Transcending Contradiction in the *Paradiso* 115
F. Regina Psaki

Appetites: Works Cited 131

III Philosophies

8. Mysticism and Meaning in Dante's *Paradiso* 143
Steven Botterill

9. The Heaven of the Sun: Dante between Aquinas and Bonaventure 152
Giuseppe Mazzotta

10. Vulgarizing Science: Vernacular Translation of Natural Philosophy 169
Alison Cornish

11. The Body and the Flesh in the *Purgatorio* 183
Robert M. Durling

12. From Plurality to (Near) Unicity of Forms: Embryology in *Purgatorio* 25 192
Manuele Gragnolati

13. *Quando amor fa sentir de la sua pace* 211
Giuliana Carugati

Philosophies: Works Cited 228

IV Reception

14. Virility, Nobility, and Banking: The Crossing of Discourses in the *Tenzone* with Forese 241
Susan Noakes

15. Scatology and Obscenity in Dante 259
Zygmunt G. Barański

16. On Dante and the Visual Arts 274
Christopher Kleinhenz

Reception: Works Cited 293

V HISTORIES

17. Dante's Jeremiads: The Fall of Jerusalem and the Burden of the New Pharisees, the Capetians, and Florence — 301
Ronald L. Martinez

18. From Francis to Solomon: Eschatology in the Sun — 320
Ronald Herzman

19. Already and Not Yet: Dante's Existential Eschatology — 334
Amilcare A. Iannucci

20. Dante after Dante — 349
Albert Russell Ascoli

Histories: Works Cited — 369

VI REWRITINGS

21. Ovid and the *Exul Inmeritus* — 389
Michelangelo Picone

22. The Re-Formation of Marsyas in *Paradiso* 1 — 408
Jessica Levenstein

23. Dante in England — 422
David Wallace

24. Moby-Dante? — 435
Piero Boitani

25. Still Here: Dante after Modernism — 451
Peter S. Hawkins and Rachel Jacoff

Rewritings: Works Cited — 465

Notes on Contributors — 474

Index — 479

INTRODUCTION

This volume is the fruit of a unique conference, "Dante2000," sponsored by the Dante Society of America and the Italian Academy of Advanced Studies in America and held at Columbia University on April 7–9, 2000. When I became the fifteenth president of the Dante Society in 1997, with a tenure that fell over the cusp of the millennium, it occurred to me that the spring of 2000 would offer an excellent symbolic vantage point from which both to assess our past accomplishments, as Dante scholars, and to outline and suggest the avenues of scholarship that we believe would be most exciting to pursue in the years to come. And I had no doubt that Dante would have considered the weekend of his vision in the year 2000 an appropriate and worthy opportunity to celebrate his poetry.

In deciding to organize and sponsor its first full-scale conference in a history that reaches back to 1881, when the poet Longfellow organized a group of friends and scholars in the environs of Harvard University into a Dante Club, the Dante Society of America hoped to capitalize on the millennial spirit in the air to serve up the best and most provocative Dante scholarship we could find: the scholarship most likely to set the agenda for "the next millennium" of Dante studies. We wanted to crystallize and highlight a moment in time—"Dante2000"—and to suggest the plenitude of this moment with respect to the future.

Our goal was to nudge the course of scholarship by suggesting new avenues of research and discussion; to accomplish this goal we invited our contributors to write on preselected topics. A Program Committee consisting of Kevin Brownlee, Robert Durling, Richard Lansing, and me chose the topics over the course of an intense weekend meeting in January 1998. My notes to that meeting show that we were asking ourselves big questions: What methodologies and approaches are particular to Dante scholarship? Why do we read Dante today? What are the topics that need to be explored in the years to come? The pages and pages of "high energy topics" that we generated at that meeting were ultimately culled into ten sessions, an extraordinarily rich program. Those original conference sessions suggest our dual goal—to synthesize and to lead—both in their titles and in the way they were arranged: the order was intended as a bridging mechanism, a way to indicate the organic links that exist between topics that are more contemporary and topics with a venerable history. For instance, we placed "Dante and Gender," a new area of research in Dante studies, before "Eros and Mysticism," an established field whose gender-related issues have perhaps not been adequately explored; for similar reasons, we had "Dante and the Body" lead into "Dante and Ovid," in order to suggest the importance of Ovid as the premier poet of the body.

Inevitably, since our invitations to participate in the "Dante2000" conference constituted an effective sounding of scholars in the field, our attempts to direct, by suggesting topics, became also an opportunity to be directed. The dialectical nature of this process is clearly exemplified by the two sessions that were ultimately needed to contain all the papers we received in the area we then called "Reception and Cultural Studies," the latter in particular being a field that benefits from an aura of innovation in today's scholarly arena. By the same token, but more in the direction of innovation within a traditional avenue of research, the hefty section devoted to *Philosophies* in this volume testifies to the vitality and robustness of one of the oldest fields of *dantismo.*

When it came time to collect the papers into this volume, a further consolidation of the themes from the conference, along the lines of the just-cited *Philosophies*, seemed appropriate. Thus, H. Wayne Storey and I, the volume's two editors, ultimately chose to abstract the topics further, into the ones that you see in the table of contents—*Philologies*, *Appetites*, *Philosophies*, *Reception*, *Histories*, *Rewritings*—hoping in this way to capture the perdurability of these themes, oriented both to the past and to the future. At the same time, we attempted to give a kind of overall chronological thrust to the volume, which begins with John Ahern's invocation of the "first copies" of the *Commedia* and ends with Peter S. Hawkins and Rachel Jacoff on the uses to which Dante has been put by today's poets.

The foundation of literary criticism is always the text: discovering it if necessary, establishing it, remaining aware of its ecdotic constructedness as we move forward on the hermeneutic journey of interpreting it. The foundation and starting point of this volume, therefore, is

Philologies, represented here by three papers that collectively offer a timely overview of what the field traditionally called "philology" can consist of today. John Ahern's title, "What did the First Copies of the *Comedy* Look Like?" provides the point of entry into an exploration that constitutes the perfect counterweight to our enterprise: to our volume's concern to probe the way we read Dante now, Ahern's essay stands as an effective guide to the way they read Dante then. Ahern takes us into the world of Dante the promoter and promulgator of his work, illuminating both what Dante expected could happen—that his texts could be corrupted—and the steps that he took in light of his expectations. Dante was his own amanuensis, his own Giovanni Malpaghini (Petrarch's favorite copyist), copying his immortal verse into fragile *fascicoli* that are the true analogue to the "foglie levi" on which "si perdea la sentenza di Sibilla" ("the light leaves on which the Sibyl's words were lost" [*Par* 33.65–66]). The miracle is that these light fascicles seem instead to have aided in the diffusion of Dante's words, which instead of being lost were thus conserved.

From the preoccupations of the author, we move, with H. Wayne Storey's essay, "Early Editorial Forms of Dante's Lyrics," to the preoccupations of the scribes, entering into the dense world of the actual manuscripts and the professional copyists who made them. How do the preferences and organizational habits of these scribes affect our reception and understanding of Dante's lyrics? How does the organization of a particular manuscript bespeak a hidden ideological agenda based on the scribe's regional and political affiliations that we have neglected to factor into our decoding of the text? These are questions that, as we go forward into a new millennium of Dante criticism, we will no longer be able to ignore. The central and continued relevance of philology as a science and discipline is strongly vindicated in the panoramic contribution of the Italian philologist Guglielmo Gorni, "Material Philology, Conjectural Philology, Philology without Adjectives." Wittily conjuring a typically myopic view of the philologist's calling—"The philologist possesses by trade certain technical skills (in ancient language, prosody, and paleography) and, thanks to this knowledge at once refined and elementary, oversees the textual tradition and examines the writings in their materiality, leaving to hermeneutics, to exegesis, and to literary criticism the pleasures of the text and what matters most"—Gorni shows us that philology is anything but technical and dry, that, in fact, it is both necessary and relative, foundational and fleeting: "Philology lives by hypotheses more than by certainties, nothing but hypotheses, more or less judicious. And therefore philology is not a trade to entrust to a corporation of technicians, generally limited in their interests and tastes, who know their job. Philology is a habit of the mind, a lesson in relativism and in the insufficiency of our knowledge to be taken into account before reading any text." The *foglie levi* of the Sibyl indeed!

The next section, *Appetites,* considers issues to do with gender, the body, and human sexuality in a variety of Dantean contexts, moving from Dante's lyrics to the *Commedia.* My essay, "Beyond (Courtly) Dualism: Thinking about Gender in Dante's Lyrics," traces the evolution in Dante's thinking about gender, in order to account for his development from a courtly poet—working in a set of conventions in which women do not speak, act, or do—into the poet of the *Commedia,* that is, into a poet who assigns moral agency to all human beings, including women. Using three poems as developmental signposts—the early sonnet *Sonar bracchetti* and two mature *canzoni, Poscia ch'Amor* and *Doglia mi reca*—I delineate the trajectory whereby Dante moves from a world that is polarized and dichotomized by gender into two rigidly separated spheres toward a more fluid and non-dualistic understanding of human beings and human desire. An insistence on non-duality is also a hallmark of "Queering Nature, Queering Gender: Dante and Sodomy," in which Gary P. Cestaro discusses the "sodomitic culture of Florence" and comes to the conclusion that "If there is a grammar of nature for Dante, it cannot be the obvious, straight-lined grammar that he left behind in the failed *De vulgari eloquentia.*"

The next two essays, Lino Pertile's "Does the *Stilnovo* Go to Heaven?" and F. Regina Psaki's "Love for Beatrice: Transcending Contradiction in the *Paradiso,*" also deal with human desire in Dante's work and form a stimulating and provocative unit, since one scholar, Pertile, essentially answers his title question in the negative, while the other, Psaki, answers it instead in the affirmative. Maintaining that there is no space for exemplary human love in the *Commedia,* Pertile argues that "the love that is punished in Hell and purged in Purgatory is shown to have nothing in common with the otherworldly love that conquers the Heavens to reach beyond space and time." Psaki maintains exactly the opposite: "For Dante, theologically as well as poetically, there is no ontological divide between *eros* and *agape,* between body and the incorporeal heaven that has no *dove* ("where" [Par 27.109–10])) other than in the mind of God (*Par* 27.109–10); the love he felt for Beatrice in the body is the love he still feels for her in Paradise." These two positions beautifully crystallize both sides of a problematic that is central not only to the study of Dante, but indeed to our understanding of the philosophical underpinnings of Christianity itself. As readers and critics we are continually negotiating precisely this foundational—and still vigorous, as these essays demonstrate—debate, a debate reflecting the ancient dialectic in our cultural heritage between what we could call, in shorthand, a more Platonic and a more Aristotelian worldview.

Philosophical issues, and ancient philosophical controversies, come into clearer focus in the next section, *Philosophies,* which provides an apt emblem for those controversies, in their medieval dress, in Giuseppe Mazzotta's title, "Dante between Aquinas and Bonaventure." Two essays probe the mystical quotient of Dante's poetic and philosophical patrimony: while Steven Botterill, in "Mysticism and Meaning in Dante's *Paradiso,*" evenhandedly considers the reasons for traditionally excluding Dante from the canon of mystical authors and finds them wanting, Giuliana Carugati offers a full-fledged Neoplatonic reading in "*Quando amor fa sentir de la sua pace*" ("When Love makes his peace felt"). Carugati argues that Dante uses amorous and erotic language in a Neoplatonic fashion to access ancient ideas that were neglected by the traditional teachings of the Church, and that, like the great Neoplatonic thinkers, Dante possesses an erotic vision of being whereby "He who falls in love, insofar as he thinks, thinks god in the only way in which god is thinkable, namely, in his intelligible hypostasis," which is to say, for Dante, in the lady. In other words, to think God is to think the lady—a view that adds further layers of complexity to the question of human desire as discussed by previous authors in this collection.

In "The Heaven of the Sun: Dante between Aquinas and Bonaventure," Giuseppe Mazzotta reconstructs the compositional tesserae that go into the complex mosaic of Dante's heaven of wisdom, thus mapping not just the cantos that make up this Heaven but also the fundamental coordinates of Dante's philosophical thought. Through his encounters with Saints Bonaventure and Aquinas, Dante "confronts the philosophical-theological speculations of the two great masters of the thirteenth century" as "through them he seeks to reconstitute the vast circle of Christian wisdom." Focusing on *Purgatorio* 5, Alison Cornish, in "Vulgarizing Science: Vernacular Translation of Natural Philosophy," shows us how Dante, in the meteorological section of that canto, "is rendering the concepts and language of natural science useful" for his contemporary readers; thus, the enterprise of writing the *Commedia* should be seen to include the task of making natural science available, or "vulgarizing science." Moving to *Purgatorio* 10–12, the terrace of pride, Robert Durling looks at "The Body and the Flesh in the *Purgatorio*," a topic that is picked up again by Manuele Gragnolati in "From Plurality to (Near) Unicity of Forms: Embryology in *Purgatorio* 25." The discourse on embryology and the formation of the souls' aerial bodies in *Purgatorio* 25 has generated a long critical debate in Dante studies: in the 1920s Giovanni Busnelli argued that Dante's account of the generation of the soul is fully Thomistic, while Bruno Nardi stressed Dante's independence from Thomas. Gragnolati intervenes in this debate by arguing that the text is deliberately ambivalent, and that Dante draws on the philosophy of both Bonaventure (for plurality of forms) and Aquinas (for unicity of forms), going on to show how Dante, in conceiving the resurrection body, "uses some principles of unicity to stress the soul's power," but at the same time "stresses that the aerial body is not enough, and that the soul without its real body is imperfect," drawing thus also on principles of plurality. We circle back in this way to the coordinates mapped by Mazzotta: "Dante Between Aquinas and Bonaventure."

The three essays representing the field of *Reception* excavate, in interestingly divergent ways, the cultural humus from which the *Commedia* grew. In "Virility, Nobility, and Banking: The Crossing of Discourses in the *Tenzone* with Forese," Susan Noakes insists on the importance of a culturally enriched reading to understand Dante's sonnet exchange with his friend Forese Donati. The attribution of these sonnets has been doubted, largely because the violent and sexually explicit world they depict is foreign to the context that most *dantisti* have come to expect as Dantean. Noakes sets out to contextualize the poems, bringing Dante studies back to social biography and history, last practiced with respect to the *tenzone* by Michele Barbi, who in 1924 "devoted forty-two pages to an explanation of Forese's remarks about Dante's father." Armed with the extraordinary advances in Florentine historiography achieved since Barbi's time, Noakes shows that "even forty-two pages were insufficient to explain, to twentieth-century ears, the complexity of what Dante's father, as invoked by Forese's tongue, meant to a late thirteenth-century Florentine audience."

In the same way as the essays in *Philologies* testify to the revitalizing of an old field that for a time was rejected as dry and merely technical but now is the fertile ground of some of our most exciting developments, in part because in the intervening years the boundary between philology and literary criticism has become more porous, allowing for the interesting hybrids exemplified by Gorni himself, so in Noakes's essay we see how profitably social history, similarly put aside for a time as too positivistic and unimaginative, is now being dusted off. Dusted off by a literary critic, social history and biography offer an excitingly original and imaginative venue for reconsidering a set of texts—the *tenzone* with Forese (newly translated here by Noakes as well)—whose opacity has resisted conventional literary critical tools.

A similar revitalizing, in this case of the venerable trade of *Quellenforschung* or source-study, is at work in Zygmunt G. Barański's essay. For Barański too, misplaced critical squeamishness regarding topics that do not conform to our expectations of what Dante should be treating—in this case, "Scatology and Obscenity in Dante"—serves as a starting point for enriching and recontextualizing our understanding of the erotic and scatological elements in *Inferno* 18. According to Barański, treatment of the excremental and the erotic diverged significantly for Dante and his culture: "the poet is prepared to talk openly about the former but not about the latter" (a prohibition that, we note, makes the *tenzone* all the more valuable). Pointing out that the Bible makes significant recourse to the scatological, Barański demonstrates the scriptural character of much of the scatological language of *Inferno* 18. In "On Dante and the Visual Arts," Christopher Kleinhenz reinforces the importance of Scripture as a Dantean cultural context, transposed however to the visual sphere, by suggesting that the idea of composing a narrative that can be read both horizontally and vertically came to the poet "from his looking, since the time he was a small boy, and ever with love, upon the mosaics in the cupola of the Florentine Baptistery."

From using historical context to better understand a literary text, we move, in Ronald L. Martinez's "Dante's Jeremiads: The Fall of Jerusalem and the Burden of the New Pharisees, the Capetians, and

Florence," to conjuring "one of the devastating catastrophes offered by history, conceived and accomplished by human actors." In this dense exploration of the ways in which Florence is compared to Jerusalem, both "cities reserved for divine vengeance," Martinez focuses on four cantos, *Inferno* 19 and 23 and *Purgatorio* 20 and 23, mapping the complex of intricate interrelations between them. The *Histories* section continues with two essays that look beyond the end of history. Ronald Herzman brings his expertise in eschatology and the apocalyptic tradition to Dante's life of Francis in *Paradiso* 11 in "From Francis to Solomon: Eschatology in the Sun," suggesting that "the events in Francis's life which are chosen by Dante are chosen in part because they are the apocalyptic events of *Purgatorio* 32 rewritten *in bono.*" Amilcare Iannucci returns to *Purgatorio* 32 (the source of the verse he cites in his title) in "Already and Not Yet: Dante's Existential Eschatology": "Given the apocalyptic nature of the scene atop the Mountain of Purgatory (*Purg* 28–33), a scene that brings the poem's historical metaphor to its close, it is more than likely that Dante thought that history was approaching its last days." And, finally, in "Dante after Dante," Albert Russell Ascoli considers the history of reading Dante from a theoretical perspective, looking at "the problem of conceiving Dante's relationship to his readers as it unfolds both textually and historically."

Ascoli's query, "What is the history of reading Dante, the story of Dante's readers?" provides the springboard to our volume's final section, *Rewritings,* which offers, first, two essays on Dante as reader and rewriter, in both cases of Ovid, followed by three essays on Dante being read and then rewritten. In "Ovid and the *Exul Inmeritus,*" Michelangelo Picone looks at "the profound influence Ovid's life and literary output while in exile had on the author of the *Divine Comedy,* undoubtedly the greatest of all medieval exile poems." The Ovidian poems of exile are meticulously canvassed for their points of contact with the *Commedia,* producing fresh insights and far-reaching claims: for instance, Picone holds that Ovid's description of intense cold in the *Tristia* is transmuted into Hell's frozen pit of ice, Cocytus, which Dante invented "relying on Ovid alone." Switching to the Ovid of the *Metamorphoses* in "The Re-Formation of Marsyas in *Paradiso* 1," Jessica Levenstein provides a strong reading of the Marsyas episode in the sixth book of the *Metamorphoses* before exploring the factors that contribute to Dante's reimagining of the myth in *Paradiso* 1; reading Marsyas as an allegory of the fragmented self, Levenstein shows how Dante employs the Marsyas story as an effective way for the poet to confront "the dominant problem of the divided self in this canto."

The story of "Dante in England," as told by David Wallace, is a fascinating account of the "comic theme of the English encountering the foreignness of Dante (who then in turn discovers the foreignness of the native scene)." Surprisingly little anxiety seems to attend Dante and his Catholicism in England; even during the Reformation "the overwhelming majority of references from this period adduce Dante positively (as an antipapal writer, a sort of Italian Lollard) or in humorously appreciative vein." A more heroic—indeed Ulyssean—Dante is embedded in Melville's epic novel, *Moby-Dick,* according to Piero Boitani. In "Moby-Dante?" Boitani introduces us to Melville as reader of Dante ("Herman Melville bought a copy of Cary's Dante, *The Vision,* on June 22, 1848"), and makes a case for the similarities between Melville's Ahab and Dante's Ulysses, for Ahab as "an ultra-Ulyssean Ulysses." Finally, in "Still Here: Dante After Modernism," Peter S. Hawkins and Rachel Jacoff leave the nineteenth-century Dante to concentrate on the dialogue of the twentieth century, focusing on T. S. Eliot, Derek Walcott, Seamus Heaney, Charles Wright, and Gjertrud Schnackenberg.

Hawkins and Jacoff conclude by citing Osip Mandelstam: "It is unthinkable to read the cantos of Dante without aiming them in the direction of the present day. They were made for that. They are missiles for capturing the future." Mandelstam could not be more right, and in our own small way, in this volume, we have endeavored to aim Dante's missiles in the direction of the present day. A similar thought may be found in the last sentence of Gianfranco Contini's classic essay "Un'interpretazione di Dante." Contini's image, which has stayed with me from my early twenties, when I first read it, perfectly captures the idea of a Dante whose words are missiles for capturing the future—of a Dante for the next millennium, indeed for all millennia: "L'impressione genuina del postero, incontrandosi in Dante, non è d'imbattersi in un tenace e ben conservato sopravvissuto, ma di raggiungere qualcuno arrivato prima di lui" ("Posterity's genuine impression, upon meeting Dante, is not of bumping into a tenacious and well-preserved survivor, but of catching up with someone who arrived before we did"). And so, confident that he arrived before us, we do not usher Dante into the twenty-first century, but hope to bump into him now that we're finally there.

I would like to thank Fordham University Press for undertaking to publish this massive volume; my co-editor, H. Wayne Storey, for graciously welcoming it into his Fordham Series in Medieval Studies; and the Council of the Dante Society of America for its support of our endeavor. Mary Beatrice Schulte has been a veritable Beatrice of editors, providentially bringing our project to a happy conclusion. To her and to Lynn Erin MacKenzie, for her stalwart and salvific research assistance, my sincere thanks.

TEODOLINDA BAROLINI
President, Dante Society of America
Columbia University, N.Y.

NOTES FOR AN INTRODUCTION

The mechanics of gathering and editing a volume of essays of this sort might seem a matter of simple collection and standardization. Instead, the politics of textual issues, both in terms of primary texts and this volume's treatment and representation of critical essays, are evermore challenging at the turn of a century in which we face the probable end of printed scholarly editions and the growing "virtualization" of our relationship to texts. Consequently, the ways in which we talk about texts, including the essays in this volume, require a greater rigor and attention to the details that constitute what we might be about to lose, or, at the very least, will have to reformulate as the primary tools of our work and the eventual results of our own scholarly activity. Ironically, the trend away from formal citation, in the form of the scholar's beloved footnote, and the reconstitution of texts rendered appropriately more problematic by more materially earnest, or at least less pseudo-scientific, methods of textual editing have left us—on the one hand—with less information, and—on the other hand—with culturally richer texts that require better prepared readers. This double bind seems inevitable since historical integrity requires that we present, for example, Dante's ancient texts in all their disputable uncertainty while trying to provide solid direction in the reading of those texts to students whose rediscovery of ancient languages and the materiality of their manuscript containers becomes increasingly more difficult. Thus, the still-lingering temptation to standardize, to insist upon one version of the *Comedy*, for example, or to adopt more so-called "reader-friendly" texts serves neither the general reader nor the specialist. In the specific case of Dante, given the current state of the emerging editorial debate surrounding not just the *Divine Comedy*, but other works as well (including the *Vita Nova*, the *Convivio*, the *Fiore*, and numerous lyrics), the idea of imposing a single edition of any one work upon the contributors to this volume would have misrepresented both the textual consciousness of current Dante studies—in

America and in those countries represented by the conference participants—as well as the editors' desire to allow the contributors' treatment of textual issues to speak for themselves. On the other hand, the diverse editions of the *Comedy* utilized by the contributors are clearly cited to encourage readers to note the differences among these editions, since different editions of the same text might indeed lead to different interpretative results.

The metamorphosis of this volume's titles reflects not only the impetus of the original international conference sponsored by the Dante Society of America (Dante2000), but also the thematic and methodological diversity that characterize current Dante studies. The penultimate title that was to have gone to press, *Dante in America: Reading Dante's Texts in the New World,* was, in its editorial development, meant to be mildly provocative. The working title had ultimately failed to capture the collective dynamic that emerged from the essays as a wide-angle photograph of the maturation of American Dante studies from their pre-Longfellow origins, brilliantly examined by Giuseppe Mazzotta (*Dante Studies* 2000), to the richly diverse scholarly approaches of *dantisti* practicing particularly in North America. While even today the study of Dante in America seems to some a field devoted exclusively to the elaboration of Singleton's allegorical approach, the broad range of topics and methods in this volume suggests anything other than a single way of reading Dante in the "New World." If there is an aspect that characterizes these essays, it is their diversity, their "multivocality," and not an implicit homage to Longfellow or Singleton. This is not to say that all the essays break with tradition, but rather that they represent more self-consciously their debts to and debates with past Dante criticism. If there ever was an "American school" of Dante criticism, many of the essays in this collection would confirm the need to reevaluate its historical and current definitions.

The final title that went to press, *Dante for the New Millennium,* reverts back to the volume's original working subtitle, *Themes and Methods for the Next Millennium,* but with less pedagogical intentionality. What at first seemed to me a rather harsh ambiguity imposed by that "new" now strikes me as emblematic of the regenerative nature of Dante studies, from the first commentaries on, thanks to a poet whose texts have for centuries provoked critical interpretation.

The decision to divide the essays into six sections whose titles reflect multiple means of defining the same disciplinary approach (*Philologies*, *Appetites*, *Philosophies*, *Reception*, *Histories*, and *Rewritings*) and virtually separate bibliographic orientations (for the same poet!) recognizes the distinct impact of each of these traditions and their continuation, modification, and renewal in the critical language of each of the sections of this volume. Notably contrasting scholarly points of view that sound not as polemic but as investigations of the evidentiary and interpretative possibilities of differing critical traditions and perspectives are represented in each section of this volume. Also within each of the six modules, if not in each of the essays, one encounters in varying degrees a reassessment of the critical origins that spawned the author's method and interpretative values.

The notion behind six separate lists of works cited was twofold. Each list would help define the subfield, both in its historical development and its future trajectory as envisaged by the contributors to each unit. Few Dante scholars would argue with the reality of such bibliographic differences, if not virtual divisions, between those who focus, for example, on *Dante philosophe* and those who study gender issues in medieval lyrics. It bears noting that when we began collecting the essays for publication, we presumed we would have been able to reduce the common bibliographical items among the six parts to a longer list of abbreviated titles. In fact, the six bibliographies demonstrate the unique trajectories of six ways of thinking about and interpreting Dante from the past and in the future. Thus, the list of common works abbreviated is perhaps shorter than one might expect. Within the bibliographies, we have followed the system of listing most pre-1500 authors according to the convention of given name rather than family name. Thus, the reader will find Dino Compagni—rather than Compagni, Dino—in the bibliographies at the close of each section. The most notable exceptions are, in fact, the four notables (Alighieri, Dante; Aquinas, Thomas; Boccaccio, Giovanni; and Petrarca, Francesco), thanks to the recognizable nature of their patronymics. A list of abbreviations for the essays and these bibliographies follows these Notes.

Those editorial formulae that were imposed have very much to do, in fact, with recent developments in the field of material studies, initiated in the 1980s by Denis Muzerelle and developed by Ezio Ornato. Throughout the volume, the Latin *charta / -ae* substitutes the imprecise "folio" still used by some to indicate one half of a *bifolium* (a folio folded in half to make two *chartae*). By the same token, all poetic verses are referred to as "verses" to avoid confusion with the "lines" of medieval manuscripts upon which multiple verses were often written. In those essays that discuss manuscripts, the unwieldy and unnecessarily specialized use of initials, even for the most common manuscripts, has been abandoned in favor of the clear indication and even repetition of their shelf marks (for example, Vat. Lat. 3793 instead of *V* or *A*). In their quality as books, rather than lexical and syntactic mines to be stripped for their variants, we do no more harm in repeating a shelf mark for the inexperienced reader than in citing in full Eco's *Nome della rosa* rather than "N" or, in its condition as his first novel, "A."

The practice of rendering the title (first verse) of all lyric poems in italics rather than in quotation marks stems from both a theoretical and a pragmatic rationale. Already used by Italian editors, this means of distinguishing the lyric composition (whether sonnet or *canzone*) recognizes the conceptual and material autonomy of the lyric as a separate composition, rather than as part of a larger poetic collection. But, especially in those essays that treat primarily Dante's lyric poetry, it became clear that the visual confusion between "titles" of lyrics and "cited verses" only hampers the reader's comprehension of the essay. Thus, the standard American editorial practice is herein abandoned in favor of a clearer graphetic treatment.

The thorny issue of translation was initially raised by one of the contributors to the volume as a matter of standardization. Of course, the interpretative values of translation would, and do, largely reflect the scholar's personal reading of a given passage and, obviously, the edition of the work in the original used by the translator and the scholar. For this reason, we encouraged contributors to provide their own translations where they felt translation was necessary given the diversity of potential readers. Many elected to rely on translations already in print. The significant problem of the relationship between the translation and the base text utilized by these translators raised again the difficult question of a standard edition of the *Comedy* and, almost as quickly, put the question to rest. As early as the fourteenth century, we find cases in which the commentary corresponds to lexical readings different from those of the text it accompanies. It is worth noting, on the other hand, that some essays, my own included, do not contain translations of the original texts due mostly to the linguistic or philological nature of the essays. This absence is not designed to discourage readers, but as a simple statement of editorial integrity.

I conclude this brief introduction by noting two aspects about the timing of the publication of this volume in the Fordham Series in Medieval Studies. The series itself was founded, among other reasons, to promote the distribution of conference papers of particular importance to the field of medieval studies. What is seldom recognized in the publication of collections of this sort is the intellectual process that is vital to our work and for which the tradition of the "conference," the gathering of specialists in a single or related fields, was founded and was certainly intended in the case of Dante2000. While the idea of the first international conference sponsored by the Dante Society of America might have led one to presume a collection of monolithic statements, the conference itself generated significant critical debate and rethinking of many of the presentations. The period between the conference and the final submission of essays to the Fordham University Press included a particularly lively editorial process of drafts, suggestions, queries, and rewritings that represents the "state of the question" far better than the conference. It would, in fact, be better to characterize this volume as the maturation of themes and methods we initially discussed in New York City in April 2000, rather than the *acta* of Dante2000. That these essays should appear the year before the numerous celebrations of the seven-hundredth anniversary of Petrarch's birth is probably significant only to the extent that the enrichment of our understanding of medieval culture ultimately depends not on the turning point of the millennium, nor the anniversary of a poet, but on the good intentions of scholars willing to question and test their own results, and then see through the lengthy process of the collective publication of essays whose appearance in separate journals would have made a less patient and, I believe, less remarkable statement.

H. WAYNE STOREY
Indiana University, Bloomington

ABBREVIATIONS

Aen	*Aeneid*
Conv	*Convivio*
DS	*Dante Studies*
DVE	*De vulgari eloquentia*
ED	*Enciclopedia Dantesca*
MLN	*Modern Language Notes*
PL	*Patriologiae cursus completus, series Latina*
RPh	*Romance Philology*
PMLA	*Publications of the Modern Language Association*
SFI	*Studi di filologia italiana*
ST	*Summa theologiae*
StD	*Studi Danteschi*
Inf	*Inferno*
Purg	*Purgatorio*
Par	*Paradiso*

PHILOLOGIES

1

What Did the First Copies of the *Comedy* Look Like?

John Ahern

THIS ESSAY contains the early results of an ongoing study of the reception and codicology of Dante's *Comedìa*—a statement that might well raise eyebrows since the poem's earliest surviving copies (Ashburnham 828 [perhaps 1335 or a little later], Landiano 190 [1336] and Trivulziano 1080 [1337]) date to the mid-1330s, about fifteen years after Dante died, which precludes examination of the first copies. Dreams of discovering manuscripts in Dante's own hand haunt even sober philologists such as Contini (1989) and Branca (1988), but remain merely dreams. Given the lack of hard evidence, my contribution might fit better in a section called "Immaterial Philology," could Guglielmo Gorni be persuaded to sanction such a category. For centuries philologists, seeking a more accurate text, have scrutinized its more than eight hundred surviving manuscripts, but rarely—and understandably—looked closely at that initial thirty-year gap. I would like to recover, to the extent possible, the shapes that the book took in Dante's lifetime and the first few years afterward, from around 1307 to the mid-1330s. Even though my question admits only the sketch of an answer, it will, I hope, focus more sharply the boldness of Dante's experimental poem, whose subsequent status as the classic of classics tends to obscure its editorial originality.

Most of the poem was widely known by Dante's death in September 1321. Publication had begun about fourteen years earlier when he sent the first copies to friends and patrons. *Da poi che la Natura ha fine posto,* the *canzone* that his longtime friend and correspondent the jurist Cino da Pistoia wrote on the death of the Emperor Henry VII in August 1313, contained echoes of *Inf* 1.69 and 10.80. Over the next eight years Cino continued to receive parts of the poem. At least one of the three sonnets critical of the *Comedy* which are attributed to him, *Infra gli altri difetti del libello,* is accepted as genuine. His *canzone* on Dante's death, *Su per la costa, Amor, de l'alto monte,* alludes to the *Comedy* (*Inf* 15.72), including the last *cantica* (*Par* 23.132; 28.97)—a situation that suggests that Cino had a nearly complete copy of the text at the time of Dante's death, perhaps a holograph. One would give much to find that copy and its probably polemical annotations, given their divergent politics after 1313 (Graziosi 1997). Another deeply engaged reader of the *Comedy,* the Florentine aristocrat and political figure Pieraccio Tedaldi, writing in Romagna, also composed a poem on Dante's death.

By 1314, if not earlier, Francesco da Barberino, a Tuscan notary writing in Mantua, mentions the poem in this well-known gloss to his *Documenti d'Amore* (1905–27, 2:275–76):

> hunc Dante Aringhierij in quodam suo opere dicitur Comedia et de infernalibus inter cetera multa tractat commendat protinus ut magistrum et certe siquis illus opus bene conspiciat videre poterit ipsum dantem super ipsum Virgilium vel longo tempore studuisse vel in parvo tempore plurimum profecisse.

> Dante Alighieri, in a certain work of his called the *Comedy,* which treats hellish matters among many others, commends this man as his teacher and, certainly, if one were to pay close attention, one would see that Dante himself had read Virgil himself over a long period or had in a short time become quite familiar with him.[1]

Francesco da Barberino knew Dante's earlier poetry, having listed him among the "moderni" along with Guittone d'Arezzo, Guido Guinizelli, Guido Cavalcanti, and Cino da Pistoia (*Documenti d'Amore* in 1905–27, 1.100). The allusion to *Inf* 1.85 suggests at the very least that early cantos of the *Inferno* circulated in the Val Padana by 1313–14.

Copies in the hands of friends and patrons soon generated other copies. In Siena around 1315 someone familiar with the *Vita Nuova, Inferno,* and *Purgatorio,* especially the later cantos, provided inscriptions in *terza rima* for Simone Martini's *Maestà* (Brugnolo 1987; Gorni 1988). By 1316, in the Franciscan monastery of Santa Croce in Florence, the friar Anastasio may well have known the *Purgatory,* perhaps from a copy sent by Dante himself, who had frequented disputations there in the mid-1290s (as noted in *Conv* 2.12). Around 1316–22, the young Florentine notary Andrea Lancia, who had met Dante probably in the Veneto between 1312 and 1318, composed an Italian summary of the *Aeneid* whose language contained reminiscences of the *Inferno* and cited *Purg* 2.81 (Valerio 1985).

Around 1317, if we accept the *Epistle to Can Grande* as authentic, Dante sent the first canto of the *Paradiso* (and possibly more) to Can Grande in Verona, hoping apparently that he would promote its copying and circulation. Corroboration of the role of patrons in the poem's early circulation is provided by the Venetian poet Giovanni Quirini, who, in a *sonetto caudato,* asked an unnamed lord (perhaps Can Grande) to release the *Paradiso.* The appearance of rhymes from *Paradiso* 9 in this sonnet suggests that Quirini knew the first third of that *cantica* as well, and probably the *Inferno* and *Purgatorio* too, since in another sonnet, accompanying the loan of a copy of the *Comedy,* he terms it "il mero / libro di Dante" ("Dante's pure book"). His wish for further cantos of the *Paradiso* apparently was granted, for his sonnet on Dante's death echoes *Par* 20.62 (as well as *Purg* 14.88 and 26.97–98).

Boccaccio (1974, 193), writing the *Trattatello in laude di Dante* in the early 1350s, confirms Dante's practice of dedicating individual *cantiche* to aristocratic patrons:

> Questo libro della *Commedia,* secondo il ragionare d'alcuni, intitolò egli a tre solennissimi uomini italiani, secondo la sua triplice divisione, a ciascuno la sua, in questa guisa: la prima parte, cioè lo '*Nferno* intitolò a Uguiccione della Faggiuola, il quale allora in Toscana signore di Pisa era, mirabilmente glorioso; la seconda parte, cioè il *Purgatorio,* intitolò al marchese Moruello Malespina; la terza parte, cioè il *Paradiso,* a Federigo III re di Cicilia.

> He dedicated this book of the *Comedy,* according to the arguments of some people, to three very important Italians, following its threefold division, to each man his own part, in this fashion: he dedicated the first part, i.e., the *Inferno,* to Uguccione della Faggiuola, who at that time in Tuscany was lord of Pisa, marvelously glorious; the second part, i.e., the *Purgatorio,* he dedicated to the marchese Moruello Malaspina; the third part, i.e., the *Paradiso,* to Frederick III, king of Sicily.

A few lines later, Boccaccio (1974, 194) complicates this picture with further, possibly contradictory, information:

> Alcuni vogliono dire lui averlo intitolato tutto a messer Cane della Scala; ma, quale si sia di queste due la verità, niuna cosa altra n'abbiamo che solamente il volontario ragionare di diversi; né egli è sì gran fatto che solenne invesitagazione ne bisogni.
>
> Some people want to say that that he dedicated the whole thing to Cane della Scala, but no matter which of these two versions is the true one, we have absolutely nothing except the free accounts of different people; nor is this so great a matter as to require a solemn investigation.

It is striking that, three decades after Dante's death, such a keen investigator could not discover the exact circumstances of the poem's early publication. In any case, his two versions are not irreconcilable. Dante may have initially dedicated the *Paradiso* to Frederick III (1272–1337) in the hope that his court would publish the poem broadly south of Tuscany, only to decide subsequently to dedicate the *Paradiso* and, eventually, the whole poem to Can Grande, because Verona offered a more prominent court from which to issue the completed poem. Again in the *Trattatello,* Boccaccio (1974, 183) confirms the piecemeal publication of the poem:

> Egli era suo costume, quale ora sei o otto o più o meno canti fatti n'avea, quegli, prima che alcuno altro gli vedesse, donde che egli fosse, mandare a messer Cane della Scala, il quale egli oltre ad ogni altro uomo avea in reverenza; e, poi che da lui eran veduti, ne facea copia a chi la ne volea.
>
> It was his habit when he had made more or less six or eight cantos of the *Comedy,* to send them, before anybody else saw them, from wherever he might be, to messer Cane della Scala, whom he held in greater reverence than any other man and then, when della Scala had seen them, he would make copies of them for those who wanted them.

From Boccaccio's account Dante appears to have functioned as a one-man *scriptorium,* making copies of recent installments for anybody who wanted one, as well as producing entire canticles.

In the decade 1317–27 the principal center of diffusion of the *Comedy* appears to have been Bologna. There, in 1317, another Tuscan notary, ser Tieri degli Useppi da San Gimignano, while testing his pen on the cover of the Register of Criminal Accusations, wrote out Virgil's rebuke to Charon (*Inf* 3.94–96). It seems probable that ser Tieri, although quoting from memory, possessed at least the first half of the *Inferno.* The city's academic and political elites knew the poem. Around 1320 Giovanni del Virgilio sent Dante a Latin eclogue in which he requests (as one shepherd to another) "ten more cheeses," usually taken to be cantos of the *Paradiso,* a request that parallels Quirini's just-cited *sonetto caudato.* This fact suggests that by the late teens an audience in possession of the *Inferno* and the *Purgatorio* and eager to have the latest installment of the *Comedy* existed in northeastern Italy. About three months after Dante died, ser Giovanni d'Antonio, a Guelph notary, inserted into the margins of a contract the vehement reprimand to Nicholas V from *Inf* 19.97–99.

When the sixteen-year-old Petrarch came to Bologna in autumn 1320 to study civil and canon law he probably knew something about Dante from his father, an exiled White Guelph like Dante. He probably also recalled the meeting of the two men nine years earlier in Pisa. If Petrarch did not already know about the *Comedy,* notaries, students, and professors in Bologna would soon have mentioned the still-incomplete poem, whose author lived in nearby Ravenna. He may well have known Dante's son Pietro, a fellow student in Bologna. Forty years later, writing to Boccaccio, Petrarch recalls disdainfully how illiterates performed parts of the poem at crossroads and theaters to applauding drapers, innkeepers, and people in shops and markets (*Familiares* 21.15; Ahern 1982b). His family's wealth and position at the papal court at Avignon had allowed him to develop into a precocious, exigent bibliophile, familiar with a variety of elegant formats, for whom the undoubtedly unprepossessing copies of individual canticles, probably in notarile script, then circulating in Bologna could only provoke scorn. During these very years he commissioned the magnificent Ambrosian Virgil, containing the *Eclogues, Georgics, Aeneid,* Statius's *Achilleid,* two commentaries on Donatus's *Ars Major*—a work beyond the means or dreams of a penniless exile like Dante (Billanovich 1975; 1996, 3–40):

> Ea vero michi obiecte calumnie pars altera fuerat, cuius in argumentum trahitur quod a prima etate, que talium cupidissima esse solet ego librorum varia inquisitione delectatus, nunquam librum illius habuerim, et ardentissimus semper in reliquis, quorum pene nulla spes superat, in hoc uno sine difficultate parabili, novo quodam nec meo more tepuerim.
>
> (*Familiares* 21.15.10 [Petrarch 1992])

> There is a second accusation leveled against me: I never owned a copy of his book, although from early youth when one usually longs for such things I enjoyed collecting books. While always hunting passionately for other books with little hope of finding them, I was strangely indifferent to this one which was new and easily available.
>
> (trans. Bernardo [Petrarch 1985])

We may doubt his claim never to have possessed a copy of the *Comedy,* because allusions to the poem and other writings by Dante—witting and unwitting—reverberate through most of his Italian and even Latin works (Baglio 1992; Trovato 1979; Santagata 1990; Orelli 1978). Other readers in Bologna shared his predilection for *Inferno* 5. The year before he arrived in Bologna, an anonymous notary had copied the opening twenty verses of that canto, as well as *Purg* 1.1, on a scrap of parchment found in a register of 1319. Even if Petrarch did not own a copy of the *Inferno* in Bologna, he assuredly read it and certainly heard parts of it performed. Once back in Avignon he appears to have had access to a copy of it, probably that of Sennuccio del Bene.

When Dante died during the second year of Petrarch's stay in Bologna, so far as we know, no complete single-volume manuscript of the *Comedy* was in circulation. In Ravenna his patron Guido da Polenta probably possessed a copy, as did members of his circle there: Dino Perini, a doctor in correspondence with Giovanni del Virgilio in Bologna, Piero Giardini, a notary active between 1311 and 1348 who, according to Boccaccio, had been Dante's disciple and also served as Boccaccio's informant (*Trattatello* 1974, 186), and Guido Vacchetta, who knew Giovanni del Virgilio. According to Boccaccio (*Trattatello,* first redaction 185–89; second redaction, 121–27), Dante's son Iacopo, then in his twenties, working from a holograph, prepared the first one-volume *Comedy* for Guido da Polenta (Francesca's uncle). In an accompanying sonnet, "*Acciò che le bellezze, signor mio,*" probably sent on April 1, when Guido assumed his duties as Capitano del Popolo in Bologna, Iacopo asked Guido to correct the text ("I'm sending it so that you might correct it"), a request that suggests that Guido knew the work, possessed authoritative copies, and would circulate the corrected version (Iacopo Alighieri 1990, 7). Iacopo appears also to have sent Guido his own Latin commentary, the *Chiose,* as well as a short verse summary, or *capitolo.*

The entire *Comedy* soon circulated freely in Bologna, awakening strong responses. In 1324 the Guelf notary and political figure Graziolo dei Bambaglioli (ca. 1290–ca. 1343), in his Latin commentary on the *Inferno,* quoted *Par* 15.10–15 (Rossi 1999). He apparently owned the whole poem, which he read as a single text. His commentary, like Jacopo's *Chiose,* reads like hastily composed notes rushed into circulation to answer the many objections raised against the poem, especially its truth claims, in the over-heated atmosphere of the 1320s. As a student of Aristotle, Cicero, Sallust, Seneca, Virgil, Ovid, and Lucan, and acquainted with Peter Lombard, Aquinas, and the *Glossa Ordinaria,* Graziolo corresponds well to Dante's ideal reader, the *philosophus* as evoked two decades earlier in Dante's *Convivio* (3.11). Between 1324 and 1328 another Bolognese, probably a theologically trained academic, Jacopo della Lana, produced for students what soon became the best-known early commentary which read the poem as a *summa* of philosophical and theological thought. In 1322–24 a university lector, Francesco Stabili (1269–1327), better known as Cecco d'Ascoli, composed a poem, *Acerba,* that aggressively challenged parts of the *Comedy.* Stabili clearly knows the poem well and appears to have exchanged epistles with Dante. The first documentary reference to a specific copy of the *Inferno* survives in a legal document dated May 6, 1325, which contains a list of books belonging to Antonio Spatiario, a Paduan resident in Bologna (Orlandelli 1959). That the list includes legal texts (*Digestum Novum* and *Digestum Vetus*) but also political (Aquinas's *De regimine principum*) and military works (Vegetius Flavius's *De re militari*), suggests that the possessor was a person of standard legal and Scholastic culture. The poem continued to win readers among the city's notaries. In 1327 ser Pace dei Terracci wrote out *Inf* 13.22–29 and *Purg* 11.1–24 in the *Memoriali bolognesi.*

Outside Bologna the *Comedy* attracted readers in the highly polarized ecclesiastical culture of the day. By 1326 a Dominican friar, the so-called Anonimo Lombardo, had composed Latin glosses on the poem for theologically literate readers unused to reading vernacular texts. The Franciscan inquisitor in Florence, Accursio Bonfantini, produced an exposition of the *Comedy,* of which a fragment survives in a manuscript of the *Ottimo Commento.* When another ecclesiastic—probably the redoubtable Guelph and Dominican archbishop of Pisa, Simone Saltarelli—established the program of the otherwise non-Dantean fresco of Hell in the Campo Santo at Pisa (1330–36), he appears to have imitated Dante by placing living enemies in a (pictorial) representation of Hell: Emperor Ludwig of Bavaria and his antipope, Nicholas V (Polzer 1964; Kreytenberg 1989). Another Dominican, Guido Vernani (ca. 1280–ca. 1340), who condemned and burned the *De Monarchia* in 1328, also read and disliked the poem: "iste homo copiosissime deliravit et, ponendo os in caelum, lingua eius transivit in terra" ("this man was abundantly delirious; while his mouth was placed in heaven, his tongue went around on earth").

Dominican reaction was divided. The *Inferno*'s popularity among novices led the Tuscan general chapter in 1336 to ban "quatenus poeticos libros sive libellos per illum qui Dante in vulgari compositos nec tenere vel in eis studere" (owning or reading poetic books or booklets composed in the vernacular by the man named Dante). The words *liber* (book) and *libellus* (booklet) suggest that both single canticles (*cantiche*) and complete *Comedies* circulated among the novices. Apparently the chapter did not expect compliance because it also stipulated that transgressors "libris predictis ex vi presentis statuti privari" (be deprived by force of the aforementioned books).

Italian Jews knew the poem in the period 1320–30. Both Immanuello Romano's sonnet on Dante's death and his account of a journey to Hell and Paradise (*Mabberet ha-Tofet weha-Eden*), guided by a Dante-like figure named Daniel, attest to his knowledge of the *Comedy*. Bosone da Gubbio (of whom more shortly) may have introduced Immanuello to the works of Dante and Cino da Pistoia when Immanuello visited Gubbio after the expulsion of the Jews from Rome in 1322. Immanuel, also known as Manoello Giudeo, wrote biblical commentaries and a lost treatise in Hebrew on the mystical nature of the Hebrew language, as well as poems in Hebrew based on Judeo-Arabic models (Alfie 1998). Either he or his cousin, Judah ben Moses ben Daniel, may have made the transliterations into Hebrew of *Purg* 16.73–75, *Par* 5.73–84, 13.52–53, and 20.49–54 that appeared in a miscellany of Christian writing owned by a Jew in Rome in the late 1320s (Bernheimer 1915).

The *Comedy* also attracted culturally unprepared readers. Merchants—a category ignored by Dante in his discussion of his audience in the *Convivio*—read the poem. Domenico Lenzi, a Florentine grain merchant in Piazza Or San Michele with no Latin and little schooling, in his *Specchio Umano,* an almost daily record of grain prices from 1320 to 1335, recounts how the poor were driven out of Pisa during a famine in 1329, and appositely quotes Ugolino's anguished cry from another episode of expulsion and death by starvation in Pisa (*Inf* 33.66): "Ahi dura terra, perchè non t'apristi?" Lenzi seems also to recall *Purg* 2.97, 3.122–23, and 20.147 (Branca 1965).

Readers of Italian but not Latin wanted to penetrate more deeply into the poem. An Italian version of Graziolo's Latin commentary appeared by 1333. An unknown Tuscan Guelph, possibly from Siena and writing no later than 1337, left random annotations on the *Inferno,* now known as the *Chiose Selmiane,* in which in a low popular tone he misconstrued the poem's literal meaning and provided misinformation about recent events (Mazzoni 1971a). Another nameless Tuscan composed a *cantare Febus el forte* (ca. 1325–35), which echoes *Inf* 5.10, 26 (Meli 1958). The sonnets that Giovanni Guerrini wrote defending Dante against Cecco d'Ascoli's *Acerba* also confirm the poem's popularity among "low-end readers." Indeed, the already noted oral performances of the poem in Bologna around 1319–25, which so displeased Petrarch and Giovanni Del Virgilio, indicate that the poem had won a following among the urban population at large, including the illiterate.

From the start, readers of modest cultural background wanted simple guides to the poem. At the end of many manuscripts appear crude summaries in *terza rima* of two or three pages, often referred to as *capitoli,* which served as tables of contents and simple interpretive keys. More than seventy manuscripts reproduce two of the earliest *capitoli,* by Jacopo Alighieri (1322) and the politician Bosone da Gubbio, which were often copied together in manuscripts. Guido da Pisa's *Declaratio Poetica,* also in *terza rima,* appeared before 1327. Around 1328 the poet Mino Vanni, a poor wool worker in Arezzo, composed a similar compendium as well as twenty-five sonnets on the *Inferno.* From this period dates an anonymous *capitolo* as well as one by Cecco di Meo Mellone.

In Rome, Siena, Gubbio, Arezzo, Florence, Bologna, Ravenna, Venice, and Verona the poem circulated widely, crossing divisions between Guelph and Ghibelline, lay and clerical, Dominican and Franciscan, Christian and Jew, often in surprising ways. Cino knew Dante, Francesco da Barberino, Bosone da Gubbio, and Immanuello

Romano; and he was in Naples when Graziolo and Boccaccio were there. Around 1328 the Dominican friar Guido Vernani dedicated his treatise, which attacked Dante's *De Monarchia,* to the poem's first commentator, Graziolo dei Bambaglioli. In 1327 the Franciscan Accursio Bonfantini, who may well have explicated the poem to an audience in the cathedral in Florence, condemned Dante's Bolognese antagonist, Francesco Stabili, to be burned at the stake.

The forty to fifty specific copies deducible from the preceding narrative suggest a far greater number in circulation. For example, in Florence ca. 1329–31, Andrea Lancia employed four commentaries (Jacopo Alighieri, Graziolo dei Bambaglioli, Guido da Pisa, and Jacopo della Lana) in the first version of his *Ottimo Commento* (Azzetta 1996). He had probably been acquiring copies of the poem since he first read it ca. 1316. And, in fact, the unprecedented number, at least for a vernacular text, of mostly non-professional copies in circulation, not to mention commentaries and *capitoli,* was not an unmitigated blessing, for just nine years after Dante's death his text had already suffered troubling corruption.

In the late summer or early fall of 1330, the rising Florentine politician Giovanni Bonaccorsi persuaded his friend Forese Donati, *pievano* of Santo Stefano at Botena in the Val di Sieve, to make what would later be called "the first critical edition of the *Comedy*" (Vandelli 1922). Exasperation with the many erroneous copies circulating in Florence and Tuscany led the two men to produce this (now lost) manuscript. Forese says in his note: "defectu et imperitia vulgarium scriptorum liber lapsus est quam plurimum in verborum alteratione et mendacitate" ("through the fault and ignorance of scribes in the vernacular the book [i.e., the *Comedy*] to a very great extent fell into the alteration of words and falsehood" [Vandelli 1922, 118]). Before beginning work, Forese assembled different kinds of manuscripts from which he selected the best readings: "Ego autem ex diversis aliis respuendo que falsa et colligendo que vera vel sensui videbantur concinna, in hunc quam sobrius potui fideliter exemplando redegi" (but rejecting what is false in various other copies, and gathering together what is true or seems to jibe with the meaning, as soberly as possible I made a faithful copy and edition). Forese seems not to have exaggerated. Already in the earliest commentaries (1322–29) errors had crept into citations from the *Comedy* (Lanza 1995, xvi).

Dante himself, had he been alive, might well have been more gratified by his poem's initial "rapid, massive diffusion," which was quite uncharacteristic of medieval vernacular works, than surprised by its rapid textual deterioration (Pomaro 1995, 497). Like other writers, he knew that all texts, Latin or Italian, lay at the mercy of copyists. Brunetto Latini, in the early 1260s, was appalled when a copy of his writing given to a friend fell into the hands of boys (*fanti*) who made so many copies that "si ruppe la bolla / e rimase per nulla" ("the seal was broken and nothing was left" [*Tesoretto,* vv. 107–108, in Contini 1960, 2:179]). Around 1314, Francesco da Barberino complained in his *Documenti d'Amore* about all the books he had seen ruined by incompetent scribes: "Vidi enim et etiam aliorum librorum ob scriptorem defectum innumeres vitiosos" ("for I saw countless books by other people corrupted by a deficient scribe" [1905–27, 1:346, as well as 1:94, 296, and 299]). Four decades later in 1356–57, Petrarch would wonder "who could remedy the ignorance of scribes and their indolence, which corrupts and confuses everything, in fear of which, I imagine, already many brilliant minds have turned away from great creative projects" (*De Remediis* 43 [Petrarch 1991, 140–41]). He preferred "ydiote quos sillaba una vel littera sepe diu tenuit perplexos omnia accuratissime nequid tale iterum patiantur, emendant; quod ingenio fidentes et maioribus intenti negligunt" ("the uneducated whom the mistake of a single syllable or letter often puzzles for a long time [and so] correct everything with great accuracy lest they suffer again in such mistakes, something which those relying on their genius and who are intent on more important matters fail to do" [*Familiares* 18.5; trans. Bernardo [Petrarch 1985]).

Dante devised original stratagems to defend his poem's textual integrity. He invented the metrical form *terza rima,* whose interlocking structure immediately exposes interpolations and omissions. He placed the significant word *stelle,* "stars," at the end of each *cantica,* to block additions at those vulnerable points (Ahern 1984). Clearly, his fears of textual tampering were justified. Maestro Antonio da Ferrara, writing around 1355 to Menghino Mezzani, who had known Dante in Ravenna, notes that he would like to erase the name of "Alberto tedesco" (*Purg* 6.97) and replace it with Carlo IV of Bohemia ("S'a legger Dante mai caso m'accaggia" [Mastro Ferrara 1972, 218–19]). To make its survival more likely, Dante obliquely encouraged readers to bind its accumulating fascicles into a single volume (Ahern 1982a).

In the long run, these devices helped to protect a poem whose traditions, relative to other fourteenth-century vernacular texts, are remarkably strong (Petrocchi 1994). And yet, in the short run, as noted earlier, all the many pre-1336 copies—both Dante's originals and the copies they generated—vanished completely. It is easy to see why. Unbound copies, copies on paper rather than parchment, copies in personal anthologies—all were easily dispersed. It was only when the poem began to attain classic status in the 1330s that copies began to survive. Indeed, the wisdom of Dante's editorial decisions is implicit in the speed with which his poem reached so many and such diverse readers.

He appears to have circulated consecutive installments whose format invited rapid, economical reproduction. Although friends and relatives may have assisted him in producing such copies, given his relative poverty and isolation from major centers of book production, it is likely that he himself produced most of the copies he sent out (Bologna 1986, 553–64). Certainly, it is unlikely that he himself possessed the scribal skills to produce luxury volumes for presentation to aristocratic patrons. The format that he chose built on textual practices familiar to the urban professionals, lay and clerical, who constituted the heart of his audience.

He would have written in the widespread relatively rapid notarile script, *cancelleresca,* rather than a cumbersome Gothic book hand. (Salutati, in fact, recalled seeing the lean script of Dante's now lost holograph epistles in the Florentine chancery.) He would have written on parchment, not paper, and in the double columns long customary in legal and other texts because of their more economical use of page space. A double-column format with twelve *terzine* (or thirty-six verses) per column would produce a single sheet holding, on its two sides, a total of 144 verses, that is one-hundredth of the total text, or a *canto per carta* (a canto on each *charta*). For reasons of editorial economy and theological-aesthetic symmetry, his own bound author's copy (which he may well never have actually seen) would have run to exactly 100 *chartae.* The fact that the three earliest surviving copies of the poem consist of about 100 *chartae* would tend to confirm this hypothesis. The text of the poem occupies 104 pages, front and back, in the codex Laurenziano Ashburnham 828, 100 *chartae* in Landiano 190, and 103 *chartae* in the manuscript Trivulziano 1080 (Roddewig 1984, 73, 261, 189). Dante, however, probably did not expect future copyists always to employ exactly 100 *chartae.* Copyists rarely if ever reproduced exactly such formats. Moreover, as an inveterate auto-commentator, he probably assumed—correctly, as it turned out—that his poem would soon elicit glosses and commentaries, which would then add many more pages to the book.

He appears to have modified some ideas about format as he went along, much as he changed aspects of his narrative—for example, the reassignment of the final prophetic encounter from Beatrice (*Inf* 10.130–32 and 15.88–90) to Cacciaguida (*Par* 15–17). Thus, as the poem progresses, the length of individual cantos became ever more regular, so that the *Purgatorio* and the *Paradiso* differ in length by only a tercet. Perhaps the decision to dedicate *grosso modo* a *canto per carta* came to him toward the end of the *Inferno* (or even later) as he began to consider the poem's final shape. Similarly, the use of the term "cantica" for the three major divisions of the poem appears to have occurred to him while writing the *Purgatorio* (Pertile 1991; 1992). And, well into the *Paradiso* (10.44), where his poem's final shape concerns him more and more, he imagines his actual—albeit ideal—reader as sitting as his desk, *banco,* implying that his poem's ultimate physical form will not be a *libro-registro* (register-book) in chancery minuscule (the kind of book most consistent with his audience of notaries, lawyers, judges, professors, merchants, and clerics) but a *libro da banco,* the sort of large-format, Latin scholastic text in a formal book hand which intellectuals prized above all other kinds of books (Petrucci 1995, 179–86). Perhaps, after a decade of hard work, seeing the first signs of success, he dared aspire to a higher status for his poem than the more accessible format (the *libro-registro*) that had served him so well. If so, he was mistaken, for even after the *Comedy* had achieved classic status, readers continued to prefer it in the form of a *libro-registro.*

To conclude this sketch, I cite a text of disputed authenticity, Brother Ilaro's *Epistle* to Dante's patron Uguccione della Faggiuola, written around 1314 or 1315 (Billanovich 1949; Padoan 1993). I say "disputed" because the sole surviving copy—itself a partial transcription—is contained in Boccaccio's *Zibaldone* in codex Laurenziano Pluteo XXIX 8. Even if, for whatever reason, Boccaccio forged this *Epistle,* he would have taken care to make the details plausibly consistent with contemporary publication conditions.

Three details are germane. First, toward the end, Ilaro tells Uggucione in a letter that Dante had encouraged him to gloss the *Inferno* and send him the manuscript:

> multi affectuose subiunxit, ut, si talibus vacare liceret, opus illud cum quibusdam glosulis prosequerer et meis deinde glosulis sotiatum vobis transmicterem.
>
> (*Epistola di Fra Ilaro* 12 [in Padoan 1993, 13–15])

> very affectionately he [Dante] added that if it were licit for me to waste time in such things, I might place some glosses on this work and that together with these glosses I send it on to you.

In other words, Dante expected his poem to generate hypertexts, as it did. Second, Dante tells Ilaro that he chose not to write in Latin because "vidi cantus illustrium poetarum quasi pro nichilo esse abiectos" (11) ("I have seen the songs of famous poets cast aside as worthless"). Quite unlike the young Petrarch, among others, who four or five years later would begin a long career of seeking out and reviving those very Latin classics in their unfamiliar formats and scripts, Dante rejected the language and textual formats of his Latin literary models. Finally, the *Epistle* provides a disarming portrait of Dante as producer and publisher of his own text. Traveling toward the Val Padana across the Apennines, Dante reached the monastery of Santa Croce del Corvo near Luni where a monk, Ilaro, eventually recognized him. Dante's fame (but not yet as author of the *Comedy*) has preceded him. Noting Ilaro's rapt attention, Dante

> libellum, quendam, de sinu proprio satis familiariter reseravit et liberaliter michi obtulit. "Ecce" dixit, "una pars operis mei, quod forte numquam vidisti. Talia vobis monumenta relinquo, ut mei memoriam firmius teneatis. Et cum exibuisset—quem libellum ego in gremium gratanter accepi—aperui et in eius presentia oculos cum affectione defixi. . . .
>
> (*Epistola di Ilaro* 8, [Padoan 1993])

> With great familiarity he took out a little book from his breast (or upper garment) and freely offered it to me. "Here," he said, "is one part of my work which perhaps you have never seen. Such monuments I leave you so that you will have a stronger memory of me." And when he showed it to me, I joyfully took the book on my lap and opened it.

Before beginning his journey, Dante must have concealed on his person a light, unbound *libellus* or booklet, conceivably consisting of some thirty *carte,* and corresponding, perhaps, to the first *cantica.* In his chance meeting with this obscure, admiring monk, he intuits a potential reader and explicator. Probably he was carrying more than one copy and had stored other copies elsewhere, for he could hardly give away his sole copy. He took a risk in bestowing on this stranger a text that cost him so much to produce. And, in fact, the holograph he gave Ilaro was lost, as were Ilaro's glosses, but the gamble paid off.

Note

1. All translations are mine except where noted.

2

Early Editorial Forms of Dante's Lyrics

H. Wayne Storey

THE STORY of Dante's lyric production is long, dense, and often complicated by thorny issues of attribution, authenticity, variant readings, and diverse regional traditions. In some cases the application of rigorous Lachmannian stemmatics has provided the path for resolving some of the most difficult *cruces* in this early tradition. However, combined with the apparent power of traditional, philological asseverations, this time-honored methodology designed to reveal an important part of the story has at times laid claim to the whole narrative and the final truth. For example, in the editing of the *Vita Nova,* Gorni pondered Barbi's asseverative position on the artificial partitioning of chapters in the early manuscript tradition of the *Vita Nova:* "I am trying to understand . . . what might have induced Barbi on the one hand to affirm things that were not true . . . and on the other to respect the vulgate tradition's 'partitioning' [of the *Vita Nova*], putting his readers on notice about the purely conventional nature [of his *paragrafi*] and warning future philologists against revisiting the issue" (1995, 209).[1] There is little doubt that Barbi's forceful recommendation that future textual scholars could emend the readings but should not tamper with his chapter divisions has, until Gorni's edition (Alighieri 1996), had the effect of limiting our understanding of Dante's *libello* and its textual strategies. My own evaluation of Barbi's treatment of *Non mi poriano giammai fare ammenda* (1993, 143–56) evaluated more the slavish reception of Barbi's determinations in light of his profound contribution to textual studies. Ultimately, however, one of the prices that scholarship has paid has been long-accepted textual foundations, fostered especially by Lachmannian principles, that actually block further investigation and discovery.

One of the problems created by the strip-mining effect of Lachmannian stemmatics applied to the study of lyric poetry has been the suppression of the multiple features and dynamics of what Stephen Nichols has called "the whole book" (Nichols and Wenzel 1996). It is, of course, a reasonable operation to investigate the evidence of a single sonnet found in, say, nine manuscripts and to assess the relationships among those nine copies of the poem based on common errors to arrive at an "ideal copy" of the sonnet. However, as cautious philology has established, the descent of a lyric poem is seldom direct; in short, few medieval readers and copyists ever got their hands on "ideal copies." Moreover, as we have seen confirmed in some of the poems of Dante's *Vita Nova,* earlier authorial versions constitute legitimate readings in the context of the *libello*'s prehistory. Nevertheless, textual editors who have mined the large lyric collections of early Italian poetry have often declared entire codices "reliable" or "good" while never assessing the internal roles of the individual compositions within each codex. Few are the works in a medieval manuscript that have *not* been put there according to the design of the patron commissioning the work or the specific interests of the codex's intended reader, perhaps the copyist himself. Thus, when we reflect on the fact that each of the nine textual containers of the nine handwritten copies of our hypothetical sonnet has been produced according to and in the context of specific scribal and cultural criteria of a reader or patron, a slightly different view of the medieval text emerges.

If there is one tenet of the growing field that has come to be called "material philology," it would be the recovery of the material relationships in the "whole book," constituted by each manuscript's constellation of intricate and occasionally coordinated internal and external forms of preparation and presentation, including—but not limited to—quiring, rulings, systems of diacriticals, rubrication and initials, and scribal practices of layout (or *mise en page*) as well as the influences of patronage and production values. The sometimes common cultural relationships among compositions spawned in these individual witnesses provide a vital part of the picture not only of the production of literary artifacts, but especially of their consumption.

When we turn specifically to the topic of the early editorial forms of Dante's lyrics, we might initially question the utility of reinvestigating textual terrain seemingly so thoroughly studied by Dante's venerable editors. As way of reply we need only consider the fact that without Gorni's questioning of Barbi's presentation of the *Vita Nova*'s "chapters" and his re-examination of the *libello*'s early editorial forms, we would still be reading a nineteenth-century *Vita Nuova* much the same way as we are still reading a fifteenth-century *Rerum vulgarium fragmenta* (Storey 1999, 232–35). An equally problematic and still, for the most part, unacknowledged problem resides in the attestation of the sonnet *Non mi poriano giammai fare ammenda.*

With a few representative examples from Dante's principal lyric genres, I would like to focus on a dimension that is a primary concern for the material philologist: the role of the copyist and / or compiler. Without going down the path of the complex topic of the nature of evidence itself, but certainly within the realm of the evidentiary, some of the questions that we must learn to develop more consciously are "Who is giving us this evidence?" and "How has this scribe possibly reshaped its systems of presentation?" In other words, what are the mechanisms employed by the scribe in producing a copy of a lyric within a given material context for a given patron? And how is editorial form reshaped by scribal intervention and to what end? As we move through our examples of early editorial forms of Dante's lyrics, we will be examining specifically the nature and influence of the copyist's *parti pris* in the shaping of the lyric's presentation within the unique context of the book or document.

In the case of some of the earliest attestations of Dante's poetry, the *Memoriali bolognesi,* we are privileged to have documentary sources regarding the cultural formation of the copyists. I have already discussed elsewhere (1993, 143–56) our first example, from *Memoriale* 69: Enrichetto delle Querce's 1287 copy of the sonnet that Barbi (Barbi and Maggini 1956, 186–90) list as Dante's poem LI, *Non mi poriano giammai fare ammenda.*[2]

The layout of this sonnet belongs to one of four "standard" formats for the sonnet in late thirteenth- and early fourteenth-century transcriptions. However, as I have noted (1993, 149), the punctuation (the virgule [/]) that serves to denote the end of some verses is also employed by the copyist to mark two interpretative pauses, in vv. 8 and 11, which distinguish this early copy from its later witness in the Vatican codex Chigiano L.VIII.305. Clearly, Enrichetto is a good Bolognese scribe, as the law prescribed, who (1) had a good exemplar of a poem, and (2) was well enough acquainted with literary forms of transcription to follow carefully the sonnet's structural features. Moreover, most of the Bolognese notaries in the thirteenth and fourteenth centuries were well versed in the political culture of their city as well as in its latest literary trends. We also know that before the final proscription in 1355 of poetry in these legal registers, numerous notaries filled unused legal space of their *chartae* with pieces of rhymes in Latin and the vernacular. Copies of lyrics reliably attributable to Dante and registered, often as fragments, in the *Memoriali* of 1292, 1310, and 1316 (Orlando 1981, 47) belong to this category of legal filler. A few scribes, such as Bonaccorsio di Rombolini (*Memoriale* 74 of 1288), simply utilize entire *chartae* to transcribe small lyric groupings. However, the 1287 copy of *Non mi poriano* belongs in a category unto itself. It neither accompanies other lyrics nor serves as legal filler. Rather, c. 203v is pure literary space in a legal document. Enrichetto did not need to fill this space; nor was he preserving some collected songs. Instead, the sonnet becomes monumental if not declaratory, not unlike the preliminary miniatures that grace the opening *chartae* of some of the fourteenth-century registers of Siena or Guittone's *canzone Vera vertù vero amore* in the codex Banco Rari 217 (c. 1r).[3] Nevertheless, it is unlikely that the monument is to a then relatively unknown twenty-two-year-old Florentine poet whose poem was so reliably copied in Bologna by Enrichetto. Rather, in 1287 we find ourselves only twenty-two short years after the founding of the *Memoriali,* which were instituted to help curb the extraordinary powers of the notaries in Bologna by forcing them to register their legal *acta* with a public authority (Orlandelli 1967, 197–99). In 1287 we also find ourselves not even a year after the decrees against the Asinelli, Orsi, and Garisendi families to quell civil unrest. From March to November 1286 homes around the Garisenda tower belonging to members of these families were selectively demolished.

Based on this early Bolognese copy, critics such as Lovarini and Sighinolfi questioned the authenticity of *Non mi poriano.* But their arguments could stand neither against the poem's editing through the filter of the later and firmly pro-Dante and stilnovist manuscript Chigiano L.VIII.305, which contains the poem's earliest attribution to Dante, nor against the contrary insistence of critical and cultural icons such as Ricci, Torraca, and Barbi.[4] Even if the poem is Dante's, it is likely that Enrichetto adopted it as an allegorical recall of the previous year's political policies and incidents surrounding the tower. Certainly, in the context of this 1287 *Memoriale,* the sonnet becomes a far more political document co-opted as a memory of recent history and a powerful reminder, if not a politically charged message, to the register's audiences: the public authority of Bologna and posterity.

Nevertheless, Enrichetto's "message" for posterity has been virtually erased, thanks to two facts. First of all, the notary unwittingly chose a poem precisely with an allusion to a tower that would be immortalized later in *Inf* 31.136–38. Worse yet, this same sonnet and its now alluringly Dantean "allusion" would catch the eye of the mid–fourteenth-century Florentine compiler of the codex Chigiano L.VIII.305 assembling a comprehensive guide to the poets of the Dolce Stil Novo. Once the later Florentine edits the sonnet and enters it on c. 59v among the correspondence of the *stilnovisti,* the poem's relationship with its lyric environment changes to form the basis for conjectures on Dante's early visits to Bologna.

Also in Bologna, but now dated 1300 and under the auspices of the institution of the Camera Actorum, is a small poetic collection assembled by the Tuscan notary Isfacciato di Montecatini on the now-mutilated covers of his register (374). The contents of the collection reveal a moment of cultivated Tuscan taste and admiration for both the latest in Stilnovist verse and its Sicilian origins (see Figure 1 [in order but, as in the *Memoriali,* without attribution]: Dante's *Ne li occhi porta la mia donna Amore,* Cino's *Sta nel piacer della mia donna Amore,* and the envoy of Guido Cavalcanti's *Donna me prega;* Figure 2: the anonymous *Io mi sono tucto dato a trager oro* [erroneously assigned by the later stilnovist Chigiano L.VIII.305 to Cino da Pistoia], Giacomo da Lentini's *Feruto sono isvariatamente*, and the sonnet's response in the so-called Abate di Tivoli's *Qual hom riprende altru' ispessamente*). Examining the four sonnets, we discover a layout that conveys the essential conventions of poetic transcription in the late Duecento. Initials are occasionally reserved to distinguish the *capoverso,* or first verse, and the beginning of the tercets (v. 9). The contrasting structures of the quatrains and the tercets are distinguished by the sole paragraph marker, which denotes the beginning of the *terzine* (v. 9). Isfacciato is particularly attentive to the tercet-based construction of the double sonnet (*Io mi sono tucto dato*), the same genre as Dante's *Morte villana, di pietà nemica* (see below). The first twelve verses are transcribed in lines of three verses each. But for the double sonnet's vv. 13–20, consisting of two four-verse units of three hendecasyllables and a concluding *settenario* (a verse whose final accent falls on the sixth syllable), Isfacciato lengthens the transcriptional lines to include the fourth verse, and then notes marginally with two paragraph markers both poetic groupings. His careful transcription is evident also in his corrections and treatment of the punctuation and spacing to denote the *rimalmezzo* (mid-verse rhyme) in the envoy of Cavalcanti's *canzone* (*laudata* and *persone*). Even more remarkable in this context is Isfacciato's maintenance of the last two of the three compositions in the Sicilian *tenzone* (literary debate) between Giacomo da Lentini and the Abate.[5]

In this atmosphere of heightened attention to the transcriptional details of these lyric poems, Dante's *Ne li occhi porta* (Figure 1) stands as a significant witness to the independent circulation of rhymes that would later be recycled and infused with new significance in the macrotext of the *Vita Nova* (where it will appear in the twelfth *paragrafo* [Barbi's XXI]).[6] This early editorial form not only documents De Robertis's (1954, 24–25) independent, or "estravagante," redaction of the poem, as opposed to the "organic" tradition of the *Vita Nova,* it also signals a cultural and historical context of contiguity that distinguishes itself from the now dominant, Cavalcantian interpretations fostered by the *Vita Nova.* This second feature potentially revises our understanding of the progression of influence traditionally supplied by literary historians less as a movement from Guido Cavalcanti to Cino da Pistoia than as a case of historical and regional reception almost in opposition, still in 1300, to Dante's revision in the *Vita Nova* of his own lyric program, a program that would be fulfilled only in Boccaccio's influential reading and editorial formation of Dante's poetic development.

From what is left of the now-lacerated parchment (Figure 1), we can identify authorial variants symptomatic of the poem's independent tradition: "sì che sbassando 'l viso" (v. 5, against the revised reading in the *libello* "bassando 'l viso"), "Tant'è novo miracolo" (v. 14, against the revised "Sì è novo"), and the unique "launche passa" (v. 3, against the revised "ov'ella passa").[7] However, it is the poem's function, in combination with Cino's sonnet *Sta nel piacer della mia donna Amore,* that amounts to the most conspicuous scribal variant, offering perhaps the most concrete proof of Dante's stylistic and thematic alignment with Cino, at least from the perspective of the copyist's reading. Sharing the same second half of the opening hendecasyllable ("la mia donna Amore") and founded on the same vocabulary, in this assemblage Dante's and Cino's sonnets serve the editorial purpose of illustrating the stilnovist poetic motifs of "angelico diporto" (Cino's v. 10) and the "novo miracul e gentile" (Dante's v. 14) carried forth in the eyes of the woman ("ne li occhi porta . . . Amore" [Dante, v.1] / "nel mover delli ochi il porge al core" [Cino, v. 3]), which the eyes of the lover cannot tolerate ("sbassando 'l viso, tutto smore" [Dante, v. 5]; "Soffrir non possan li ochi lo splendore" in v. 5 of Cino's *Sta nel piacer*). This historical witness of the earlier, pre-1301, reception of Dante's sonnet in thematic-linguistic combination with Cino's *Sta nel piacer* stands in contrast to the later, canonical reading of Dante's poem within the critically interpretative context of Guido Cavalcanti's *Chi è questa che ven, ch'ogn'om la mira* (cf. Pazzaglia 1973, 33–34). Rather, the thematic grouping of Dante's *Ne li occhi* and Cino's *Sta nel piacer* in our 1300 Bolognese fragment not only corroborates microscopically the trend suggested by Brugnolo (1989, 18–20) and Balduino (1984, 160–61) of thematic-linguistic linkage in the compilation of early anthologies, it especially underscores the diverse uses of lyric poems instituted by medieval poets, copyists, and patrons who copied, edited, and read differently the same poems and poetics we interpret today as solidly canonical.

This same editorial linkage between the independent tradition of *Ne li occhi* and the profound presence of Cino da Pistoia in the literary heritage of northeastern Italy is pivotal also in the fragmentary Italian section of codex Escorial e.III.23, produced probably near Padua (De Robertis 1954, 19–20) sometime during the first two decades of the fourteenth century, where we see similar systems of ordering and editorial selection at work.[8] While the entire *ordinatio* of this manuscript has yet to be examined—inasmuch as its fragmentary conditions allow—from a material point of view, previous work has revealed, especially in the case of Guittone's *libellus* on *chartae* 74r–v, that the individual *charta*—recto to verso—is the primary unit for presenting linked compositions (Storey 1993, 171–92).[9] The rubric in the hand of c. 73r announces the collection of sonnets (*soniti*) by Dante, Guido

Cavalcanti, "misser cino," and others, with the poems on the recto attributed to "Dante algieri da flor[enza]" and on the verso to "Guido chavalchanti da flor[enza]." Eight sonnets are attributed to Dante and copied systematically in a six-line format, two verses per line for the octave and three verses per line for the tercets, even when the length of the tercet's transcription compromises the external margin and approaches, or invades, the prickings. This rigorously standardized format for the *terzina* serves to unite the hands of the codex, which possibly worked in collaboration or followed precise models or a common exemplar.[10] However, in addition to the matrices of authorial attribution and the methodical *mise en page*, the eight sonnets are grouped according to another, overriding compilational rationale: the eyes, vision, the *optique amoureuse.*[11]

Each of the eight sonnets evinces not only the linguistic and thematic centrality of the eyes (*oggi* [*occhi*]) and the act of vision in the process of love, but also the subtlety of an original compiler's reading, which begins with the sonnet whose doubled use of the verb "to see" (*vedere* [vv. 1–2 "Vede . . . / chi . . . tra le donne vede"]) serves as a caption:

1. *Vede perfectamente ogni salute*
2. *Ne li oggi porta la mia dona amore*
3. *Dei oggi di quella gientil mia dama*
4. *Dei oggi de la mia dona se move*
5. *Tanto gientil e tanto honesta pare*
6. *Se 'l visso mio a la terra s'enchiena*
7. *Lo fin piaçer de quello adorno visso*
8. *Gientil pensero che [parla di voi].*

While our sense of caution in attribution and the material constitution of the artifact, as either a book or a *libellus,* did not concern so much the medieval reader / copyist, it is noteworthy that sonnets that today we assign to other poets (*Lo fin piacer di quell'adorno viso* to Cino and *De gli occhi di quella gentil dama* to an unknown poetaster) or with doubt to Dante (*Se 'l viso mio a la terra si china,* for which there is equally authoritative attribution to Cino [Contini 1995, 245]) have been integrated into what would seem to be mostly a selection of sonnets from the *Vita Nova* (nos. 1, 2, 5, 8). But four features concertedly point instead to the remnants of a song cycle that probably predated the *Vita Nova* and demonstrated different interpretative values and associations for some of the lyrics that would be recycled in the *libello*. First of all, the distance between *Vede perfectamente* and *Tanto gientil e tanto honesta pare,* reversed in order and linked in the same *paragrafo* of the *Vita Nova* (17), is enforced by the material and thematic proximity of *Se 'l visso mio* (no. 6) to *Dei oggi de la mia dona se move* (no. 4) (both noted for their thematic "fearfulness") and by the strategic variant in *Se 'l visso mio* ("la beltà vostra, pellegrina / quassi giù fra nuy" [vv. 5–6]) of "una cossa venuta / de ciello en terra a mirachol mostrare" in the thematically oppositional *Tanto gientil e tanto honesta pare* (no. 5).

The second determining feature is found in the strong linkage in the Escorial grouping between the first two sonnets, *Vede perfectamente* and our *Ne li oggi porta.* While these two sonnets will later be materially separated in their reapplications in the *Vita Nova,* here we see evidence of their prosodic, linguistic, and thematic ties. The rhymes of the tercets of *Vede perfectamente* (*-ile, -ente,* and *-ore*) are redistributed in *Ne li oggi porta* (*-ore* in vv. 1, 4, 5, 8; *-ile* [*-ille*] in vv. 9, 14; and *-ente* in vv. 10, 13), utilizing five of the same rhyme words (*amore, onore, umile, gentile,* and *mente*) and repeating, in variation, the motif in the negative of drawing to mind the overpowering spiritual nobility (note the proximity of *gentile*) of the beloved: "Et hè nnej acti soy tanto gientille, / che nexun la si pò *richar a mente*" (*Vede perfectamente,* 12–13; emphasis added) // "non se pò dicer né *tenir a mente,* / tant'hè novo mirachol e gientille" (*Ne li oggi porta,* 13–14; emphasis added). Both sonnets address the relationship between vision / greeting and beatitude, honor and humility instilled in the inextricable word play between *salute* (spiritual health) and the *saluto* (the greeting also in the form of the verb *salutare*): "La sua vista facie ogni cossa humille" (*Vede perfectamente,* v. 9), "e cuy saluta fa tremar lo core" (*Ne li oggi porta,* v. 4).

Additionally, the third and fourth factors in determining our fragment cycle are the pre–*Vita Nova* forms—mentioned earlier and found in both poems—and the unifying standardized, six-line editorial layout that defines the cohesiveness of the groupings. Taken as a whole, these four elements suggest an early relationship between the two sonnets, generated from the common theme of the nobilizing effects of Beatrice, which is disrupted and redistributed in paragraphs 12 and 17 of the *libello.* Traces of their similar thematic goals are, instead, transferred to the introductory prose that offers the rationale for each poem.[12]

In the context of the independent circulation of the lyrics of the *Vita Nova,* the mid–fourteenth-century Vatican codex Barberiniano Latino 4036 documents the problematic editorial interaction of the *libello* with earlier editorial forms of individual lyrics. Among the *chartae* of this manuscript we find evidence of some poems' *mise en page* as demonstrated in roughly contemporaneous manuscripts of the *libello* (such as Laurenziano Martelli 12, Vatican Chigiano L.VIII.305, and BNCF Magliabechiano Cl. VI 143), while the transcription of sonnets based on the *terzina* (such as *Voi che per la via d'amor passate* and *Morte villana di pietà nemica*) relies upon an older, more conventional layout which emphasizes the unique prosody of the *sonetto rinterzato.*

As we see in Figure 3 (Vatican, Barberiniano Latino 4036, c. 123), the copyist adopts the format of a single verse per line to copy the first sonnet *Piangete, amanti, poi che piange amore.*[13] On other *chartae* the scribe repeats the same format for sonnets of the *Vita Nova,* such as *A ciaschun'alma presa in gentil core* (c. 121) and *Venite ad intender li sospiri miei* (c. 130). However, to transcribe *Morte villana* the copyist turns, as he does also at c. 122, to a more traditional—if not antiquated—presentation in which the sonnet's traditional two-verse sections, or hemistiches, are extended to tercets but always in the larger context of a six-, rather than four-, verse rhyme cycle: AaB / BbA. While we have evidence of late thirteenth-century scribes contending with sixteen-verse sonnets by Monte and Guittone always within the framework of the standard two-verse-per-line transcriptional format, the dominant tercet structure of *Morte villana* requires the editorial solution utilized by the copyist of Latino 3793 for Monte's *sonetto rinterzato Coralment'ò me stesso 'n ira, cappo* (c. 168v [Storey 1993, 71–109, Fig. 2.1 for the plate]). And, as we see at lines 5–8 of Barberiniano Latino 4036 (Figure 3), the sonnet's usual tercets have been extended to four verses but are still transcribed as a *terzina* on one long line followed by a single verse on the next (CDd / C). But why has the scribe adopted this *retro* format in the midst of the relatively new, single-verse-per-line presentation for the *Vita Nova*'s sonnets? Certainly, documentation reveals that at mid-century, thanks to the *Divine Comedy,* the *terzina* had come into its own as a metrical unit that was invariably transcribed one verse per line.[14] Also at mid-century the reliable Laurentian codex Martelli 12 reveals a *Vita Nova* and independent transcriptions of its short lyrics in a single-verse-per-line format, even for *Morte villana* (c. 38r). The contemporaneous manuscript Vatican Chigiano L.VIII.305 (c. 9v) adopts a two-verse-per-line format typical for sonnets.

The principal effect of the shift in transcriptional layout is, of course, contrastive on the *charta,* highlighting the different metrical structure of the *sonetto rinterzato,* a contrast reduced—if not eliminated—in contemporary and, certainly, in subsequent copies of the *Vita Nova.* The copyist of Barberiniano Latino 4036 utilizes the format to negotiate especially the metrical and prosodic balance of the extended quatrains, presenting on the first line the A rhyme in its hendecasyllable and *settenario* variations and the tercet's concluding hendecasyllable B rhyme (AaB), which anticipates the larger unit's, the "quatrain's," resolution in variation (Bb) and final closure in its return to the initial A rhyme (thus BbA). This *mise en page* also reflects the syntactic construction instilled in the tercets (vv. 1–3, 4–6, etc.) and "quatrains" as enclosed sense units (vv. 1–6, 7–12). The contrasting formula of the two-verse-per-line layout in Chigiano L.VIII.305, c. 9v, de-emphasizes the cohesiveness of the extended quatrain's structure by highlighting first the couplets and then the refrain of the A and B rhymes: Aa / BB / bA. But it is in the extended *terzine,* now constituted by four verses on two disproportionate lines of 3 + 1, that the dominant opening and closural resonance of the C rhyme is matched and underscored by the transcriptional strategy adopted by the copyist of Barberiniano Latino 4036. The C rhyme (*-ia*) links the two extended *terzine* (vv. 13–16 and 17–20), supplies the essential rhyme words and the pivotal qualities and conditions (*cortesia, leggiadria, compagnia*) destroyed by Death, and ultimately offers the visually isolated verses which close, like death, the woman's "loving nobility" ("amorosa leggiadria") and the possibility of seeing her presence ("compagnia").

The decision of the copyist of Barberiniano Latino 4036 to use the older, *terzina*-based format, which might have even been germane to his exemplar, to copy *Morte villana* does not reflect a version that changes the thematic substance of the poetic lament. Aside from the contiguous nature of *Morte villana* and *Piangete amanti* in both the *Vita Nova* and in Barberiniano Latino 4036, we have no way of knowing if *Morte villana* served before the *Vita Nova* its later function as a prosodic variation of the preceding *planctus Piangete, amanti, poi che piange Amore.* The several editorial versions of the poem that have come down to us would thus be indifferent if it were not for Dante's prose explanation (4, 12) of the four parts of *Morte villana* which fall not according to the syntactic-prosodic divisions emphasized by the layout of Barberiniano Latino 4036, but at vv. 1, 4, 7, and 19.

One of the features that probably made the *Vita Nova* so unique to medieval copyists was its material closure. It is a self-contained booklet closed in its form and unopenable in its narrative instructions to the inclusion of extraneous lyric materials. The *Vita Nova* should have been a medieval scribe's dream text to copy. A macrotext composed and arranged under the guiding metaphor of transcription and glossing, the *Vita Nova* also provides the scribe with clear indications of literary form (sonnet, *canzone, ballata*), rubrics and sections ("cominciamento," "proemio," and the all important "paragrafi maggiori"), interpretative divisions within the text (for punctuation, capitals, and *mise en page*), and even the placement of glosses.[15] For a text that communicated so much through the language of the craft of the medieval scribe, it is amazing to see the diverse levels of quality in the work's fourteenth-century copies. Suffice it to say here that one of the copyists most responsive to the forms of the *Vita Nova* and other Dantean lyrics is the scribe of Martelli 12 in the Biblioteca Laurenziana.

Produced between 1330 and 1340, the probably Umbrian Martelli 12 is a miscellany that contains, among other compositions, an *Expositione de songni,* a treatise on dreams, in Latin (cc. 22r–25r) and, in a different hand, the vernacular (cc. 32v–34r).[16] Between these two treatises, in a new gathering compiled by a new hand, we find a section of *canzoni* and *ballate* by Dante, Cavalcanti, and Caccia da Castello beginning at the top of a recto with the annunciative six-line painted initial C of *Così nel mio parlare vollio esser aspro* (c. 26r).[17] These poems are preceded at the close of a quaternion, on cc. 25r–v, by a copy in order of poems 2 through 7 of the *Vita Nova,* that is from *O voi che per la via d'Amor passate* to *Tucti li miei penser parlan d'Amore,* in the same two-column presentation transcribed—by a hand different from the B hand responsible for the extended Dante section—one verse per line.[18] These transcriptions do not reveal a radically different tradition or significant changes in editorial format from the same lyrics enclosed in the *libello* which follows in two final gatherings, cc. 35–51.[19] Rather, given especially their order of presentation and the layout of sonnets and the *ballata* in one verse per line, these "extracted" copies seem to come directly from a copy of the *Vita Nova* (Barbi 1932, xxviii), suggesting that early on in the tradition of the *libello* the editorial forms of the poems were solidified and somewhat protected by the little book's multiple literary and material mechanisms of closure. The Martelli copy of the *Vita Nova* corroborates this fundamental, historically early shift in editorial form, particularly in light of the formats in which we find Dante's independent lyrics. When we compare the single-verse-per-line scribal format of both copies of Dante's *Ballata, i' vo che tu ritrovi Amore* in Martelli, c. 25v, with the Martelli copy of Cavalcanti's *ballate mezzane, La forte e nova mia disaventura* (c. 29v) and *Vedete ch'io son un ke vo piangendo* (c. 29v), we notice that the copy of Cavalcanti adopts the same diacritical and unit distinctions but in a generally prose-like transcriptional style similar to the strategy for the *canzone* in most Due- and Trecento manuscripts. This scribal convention for the *ballata* is corroborated in Chigiano L.VIII.305 and dates back to an even more articulated system of marking the stanza's *piedi* (for example: AbC AbC), spatially separating the *piedi*'s two parts or *mutazioni,* and double marking the *volta* (for example CDDX), as we see in the copy of the *balata Rosa fresca novella* in the late thirteenth-century codex Banco Rari 217 (c. 70r [cf. Leonardi 2000]).

Often revered for its attributions and accuracy, Chigiano L.VIII.305, also from the mid–fourteenth century, reveals in its transcription of the *ballata* the cultural collision of the two transcriptional forms of the poem. The Florentine copyist organizes his transcription (cc. 12r–v) according to the divisions of the prosodic units of refrain (XYYX), *piedi* as a single grouping (AbCAbC), and *volta* (CDDX), distinguishing the opening refrain with a two-line initial which extends well past the *colonnina* (*Ballata i' vo' che tu ritrovi*) and marking the subsequent units into *piedi* and *volta* with a paragraph marker. Copying the verses of each unit as run-on prose with verse markers (or commas [/]), this transcriptional method emphasizes, like its late-Duecento ancestor Banco Rari 217, the traditional prosodic parts of the genre. Yet, the influence of Dante's prose explanation of the three parts of the poem alters that traditional transcriptional layout.

As we see in Figure 4 (c. 11v), at the close of v. 30 (line 10: "di che domandi amor, che sedegle vero"), the copyist fails to start a new line of transcription for the *volta* (vv. 31–34) and inserts a paragraph marker in the left margin at v. 30. The next paragraph marker correctly signals the beginning of the next unit, the *piedi* (vv. 35–40), but the scribe concludes the stanza at v. 39 (notice the space after "reman tu qui collei"), copying v. 40 ("e del tuo servo ciò che vuoli ragiona"), rather than 41 (the initial verse of the concluding *volta* [41–44]), on a new line of transcription. The copyist concludes this final unit at v. 42, leaving space after *pace* and starting a new line, with a new paragraph marker, for the *ballata*'s envoy and final hemistich on a single line: "Gentil ballata mia . . . / . . . che tu n'aggie honore" (43–44).

The copyist's apparent compromise of the prosodic units that his layout is intended to highlight is not, as it first appears, purely a moment of inattentiveness (line 10) which throws off the diacritical marking and transcriptional spacing of the *ballata.* Rather, the error suggests that the copyist of our Chigiano codex was working from an exemplar in which the verses of the *ballata* were transcribed, as in the Martelli copy, one verse per line, and that he was recasting the *ballata* in the older transcriptional format. The error at vv. 39 and 40 reveals our scribe trying to reconstitute three prosodic units of relatively equal length between vv. 30 and 44. But the influence of the exemplar and Dante's explanatory prose ultimately controls his transcription. In its address to the poem, the envoy ("Gentil ballata mia") in his exemplar is marked and separated by the copyist from its prosodic unit (the final *volta*) to adhere to Dante's declared structure for the *ballata:* "The second part begins here 'Con dolce sono'; the third here 'Gentil ballata'" (5, 23 [Barbi XII, 16]). Notably, this same separation of the final two verses from the body of the *ballata* is corroborated by the equally problematic, and contemporary, Magliabechiano Cl. VI 143 (c. 3v).[20] This moment in the scribe's negotiation of the influence of interpretation on his own transcription, especially in light of Dante's prose instructions, marks a significant crux in the treatment of Dante's prosody in the revised context of the *Vita Nova.* For the microscopic evidence of the treatment of the *ballata* suggests distinct textual and material changes in the function and interpretation of Dante's lyrics within the frame of the *libello.*

Certainly, one of the primary "tensions" of the *Vita Nova* is the relationship between the explanations and historical narrative of the prose on the one hand and the lyrical meditations of the poetry on the other. While we have evidence that lyric poems circulated in the "containers" of prose letters, equally important witnesses suggest that independent books of poetry, probably circulated in what we think of as pamphlets today, likely bore lyric collections of a single poet or poets in correspondence in a quire or two. Like that of the *razos* and *vidas* of the Provençal tradition, the prose frame of the *Vita Nova* ultimately forces the historicization, the narrative integration of lyric meditation into the *libello*'s larger purpose of telling a story that supersedes each poetic microtext but to which each poem must contribute. At one point in that narrative, Dante makes the rationalization for the longer form of the *canzone* over the sonnet on the ground that the shorter form is inadequate for his narrative intentions: "E non credendo poter ciò narrare in brevitade di sonetto, cominciai allora una canzone, la quale comincia *Sì lungiamente*" (18, 2 [Barbi XXVII]). This more narrative contribution does not mean the elimination of the purely lyric markers that distinguish, for example, the sonnet. Rather, as we have noted, Dante attempts to safeguard the exact lyric content of his little book with repetitive constructions in the prose. However, for those lyrics produced before the compilation of the *Vita Nova* and reutilized in its macrotextual structure, the challenge of (re)narrativizing the poems involved also the alteration of their material poetics in relation to the larger and now hosting material construction of the *libello*'s "story."

The final lyric genre we shall briefly examine is Dante's *canzone*, the long, stanzaic form often used for more doctrinal meditations, such as *Donne ch'avete intellecto d'amore* or *Le dolci rime d'amor ch'i' solia.* The pre-Petrarchan transcriptional layout of this genre represents perhaps the only legitimate recipient of the once-standard formula used by traditional philologists to describe medieval scribal forms: *a mo' di prosa* (in run-on prose form).[21] Yet this does not mean that the *canzone* did not appear in more prosodically articulated layouts. The two distinct transcriptional formats for two *canzoni* in the *Vita Nova, Donne ch'avete intellecto d'amore* and *Donna pietosa e di novella etate,* in Magliabechiano Cl. VI 143 (respectively on cc. 6r and 8v) as well as the cautiously standardized *mise en page* of the same *canzoni* in Chigiano L.VIII.305 (respectively on cc. 14v–15r and 18v–19r) demonstrate fundamentally similar scribal criteria applied to the genre: (1) a painted initial for the first verse, or *capoverso,* (2) distinction by space and / or paragraph markers of the two principle prosodic units of the *canzone:* the stanzas and the envoy, and division of verses by commas (/) with an occasional *punctus* (.) to close the stanza or, rarely, a verse.[22] This format goes back to the oldest transcriptions of *canzoni* in the Italian Duecento tradition and is, I believe, probably imposed by most copyists, including Boccaccio, on the *canzoni* of the *Vita Nova.* Even Martelli 12 abandons its usual single-verse-per-line presentation for the *canzoni* of the *Vita Nova,* adopting instead the prose format with stanza markers of the *canzoni* transcribed outside the *libello*'s frame in the preceding quinternion (on cc. 26r–32r).[23]

In transcriptional formats such as those of the Martelli and Chigiano L.VIII.305 codices, the burden of distinguishing poetry from prose, confronted by most fourteenth-century copyists, is carried by the stanzaic layout, paragraph markers, and a minimal use of initials, not to mention Dante's prose apparatus of repeated formulae to signal the shifts. In fact, it is the uncertainty of the copyist's handling of these diacritical and presentational features in Magliabechiano Cl. VI 143 that confirms the importance of the *Vita Nova*'s material dynamic. Consequently, alterations in the *canzone*'s *mise en page* tend to suggest the interference of a strong material tradition in the exemplar. One such case would be the apparently fourteenth-century interpretation of the first four verses of the opening stanza of *Donne ch'avete intellecto d'amore* (Martelli 12, c. 41r [Figure 5]) copied purposefully as a proem to the poem. The copyist transcribes these first four verses not only as a separate prosodic unit but also in a single-verse-per-line presentation. He closes the four-verse proem with a full stop after *mente* and starts a new line of transcription with a paragraph marker and indentation at v. 5, "Io dico che pensando 'l suo valore," and continues the rest of the stanza in a run-on prose transcription. This presentational method does not appear in either *Donna pietosa* (c. 44r) or *Li occhi dolenti* (c. 47v), ruling out the influence of Dante's prose divisions which follow in the *paragrafo,* or in the *canzoni* of the preceding quinternion, and not even in Cavalcanti's emblematic *Donna me prega* (c. 28r).[24] Rather, the copyist either sets off the proem in the distinctive single-verse format as a form of interpretative recognition of the *canzone*'s notoriety or follows an exemplar in which the proem was separate from the rest of the stanza and, more important, was in a single-verse-per-line layout. Such a moment of distinction between the two formats within the transcription of a *canzone* represents the tension in the relationship between transcription and poetics. The proem's very recognizable opening verses, already historicized particularly by *Purgatorio* 24, override the *canzone*'s conventional format and the issue of writing space in the codex.

But, as we remember, the third *canzone* in the *Vita Nova* is a stanza of a *canzone* interrupted by the revelation of Beatrice's death, *Sì lungiamente m'à tenuto Amore,* which potentially changes our understanding of the role and general interpretation of genre and its transcription in this century of cultural transition. The case of this stanza presents numerous difficulties for medieval and modern readers alike, first in the identification of its genre and secondly in its role at the critical moment in the *Vita Nova*'s poetic and narrative trajectory, a moment of structural and poetic *ruptio.*

The copyists of Martelli 12 and Chigiano L.VIII.305 and Boccaccio in his two copies, Archivo y Biblioteca Capitulares (Toledo) 104.6 and Chigiano L.V.176, recognize the genre and follow the standard transcriptional formula (stanzaic) for *Sì lungiamente.* Once again, however, the difficulties encountered by Magliabechiano Cl. VI 143's copyist prove instructive. In fact, his transcription of the fourteen-verse stanza as a sonnet could suggest two culturally fundamental scenarios. The first is that in his exemplar the stanza is written in the traditional, prosaic form, which he then, reading the fourteen verses, attempts to interpret and restructure as a sonnet, alas with a *settenario* (the d rhyme at v.11 and a concluding rhyming couplet [EE: vv. 13–14]). The alternative recalls the Martelli transcription of the four-verse proem of *Donne ch'avete intellecto d'amore* and suggests that our challenged Magliabechiano scribe found in his exemplar a stanza copied in the same format as a sonnet, that is, one verse per line, and attempted to convert the transcription to make the poem fit into his planned space. This second scenario is supported by the stanza's transcription in Barberiniano Latino 4036 (Figure 6), a contemporary of Magliabechiano Cl. VI 143. Barberiniano Latino 4036 reflects a unique interest in the genre of the sonnet, copying in order all but one of the sonnets in the *Vita Nova.*[25] The inclusion of *Sì lungiamente* among the carefully selected and ordered sonnets suggests that, like the Magliabechiano scribe, this copyist, Gino Guidinelli, also interpreted his exemplar as a sonnet in spite of Dante's clear indication of its genre, if Gino had a *Vita Nova* before him.[26]

The *Vita Nova* is, among other things, an open experiment in the craft of representing the relationship between a life, filled with still-uninterpreted signs, and the poetic production that serves as a vehicle for its interpretation. Like the purposeful inclusion of both beginnings of *Era venuta nella mente mia* (23, 7 [Barbi XXXIV]), to which medieval copyists reacted in different ways, the fragmenting of the stanza by the citation from the Lamentations of Jeremiah ("Quomodo sedet sola civitas"), a bold narratological strategy analogous to Cavalcante's interruption of Farinata, must have proved difficult for all but the most careful readers and copyists. Because of its narratological status as a fragmented text, necessarily interrupted by the story the *Vita Nova* has to tell, *Sì lungiamente* is subsequently defined by its poetic representation of a narrative trajectory no longer tenable in the context of the *libello.* Instead, its role in the *libello* is, narratively speaking, a place to which the poet's story can never return. Thus the confusion of the genre of *Sì lungiamente* is not just the symptom of a materially challenging presentation in the exemplars used by the copyists of Magliabechiano Cl. VI 143 and Barberiniano Latino 4036, but also a reflection of its textual unimportance relative to the context of the larger story of the *Vita Nova* which it serves within the frame of the *libello. Sì lungiamente* answers the question of what Dante was writing when he heard the news of Beatrice's death. But, like the question "what were you doing when you heard the big news?" it is transcended by the news itself; its "value" is oriented completely toward the event that interrupts it. Even outside the narrative frame of the *Vita Nova,* as we find the text in Barberiniano Latino 4036, the stanza *qua* sonnet defines itself still according to the structure of the macrotext. It is the beginning of a longer text (*canzone*) motivated, according to Dante's prose explanation, precisely by the need to narrate a longer part of the story of the poet's openness to Beatrice's goodness and how that goodness took root in him because the shorter sonnet form was inadequate (*Vita Nova* 18, 2). Dante's especially careful linkage of transcriptional form and genre to thematic and narrative structures in the context of *Sì lungiamente* proves in the *Vita Nova* an ironic narratological set-up as we settle in for the *canzone*'s long, and never delivered, exposition. In its actual brevity and textual suspension, *Sì lungiamente* renders its poetic condition uncertain (Barberiniano Latino 4036), open to additional fragmentation (Martelli 12), and even reformulated as the sonnet it was intended to supersede (Magliabechiano Cl. VI 143).

From the earliest forms and circulation of Dante's lyrics to the seemingly more protected constructs of the *Vita Nova* in its subtle permutations at the hands of early copyists, it is the scribe's relationship both to the use of the lyrics he has to copy and to the material mechanisms of production in the context of his document that mediates the forms in which these poems were actually read by medieval readers. While the materiality of these early lyric forms does not represent to our modern editorial eyes an orderly and schematic system of presentation, it is nevertheless the shape that lyric poetry took before the scribal reforms of the early fifteenth century.

Notes

1. We should keep in mind the contexts of Barbi's insistence upon the artificial "chapters" imposed on the text of the *Vita Nova* in order to standardize a system of reference for its sections. The first context is the cultural environment of Barbi's stand on behalf of his nascent neo-Lachmannian stemmatics in Italy and in opposition to Italian proponents of best-text critical editing, a stand reflected in his 1907 edition of the *Vita Nova*, but especially in his 1893 article in the first issue of the *Giornale dantesco* on the future of Dante studies in Italy. His cultural mission of a systematic recovery of historically authentic Dantean texts was bolstered by a nationalistic agenda focused on the homecoming of Dante studies ("il desiderio di evitare in futuro il biasimo che i lavori più importanti e proficui si compiessero altrove che da noi" [Barbi 1934, 1]). However, still in 1897, in a review signed only as "Z," Barbi's method of reconstructing a new text, the conjectured archetype, was deemed to present "very grave dangers" (515). The second context is editorial. In truth, the practice of dividing the work into forty-two or forty-three chapters dates back even to before Alessandro Torri's 1843 edition, and represents more Barbi's attempt to settle arbitrarily the problem of diverse critical apparatuses. However, that Barbi was blind to the hermeneutic impact of such arbitrary decisions regarding the verifiable materiality of a medieval artifact such as the *Vita Nova* demonstrates the necessity of integrating material philological analyses into our philological and interpretative assessments.

2. See Storey 1993, 148 for the photographic reproduction of c. 203v.

3. See Storey 2000, 93–96, for a discussion of the first *charta* in the context of the overall program of the quires of Banco Rari 217. For the photographic reproduction of the *charta*, see Leonardi 2000.

4. For a review of this debate, see Storey 1993, 147–55.

5. Typically, as we see from the *siciliani* and the *siculo-toscani* to Petrarch, the otherwise tenuous material cohesion of the multiple contributions to *tenzoni* is consistent only in those quires of medieval anthologies

devoted to the *tenzone* as a genre or in authorial working copies (for example, Petrarch's Vaticano Latino 3196).

6. All citations not taken from manuscripts of the *Vita Nova* come from Gorni's edition (Alighieri 1996) according to his suggested paragraphs (in bold) followed by the line numbers in lightface (example: 28, 2). Where helpful, the chapter divisions devised by Barbi (1907 and 1932) are indicated parenthetically.

7. De Robertis (1954, 25) declares "launche" the genuine reading in the tradition in opposition to scribal trivialization of the redaction in "là dove" (Escorial e.III.23).

8. Though a fragment, the Italian section of the codex demonstrates not only a statistical preponderance of Cino's poetry but especially a distribution of attributions to Cino in diverse scribal circumstances, including poetic correspondence and small regionally representative compilations. For a broader and yet more microscopic examination of Cino in Dante's poetic production, see Brugnolo's recent reassessment (1993).

9. This orientation is particularly evident on *charta* 83 in the renewal of the attribution to "Dante algieri" at the top of the verso after the entire recto has been devoted to sonnets attributed to Dante and before the section on 83v dedicated to Cino's poems.

10. I am indebted to Roberta Capelli for her firsthand assessments of the manuscript and for posing the question of the possible contemporaneity of the hands, as well as possible revisions for the codex's dating. The similarity of the treatment of the *terzina* in the hand that copies Guittone's *Trattato,* c. 74r–v, corroborates this standardizing model.

11. The organizing principle of the selections reliably from Cavalcanti on *charta* 73v would seem to be similar but far less rigorous in light of the presence of *Tu m'ay sì piena de dolor la mente, S'io prego questa dona che pietate,* and especially *Beltà de dona e de saccente core,* in which vision either plays no central role or, as in *Beltà,* does not appear.

12. In the *Vita Nova* it is Dante's prose commentary that often supplies the temporal and prefatory linkages. For *Ne li occhi porta la mia donna Amore* Dante notes that his lyric is designed "to demonstrate how she awakens Love . . . even when it is not present, how she brings it into being through her miraculous works" (v. 12), and for *Vede perfectamente ogne salute* he introduces his intention to "relate how her spiritual qualities [*virtute*] took root and grew in other women" (v. 17).

13. The numbering of the paper *chartae* of Barberiniano Latino 4036 is actually a later pagination which counts each side of the *charta.* Consequently, the manuscript's 98 *chartae* are numbered 1–196. See De Robertis 1960–70, no. 323 (42 [1965], 435).

14. Petrarch's experimentation with the *terzina* in the *Triumphi* in Vatican Latino 3196 shows its development as a strictly single-verse-per-line construction (Storey 1999).

15. We recall, for example, Dante's clear instructions on the placement of the *divisioni* in 20 [Barbi XXXI]: "la dividerò prima che io la scriva; e cotale modo terrò da qui innançi," a phraseology echoed in the scribe's marginal admission of changing his transcriptional strategy in Riccardiano 1088 (see Storey 1993, 226–27).

16. While I will treat more fully the problematic description and interpretation of this important manuscript in a separate study of the fourteenth-century manuscripts of the *Vita Nova,* it should be noted here that I follow the modern numbering of the *chartae* found in the lower right corner of the recto and proposed by Papa (1884, 193–94) and De Robertis (1962, no. 243) rather than the erroneous numbering in Barbi (1932, xxvii–xxviii) and *Mostra* (1957, 30–31), in which the ancient guard leaf plays a significant role (cf. Maniaci 1996, 136). However, given the importance of the scribal participation in the compilation of this codex, we should rapidly note that the codex's three principal hands correspond to the three basic units of production in seven, not four, fascicles. Hand A is responsible for cc. 1–9 (one gathering); hand B pens cc. 12–25 (two gatherings); and hand C seems to have copied most of the Dantean material, cc. 26r–31v; hands D and E—in the same quinternion with C and F—complete Dante's *canzoni* through c. 32r; hand F adds the treatise on dreams in the vernacular (cc. 32r–34r); and hand G copies cc. 35r–51r (three gatherings). The blank verso of c. 34 announces the incipit of the *Vita Nova* in the next gathering (cc. 35–43, a quinternion missing the first half of the bifolium of c. 43).

17. The codicological construction of the fascicles of Martelli 12 is not, as Barbi (1934, xxvii–xxviii) proposes (and *Mostra* 1957 [30–31] follows), in four quinternions, but rather a far more complex compilation composed of irregular and regular quinternions, ternions, quaternions, and an inserted bifolium. The implications of this construction on the composition of the manuscript is considered in my study on the fourteenth-century material tradition of the *Vita Nova.*

18. The scribes of Martelli 12 looked to complete the quaternion with material that would anticipate the next section, the quinternion that would contain longer poems by Dante, Cavalcanti and Caccia.

19. Significantly, the *libello* is copied on two quires of five and then three bifolia each, that is, a quinternion missing a charta and a quaternion (see below and cf. Barbi's description [1932, xxvii–xxviii] of cc. 36–52 [*sic*]). This seemingly technical distinction, and correction of our previous understanding of the manuscript's material composition, reveals an important cultural orientation, around 1340, toward a problematic text attached to courtly and scientific (philosophical) works.

20. The initial two-column presentation of Magliabechiano Cl. VI 143 hosts sonnets in single-verse-per-line layout. However, the *ballata* is transcribed as run-on prose without distinguishing the poem's prosodic units, except for the envoy.

21. Petrarch's diverse transcriptional formats for the *canzone* reflected subgenres, such as the *canzone unissonas,* and differentiated between stanzaic constructions of varying lengths (see Storey 1993, 283–314).

22. The Magliabechiano copy of *Donne ch'avete intellecto d'amore* distinguishes only the first verse and the envoy. The stanzas are run together. *Donna pietosa* in the same codex follows the more conventional method of separating stanzas.

23. These *canzoni* include, among others, *Così nel mio parlar vollio essere aspro, Io son venuto al puncto dela rota, Tre donne entorno al cor mi son venute,* as well as *canzoni* by Guido Cavalcanti.

24. One occurrence of the insertion of a paragraph marker does appear at v. 5 of the sonnet *Videro li occhi miei quanta pietate* (Martelli 12, c. 49r).

25. *Gentil pensero che parla di voi* is missing in the ordered compilation as are four of the *canzoni,* the *ballata,* and the prose.

26. Additionally, the Barberiniano Latino 4036 copy uniquely aligns itself with the defective copy of *Sì lungiamente* in Martelli 12, opting for the reading of "sento" as the principal verb in v. 10 ("chi i mei spiriti sento gir parlando"). Martelli reads "suspiri sento gir parlando," similar to Magliabechiano Cl. VI 143: "gli miei sospiri gir parlando." Martelli 12 is missing v. 14.

Figure 1: Bologna, Archivio di Stato, Camera Actorum 374 (1300). Reprinted by permission.

Figure 2: Bologna, Archivio di Stato, Camera Actorum 374 (1300). Reprinted by permission.

Figure 3: Vatican, Barberiniano Latino 4036, c. 123. Reprinted by permission.

Figure 4: Vatican, Chigiano L.VIII.305, c. 11v. Reprinted by permission.

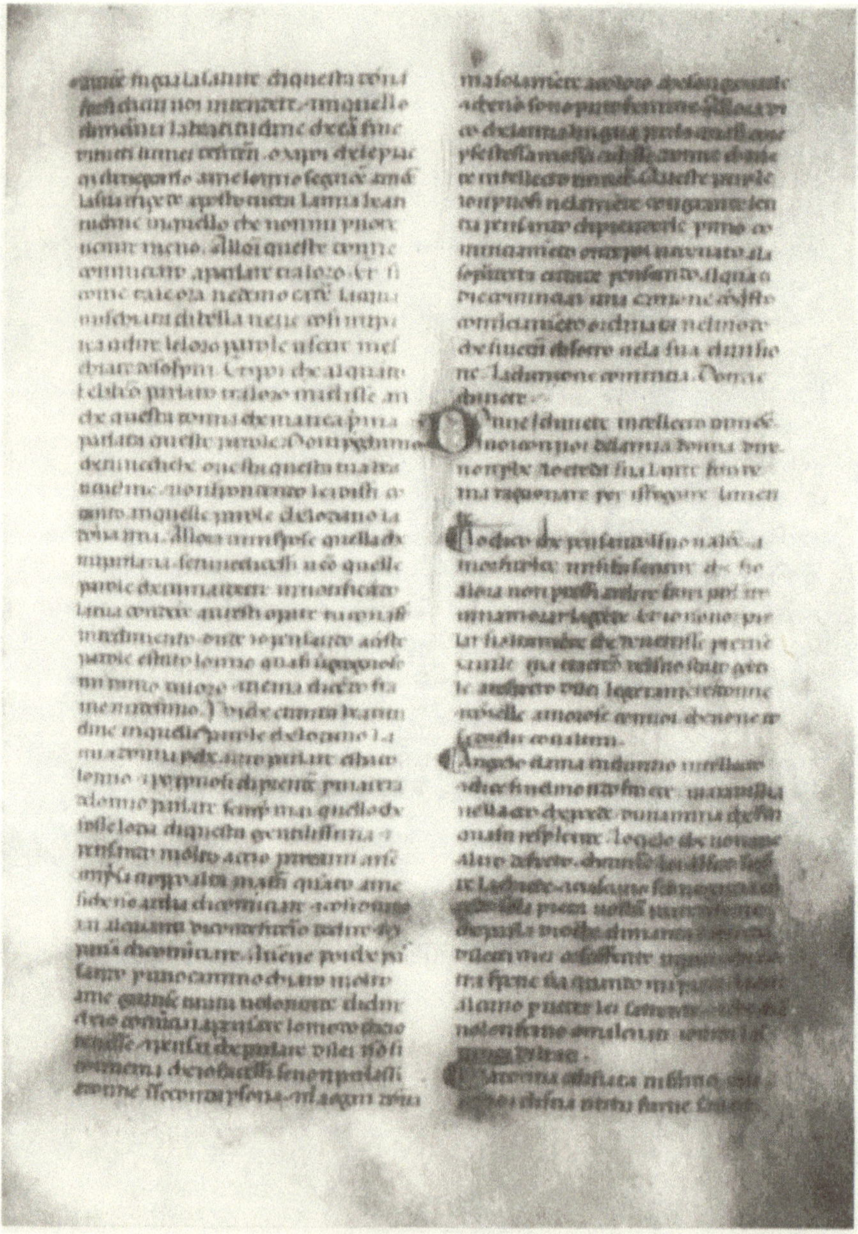

Figure 5: Florence, Biblioteca Mediceo-Laurenziana, Martelli 12, c. 41r. Reprinted by permission.

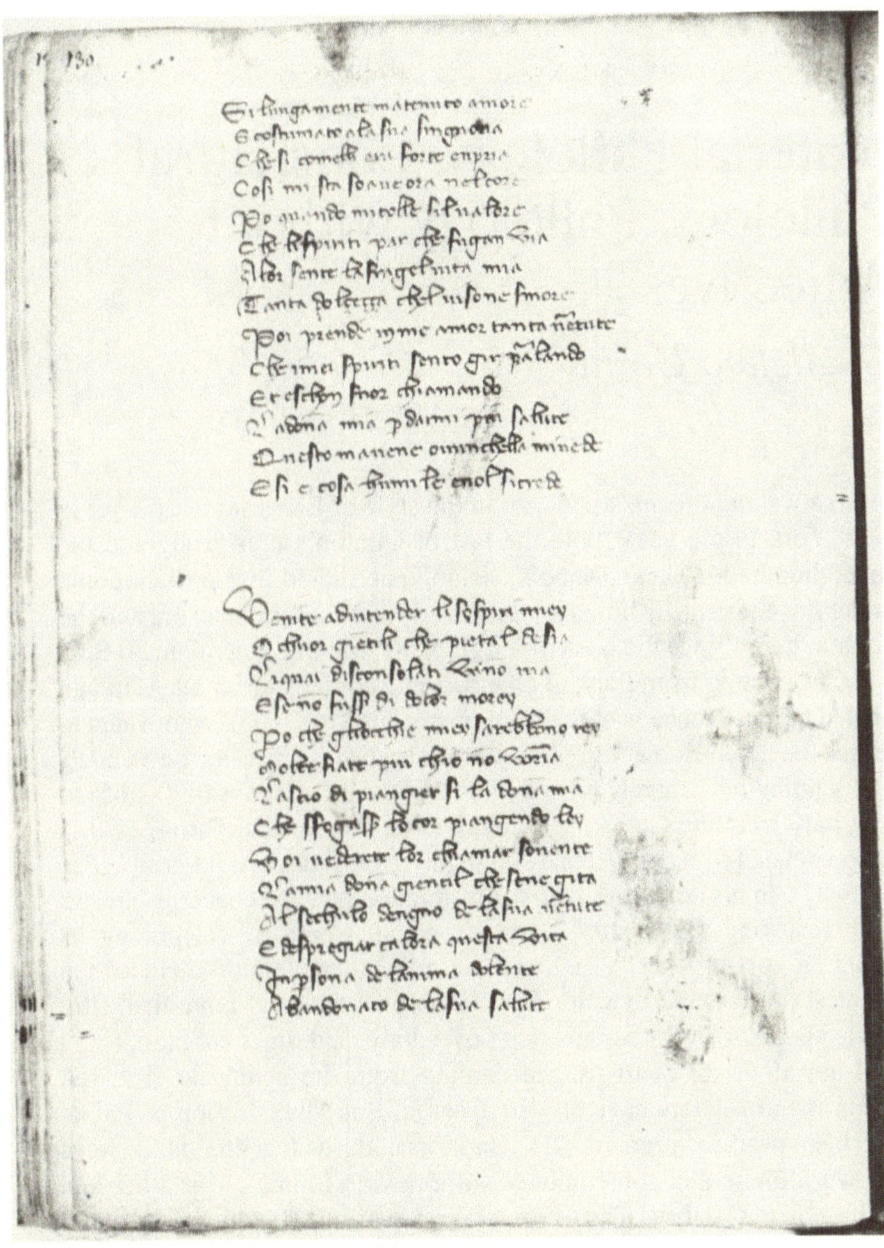

Figure 6: Vatican, Barberiniano Latino 4036, c. 130. Reprinted by permission.

3

Material Philology, Conjectural Philology, Philology without Adjectives

Guglielmo Gorni

I HAD a waking dream, somewhat in the style of Borges. I wasn't yet in New York in the year 2000, the last of Clinton's presidency and the seven-hundredth since Dante's vision, but rather in Constantinople under the emperor Justinian, in the year 530 of the Christian era and the six-hundredth since the birth of Virgil, who "Mantua genuit" in 70 B.C.

I was coming from Italy, to take part in a conference on the Mantuan poet. The conference is at the wish of Justinian (527–65), who wants to revive the fallen Roman Empire from the east. He is battling the Vandals and sending his generals Narses (478–574) and Belisarius (490–565) to free Italy from the Goths: "e al mio Belisar commendai l'armi, / cui la destra del ciel fu sì congiunta, / che segno fu ch'i' dovessi posarmi" (*Par* 6.25–27). In his ambitious plan for restoration he even concerns himself with renewing the literary glory of ancient Rome by celebrating its supreme poet-prophet, Virgil, six centuries after his birth. "Honor the greatest poet" is the byword. The Western Empire fell more than fifty years ago, in 476. Barbarians reign over Italy, and times are hard.

I am alone, or nearly so, in coming from the peninsula. The last Latin men of letters have all disappeared. Ennodius, bishop of Pavia, has been dead for years (d. 521), and Cassiodorus (ca. 485–580) shuns all worldliness and contemplates withdrawing to one of his *Vivarium* in his native Calabria. The gravest loss, Severinus Boethius, was put to death by King Theodoric in 524. He would indeed have honored Virgil as befitted him, but his body "giace / giuso in Cieldauro" (*Par* 10.127–28) for six years now. My teacher and the teacher of "my betters" at Pavia: but who could reclaim his legacy? No, from Italy there no longer comes the voice of any master. From the shores of Africa Fulgentius might join us here; his *Expositio virgilianae continentiae* has stirred a lot of discussion because of its deconstruction of the books of the *Aeneid* as an allegory of human life, in four groups of three. But not even Fulgentius roused himself to come to our Virgilian conference, proclaimed in the old Byzantium or new Rome, that was rebaptized Constantinople a couple of centuries ago and is also called, familiarly, the *Big Apple*.

Justinian, at this time, has not yet extracted "d'entro le leggi il troppo e 'l vano" (*Par* 6.12), a work he will undertake later. Right now the emperor is engrossed in dreams of a Latin restoration. He has not yet converted to orthodoxy and believes that Christ has only one nature, the divine:

> E prima ch'io a l'ovra fossi attento,
> una natura in Cristo esser, non piùe,
> credea, e di tal fede era contento;
> ma 'l benedetto Agapito, che fue
> sommo pastore, a la fede sincera
> mi dirizzò con le parole sue.
> Io li credetti . . .
>
> (*Par* 6.3–18)

and all around him revolve heretics, schismatics, and innovators: Arians, Monophysites, Nestorians, Pelagians, Montanists, and Aphthartodocetists, with a thousand abstract claims and endless clamor. Who understands anything anymore? Where does the truth lie? In Italy, Queen Theodolinda (d. 625) is still too far in our future to impose Roman orthodoxy on her subjects. Soon, by all accounts, the Nika revolt (January 532) will break out here, the Blues against the Greens at the hippodrome: they shout "Nika" (conquer) as one would shout "Go Italy" at the stadium: a sports cheer that becomes a political slogan. It has never been seen, and who knows if it will happen again.

I am among the few, as I was saying, to come from Italy, and the only one, or nearly so, allowed to deliver my discourse in Latin, the language of the poet we are all honoring, at a conference that speaks Greek, the master language of the Mediterranean. I do not know if it is a privilege or a condemnation, if my speech is the echo of a deathbound language, tolerated out of curiosity or condescension, or if it is rather the sign of neo-Latin hope. The fact remains that I am here, on the shores of the Bosporus, to ponder the difficult times that we are called upon to live, adapting the topical theme of the *Ubi sunt?* Rome has fallen. Will we be able to save Virgil? And will Virgil be able to deliver civilization and the humanities from the barbarians?

The title of my contribution is "Utrum philologia rectae verborum interpretationi prosit an non," whether philology is of use in the study of texts—whether it belongs to a now-outmoded world, like the geomancer's art ("quando i geomanti lor Maggior Fortuna / veggiono in orïente, innanzi a l'alba, / surger per via che poco le sta bruna" [*Purg* 19.4–6]), or, like astrology, once so esteemed by Dante and now proscribed by modern science. Or whether, instead, some utility may be found in it, albeit limited, such as the customary maintenance of the patrimony: a necessary but tiresome activity, to be delegated to those who have no ideas, or who do not venture to have any. The philologist possesses by trade certain technical skills (in ancient languages, prosody, and paleography) and, thanks to this knowledge at once refined and elementary, oversees the textual tradition and examines the writings in their materiality, leaving to hermeneutics, to exegesis, and to literary criticism the pleasures of the text and what matters most. Having verified the textual correctness, cleared up, or at least circumscribed certain obscure points of language or complex tradition, the philologist should step aside, his work complete. It was good that I came here not to resolve or to complicate a *crux,* but to perform something of a public examination of conscience.

I am exaggerating somewhat, perhaps mine is more a caricature than a portrait. But current opinion is that philology should be treated with care, like an elderly and respectable lady; and having once paid her the homage she is due, it is better to keep one's distance and leave that tedious, drawn out, and contentious jurisdiction to those born with such a vocation or fancy. It is a science, say its devotees, but so controversial and litigious a science that the profane have the right to wonder what its heuristic bases are. Physicists also disagree among themselves, but some certainties are in the public domain. They may quarrel for decades, but then they will all agree on certain points and turn to something else. In philology, no; it is not that simple. It has been more than thirty years since Petrocchi published his critical edition of the *Commedia,* and the debate is not over yet. Not only do individual textual points, or *cruces,* resurface unresolved, or resolved in another fashion. This is to be expected in a normal dialectic. But there are those who actually start over from the very beginning of the question, with other criteria and on a different basis: Antonio Lanza, for example, who has already published two editions of the *Commedia* (1995; 1996) and is preparing a third. Petrocchi based his text on the "antica vulgata" (his death did not permit him to obtain the most recent *varia lectio*). Lanza is preparing his "according to the oldest Florentine manuscripts." And there is a third who has undertaken the work, Federico Sanguineti (2001), who proposed a different *stemma codicum* from Petrocchi's and, in my opinion, one better founded, listing conjunctive and even archetypal errors heretofore unnoted. You cannot even agree on the errors in the archetype? might object someone worthy of voicing doubt. What kind of science is this? The earth circles around the sun for everyone: it was hard to have this fact accepted, but now the matter is clear. And philologists, in seven hundred years, have not produced a *ne varietur* edition of the *Commedia,* and they are still wrangling?

It must be said that a clear inspection of the material sources always holds surprises. If the manuscript witnesses, barring unforeseen discoveries, are all basically cataloged, elements that were once overlooked can give specialists very valuable and unexpected information. The study of anthologies and of single *canzonieri* as autonomous organisms is back in vogue. And a text that appeared final and definitive like Barbi's *Vita Nuova* (1907), the first scientific edition of a work in the vulgate with multiple manuscript traditions, has been contested both in choices of language and in chapter divisions, inherited from the eighteenth-century. In the light of new assessments, there can no longer be, according to the once accepted convention, forty-two chapters, but rather, according to the *stemma,* thirty-one *paragrafi.* It must be said immediately that this is not a more elegant partitioning that we gladly adopt as superior. But the critical editor is at the service of the text and its tradition, and does not indulge in intuitions of his own, however brilliant in his estimation. The "paragraphs" are thirty-one in number because the manuscripts say so to anyone who knows how to read and understand them, not because the editor says so himself. Logic, on which the philological method must be based, requires such a revised division if it is true that identical paragraphing in independent manuscript witnesses cannot be attributed to chance, but goes back to a common source that can be shown to be the archetype or the original. Thus, I would not welcome the approval that, with a certain amount of disagreement,[1] has been accorded the *libello*'s new division into thirty-one *paragrafi* if one believed the idea were mine. I regret having to be apodictic: but either the invention is Dante's, and one that Barbi did not trouble himself to pursue for various reasons and that has surfaced only now, or else it is not. The logic of the *stemma* is inescapable; it does not permit exceptions or cunning.[2]

It is indeed true that textual philology is not only the science of the certain. It is also, and has been for centuries, the field of emendations based on conjecture, mental operations that postulate a certain textual reality by an intuitive process. In this, *si parva licet,* philology shares the statute of theoretical physics, which explains certain facts with heuristic and probable models. Thanks to these attempts to account for a reality removed from our observation, it arranges and justifies the majority of phenomena within a coherent theoretical framework, however, without being able to prove it through experimentation. The ancients designated this intuitive restoration of the document, where one believes it to be corrupted or incomplete, by the telling name of *divinatio.* And philologists have, not infrequently, abused this quasi divine (re-)creation. The example of *Vita Nova* 30.6 (XLI 6) will have to suffice. We should keep in mind that the passage in question is one with which not even the shrewdest reader could find fault:

> [. . .] lo mio pensero sale nella qualità di costei in grado che lo mio intellecto nol può comprendere, con ciò sia cosa che lo nostro intellecto s'abbia a quelle benedecte anime sì come l'occhio debole al sole: e ciò dice lo Phylosofo nel secondo della Metafisica
>
> (Gorni 1996)

> My thought ascends so far into the quality of her being that my intellect cannot follow it; for our intellect in the presence of those blessed souls is as weak as our eyes before the sun; and this is confirmed by the Philosopher in the second book of his *Metaphysics*
>
> (trans. Reynolds [Alighieri 1969])

Nevertheless Friedrich Beck (1920, 279), the first critical editor of the *Vita Nova* (1896), postulated a lacuna and claimed that one ought to read "sì come l'occhio debole [de lo vipistrello] al sole." And to make this *vipistrello* of his fit into the *Vita Nova* ("*vipistrello,* nicht *pipistrello* schreibt Dante," he believes in good faith) and to find a niche for it in some supposed lacuna, he mobilized Boethius, Albertus Magnus, St. Thomas Aquinas, and Cardinal Bessarion. It is, in effect, what Aristotle affirms in a detailed passage that the *Convivio* paraphrases quite simply "la quale soverchia li occhi della mente umana, sì come dice lo Filosofo nel secondo della Metafisica" (2.4.16), citing only further on "le pupille del pipistrello" (but, according to Ageno [Alighieri 1995], "le pupille del palpastrello," that is, 'della palpebra') of the Aristotelian source:[3] a bat in the *Vita Nova,* introduced by philological decree; Beatrice with a *vipistrello* or with *civetta,* according to certain Latin sources, as in a surrealist painting. Beck opted for the *Fledermaus,* which brings to mind Johann Strauss II (1874) sooner than Dante. Here the *Metaphysics* is turned into an operetta and philology into a scholarly interpolation, from which neither the copyist nor the philologist is safe if either loses his sense of discretion and denies the historical respect due to the facts of the document.

Professor Ageno was, on the contrary, wary of bats, so much so that she removed from the *Convivio* the only one that, in homage to the "maestro di color che sanno," fluttered about its pages. She chased it out mistakenly, in my opinion. In contrast to the *Vita Nova,* the treatise is indeed inhabited by a philosophical bat. And in matters of emendation *ope ingenii,* it is not that Ageno holds back.[4] Her *Convivio* enumerates nearly a thousand errors in the archetype, an unheard-of number of archetypal errors. A thousand errors and hence a thousand conjectures—that is to say, words and parts of the text that are not in any manuscript—are fearlessly devised by the editor with undoubted competence, but still the product of her own mind. It seemed right to ask myself whether a thousand errors and lacunae were to be imputed to the archetype, and whether they did not go back to the original instead. If the second scenario were true, the achievement of Ageno would be to correct not the archetype, but the author. The prospect is unsettling and casts a shadow on the actual condition of the work left unfinished by Dante. Was the *Convivio* really left, as I have written, in the "'gaseous,' rather than the 'solid' state," in the form of scattered glosses or notes, not continuous prose? The hypothesis of a restoration promises insurmountable difficulty.

More restraint is imposed on conjecture today than in the past. When I hypothesized (2000) in the canto of Ulysses that rather than "poi che 'ntrati eravam ne l'alto passo" (*Inf* 26.132), the passage should read (as a correction of the archetype) "arto passo" (which is also the "foce *stretta* / dov'Ercule segnò li suoi riguardi" [107–8]), I trust that I accompanied my *divinatio* not only with good reasons, as was my duty, but also with the prudence, relativism, and skepticism which seem to me to be connatural with the temperament of a good philologist.

I shall touch on the most conspicuous case of conjectural philology in our studies, the attribution of the anonymous *Fiore* and *Detto d'Amore* to Dante. Contini (1984) produced a demonstration of marvelous wit on the subject, which left everyone dazzled, but convinced few. Regarding the presence of Dante as the author of the *Fiore,* one might say what Ariosto wrote of the virginity of Angelica, "perhaps it was true, but not, however, believable." For my part I have tried to believe, but I do not deny the difficulties unleashed by so massive an intrusion into Dante's *corpus.* Putting down the *Fiore,* I do not ask myself "if it is not Dante's, whose is it?" but "where do we situate it, what do we do with it, if it is not Dante's?" It is only in the context of the work that we can with certainty assign to Dante that the parameters of parody, palinode, and intertextuality function in the *Fiore* (cf. Leonardi 1996); the text's relationships with other stylistic personalities prove fragmentary and, in my estimation, often illusory as well, or founded on pretensions. The conjecture of Contini is onerous, but at least as conjecture it stands on its own feet. The same cannot be said of other hypotheses that have been expounded. As far as I am concerned, either we attribute the *Fiore* and the *Detto* to Dante, or we resign ourselves to leaving them to the mysterious Durante who signed the poem, without proposing other names. Recently Maurizio Palma di Cesnola (1999) advanced the candidacy of the French Guillaume Durant. Palma was my student and he remains my esteemed collaborator at Geneva. But I am obliged to dismiss this rash linguistical hypothesis, which appears to have a certain following, because, I regret to say, elementary grammatical rules have been forgotten, such as the rule (in effect at least until the age of Bembo) which privileges the first name over the patronymic or family name. It would make no sense today to write that the *Promessi sposi* is by Alessandro, the *Ossi di sepia* by Eugenio, or *Ragazzi di vita* by Pier Paolo. However, such was the standard imposed by the rule in the past according to which the *Fiore* by (ser) Durante could not be the work of someone of the house Durand, but of one who bears it as a first or given name. Gu(i)glielmo (Durante or at most Durando) could never sign himself with a curt Durante.

In *filologia dantesca,* the study of Dante's works in the context of his medieval culture, the greatest problems stem from two facts: no holograph of Dante's has been preserved, and for a number of his works the distance between the date of composition and that of the oldest manuscript is great indeed, especially in an age of extremely rapid linguistic change: for the *Vita Nova* the gap is about sixty years; for the *Convivio,* more or less a hundred years; for the *Commedia,* fortunately only a decade and a half, but the text has been affected by the interference of the concurrent linguistic systems of copyists, recipients, or even the exemplars. I cannot document here what in any case Dante scholars already know: the original of every work of Dante's is unattainable. The philologist, at the bow of a sinking boat, beats down the wave that prevents him from sighting dry land; he sees only from afar, guesses at the original, suspects, but never touches it.

Years ago I encountered a manuscript from the Bodmer Foundation of Cologny (Geneva) with the shelfmark 132.[5] It is a miscellany of Latin writings in many hands, which includes an ample anthology of the letters of Pier della Vigna. The manuscript is from the end of the Duecento. It is Florentine and in its early centuries never circulated outside Florence. Above all, it belonged to ser Andrea Lancia, the author of the *Ottimo Commento* on the *Commedia.* It had been my fond dream that among the glossators who wrote in its margins was Dante himself. Dante would indeed have read the *Epistule* of Pier della Vigna, of whose curial style there is a splendid imitation in *Inferno* 13. On which pages would he have made his illustrious acquaintance through his Latin prose? Better than anywhere else, I mused, on those *chartae* of the Florentine codex of ser Andrea Lancia now at the Bodmer Foundation. Perhaps Dante did leaf through those pages and somehow leave his mark on them. But who now would be able to recognize the possible traces of his hand? Let us resign ourselves to the fact that we are not left with any holograph of his.

I like to imagine for myself an absolute philology, a philology without adjectives. (I borrow the formula from one who could not abide philology as a textual practice, Benedetto Croce, who spoke of a poetry without adjectives.) And I illustrate my point of view with a somewhat provocative question. What is the position that, within the *stemma codicum,* is the domain of the critical text in relation to the original? The ideas on this matter have changed in the course of the century.[6]

For traditional philology, the modern critical text (T), established in accordance with the *stemma,* was the true and conformant image of the lost original. When possible, one reconstructed the archetype ω on the basis of the tradition, and then *ope ingenii* the editor tended to its errors, faithfully restoring the original O, according to the scheme:

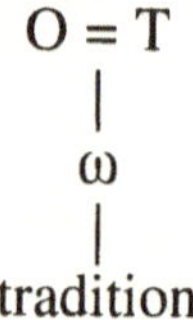

The agnostics of philology, often in the footsteps of the great but nonetheless perilous lesson of freedom imparted by Joseph Bédier (cf. Stussi 1994), consider it instead an utter illusion to want to make O coincide with T, and place T as low as possible in the schematic representation of the "integrity" of the witnesses. In their eyes, T is a *descriptus,* or, better, it is the most recent of the *descripti.* And not only that: T is contaminated, given that the modern editor does not hesitate to draw on one branch or another of the tradition, known to him in its totality. And T is also interpolated, because the philologist does his share too, and slips in readings of his own invention and his own taste. By this standard, T is less authoritative than every other historical witness of the text, even the most humble. A text in pen and ink is, if nothing else, a concrete document. It has served as a text for a certain number of readers, it exists, it is not an abstract reconstruction of the work. The tradition, in each of its representatives, is above T:

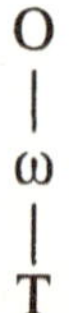

In my opinion, the most appropriate collocation of the critical text T is not, in fact, at the same level, but below O, which remains unattainable to the textual scholar and cannot be substituted. T is in an intermediary position between the original and the archetype, O and ω:

T approaches O, tends toward O, but will never coincide with O. On certain points, for given readings, it cannot raise itself above the archetype ω. T is a prisoner of the evident inaccuracy that defines the archetype as such. In other cases it can reclaim a possible—or even a plausible—conformity with O without being able to be sure of it.

This insurmountable hiatus between T and O is evident and active above all in every point of analysis of textual forms. If the choice of the reading can be facilitated by certain historical criteria (of meaning, of language, of style, of tradition within a given literary genre), what criteria are we to adopt in the choice of the most common linguistic forms? The historical analogy with the language of the time is illusory and inoperative, because Dante's language is not reducible to that evidenced by the surviving documents of his age (pages of archives, statutes, and writings of a practical nature). Just as today the language of Gadda or Calvino is not that of notarial deeds, nor of the proceedings of the *carabinieri.*

It is here that the philologist more often finds himself making decisions that are in varying degrees subjective, with responsibilities that are laden with consequences. In this domain the philologist has the impression of working with choices that are of seemingly modest importance but that, taken as a whole, radically alter the physiognomy of a text. *Fue* or *fu, apresso* or *appresso, ogni, ogne,* or *onne, li* or *gli, signore* or *segnore,* Latinizing or vulgate spelling? Maintaining the forms of a single manuscript in these options ensures that one will not depart from an established reality. But in so doing one will have maintained the language of a copyist: one cannot presume to have restored that of Dante. On the other hand, to pick and choose among manuscripts the oldest and rarest forms, as Barbi has done, is a fine work of restoration, but the result is a false historical composite, which introduces into Dante's texts *etterno* or *canoscenza, canosciute* and even *caunosciute:* isolated and combined forms, ascribed to Dante on the *a priori* basis of their archaic flavor for the sake of neo-Gothic aestheticism, not for reasons of science.

In my edition of the *Vita Nova* (Alighieri 1996), I have adopted other criteria. In the first place, I have carefully documented in the Notes to the Text all the formal differences that one notices in the old witnesses, rather than concealing them as Barbi unfortunately did. As far as the selection of forms is concerned, I determined to avoid following one single manuscript witness both for reasons of principle (see 1998)[7] and on account of the proven unreliability of each of these manuscripts in the specific case of the *Vita Nova.* I prepared the edition "not [on] the criterion of the majority, but the rejection of the singularities (even if archaicizing) with the greatest consistency possible, even if I then happen to specify that the one chosen is the majority reading."

The operation, clear in theory, shows itself difficult in practice. The array of cases that one faces cannot be reduced to a perfectly consistent criterion. I do not say this as a personal apology, to try to shield myself. Rather, it is to show how misguided anyone is who believes that philology is a reassuring work that affords modest but secure satisfactions to those who actively engage in it, as well as excellent guarantees of readability to those who passively enjoy its benefits. Dates and documents are, in philology, an insurmountable limit, the barrier against idle talk, and the pretensions of incompetent bunglers. In the defense of the certain, philology is severe, and may appear intolerant as well, when it must respond to alternative hypotheses lacking a textual foundation: as in the defense, let us say, of a *Vita Nova* divided into thirty-one "paragraphs," according to the *stemma.* But in so many respects objectivity is an illusion, and the margin of discretion is at once appealing and agonizing for the philologist. If the critical editor is not an arrogant rewriter of the text, he is constitutionally a desperate man. Philology lives by hypotheses more than by certainties, nothing but hypotheses, more or less judicious. And therefore philology is not a trade to entrust to a corporation of technicians, generally somewhat limited in their interests and tastes, who know their job. Philology is a habit of the mind, a lesson in relativism and in the insufficiency of our knowledge to be taken into account before reading any text. It is not only a practice or an art; it is also a theory. And it is for everyone. Not that it is for everyone to exercise it, because it is unfortunately a difficult and a jealous science. But no one can declare himself truly free of it. A critical text is always in the care of the editor concerned, but it concerns us all.

Translation by Tamara Pollack

NOTES

1. To which I reply in Gorni 1994 and 1995. The justification for the new paragraphing was given in Gorni 1995.

2. Regrettably, one concedes it readily, having to change the vulgate paragraphing of the *Vita Nova* entails many difficulties in citations and the use of bibliography, but one cannot close one's eyes to the evidence with this excuse.

3. A discussion of this passage, according to Ageno (Alighieri 1995) is in Gorni 1997a, from which I am drawing freely for these observations.

4. I have attempted an appraisal of the late *dantista*'s philological work in Gorni 1997b.

5. See Gorni 1988. The codex is parchment of a large format, made up of forty-eight *chartae* and produced in the last quarter of the thirteenth century. It belonged to the collection of Giuseppe Martini di Lugano and has been the property of the Bodmer Foundation since 1948, acquired through the H. P. Kraus bookseller in New York.

6. The considerations that follow arise in the margins of Pasquali 1962.

7. On the theoretical plain, the formal restitution (not reconstruction) "is entrusted, as is every other element of the text, to the responsibility of the editor, a role that is difficult to assume, but which, in my opinion, barring exceptions cannot be delegated to the merely apparent reliability and to the materiality of a single textual witness. Philology is above all a mental process of reasoning about dates and of a probabilistic search for solutions, not simple diligence and acquiescent resignation to the naked facts" (Gorni 1998, 6). In practice "I have come to the conviction that I cannot delegate to K [Chigiano L. VIII. 305] the analysis of the forms, though it affords so little intellectual satisfaction to the editor, and its realization is so tedious if enacted case by case, holding in reserve the singular substance of the text, which Contini judged inseparable from the first" (Gorni 1998, 16).

PHILOLOGIES: WORKS CITED

Ahern, John. 1982a. "Binding the Book: Hermeneutics and Manuscript Production in *Paradiso* 33." PMLA 97:800–809.

______. 1982b. "Singing the Book: Orality in the Reception of the *Comedy.*" *Annals of Scholarship* 2.4:17–40. 1997. Reprinted in *Dante: Contemporary Perspectives.* Ed. Amilcare A. Iannucci. Toronto: University of Toronto Press. 214–37.

______. 1984. "Dante's Last Word: the *Comedy* as a *liber coelestis.*" DS 102:1–14.

Alfie, Fabian. 1998. "Immanuel of Rome, Alias Manoello Giudeo: The Poetics of Jewish Identity in Fourteenth-century Italy." *Italica* 75:307–29.

Alighieri, Dante. 1969. *La Vita Nuova: Poems of Youth.* Trans. Barbara Reynolds. Baltimore: Penguin Books.

______. 1995. *Convivio.* Ed. Franca Brambilla Ageno. 3 vols. Florence: Le Lettere.

______. 1996. *Vita Nova.* Ed. Guglielmo Gorni. Turin: Einaudi.

Azzetta, Luca. 1996. "Per la biografia di Andrea Lancia: Documenti e autografi." *Italia medioevale e umanistica* 39:121–70.

Baglio, Marco. 1992. "Presenze dantesche nel Petrarca latino." *Studi petrarcheschi* 9:76–136.

Balduino, Armando. 1984. *Boccaccio, Petrarca, e altri poeti del Trecento.* Florence: Olschki.

Bambaglioli, Graziolo. 1998. *Commento all' "Inferno" di Dante.* Ed. Luca Carlo Rossi. Pisa: Scuola Superiore Normale di Pisa.

Barbi, Michele. 1893. "Gli studi danteschi e il loro avvenire in Italia." *Giornale dantesco* 1:1–19. 1934. Reprinted and expanded in *Problemi di critica dantesca, prima serie (1893–1918).* Florence: Sansoni. 1–27.

______. 1934. *Problemi di critica dantesca, prima serie (1893–1918).* Florence: Sansoni.

______, ed. 1907. *La Vita Nuova di Dante Alighieri.* Florence: Bemporad.

______, ed. 1932. *La Vita Nuova di Dante Alighieri.* Florence: Bemporad.

Barbi, Michele, and Francesco Maggini, eds. 1956. *Rime della "Vita Nuova" e della giovinezza.* Florence: Le Monnier.

Beck, Friedrich. 1920. "Textkritische und grammatisch-exegetische Bemerkungen zu Dantes *Vita Nova.*" *Zeitschrift für romanische Philologie* 40:257–85.

Bernheimer, Carlo. 1915. "Una trascrizione dalla *Divina Commedia* sugli inizi del sec. XIV." GSLI 66:122–27.

Billanovich, Giuseppe. 1949. "La leggenda dantesca di Boccaccio: Dalla lettera di Ilaro al *Trattatello in laude di Dante.*" StD 28:45–144.

______. 1975. "Dalle prima alle ultime letture del Petrarca." In *Il Petrarca ad Arquà.* Ed. Giuseppe Billanovich and Giuseppe Frasso. Padua: Antenore.

______. 1996. *Petrarca e il primo umanesimo.* Padua: Antenore.

Boccaccio, Giovanni. 1974. *Trattatello in laude di Dante.* Ed. Pier Giorgio Ricci. Vol. 3 of *Tutte le opere di Giovanni Boccaccio.* Ed. Vittore Branca. Milan: Mondadori.

Bologna, Corrado. 1986. "Traduzione testuale e fortuna dei classici." In Vol. 6 of *Letteratura italiana.* Ed. Alberto Asor Rosa. Turin: Einaudi, 1986. 538–64.

Branca, Vittore. 1965. "Un biadaiuolo lettore di Dante nei primi decenni del '300." In *Studi in onore di Alfredo Schiafini.* Ed. Ettore Paratore. 200–208. Special issue of *Rivista di cultura classica e medievale.*

______. 1988. *Ponte Santa Trinità: Per amore di libertà, per amore della verità.* Venice: Marsilio.

Brugnolo, Furio. 1987. "Le terzine della *Maestà* di Simone Martini e la prima diffusione della *Commedia.*" *Medioevo romanzo* 12:153–54.

______. 1989. "Il libro di poesia nel Trecento." *Il libro di poesia dal copista al tipografo.* Ed. Amedeo Quondam and Marco Santagata. Modena: Panini. 9–23.

______. 1993. "Cino (e Onesto) dentro e fuori la *Commedia.*" In Vol. 1 of *Omaggio a Gianfranco Folena.* Ed. A. Danielle. Padua: Programma. 369–86.

Cioffari, Vincenzo. 1989. *Anonymous Latin Commentary on Dante's "Commedia": Reconstructed Text.* Spoleto: Centro italiano di studi sull'alto medioevo.

Contini, Gianfranco. 1989. *Diligenza e voluttà: Ludovica Ripa di Meana interroga Gianfranco Contini.* Milan: Arnoldo Mondadori.

______, ed. 1960. *Poeti del Duecento.* 2 vols. Milan and Naples: Ricciardi.

______, ed. 1984. *Il "Fiore" e il "Detto d'Amore" attribuibili a Dante Alighieri.* Milan: Mondadori.

______, ed. 1995. *Le rime di Dante Alighieri.* Turin: Einaudi.

De Robertis, Domenico. 1954. *Il canzoniere escorialense e la tradizione "veneziana" delle rime dello stil novo.* Turin: Loescher-Chiantore. Supplement 27 of GSLI.

______. 1960–70. "Censimento dei manoscritti di rime di Dante." SD 37 (1960):141–273; 38 (1961):167–276; 39 (1962):119–209; 40 (1963):443–98; 41 (1964):103–31; 42 (1965):419–74; 43 (1966):205–38; 44 (1967):269–78; 45 (1968):183–200; 47 (1970):225–58.

Francesco da Barberino. 1905–27. *Documenti d'amore secondo i manoscritti originali.* Ed. Francesco Egidi. 4 vols. Rome: Società filologica romana.

Gorni, Guglielmo. 1979. "Sull'origine della terzina e altre misure." *Metrica* 2:44–60.

______. 1988. "Notizie su Dante, Andrea Lancia, e l'Ovidio volgare." *Studi Medievali,* ser. 3, 29:761–69.

______. 1994 [1996]. "Il *copyright* della *Vita Nuova.*" *Rivista di letteratura italiana* 12:481–90.

______. 1995. "*Paragrafi* e titolo della *Vita Nova.*" SFI 53:203–22

______. 1995 [1997]. "Ancora sui *paragrafi* della *Vita Nova.*" *Rivista di letteratura italiana* 13:537–62.

______. 1997a. "Appunti sulla tradizione del *Convivio:* A proposito dell'archetipo e dell'originale dell'opera." SFI 55:5–22.

______. 1997b. "La filologia di Franca Ageno: Dal manuale di critica testuale all'edizione del *Convivio.*" In *Schede umanistiche: Rivista semestrale dell'Archivio Umanistico Rinascimentale Bolognese.* N.S. 1:7–31.

______. 1998. "Restituzione formale dei testi volgari a tradizione plurima: Il caso della *Vita Nova.*" SFI 56:5–30.

______. 2000. "I *riguardi* di Ercole e l'*alto passo* di Ulisse." *Letteratura italiana antica* 1:43–58.

Graziosi, Elisabetta. 1997. "Dante a Cino: sul cuore di un giurista." *Letture classensi* 26:55–91.

Iacopo Alighieri. 1990. *Chiose all' "Inferno."* Ed. Saverio Bellomo. Padua: Antenore.

Kreytenberg, Gert. 1989. "L'Enfer d'Orcagna: La première peinture monumentale d'après les chants de Dante." *Gazette des Beaux Arts* 114:243–62.

Lanza, Antonio, ed. 1995. *La "Commedìa" di Dante Alighieri: Testo critico secondo i più antichi manoscritti fiorentini.* Anzio: De Rubeis.

______, ed. 1996. *La "Commedìa" di Dante Alighieri: Testo critico secondo i più antichi manoscritti fiorentini.* 2nd ed. Anzio: De Rubeis.

Leonardi, Lino. 1996. "*Langue* poetica e stile dantesco nel *Fiore:* Per una verifica degli *argomenti interni.*" In *Studi di filologia medievale offerti a d'Arco Silvio Avalle.* Milan and Naples: Ricciardi. 237–92.

______, ed. 2000. *Il canzoniere palatino.* Florence: SISMEL.

Maniaci, Marilena. 1996. *Terminologia del libro manoscritto.* Rome: Istituto centrale per la patologia del libro.

Mastro Ferrara (Antonio Beccari). 1972. *Le rime.* Ed. Laura Bellucci. Bologna: Pàtron.

Mazzoni, Francesco. 1965. "La critica dantesca del secolo XIV." *Cultura e scuola* 13–14:285–97.

______. 1971a. "Chiose Selmiane." In ED 1:973–74.

______. 1971b. "Chiose Vernon." In ED, 1:974.

Meli, Elio. 1958. "Riecheggiamenti danteschi in un cantare toscano del secolo XIV." *Filologia romanza* 5:82–87.

Mostra. 1957. *Mostra di codici romanzi delle biblioteche fiorentine.* Florence: Sansoni.

Nichols, Stephen G., and Siegfried Wenzel, eds. 1996. *The Whole Book: Cultural Perspectives on the Medieval Miscellany.* Ann Arbor: University of Michigan Press.

Orelli, Giorgio. 1978. "Dantismi nel *Canzoniere.*" In *Accertamenti verbali.* Milan: Bompiani. 67–81.

Orlandelli, Grianfranco. 1959. *Il libro a Bologna dal 1300 al 1330: Documenti con uno studio su Il contratto di scrittura nella dottrina notarile bolognese.* Bologna: Zanichelli.

______. 1967. "I Memoriali bolognesi come fonte per la storia dei tempi di Dante." In *Dante e Bologna nei tempi di Dante*. Bologna: Commissione per i testi di lingua. 193–205.

Orlando, Sandro, ed. 1981. *Rime dei Memoriali bolognesi (1279–1300)*. Turin: Einaudi.

Padoan, Giorgio. 1993. *Il lungo cammino del poema sacro: Studi danteschi*. Florence: Olschki.

Palma di Cesnola, Maurizio. 1999. "La battaglia del *Fiore:* Omaggio a Remo Fasani." In *Studi e problemi di critica testuale* 59:5–42. 1999. Also in *Tra due mondi: Miscellanea di studi per Remo Fasani*. Ed. Giovanni Cappello, Antonella Del Gatto, and Guido Pedrojetta. Locarno: Dadò. 59–102.

Papa, Pasquale. 1884. "Conti di antichi cavalieri." GSLI 3:192–217.

Pasquali, Giorgio. [1934] 1962. *Storia della tradizione e critica del testo*. 2nd ed. Florence: Le Monnier.

Pazzaglia, Mario. 1973. "Ne li occhi porta la mia donna Amore." In ED 4:33–34.

Pertile, Lino. 1991. "'Canto,' 'cantica,' e 'Comedìa' e l'*Epistola a Can Grande*." *Lectura Dantis* 9:105–23.

______. 1992. "'Cantica' nella tradizione medievale e in Dante." *Rivista di storia letteratura religiosa* 27:389–412.

Petrarch, Francesco. 1985. *Letters on Familiar Matters: Rerum familiarium libri XVII–XXIV*. Trans. Aldo S. Bernardo. Baltimore: Johns Hopkins University Press.

______. 1991. *Petrarch's Remedies for Fortune Fair and Foul: A Modern English Translation of "De remediis utriusque Fortune."* Vol. 1. Bloomington: Indiana University Press.

______. 1992. *Opere: Canzoniere, Trinofi, Familiarium rerum libri*. Florence: Sansoni.

Petrocchi, Giorgio. 1994. *Itinerari danteschi*. Ed. Carlo Ossola. 2nd ed. Milan: Francoangeli.

______, ed. 1966–67. *La Commedia secondo l'antica vulgata*. 4 vols. Milan: Mondadori.

Petrucci, Armando. 1995. *Writers and Readers in Medieval Italy: Studies in the History of Written Culture*. Ed. and trans. Charles M. Radding. New Haven, Conn.: Yale University Press.

Polzer, Joseph. 1964. "Aristotle, Mohammed, and Nicholas V in Hell." *Art Bulletin* 46:457–69.

Pomaro, Gabriella. 1995. "I copisti e il testo: Quattro esempi dalla Biblioteca Riccardiana." In *La Società Dantesca Italiana, 1888–1988: Atti di Convengo internazionale, (Firenze, 24–26 novembre 1988)*. Ed. Rudy Abardo. Milan and Naples: Ricciardi. 497–536.

Roddewig, Marcela. 1984. *Dante Alighieri: Die göttliche Komödie—Vergleich und Bestandaufnahme der Commedia-Handschriften.* Stuttgart: Hiersemann.

Rossi, Luca Carlo. 1999. "Il commento dantesco di Graziolo dei Bambaglioli. *Letture classensi* 28:43–54.

Sanguineti, Federico, ed. 2001. *Dantis Alagherii "Comedia."* Tavarnuzze–Florence: Galluzzo.

Santagata, Marco. 1990. *Per moderne carte: La biblioteca volgare di Petrarca.* Bologna: Il Mulino.

Storey, H. Wayne. 1993. *Transcription and Visual Poetics in the Early Italian Lyric.* New York and London: Garland.

______. 1999. "Voce e grafia nei *Triumphi.*" In *I "Triumphi" di Francesco Petrarca.* Ed. Claudia Berra. Milano: Cisalpino. 231–53.

______. 2000. "Sulle orme di Guittone: I programmi grafico-visivi del codice Banco Rari 217." In *Studi vari di Lingua e Letteratura italiana in onore di Giuseppe Velli.* Ed. Claudia Berra. Milano: Cisalpino. 93–105.

Stussi, Alfredo. 1994. "Cenni storici." *Introduzione agli studi di filologia italiana.* 3rd ed. Bologna: Il Mulino.

Trovato, Paolo. 1979. *Dante in Petrarca: Per un inventario dei dantismi nei "Rerum vulgarium fragmenta."* Florence: Olschki.

Valerio, Giulia. 1985. "La cronologia dei primi volgarizzamenti dell'*Eneide* e la diffusione della *Commedia.*" *Medioevo romanzo* 10:3–18.

Vandelli, Giuseppe. 1922. "Il più antico testo critico della '*Divina Commedia.*'" StD 5:41–98. Rpt. in his *Per il testo della "Divina Commedia."* Ed. Rudy Abardo. Florence: Le Lettere. 111–44.

Z. 1897. Review of Friedrich Beck, *Dantes "Vita Nova"* and Lewis Fr. Mott, *The System of Courtly Love Studied as an Introduction to the "Vita Nuova."* GSLI 29:513–16.

APPETITES

4

Beyond (Courtly) Dualism: Thinking about Gender in Dante's Lyrics

Teodolinda Barolini

DANTE wrote eighty-eight lyric poems of different genres (sonnets, ballads, *canzoni*), beginning when he was about eighteen and continuing right up to the threshold of the *Commedia*.[1] Writing lyric poems thus constituted his poetic apprenticeship, both formal and ideological; the Dante of the *Commedia*, the Dante we all know, came out of those lyrics.

And yet, the world of Dante's lyrics is frequented by very few. Even within the scholarly precincts of *dantismo,* it is a field apart, cultivated mainly in Italy, and guarded by philological and editorial difficulties that make this part of the canon forbidding and inaccessible. Moreover, the commentary tradition on the lyrics has become encrusted and repetitive, offering very little in the way of genuine interpretation despite the fact that it is here that the wellsprings of Dante's ideological convictions are to be located. These are poems that harbor implicit and at times explicit debates on cultural and societal issues of great immediacy for Dante's mercantile audience: issues such as the nature of chivalry and nobility, the desire for wealth and its relationship to avarice, the limits and constraints of political loyalty, and—intertwined with everything else—the role of women and, implicitly, the construction of gender. Dante's developing views on the construction of gender are my topic in this essay.

Because many of Dante's lyrics deal with desire that is filtered through a cultural system that we know as "courtly love," in which the male lover aspires to the love of a lady worshiped as an ennobling ideal, attention to issues of gender seems an obvious enough critical move. If it has not previously been attempted, we must bear in mind not only the immediate context as it pertains to scholarship on Dante's lyrics but also the broader context in which the word "gender" in the sense of "gender studies" is not even easily translated into Italian. Courtliness, the set of values associated with what Dante calls *cortesia,* is by definition a gendered issue, since its logic is constructed around a male / female binary. In the courtly lyric, the lover, who has a voice (as a matter of course, since the male poet takes on the role of the male lover), aspires to that which the female represents—to possess it, to understand it, to be identified with it—and uses his voice to express this aspiration: to express his desire, his striving, his anguish, his hopes, his frustration, his fears. On the other side of this binary stands the courtly lady, who represents the pinnacle of unattainable perfection for which the lover yearns. She represents, she embodies, she serves as goal and point of reference; in the courtly lyric, she does not do, act, or speak. From this perspective, the question that took shape for me was how to account for Dante's development from a courtly poet into the poet of the *Commedia,* that is, into a poet who assigns moral agency to all human beings, including women.

Now, again from this perspective, what Dante does in the *Commedia* is genuinely remarkable, for Beatrice develops from the silent icon of his courtly verse to the very talkative figure I once labeled *Beatrix loquax* (1992, 303*n*36).[2] Her speechifying has put off (the mostly male) commentators: to the claim that the "Beatrice [of the *Vita Nova*] appears far more persuasive, enigmatic, explosive, than the recreated and cantankerous figure" of the *Commedia* (Harrison 1988, 19), we must reply that the "explosive" Beatrice of the *Vita Nova* is silent, while the "cantankerous" Beatrice of the *Commedia* speaks. It is interesting to note how little critical appreciation there has been for Dante's radically new creation. The traditions he inherits boast female abstractions like Boethius's "Philosophia" who speak authoritatively in a voice that is coded as non–gender-specific (i.e., masculine) and female non-abstractions who either do not speak or speak within the province of the gender-specific. In the Beatrice of the *Commedia* Dante creates something new: a historicized object of desire—not a personification—who, at the same time as she is portrayed as the embodiment and pinnacle of all his desire, yet speaks, indeed, in the *Paradiso,* speaks "like a man," unconstrained by the content or modality normatively assigned to female speech. In this ability at least imaginatively to reconcile woman as simultaneously sexual and intellectual, desirable and magisterial, Dante found few imitators.

But Dante was in every respect highly unusual in his drive to get beyond dualisms. In the same way as the work of cultural historians like Caroline Bynum has shown that medieval religious thinking was less dualistically imprinted than we thought, we are now in a position to see that much of the dualism characteristic of Dante studies is our imposition on the past. The particular local dualisms dear to *dantisti*—*poeta* versus *theologus, amore corporale* versus *amore spirituale*—will one day be as outdated as a rigidly conceived body / soul dualism has become among cultural and religious historians of the Middle Ages.[3] Similarly, another fundamental binary, woman / man, may turn out to have been more flexibly construed by Dante than we had supposed.

I did not expect, as I began work on a historical reconstruction of Francesca da Rimini, the young woman who was killed by her husband, Gianciotto Malatesta, ca. 1285, because of her affair with his brother Paolo Malatesta, to come to the conclusion that "Francesca's story, as told by Dante, is . . . one in which unusual value is placed on the personhood of the dynastic wife" (Barolini 2000a, 3). Nor did I expect to come to the view that the obnoxiously paternalistic late *canzone Doglia mi reca* harbors an unusually progressive perspective on gender roles, in the sense that women are held to the same moral standards as men. These instances are, I believe, symptoms of a larger truth: not necessarily that Dante is a proto-feminist—a case that I would rather make, and have made, for the much more dualistically inclined Boccaccio (see Barolini 1993)—but rather that Dante is not a dualist. Dualisms attract him—body versus soul, love versus intellect, Francis versus Dominic, Aristotelianism versus Neoplatonism, form versus content—precisely as that which requires integration, in a process that must be accomplished with nuance, detail, specificity, and difference preserved and intact. Dante's poetic identity is founded on this double-pronged need: the need to uncover aporias and dualisms and the need to reconcile them through paradox and metaphor. One could say of him what he says of love in *Doglia mi reca.* Like love, Dante has the power to make one out of two: "e a costui [fu dato] di due poter un fare" (v. 14).

While the *Beatrix loquax* of the *Commedia* is the most obvious example of Dante's mature reconfiguration of the gender paradigm he inherited from the courtly lyric, his treatment of Francesca da Rimini is also relevant to our topic (see Barolini 2000a). To reconstruct the cultural significance of *Inferno* 5 from the perspective of gender we need to recall that the historical record is silent about Francesca. The first and most authoritative chronicler of Rimini was Marco Battagli, whose history *Marcha* contains "On the Origins of the Malatesta," composed in 1352. Battagli (1913) alludes to the event in which Francesca died without naming her, indeed without acknowledging her existence, except as an implicit cause of Paolo's death, which occurred "causa luxuriae": "Paolo was killed by his brother Giovanni the Lame on account of lust." Like Battagli, the anonymous author of the later fourteenth-century *Cronaca malatestiana* (1922) also dispenses with Francesca's name, referring to her merely as "wife" ("la donna sua"). The only historical document that records Francesca's name is the will of her father-in-law, the founding patriarch Malatesta da Verucchio, in which he refers to "the dowry of the late lady Francesca." Otherwise, silence.

However, Dante does not observe this silence, preserving Francesca, recording her name, giving her a voice, and saving her from historical oblivion. And, as though to make this point crystal clear, Francesca's is the *only* name from her story registered in *Inferno* 5; Paolo's name is absent, as is Gianciotto's. In canto 5, *she* is the protagonist, *she* is the agent, *she* is the one who speaks, while Paolo stands by weeping. Through the intervention of *Inferno* 5, Francesca becomes a cultural touchstone and reference point, achieving a dignity and a prominence—a celebrity—that in real life she did not possess. The woman who in real life was merely a dynastic pawn, whose brutal death did not even cause a serious rupture between the Malatesta of Rimini and the Polentani of Ravenna, emerges in Dante's version as the canto's unchallenged protagonist; the woman who in history had no voice and no name emerges as the canto's only voice and only name. How did a courtly poet, that is, a poet raised in the conventions of female silence, reach this point? The traces of this evolution are to be found in his lyrics.

To sketch the development of Dante's thinking about gender in the *Rime,* I turn to three poems as developmental signposts: the early sonnet *Sonar bracchetti* and two mature *canzoni, Poscia ch'Amor* and *Doglia mi reca.* Written most likely when Dante was in his early twenties, *Sonar bracchetti* offers a clear vision of the world as polarized and dichotomized by gender; indeed, female and male serve as the poles around which two totally divergent ideologies crystallize.

Sonar bracchetti takes off with a verbal explosion of enormous vitality, presenting a male world of action through seven infinitives that evoke hunting as a swirl of activity:

> Sonar bracchetti, e cacciatori aizzare,
> lepri levare, ed isgridar le genti,
> e di guinzagli uscir veltri correnti,
> per belle piagge volgere e imboccare . . .
> (vv. 1–4)

> Baying of hounds, hunters goading them on, hares leaping from cover, shouting people, swift greyhounds slipping the leash, dashing about through beautiful meadows and snatching prey . . .

All this—the baying hounds, pursuing hunters, leaping hares, screaming crowds, greyhounds slipping their leashes to turn and grasp their prey—all this, declares the poet, must delight a heart that is free and unburdened by love: "assai credo che deggia dilettare / libero core e van d'intendimenti!" ("such things must greatly delight, I think, a heart that is free and empty of amorous understandings" [vv. 5–6]). Love and its stylized lexicon (*core, intendimenti*) enter this poem as that which the hunt is not, for the hunt and the world it stands for can be enjoyed only by one who possesses a "libero core"—a free heart.

Dante thus introduces love in opposition to the male world of action portrayed in the opening verses; love could transform someone free and unburdened into someone unfree and burdened, and thereby prevent him from taking delight in the activities of the hunt. Love is on one side; freedom, the world out of doors, and maleness are on the other. Grammatically, the male domain is signified by verbs, by the seven successive infinitives that conjure the hunt, culminating in an eighth infinitive associated with the male poet, *dilettare,* expressing his belief that such things should be able to delight him. Infinitives that signify male freedom are used by Boccaccio, perhaps influenced by Dante's sonnet, in the Proem of the *Decameron,* where we find the alignment of deeds and their verbs with men.[4] The pains of love are alleviated for men, because they have access to a host of distracting activities expressed by nine successive infinitives: "per ciò che a loro, volendo essi, non manca l'andare a torno, udire e veder molte cose, uccellare, cacciare, pescare, cavalcare, giucare o mercatare" ("because men, if they wish, are able to walk abroad, hear and see many things, go fowling, hunting, fishing, riding and gambling, or attend to their business affairs" [*Proemio* 12; in Boccaccio 1980]).

In the case of *Sonar bracchetti,* however, our male poet is unable to enjoy his birthright. Using the sonnet's formal dichotomy as a template for presenting ideological dichotomy, the poem swerves in v. 7, slightly before the conclusion of the octave, to engage a different reality. With the subtle adversative "Ed io" which sets the poet apart from the delights enumerated in the opening quatrain, we learn that one of his amorous thoughts has intruded onto his consciousness and speaks to him: "Ed io, fra gli amorosi pensamenti / d'uno sono schernito in tale affare, / e dicemi esto motto per usanza" ("And I, among thoughts of love, find myself mocked in this affair by one of them who habitually speaks to me thus" [vv. 7–9]). And what does the mocking thought say? It upbraids him for abandoning the courtly world of women and love for the "sì selvaggia dilettanza"—the "so rustic pleasure"—of the hunt: "Or ecco leggiadria di gentil core, / per una sì selvaggia dilettanza / lasciar le donne e lor gaia sembianza!" ("O here indeed is the gallantry of a noble heart! For so rustic a pleasure to leave the ladies and their happy ways!" [vv. 10–12]). As a result of love, he is now fearful, ashamed, emotionally and psychologically weighed down, quite the opposite of *libero:* "Allor, temendo non che senta Amore, / prendo vergogna, onde mi ven pesanza" ("Then, fearing that Love may overhear, I grow ashamed, and thence comes heaviness" [vv. 13–14]).

The poet's thought reproves him by feigning, sarcastically, to find in him the key courtly virtue, *leggiadria,* which in fact he lacks: "Or ecco *leggiadria* di gentil core"—"here indeed is the *leggiadria* of a noble heart!" (*Leggiadria* comes from *leggero,* "light," and is a quality of lightness or grace of being possessed by the courtly knight.) The male lover is here denounced for lacking a key courtly attribute, for lacking the *leggiadria* possessed by a *gentil core;* the sign of his defective nature is that he would abandon the refined and courtly world of ladies for the "sì selvaggia dilettanza" of the hunt (in "selvaggia" we catch overtones of both "sylvan" and "savage"). How could he, the thought wants to know, "for so rustic a pleasure"—so suspect a pleasure—"leave the ladies" ("lasciar le donne")? How could he choose the hunt rather than "the ladies and their happy ways"? How could he choose the hunt and thus abandon the ladies and their happy ways—"lasicar le donne e lor gaia sembianza"?

This implicit question, posed by way of the reproof administered by the poet's thought, serves to delineate two clearly defined spheres. The world of women and love is emphatically the sphere of courtliness by virtue of its unambiguous association with *leggiadria*, the courtly virtue par excellence. It is also emphatically an inner world, a passive world.

Indeed, the sonnet's second half—we could say its "female half"—is as replete with static nouns and adjectives as its first—male—half is replete with dynamic verbs. Moreover, whereas the lexicon of the poem's opening section is realistic, specific, and concrete, the later lexicon is generic and coded. Just comparing nouns, we move from "hounds," "hunters," "hares," "people," "leashes," "greyhounds," "meadows" (*bracchetti, cacciatori, lepri, genti, guinzagli, veltri, piagge*) to "heart," "amorous understandings," "thoughts," "gallantry," "delight," "ladies," "appearance," "[the god of] Love," "shame," "heaviness" (*core, intendimenti, pensamenti, leggiadria, dilettanza, donne, sembianza, Amore, vergogna, pesanza*). If the male world is built with the contagiously tumultuous verbs we noted above ("to bay," "to goad," "to leap out," "to shout," "to slip," "to dash," "to snatch") and concrete nouns drawn from everyday life and the world as we know it (even if we do not all go hunting, we all know about dogs, rabbits, and yelling onlookers), the female world is instead constructed with a generic and stylized vocabulary associated with the value system that we have come to label courtly love.

These two worlds stand opposed; what works in one does not work in the other. This point is clearly made by the denunciation of the male lover for his lack of *leggiadria;* as we saw, the sign of his defective nature is that he would abandon the world of ladies for the rustic pleasure of the hunt. He stands self-accused by that part of himself associated with love (and, therefore, with the female sphere) of abandoning the world of women for the world of men. How could he "lasciar le donne e lor gaia sembianza"? The oppositional nature of the male / female binary sketched by this sonnet is summed up in this verse, in the thought of "leaving the women"—"lasciar le donne." This is an either / or universe: either you take the "donne" or you leave them. The young Dante has here given an edgy gendered spin to his version of courtly dualism.

Now let us put *Sonar bracchetti*'s oppositionally gendered world into context. Commentators routinely cite Folgore da San Gimignano's sonnet cycle on the months of the year and, in particular, February's sonnet *E di febbraio vi dono bella caccia.* They then just as routinely note that, hunting thematics aside, the truer precursor is Cavalcanti's sonnet *Biltà di donna e di saccente core,* because of the similar build-up of juxtaposed elements in infinitive clauses, structured to make the point that none of this beauty and grandeur can rival the beauty of the poet's lady. Both Folgore and Cavalcanti are valid references, but the point that needs to be made here—as so often with Dante's lyrics, in which experimentation is always on the agenda—is that Dante's opening gambit fuses these diverse registers, combining the themes of Folgore's so-called bourgeois realism with the stylistic recall of Cavalcanti's idyllic paean to love. All this adds up to a sonnet that is a hybrid with respect to the conventions with which Dante was working; in fact, speaking thoughts, a thoroughly stilnovist convention, do not typically coexist with hunt scenes. This rhetorical hybridity is functional; it reinforces the gendered split that is at the core of *Sonar bracchetti* and is its most interesting feature.

Another way to make this point is to consider another sonnet from Dante's youthful period which is closely linked to Cavalcanti, the sonnet addressed to him: *Guido, i' vorrei che tu e Lapo ed io.* Here we find not the dichotomous courtly realism of *Sonar bracchetti* but a homogeneous courtly idealism much more in line with Cavalcanti's *Biltà di donna,* the sonnet to which *Sonar bracchetti* is indebted. The courtly idealism of *Guido, i' vorrei* offers not dichotomy but homogeneity, a world in which all tensions and divides are lulled into a quiescent dream of oneness and delectation. By contrast (and, given the Cavalcantian pedigree of both, it is a contrast of which Dante would have been highly conscious), the delectation of *Sonar bracchetti* is not fused and unified but polarized and gendered, boasting the "selvaggia dilettanza" of the male sphere on the one hand and the "gaia sembianza" of the ladies on the other. Dante is certainly aware of gender as a source of tension even in *Guido, i' vorrei,* as the poem's structure makes clear: first, the octave figures the harmony of the male poets; then, in a second act as it were, the tercets fold into this ethereal stilnovist soufflé the poets' ladies, with the hope (the Freudian hope, one is tempted to say) that "ciascuna di lor fosse contenta" ("each one of them would be happy"). But this structural awareness of dichotomy only emphasizes this poem's commitment to evade and transcend it. *Guido, i' vorrei* is a dream of oneness; it is about floating beyond dichotomy, floating beyond the divisions that could sunder a man from a woman, or indeed—given the two male identities that frame its incipit—a man from a man.

Sonar bracchetti is, instead, about dichotomy, and specifically about male / female dichotomy. Far from being a trivial bit of youthful froth, *Sonar bracchetti* is a forthright exposition of courtly society's gendered faultline, noteworthy in particular for its clever deployment of the sonnet's dichotomized form to make an argument about dichotomy. However, *Sonar bracchetti* never challenges the ideological legitimacy of the dichotomized courtly world that it so acutely renders. It is all the more interesting, therefore, to find Dante's handling of gender evolve along the arc of his lyrics in a wholly other direction. He will ultimately, in the late *canzone Doglia mi reca,* configure gender within a context that is not just non-courtly but explosively anti-courtly. The move away from a courtly ideology is significant, since it makes possible the construction of woman as a moral agent in her own right. It results in taking woman off the pedestal on which her sole occupation is to arbitrate man's behavior, and allows a shift away from an exclusive focus on the man: his *vergogna,* his *pesanza,* his *paura,* and even—occasionally—his *baldanza.* Once this shift has occurred, the female can come into focus as a subject (albeit an errant subject), rather than serving solely as backdrop for male subjectivity and commentator on male behavior. Anti-courtliness is the signature move of *Doglia mi reca,* and it makes possible a new approach to the construction of gender.

But before reaching Dante's anti-courtly apogee, our trajectory requires a stop at the *canzone Poscia ch'Amor,* dedicated to analyzing the courtly attribute of *leggiadria* (we remember that the poet's fall from courtliness in *Sonar bracchetti* was signaled precisely by his failure to demonstrate "*leggiadria* di gentil core"). In this important *canzone* the more mature Dante, whose lyrics now broach explicitly moral and ethical concerns, attempts to wed courtly values with moral and ethical values, and so to preserve courtliness. In the short term, this experiment must not have proved fully satisfactory, for Dante moved on to *Doglia mi reca,* where ethics trumps courtliness. But in the longer term, this *canzone* foretells the *Commedia,* where courtly values, morphed and reinvigorated, will resurface, as indicated by the presence in the *Paradiso* of two of *Poscia ch'Amor*'s quintessentially courtly terms, *donneare* and *leggiadria.* The verb *donneare* ("to pay court to a lady"; "hold amorous communication with a lady") from the Provençal *domnejar,* which is used in *Poscia ch'Amor* to describe the correct form of interaction between the sexes, reappears in the *Paradiso,* where it limns the interaction between Dante's mind and God's grace and between Dante's mind and Beatrice.[5] And *leggiadria* is the hallmark of the third canticle's transfigured courtly mysticism, used to describe the angel Gabriel in *Paradiso* 32: "Baldezza e *leggiadria* / quant'esser puote in angelo e in alma, / tutto è in lui" ("Confidence and grace, as much as can be in angel or in soul, all are in him" [32.109–11]).[6]

Poscia ch'Amor shows us Dante struggling to accommodate courtly values he cherishes within a moral system already influenced by Aristotelian and Scholastic ethics. To this end he tackles the definition of *leggiadria,* first instructing us as to its misapplication and then turning to a positive definition. Despite what could seem like the rather severe obstacle of having to admit that *leggiadria* is not suitable to honorable men of a religious or philosophical disposition, and therefore is not an absolute virtue, since absolute virtue is suitable to everyone, he recovers well, arguing that it is a composite virtue.[7] "Sarà mischiata," he opines, "causata di più cose" (vv. 84–85):

> Dunque, s'ell'è in cavalier lodata,
> sarà mischiata,
> causata di più cose; per che questa
> conven che di sè vesta
> l'un bene e l'altro male,
> ma vertù pura in ciascuno sta bene.
> (vv. 83–88)

> Therefore, if *leggiadria* is praised in a gentleman, it must be something mixed, caused by several factors: and this is why it must clothe one man well, another badly, whereas simple virtue is becoming in everybody.

This notion of a composite virtue—"mischiata" in Dante's word—provides the perfect emblem for *Poscia ch'Amor,* which is itself "mischiata," a mixed *canzone,* fully committed to courtly values yet already betraying the pressure that will ultimately lead to the anti-courtly stance of *Doglia mi reca.* This pressure to adopt a competing set of values manifests itself precisely around the issue of gender, where indeed *Poscia ch'Amor* is mixed to the point of confusion, both exalting and castigating women.

On the one hand, *Poscia ch'Amor* fulfills its courtly mandate by offering the type of the courtly lady. False knights, the poet tells us, are revealed in part by whom they choose to love: "non sono innamorati / mai di donna amorosa" ("they are never in love with an amorous lady" [vv. 48–49]). The unworthiness of false knights, who do not live up to the courtly ideal, is reflected in the unworthiness of the women they choose; they never love a "donna amorosa"—that is, in this coded and stylized language, a lady who is refined, noble, inclined to love, and worthy of love, the bearer of the courtly standard. By implication there are some women who are worthy, who do conform to the type of the *donna amorosa.* In fact, the poet holds up a specific but unnamed woman as the embodiment of *leggiadria* and claims that, because he lives in a society in which *leggiadria* has gone astray, she was the sole means of his own familiarity with it. The exaltation of this lady, "una gentile / che la mostrava in tutti gli atti sui" ("a gentle lady who revealed *leggiadria* in all her acts" [vv. 62–63]), is striking, because she is the only individual in a poem without contemporary interlocutors. For this reason, Dante deprives *Poscia ch'Amor* of the *congedo* that typically sends the poem to a contemporary recipient. Rather, this *canzone* on *leggiadria* has no worthy recipients, since, as the last verse declares, "Color che vivon fanno tutti contra" ("Those living all do the contrary")—that is, no one currently lives according to *leggiadria*'s precepts and standards.

So far *Poscia ch'Amor* seems conventionally courtly in its gender configuration. But the section on the poor courtship skills of the knights of today leads in an unusual direction. It seems that these false knights are vile seducers who do not court ladies in the fashion of someone equipped with *leggiadria,* but rather entice them into base delights. These are men who would not move a foot to court a woman in a graceful and civilized fashion, but rather, like a thief to his theft, go after sensual pleasure. What follows is fascinating, because the moralizing Guittonian strain of the verse (we should not forget that Guittone's *canzone Altra fiata aggio già, donne, parlato* exhorts women to vigilance against male seduction) seems to cause Dante's ideological bearings momentarily to slip. At the end of the third stanza, as he passionately pursues the theme of the vile seducers (eliciting from Contini the comment "Dante contro don Giovanni" [Alighieri (1946) 1970, 101]), despite the fact that the fourth stanza will soon present the epitome of female courtliness, "che [leggiadria] mostrava in tutti gli atti sui," Dante violates courtly logic by entertaining the notion that women are part of the general moral turpitude: they are not blameless. These are the verses that make *Poscia ch'Amor* truly "mixed"—"mischiata"—not just a reaffirmation of courtly values in their pure form but also a vehicle toward the virulently anti-courtly *Doglia mi reca:*

> non moverieno il piede
> per donneare a guisa di leggiadro,
> ma, come al furto il ladro,
> così vanno a pigliar villan diletto;
> e non però che 'n donne e sì dispento
> leggiadro portamento,
> che paiono animai sanza intelletto.
> (vv. 51–57)

> Never would they stir themselves to court ladies in a graceful and civilized way, but like a thief to his theft they go after base sensual delight; and this not because courtly comportment has so completely been extinguished in women that they seem animals without intellect.

Dante's less than transparent syntax requires us to pay close attention to construing the literal meaning of these verses. Let me be clear: Dante does *not* say in this passage that ladies are animals without intellect. What he does do is bring ladies into a discursive space in which it is held possible that they could potentially degrade to that degree. He says that false knights go to steal sensual pleasure from women, and that this occurs not because courtly behavior is so lacking in women that they have become animals without intellect. In other words, the false knights must take the blame for their own corrupt behavior, not seek simply to blame the corruption of women. Technically, the sentence negates that women have degraded to the point of becoming animals, telling us that, yes, "leggiadro portamento" ("courtly comportment") in women has been somewhat extinguished, but it is not "sì dispento" ("so extinguished") as to make them animals! Dante thus imports a defense that functions as an offense, all the more telling in that there was no apparent need for this line of reasoning, no previous suspicion of an attack on the courtly integrity of the "donna amorosa."

Responding to an internal logic and pressure that are in conflict with the governing—but internally conflicted—logic of the poem, Dante introduces the possibility that *donne* can degrade, that in theory they could even degrade to the point of being "animai sanza intelletto." So ends stanza 3 of *Poscia ch'Amor,* striking a note that will be a major motif of *Doglia mi reca:* humans degraded to the point that "they seem animals without intellect." Thus, the closer we get to *Doglia mi reca* the further we get from the courtly paradigm, including the theologized courtly paradigm of the *Vita Nova,* the early book whose most famous *canzone* begins *Donne ch'avete intelletto d'amore* ("Ladies who have intellect of love"): "donne . . . che paiono animai sanza intelletto" is a long way from "Donne ch'avete intelletto d'amore."

The male narcissism of courtly lyric requires the sustaining presence of the lady, available as the backdrop and foil, even occasionally censurer, of the man, but not as a subject with her own inner life and moral choices—in short, not with her own desires. *Doglia mi reca,* a late *canzone* written shortly before the transition to the *Commedia* and fully committed to moral themes, signals at once its aggressively anti-courtly posture, taking the moral critique of women that briefly surfaced in *Poscia ch'Amor* and making it programmatic. This poem, an expansive meditation on desire, opens with female desire, already anomalous as a focus of attention, and makes its anti-courtly agenda even more explicit by focusing on base female desire—"il vil vostro disire":

Doglia mi reca ne lo core ardire
a voler ch'è di veritate amico:
però, donne, s'io dico
parole quasi contra tutta gente,
non vi maravigliate,
ma conoscete il vil vostro disire.
(vv. 1–6)

Grief brings boldness to my heart on behalf of a will that is friend to truth. If then, ladies, I speak words against almost everyone, do not wonder at this, but recognize the baseness of your desires.

As truth's friend, Dante tells us, he will utter "words against almost everyone"; in other words, he views his program in this *canzone* as profoundly unconventional. Dante is here signaling that in *Doglia mi reca* he will stake out an anti-courtly position. Moreover, he is letting us know that he is starting within the courtly framework and working against it, rather than operating within a different framework altogether. This is an important distinction for, were *Doglia mi reca* operating within the set of conventions we associate with misogynistic writing, for instance, an attack on female desire would be utterly conventional. Thus, in the explicitly misogynistic *Corbaccio,* where female desire is routinely construed as vile and base, Boccaccio is not worried that he will be perceived as antagonistic or unconventional, as Dante is in *Doglia mi reca.* While Dante may say some things in *Doglia mi reca* that today strike us as misogynistic, it is important to grasp that he is not adopting misogynistic conventions, but rather exploding courtly conventions from within: he is following his own moral logic to a place that coexists ever more uneasily with his courtly point of departure. The development in his thinking could be described with the following analogy: if the conventional courtly framework is the ocean, and *Poscia ch'Amor* and *Doglia mi reca* are ships, then the lines about the "donne . . . che paiono animai sanza intelletto" are a ticking time-bomb that in *Doglia mi reca* finally explodes, threatening the integrity of the vessel and totally changing our perspective on the courtly *mare magnum* that still surrounds us.

I have written previously (1997) about Dante's radical treatment of male desire in *Doglia mi reca.*[8] In the tradition of the Provençal *sirventes,* Dante frequently signifies the degradation of the courtly world through juxtapositions that carry shock value; we think of the Provençal poet Giraut de Borneil, who in *Per solatz reveillar* (1989) calls "Shame on the knight who pays court to a lady after laying hands on bleating sheep and robbing churches and travelers!" (vv. 27–30). In *Poscia ch'Amor* Dante follows Giraut, deploring the retreat from courtly values and, like Giraut, comparing the corrupt courtship of false knights to thieves plying their trade.[9] But in *Doglia mi reca* Dante goes further: by conflating courtship with lust and lust with avarice he endangers the courtly paradigm that privileges love over baser desires and illuminates the common ground of all concupiscence. *Doglia mi reca*'s juxtaposition of the desire experienced by a lover with the desire experienced by a miser serves not just as a condemnation of false courtliness in the hope of a return to true courtliness, as in Giraut's model, but also as the springboard for an analysis of desire that is new to the lyric tradition. In fact, in his mature lyrics Dante is elaborating an analysis of desire that anticipates the *Commedia* in its move away from the dualistic courtly paradigm toward a unified Aristotelian template (see Barolini 1997 and 1998).

If *Doglia mi reca* explodes the courtly paradigm in the context of male desire, it does so also by allowing female desire to exist as a context, no longer holding women harmless as passive recipients of male love, but forging them as desirers and moral agents in their own right, and starting down a path that will lead eventually to Francesca and Piccarda. But at this point in his development, Dante is not yet incorporating courtly issues into a broader moral framework, as he does in *Inferno* 5, but rather importing all these moral issues into a constraining courtly framework, which is why his thinking sometimes appears contradictory and muddled. Thus, *Doglia mi reca* begins by bringing female agency to the fore, as we have seen, but then confuses the issue as the first stanza continues. Making female beauty the correlative of male virtue and love the force that unifies the two—"se vertute a noi / fu data, e beltà a voi, / e a costui di due poter un fare" ("if virtue to us was given, and beauty to you, and to Love the power to make of two things one" [vv. 12–14])—Dante holds that it is a woman's duty to deny her love to men who cannot match in virtue what she offers in beauty. He instructs women not to love, and to cover up their beauty, since virtue, which was beauty's target, is no more:

> voi non dovreste amare,
> ma coprir quanto di biltà v'è dato,
> poi che non c'è virtù, ch'era suo segno
> (vv. 15–17)

you should love no more, but rather hide the beauty given you, since virtue, which was its goal, is found no more[10]

By engaging a gendered duality that assigns beauty to women and virtue to men, thus associating women with exteriority and superficial values and men with interiority and ethical values, the *canzone*'s implicit program of non-dualistic gender construction seems to falter. Charting territory that is new to him, Dante does indeed falter. But his attraction to the idea of female agency and responsibility is strong and manifests itself again before the stanza concludes. The first stanza of *Doglia mi reca* ends by declaring that it would be particularly laudable for a woman to bid farewell to her beauty of her own accord:

> Dico che bel disdegno
> sarebbe in donna, di ragion laudato,
> partir beltà da sè per suo commiato.
> (vv. 19–21)

I say it would be an act of fine scorn in a woman, and rightly praised, to sever beauty from herself—bidding it farewell of her own accord.

Dante here puzzles the English editors Foster and Boyde who wonder what is "the special point of adding 'of her own accord'?" (Alighieri 1967, 2:300). But precisely these words, "per suo commiato," hold the key to Dante's thought process. These words bring Dante back—perhaps he too was surprised at this—to her will, her agency. Moreover, his apparent need to go in this direction gets him all tangled up. Let us consider: if women should cover themselves of their own will (in a kind of self-imposed chador), then women are to make a moral choice to hide their beauty from immoral men. So, though this passage began with the equation virtue:men = beauty:women ("se vertute a noi / fu data, e beltà a voi" [vv. 12–13]), it soon gets severely tangled, as Dante exhorts women to deploy the virtue that they theoretically lack against the men who theoretically possess it.

Although *Doglia mi reca* never fully overcomes this initial confusion, it develops always in the direction of assigning more and more choice to women, and as a result takes an anomalous interest in communicating with them and instructing them. Whereas the courtly *canzone* frequently opens with a conventional address to ladies who then disappear from the poem (Cavalcanti's *Donna me prega,* Dante's *Donne ch'avete intelletto d'amore*), the female addressees whom Dante enlists in the struggle against male vice in stanza one of *Doglia mi reca* do not disappear from view but are summoned again prior to the *canzone*'s midpoint and again at its conclusion. Dante comes back to his female audience midway through the third stanza. The passage starts out in a metapoetic key, announcing a change in style toward greater clarity in order best to serve his female audience, and then reaffirms the poet's role as moral guide, whose compensation will be his audience's compliance:

> Ma perchè lo meo dire util vi sia,
> discenderò del tutto
> in parte ed in costrutto
> più lieve, sì che men grave s'intenda:
> che rado sotto benda
> parola oscura giugne ad intelletto;
> per che parlar con voi si vole aperto:
> ma questo vo' per merto,
> per voi, non per me certo,
> ch'abbiate a vil ciascuno e a dispetto.
> (vv. 53–62)

> But that my speech may be of use to you, I'll come down from the general to the particular, and to a lighter form of expression, so that it may be less hard to understand; for seldom under a veil do obscure words reach the intellect, hence with you one must speak openly. But this I want in recompense (for your own good, certainly not for mine) that you hold every man as vile and object of scorn.

No doubt the patronizing tone of this passage is annoying. At the same time we do well to keep in mind that these verses testify to Dante's genuine concern that the women to whom he writes understand him, that they be authentic comprehenders and recipients of his message, maybe even authentic interlocutors, given that this poem's *congedo* explicitly sends it to a woman. There can never be problems of communication in dealing with an idealized projection of our own desires; problems of communication arise only when we deal with an authentic other, like the women of this *canzone.* And, again, we can see how far *Doglia mi reca* has moved beyond *Poscia ch'Amor,* where the moral focus is still almost exclusively on men, and where the metapoetic core is not gender-specific.[11]

There is a lot that one could say about the metapoetic verses addressed to women in *Doglia mi reca,* although ultimately I think the most important point about them is that they exist at all. The women of this *canzone* are neither like animals, "sanza intelletto," or idealized, possessing "intelletto d'amore"; rather, they have plain "intelletto," enough to receive the poet's instruction, if not in its obscure form, as "parola oscura," then as "parlar . . . aperto." Dante combines technical poetic jargon rooted in Provençal (*trobar clus, trobar leu,* and so on) with a pedagogic pragmatism that may be a hallmark of texts addressed to women: the emphasis on the utility of discourse ("perchè lo meo dire util vi sia") reminds one again of the *Decameron*'s Proem. This double focus accounts for the insecurity of the commentary tradition regarding "sotto benda" in v. 57: does "under a veil" refer to a literal article of clothing and, therefore, to those who wear it (i.e., women)? Or does it refer to an allegorical veil, a veil of language? I take it to mean both. In a deliberate recall and inversion of the exhortation that women veil their physical beauty, the poet will throw the veil of obscurity off the text and speak openly, unveiling the truth for his female audience: "I have unveiled for you, ladies"—"Disvelato v'ho, donne" (v. 127)—says the poet later, using the same trope. Here the male poet does the work of unveiling for his veiled female audience; in the *Commedia* Beatrice will unveil both herself and then, through her speech, the mysteries of the universe for her audience, both female and male.

In the *congedo* Dante instructs his *canzone* to await the commands of its female recipient (we note the highlighted female pronouns in "a costei," "prima con lei," "prima a lei"), who is not an idealized *senhal* but a specific "lady from our country: beautiful, wise, and courteous" ("donna / ch'è del nostro paese: / bella, saggia e cortese" [vv. 148–50]). She will dispose of the *canzone:* "prima con lei t'arresta, / prima a lei manifesta / quel che tu se' e quel per ch'io ti mando; / poi seguirai secondo suo comando" ("stay first with her, to her manifest what you are and why I send you; then continue as she commands" [vv. 155–58]). Commentators show some surprise at the *congedo*'s praise of a woman ("a perhaps rather surprising conclusion to the stern exhortations preceding it," say Foster and Boyde [Alighieri 1967, 2:296]). But it is all of a piece with *Doglia mi reca*'s treatment of women as moral agents who are held accountable for their desires and actions. As moral agents, they are individual subjects and, like the lady to whom the *canzone* is addressed, even receive names: in this case she is "Bianca, Giovanna, Contessa" (v. 153), later she will be Francesca, the only contemporary named in her canto. At stake are discretion, choice, responsibility, agency. To the degree that a woman is "wise" ("saggia"), she will make appropriate decisions, in this case the decisions regarding the *canzone.* If she is not *saggia,* she may make inappropriate decisions, and—despite the poet's best efforts—may perish. This strong sentiment from *Doglia mi reca*'s seventh and conclusive stanza anticipates the *Commedia,* in which a woman's moral choices, like a man's, may in fact cause her to perish. The stanza begins "Disvelato v'ho donne," and the point of that unveiling becomes successively clearer as the stanza unfolds: once beyond moral ignorance, women become moral agents.

Not only the women, but the poet too seems to have moved beyond his initial intellectual position. Rather than the rigorous separation between virtue and beauty, male and female, that we saw in stanza one, in stanza seven Dante works against dualism, elaborating on his earlier claim that love has the power to make one out of two ("e a costui di due poter un fare" [v. 14]). Love is the process whereby two become one. It is the means of forging unity, of destroying dualism. In this instance, love is the process whereby the two goods, virtue and beauty, are commingled and thus degendered, growing into leafy fronds of love that have drawn equally from the roots of both male and female: "che l'amorose fronde / di radice di ben altro ben tira" ("for from one good root another good draws out the leaves of love" [vv. 134–35]). As in the *Paradiso,* where Dante uses metaphor to capture paradoxical unities that lie outside the purview of discursive language, here the metaphor of the "amorose fronde" figures a holistic and degendered vision of beauty grounded in ethics, and vice versa.

However, this vision of potential unity should not result in complacency, for women must remain on their guard against all the non-virtuous men with whom their roots would yield not "amorose fronde," leaves of love, but only animal appetite, lust. Love, properly understood, is inseparable from virtue. Therefore, a woman can consider herself loved by a vicious man only if she redefines love, giving the name of love to what is mere bestial appetite: "chiamando amore appetito di fera" ("calling the appetite of a beast by the name love" [v. 143]). Such a woman should perish, since she disjoins her beauty from natural goodness and believes love to be "outside the garden of reason":

> Vedete come conchiudendo vado:
> che non dee creder quella
> cui par bene esser bella,
> esser amata da questi cotali;
> che se beltà tra i mali
> volemo annumerar, creder si pone,
> chiamando amore appetito di fera.
> Oh cotal donna pera
> che sua biltà dischiera
> da natural bontà per tal cagione,
> e crede amor fuor d'orto di ragione!
> (vv. 137–47)

See how I reach my conclusion: she who thinks it good to be beautiful should not believe herself loved by such as these; though if we wanted to number beauty among the evils, then one could believe that—provided one give the name "love" to bestial appetite. O let such a woman perish, who for such reasons sunders her beauty from natural goodness and believes that love exists outside the garden of reason!

This passage holds that it is the responsibility of the woman to distinguish between lovers, and to make sure that she is not "amata da questi cotali" ("loved by such as these"), desired by the men of vice whom the *canzone* has savaged. If she does give her love to such a man, disjoining her beauty from virtue, she deserves to perish.[12] We can see now why Dante apologizes in advance for his "parole quasi contra tutta gente": nothing could be less courtly than "Oh cotal donna pera" ("Oh, let such a woman perish").

I have discussed elsewhere how this final stanza of *Doglia mi reca* adumbrates *Inferno* 5, both in considering whether the use of the name "love" is sufficient guarantee that we are in fact talking of love and in raising the possibility that someone who desires—a woman who desires, no less!—could define love in a self-serving way, and could justify her appetite by calling it with the name love. As with Francesca, although she may use the word *amore,* the *donna* of the last stanza of *Doglia mi reca* misapplies the signifier, for the impulse that grips her is an "appetito di fera." Her mistake comes from the fact that she believes—wrongly, according to Dante—that love is disjoined from reason, that love is outside the garden of reason: "crede amor fuor d'orto di ragione" (v. 147).[13] The triple use of *credere* in this stanza is significant: the point is that women have beliefs, values, and ideas for which they, like men, will ultimately be held accountable.

Although at first it seems counter-intuitive to read the harsh paternalism of *Doglia mi reca* in a progressive light, Dante accomplishes quite a lot in this *canzone.* The ladies of *Doglia mi reca* are definitely off the courtly pedestal. They now have more to worry about than the behavior of their male lovers: they have their own selves, including their immortal souls, to take care of. They have acquired the status of moral agents and although they do not yet speak—an activity for which we have to await the *Commedia*—they are expected to be able students, fully receiving and intellectually digesting the poet's message.[14] Moreover, if we put *Doglia mi reca* into the context of options available to the courtly poet, we see that Dante here bypasses altogether the courtly paradigm, according to which a lady is conceived in negative terms not on moral grounds but on the basis of her perceived cruelty to her male lover (in Dante's personal lyric constellation, this would be the stony lady of the *rime petrose*). In *Doglia mi reca* a woman possesses her own actions and her own desires and it is up to her whether she develops into "Bianca Giovanna Contessa" or someone else.

I would like to conclude by coming back to dualism as a powerful prism that leads Dante's readers to distort what Dante is saying, even to misconstrue the literal meaning of his words. My example in this context is Antonio Gagliardi's stunningly incorrect reading of *Doglia mi reca,* noteworthy because his book *Guido Cavalcanti e Dante* (1997) has much that is valuable in it, including his bringing *Doglia mi reca* into play in a discussion of desire. But, starting from the position that Dante is a cultivator of intellectual love only, Gagliardi profoundly misreads the *canzone* as denying all value to human love, viewing it as "desiderio animalesco" ("animal desire") and the *canzone* as establishing "un'ermeneutica negativa di qualsiasi desiderio funzionale all'eros" ("a negative hermeneutic with respect to all erotic desire" [73]). He misconstrues the literal meaning of the text, as when he writes that "Il desiderio di per sé è vile" ("Desire in and of itself is vile" [74]), sustaining that for Dante "la virtù non si colloca nella medietà del desiderio erotico, come sarebbe possibile in Aristotele, ma mira alla sua negazione radicale. . . . Oltre ad 'amore appetito di fera' non c'è altro" ("virtue is not located at the median with respect to erotic desire, as would be possible in Aristotle, but aims for its radical negation. . . . Other than 'love that is bestial appetite' there is nothing" [86]).

We know that this is wrong: Dante was not a dualist, and he did indeed construe desire, including erotic desire, according to an Aristotelian and Thomistic paradigm (see Cogan 1999 and Barolini 2000b). Gagliardi's comments are worth citing at length, however, because they are—in their general thrust, if not in their specific application—far from uncommon. Unified theories of desire seem in general to withstand with difficulty what seems to be an almost instinctive human reversion to moral Manichaeism, with the result that dualism pervades our interpretation of our moral universe. It is not surprising that, as a by-product, dualism would pervade also our reading and reception of a morally saturated poet like Dante.

With respect to Gagliardi's remark "Other than 'love that is bestial appetite' there is nothing," the opposite is true. By the time Dante reaches *Doglia mi reca* he believes that only the impulse that dwells within reason's garden may be granted the name love. What Dante is saying in *Doglia mi reca* is that desire exists on a continuum, that on this continuum may be found both love and animal appetite, and that it is up to us to choose between them. In this *canzone* Dante outlines a continuum of human appetite by sketching in the two poles, the two extremes: *appetito di fera* and *amore d'orto di ragione.* Appetite divorced from reason is often mistakenly called love, whereas appetite in accord with reason is correctly called love. Dante's mature view of desire is thus not dualistic, for it is not appetite that is bad or good, but how we direct it. The integrated view of desire that Dante achieves in *Doglia mi reca* shows in the language of the seventh stanza, not only in the metaphor of the "amorose fronde" but in the repeated yoking of the good and the beautiful: "cui par *bene* esser *bella*" (v. 139), "che sua *biltà* dischiera / da natural *bontà*" (vv. 145–46). What troubles the poet is precisely that anyone would seek to unyoke beauty from virtue—"che sua biltà dischiera / da natural bontà"—and thus produce dualism. Reason and appetite are constants of our identities; the goal—and the challenge—is to keep them unified and aligned.

Given his dualistic template, it is not surprising that Gagliardi also misreads what Dante says about women in *Doglia mi reca*, writing that "La donna è pura animalità coperta dalla bellezza" ("Woman is pure animality covered by beauty" [1997, 75]) and deducing from Dante's initial alignment of virtue with men and beauty with women that "la donna non può essere virtuosa" ("woman cannot be virtuous" [74]). Here, too, as I have tried to show, quite the opposite is true. In *Doglia mi reca* Dante overcomes the polarized world of the Beatrice-versus-*donna petra* paradigm, in which the anti-Beatrice is conceived as negative not on substantive moral grounds but because of erotic rejection, and begins to put women and men on an equal footing before God. Dante's treatment of women in these later lyrics tracks his mature conception of desire, which is neither completely intellectualized nor completely bestial, but a continuum that embraces both extremes. Women for him are not located at one pole or the other, but are somewhere much more complex—and human—in between.

Notes

1. There are eighty-eight poems in the editions prepared by Barbi (Alighieri 1956 and 1969) and Contini (Alighieri [1946] 1970); Foster and Boyde (Alighieri 1967) count eighty-nine because, in reversing the attributions in an exchange between Dante Alighieri and Dante da Maiano, they gain an additional composition for Dante. I cite from Alighieri 1956 and 1969 (ed. Barbi); translations are my own.

2. On the importance of Beatrice's speech, and the unorthodox roles that Dante assigns to her, see Ferrante 1992.

3. See Bynum 1991 and 1995. Getting past the *poeta / theologus* binary was very much my goal in *The Undivine "Comedy"* (1992).

4. For the alignment of deeds with men and words with women in the *Decameron,* and the way that Boccaccio programmatically contaminates his categories, see Barolini 1993.

5. In these verses Dante manages to put his mind both in the female position, being courted by grace, and in the male, courting Beatrice: "La Grazia, che donnea con la tua mente" ("Grace that discourses amorously with your mind" [*Par* 24.118–19]); "La mente inamorata, che donnea / con la mia donna sempre" ("My enamored mind that always holds amorous discourse with my lady" [*Par* 27.88–89]).

6. *Leggiadria,* used only once in the *Commedia,* occurs in five lyrics: *Per una ghirlandetta, Sonar bracchetti, Morte villana, Due donne in cima, Poscia ch'Amor.*

7. The gloss of Foster and Boyde (Alighieri 1967, 2:230) on this passage is worth citing, since it hits on the key issue—the move from (courtly) dualism to (Aristotelian) non-dualism: "Dante is not a dualist for whom *levitas* is bad because *gravitas* is good, or vice versa. He is an Aristotelian, for whom virtue resides in the mean, and it is not difficult for him to distinguish and condemn excessive or misguided 'lightness' of behaviour, without condemning 'lightness' of behaviour as such."

8. As my work on this *canzone* has proceeded I have become progressively more aware of its boldness and subtlety. Thus, in the 1997 essay I dealt with Dante's handling of desire in the *canzone, tout court,* and did not yet qualify it as his treatment of "male desire." The gendered aspects of *Doglia mi reca*'s analysis became apparent only in a later stage of my work.

9. Giraut's *Per solatz reveillar* is an important and insufficiently studied intertext of *Poscia ch'Amor.* Although Contini (Alighieri [1946] 1970, 98) notes the generic relationship between the two *canzoni,* commenting that Dante, "come Guiraut de Bornelh, lamenta la decadenza del *Joi,* del *Pretz,* del *Solatz,*" he does not note *Poscia ch'Amor*'s close verbal dependence on *Per solatz reveillar.* I suggest that vv. 51–54 of *Poscia ch'Amor*—"non moverieno il piede / per donneare a guisa di leggiadro, / ma come al furto il ladro, / così vanno a pigliar villan diletto"—are modeled on Giraut's vv. 27–30: "Cavalliers si'aunitz / Que·s met en doneiar, / Pois qe tocha dels mans moutons belanz / Ni qe rauba gleisas ne viandanz!" (468) ("Now is renown won through robbery and through snatching sheep from the flock. Shame on the knight who pays court to a lady after laying hands on bleating sheep and robbing churches and travelers!" [Shaman 1989]). Both passages are marked by the presence of the verb *donneare,* and, in both, corrupt lovers are compared to thieves.

10. The context in no way supports Pézard's thesis that this passage exhorts women to self-blinding, a thesis given undue credibility by Foster and Boyde in their commentary (Alighieri 1967, 2:299–300). The key word here is "coprir," and the key trope is veiling / unveiling. Thus, "ma coprir quanto di biltà v'è dato" in stanza 1 is echoed by "rado sotto benda" and "aperto" in stanza 3. The trope is common in moralizing discourses on female chastity. We find *coprire* used by Guittone (1940) in a similar context in the *canzone Altra fiata aggio già, donne, parlato:* "Donne, se castità v'è in piacimento, / covra onestà vostra bella fazone" (vv. 157–58).

11. Rather than make a point about gender, the metapoetic core of *Poscia ch'Amor* develops the theme of the poet's lack of interlocutors: "per che da questo punto / con rima più sottile / tratterò il ver di lei, ma non so cui" ("so that from this point on, with more subtle verses, I will treat the truth regarding her [*leggiadria*], but I know not for whom" [vv. 67–69]). This note of existential loneliness will also furnish the *canzone*'s disillusioned final verse, "Color che vivon fanno tutti contra" ("Those living all do the contrary").

12. There is a precedent for female unchastity leading to death in Guittone d'Arezzo's *Altra fiata aggio già* (1940). Dante's complex Scholastic analysis of different kinds of desire concludes with the idea that a woman who fails to discriminate between lovers deserves to perish. Guittone simply exhorts women to remain chaste at all costs, for even death is better than taking a lover:

> Ohi, quanto fòrate, donna, men male,
> se l'amadore tuo morte te desse,
> che ben tal te volesse!
> Chè pregio vale ed aunor più che vita.
> Oi donna sopellita
> in brobio tanto ed in miseria, aviso
> che peggio d'onne morte è vita tale.
> (vv. 108–14)

("Oh, how much less evil it would be for you, lady, if your lover were to give you death rather than love you thus! For esteem and honor are more valuable than life. O lady buried in such shame and misery, I hold that worse than any death is such a life.")

13. The last stanza of *Doglia mi reca* is critical for understanding Dante's anatomy of desire: "The idea of a love that is 'appetito di fera' and 'fuor d'orto di ragione' allows us to postulate its converse, namely, a love that is human rather than feral and that is *within* reason's garden. In other words, these verses supply the crucial discriminant between types of 'love,' or more properly between lust and love, namely reason, the faculty that renders us human rather than bestial. The anatomy of love that results, with its two

opposing categories—'amore appetito di fera' versus 'amor . . . d'orto di ragione'—will find confirmation in the *Commedia*" (Barolini 1997, 16). I would now stress that these two categories should be conceived as opposing extremes along a single continuum of desire. For *Doglia mi reca* in the context of *Inferno* 5, see Barolini 1998.

14. Is Guittone a precursor here? In other words, does Guittone's harsh paternalism toward his female audience in *Altra fiata aggio già, donne, parlato* open the door to their free agency as well? To what degree does Guittone pave the way for Dante's handling of gender in *Doglia mi reca?* My impression is that *Altra fiata* does indeed offer an early model of the *Doglia mi reca* paradigm whereby paternalistic morality defeats courtliness and ironically enhances the status of women by conceiving them as moral agents. But Guittone's anti-courtliness is also quite different from Dante's, and would repay study as a model that Dante both attended to and rejected. Guittone is more attuned to popular religiosity and less to philosophical models than Dante is (for instance, in his adoption of an explicit Eve / Mary template for female behavior). And he differs from Dante in using an autobiographical stance: the premise for his sermon is that he himself was once a seducer who entrapped and deceived women (much like the false knights of *Poscia ch'Amor*).

5

Queering Nature, Queering Gender: Dante and Sodomy

Gary P. Cestaro

> Comunemente, designiamo l'omosessualità sotto il nome di vizio contro natura, mentre in realtà è vero il contrario: l'omosessualità è nella natura, che accetta tutto e contiene tutto; è la Morale che, in questo caso come in molti altri, si oppone alla natura per ragioni che le sono proprie, rifiutando e condannando l'omosessualità.
>
> (Rossi Barilli 1999, 39)

> We commonly designate homosexuality as "the vice against nature," when really just the opposite is true: homosexuality is in nature, which accepts everything and contains everything; it is Morality that—in this case as in so many others—opposes nature for reasons all its own by refusing and condemning homosexuality.
>
> (my translation)

THE WORDS are Alberto Moravia's in a 1961 defense of Pier Paolo Pasolini, who had been charged with armed robbery and sentenced to twenty days' confinement for having done nothing more, it seems, than admire a young *barista* whose acquaintance he wished to make. Moravia's remark that nature "accepts *everything* and contains *everything*" is, perhaps, not a ringing endorsement of gay male sex. Nonetheless, it is 1961—the year of my birth—and we are grateful to Moravia for his sympathetic defense.

By citing the common acceptation of "homosexuality" as the "vice against nature," Moravia evokes a common medieval definition of sodomy. As Mark Jordan (1997, 45–66) has recently taught, we owe the invention of *sodomia*—the word and in some ways the crime—to the eleventh-century Italian saint Peter Damian in his rabid and anxious harangue against monastic sodomy, the *Liber gomorrhianus*. The construction of sodomy as the *vitium contra naturam*, already suggested by Paul (Rom 1:26–27), becomes common in the later Middle Ages. This is the definition apparently promoted by Alan of Lille in the playful *De planctu naturae*—although Jordan (1997, 67–91) has his doubts about what's really going on there. In any event, this is the definition registered and made official by the Scholastics, by yet another Italian saint, Thomas Aquinas, in the *Summa Theologica* (Boswell 1980, 314–28; Jordan 1997, 114–58).[1] It is this very definition that Virgil cites in *Inferno* 11 to seal with the sign of Sodom the wanderers on the desert plain of cantos 15–16.

> Puossi far forza nella deitade,
> col cuor negando e bestemmiando quella,
> e spregiando ['n] natura sua bontade;
> e però lo minor giron suggella
> del segno suo e Soddoma e Caorsa
> e chi, spregiando Dio col cor, favella.
> (*Inf* 11.46–51).[2]

Violence against the Deity, too, exists: / To deny and blaspheme Him in the heart does this, / As does despising Nature and her gifts: / Therefore the smallest ring imprints its mark / On Sodom and Cahors and him who speaks / Contemptuously of God with all his heart.

Marvelously free of the pseudo-Foucauldian reservation so automatic among many current scholars, Moravia simply replaces Thomas Aquinas's *sodomia* with the nineteenth-century coinage *omosessualità*. Foucault did indeed insist on the historical specificity of ways of knowing and the production of knowledge / power; the important distinction between Dante's "sodomy" and our modern "homosexuality" needs to be kept in mind. But my essay ultimately moves in an opposite—or, if not opposite, "queerer"—direction. I will suggest that, despite Virgil's Scholastic tendencies in *Inferno* 11, we find something akin to Moravia's affirmation of "homosexuality" as part of nature in the poetry of *Inferno* 15–16. I take the word "queer" from the field of queer theory, where it intends a practice of reading that is not so much interested in discovering "homosexual" identities in history or outing historical figures, but nonetheless challenges the equally ahistorical notion of a universal benevolent, procreative heteronormativity across time. While I cannot and will not claim that Dante's *Natura* is "homosexual," I will argue that she is, at the very least, queer.

But first I would like briefly to consider the debate over homosexual identity—according to Foucault (1976) really possible only since the nineteenth century—versus sodomitic acts, which boast an ancient and medieval pedigree but do not necessarily say anything about an individual's self-definition or identity, much less gender. I would like to point out some of the ways in which this distinction, generally significant and useful, is nonetheless problematic, particularly when it comes to reading Dante.

We are now fortunate to possess a serious scholarly investigation of what we might call the sodomitic culture of Florence during a period that begins a century after Dante's death. I refer to Michael Rocke's *Forbidden Friendships: Homosexuality and Male Culture in Renaissance Florence* (1996). The core of Rocke's evidence lies in the Florentine archives, in the records of an extraordinary magistracy called the "Ufficiali di notte," whose sole competency was to prosecute acts of male-male sodomy. The "Ufficiali" were active from 1432 to 1502, but Rocke reaches back to the Due- and Trecento for additional legal as well as other anecdotal (including literary) evidence and suggests that the Renaissance culture he describes developed during the earlier *comune.* Archival evidence for the legislation of sodomy in Florence begins, in a small way, during Dante's lifetime and then emphatically in 1325, four years after Dante's death. Clearly, sodomy was from early on a "problem" for Florentine officials. The special magistracy was created only in the fifteenth century when leaders perceived that the amount of sodomitic activity in the city had reached a critical point and worried that Florence's reputation for male-male sex had grown to international dimensions. The German word *Florenzer,* it seems, was a synonym for "sodomite."

Rocke's major revelation is that sodomy—if not legal, or morally acceptable exactly—was nonetheless normative for a great many Florentine males of the period. If we are to believe his statistical reading of the archives, most Florentine men had sex with other men at some point in their lives. Reflecting ancient Mediterranean models of what has sometimes been called "pedagogical sodomy," most of these relationships featured an adult over the age of eighteen in bed with (or, perhaps more often, in some dark alley with) an adolescent boy. While many of these relationships were occasional and / or mercenary, some were more long-term. What is most significant from our modern perspective, this activity in no way invalidated or prevented the man's eventual acceptance of a wife and the civic responsibilities of the heterosexual family unit. Occasional, discreet sodomy was a fact of life for many Florentine males, who did not then necessarily become identified as "sodomites." Regarding the general conceptualization and social function of sodomy, Rocke's investigation can at least begin to suggest a real social context for sodomy in Dante.

And the first tentative conclusion we may draw regarding sodomy and gender here is that, for the adult, active male, sodomy did not have an impact on gender. Many Florentine males could enjoy sex with younger men without compromising their privileged status as male and eventual *paterfamilias,* although the comfortable inclusion of sex with younger men into adult male sexuality certainly reconfigures the category "male" in ways that would not be considered normative by many today. On the other hand, we know from a long, parodic literary tradition (which includes Alan of Lille's *De planctu*), as well as some of Rocke's own evidence, that the passive partner was commonly characterized as a woman, "donna" or "femina." In *Purg* 26.76–81, Dante himself recalls Caesar's liaison with—indeed, submission to—King Nicomedes of Bithynia and his subsequent triumph in Rome to the cry of "Regina!"

I think it is fair to assume that sex between men was relatively commonplace in Dante's Florence in a way that anticipates the society of a century or so later that Rocke describes. But to the extent that Rocke posits a theoretical framework for this impressive evidence, he offers the sort of automatic Foucauldianism I referred to in my opening: late-medieval sodomy and modern homosexuality are radically different constructions; sodomy refers to occasional acts and was often (at least in his sample) a part of normative male gender; homosexuality is a modern identity that challenges heteronormativity and normative gender. Rocke repeatedly warns us against self-recognition.

I would simply like to call into question the absoluteness of such pronouncements. As Louise Fradenburg and Carla Freccero (1996, xiii–xxiv) argue in the Introduction to their collection on *Premodern Sexualities,* while historians and literary critics are appropriately suspicious of the pleasure implied by simple identification with the past, equally suspect is the tendency to draw a line between modern and premodern and set them in absolute, symmetrical opposition. They ask us to question what exactly is at stake in the currently fashionable distinction between acts and identities. They remind us of Foucault's own emphasis on the ways in which the "confessional regimes" of early Christianity continue to inhabit the modern discourse of sexuality.[3]

After all, much of what Rocke describes is apparently familiar: well-known cruising areas, habitual meeting places, even taverns, and at least some individuals who continued to prefer men to women throughout their lives. Clearly, some men developed public reputations or—what else shall we call them?—identities as inveterate sodomites. Perhaps it is this minority group that should most interest those of us willing to run the risk of an identification, however careful and qualified, and indulge in the pleasures of genealogy.

But we hardly needed Rocke's careful sifting through the archives to know that some men in medieval and Renaissance Italy always preferred to have sex with other men. Surely, readers of Boccaccio have known this all along. In the very first tale of the *Decameron,* a parody of the Christian confessional discourse so central to Foucault, Panfilo tells us that ser Cepparello likes having sex with women "about as much as a dog likes getting beaten with a stick" (Boccaccio 1976, 34).[4] In the last novella of Day Five of the *Decameron,* Pietro di Vinciolo does not let his marriage to a beautiful maiden get in the way of his real desire for young men. In the end, of course, Pietro's proto-feminist wife accommodates his differing desire while insisting upon her own right to pleasure, in a novella that attests to the complexities of sexuality and gender in the period.

The distinction between acts and identities, however, is particularly problematic when we come to Dante's sodomites, especially in the *Inferno.* The modern commentary tradition has repeatedly noted that there is no independent written record of Brunetto Latini (or Priscian, for that matter) having been a sodomite. But the poetic logic of the *Inferno* bestows upon all the sinners in cantos 15–16 eternal identities as sodomites as it imposes eternal identities upon all its sinners. The sinner steps up to Minos and "tutta si confessa"—out comes the eternal character (see *Inf* 5.1–15). In Dante's universe, ser Brunetto takes on an essential identity as a sodomite, no matter that he had a wife and children in his earthly life (*pace*—most recently—Peter Armour).[5] In this poetic sense, at least, Dante gives us "homosexuals" *avant la lettre,* without the help of nineteenth-century medical or legal discourse.

And it is to Dante's poetry—to the poetry of *Inferno* 15–16 in particular—that I would like to turn in the remainder of this essay.[6] I will argue that, while there is undoubtedly in Dante a rational—what I would like to call grammatical—model of gender and sexuality, his poetry sometimes tells a different story. Risking a kind of neo-Crocean dualism, I am saying that there are poetic moments—or, if you will, queer moments—in tension with straight, straight-lined, "grammatical" thinking.[7] The moments I am thinking of blend a medieval horror of biological process with a kind of empirical wonder before the often enigmatic workings of the physical universe, *Physis, Natura.*

In *Conv* 4.24, for instance, Dante clearly articulates a rational grammar of gender based on binary opposition.[8] One exemplary quality of adolescence is obedience to one's father and father-figures. The adolescent must obey his father just as the bawling infant—as soon as reason begins to appear—must turn away from the mother's breast, the dispersive flow of milk, and female corporeality in order to embrace the law of the father, symbolic language, male reason. The metamorphoses of *Inferno* 24–25, on the other hand, overflow—albeit in the context of divine justice—with images from the natural world that resist any clear-cut notion of gender, indeed images that pronounce *Natura*'s general preference for gradual transformation over binary division and opposition. Thus, we get the gradual dissolution of frost on grass (*Inf* 24.1–15); the mysterious intermingling of black and white as paper burns (*Inf* 25.61–66); the *entrelacement* of ivy on bark (*Inf* 25.58–60); intertwined, copulating snakes in poignant reference, at last, to human nature and the queered gender dramas of Ovid's Hermaphroditus and Tiresias.[9]

Likewise in *Inferno* 11 Virgil gives us something like a Scholastic grammar of sexuality which plots a benevolent, procreative Nature against a violent, destructive sodomy and draws a line between the two. But *Inferno* 15–16 is again filled with images of flow and transformation from the natural world that blur this line while queering nature and sexuality in the process. Each of Dante's two encounters with sodomites in cantos 15 and 16 begins and ends with an image of flowing water making its way to the sea. Indeed, read together, these images convey an implied narrative, a story of water flowing inexorably around and through human constructs.

At the opening of canto 15, in imitation of God and Nature, the poet-artisan expends no less than four full tercets to describe the stone embankments that carry the travelers out across the hot desert plain aside the stream of blood toward the pit of Malebolge and the central abyss.

> Ora cen porta l'un de' duri margini;
> e 'l fummo del ruscel di sopra aduggia,
> sì che dal foco salva l'acqua e li argini.
> Quale i Fiamminghi tra Guizzante e Bruggia,
> temendo il fiotto che 'nver lor s'avventa,
> fanno lo schermo perché 'l mar si fuggia;
> e quale i Padovan lungo la Brenta,
> per difender lor ville e lor castelli,
> anzi che Chiarentana il caldo senta;
> a tale imagine eran fatti quelli,
> tutto che né sì alti né sì grossi,
> qual che si fosse, lo maestro felli.
>
> (*Inf* 15.1–12)

Now the firm margin bears us, under the vapor / Rising from the stream to form and fend / The fire off, sheltering both banks and water. / As Flemings between Wissant and Bruges, to defend / Against the tide that rushes in on them, / Construct a bulwark to drive the sea from the land; / And Paduans on the Brenta do, to stem / The water and protect their castle and town / Before Carentana feels the heat—in the same / Manner those banks were made, except the one / Who built them did not make them as high or thick, / Whoever he was.

These similes picture real-life dikes and dams constructed by the Flemish and then the Paduans to protect their cities from Nature's destructive power at high tide and spring thaw. A straight reading sees here reflected a reactionary strain of thought regarding the city in the Middle Ages: the city, *locus par excellence* of usury and sodomy, like linguistic grammar the elaborate construct of human artifice and industry, a direct affront to the cyclical and generational flow of *Natura* (Freccero 1991). Still, it has always struck me as odd that—in these cantos that are supposed to be about a violence against Nature—the violence here is entirely on Nature's side.

Of course, the story of *Natura* as told by Economou (1972) and others is long and complex, and we cannot hope to do justice to it here. In his *Christianity, Social Tolerance, and Homosexuality,* John Boswell

(1980) surveys this story from Plato and Aristotle through Boethius, and relates that Nature is largely defined as all that is, all that exists, or all that is inborn in the individual. While certain early Christian and Neoplatonic thinkers promoted a concept of Nature as an ideal, forever benevolent, and procreative force, such notions never really took hold intellectually or popularly, particularly "among people struggling to keep alive in the face of the destructive powers of 'nature'" (303). For Boswell (303–304), it is twelfth-century allegory, specifically Alan of Lille in the *De planctu,* that struggles to appropriate Nature into Christian ethics, where as divine minister she becomes the champion of an exclusively heterosexual fecundity. From here the idea passes to the Scholastics. Albert and Thomas, with sometimes confused appeals to Roman natural law and zoology, can thus condemn sodomy as a crime *contra naturam.* Boswell espies a significant shift in public opinion with urbanization from the twelfth to the thirteenth century, so that by the middle of the thirteenth century, as Dante enters the world, the "opposition between 'nature' and homosexual behavior was a common assumption of Europeans" (315). The older, broader idea of nature as all creation was still very much in reach of a thinker like Dante. It's just that city life did not make for keen observers of nature; that Dante-poet was a keen observer of nature, however, is by now a commonplace. Dante is caught between an idealized, eternally generative *Natura* and a more empirical appreciation for her immense variety.

To be sure, there is an attempt in *Inferno* 15–16 to assimilate *Natura* to *Fortuna,* that other *vicaria dei* about whom Dante is much more explicit (*Inf* 7.67–96).[10] The pilgrim is strong in the face of Brunetto's prophecy of hard times: "As Fortune pleases let her wheel be turned, / And as he must let the peasant turn his spade" (*Inf* 15.95–96), verses that superimpose the cycles of Fortune upon the fertile cycles of man-in-Nature. In this ideal logic, Nature reflects God just as man's art must reflect Nature. Nature's apparent missteps are explained away Neoplatonically by her proximity to inherently imperfect matter, which differs in its capacity for divine light, as Thomas himself explains in *Par* 13.76–78. Nature is an artisan whose fleshy hand trembles. In this reading, sodomy is simply a mistake—a slip of the pen or, if you will, slip of the penis. Still, I feel that Dante's insistent descriptions of the excessive and threatening flow of nature in *Inferno* 15–16 betray doubt over the possibility of containing nature in reason—doubt, that is, over making nature correspond to what some men construe as divine reason. After all, in *Par* 13.112–42, Thomas also warns the pilgrim to refrain from rash judgments, to beware of the accepted wisdom, and to remember the limitations of human reason when it comes to reading the text of creation.

At the end of *Inferno* 15, we learn from Brunetto that the infamous bishop Andrea de' Mozzi is among the sodomites, a bishop who—if we are to take Boccaccio's word—was transferred from Florence to Vicenza because of his abominable sexual misconduct.

> Priscian sen va con quella turba grama,
> e Francesco d'Accorso; anche vedervi,
> se avessi avuto di tal tigna brama,
> colui potéi che dal servo de' servi
> fu trasmutato d'Arno in Bacchiglione,
> dove lasciò li mal protesi nervi.
> (*Inf* 15.109–14)

Priscian trudges in that unhappy band, / As does Francesco d'Accorso. And if you crave / To see such scurf, among them you can find / One whom the Servant of Servants asked to leave / The Arno for Bacchiglione; and there / He left his body, distended in its nerve / And muscle.

But Dante the poet tells us not that he was transferred from Florence to Vicenza, but rather, in an Ovidian turn of phrase, that Andrea was "transmuted" ("trasmutato" [cf. *Inf* 25.142–43]) from one river to another, from the Arno to the Bacchiglione, where he died and left his corporeal "nervi," which were somewhat enigmatically *mal protesi.* Thus, we have moved in canto 15 from the open North Sea and then the Arno to the Brenta and the Bacchiglione, two related streams, part of the same family of tributaries on Italy's eastern seaboard, the "left" side of the peninsula divided by the Appenine ridge, according to the *De vulgari eloquentia* 1.9.4.

As it happens, the Bacchiglione eventually flows into the Brenta as they both move with all other streams toward assimilation into the sea. Dante's implied image here—one flow of water under two different names—participates in one of the poet's favorite metaphorical themes, one that recurs in his writing with some frequency (cf., for instance, *Inf* 16.94–99; 20.76–78; *Purg* 5.94–99, 124–26). Proper names—grammatical language—can never quite contain the flow of natural reality. But in cantos 15 and 16, Dante blends sexuality into the metaphorical mix.

Throughout the encounter with Brunetto, the pilgrim and his guide move steadily across the desert plain toward the center abyss, so that at the beginning of *Inferno* 16 we are told they can already hear the roar of the waterfall over the edge of the seventh circle. "Già era in loco onde s'udìa 'l rimbombo / dell'acqua che cadea nell'altro giro, / simile a quel che l'arnie fanno rombo" ("I was already where we heard the noise / Of water winding downward as it spilled / To the next circle with a sound like bees" [*Inf* 16.1–3]). This sound is similar to the buzz around beehives, as in birds and bees perhaps; but one is also reminded of the bee's sting, the violence and aggression inherent in the natural world. We must imagine Dante's meeting with the sodomites in *Inferno* 16 against this auditory background, a crescendo that precisely matches the travelers' continual path closer to the falls. When about two-thirds of the way into the canto the sodomites disappear and the travelers are at the edge of the circle overlooking the falls, the roar is so thundrous that speech is nearly drowned out, revealing again the tension between human constructs—linguistic and otherwise—and natural flow: "Io lo seguiva, e poco eravam iti, / che 'l suon dell'acqua n'era sì vicino, / che per parlar saremmo a pena uditi" ("[And then my master left,] I after him; / And we had traveled but a little distance / Before the sound of falling water came / From so near we could scarcely hear our voices" [*Inf* 16.91–93]).

And just here at the end of the sodomy episodes, the poet intervenes to describe the waterfall in another four-tercet simile that recalls the opening of *Inferno* 15.

> Come quel fiume c'ha proprio cammino
> prima da Monte Veso inver levante,
> dalla sinistra costa d'Apennino,
> che si chiama Acquaqueta suso, avante
> che si divalli giù nel basso letto,
> e a Forlì di quel nome è vacante,
> rimbomba là sovra San Benedetto
> dell'Alpe per cadere ad una scesa
> ove dovrìa per mille esser recetto;
> così, giù d'una ripa discoscesa,
> trovammo risonar quell'acqua tinta,
> sì che 'n poc'ora avrìa l'orecchia offesa.
> (*Inf* 16.94–105)

> As that river which is first to carve its course / East down the Apennines from Viso's sources— / Called Acquacheta up high, before it pours / To its low bed at Forlì—clears the spine / Above San Benedetto dell'Alpe and roars / In a single cataract that might have been / a thousand; just so, down a precipitous bank, / Dark water drummed so loudly it would pain / Our ears before much longer.

We are again on Italy's eastern seaboard, now in the Emilian Appenines, near Forlì, where, once again, the water flow changes names from Acquaqueta to Montone. That river name, Acquaqueta or "Still Water," is—as often in Dante—at once geographically precise and ironically poetic. It gestures toward the effort of names and grammatical language to still the flow of language and time in the context of a simile that underscores the futility of just such an effort. The simile is painstakingly elaborate, "troppo lunga e minutamente analitica," comments Sapegno (Alighieri 1957, ad locum). But here again is Dante-poet, descriptive linguist and at the same time tireless descriptor of nature's minute variations and perplexing details. It is not nearly enough for Dante to convey that the flow of water changes names near Forlì. This same flow becomes a roaring cascade like the one now before the travelers. Somewhere above the monastery of San Benedetto dell'Alpe, there where such a volume of water might normally be expected to change elevation by means of a thousand more gradual, gentle pools, *Natura* has—shockingly—opted for a single, violent plunge. The poet-naturalist's awe and frank wonder is unmistakable.

But we have not yet finished with this one simile, whose absurd over-elaboration stands as if in defiance of comfortable, easy reading. It is as if the poet admonishes us not to be simplistic or naive readers of the complex text of nature. As a kind of epilogue to his treatment of sexual sodomy, the poet feels it necessary to convey in addition that this river, known variously as Acquaqueta or Montone, is the first along that seaboard, moving north to south, to resist the powerful draw of the Po delta. Here Dante sees confirmed in the text of nature what he had read in the text of Boethius's *Consolation of Philosophy:* all things in the great cycle of nature seek their own individual paths back to origin and reassimilation, "repetunt *proprios* quaeque *recursus*" (III.poem ii.34; emphasis added). In *Inferno* 16, the Acquaqueta / Montone resists the mainstream, forges its own independent path—its *proprio cammino*—to the Adriatic Sea, but is surely no less a part of nature, or divine reason, for that.

The poet-naturalist—one with the poet of fluvial linguistics—insists on this detail: this stubborn stream that at least for a time resists the larger flow and defies simple identity in a proper name as it moves toward an extraordinary and, in this context, extraordinarily erotic release and reassimilation. Physical life is indeed a mystery, but inexplicable only to a simple and imperfect human reason. Like the myriad dialects of the Italian peninsula whose number reaches one thousand and beyond, it divides and subdivides with seemingly perverse pleasure (*DVE* 1.10.7).

If there is a grammar of nature for Dante, it cannot be the obvious, straight-lined grammar that he left behind in the failed *De vulgari eloquentia.* If there is a grammar of nature for Dante, it must be akin to the poet's most extensive, and most mysterious, treatment of grammar in the second book of the *Convivio,* where he describes in scientific detail yet another enigmatic natural body. In the second book of the *Convivio,* Dante offers his famous analogies between the seven liberal arts and the seven planets. Grammar is like the moon, the very emblem of infinite variability (*Conv* 2.13.9–10). Just as the moon waxes and wanes, grammar—here virtually one with natural language—constantly changes form as it accepts and rejects words, declensions, and syntax over time. Just as the moon is spotted with light and dark, grammar has areas of light and dark, for "the rays of human reason can never penetrate it in its entirety." This is the grammar of nature that spreads throughout Dante's writing: the grammar of unending linguistic variation, the grammar of leafy tree branches forever shooting off in different directions, the grammar of ocean tides and the flow of water on earth.[11] This is the grammar that we discover in such high relief in the sodomy cantos. If we can extrapolate from this a grammar of sexuality in *Inferno* 15 and 16—as I believe we can—it is surely not the straight grammar of linguistic prescription. The grammar of sexuality for Dante must, like the moon, always remain a bit mysterious, partially veiled to human intellect. It is the grammar of a natural world replete with polymorphous life whose only constant is change. Like human language and Andrea de' Mozzi, it is always subject to "transmutation." Like the flow of a river, its twists and turns in space and time are numberless and sometimes baffling as each and every element forges its *proprio cammino* toward release.

Notes

1. There are three significant passages on sodomy in Aquinas's *Summa:* 1a.2ae.31.7; 1a.2ae.94.3; and 2a.2ae.154.11–12, which is the best known for its condemnation of several sexual acts, including sodomy, as vices against nature. Most relevant to the present discussion, however, is 1a.2ae.94.3, where Aquinas allows that same-sex desire may be inborn and thus "natural" for some individuals.

2. Virgil is explaining the moral topography of *Inferno* to the pilgrim; the innermost round of the seventh circle (violence) contains souls who were violent against God (blasphemers), against God's daughter, Nature (sodomites), and against God's granddaughter, Art (usurers). All citations of the *Comedy* are from Sapegno's edition (Alighieri 1957); English translations of the *Comedy* are Robert Pinsky's (Alighieri 1994b). All other translations are my own unless otherwise noted.

3. "Let us be clear: we do not urge a return to transhistoricist nostalgia. We urge instead continuing attention to the role played by desires, residues, and repetitions in the historical construction of sexuality, and in particular to the fantasmatic figure of a modernity symmetrically and absolutely opposed to premodernity. . . . The past may not *be* the present, but it is sometimes *in* the present, haunting, even if only through our uncertain knowledges of it, our hopes of surviving and living well" (Fradenburg and Freccero 1996, xix–xxi).

4. For a similar usage, see the tale of Pietro di Vinciolo, in which Pietro's wife proclaims to him: "se' così vago di noi [donne] come il can delle mazze" ("you desire us [women] as much as dogs like getting beaten" [Boccaccio 1976, 525]).

5. Somewhat in the tradition of Pézard 1950 and R. Kay 1978, Armour has worked hard in a series of articles (1990, 1991, 1994) to erase same-sex desire from canto 15 and thus "clear" Brunetto's name of the charge of sodomy.

6. The bibliography on these cantos is immense. Despite its flawed thesis, Pézard 1950 remains one of the most sensitive, insightful, and certainly extensive treatments. I have found the following most useful, particularly with regard to the question of sexuality in these cantos: Ahern 1990a, 1990b; Boswell 1994; Durling and Martinez 1996; Freccero 1991; Holsinger 1996; Pequigney 1991; Vance 1984.

7. We recall here the etymology of *grammatica* from the Greek *gramma* ("line" or "letter").

8. See esp. *Conv* 4.24.14: "Onde, sì come, nato, tosto lo figlio a la tetta de la madre s'apprende, così tosto, come alcuno lume d'animo in esso appare, si dee volgere a la correzione del padre, e lo padre lui ammaestrare" ("So as a child clings to the mother's breast as soon as it is born, likewise as soon as

some light appears in his mind he ought to turn to the correction of his father, and his father should give him instruction"). All quotations from the *Convivio* are from Alighieri 1954; translations of the *Convivio* are Richard Lansing's (Alighieri 1990).

9. In effect, most of canto 25 resonates on some level with the Ovidian episodes of Tiresias (*Metamorphoses* 3.322–31) and Hermaphroditus (*Metamorphoses* 4.373–79). For Tiresias, see *Inf* 20.40–45.

10. Cf. *Natura*'s self-presentation as God's servant, worker, and "vicaria" in the *Tesoretto,* vv. 289–320 (Brunetto Latini 1960). I agree that Dante aims to define a restored nature in history, a middle ground between the ideal prelapsarian *locus amoenus* and corrupt fallen nature (Mazzotta 1979, 130–31, 184–85, 326–27). But empirical doubt remains. How does one distinguish corruptions in the observable natural universe, particularly where human will is not involved?

11. Of course, the waxing and waning moon is directly connected to the movement of water on earth in the ocean tides, which Brunetto discusses in his *Tesoretto,* vv. 1030–42 (Brunetto Latini 1960, 212), a text very much present in *Inferno* 15. See also Brunetto's *Tesor* 1.124.7–9 (Brunetto Latini 1947), where he insists again on the ultimate mystery of tidal movement and the limitations of human reason. On Brunetto's works in the text of *Inferno* 15, see Della Terza 1978.

6

Does the *Stilnovo* Go to Heaven?

Lino Pertile

SOMETHING IS MISSING from Dante's portrayal of love in the *Commedia.* At the beginning of the *Inferno* and at the end of the *Purgatorio* we find, respectively, love condemned (Francesca) and love reformed (Guinizzelli), but where is love rewarded, blessed, sanctified? Where is exemplary love?

The intellectual light that surrounds Dante's universe outside space and time is full of love (*Par* 30.40); love is what causes the angelic choirs to spin around God and, consequently, to turn the nine heavenly spheres; love is what makes the blessed want to come down to talk to the pilgrim, while in Paradise the pilgrim's mind in its turn appears more than ever in love with Beatrice. Moreover, as I have shown elsewhere, the language of desire permeates the third canticle to the point that even Dante's intellectual efforts to grasp a reality that is beyond his understanding is often portrayed in daringly erotic terms (Pertile 1990, 1993b, 1998).[1] But where is *earthly* love, the love in whose name God's creatures join together to be fruitful and multiply on earth (Gen 1:22, 8:17, 9:1 and 7)?

Its natural locus within the physical and moral structure of Dante's other world should be the sphere of Venus. But in point of fact, against all reasonable expectation, love is hardly mentioned in the Venusian sphere. The term *amore* naturally appears much more frequently in the text of the third canticle than anywhere else in the poem: to be precise, it occurs 85 times in the *Paradiso,* 50 in the *Purgatorio* and 19 in the *Inferno.* These figures become even more significant if we consider the textual segments from which the word *amore* is absent: 26 cantos in the *Inferno,* 11 in the *Purgatorio,* and 4 in the *Paradiso.* Oddly enough, however, one of the four *Paradiso* cantos from which *amore* is absent is canto 9, which is one of the two cantos set in the Heaven of the *bella Ciprigna.* What is the meaning of this paradoxical fact?

The souls of Venus are so full of love ("sem sì pien d'amor") that, to satisfy Dante's desires, they are ready to interrupt the singing and dancing with which they accompany the circular motion of the Principalities (*Par* 8.34–39). However, this *amor* corresponds more closely to charity or kindness than to love. In any case it is hardly a distinguishing feature of this Heaven, for it is common to all the spirits of Dante's Paradise. In fact, Charles Martel, the first spirit the pilgrim meets in the sphere of love, does not seem to be there, as far as we know, as a result of any special association with love. The son of Charles d'Anjou, Charles Martel died in 1295 at the age of twenty-four. In a lovely *terzina* he mentions Dante's affection for him and his affection for Dante:

> Assai m'amasti, e avesti ben onde;
> che s'io fossi giù stato, io ti mostrava
> di mio amor più oltre che le fronde.
> (*Par* 8.55–57)

You loved me much and had good cause for that; for had I stayed below, I should have showed you more of my love than the leaves alone.[2]

But he moves on swiftly to talk about other things—the lands he was due to inherit when he died, and the cause why so often parents and children differ so much in disposition. Why then should he be in the Heaven of Venus? Some commentators argue that Charles is rewarded here for his love of justice and good government, a love that is clearly evident from his discourse, and seems to be associated with the "good" influence of Venus. However, this kind of love has nothing in common with the phenomenon to which Dante devotes one circle in Hell and a terrace in Purgatory.

The other three souls we encounter in the Heaven of Venus (*Par* 9) are Cunizza, Folquet, and Rahab. All three clearly belong to the venereal type. However, it is not as love heroes that they are rewarded here, but as repented lovers. Cunizza's love affairs were all too well known before she converted in old age: here she deplores the Venetian population's indifference to any kind of goodness; Folquet admits he loved with greater ardor than Dido had: here, however, he denounces the accursed florin "c'ha disvïate le pecore e li agni" ("that turns both sheep and lambs from the true course" [*Par* 9.131]); finally, Rahab is the biblical prostitute who saved herself not through an act of love, but by favoring Joshua's capture of Jericho. In short, these souls do not find themselves in Paradise *because* they loved, but *in spite of* their having loved. They are here because, though "il folle amore" ("frenzied love" [*Par* 8.2]) ruled their lives, they eventually were able to free themselves of its yoke. They are not unlike Francesca and Paolo, but, in contrast to them, they survived their sin and conquered it. The Heaven of Venus is unique in Dante's Paradise in that it seems to be inhabited only by those spirits who *resisted* the influence of *folle amore.*

In *Purgatorio* 18 Virgil explains that, while all love is natural and potentially good, only love that is governed by reason is morally praiseworthy (vv. 40–75). Virgil's discourse represents a significant correction of Francesca's fatalistic view of love as a totally irresistible natural force—a view that Dante himself had expressed in both the *Vita Nova* and some of his late lyrics such as the so-called *canzone montanina, Amor, da che convien pur ch'io mi doglia,* and the sonnet to Cino da Pistoia, *Io sono stato con Amore insieme.* Conversely, what seems to triumph in Virgil's speech is the view ostensibly espoused by Dante in another of his late lyrics, *Doglia mi reca,* where the ideal of a rational love, "d'orto di ragione" ("of reason's garden" [v. 147]), is opposed to the practice of lustful love as "appetito di fera" ("bestial appetite" [v. 143]).[3] Thus, *Purgatorio* 18 seems to bring to a final and positive resolution a conflict that existed in Dante's mind as late as 1307–8 when he is believed to have written both the lyrics mentioned above and the first cantos of the *Inferno.* But, if a "giusto amor" (*Purg* 18.96) does indeed exist, where is it to be found in Dante's Heaven?

There is no exemplary husband or wife in the sphere of Venus, no positive correlative of Francesca's negative model. To put it in Boccaccian terms: in Dante's Heaven of Love we do not find a Griselda, a Lisabetta da Messina, or a pair of chaste but unlucky lovers such as Girolamo and Salvestra. Dante does not think of a love in which *eros* and *agape* might be joined in a just and harmonious equilibrium. He does not even suggest that there might be a middle way between adulterous and mystical love. Indeed, if we consider the three most memorable female figures of the *Comedy*—Francesca, Pia, and Piccarda, excluding for the time being Beatrice—we are bound to conclude that Dante must have had a rather grim idea of marriage, conjugal relationships, and physical love in general. That is why, after all, the space allotted to love in Dante's Heavens still lies within the shadow of the earth—that is, below the line where untainted goodness starts. This point becomes even more apparent if we consider a detail in the seventh terrace of his Purgatory.

We know that, for each vice it corrects, Dante's Purgatory exhibits examples of the opposite virtue. In the seventh terrace the souls of the lustful purge themselves of Venus's poison by crying out examples of chastity. The first two are canonical examples of total chastity, one Christian and historical—the Virgin Mary—and the other pagan and mythological—the goddess Diana. However, the third example is different and rather problematical: "indi donne / gridavano e mariti che fuor casti / come virtute e matrimonio imponne" ("and they praised aloud those wives and husbands who were chaste, as virtue and as matrimony mandate" [*Purg* 25.133–35]). It is not clear whether the lustful cry out specific *names* of exemplary husbands and wives without mentioning them in the text, or whether they actually invoke, as seems to be the case, the entire category of chaste spouses. This occurrence is unique in the poem, and goes against its internal rules: Dante quotes a general example that by its nature is devoid of exemplary value and therefore useless—as Cacciaguida will explain at the end of *Paradiso* 17. But why? Quite simply because he cannot conjure up one single exemplary instance of blessed earthly love.

This absence contrasts sharply with the glorification, for instance in *Tundale's Vision,* of "the married, both men and women, who did not mutually befoul their marriage by the stain of illicit adultery and who served the faith of legitimate union" (ch. 19: The Glory of the Married). It is indeed significant that, compared to the popular visions, Dante is much less harsh in punishing the lustful, but he totally neglects to reward legitimate lovers.

It is surprising to discover that there is more love in the Heaven of the Sun than in that of Venus. *Paradiso* 10, the first devoted to the Sun after the two Venusian cantos, begins by singing the love that makes the world go round with such marvelous order:

> Guardando nel suo Figlio con l'Amore
> che l'uno e l'altro etternalmente spira,
> lo primo e ineffabile Valore
> quanto per mente e per loco si gira
> con tant' ordine fé, ch'esser non puote
> sanza gustar di lui chi ciò rimira.
> (*Par* 10.1–6)

Gazing upon His Son with that Love which One and the Other breathe eternally, the Power—first and inexpressible—made everything that wheels through mind and space so orderly that one who contemplates that harmony cannot but taste of Him.

It ends with the dance and song of the wise spirits celebrating their love for each other and for God. Their circular motion is described in suggestively erotic terms that perhaps might have been more appropriate under Venus. Indeed, it is as though the poet were releasing now the kind of language that he had suppressed in the previous Heaven:

Indi, come orologio che ne chiami
ne l'ora che la sposa di Dio surge
a mattinar lo sposo perché l'ami,
che l'una parte e l'altra tira e urge,
tin tin sonando con sì dolce nota,
che'l ben disposto spirto d'amor turge;
cosí vid' ïo la gloriosa rota
muoversi e render voce a voce in tempra
e in dolcezza ch'esser non pò nota
se non colà dove gioir s'insempra.
(*Par* 10:139–48)

Then, like a clock that calls us at the hour in which the Bride of God, on waking, sings matins to her Bridegroom, encouraging His love (when each clock-part both drives and draws), chiming the sounds with notes so sweet that those with spirit well-disposed feel their love grow; so did I see the wheel that moved in glory go round and render voice to voice with such sweetness and such accord that they can not be known except where joy is everlasting.

In this context Saint Francis of Assisi becomes Dante's champion of perfect love. Significantly, Francis's marriage to Lady Poverty is the only example of conjugal love that the *Comedy* celebrates and exalts. Physical love becomes acceptable at last, though only as a metaphor which is spiritually fulfilled after the death of the body in a relationship with God in which desire is always satisfied without ever being extinguished.

Thus, it seems that for Dante no heavenly Venus is to be found either alongside, or in opposition to, the earthly, sensual, sinful, and socially disruptive one. The *maritalis affectio* or *conjugalis amor* so often celebrated by the Fathers of the Church does not seem to exist for him. The matrimonial variety of love is represented in the *Comedy*, and only incidentally, by Nella Donati, Forese's "vedovella" ("gentle widow" [*Purg* 23.92]). However, apart from the ironically palinodic quality of the episode—if the *tenzone* is indeed authentic—Nella's example is evoked in the context as the exception that confirms the rule. In fact, we owe to Forese the most ferocious and sinister of Dante's invectives against women in general and Florentine women in particular. In sum, sensual love, in all its forms and gradations, is viewed in the poem as an essentially pathological condition, a perverse affliction ("mal perverso" [*Inf* 5.93]) from which the soul must be released if she is to climb to Heaven. Was the Cavalcanti of *Donna me prega* right then, and does Dante acknowledge it *de facto* if not verbally?

Of course, there is love in the *Paradiso,* but compared to the two earthly realms, it seems to be a radically different phenomenon. As we proceed from canto 9, in the Heaven of Venus and Love, to canto 10 in the Heaven of the Sun and Wisdom, the brightness of the blessed is such, even in relation to the sun's, that the poet is unable to portray it. Beatrice invites him to thank God for having raised him so high, and Dante obeys with such ardor that he forgets her: "e sì tutto 'l mio amore in lui si mise / che Bëatrice eclissò ne l'oblio" ("and all my love was so intent on Him that Beatrice was then eclipsed within forgetfulness" [*Par* 10.59–60]). However, far from taking offense for this forgetfulness, Beatrice smiled, being obviously pleased at her pupil's signs of spiritual progress. Thus, Minerva replaces Venus, Wisdom replaces Love.

This episode is very significant. On the one hand, it corrects the case of Dante's retrograde neglect of Beatrice as related in the *Vita Nova* and condemned in the Earthly Paradise; on the other, it anticipates the journey's and the poem's final moments, when Dante will find himself alone before the ultimate vision. Forgetting Beatrice is acceptable and positive, and may even be necessary, as we will see, as long as it is as a result of a flight *in suso,* a motion heavenward, not *in giuso,* downward, the direction Dante had moved morally after the death of the *beatissima:*

> e se 'l sommo piacer sì ti fallio
> per la mia morte, qual cosa mortale
> dovea poi trarre te nel suo disio?
> Ben ti dovevi, per lo primo strale
> de le cose fallaci, *levar suso*
> di retro a me che non era più tale.
> Non ti dovea gravar le penne *in giuso,*

ad aspettar più colpo, o pargoletta
o altra novità con sì breve uso.
(*Purg* 31.52–60; emphasis added)

and if the highest beauty failed you through my death, what mortal thing could then induce you to desire it? For when the first arrow of things deceptive struck you, then you surely should have lifted up your wings to follow me, no longer such a thing. No green young girl or other novelty—such brief delight—should have weighed down your wings, awaiting further shafts.

In other words, with her body out of the way, Dante was expected to love Beatrice more, not less. The implication is that true love must ultimately surpass the object of its desire. To achieve the ultimate purpose of the journey, the pilgrim must learn to direct all his love toward God, thus leaving behind not only Virgil but even Beatrice, to the point of forgetting her. The aim of true love is to reach beyond human love. Only then does it reach the love of God, for "*Regnum celorum* vïolenza pate / da caldo amore e da viva speranza / che vince la divina volontate" ("*Regnum celorum* suffers violence from ardent love and living hope, for these can be the conquerors of Heaven's Will" [*Par* 20.94–966]).

This is what happens in the Empyrean, when Dante suddenly realizes that Beatrice is no longer with him. As the old man who has replaced her tells him, Beatrice has once more taken her place in the great rose of the blessed. Dante gazes at her from afar, and the last words he addresses to her are not a lover's adieu, but the prayer of one of the faithful (*Par* 31.79–90). He thanks her as one thanks a saint who has granted a grace. There is no mention in his speech of his love for Beatrice or of her love—but was it love?—for him. Veneration and gratitude, yes, but not earthly love. The ancient flame that flared up the moment he intuited her presence in the Earthly Paradise, where is it now?

Beatrice smiles and for a moment she looks toward Dante, "poi si tornò a l'etterna fontana" ("Then she turned back to the eternal fountain" [*Par* 31.93]). Borges writes that these are "los versos más patéticos que la literatura ha alcanzado," for at the end of the poem written for her they say that Beatrice is irretrievable. The truth, of course, is that it is Dante the writer who decides to distance Beatrice to the point of removing her from the stage before the pilgrim reaches his final destination. The question is why does he do it, and why will Saint Bernard do where Beatrice will not: what strategy lies behind these changes?

I would like to suggest that, if Dante removes Beatrice, it is because her presence is no longer necessary; it may, in fact, even get in the way of Dante's final achievement. Ultimately, Beatrice must go, not because she loves God more than Dante, as Borges seems to imply, but because Dante must be shown to love God more than he loves Beatrice. All love becomes love of God in Heaven, and it excludes *stilnovo* love as much as *maritalis affectio.* This is why Beatrice's replacement cannot take place directly on the axis of sublimated eroticism—for example, through the Virgin Mary—but on that of sanctity, through a *sene* who, being holy, old, and male, is above all suspicion of concupiscence. Let me clarify this point.

When he unexpectedly materializes, Saint Bernard appears not as a *deus ex machina* but as another link, a new mediator between Dante and the Virgin, and therefore his apparition, justified as it may be externally on the basis of his well-known Marian devotion, does not seem to be narratologically cogent. The question is: why could not Beatrice herself recommend Dante directly to Mary? A question that becomes even more disturbing if we consider that, as a result of this change of mediator, the last words entrusted to the *beatissima,* at the end of *Paradiso* 30, turn out to be a prophetic condemnation of Pope Clement V, who, she says, by joining the simonists, will push further down the soul of Boniface VIII—hardly a suitable parting speech from the lady who has shaped the entire life of her poet.

My feeling is that something does not quite jibe in this final section of the poem. Indeed, I would like to try out a conjecture of mine that may help us to better understand what is going on here. My hypothesis is that Saint Bernard may not have been in Dante's original plans for the conclusion of his poem. The evidence I can summon up in support of this idea is circumstantial, but compelling.

In the second canto of the *Inferno* Virgil tells Dante that "tre donne benedette" ("three blessed women") are concerned for him "nella corte del cielo" ("within the court of Heaven" [*Inf* 2.24–25]): the Virgin Mary, Saint Lucy, and Beatrice. The initiative to save Dante is triggered by the Virgin, who tells Saint Lucy, who in turn tells Beatrice. Finally Beatrice comes down and tells Virgil, who moves from Limbo to rescue the beleaguered poet. Many readers have noticed the exquisitely courtly atmosphere that characterizes the heavenly operations at this stage of the poem: the *stilnovo* register that so deeply colors the

Virgin's speech to Lucy, Lucy's speech to Beatrice, Beatrice's speech to Virgil, and her parting tears.

This model is not taken up at the end of the poem. The court the pilgrim sees with his own eyes is not the court that Beatrice had described to Virgil and Virgil to Dante at the outset of the journey. However, what truly disrupts the model is Saint Bernard, for in the final chain of mediators between Dante and God, Saint Bernard takes over the position that at the beginning of the story was Saint Lucy's.

There is something odd about Saint Lucy. She is given quite a substantial role in the first two canticles. In *Inferno* 2 the Virgin speaks directly to her, describing Dante as her *fedele* (v. 98), while Lucy speaks directly to Beatrice, urging her to go to help Dante who loved her so (v. 104). In *Purgatorio* 9 she transports the dreaming pilgrim from the Valley of the Princes to the gates of Purgatory, which she points out to Virgil with her beautiful eyes (*Purg* 9.52–63), thus prefiguring Dante's final approach to the ultimate vision in Paradise. Now, if at the end of the journey we found Saint Lucy instead of Saint Bernard, we would have no reason to be surprised at all. Indeed, Lucy would thus appear in three episodes, one in each canticle, and in the third she would hand over her *fedele* to the Virgin, thus completing the mandate she had received from the Virgin at the start of the action. The cycle would come to a close just where it started; the rescue operation would appear to be fully completed. We would have at the beginning Mary, Lucy, Beatrice, Virgil, and at the end Virgil, Beatrice, Lucy, Mary. Instead nothing of the sort. The third time Lucy appears, she is sitting idle in the Rose of the Blessed. Bernard points her out to Dante in a very concise tercet:

> e contro al maggior padre di famiglia
> siede Lucia, che mosse la tua donna
> quando chinavi, a rovinar, le ciglia.
> (*Par* 32.136–38)

And opposite the greatest father of a family, Lucia sits, she who urged on your lady when you bent your brows downward, to your ruin.

As a matter of fact, Lucy did much more than Bernard says; she is one of Dante's active "movers," yet Dante does not devote a glance or a word to her. Too little, in my opinion, for a character of such importance in the process of Dante's redemption. Lucy's failure to appear for a third time in an active role and to close the chain opened at the beginning strikes me as odd. I suggest it betrays a structural adjustment, a little earthquake that must have occurred after the writing of *Purgatorio* 9, where Lucy's position in the poem had been consolidated, and we had been given every reason to expect a third and final intervention on her part.

There is another notable and real structural adjustment in the third canticle. It concerns Beatrice, and it seems to go hand in hand with my hypothetical adjustment regarding Saint Lucy. As we know from *Inf* 10.130–32 and 15.88–90, Dante had originally planned that his exile would be fully revealed by Beatrice in Paradise. However, when he gets to Paradise, it is Cacciaguida who explains the dark prophecies the pilgrim heard from Farinata, Brunetto, and other characters. No doubt, Dante considers the change so necessary that he is willing to contradict himself in order to make it. But why make it?

Between *Inferno* 2 and *Paradiso* 31 lie practically the whole poem and probably about twelve years of exile. It is this experience in the poet's life, the new maturity he achieves through it, that makes him change his original plans. My suggestion is that the conception of love that characterized the *stilnovo* and determined the writing of *Inferno* 2 does not survive beyond Purgatory. The Beatrice whom Dante finds on the other side of the river Lethe goes already beyond the *stilnovo*—and, by guiding Dante through the heavenly spheres, she teaches him the same transcendence. But her replacement by Cacciaguida, followed by her, or more likely Lucy's, replacement by Saint Bernard—significantly, two female characters replaced by two male ones—are two much more radical adjustments. Perhaps Saint Bernard embodies an ideal of chastity, spirituality, and mystical ardor that, deep in his consciousness, Dante feels unable to fully associate with Beatrice—or any woman for that matter. Be this as it may, the Empyrean, initially imagined as a ladies' court, is no longer a court at the end of the journey—let alone a ladies' court—and the love that is punished in Hell and purged in Purgatory is shown to have nothing in common with the otherwordly love that conquers the Heavens to reach beyond space and time. Between these two forms of love there is no mediation, no rational love capable of reconciling the love of the creator with the love of the creature. Which must imply—though I doubt this was Dante's intention—that Virgil's discourse in *Purgatorio* 18 was over-optimistic. In the *Comedy* rational love is a rarer phenomenon than the love of God.

Dante set off perhaps with the idea of consecrating the *stilnovo* at the end of his journey. In the event, he changed his mind, because on the way he discovered—he learned, he decided, he chose to show—that there is no room for earthly love in Paradise: *l'amor che move il sole e l'altre stelle* and *amor ch'a nullo amato amar perdona* remain to the end powerful and irreconcilable adversaries.

Notes

1. This essay is part of my ongoing research on Dante's language of desire: see Pertile 1990, 1993b, 1998. My views on the *stilnovo* are set out in Pertile 1993a. My warmest thanks to Tony Oldcorn whose reading considerably improved this essay.

2. Citations from Dante's *Comedy* are from Alighieri 1966–67; translations are from Mandelbaum 1982 and 1984.

3. The connection between *Inferno* 5, the *canzone Amor, da che convien,* the sonnet *Io sono stato con Amore insieme,* and *Purgatorio* 18 has been recently examined by Teodolinda Barolini in two innovative essays; see Barolini 1997 and 1998. In *Doglia mi reca* Dante writes of "amor fuor d'orto di ragione" ("love outside of reason's garden" [147]); Barolini argues that he thus "allows us to postulate its converse . . . an appetite that is human rather than feral and that resides *within* reason's garden" (Barolini 1998, 53). See also chap. 4 above. The link between Francesca's speech and *Io sono stato con Amore insieme* is particularly compelling as the sonnet implicitly compares love to a tempest that no amount of bell ringing (i.e., rational debate and counseling) will abate. On the custom of ringing bells to quell storms see Pertile 1996. The idea of love as a tempest that reason cannot restrain is present also in *Amor, da che convien,* vv. 26–27.

7

Love for Beatrice: Transcending Contradiction in the *Paradiso*

F. Regina Psaki

THE FIGURE of Beatrice and the poetry that Dante dedicated to her have been the object of critical scrutiny for as long as the *Divine Comedy* has existed—indeed, longer, to go by the poet's claim in the *Vita Nuova* that he submitted his first sonnet about her to the judgment and interpretation of other poets. To this day Beatrice's very identity remains an object of speculation and controversy (e.g., De Vita 1998), and to say that her role and ethical status in Dante's spiritual and poetic itinerary have been variously interpreted is a flat understatement. I believe, however, that for most readers of Dante Beatrice is bound up in an economy of spiritual maturation that has seemed to entail her association with the physical world and *cupiditas* and thus with all that the Christian soul is urged to supersede in its progress toward beatitude. The protagonist's love for her has been read in a key of transition from human to divine love and of relegation to a superseded past.

If this paradigm has enjoyed credibility in Dante studies, the critical "turn toward the body" of the last decades has begun to modify it in many contexts.[1] Emerging first in philosophical critiques of the binary oppositions that characterize metaphysics, and indeed Enlightenment and post-Enlightenment thought in general, a new attention to the material stratum of reality has led to post-structuralist and deconstructionist readings of literary texts, readings that contest the fundamentally dualist orientation of modernity.[2] Recent scholarship on the body is so voluminous and varied that for each category I offer only two or three exemplary titles; still it is intriguing to note the variety of disciplines that enable a rethinking of the body and its valences for medieval intellectuals, both lay and ecclesiastical. Research on the body in modernity as a stratum subject to social, political, and discursive construction, not merely as a natural object (Foucault 1976; Bordo 1993; Butler 1993), urges a reconsideration of the body throughout history (e.g., Feher et al. 1989; Laqueur 1990) and in particular periods. Essay collections consider constructions of the body in classical antiquity (Montserrat 1998 and Porter 1999), and detailed reconsiderations of the body and its claims in late antiquity and the Middle Ages have been undertaken by Peter Brown (1988), Margaret Miles (1979), Elaine Pagels (1988), and Caroline Walker Bynum (1987, 1991, 1995). Research is abundant on the practices and value of the body in comparative religion (Coakley 1997a) and in medieval Western Christianity (Bottomley 1979; Bynum 1987; Joubert 1991; Biller and Minnis 1997; Louth 1997; and Coakley 1992 and 2000), as well as in the medieval and early modern periods in general (Kay and Rubin 1994; Grantley and Taunton 2000). The representations and roles of the female body in particular have been a productive research focus (Suleiman 1986; Miles 1989; Lomperis and Stanbury 1993). Research on historical constructions of sexuality and sexual identities has flourished in the past decade (Lees and Fenster 1994; Cohen and Wheeler 1997; Hadley 1999; and Murray 1999). The body in extreme situations, including torture and pain, has been the focus of influential work by Elaine Scarry (1985), moving out into specific epochs and areas (Peters 1985; DuBois 1991; Enders 1999).

This attention to the body and its role in politics, society, spirituality, sexuality, and identity has, of course, affected Dante studies as well. The body, from the earthly body to the aerial bodies of the preresurrection dead and the resurrected body, has been the focus of excellent recent scholarship on medieval Christianity and Dante (Bynum 1991 and 1995; Dinzelbacher 1993; Moevs 1994; Shapiro 1998; Trottmann 1999; Jacoff 2000; Gragnolati 1999). And on the principle that the body is an exemplary figure for the physical world and for life on earth, it has featured in explorations of the value of earthly life, earthly achievement, and earthly love from the vantage point of eternity (Barolini 1984 and 1992; Harrison 1988; Schnapp 1991; Sowell 1993; Kirkpatrick 1994). Love as a driving force in paradise is explored from a variety of perspectives (Waller 1989; Zupan 1990; Boyde 1993; Chiavacci Leonardi 1998; Pertile 1993b and 1997). The widespread interest in reevaluating how premodernity viewed the body has set the stage for a reading of Dante's Beatrice as an even more complex and polysemous figure, and for the consideration of his love for her as both fully sexual and fully valorized.

In this essay I will offer an interpretation of the value the poet Dante assigned to the figure of Beatrice and to human sexual love in the *Comedy*. First, I will schematically summarize my own understanding of the unique role that Beatrice retains in the pilgrim's bliss and the poet's aesthetics, which I have presented in previous studies. In the second section I will link Dante's reconciliation of human sexual love and divine love to the series of other reconciliations—theological, epistemological, eschatological, and more—which give the *Paradiso* one of its most prominent thematic programs. In the last part of the essay, I will compare this project of Dante's with the modern tendency to delimit the medieval within a set of parameters that we will not allow the period to transgress, even if that means that we have to distort or discard evidence that it does indeed transgress them.

A vivid example of how modernity cramps the medieval and artificially limits its possibilities is the sanitization that has been visited on the love of Dante for Beatrice (and for that matter on the love expressed in troubadour and *trouvère* lyric [Paden 1999]). In three essays I have explored what Dante posited as the role of the sexual body in perfected human nature and what function and nature his love for Beatrice might have in beatitude. In one article I surveyed the critical reception of Dante's coopting of the language of erotic love in his *Paradiso* (Psaki 1996a). I argued that critics tend to conclude that Dante feels free to adopt this language of love precisely because he intends for it to signify differently in the *Paradiso* than in its original matrix of lyric love poetry. Indeed, it is often maintained that the force of this language of erotic love in the *Paradiso* depends upon the assumption of a new meaning in dynamic tension with its original one.

In a second article, I argued that the ideal relationship posited in the *Comedy* between Beatrice and Dante derives in part from the way the poet construes the ideal condition of man in the earthly paradise, before the fall (Psaki 1996b). Dante's ideal of humankind in the celestial paradise, I believe, departs substantially from both orthodox and heterodox exegesis of the earthly paradise, while still having discernible roots in it. The patristic and literary accretions around the Eden narrative offer a complex genealogy for what I call Dante's redemptive erotics. Here too, however, modernity entertains a default notion of what medieval people understood the earthly paradise to be, a version nearer to the *contemptus mundi* tradition than to what Dante actually says.

In my third article I examined very specific lexical and poetic choices in the *Paradiso* by which Dante adumbrates an eroticized relationship between the pilgrim and Beatrice, one that is simply not congruent with earthly dichotomies of soul and body, *caritas* and *cupiditas,* pure and impure (Psaki 2000). Dante's *Paradiso* reconciles the contradictory yet coexistent verities of his own historically specific love for and with Beatrice under the sign of the contradictory yet coexistent verities of Christian doctrine, the harmonization of which he effects through the challenging and polysemous medium of poetry.

If we rely on the information given us in the *Vita Nuova* and the *Comedy,* we are to understand that Dante loved Beatrice from the moment he saw her and that this love was characterized by intense sexual desire (Williams 1941, 7). But this love has somehow been decorously shrouded in protective wrapping to the point that in Dante criticism it is often described as romantic and pure in the *Vita Nuova* and safely transcended in the *Comedy,* at least after one dangerous moment late in the *Purgatorio.* Such desexualization of what is demonstrably a bodily as well as an emotional love is far more congruent with ideologies of love in the nineteenth century than with Dante's texts, and it has the unfortunate effect of occluding part of what really is astonishing in his poetic achievement.

Dante's erotic language in the *Paradiso* is ubiquitous and well documented, particularly in English-language criticism, and I explored it in some detail in my third article. Dante deploys a register strongly marked for erotic love, in describing both the bond between himself and Beatrice, and that among the souls of the blessed, as well as between the blessed and God. In innumerable single phrases (such as *dolce amor*) and in implied poetic contexts (the erotic *alba* in *Paradiso* 10), Dante adopts exactly the same language of love poetry. Allegorical scenarios such as the marriage of Francis and Poverty, of Dominic and Faith, invoke the mystical conflation of erotic and spiritual love (and not, I argue, merely the metaphor of erotic for spiritual love). The famed neologisms of this canticle include powerfully interpenetrative linguistic inventions ("s'io m'intuassi, come tu t'inmii" [*"if I could en-you myself, as you en-me yourself"* (*Par* 9.81)]).[3] The language Dante uses to describe the love that we cannot begin to understand, the machine that powers the pilgrim's ascent and the entire universe's motion, is the language of bodily, sexual love.

Critics acknowledge this language of love, but all seem to end up reinstating a decontamination zone between the erotic vocabulary of salvation and erotic vocabulary *tout court.* Dante uses this language, they say, deliberately and audaciously, to mean everything except what it says; the pre-existing language of love is applied to a new and disembodied kind of love. As I noted above, in fact, the logic seems to run that he can apply this pre-existing language of love only because its object has been superseded, or transformed. This insistent qualification of amatory language as a *redeemed* vocabulary betrays a cultural nervousness about the notion that sexual love may be sacred.

My argument is essentially that Dante's colonization of the language of courtship, caress, intercourse, and orgasm as components of divine bliss is striking not because it was unprecedented, but precisely because it is not deployed in familiar fashion as simply a figure for the love that joins risen mankind and God. Instead, it serves to solidify and legitimize the specific human relationship that frames and generates the entire poem: the unique and permanent pairing of Dante and Beatrice. I claim that Dante hypothesizes a redeemed or even redemptive eroticism that makes a place for human sexual love not only in earthly life but in beatitude, that he posits for and with Beatrice a love that is no less sexual than blessed, no less erotic than salvific. I cannot conclude that for Dante ideal erotic love is desexualized, purged of the corporeal, superseded by a generalized and purely mental communion. The individual matters; the relationship with Beatrice powers the entire journey; and Dante insists too heavily on the return of the body for his experience of Beatrice to remain aphysical. I believe that Dante's paradigm of bliss includes the specific, corporeal bliss of love in all the dimensions we now know and others of which we can only dream. Dante's innovation is not, in other words, that divine love has corrected or replaced sexual love; it is that in his poem the concepts of sex and sin have been untangled, and sex can inhabit the sacred.

The conceptual adjustment by which Dante makes oppositional constructs compatible is a sleight-of-hand accomplished through the medium of poetry. Poetry is the form of language most able to encompass and to reconcile contradiction and polysemy, and thus to do justice to the intricate complexities of the Christian faith.[4] Christianity rests on a set of logically untenable postulates that it is the work of the *Paradiso* to reconcile, or at least to claim will be reconciled in an afterlife that we cannot now fully understand. Certain terms appear contradictory and thus irreconcilable in terms of earthly logic: "come tu vedi / ogne contradizione e falsa e vera" ("as you with contradictories / can see that one is true and one is false" [*Par* 6.20–21]). But as Rachel Jacoff (2000, 125) aptly notes, "Dante complicates and even deconstructs categories we normally assume incompatible." Throughout the "ascent" through the spheres to the vision of God, Dante thematizes the reconciliation in Paradise of concepts, institutions, and values which on earth were opposites.

For my purposes, the first major such scene is the pilgrim's arrival in the sphere of the moon. The poet links the physical nature of the moon to both the mysteries of paradisal being and the mystery of the double nature of Christ—human and divine. The pilgrim's tentative explanation of the moon spots and Beatrice's extensive correction of it has had its detractors, seeming as it does a digressive moment of erudition, though Dante critics have tended to respect the poet's assurance that the topic is on the contrary absolutely central:

> S'io era corpo, e qui non si concepe
> com' una dimensione altra patio,
> ch'esser conviene se corpo in corpo repe,
> accender ne dovria piú il disio
> di veder quella essenza in che si vede
> come nostra natura e Dio s'unio.
> Lí si vedrà ciò che tenem per fede,
> non dimostrato, ma fia per sé noto
> a guisa del ver primo che l'uom crede.
> (*Par* 2.37–45)

If I was body (and on earth we cannot see / how things material can share / one space—the case, when body enters body), / Then should our longing be still more inflamed / to see that Essence in which we discern / how God and human nature were made one. / What we hold here by faith, shall there be seen, / not demonstrated but directly known, / even as the first truth that man believes.

What the poet will "demonstrate" in portraying the vast panorama of Paradise is precisely how the reconciliation of earthly impossibilia—such as two bodies sharing one space—is necessary to a proper understanding of the mystery of the Incarnation, or, in other words, how the earthly intersects with the divine. That proper understanding must remain a matter of faith to us here on earth, but in heaven we shall apprehend it directly, "facie ad faciem," and, indeed, it is this understanding that flashes upon the pilgrim at the very end of the poem.

The pilgrim's first encounter in Paradise, with Piccarda Donati, is organized around an interrogation of the contradictions of the human will. Beatrice gives voice to the pilgrim's confusion over those who break vows against their will and are penalized:

> Tu argomenti: "Se 'l buon voler dura,
> la vïolenza altrui per qual ragione
> di meritar mi scema la misura?"
> (*Par* 4.19–21)

You reason: "If my will to good persists, / why should the violence of others cause / the measure of my merit to be less?"

By positing a subtler distinction in "the will" into absolute and contingent will (*Par* 4.109–11), Beatrice vindicates the justice of the divine assignment of these souls to the lowest rank of Paradise. More crucial, however, is the previous doubt the pilgrim had expressed to Piccarda herself: do the souls in this first heaven wish for a loftier place (*Par* 3.64–66)? Piccarda's explanation exposes an unexamined assumption of the pilgrim's that the souls' wills are, like mortal wills, unmoved by and indeed antagonistic to that divine will that places them in the first sphere. Her answer dissolves that antagonism:

> Anzi è formale ad esto beato *esse*
> tenersi dentro a la divina voglia,
> per ch'una fansi nostre voglie stesse. . . .
> (*Par* 3.79–81)

The essence of this blessed life consists / in keeping to the boundaries of God's will, / through which our wills become one single will. . . .

Piccarda's conclusion that "'n la sua volontade è nostra pace'" ("in His will is our peace" [*Par* 3.85]) reconfigures the earthly notion of human desire as isolated, self-directed, and self-serving into a new and paradisal notion of human desire as cooperative with other desires (*voglie*) and concordant with divine will (*volontade*). Thus, the poet's reconfiguration of our understanding of the will rests both on adjustments that are transparent in terms of earthly logic (subtler distinctions between categories of will) and on adjustments that are opaque (a revised understanding of what will is and how it functions).

The transcendence of these contradictions in the sphere of the moon sketches in miniature this thematic strand of the *Paradiso,* as beginnings typically do adumbrate the content and concerns of literary works. The episodes of doubt and clarification (immediate or promised, but suspended) define the trajectory of the pilgrim's progress "up" through the heavenly spheres toward God. The logical contradictions that puzzle him are both powerful and obvious; their resolution constitutes the pilgrim's final education and, to the degree that he stands in for us, ours as well. They run the gamut from the most basic to the most subtle complexities of Christian doctrine. An early uncertainty of the pilgrim's is how Christ's death can be both "giusta vendetta" and "giustamente punita" ("how just vengeance can deserve just punishment" [*Par* 7.20–21]); Beatrice's explanation hinges on the fact that God is both just and merciful, and his justice must operate in occult harmony with his mercy (*Par* 7.25–51).

When Dante claims, or effects, a resolution of contradictories and a transcendence of their opposition, he often does so on the basis of what lies beyond the boundaries of human understanding. Salvation is a function of both merit and grace (*Par* 25.69; 29.61–66), in what proportion and in what causal relation we cannot know. A man's choices are foreknown and yet wholly in his own power (*Par* 17). Divine justice is infallible if unfathomable (*Par* 19); souls can be Christian before Christ, although apparently pagan (*Par* 20); predestination can coexist with freedom of the will, though we cannot see how (*Par* 20.130–32; 21.94–96).

More than once we may suspect that the lesson is shifting as we go. In one passage Cacciaguida tells the pilgrim that divine foreknowledge imposes necessity upon human behavior no more than the eye that watches a boat downstream (*Par* 17.40–42); the analogy of the observing eye and the autonomous boat neatly separates divine foreknowledge from necessity or predestination. In another passage, however, in the context of the way time and place can determine salvation or damnation, the Eagle tells the pilgrim that earthly vision "ne la giustizia sempiterna / . . . com' occhio per lo mare, entro s'interna" ("can penetrate into eternal justice / no more than eye can penetrate the sea" [*Par* 19:58–60]). Here the Eagle acknowledges that God has in some way predetermined the fate of some souls by causing them to be born outside the spatial or temporal range of Christianity. The pilgrim's doubt that it is just for souls to be damned who had in life no opportunity to hear the salvific word of Christ is rational in terms of earthly logic; but some deeper justice that we cannot know (and the poet cannot explain) makes his doubt irrelevant and indeed presumptuous:

> Or tu chi se', che vuo' sedere a scranna,
> per giudicar di lungi mille miglia
> con la veduta corta d'una spanna?
> . . . .
> Oh terreni animali! oh menti grosse!"
> (*Par* 19.79–81, 85)

Now who are you to sit upon the bench, / to judge events a thousand miles away, / when your own vision spans so brief a space? . . . / O earthly animals, o minds obtuse!

This magisterial scolding notwithstanding, the pilgrim has not learned why his doubt is wrong, only that the limited scope of human intellect cannot understand why it is just for a man predestined never to hear or know of Christ to be damned (*Par* 19.70–78).

A similar uncertainty applies to the ontological status of Earth in the *Comedy*. The "little threshing-floor" (*aiuola* [*Par* 22.151 and 27.86]) should be considered both "the least" (*per meno* [*Par* 22,137]) and the most important, determining as it does a soul's fate in eternity. Uncertain, too, is the ontological priority the poet assigns to apprehension and love in effecting blessedness. We are drawn to God through knowledge and desire (*Par* 26.25–66; 28.106–14); Beatrice states clearly that "a l'atto che concepe / segue l'affetto" ("affection follows the act of knowledge" [*Par* 29.139–40]), and Solomon clarifies that vision determines the intensity (*ardore*) of love (*Par* 14.40–42, 49–51). Yet other passages complicate the relation between knowledge and love in summoning us to God. Marco Lombardo had explained how the motion of the soul makes it turn to things it perceives and thus to desire them (*Purg* 16.88–93). But what is that initial motion, instilled by its maker, if not love? In *Par* 24.64–65 as well the Pauline definition of faith as the substance of things hoped for, and the evidence of things not seen, troubles the sequence of apprehension and desire, positing rather a non-linear, and non-dualist, relation between them. Dominic and Francis, aligned with knowledge and love respectively, are treated as functionally interchangeable:[5]

> De l'un dirò, però che d'amendue
> si dice l'un pregiando, qual ch'om prende,
> perch' ad un fine fur l'opere sue.
> (*Par* 11.40–42)

I shall devote my tale to one, because / in praising either prince one praises both: / the labors of the two were toward one goal.

The distinction between knowledge and love, then, is both essential and infinitely complex.

The contradictions that require healing intensify as the pilgrim nears the beatific vision, and the poet faces the challenge of describing the nature of the divinity and of beatitude. God can be conceived as a dimensionless point (*Par* 28.16) that nonetheless encompasses the created universe (*Par* 27.114). The created universe is simultaneously geocentric and theocentric (*Par* 28). Heaven is both desire and satiation (Bynum 1995, 304–305; Pertile 1993b and 1997; Chiavacci Leonardi 1998). Mary's nature is a dizzying paradox on multiple levels:

> Vergine Madre, figlia del tuo figlio,
> umile e alta più che creatura. . . .
> (*Par* 33.1–2)

Virgin Mother, daughter of your Son, / more humble and sublime than any creature.

The Trinity, the highest example of paralogism, is both three and one:

> Quell'uno e due e tre che sempre vive
> e regna sempre in tre e 'n due e 'n uno . . .
> (*Par* 14.28–29)

That One and Two and Three who ever lives / and *reigns ever* in Three and Two and One.

How Christ, wholly divine and wholly human, reconciles both contrary natures within himself is the pilgrim's last, passionate question, answered by a flash of simultaneous knowledge and love (*Par* 33.127–41). It is with this revelation of how human and divine nature are reconciled that the poem falls silent.

Paradoxically, it is as the poet falls silent that the pilgrim finally completes his evolution into the poet-figure who is now ready to begin writing the *Comedy* we have just finished reading. A final paradox of the *Paradiso* is that poetry is both repeatedly called insufficient to describe the divine and repeatedly shown to be the only verbal form adequate to adumbrate it to any degree. It is indeed the form that the poet adopts to describe it. The last element to mention, then, in this programmatic reconciliation of oppositions is the specifically *poetic* nature of this reconciliation. The *Comedy* could not have been conceived, in other words, as a prose treatise; only poetry, with its compactness (the connective tissue suppressed), its formal constraints, formal beauty, and multiple meanings, is adequate to render (and heal) contradictions that in terms of earthly logic are intransigent. By this I do not mean that Dante uses poetic language in order to speak imprecisely, but rather that he makes razor-sharp use of its polysemous qualities. Rachel Jacoff (2000, 125, 128), for example, analyzes the careful use Dante makes of the plural possibilities of poetic language in differentiating (and assimilating) aerial bodies and earthly bodies.

From the question with which I began—what is the nature of the love the poet tells us he retains for Beatrice to the very end of the *Paradiso?*—I may seem to have wandered very far. Yet this brief survey of the third canticle's project of transcending contradiction is intimately tied to that very question. For Dante, theologically as well as poetically, there is no ontological divide between *eros* and *agape,* between body and the incorporeal heaven that has no *dove* ("where" [*Par* 27.109–10]) other than in the mind of God; the love he felt for Beatrice in the body is the love he still feels for her in Paradise:

Io dissi: "Al suo piacere e tosto e tardo
vegna rimedio a li occhi, che fuor porte
quand' ella entrò col foco ond' io sempr' ardo."
(*Par* 26.13–15)

I said: "As pleases her, may solace—sooner / or later—reach these eyes, her gates when she / brought me the fire with which I always burn."

The distinction that the pilgrim makes between twisted love (*l'amor torto* [*Par* 26.62]) and right love ([*l'amor*] *diritto* [*Par* 26.63]) does not entail an association of sexual with selfish love, or spiritual and selfless love; sexual / bodily love can indeed be selfless, the "right love." Between the corporeal body and the incorporeal heaven that has no "where" [*dove*] other than in the mind of God there is no incongruity, for corporeal body will, in fact, inhabit that heaven, though we do not know how this can be. The love that Dante felt for Beatrice in the body will unite with, not be superseded by, the love for God to which she drew him (*Par* 26.13–18). There is no need to leave one love behind to reach the other, for they both are one:

> Le fronde onde s'infronda tutto l'orto
> de l'ortolano etterno, am' io cotanto
> quanto da lui a lor di bene è porto.
> (*Par* 26.64–66)

> The leaves enleaving all the garden of / the everlasting Gardener, I love / according to the good He gave to them.

This declaration of love on the pilgrim's part, and the understanding it articulates, is endorsed when Beatrice and the souls of the heaven of the fixed stars sing "Santo, santo, santo!" ("Holy, holy, holy!" [*Par* 26.69]).

Dante's entire poetic career was devoted to rehabilitating his loves from classical literature and myth and integrating them into a Christian economy. If we imagine him unable to integrate his love for Beatrice without simply dematerializing it or superseding her, we limit the force of that integrative mind in a way that is inconsistent with the near-omniscience that modern criticism otherwise tends to attribute to him. Because Dante is a medieval Christian, we seem to assume a set of limits beyond which he cannot range, despite the overt evidence in his poem to the contrary.

I will conclude this discussion of Dante's unexpected postulates with a glance at how modernity conditions itself to see certain reflexes in medieval culture and not others. Giuseppe Sergi (1998, 14) has noted the divergence between generalist and specialist ideas of the Middle Ages: "We must attest then that the Middle Ages of today's popular culture is very little affected by the research of historians, but rather responds to tenacious needs of collective psychology, which are fed and confirmed by the popular media. . . ." Although his book aims to correct the inaccurate conflations and generalizations of popular culture, Sergi does not explicitly address the extent to which specialists might be influenced, even unconsciously, by popular culture. One corrective is particularly useful; Sergi reminds us that conditions in the past are not increasingly more alien the further back we look. Indeed, the more recent past can be far more alien, depending upon the category we are examining (1998, 11–12).

I noted above that for highly complex theological matters and subtle logical distinctions, no other language could serve Dante like poetry, and the category of poetry is one that links the medieval and the modern periods. Medieval and modern literary texts alike share that tendency to stage important debates in imagistic rather than analytical language; we need to read this imagistic language carefully, not perfunctorily. An illustrative episode of the *Purgatorio* explores how expectations condition perception and interpretation. When the pilgrim first encounters souls undergoing actual penance, he fails to read their physical posture and facial expressions correctly:

> Vero è che più e meno eran contratti
> secondo ch'avien più e meno a dosso;
> e qual più pazïenza avea ne li atti,
> piangendo parea dicer: "Più non posso."
> (*Purg* 10.136–39)

They were indeed bent down—some less, some more— / according to the weight their backs now bore; / and even he whose aspect showed most patience / in tears, appeared to say: "I can no more."

The pilgrim misreads these sinners, however, as the next canto makes clear: they are praying an extended version of the Lord's Prayer, and their emotions are not desperation or sorrow, but rather love, altruism, and exaltation (*Purg* 11.1–24). This particular error, though only one of many that the pilgrim makes, is useful for my purposes because of its placement and its foundation. Why does the pilgrim misunderstand what he is seeing? First, because he extrapolates from the souls' posture and their tears the emotions a mortal would be feeling: he sees what his mortal preconceptions allow him to see. Because he is conditioned by his recent experience, he assumes that the semiotics of Purgatory parallel those of Hell. The poet does not comment at all when the pilgrim's error is revealed; he does not need to. Because this is a moment of education for the pilgrim, in which he begins to learn the rules of the Mountain of Purgatory, the poet expects readers to pay careful attention to the pilgrim's mistake, and apply it to ourselves. The entire passage is constructed to focus on the problem of precognitive assumption, preexisting assumptions that color—or even determine—how evidence is perceived and interpreted, and persist even when the evidence militates against them. The pilgrim does not recognize that these souls rejoice, because his grid of assumptions, expectations, and experience blinds him to the evidence before his eyes. For him suffering *cannot* be joyful, so he does not see that suffering *is*.

Expectations govern perceptions both within and around the *Comedy*. Though lionizing the *Comedy* and its author, modernity has tended to approach the text and its entire cultural matrix with prior assumptions about what it can and cannot mean. This can lead to a dismissal of its evidence or, at the very least, surprise at it. If we are surprised by the evidence that the historical record affords us, then we should adjust our conceptual categories, not the historical record. Nevertheless, the historical record—not our spectrum of admitted possibility—is what often gets the tweaking. In a variety of cases evidence of the past is discounted, revised, or—in extreme cases—destroyed to make it conform to modern expectations.

As a shorthand for, or epitome of, the way medieval people differed from moderns, it is often repeated that medieval artists did not tend to sign their work. An array of conclusions is drawn from this "fact": for example, that medieval artists offered up their work to the glory of God, not their own; that medieval individuality was much attenuated compared to modern; that medieval artists felt no sense of individual merit or individual style. These all lead back to the notion that medieval people were simply not like us. It is for many reasons problematic to equate a lack of signature with a lack of individuality, not the least of which is the fact that such lack of signature is, if not invented, grossly exaggerated. Marcel Durliat (1982, 586) confirms not only that there are many signatures on sculptures, frescoes, and manuscripts, but also that these signatures evoke a personal style, calling the anonymity of the medieval artist a myth: "As soon as we relinquish the myth of the anonymity of Romanesque creation to observe, objectively, the conditions of its production, we realize that it was in fact extremely 'personalized.'" But the expectation of anonymity that pervades modernity's construction of the medieval artist conditions us to see "exceptions" in the plethora of signatures medieval artists have left to us.

Happily, even rarer is the irrevocable destruction of the historical record practiced in pursuit of an imagined medieval ideal, as when nineteenth-century restorers "re-medievalized" churches to bring them into line with a modern notion of the period's aesthetic:

> With the aim of recovering, beneath the patina of successive layers, the authenticity of the rough material that, in their eyes, revealed the deep rationality of the monumental Romanesque and Gothic system, and too often imbued with the dogma of bare stone (which alone was capable of expressing what they thought to be the ascetic essence of Romanesque religious building), they scraped away these layers, for the most part without further investigation. They did not know that these had been applied systematically by the Romanesque builders, who—no matter what is said of them—were not great admirers of the effect of bare stone; they scraped these worn skins down to the bone, without ever knowing that in more than one case the sheets of plaster were carrying away paintings that were sometimes overlaid by various layers that had been added on. How many of them? It is impossible for us now ever to know.
> (Oursel 1980, 217)

These despoiled frescoes represent the worst-case scenario. But although the historical record is not destroyed when we ignore it or second-guess it, it is certainly misrepresented, temporarily or permanently. A modest cottage-industry in the debunking of myths about the Middle Ages has sprung up, both in austere print (Heers 1992) and on the ebullient internet (ORB 2000). Such fictions as the "right of the first night" (Boureau 1998), the chaste love of the troubadours (Paden 1999), and the belief that the earth was flat (Russell 1991) are being briskly dismantled.

We must ask, though, what myths are being introduced? How are we deforming the Middle Ages now? We cannot count on time, distance, and additional analysis eventually to generate a true picture of "the medieval mind." On the one hand, as we can see from the evidence that has been either destroyed or overlooked, our expectations determine what we will see. On the other hand, no one is able to step outside that loop of expectation and assumption to perceive and, only then, interpret the data. Still, to do justice to the full evidence of the historical record, we need to readjust our notions of what people in the past can have thought or done. This exploration of both Dante's construction of Paradise's love and the obstacles to our taking him at his word has sought to make visible evidence that otherwise had to be overridden, or read past, or, as in the case of those frescoes, effaced.[6]

Notes

1. This "turn toward the body" has a strongly integrative tendency, in that very few studies examine body utterly divorced from mind or soul. The impulse behind this trend seems thus to be to recuperate the body into identity rather than to keep it separate from, or privilege it at the expense of (formerly privileged), mind.

2. Useful introductions to this long critical history are in Warner and Szubka 1994; Cahill 1996; and Coakley 1997b. On modernity as a "promiscuous concept" and on its implicit dualism, see Ferguson 2000.

3. Citations from the *Divina Commedia* are taken from Alighieri 1994a. I use Mandelbaum's translation (1982; 1984) for most passages. Italics in the translation indicate either my own translation or my adaptation of Mandelbaum's. All translations of critical studies are mine.

4. Jacoff (1991, 193) links binary oppositions to the contradictory verities of theology: "The virgin mother, like the squared circle, forces us to the limits of language in order to communicate that which is beyond the human: 'Trasumanar significar *per verba* / non si poria. . . . ' . . . Dante reveals and revels in the potential intersection of transgression and transcendence . . . displays, compresses, and masters the paradoxes at the heart of language and theology."

5. The praise of each saint by a representative of the other's order is matched by the speaker's deprecation of his own order. Paradoxically, the Franciscan and Dominican orders too are reduced to one, in their depravity and shortsightedness (*Par* 11–12).

6. I would like to thank colleagues at the University of Oregon and interlocutors at the Dante2000 conference for feedback, insights, objections, and encouragement.

APPETITES: WORKS CITED

Ahern, John. 1990a. "Nudi Grammantes: The Grammar and Rhetoric of Deviation in *Inferno* XV." *Romanic Review* 82:466–86.

______. 1990b. "Troping the Fig: *Inferno* XV, 66." *Lectura Dantis* 6:80–91.

Alighieri, Dante. [1946] 1970. *Rime.* Ed. Gianfranco Contini. 2nd ed. Milan: Einaudi.

______. 1954. *Convivio.* Ed. G. Busnelli and G. Vandelli. 2 vols. Florence: Le Monnier.

______. 1956. *Rime della "Vita Nuova" e della giovinezza.* Ed. Michele Barbi and Francesco Maggini. Florence: Le Monnier.

______. 1957. *La Divina Commedia.* Ed. Natalino Sapegno. Milan and Naples: Ricciardi.

______. 1966–67. *La Commedia secondo l'antica vulgata.* Ed. Giorgio Petrocchi. 4 vols. Milan: Mondadori.

______. 1967. *Dante's Lyric Poetry.* Ed. Kenelm Foster and Patrick Boyde. 2 vols. Oxford: Oxford University Press.

______. 1969. *Rime della maturità e dell'esilio.* Ed. Michele Barbi and Vincenzo Pernicone. Florence: Le Monnier.

______. 1990. *Dante's Il Convivio: The Banquet.* Trans. Richard H. Lansing. New York and London: Garland.

______. 1994a. *La Commedia secondo l'antica vulgata.* Ed. Giorgio Petrocchi. 2nd ed. Florence: Le Lettere.

______. 1994b. *The Inferno of Dante: A New Verse Translation by Robert Pinsky.* New York: Farrar, Straus and Giroux.

______. 1996. *De vulgari eloquentia.* Ed. and trans. Steven Botterill. Cambridge: Cambridge University Press.

Armour, Peter. 1990. "*Inferno* XV." In *Inferno.* Vol. 1 of *Dante's "Divine Comedy": Introductory Readings.* Ed. Tibor Wlassics. Charlottesville: University of Virginia Press. 189–208.

______. 1991. "The Love of Two Florentines: Brunetto Latini and Bondie Dietaiuti." *Lectura Dantis* 9:11–33.

______. 1994. "Brunetto, the Stoic Pessimist." DS 112:1–18.

Barolini, Teodolinda. 1984. *Dante's Poets.* Princeton, N.J.: Princeton University Press.

______. 1992. *The Undivine "Comedy": Detheologizing Dante.* Princeton, N.J.: Princeton University Press.

______. 1993. "'Le parole son donne e i fatti son maschi': Toward a Sexual Poetics of the *Decameron* (*Dec.* II 10)." *Studi sul Boccaccio* 21:175–97.

______. 1997. "Guittone's *Ora parrà,* Dante's *Doglia mi reca,* and the *Commedia*'s Anatomy of Desire." In *Seminario Dantesco Internazionale: International Dante Seminar* 1. Ed. Zygmunt B. Barański. Florence: Le Lettere. 3–23.

______. 1998. "Dante and Cavalcanti (On Making Distinctions in Matters of Love): *Inferno* V in Its Lyric Context." DS 116:31–63.

______. 2000a. "Dante and Francesca da Rimini: Realpolitik, Romance, Gender." *Speculum* 75:1–28.

______. 2000b. "Medieval Multiculturalism and Dante's Theology of Hell." In *The Craft and the Fury: Essays in Memory of Glauco Cambon.* Ed. J. Francese. 82–102. Special issue of *Italiana* 9.

Battagli, Marco. 1913. *Marcha.* Ed. Aldo Francesco Massèra. Rerum Italicorum Scriptores 16.3. Città di Castello: Lapi.

Biller, Peter, and Alastair Minnis, eds. 1997. *Medieval Theology and the Natural Body.* Rochester, N.Y.: York Medieval Press.

Boccaccio, Giovanni. 1976. *Decameron.* Ed. Vittore Branca. Vol. 4 of *Tutte le opere di Giovanni Boccaccio.* Milan: Mondadori.

______. 1980. *Decameron.* Ed. Vittore Branca. Turin: Einaudi.

Boethius. 1973. *Tractates and the Consolation of Philosophy.* Eds. H. F. Stewart, E. K. Rand, and S. J. Tester. Cambridge, Mass., and London: Harvard University Press.

Bordo, Susan. 1980. "The Cartesian Masculinization of Thought." *Signs* 2:439–56.

______. 1993. *Unbearable Weight: Feminism, Western Culture, and the Body.* Berkeley: University of California Press.

Boswell, John. 1980. *Christianity, Social Tolerance, and Homosexuality: Gay People in Western Europe from the Beginning of the Christian Era to the Fourteenth Century.* Chicago and London: The University of Chicago Press.

______. 1994. "Dante and the Sodomites." DS 112:63–76.

Bottomley, Frank. 1979. *Attitudes to the Body in Western Christianity.* London: Lepus Books.

Boureau, Alain. 1998. *The Lord's First Night: The Myth of the Droit de Cuissage.* Trans. Lydia Cochrane. Chicago: The University of Chicago Press.

Boyde, Patrick. 1993. *Perception and Passion in Dante's "Comedy."* Cambridge: Cambridge University Press.

Brown, Peter. 1988. *The Body and Society: Men, Women, and Sexual Renunciation in Early Christianity.* New York: Columbia University Press.

Brunetto Latini. 1947. *Li livres dou Tresor de Brunetto Latini.* Ed. Francis Carmody. Berkeley: University of California Press.

______. 1960. *Il tesoretto.* In Vol. 2 of *Poeti del Duecento.* Ed. Gianfranco Contini. Milan and Naples: Ricciardi.

Butler, Judith. 1990. *Gender Trouble: Feminism and the Subversion of Identity.* New York: Routledge.

______. 1993. *Bodies That Matter: On the Discursive Limits of "Sex."* New York: Routledge.

Bynum, Caroline Walker. 1987. *Holy Feast and Holy Fast: The Religious Significance of Food to Medieval Women.* Berkeley: University of California Press.

______. 1991. *Fragmentation and Redemption: Essays on Gender and the Body in Medieval Religion.* New York: Zone Books.

______. 1995. *The Resurrection of the Body in Western Christianity, 200–1336.* New York: Columbia University Press.

Cahill, Lisa Sowle. 1996. "The Body—in Context." In *Sex, Gender, and Christian Ethics.* Cambridge: Cambridge University Press. 73–107.

Chiavacci Leonardi, Anna Maria. 1998. "Il *Paradiso* di Dante: L'ardore del desiderio." *Letture classensi* 27:101–12.

Coakley, Sarah. 1992. "Visions of the Self in Late Medieval Christianity: Some Cross-Disciplinary Reflections." *Philosophy* 32:89–103.

______. 1997a. *Religion and the Body.* Cambridge: Cambridge University Press.

______. 1997b. "Introduction: Religion and the Body." In *Religion and the Body.* Ed. Sarah Coakley. Cambridge: Cambridge University Press. 1–12.

______. 2000. "The Eschatological Body: Gender, Transformation, and God." *Modern Theology* 16:61–74.

Cogan, Marc. 1999. *The Design in the Wax.* Notre Dame, Ind.: University of Notre Dame Press.

Cohen, Jeffrey Jerome, and Bonnie Wheeler, eds. 1997. *Becoming Male in the Middle Ages.* New York: Garland.

Cronaca malatestiana. 1922. Ed. Aldo Francesco Massèra. In Rerum Italicorum Scriptores 15.2. Bologna: Zanichelli.

Della Terza, Dante. 1978. "Il canto di Brunetto Latini." In *Orbis medievalis: Mélanges de langue et de littérature médiévales offerts à Reto Raduolf Bezzola à l'occasion de son quatre-vingtième anniversaire.* Ed. Georges Güntert, Marc-René Jung, and Kurt Ringger. Berne: Francke. 69–88.

De Vita, Daria. 1998. "'Fu chiamata da molti Beatrice.'" *Belfagor* 53:1–25.

Dinzelbacher, Peter. 1993. "Il corpo nelle visioni dell'aldilà." *Micrologus* 1:301–26.

DuBois, Page. 1991. *Torture and Truth.* New York: Routledge.

Durliat, Marcel. 1982. *L'Art roman.* Paris: Mazenod.

Durling, Robert M., and Ronald L. Martinez. 1996. "Dante and Homosexuality." In *Inferno.* Vol. 1 of *The Divine Comedy of Dante Alighieri.* Ed. and trans. Robert M. Durling. Introduction and notes by Ronald L. Martinez and Robert M. Durling. New York and Oxford: Oxford University Press. 559–60.

Economou, George D. 1972. *The Goddess Natura in Medieval Literature.* Cambridge, Mass.: Harvard University Press.

Enders, Jody. 1999. *The Medieval Theater of Cruelty: Rhetoric, Memory, Violence.* Ithaca, N.Y., and London: Cornell University Press.

Feher, Michel, with R. Naddaff and N. Tazi. 1989. *Fragments for a History of the Human Body, Zone 3* (Part I), *Zone 4* (Part II), and *Zone 5* (Part III). New York: Urzone.

Ferguson, Harvie. 2000. *Modernity and Subjectivity: Body, Soul, Spirit.* Charlottesville: University of Virginia Press.

Ferrante, Joan M. 1992. "Dante's Beatrice: Priest of an Androgynous God." In *CEMERS Occasional Papers* 2. Binghamton, N.Y.: Medieval and Renaissance Texts and Studies.

Foucault, Michel. 1966. *Les mots et les choses: Une archéologie des sciences humaines.* Paris: Gallimard.

______. 1975. *Surveiller et punir: Naissance de la prison.* Paris: Gallimard.

______. 1976. *La volonté de savoir.* Vol. 1 of *Histoire de la sexualité.* Paris: Gallimard.

Fradenburg, Louise, and Carla Freccero, eds. 1996. Introduction to *Premodern Sexualities.* New York and London: Routledge. xii–xxiv.

Freccero, John. 1991. "The Eternal Image of the Father." In *The Poetry of Allusion: Virgil and Ovid in Dante's "Commedia."* Ed. Rachel Jacoff and Jeffrey T. Schnapp. Stanford, Calif.: Stanford University Press. 62–76.

Gagliardi, Antonio. 1997. *Guido Cavalcanti e Dante: Una questione d'amore.* Catanzaro: Pullano.

Gardiner, Eileen, ed. 1989. *Visions of Heaven and Hell before Dante.* New York: Italica.

Giraut de Borneil. 1989. *The Cansos and Sirventes of the Troubadour Giraut de Borneil: A Critical Edition.* Ed. Ruth Verity Sharman. Cambridge: Cambridge University Press.

Gragnolati, Manuele. 1999. "Identity, Pain, and Resurrection: Body and Soul in Bonvesin da la Riva's *Book of the Three Scriptures* and Dante's *Commedia.*" Ph.D. Diss., Columbia University.

Grantley, Darryll, and Nina Taunton, eds. 2000. *The Body in Late Medieval and Early Modern Culture.* Aldershot, England, and Burlington, Vermont: Ashgate.

Guittone d'Arezzo. 1940. *Le rime di Guittone d'Arezzo.* Ed. Francesco Egidi. Bari: Laterza.

Hadley, D. M. 1999. *Masculinity in Medieval Europe.* London and New York: Longman.

Harrison, Robert Pogue. 1988. *The Body of Beatrice.* Baltimore and London: Johns Hopkins University Press.

Heers, Jacques. 1992. *Le Moyen Âge, une imposture.* Paris: Perrin.

Holsinger, Bruce. 1996. "Sodomy and Resurrection: The Homoerotic Subject of the *Divine Comedy.*" In *Premodern Sexualities.* Ed. Louise Fradenburg and Carla Freccero. New York and London: Routledge. 243–74.

Jacoff, Rachel. 1991. "Transgression and Transcendence: Figures of Female Desire in Dante's *Commedia*." In *The New Medievalism*. Ed. Kevin Brownlee, Marina Brownlee, and Stephen Nichols. Baltimore: Johns Hopkins University Press. 183–200.

______. 2000. "'Our Bodies, Our Selves': The Body in the *Commedia*." In *Sparks and Seeds: Medieval Literature and Its Afterlife: Essays in Honor of John Freccero*. Ed. Dana E. Stewart and Alison Cornish. Turnhout: Brepols. 119–37.

Jordan, Mark D. 1997. *The Invention of Sodomy in Christian Theology*. Chicago and London: The University of Chicago Press.

Joubert, Jacques. 1991. *Le corps sauvé*. Paris: Les Éditions du Cerf.

Kay, Richard. 1978. *Dante's Swift and Strong: Essays on "Inferno" XV*. Lawrence: Regents Press of Kansas.

Kay, Sarah, and Miri Rubin, eds. 1994. *Framing Medieval Bodies*. Manchester: Manchester University Press.

Kirkpatrick, Robin. 1994. "Dante and the Body." In *Framing Medieval Bodies*. Ed. Sarah Kay and Miri Rubin. New York: Routledge. 236–53.

Laqueur, Thomas. 1990. *Making Sex: Body and Gender from the Greeks to Freud*. Cambridge, Mass.: Harvard University Press.

Lees, Clare A., and Thelma S. Fenster, eds. 1994. *Medieval Masculinities: Regarding Men in the Middle Ages*. Minneapolis: University of Minnesota Press.

Lomperis, Linda, and Sarah Stanbury, eds. 1993. *Feminist Approaches to the Body in Medieval Literature*. Philadelphia: University of Pennsylvania Press.

Louth, Andrew. 1997. "The Body in Western Catholic Christianity." In *Religion and the Body*. Ed. Sarah Coakley. Cambridge: Cambridge University Press. 111–30.

MacDonald, Diane L. Prosser. 1995. *Transgressive Corporeality: The Body, Poststructuralism, and the Theological Imagination*. Albany: State University of New York Press.

Mandelbaum, Allen, trans. 1982. *The Divine Comedy of Dante Alighieri: Purgatorio*. Berkeley: University of California Press.

______, trans. 1984. *The Divine Comedy of Dante Alighieri: Paradiso*. Berkeley: University of California Press.

Mazzotta, Giuseppe. 1979. *Dante, Poet of the Desert: History and Allegory in the "Divine Comedy."* Princeton, N.J.: Princeton University Press.

Miles, Margaret. 1979. *Augustine on the Body.* Missoula, Mont.: Scholars Press.

______. 1989. *Carnal Knowing: Female Nakedness and Religious Meaning in the Christian West.* Boston: Beacon Press.

Moevs, Christian. 1994. "The Metaphysics of the *Primo Mobile*: Love, Mind and Matter in Dante's *Comedy.*" Ph.D. Diss., Columbia University.

Montserrat, Dominic, ed. 1998. *Changing Bodies, Changing Meanings: Studies on the Human Body in Antiquity.* London and New York: Routledge.

Murray, Jacqueline, ed. 1999. *Conflicted Identities and Multiple Masculinities: Men in the Medieval West.* New York and London: Garland.

(ORB) Online Reference Book. 2000. *Misconceptions about the Middle Ages.* http://orb.rhodes.edu/non_spec/missteps/Con.html

Oursel, Raymond. 1980. *Révélation de la peinture romane.* St. Léger-Vauban: Zodiaque.

Paden, William. 1999. "The Troubadour's Lady as Seen Through Thick History." *Exemplaria* 11:221–24.

Pagels, Elaine. 1988. *Adam, Eve, and the Serpent.* New York: Random House.

Pequigney, Joseph. 1991. "Sodomy in Dante's *Inferno* and *Purgatorio.*" *Representations* 36:22–42.

Pertile, Lino. 1990. "'La punta del desio': Storia di una metafora dantesca." *Lectura Dantis* 7:3–28.

______. 1993a. "Dante's *Comedy* beyond the *Stilnovo.*" *Lectura Dantis* 13:47–77.

______. 1993b. "*Paradiso*: A Drama of Desire." In *Word and Drama in the "Divine Comedy."* Ed. John Barnes and Jennifer Petrie. Dublin: Foundation of Italian Studies / Irish Academic Press. 143–80.

______. 1996. "Bonconte e l'anafonesi." *Filologia e critica* 21:118–26.

______. 1997. "A Desire of Paradise and a Paradise of Desire." In *Dante: Contemporary Perspectives*. Ed. Amilcare A. Iannucci. Toronto: University of Toronto Press. 148–166.

______. 1998. *La puttana e il gigante*. Ravenna: Longo.

Peters, Edward. 1985. *Torture*. New York: Basil Blackwell.

Pézard, André. 1950. *Dante sous la pluie de feu (Enfer, chant XV)*. Paris: J. Vrin.

Porter, James I., ed. 1999. *Construction of the Classical Body*. Ann Arbor: University of Michigan Press.

Psaki, F. Regina. 1996a. "Dante's Redeemed Eroticism." *Lectura Dantis* 18–19:12–19.

______. 1996b. "The Sexual Body in Dante and the Medieval Context." *Annali di storia dell'esegesi* 13:539–50.

______. 2000. "The Sexual Body in Dante's Celestial Paradise." In *Imagining Heaven in the Middle Ages: A Book of Essays*. Ed. Jan S. Emerson and Hugh Feiss, O.S.B. New York: Garland. 47–61.

Rocke, Michael. 1996. *Forbidden Friendships: Homosexuality and Male Culture in Renaissance Florence*. New York: Oxford University Press.

Rossi Barilli, Gianni. 1999. *Il movimento gay in Italia*. Milan: Feltrinelli.

Russell, Jeffrey Burton. 1991. *Inventing the Flat Earth: Columbus and Modern Historians*. New York: Praeger.

Scarry, Elaine. 1985. *The Body in Pain: The Making and Unmaking of the World*. New York: Oxford University Press.

Schnapp, Jeffrey. 1991. "Dante's Sexual Solecisms: Gender and Genre in the *Commedia*." In *The New Medievalism*. Ed. Kevin Brownlee, Marina Brownlee, and Stephen Nichols. Baltimore: Johns Hopkins University Press. 221–25.

Sergi, Giuseppe. 1998. *L'idea di medioevo tra senso comune e pratica storica*. Rome: Donzelli.

Shapiro, Marianne. 1998. *Dante and the Knot of Body and Soul*. New York: St. Martin's Press.

Sharman, Ruth Verity, ed. 1989. *The* Cansos *and* Sirventes *of the Troubadour Giraut de Borneil: A Critical Edition*. Cambridge: Cambridge University Press.

Sowell, Madison U. 1993. "Dante's Poetics of Sexuality." *Exemplaria* 2:435–69.

Suleiman, Susan Rubin, ed. 1986. *The Female Body in Western Culture: Contemporary Perspectives.* Cambridge, Mass.: Harvard University Press.

Trottmann, Christian. 1999. "Sulla funzione dell'anima e del corpo nella beatitudine." In *Anima e corpo nella cultura medievale: Atti del V Convegno di Studi della Società Italiana per lo Studio del Pensiero Medievale (Venezia, 25–28 settembre 1995).* Ed. Carla Casagrande and Silvana Vecchio. Tavarnuzze (Florence): SISMEL. 140–55.

Vance, Eugene. 1984. "The Differing Seed: Dante's Brunetto Latini." In *Vernacular Poetics in the Middle Ages.* Ed. Lois Ebin. Kalamazoo, Mich.: Medieval Institute Publications. 129–52.

Waller, Marguerite. 1989. "Seduction and Salvation: Sexual Difference in Dante's *Commedia* and the Difference It Makes." In *Donna: Women in Italian Culture.* Ed. Ada Testaferri. Toronto: Dovehouse. 225–45.

Warner, R, and T. Szubka, eds. 1994. *The Mind–Body Problem: A Guide to Current Debate.* Oxford: Blackwell.

Williams, Charles. 1941. *Religion and Love in Dante: The Theology of Romantic Love.* Westminster: Dacre Press.

Zupan, Patricia. 1990. "The New Dantean Alba." *Lectura Dantis* 6:92–99.

PHILOSOPHIES

8

Mysticism and Meaning in Dante's *Paradiso*

Steven Botterill

Let us begin at the beginning, with the word.

Gentile
Ettore Serra
poesia
è il mondo l'umanità
la propria vita
fioriti dalla parola
la limpida meraviglia
di un delirante fermento

Quando trovo
in questo mio silenzio
una parola
scavata è nella mia vita
come un abisso
(Ungaretti 170, 58)

Dear / Ettore Serra / poetry / is the world humanity / one's own life / flowering from the word / the limpid marvel / of a delirious ferment. // When I find / in this silence of mine / a word / it is dug out of my life / like an abyss.
(my translation)

NOT, OF COURSE, the word of Dante Alighieri; still less that of God; but, as my readers will recognize, the word of Giuseppe Ungaretti: the poem, entitled "Commiato" and dated "Locvizza il 2 ottobre 1916," that concluded his first collection, *Il porto sepolto,* published at Udine in 1916, and, later, the section of the same name in the definitive version of *L'allegria.* If I risk anachronism by citing at the outset a text so distant from any of Dante's, the product of a world and a culture that he could not have known, might not have understood, and would most certainly have despised whether he understood them or not, it is not so much because I believe that poetry, in the right hands, is at least partially capable of transcending barriers of historical time and cultural space—though I do—as because this poem, whose mysteriously evocative power has haunted me since I first read it as an undergraduate, seems to me to offer a curiously appropriate point of departure for my brief consideration of a still controversial topic in Dante studies: his relationship with—or practice of?—mysticism.

"Commiato" is clearly an *ars poetica.* After the opening *salutatio* to Ettore Serra, Ungaretti's publisher (and, by Ungaretti's own account, the "onlie begetter" of his poetic debut),[1] the next six lines offer a series of propositional statements about—or, better, definitions of—poetry. Indeed, in its earliest editions the poem itself is entitled "Poesia," acquiring the name by which we know it only in the Mondadori edition of *L'allegria* in 1942.[2] What we need to notice right away is, first, the all-encompassing scope of these definitions—poetry inappellably *is* the world, humanity, one's own life; second, the organic (rather than crafted) relationship between poetry and the word from which it flowers (rather than is constructed); and, third, the ecstatic nature of the achieved poetic experience, "la limpida meraviglia / di un delirante fermento." If poetry is to be seen in these terms, we are perhaps justified in concluding, from its universalizing aspirations, its non-rational coming into being, and its overwhelming transformative effects, that it is an essentially mystical phenomenon. This conclusion can only be reinforced by consideration of the poem's second stanza, in which, for the first time in this text, a poet enters upon the scene of poetry: a poet whose habitual mode is silence ("questo *mio* silenzio"), but who sometimes finds—not, clearly, through any willed or conscious act of his own creative intelligence—a word, which must be dug or hollowed out of the depths of his silent life with, we may imagine, difficulty and anguish. The comparison with a familiar tradition of accounts of mystical experience along the *via negativa* of apophatic mysticism, is, I think, much more than superficially striking.

I have said that "Commiato" is an *ars poetica;* and the same, as we have been taught of late by many outstanding scholars, is true of Dante's

Commedia.[3] Yet comparison soon reveals that this outward identity of purpose between the two texts is deflected, almost concealed, by profound differences of assumption and approach, not to mention genre. "Commiato" flaunts its ambition to delineate and define the poetry that is its subject, isolating the key word "poesia" on a single line, following it up with an appositional series of nouns connected to it by a definitional usage of the verb "to be," and openly voicing, through its poet-speaker, a description of the technical means and existential conditions by which and in which poetry comes into being. The *Commedia* does none of this. Its approach to the concept and definition of poetry is sometimes explicit and sometimes implicit, but always indirect, either distanced through attribution to multiple speakers and dramatized in the encounters among them, or only derivable, at best, from observation of its poetic principles in the process of being actualized in the poem's own practice. The *Commedia* may *show* us what poetry is, but it never actually *tells* us.

More important still, it would seem—at least at first sight—is that what the *Commedia* shows us about poetry has little to do with what Ungaretti's "Commiato" posits as its nature. It may be tempting to see, in the subject matter of the *poema sacro,* "the world humanity one's own life flowering from the word," but most readers, I suspect, would find it harder to recognize the *Commedia* as "la limpida meraviglia / di un delirante fermento." Marvel there may be, but it is as complex, intricate, and, not infrequently, mysterious as it is limpid; and delirium and ferment, though they are of course represented at key points of the narrative and attributed to that narrative's characters, are, poetically speaking, kept under the firm and consistent control of an overarching creative intelligence, allocated to their proper place within a lucid and elegant verbal construct. Surely, what impresses most readers of the *Commedia* is the heroically *ordered* design of its narrative and thematic structure, the copious abundance of its verbal texture, the apparently inexhaustible richness of its invention and the seemingly untroubled facility of its expression. Dante, it is safe to say, seldom gives the impression of having had to dig deep into the habitual silence of his life, as into an abyss, to find the word he needs.[4]

Narratologically fluent, representationally audacious, intellectually committed, Dante's poem appears, if anything, as a monument of a supremely *rational* engagement with the universe, one whose confident linguistic disposition and categorization of all forms of experience is based on the *De vulgari eloquentia*'s ringing declaration that "since . . . human beings are moved not by their natural instinct but by reason, and since that reason takes diverse forms in individuals . . . it was necessary that the human race, in order for its members to communicate their conceptions among themselves, should have some signal based on reason and perception" (1.3.1–2). Not for Dante, then, the incommunicable ecstasy of an individual experience, the word suffused with personal meaning prised painfully out of silence, but precisely the reverse: poetry as the triumph of clear and accurate communication among rational beings for the greater benefit of the human community. In these terms, it appears—despite the curious persistence of authors and publishers in issuing books with titles like *Dante and the Mystical Tradition*—that Dante himself is not a mystic.[5]

Such, at all events, is certainly the received wisdom among the leading scholars of mysticism itself who have been undertaking, over the last few years, a radical rethinking of that whole concept in the light of recent developments in theology, criticism, and theory, both historicist and postmodernist. Dante's name inevitably crops up at some point in this debate, and equally inevitably is promptly ruled inadmissible as evidence.

Take, for example, the recent work of Don Cupitt. Cupitt had his Warholian quarter-hour of fame some twenty years ago, as a fleetingly scandalous priest of the Church of England who had decided—with rather less originality than he seemed to want to claim—that God was no longer a necessary hypothesis. Since then he has continued to develop, in print and—*horribile dictu*—on television, his very personal conception of religious faith—a conception that has progressively voided itself of doctrinal content or claims to propositional validity, to the point where it can easily, and by Cupitt enthusiastically, be integrated with what he takes to be the almost unlimited intellectual flexibility of postmodernism. Cupitt has always been drawn to mysticism, though usually of an Eastern rather than a Western variety, and his recent book *Mysticism after Modernity* (1998) usefully summarizes, though one could wish that it also clarified, his thinking on the subject.

Most pertinent to us today is the fact that in this book Dante's *Commedia* is wheeled on almost immediately, before we are even out of the author's introduction, as the primary instance of an axiomatically non-mystical text. "Most people, surely," says Cupitt, "recognize that Dante's *Divine Comedy* is not a straightforward travel book, but an epic poem. So, if in the case of Dante we do not think of the poet as claiming to have enjoyed special supernatural experience, why should we not learn to read John of the Cross and the other great mystics in the same way?" (11). Why not, indeed? Remembering the terms in which we defined the *Commedia* above, and the distinction we drew between it and even a modern, non-religiously mystical text like Ungaretti's "Commiato," we may very well be inclined to agree that a great gulf of some kind is indeed fixed between Dante and the apophatic lyricism of, say, John of the Cross. But, having dragged Dante into his argument only to throw him out again, a few chapters later Cupitt comes to define that very mysticism as a practitioner of which Dante does not qualify (66). Mysticism, for Cupitt, is art; specifically, it is writing. (We might note in passing that Cupitt never tackles the historical question of how mystical texts, especially those of the late-medieval women in whom he is most interested, actually come to be written down, in their largely non-literate society of origin; and, indeed, his general grasp of the historical context is not unfairly illustrated by his claim [30] that Pope Urban VIII was the author of the Bull *Unam sanctam*.)[6] In Cupitt's own words: "in the monotheistic faiths at least, [mysticism] is a tradition of devotional writing which commonly uses the vocabulary of Plato and the neoplatonists, and is rather consciously paradoxical. It discourses at length about the Ineffable, uses erotic metaphors to describe matters purely spiritual, and speaks in visual terms about the Invisible. In mystical experience, we learn, the subject–object distinction is transcended; yet such experience is always described as noetic" (25).

This, remember, is the mysticism that Dante's work does *not* exemplify; and yet it would be hard to beat this paragraph as a summary description of *Paradiso*. Everything is there, from the Neoplatonist vocabulary (we can argue as much as we want about the way that vocabulary actually reached Dante, but reach him it most certainly did) to the erotic metaphors to the lengthy—or at least frequent—discourses about the Ineffable to the visual description of the Invisible (in the astonishing imagery of *Paradiso* 33). And these are indeed the means through which Dante *poeta* represents Dante *personaggio*'s achievement in noetically transcending the subject–object distinction, so that his perfect knowledge, become perfect love, brings about the perfect alignment of wills with which the poem ends. Why, then, does Cupitt deny mystical status to at least the final episode of *Paradiso,* if not to the *cantica* as a whole?

Before sketching a reply to that question, let me look briefly at another authoritative denial of Dante's mystical qualifications that emerges from a very different neck of the theological woods. Bernard McGinn's exhaustive history of Western Christian mysticism, *The Presence of God,* has been emerging volume by volume over the last decade or so, and the most recent installment (McGinn 1998) deals, as its subtitle proclaims, with a period including that of Dante's life and cultural activity. McGinn is not as theologically advanced as Cupitt—which is to say, he seems still to believe in God. At any rate, Cupitt himself seizes upon McGinn's historical treatment of the mystical phenomenon as antithetical to his own, and, moreover, as representing a "Modern" phase in the treatment of the subject, in which people still believe in mystical writing as a representation of actual, primary experience (1998, 106)—a phase to be courteously but firmly distinguished from Cupitt's own "postmodern" treatment, in which there is no primary experience, indeed nothing primary at all, so that "mysticism is a kind of writing and we do not need to invoke 'experience' in order to explain it, when its literary pedigree is so easy to trace" (10–11). (That is, in fact, the sentence that immediately precedes the denial of mystical status to Dante's *Commedia* quoted above.) But even if McGinn, for Cupitt, is the threatening pre-postmodern Other who must be vanquished, or at least discarded, the two speak with one voice on the subject of Dante. In a splendid piece of *praeteritio,* explaining why for him Hadewijch, Mechthild of Magdeburg, and Jacopone da Todi make up the triumvirate of major mystical poets of the period under consideration, McGinn consigns to a footnote (1998, 430*n*161) his observation that "I exclude Dante for the moment—a supreme poet with mystical elements in his writing, but not a mystic." And since by "I exclude Dante for the moment" McGinn actually means "I won't be mentioning him again"—as indeed he does not—we can safely take this dismissal of Dante's claims as final.[7] And yet McGinn himself, as a recent review of his book correctly points out, defines mysticism as "that part of [Christianity's] beliefs and practices that concerns the preparation for, the consciousness of, and the reaction to what can be described as the immediate or direct presence of God" (Katainen 1999, 523), which again sounds to me very much like a description of the unfolding narrative line of the *Commedia* itself.[8]

So it seems that historians and theorists of mysticism, modern and postmodern alike, will have none of the idea that Dante's poem, even in the *Paradiso,* even in the very last lines of the *Paradiso,* can aspire to being considered a mystical text. Must we then, as Cupitt would have us, "not think of the poet as claiming to have enjoyed special supernatural experience," and regard the experience of reading the *Commedia,* even *Paradiso,* as qualitatively different from that of reading John of the Cross?

In a word, no. Let me, in conclusion, try to pull together the threads of my argument and suggest a thought-experiment that may lead in the direction of a better, or at least a different, understanding of the sense in which the experience of some at least of the *Paradiso*—for I will gladly concede to the skeptics the first two *cantiche* and perhaps even most of the third—can be seen as bodying forth, in language, the mystical.

It seems to me that the denial of mystical status to all or part of the *Commedia* is based on a series of *a priori* judgments that a reader less irenic than I might very well call prejudices. One of these is the assumed superiority of the *via negativa* over the *via positiva* or *affirmativa,* the assumption that silence, expressive difficulty, ineffability, are always more tellingly indicative of mystical substance than the boldly confident, assertive use of language characteristic of Dante. I have argued elsewhere, perhaps *ad taedium* though I hope not yet *ad nauseam,* that confidence in—rather than diffidence about—language's capacity not only to constitute mystical discourse but to represent and / or express mystical experience is one of the defining novelties of Dante's approach to the whole question.[9] Second, there is a simple but damaging formalist assumption, not quite sufficiently concealed, in Cupitt's argument that the *Commedia* is "an epic poem. *So,* if in the case of Dante we do not think of the poet as claiming to have enjoyed special supernatural experience . . ." (Cupitt 1998, 11; emphasis added). It remains to be demonstrated—certainly, it is not demonstrated by Cupitt himself—that the (in itself questionable) generic identification of the *Commedia* as an epic poem automatically denies it the possibility of stating a claim to have enjoyed "special supernatural experience" or of being a representation thereof. Finally, and more generally (but also therefore more pervasively and perniciously), there is the basic philological prejudice that dictates that our reading of a text must be circumscribed by the presence and arrangement of the signs—let us skirt, for now, the theoretical quicksands and just call them words—of which that text is composed. Of course, there are limits to the semantic resonance of individual words, and therefore to the interpretative resonance of a text composed of words—there is no sense in which the *Paradiso* is a treatise on the nature and function of the internal combustion engine—but it does seem to me true, and perhaps even to some degree definitive of the workings of poetry as an instantiation of linguistic usage, that such resonance exists, that its existence should be acknowledged and available for critical inspection, and that, for example, texts should be allowed to be made to point, through acts of interpretation, beyond their own philologically determined confines. In short, I think that the *Paradiso* can be held to extend its meaning beyond the last word of its last line—and that we have, indeed, been fooled by the perfect symmetry of its closure (made concrete in the ternary repetition of *stelle* across the three *cantiche*) into forgetting this crucial fact. Moreover, I would suggest that the extension of *Paradiso* into the textual—but not interpretative—void that follows the last line of canto 33 is signaled by the *cantica* itself, from the moment of Dante *personaggio*'s "trasumanar" in canto 1, through the invocations of the ineffability *topos* and the introduction into the narrative of Bernard of Clairvaux to the final image, as being an extension not only in the direction of, but as far as an arrival at, the mystical. The place where that arrival occurs, however, is not in the text of the poem; it is in the understanding of the reader.

Here's my thought-experiment. Imagine the end of *Paradiso* as, like so much else in the *Commedia,* an essentially (if proleptically) cinematic experience. The images fade; the screen goes dark; the words "The End"—or perhaps "Fine"—flare out and then vanish into nothingness. Does your interpretative experience terminate at that point? Do you gather your belongings, leap to your feet, and rush, unthinking and unmoved, for the exit? Not, I suggest, if the film—or the poem—is any good at all; not, that is, if it has made any serious claim on your attention, understanding, or capacity for reflection; if, in short, it has enabled you yourself to create meaning. Instead, the signs that compose the film—like those of any other text—continue to signify even in their absence, their pastness, their renunciation of substance, for a period and to a degree that are determined by the (infinitely variable) power of each individual text to exact response from the sensibility of each individual reader. It is out of that textual void that, after it is "over," *Paradiso* continues to speak, though no longer as it spoke before; now its words are unspoken, its poetry is silence—and its meaning is mystical.

Notes

1. "*Il Porto Sepolto* fu stampato a Udine nel 1916, in edizione di 80 esemplari a cura di Ettore Serra. La colpa fu tutta sua" (Ungaretti 1970, 521).

2. For an account of the collection's various orderings see Ungaretti 1970, 591–94; for a list of textual variants in "Commiato" itself see Ungaretti 1970, 634.

3. See Barański 1997 for an introduction to the most recent work done in this area, much of it by Barański himself.

4. Ungaretti's own elucidation of "Commiato" likewise reinforces an image of poetic activity whose ending in (perhaps only apparent?) failure seems far indeed from the triumphant Dantean arrival at self-understanding: "Trovare una parola significa penetrare nel buio abissale di sé senza turbarne né riuscire a conoscerne il segreto" (Ungaretti 1970, 524–25).

5. Apart from Botterill 1994—the first half of whose title was in fact owed to its publisher, not its author—see such recent works as Colombo 1987; Carugati 1991; Cozzoli 1993; and Prandi 1994.

6. The author was of course Boniface, not Urban, VIII.

7. In fairness to McGinn, whose extraordinary achievement in *The Presence of God* I much admire and have frequently drawn on in my own work, I should point out that his preface to *The Flowering of Mysticism* (McGinn 1998, x) explains that he had originally intended to deal with the period 1200–1350 in a single volume, but later decided to split it into two separate volumes, only the first of which (*The Flowering of Mysticism* itself) had appeared at the time of the Dante2000 conference (or indeed at the time of this volume's publication). It thus remains possible that McGinn will return to Dante in the next volume of the series. Indeed, the foretaste of that volume in the preface to *The Flowering of Mysticism* makes it clear that "[t]he important male mystics who lived and wrote between 1300 and 1350 will appear in the next volume" (x). However, given that for McGinn (as quoted above) Dante is apparently *not* a mystic, important or otherwise, my inference that his disappearance from the text of *The Presence of God* seems likely to be permanent strikes me as not at all unreasonable.

8. Katainen goes on to conclude—quite wrongly, in my view—that "[g]iven this definition of mysticism, it is clear that while Dante wrote about a spiritual journey, he did not himself practice mysticism in the same way that Francis and Jacopone and other mystics did."

9. See, as well as Botterill 1994, 242–53, two other articles of mine: Botterill 1996 and 1997.

9

The Heaven of the Sun: Dante between Aquinas and Bonaventure

Giuseppe Mazzotta

DANTE'S ENCOUNTER with Saint Bonaventure and Saint Thomas Aquinas in the heaven of the sun (*Paradiso* 10–14) marks a radical turning point in the poet's thinking. He confronts the philosophical-theological speculations of the two great masters of the thirteenth century. With them, he focuses on a number of doctrinal controversies in which their fraternal orders and they themselves were engaged. And through them he seeks to reconstitute the vast circle of Christian wisdom: wisdom as a whole and the whole of wisdom.

Scholars have long examined the rhetorical construction and some of the themes unfolded over these cantos. Above all, they have underlined the chiasmus that shapes *Paradiso* 11 and 12: Saint Thomas and Saint Bonaventure tell the lives of, respectively, Saint Francis and Saint Dominic and attack the degeneration of Dominicans and Franciscans. One scholar in particular, Charles T. Davis, has studied the controversy over the poverty of the mendicant orders and its implication for the orders' self-understanding and role they expect to play in history.[1] Are they the prophetic sign of the spiritual, chiliastic new age heralded by Joachim of Flora's *Evangelium Aeternum?* Is a new age of the Spirit, which supersedes the age of the Son, the apocalyptic time of the end and of renewal, really at hand? Are the friars utopian visionaries bent on escaping the demand of history? Or are they impostors?

The fierce opposition by Guillaume de Saint Amour to the friars as pseudo-apostles; the Joachistic rigorism of Gerardo da Borgo San Donnino; the satire by Jean de Meun, which finds its prolongation in the attacks against the Franciscans in *Il Fiore*—all triggered impassioned refutations by both Saint Bonaventure and Saint Thomas. Their opuscules, *Apologia pauperum* and *Contra impugnantes Dei cultum,* witness their concerted effort to offset the challenges mounted against the religious orders from many fronts—intellectual, moral, and theological.

In the wake of Saint Thomas and Saint Bonaventure, Dante rejects the anti-fraternal attacks by the secular masters. Like them, he also rejects the millennial prophecies endorsed by the Spirituals, as if their millennialism short-circuited history and time. But Dante also goes to the very roots of the theological, philosophical, and moral crisis. The novelty of his discourse, his deliberate self-insertion into the philosophical-theological debates of the thirteenth century, which are crystallized in the thought of Aquinas and Bonaventure, has not yet been fully grasped. To do so, it is necessary to highlight the three major conceptual-metaphorical patterns organizing the cantos in the heaven of the sun.

One of them is Dante's reconstitution of a new Christian *mathesis.* I have discussed this issue in *Dante's Vision and the Circle of Knowledge* (Mazzotta 1993, especially 96–115). I did not show there, however, the imaginative and logical links existing between this question and the other two conceptual concerns in the cantos. One of them is the sustained theological discussion of the Trinity. The other is the economy of gifts, which involves the insight into the generosity of creation as well as the practice of poverty. The purpose of this essay is to unveil these three discursive patterns in these cantos, argue for their purposes, and show how they shed light on one another.

The new Christian *mathesis* Dante envisions would exceed both the classical model of knowledge (i.e., the Aristotelian division of the sciences and the tripartite Platonic scheme of philosophy) and the medieval rhetorical-grammatical models of education (i.e., Isidore of Seville, Brunetto Latini, etc.). In the heaven of the sun Dante represents the encyclopedic order of the arts and sciences rooted in the teachings of both Bonaventure and Aquinas. Dante wants to overcome and heal the deep rifts that separate philosophers and theologians. The philosophers (who are the neo-Aristotelians and, as far as the Oxford Franciscans go, they would include Saint Thomas Aquinas himself as a neo-Aristotelian) entertain grave doubts on the epistemological value of theology.

The reason for these doubts is clear. It is said to produce uncertain knowledge. Over and against the theologians, the philosophers affirm the primacy of philosophy as the only reliable rational activity and cast theology as a province of philosophy. On the other hand, the theologians, such as Bonaventure, enthrone theology as the queen of the sciences; they are equally skeptical about the claims of philosophy's reliability and rigor. For Dante, the epochal rift (which goes back to Alfarabi, Averroës, and Maimonides) is solved through poetry, the art variously slandered by philosophers and theologians alike.

Dante features the new *mathesis,* more than an artificial inventory of subdivisions and classifications of sciences that would cover and arrange the hierarchy of arts and sciences, as a cosmic dance by the chorus of souls in *Paradiso* 10. We are in the cosmology of the *Timaeus* read through the commentary by Chalcidius.

As in Chalcidius, the dance represents an orderly, circular arrangement that would reflect the musical perfection of the cosmos. The heaven of the sun is also the heaven of arithmetic. Since Pythagoras, it was thought that the most profound mysteries of knowledge were hidden in numbers and that the empire of number was sovereign. The dance of the wise spirits around the sun captures the rhythm (which is number) of the cosmos. It identifies knowledge as a playful dance of wisdom: a round knowledge, as in a circle, wherein knowledge's origin is knowledge's end. If the circle tropes the endless circulation of knowledge, a totality made of distinct points, the chorus blends the various voices into the harmony of the unison.

These voices belong to and evoke real, historical figures. Saint Thomas and Saint Bonaventure proceed to enumerate them one by one. In the first wheel we find Albert the Great, Aquinas himself, Gratian, Peter Lombard, Solomon, Dionysius the Areopagite, Orosius, Boethius, Isidore of Seville, Bede, and Richard of Saint Victor. The twelfth spirit is Siger of Brabant, who is said to have lived in Paris. His radical Aristotelian views about the unity of the separate intellect were refuted by Aquinas in his *De unitate intellectus contra Averroistas* and by Bonaventure in his *Collationes in Hexaemeron.*[2]

On his part, Saint Bonaventure enumerates a second ring of wise spirits that symmetrically completes Saint Thomas's list. He names Hugh of Saint Victor (whose *Didascalicon* is the model for Bonaventure's own *De reductione artium ad theologiam*); Peter of Spain; Peter Lombard; the prophet Nathan (whose Hebrew etymology is translated as "dans sive dantis" [see Sarolli 1971, 231]); Chrysostom; Anselm; Donatus; and Rabanus Maurus. The last figure he mentions—as a symmetrical counterpart to Siger of Brabant—is Joachim of Flora. His commentary on the Apocalypse (*Expositio in Apocalypsim*) interprets history according to a Trinitarian model, as a tripartite succession of ages—the age of the Father, the Son, and the Holy Spirit. Bonaventure had found Joachim's Trinitarian scansion of history heretical.

The presence of Siger of Brabant in the encyclopedic compass traced by Saint Thomas obeys the principle of wisdom as a reconciliation of contradictory viewpoints. I have given a detailed analysis of Dante's representation of Siger in *Dante's Vision* and, for the sake of clarity, will recapitulate here the main points of my argument. Siger is said to have lived in Paris, the city of philosophy, where he spent his time "leggendo" (*Par* 10.137). *Lectio* is a technical term for comments and glosses on philosophical texts. He reads in the "Vico de li Strami." He is literally on the way. Why does Dante give the philosopher's domicile?

We are only too familiar with the idea of philosophy as a journey and a quest: the route of Parmenides, the Odyssey of the soul, Ulysses' sea-journey, the pilgrim's exodus, etc. Thinking—this is the meaning of the metaphor—is an adventure, a risky exploration of unknown and unfamiliar regions of the mind, and it entails error and possible shipwreck. Aquinas had theorized about the "quinque viae" by which he comes to know God's existence. Siger is a logician, and logic conventionally provides a *method* or way. "Vico" is a metaphor that places Siger on a spiritual itinerary; it describes the movement of the mind engaged in syllogisms and in the pursuit of "invidïosi veri" (*Par* 10.138).

In the "rue de la Fouarre" Siger was absorbed in deep thoughts ("pensieri gravi" [*Par* 10.134–35]). "Pensiero," etymologically, means suspension; it conveys the sense of the *impasse* of the mind caught in irresolvable paradoxes as it journeys to the realm of the truth. The "veri"—the object of the logician's quest—are the questions of the eternity of the world, the unity of the intellect, and the relation between necessity and free will. Dante calls them "invidïosi," and the adjective, from *non-video,* suggests that the truths Siger seeks are not logically *evident* or demonstrable. In short, Siger—like Aquinas himself—casts logical reason as the preamble of faith and philosophy as a necessary step to theology. The inclusion of Joachim of Flora in the dance of the wise spirits is no less surprising than that of Siger. Historians have documented the critical role Joachim's doctrines played in Franciscan circles. They have especially stressed its impact on the rigorism of the Spirituals. Both Salimbene in his *Cronica* and Angelo Clareno suggest that John of Parma, Saint Bonaventure's predecessor as general of the Order, held Joachistic views. These views came to be considered heretical by Pope Alexander IV and by Bonaventure. Joachim's announcement of the imminent advent of a new, third age of the Spirit signaled a *de facto* dissolution of the doctrine of the Trinity.[3]

The mystical monism of Joachim's apocalyptic vision—at least the way the Spiritual Franciscans understood him—bears no real affinity with Plotinus's Mystical One, who is beyond all being, is unnamable, but still produces all things. But Bonaventure draws a parallel between Joachim's vision of a pure, new age of the Spirit and Plotinus's claim of philosophical illumination. Both bring about a "false beatitude," a premature divinization or perfection of man. And both strip life of the infirmity of mendicancy, which, for the Franciscan Bonaventure—a true follower of the "poverello"—is the realistic, authentic mark of the human condition. The parallelism between Joachim and Plotinus is put forth in Bonaventure's *Collationes in Hexaemeron.* The text is an important, though so far unacknowledged, source for Dante's representation of the heaven of the sun.

Left unfinished, the *Collationes* contain twenty-three lectures Bonaventure delivered at the University of Paris during the Easter season of 1273. Like some of his other works, the *Collationes* have a synthetic character. Arranged according to an encyclopedic principle, they gloss primarily Solomon's Book of Wisdom as well as the philosophy of Socrates and Aristotle. The commentary encompasses the fundamental themes constantly engaging Bonaventure's thought: the relation between theology and philosophy or the secular sciences and revelation; subtle speculations on the Trinity and arithmetic (above all, on the numbers 12 and 7); meditations on the freedom of God's creation of the world out of nothing; the Incarnation, with Christ the mathematical center of the cosmos; the gifts of the intellect; the "defects" of the philosophers; the light of the sun; the gates of wisdom; etc. Two of the conferences—6 and 7—focus on a radical critique of both the Parisian neo-Aristotelians and Plotinus's idea of intellectual illumination. Bonaventure singles out Averroës, "the commentator," and "his followers" (such as Siger of Brabant, who, however, is not mentioned by name) for their doctrines about the eternity of matter and the world and their skepticism about the resurrection of the body and the immortality of the soul. Plotinus's notion of intellectual or philosophical beatitude, on the other hand, is said to falsify the hardships and miseries of physical reality.

Dante accepts the Franciscan substance of Bonaventure's vision about the mendicancy or poverty of the human condition. Like Bonaventure, moreover, he rejects the principle of an autonomous philosophical knowledge: Siger's own philosophical work is seen as a preparatory journey on the way to truth. And, like Bonaventure, Dante "reduces" the encyclopedic ladder of arts and sciences to theology. There are cracks, however, in Bonaventure's model, and Dante exposes them in order to repair them.

The *Collationes in Hexaemeron* polemically juxtapose to one another three distinct theologies of history. One intuits, let it be said *en passant,* the influence of Joachim of Flora's tripartite division of history. Bonaventure dismisses the linear succession of the Joachistic pattern. He presents, rather, the Averroist or Muslim theology of history, wherein the whole of creation and history is shaped by a wholly transcendent creator. The second theory of history is the Plotinian-Joachistic speculation about God's total immanence in creation. For Plotinus there may be an infinite gulf separating the One from the world. Yet his insistence on intellectual beatitude—just like Joachim's third age of the Spirit—promises an apocalyptic, millennial time when evil is conquered and every hierarchical difference is abolished.

Between these two radically polarized conceptions stands Bonaventure's Incarnational Trinitarian theology as the mathematical "median" of reconciliation. The sharp, irreducible dualism of Averroës and the notion of God's diffusiveness everywhere are mutually exclusive. The Averroistic principle of an impassable abyss between the truth of faith and the truth of reason, God and man, immobilizes knowledge into separate spheres; it expresses itself as contempt for the human world, for it is unable to even posit that one can ever know the divine. Such a thesis is refuted by the very Neoplatonic principle of the diffusiveness of God through all the mobile gradations of being.

Dante accepts Bonaventure's Trinitarianism. Yet, he takes his distance from Bonaventure's assessment of Siger of Brabant and Joachim of Flora. Why? One answer lies in his insight into the dance of wisdom, wisdom as the whole he delineates. The more basic theological rationale for Dante's inclusion of mutually contradictory opinions is to be found in his version of the Trinitarianism he thematizes in the heaven of the sun. As the pilgrim ascends to the planet that radiates itself freely through the cosmos, he envisions a solar theoeconomy, which he derives from Franciscan spirituality. It is an economy of gifts that, gratuitously given, escape any possible commensurability and exclude only the principle of exclusion.

This Trinitarian pattern sheds light on the wisdom that is hidden in numbers. The text is punctuated by a lexicon that highlights numbers as well as the logical paradox of the one that is three and the three that are one. More than that, it evokes the heretical doctrines on the Incarnation by Sabellius and Arius (*Par* 13.127–29), while a hymn to unitrinitarianism is intoned:

> Lì si cantò non Bacco, non Peana,
> ma tre persone in divina natura,
> e in una persona essa e l'umana.
> (*Par* 13.25–27)

> They they sang not Bacchus, and not Paean, but Three Persons in the divine nature, and it and the human nature in one Person.
> (trans. Singleton [Alighieri 1975, 143])

The hymn anticipates the melody—Neoplatonic in substance—which is sung while the pilgrim leaves behind the heaven of the sun and is about to enter the planet Mars:

> Quell' uno e due e tre che sempre vive
> e regna sempre in tre e 'n due e 'n uno,
> non circunscritto, e tutto circunscrive,
> tre volte era cantato da ciascuno
> di quelli spirti . . .
> (*Par* 14.28–32)

> That One and Two and Three which ever lives, and ever reigns in Three and Two and One, uncircumscribed, and circumscribing all things, was thrice sung by each of those spirits . . .
> (trans. Singleton [Alighieri 1975, 155])

This Trinitarian motif, as a matter of fact, is ushered in at the very opening of *Paradiso* 10, where Dante celebrates the inner life of the

Godhead, whose "spiration" displays itself as the process of production of the work of art:

> Guardando nel suo Figlio con l'Amore
> che l'uno e l'altro etternalmente spira,
> lo primo e ineffabile Valore
> quanto per mente e per loco si gira
> con tant' ordine fé, ch'esser non puote
> sanza gustar di lui chi ciò rimira.
> Leva dunque, lettore, all'alte rote
> meco la vista, dritto a quella parte
> dove l'un moto e l'altro si percuote;
> e lì comincia a vagheggiar ne l'arte
> di quel maestro che dentro a sé l'ama,
> tanto che mai da lei occhio non parte.
> (*Par* 10.1–12)

> Looking upon His Son with the love which the One and the Other eternally breathe forth, the primal and ineffable Power made everything that revolves through the mind or through space with such order that he who contemplates it cannot but taste of Him. Life then your sight with me, reader, to the lofty wheels, straight to that part where the one motion strikes the others; and amorously there begin to gaze upon that Master's art who within Himself so loves it that His eye never turns from it.
> (trans. Singleton [Alighieri 1975, 107])

The total order of the universe comes into being through God's creative, generous fecundity. The order, which is a term for beauty, does not exist just in the mind: it has an objective existence (see Foster 1972, 109–24; Mazzotta 1993, 277). The reader is invited to lift up his sight to the cosmic cross formed by the intersection of the celestial equator and the ecliptic, the two oblique virtual circles traced by the sun's diurnal and annual motions.

Most simply, we are asked to be stargazers, to behold with a sense of wonder the spectacle of creation as a total gift of being, and so come to terms with the *givenness* of creation, its reduction to the perfection of art. What sustains this cosmic theodrama is the inner life of the Trinity. Bound by the breath of love, Father and Son gaze at each other. Their oneness exceeds number: they are at once one and three. From this theoeconomy of coincidence of opposites a different form of knowledge emerges. The human eye—which for Plato is the most sunlike of the organs of sense (*Republic* 508b)—can now see the source of all thought and life, which is the vital generosity of God. The metaphor of "filiation" (*Par* 10.1) suggests this much. In turn, the Father is called "primo e ineffabile valore" (v. 3): without a name, this Power has primacy. It is "primo" in that it is the first principle. Multiplicity comes from the "first." It is first, moreover, because it precedes and transcends every number and accounting just as it gives life but is before all life. More than "something," it is a no-thing from which all things and beings derive.

This Trinitarian theology at the opening of *Paradiso* 10 differs markedly from Saint Augustine's *De Trinitate* as well as from Boethius's *De Trinitate* and Aquinas's commentary on it.[4] Dante's view of God as generous source or inexhaustible *fons* appropriates Saint Bonaventure's doctrine in the *Collationes,* wherein creation as well as man emerge *ex nihilo.* Bonaventure, to be sure, echoes Augustine's view of creation out of nothing (*Confessions* 2.5–7; as well as *De Genesi ad litteram*). But he borrows the idea from Plotinus's metaphysics of the One as well as from the mystical theology of the pseudo-Dionysius in the *Divine Names.*

These texts do not merely add a mystical hue to the essentially rationalist façade of Dante's theology. They subsume his rationality in the larger view of knowledge as love. In both doctrines, the One, which is not a number, of its own nature, gives itself out without any jealous grudging and without ever exhausting the power of the source. The symbolic counter of this pure giving of oneself is the goodness of the sun. Plotinus echoes Plato's classic comparison of the sun with the good (cf. *Republic* 508 b–c; *Enneads* 5.16). In turn, the pseudo-Dionysius writes (*De divinis nominibus* 693b–696a):

> Think of how it is with the sun. It exercises no rational process, no act of choice, and yet, by the very fact of its existence it gives light to whatever is able to partake of its light, in its own way. So it is with the good. Existing far above the sun, an archetype far superior to its dull image, it sends the rays of its undivided goodness to everything with the capacity, such as this may be, to receive it. . . . Such beings owe their presence and their uneclipsed and undiminished lives to these rays. . . . They abide in the goodness of God and draw from it the foundation of what they are, their coherence, their vigilance, their home. Their longing for the good makes them what they are, and confers on

> them their well-being. Shaped by what they yearn for, they exemplify goodness and, as the law of God requires of them, they share with those below them the good gifts which have come their way.
>
> (trans Luibheld [Pseudo-Dionysius 1982, 72])

In the pseudo-Dionysius's solar theology, creation is a divine economy of gifts wherein all entities are bound by mutual relationships. This theme runs through the *Celestial Hierarchy* (cf. *Paradiso* 28). It is the doctrinal watershed between Bonaventure, who in this case is close to Dionysius, and Aquinas, who is close to Saint Augustine. Aquinas's polemic with *On the Divine Names* (which he read in the translation of Scotus Eriugena) is best formulated by Étienne Gilson: "For Saint Thomas, God gives existence because he is the Act-of-Being. For Denis, God is beyond existence and being: the One gives being because it itself does not exist. . . . Hence . . . the invisible things of God (*invisibilia Dei*) cannot be known, if one begins from the created world" (1956, 139).

Over the five cantos comprising the heaven of the sun, Dante pulls together the negative theology of the pseudo-Dionysius and the Aquinas / Augustinian theology of creation out of nothing. God is both the first principle or no-thing and the Creator-Father. The harmonization hinges on the understanding of the divinity in terms of radical self-giving.

A question is in order. Why does Dante reflect on the Trinity at this point of the poem? The answer is as clear as it is compelling. The pilgrim is leaving behind the spheres touched by the earth's shadow. He stands at the threshold of the vaster universe beyond the sun. As Ulysses' "flight" beyond the sun showed, knowledge can be a tragic transgression. For Dante, this juncture of experience requires a turning point in consciousness: a more creative and incandescent phase of the imagination is needed. Now, more than ever before, he must grasp the meaning and place of man in the cosmos; he must rethink the nature and purpose of all traditional knowledge as well as the theological speculation bequeathed to him. While the vast infinity of space opens up before his eyes he asks what is man's vocation, whether man is still the measure of creation, and what does it mean to say, as the Trinitarian theoeconomy says, that man is in God's mind from the beginning, even from before the creation of the world.

These questions lie at the heart of the biographical accounts of Francis and Dominic. *Paradiso* 11 opens with an apostrophe against syllogisms that have slid into sophistry and weapons of power:

O insensata cura de' mortali,
  quanto son difettivi silogismi
  quei che ti fanno in basso batter l'ali!
Chi dietro a iura e chi ad amforismi
  sen giva, e chi seguendo sacerdozio,
  e chi regnar per forza o per sofismi . . .
(*Par* 11.1–6)

O insensate care of mortals! How false are the reasonings that make you beat your wings in downward flight. One was following after the laws, another after the *Aphorisms,* one was pursuing priesthood, and one dominion by force or craft . . .
(trans. Singleton [Alighieri 1975, 119])

The lines cast, from a Franciscan perspective, a skeptical light on the logical-legal representation of knowledge. The epithet, "difettivi," with its Bonaventurian resonance, draws the artifices of the logical method—the "silogismi"—within the specifically Franciscan insight into the poverty of philosophy and language. The two technical terms—"silogismi" and "sofismi"—deployed also by Cavalcanti[5]—convey specious arguments by which the discipline of logic is transformed into a strategy for the legitimation of the icons of power.

At stake in Dante's text is the *disowning* of knowledge in the recognition that reality, in its rich givenness, outstrips political and logical manipulations. To know the world is not to own it. At one extreme of Franciscan spirituality, Iacopone da Todi celebrates the necessary expropriation of reason, the necessary opposition between Paris and Assisi, as the sign of the madness of divine love. At the other extreme, Dante stages his provisional Franciscan skepticism about reason's self-degradation. He represents Saint Thomas, who, as if he had read Bonaventure's *Legenda,* tells the life of Saint Francis. Stripped of every ornament, the naked, poor life of the saint puts to work a simple truth: a man is what he loves and what he does.

In a transparent acknowledgment of Francis as poet of the "Canticle of Brother Sun" (or "Canticle of the Created Things") and because we are in the heaven of the sun, Francis's birth is described as the rising of the sun at the Ganges and the world, "al mondo" (*Par* 11.50–51).

These global coordinates are connected by a local topography, a particular "loco" (v. 52), the "Porta Sole" at Perugia and Assisi. At least since Cassiodorus, who at Vivarium rescues the texts of tradition from total effacement, the West questions itself and finds itself by looking at (in) the light of the East. Assisi's "proper" sense, we are told, is Orient (v. 54). The etymology places us at the threshold of a world he lets appear in the light of new, fresh perspectives.

Saint Francis ushers in the dawn of the world. He opens the gates on new horizons and starts up a global perspective on the local regions of the earth. In a lyrical passage of the *Collationes,* Bonaventure defines the sun as the "heart of the world" (1.19). For Dante, this is Francis, the "sun" on the world, who invites us to see in the light of good and peace. Francis "orients" and re-orients the world: he challenges those who on the face of the earth have lost their way to see what they are and where they are. He asks those who do not know their way about what is man's place. To be like the sun is to be everywhere and belong nowhere. More than that, to be like the sun is tantamount to giving of oneself and to being nothing.

In Dante's text, this act of giving oneself is inseparable from the experience of being free. "Franciscus," etymologically, means free. He is a free spirit who, in freeing himself of the empire of things, is a scandal to the laws of the world, turns upside down the "proper" values of the world. The pure emblem, in this solar, free economy of gifts, is found in the representation of Francis who strips away his clothes and marries Lady Poverty.[6] As if to imitate the spiritual power of Francis's nakedness, Dante himself tears up the veil of the allegory and lets us grasp its sense as the imitation of Christ. In this absolute nakedness (which contrasts with the apparent nakedness of philosophy, which, in fact, wraps itself in sophistical conceits and mysteries) Francis owns nothing and loves literally no-thing. This will to nothingness climaxes in the spectacle of his *Christo-mimesis.* He divests himself of his very identity, no longer belongs to himself, and, like an actor in a theatrical *ludus,* impersonates Christ.

Francis's ludic questioning of the values of the world has a counterpart in the canto of Saint Dominic. The birthplace of Francis evokes the East. Dominic is variously called "atleta"—athlete of God—"campione," and, as if he were a knight errant in a love romance, "amoroso drudo" (*Par* 12.44–56). His birthplace is in the West, where the sun sets (*Par* 12.50). What seems to suggest decadence or the end of the day (or presage of the night) hides a new beginning. From the sunset a message of a new thought reaches the world: the announcement of a new knowledge that will reconcile the violence of factions.

In symmetry with the dramatic action in the preceding canto, *Paradiso* 12 stages the marriage between Faith and Dominic, faith and the "cherub" of knowledge. In the Thomist scenario of the encyclopedia, faith or theology is not juxtaposed to the sciences. Rather, it marks the road the philosophical sciences have to take. In this cherubic itinerary toward wisdom Dominic—like Francis earlier—loses all self-possession. The etymology of his name reveals it: he belongs and gives himself to his lord. And like a farmer in the fields of the Church, he is engaged in radical performances: he goes to the roots of evil, he uproots the "sterpi eretici" (*Par* 12.100), digs to the foundations of philosophical errors encapsulated by the Albigensian heresy in *languedoc.*

Saint Francis preaches to the sultan. Unlike the crusaders, he wants to tear down by peaceful speech the theological barriers dividing Christians and Muslims. Bonaventure follows Francis's example as he denounces the errors of Averroës. Saint Dominic turns against the asceticism of the Cathars, the *bons hommes* of mythical Provence. Caught in a doctrinal war, which Dante calls "civil war" (*Par* 12.108), Dominic is fierce with his enemies and finally wins. Chivalric love (which is not love of one's enemies) and war define the burning passion of his life.

In the legends of the Cathars of Provence, amorous discourses and religious sectarianism overlap. As happens in the love poetry in *languedoc,* with its cult of adultery (which is the cult of a privileged, secret, even illicit and exclusive knowledge), the infidelity of the heretics comes forth as the impoverishment of universal ideas and shared knowledge. Their hidden sectarianism marks the triumph of surreptitious plots and private designs. Dominic, by contrast, asserts the solar transparency of language: in his universe names, if correctly interpreted, truly mean what they say. Consistently, he wants to challenge all sophistry and abolish all differences and equivocations of language and beliefs. His warlike disposition in pursuing the eradication of religious differences ends up paradoxically in perpetuating conflict. In point of fact, Dominic's spiritedness and relishing of the clash of ideas shows that the quest for wisdom is not a univocally irenic exercise by which contradictions and antagonisms are reasonably worked out. Nonetheless, courageous action comes forth as the passionate nexus between philosophy and religious faith.

Dante's text moves on to present an alternative to this logical model of thought by a bold appropriation of views formulated by Bonaventure and Thomas. As if in response to Bonaventure's biography of Saint Dominic (in which the paradoxical logic of destruction prevails), Aquinas reappears on the scene. There is never, so he argues, an absolute knowledge, nor does a purely theoretical knowledge stand above practical reason. Instead, there is the need to join together the practical and the theoretical dimensions of philosophy. Ethics plays the role of joining theory and practice, philosophy and life. The reader is, thus, admonished not to judge prematurely (as both Aquinas himself and Bonaventure did with Siger and Joachim). Saint Thomas evokes the speculative errors of the Eleatics—Parmenides, Melissus, and Brison—as well as the evasiness of their judgments (*Par* 13.126). Against Bonaventure, he picks up arguments he had laid out in *Super Boetium de Trinitate.* He stresses that the dissolution of the Trinity (which Bonaventure attributed to Joachim of Flora) was attempted by philosophers such as Sabellius and Arius.

In short, philosophical knowledge, separated from or closed to theological reflection, gets lost in the labyrinths of thought. By the same token, theology that is not buttressed by philosophy slides into fideism or mere opinion. The same thing occurs in those judgments that follow the winds of opinion and in the vulgar convictions that the depths of God's wisdom may be wholly fathomed. Aquinas asserts that we need prudence. This ethical virtue (akin to the virtue of art) was granted to Solomon, who appears here as the emblem of wisdom.[7] Thomas's speech turns at this point into an explicit warning:

> Non sien le genti ancor troppo sicure
>   a giudicare, sì come quei che stima
>   le biade in campo pria che sien mature;
> ch'i' ho veduto tutto 'l verno prima
>   lo prun mostrarsi rigido e feroce,
>   poscia portar la rosa in su la cima;
> e legno vidi già dritto e veloce
>   correr lo mar per tutto suo cammino,
>   perire al fine a l'intrar de la foce.
>
> (*Par* 13.130–38)

> Moreover, let folk not be too secure in judgment, like one who should count the ears in the field before they are ripe; for I have seen first, all winter through, the thorn display itself hard and stiff, and then upon its summit bear the rose. And I have seen ere now a ship fare straight and swift over the sea through all her course, and perish at the last as she entered the harbor.
>
> (trans. Singleton [Alighieri 1975, 149])

The admonition hinges on the connection between ethics and time. By picking up the central metaphor of the journey in the poem, it reminds us that we are at sea. And while we are at sea, our certainties are incomplete knowledge, likely to shipwreck in the risky turbulence of the voyage. Saint Thomas, the speculative thinker, focuses on the value of contingency (for which cf. ST 1a.82.1) and makes ethics (or prudence) the ground where theology and philosophy meet.

The grand philosophical-theological meditation that has been carried out over the heaven of the sun comes to a head with a humbling view of human beings caught in the tangle of contingencies. Dante proposes an ethics, evinced from his own poem, which grapples with the uncertain, risky outcome of time-bound experiences. The awareness of the adventurous quality of every endeavor is not meant to arouse terror. Rather, it defines Dante's ethics of freedom. For to be at risk is to be free from the chain of causality and to share in the radical freedom and playfulness of God's creation.

I have argued in *Dante's Vision and the Circle of Knowledge* that Dante delineates a *theologia ludens.* The point is simple. In the *Inferno* and the *Purgatorio* Dante affirms the sovereignty of an ethics of laws and prohibitions. But because every authentic ethics tends to its liquidation or eclipse, in the *Paradiso* (where there is no question of moral error) ethics is subsumed in *kalokagathia,* in the conjunction of the beautiful and the good of art. This conjunction crystallizes God's playfulness. Accordingly, the representation of *Paradiso* encompasses angelic "ludi": the play of God's creation, songs, cosmic dances, music, colors, and the aesthetics of the beautiful as well as the extended playful language in the cantos of Saint Francis and Saint Dominic. "Comedy," indeed, catches the ludic and joyful essence of God. In short, play, as an expression of freedom and pleasure, binds God to the chorus of his creation.

It is usually believed that the God of the Middle Ages is too stern to play or that, if he plays, he does not do it at random. But for Dante God plays. He is even a gambler. In *Purg* 16.90 the creation of the soul displays God's play. In *Purg* 6.1–9 God plays dice, "il gioco de la zara," and the stake consists in the salvation of the souls. The image primarily conveys the inscrutability of God's plan (just as inscrutable are the aleatory games played by Fortune in *Inferno* 7). It even suggests God's arbitrariness, his total freedom from the logical procedures that rule the most reasonable human constructions. There is even more, however, in the image of God's playing dice.

In the neo-Aristotelian debates of the thirteenth century, the questions of contingency, necessity, and chance figure prominently (see Maier 1983, 339–82). In 1277 Étienne Tempier condemns the proposition that denies that "nihil fit a casu" (article 21). The condemnation is directed against the natural philosophers who, in the wake of Aristotle's *Physics,* probe the principle of causality, chance, fate, and necessity. The figures who are involved in these debates are Avicenna, Averroës (*De fato et casu*), Siger of Brabant (*De necessitate et contingentia causarum*), and Saint Thomas Aquinas. The Scholastics investigate the logical relations linking causes and effects in the chain of nature, as well as the uncertainty in determining the consequences of an event. Dante shifts the debate from the order of nature to the order of love. In the love relation joining together God and man, the relation—as happens in every love experience—is always at risk. The risk is man's freedom. So that man may be truly free, the love God freely gives must be at risk.

In the vast arc of the heaven of the sun, Dante questions man's role in the borderless spaces of the universe. And he envisions a new, radical poetic-theological discourse that is not circumscribed within the context of millennial expectations. It is open to the possibility of the encounter between man and God in the thousand-year–long voyage of the souls. Homeless on earth, man, who is always *en route* toward some distant destination, discovers that the universe, where he does not yet dwell, is where he belongs. The theology of both Saint Thomas and Saint Bonaventure agrees with this poetic insight.

These cantos have shown the pilgrim poised between the two masters of philosophy and theology. As biographers of Saint Francis and Saint Dominic, they are above all teachers of life. Dante chooses them as his interlocutors, takes them along in his celestial journey but remains eccentric to their respective circles of knowledge. And he goes beyond them. He moves beyond the sun. By his poetry he opens up new vistas for theology as he crosses the unmapped spaces of the cosmos. Saint Francis, the Jongleur of God, goes to pray in the darkness of the night along the deep, scary precipices of Monte della Verna, where he receives his stigmata (*Par* 11.107). In this bare landscape of the soul, Francis captures the mortal risk of prayer, during which the soul hovers over the abyss of God's dark light.

By this intense rethinking of the Trinity, man's scope of knowledge, and man's ethics of freedom and giving, the *Divine Comedy* presents itself as a gift. The poet has received the gift by God's grace and, true to his name, he gives it to us. The gift does not belong to us. If anything we belong to it. As we are drawn into a circle of gifts, gift-giving appears to be more profound than any possession. It reveals to us that we share in a bequest, a legacy or pardon we can only pass on. As we stand with the poet at the threshold of a new millennium, he asks that we take his gift of the book as the book of forgiving.

Notes

1. The fraternal controversies have been much examined in recent years. See Reeves 1964 and Davis 1980, 59–85 for further bibloiography.

2. On Saint Bonaventure's thought see Guardini 1921; Bougerol 1961; Steenberghen 1966, 193–271; Vanni Rovighi 1974; Biffi 1984.

3. On this controversy cf. Ratzinger 1971.

4. The Boethian text is cited frequently in the *Collationes*. See, for instance, 4. 12. For Aquinas's commentary on Boethius see Aquinas 1961.

5. "Da più a uno face un sollegismo . . . e come far poteresti un sofismo" (vv. 1, 7)

6. On this standard motif of Franciscan iconography see Bonaventure 1934, V, 5.

7. On Solomon (and his "radiant and indefectible wisdom") see Bonaventure 1934, 2:6. The context of the discussion is the Book of Wisdom 6:12, which, clearly, is the theme of the heaven of the sun.

10

Vulgarizing Science: Vernacular Translation of Natural Philosophy

Alison Cornish

THE POPULARIZATION of science is sometimes seen, especially by practicing scientists, as a necessary evil. A layman's account must first simplify and thereby distort scientific precepts, and it must also try to persuade the public of the importance or relevance of a concept or new finding. Jeanne Fahnestock (1993, 18) has shown that modern pop science consistently uses epideictic rhetoric in its efforts to praise a scientific discovery by attaching it to some already deeply held value, such as progress or tangible health benefits. In France, *la vulgarisation des sciences* was historically linked to the project of the Enlightenment and the Revolution. In such a context, popularization could become, rather than dilution or misrepresentation, the ultimate purpose of science. As one late nineteenth-century chemistry instructor put it in the publication of his *Leçon de chimie élémentaire* ("Elementary Chemistry"), "Science is not really useful until it becomes *vulgaire*," which is to say, common, diffused, not high-brow, exclusive, or elite (Raichvarg and Jacques 1991, 25).

In Dante's time, the "essential tension" (as Thomas Kuhn [1997] called it) between science and the public, was already not simply between the literate and the unlettered. Rather, vernacular literacy was opening up its space of lay culture and lay literacy that began to demand access to Latin learning. Although *volgarizzamento* is a term usually reserved for prose attempts at bringing Latin works into Italian (or "service" translations as they are sometimes called), in the late-medieval context it is often difficult to make distinctions between translations and adaptations, re-elaborations, compendia, compilations, imitations, and original works (Dembowski 1986, 257; Crespo 1986, 462). As Cesare Segre (1963, 49) once pointed out, translation is a mentality at the very origins of Italian literature.

As the vernacular made inroads in areas previously confined to Latin, limits were sometimes articulated by writers and translators. The vernacular was said to be categorically incapable of expressing abstract or complex philosophical truths. Dante's contemporary Giles of Rome, in his educational handbook for princes, explained that Latin was in fact invented to express "the nature of things, the customs of men, and the courses of the stars" since no "vulgar idiom" could fully do so (Aegidius 1556, 180v). Even the *volgarizzatori,* or translators into the vernacular, themselves, such as Bono Giamboni in his rather loose, late thirteenth-century translation of the pseudo-Ciceronian *Rhetorica ad Herennium,* confess the insufficiency of their target language: "subtle things cannot be exposed very well in the vernacular" ("le sottili cose non si possono bene aprire in volgare" [Bono Giamboni 1994, 5]).

Natural science, which at this time was frequently being translated from Greek and Arab into Latin, was not the first choice of the prose *volgarizzatori,* although its presence was felt in poetry even before Dante, from the vocabulary and repertory of natural science in Sicilian lyrics to the "philosophizing" of Guido Guinizzelli and Guido Cavalcanti. Works of rhetoric, history, and ethics were more likely to be translated from Latin into the vernacular, perhaps because of their perceived utility in the political discourse of the northern Italian city-states. A rare attempt at pop science in the thirteenth century was Restoro d'Arezzo's *La composizione del mondo,* which advertises the importance of and nobility of its subject (1997, 3). Dante's presumptive teacher, Brunetto Latini, in contrast, called the theoretical sciences the "petty cash" ("deniers contans") of his vernacular encyclopedia (*Tresor*), as opposed to the "fine gold" of rhetoric and ethics, necessary to the government of people. Yet it is to be noted that Brunetto's "small change" or "pocket money" is in one sense more useful than gold, since it is for spending on everyday necessities ("pour despendre tousjours es coses besoignables" [Brunetto Latini 1948, 90]). At least an elementary knowledge of the theoretical sciences can thus be seen as the foundation and prerequisite for the civic, practical sciences of rhetoric and ethics.

Dante's *Commedia* has been both praised and denigrated for its incorporation of scientific material. Some of his earliest imitators, such as his own son Iacopo Alighieri seemed to take that aspect of it as essential. Quite the opposite opinion characterizes modern assessments of Dante's achievement, most famously in Benedetto Croce's relegation of science and theology to the category of structure, or *nonpoesia* (1921, 67–68). Recent criticism has worked, however, toward reintegrating Dante's science into his poetry (Boyde 1981, 1993; Boyde and Russo 1995; Cornish 2000; Durling and Martinez 1990; Freccero 1968; S. Gilson 1997b, 2000; Stabile 1981, 1983; and Stewart 1993).

This essay will be devoted to the science of meteorology as it is expressed in a particular passage of the poem; then will briefly consider the implications of Dante's "vulgarization" of science also in the context of embryology. My purpose is not to find the single source of his scientific information, nor to claim that scientific exposition is the purpose of the passage. Rather, I hope to show how vulgarization seeks the relevance of science to the human condition, a relevance that can be suggested to the vernacular imagination by the technical terminology itself. My point is that Dante is not translating; he is "vulgarizing," by which I mean he is rendering the concepts and language of natural science useful here, now, and for us—or at least for his contemporary readers.

In *Purgatorio* 5, Bonconte da Montefeltro serves as an *exemplum* of the riskiest way of attaining salvation: a last-minute conversion *in articulo mortis* on the field of battle. Yet, the focus of his speech is not on the uncanny efficacy of a last-minute pronouncement of the name of Mary accompanied by a single tear (in stark contrast to his father's careful but vain preparations for death we learned of in *Inferno* 27), but rather on the fortune of the soldier's body after his soul has departed. The posthumous fate of bodies is a *topos* of the early *Purgatorio.* In canto 3, we learn both that Virgil's remains were transferred from Brindisi to Naples by order of the Emperor Augustus, and that Manfred's corpse was exhumed and removed from the kingdom because of his excommunication by Pope Clement IV. The displacement of Bonconte's cadaver, which lost its soul from battle wounds on the bank of a river, was not determined by the human intervention of emperor or pope, but by a terrible storm, raised by a devil. It is a story of weather that has, in medieval meteorological understanding, both natural and supernatural causes.

Deprived of Bonconte's soul by one tiny tear of repentance, the devil takes revenge on his body:

Io dirò vero, e tu 'l ridì tra ' vivi:
l'angel di Dio mi prese, e quel d'inferno
gridava: 'O tu del ciel, perché mi privi?
Tu te ne porti di costui l'etterno
per una lagrimetta che 'l mi toglie;
ma io farò de l'altro altro governo!
(*Purg* 5:103–108 [Alighieri 1994])

I will tell the truth, and you will retell it among the living: the angel of God took me, and the one from hell cried out: "Oh you from heaven, why do you cheat me? You carry off with you the eternal part of him for one small tear that takes him away from me; but I will make other arrangements for the other part."

By means of his evil will and powerful intellect, the devil moves vapors and gales (vv. 112–14). The "smoke" and wind produce fog and great clouds, which then turn into water; it rains so much that the earth refuses to soak up the flood; the swollen tributary sweeps up the body that had fallen on its bank as it rushes to join the royal river, the Arno, where the soldier's limbs receive a watery grave (vv. 119–29).

The extravagance of the description of the rainstorm in *Purgatorio* 5 is in proportion to the rage of the devil, cheated of the better part, who makes spoils of what is left to him. Even this supernatural intervention is part of the medieval science of meteorology, since devils were thought to manipulate the elements, to inhabit the air, and to have particular jurisdiction over its coldest region, which is precisely where rain is formed (Ducos 1998, 389; Thomasset 1998, 249). As Albertus Magnus tells us in his commentary on the Aristotelian treatise, meteorology comes from two Greek words (*meta* and *theoros*), meaning *trans* and *contemplatio*. Meteorology is the science that contemplates things that are mutable and transient (like all sublunar things) but that are—at the same time—high, close to the stars (Albertus 1890, 478–79). These elements include things which we would now consider part of the realm of astronomy, such as galaxies and comets, but which, because of their diversity and variability, could not belong to the category of "simple mobile objects": the planets and stars, immune to change. Meteorology is also the science of weather, caused by watery and earthy exhalations that produce clouds, rainbows, precipitation, wind, and earthquakes. Weather is one of those natural processes by which Aristotle's four elements can be transformed one into the other. Fire, air, water, and earth are generated and corrupted and can, by being sufficiently heated, cooled, dried, or moistened, be changed into one another. When water becomes vapor, for example, it receives more and more of the nature, and hence the natural location, of air, and thus rises above its own proper site ("quia quando vaporat, quantum recipit de natura aeris, tantum etiam recipit de loco aeris, et tantum separatur a loco suo naturali" [Albertus 1890, 481]). When vapor is "converted" back into water, it seeks its own place and falls down as rain from the air to earth. This science, which pervades Dante's works, enjoyed what may seem to us a disproportionate interest in the high Middle Ages, and was the first of Aristotle's treatises to be translated into the vernacular languages, starting with Mahieu de Vilain's French version around 1280 (Ducos 1998, 14).

Bonconte assumes Dante's common meteorological knowledge: "well you know how in the air is collected that wet vapor that turns back into water as soon as it rises to the part where the cold receives it" ("Ben sai come ne l'aere si raccoglie / quell' umido vapor che in acqua riede, / tosto che sale dove 'l freddo il coglie" [vv. 109–11]). The cold that "receives" wet vapor and turns it back into water is a middle region of air, cooled by winds to become "valde frigidus" ("very cold"), as Albertus says (1890, 486). This cold strip, also called "le voie as diables" (devils' path) by the French translators of the *Meteorologica,* lies between the hot, dry region, called the *aestus,* bordering on fire, and the hot, wet region of elemental air in its natural state (Thomasset 1998, 249). It is in this region that vapors, diffused into the air by heated water, congregate and thicken. Once thickened by the cold, these vapors then revert to the nature of water and fall, heavily, from the region of air back down to earth (Albertus 1890, 486).

The elaborate disaster that befell Bonconte's body emphasizes the strikingly divergent fates of a saved soul and its abandoned corpse. His watery end turns his death on a battlefield into a kind of shipwreck, like that of Palinurus in the *Aeneid* (see Cioffi 1992, 192). The ultimate inconsequentiality of his unburied cadaver is one of the deliberate contrasts Dante is drawing between the pagan religion, concerned with community rituals regarding the disposal of corpses, and the Christian religion, which focuses on the will of the individual soul while still joined to its body. It is the repentance of souls, not the burial of bodies, that gets people in the door of the afterlife.

Repentance was already linked with the figure of shipwreck in theological tradition, since Saint Jerome (*Ep. 130*) had called it "the second plank after shipwreck" ("Poenitentia est secunda tabula post naufragium"). As the fourteenth-century *volgarizzatore,* Jacopo Passavanti, explained it, the ship meant to carry us safely was our baptism, broken by sin, and repentance is the plank by which we might still hope to make it to shore:

> la penitenzia è la seconda tavola dopo il pericolo della nave rotta. Parla il santo dottore della penitenzia, per somiglianza di coloro che rompono in mare, de' quali spesse volte interviene che, rotta la nave per grande fortuna e per tempestade che sia commossa in mare, coloro che sono più accorti prendono alcuna delle tavole della rotta nave, alla quale attegnendosi fortemente, soprastando all'acqua, non affondano; ma giungono al rivo o al porto, iscampati del periglio del tempestoso mare[.]
> (Jacopo Passavanti 1925, 1).

> Penitence is the second plank after the danger of the broken ship. The holy doctor is speaking about penitence by using a comparison with those who shipwreck at sea. Often it happens that, when a ship wrecks through terrible bad luck and a storm that has been raised up at sea, those who are more careful take one of the boards from the broken ship, to which they cling tightly and stay afloat without sinking and reach the shore or port, having escaped the danger of the stormy sea.

In the *Aeneid,* for example, vengeful and meddling gods produce inclement weather which provokes shipwreck to favor their grand schemes which have little to do with individual will or merit. By contrast, the vengeance of the devil who lost the tug-of-war for Bonconte's soul is fierce but ultimately impotent since storms do not determine men's fate; inner storms do. (The rainstorm in *Purgatorio* 5 is no doubt meant to recall the windstorm that continually buffets Francesca and Paolo in *Inferno* 5.) Penitence is both the plank to hang onto during the storm and the punishing, vengeful storm itself. According to a medieval etymology, penitence is a kind of vengeance, as a person punishes himself for what he is sorry he did ("Poenitentia est quaedam dolentis vindicta, puniens in se quod dolet commisisse" [Pseudo-Augustine 1865, 1129]).

Penitence is also a kind of water that washes sins and quenches fires. The Dominican preacher Giordano da Pisa, in one of his Lenten sermons delivered in Florence in 1305–1306, says that penitence is like a river, related somewhat like a tributary to the larger or "royal" river of grace, without which no sin can be washed, and with which all sin and every stain can come clean ("Di verità questi fiumi sono, chi bene volesse considerare, non sono che uno: questo fiume è la grazia di Dio, sanza la quale nullo peccato si può lavare in nullo modo, e colla quale ogne peccato si può lavare e ogne macula. Il primo fiume si è *penitentie*" [Giordano 1974, 194–95; emphasis added]). In another sermon Giordano shows how the river water of grace reverses the relative potency of elements in the natural world. Fire is the most powerful thing in this world; only a small fire can be put out by a great quantity of water, he says (to paraphrase in the manner of the *volgarizzatori*). If a great fire were next to the sea, the sea could conquer it because it has so much water. But the fire of Hell is so strong that if the whole sea were in it, not only would it not quench it, it would not even cool it down in the slightest, or extinguish one spark. "Now behold a great thing!" Giordano exhorts his hearers, "Now I want to show you how the force of repentance surpasses all the forces of this world one could name: not a sea, no, but a single tear of grief for sin, that comes from a good heart, just one, do you see the strength it has?" ("Or vedi grande cosa! Or ti vo' mostrare la virtù de la penitenzia come passa tutte le virtudi di tutte le cose di questo mondo, che non si potrebbe dire: non dico mare, no, ma una sola lagrima di dolore del peccato, che venga di buon cuore, sola una, vedi vertù c'hae?" [80]). Such a tear has the strength to quench and put out all the fire of Hell in a single moment. And if that tear comes from perfect contrition, Giordano says, it can extinguish not only the fire of Hell but also that of Purgatory.

One drop of salty water suffices to transport Bonconte's soul across the sea to safe haven in Purgatory, whereas the devil must employ gale force winds and torrents of water simply to displace a dead body from one riverbank to another riverbed. The scientific portion of this account serves not only to naturalize supernatural agency, but to limit the range of the devil's power, that is, his governance ("altro governo"). His jurisdiction is reduced to corpses, air, water, earth, and weather: he can wield transformations only in the elemental world—which is already more than any human agent can do. Giordano (1974, 187–88) mocks the presumed power of earthly lords who have no control even over the elements ("Che segnoria hae egli ne l'elimento del fuoco o ne l'aria o ne' venti? Va' di' che soffino a sua posta, va' di' che piova a suo comandamento" ["What lordship does he have in the element of fire or in the air or in the winds? Go tell them that they should blow on his account, go tell them to rain at his command"]).

The Aristotelian explanation of precipitation provides a natural analogue for damnation. Just as bloated vapors rise until they encounter extreme cold which sends them crashing back down to earth, so does puffed-up arrogance go before the precipitous fall into Hell, drained of all warmth by the wind produced by Satan's flapping wings. Several sinners in the *Inferno* speak, in fact, of having "rained down" into Hell. When Guittone d'Arezzo utilized a meteorological metaphor in one of his sonnets it was to make an analogy between the formation of rain and the sin of *superbia:*

> Pare che voglia dicere l'autore:
> per la vertude che lo sole rende,
> sovra la terra dissolve vapore
> e levandolo in alto lo distende;
> volendoli sottrare lo calore,
> reconvertese 'n acqua e'n terra scende.
> Cusí avene de lo peccatore:
> in ciò che deveria servire offende.
> Per caldo di superbia si leva,
> salendo in alto, cade 'n terra plana,
> ché non ha movimento da regnare;
> credendo allegerire, pur agreva.
> Ma se servasse la coscenza sana,
> lo sole lo farea fruttificare[.]
>
> (1940, 166)

It seems that the author wants to say that, by the virtue that the sun provides, it dissolves vapor above the earth and lifting it on high spreads it out; if this warmth is taken away, it is converted back into water and descends to earth. So it happens with the sinner who offends where he should serve. He is lifted up by the heat of pride; rising high, he falls onto the flat earth, so that he has no movement with which to govern; thinking he is getting lighter, he is actually weighted down. But had he made use of a healthy conscience, the sun would have made him bear fruit.

Guittone uses the scientific example as a metaphor for a spiritual condition that is the opposite of Bonconte's. In *Purgatorio* 5, the rainstorm is an actual climatic event. Yet, the disaster that befalls the body is not just in contrast to the safety of the soul repented in the nick of time; the scientific language can also be read as an analogue, not for pride but for positive spiritual metamorphosis: conversion. In their vernacularizations of the term *convertere* to express the transformation of damp air back into its original nature as water, both Guittone and Dante show their dependence on the so-called "old version" of the *Meteorologica,* translated from the Arabic by Gerard of Cremona and mediated through the commentary of Albertus Magnus. Guittone says that the vapor "reconvertese 'n acqua," and Dante's Bonconte explains that the pregnant air converts itself into water ("sí che 'l pregno aere in acqua si converse" [5.118]).

Albertus (1890, 486) explains that when vapor is in the middle region of air, it gets thickened by the cold and returns to its nature and is converted to water: "Quando ergo vapor est in illa media regione, tunc inspissatus frigore recedit ad naturam suam, et convertitur in aquam." So, too, Ristoro d'Arezzo (1997, 217) says that, "e l'aere se convertarà in acqua, e parrà che 'l cielo se facia tutto acqua et vegnane in terra" ("and the air will be converted to water, and it will seem that the sky has turned all to water and has come down to the earth"). And in the fourteenth-century *volgarizzamento* of the *Meteorologica,* we find similar use of the term *convertere:*

> Alcuno [vapore] è caldo e umido, e quello le più volte si converte in aere se nolli si para dinanzi alcuno freddo che 'l costringa e ingrossi e faccialo convertire in natura d'acqua[.]
>
> (Aristotle 1995, 168)

> Some [vapor] is hot and wet, and this kind usually is converted into air unless it encounters some cold that condenses and thickens it and makes it convert to the nature of water.

Thomas Aquinas's commentary, which is instead based on the so-called new version of the *Meteorologica,* translated directly from the Greek by William of Moerbeke, has no cognate of the verb *convertere,* in the explanation of how aqueous vapor "returns to its own nature":

> Sic igitur deficiente calore calefaciente et elevante vaporem aqueum, vapor aqueus redit ad suam naturam, coadunante etiam frigiditate loci; et sic infrigidatur, et infrigidatus inspissatur, et inspissatus cadit ad terram[.]
>
> (Aquinas 1886, 365)

> Therefore as the heat that warms and lifts the watery vapor diminishes, it goes back to its own nature, in conformity with the coldness of the place; thus it cools down, and once cooled it thickens, and once thickened it falls to earth.

Dante was aware of the two versions of the *Meteorologica.* In the *Convivio* he took advantage of the discrepancies to attribute his own apparent divergence from Aristotle's opinion on the Milky Way to "errors of the translators" (Berti 1984, 364).

The description of rain formation in *Purgatorio* 5 may also echo Aquinas's "vapor aqueus redit ad suam naturam" in the phrase "quell' umido vapor che in acqua riede" (*Purg* 5.110). But it is elemental conversion, in the language of the old translation, when water that has become air reverts to its original nature, that best matches the distillation of Bonconte's whole sinful life into a single salty tear of remorse. Conversion is the radical change brought on by repentance. As the author of a medieval tract on true and false penitence put it, someone who wants to put away sin is turned from it; converted is the person who is turned completely and totally, not so much because he fears pain, but so that he might hurry to reach his good God ("Vertitur peccato, qui jam vult dimittere peccatum; convertitur, qui jam totus et omnino vertitur, qui jam non tantum poenas non timet, sed ut bonum Deum festinat tendere" [Pseudo-Augustine 1865, 1128]). From the vantage point of the *Purgatorio,* the term "converse" suggests a spiritual parallel overlooked by Guittone, and out of reach of the enraged devil. Guittone used the Scholastic analysis of inclement weather as an explicit analogy for pride, a metaphor for the swollen sinner who puffs up and floats only to come pounding back down to earth. In the *Purgatorio,* the violent storm, the raging rivers, and the damage they do, are real not metaphoric. And yet the watery conversion that is no less real and matters more is the one that impels Bonconte's soul along the tributary of penance to the royal river of grace that washes all sin.

Lino Pertile (1996) has recently argued that learned sources, such as Albertus and Thomas, that the critics brought to bear on Bonconte's account of the devilish storm ascribe excessive erudition to the speech of Bonconte the soldier. Pertile argues that Bonconte must have been rough and uneducated, and certainly no scholar. As an example, he points out that modern readers misunderstand the word *intento* in the description of the sky in the Appenine valley covered with fog as a

Latinism ("intense" or "dense") which would have referred to the thickened vapors discussed in the meteorological tracts.

Indi la valle, come 'l dì fu spento,
da Pratomagno al gran giogo coperse
di nebbia; e 'l ciel di sopra fece intento
(*Purg* 5.115–17)

Whence, as day was extinguished, he covered the valley with fog, from Pratomagno to the high peak; and made dense the sky above.

Pertile points out that the fourteenth-century commentator Benvenuto da Imola understands *intento* as a variation of the northern dialect form *intinto,* meaning "dark." This linguistic variation would mark Bonconte's speech as un-Latin and his ideas about rainstorms as popular rather than learned, akin to the kind of superstitions about stormmakers Dante had mocked in an earlier lyric poem *Io sono stato con Amore insieme.*

As we have seen, belief in the supernatural origin of storms is part of meteorological science in the high Middle Ages. Moreover, the specification of the mountain valley in Dante, however particular to the local geography of the battle of Campaldino where Pertile finds regional dialect, might be a further echo of Albertus's discussion of how clouds form: "for there does the thin vapor gather and thicken, and especially when it is between very high mountains, because there it chokes and chills more than elsewhere" ("ibi enim congregatur rarum vaporis et inspissatur, et praecipue quando est intra montes altissimos, quia ibi praefocatur et infrigidatur magis quam alibi" [Albertus 1890, 486]). What is essential, however, in the context of translation and adaptation of which the *Commedia* is a part, is that the presence of dialect terms, Florentine or non-Florentine, or terms alien to the terminology of Scholastic science, does not negate the underlying scientific source; it is simply a characteristic of vulgarization.

Indeed, in the following verse containing the recognizably meteorological term *converse,* there is also an adjective that is purely vernacular in its application to rain formation, and might, in fact, be coined by Dante: "sí che 'l pregno aere in acqua si converse" ("so that the pregnant air was converted to water" [v. 118]). Although Patrick Boyde (1981, 74–75) suggests that "impregnated" air is part of the Aristotelian account of condensation and evaporation, only Dante seems to have used that terminology. In the Latin Aristotle and its subsequent commentators, the air is said to become thickened by the collecting vapors: "inspissatus or ingrossatus" (*ingrossato* in the *Metaura*). The *Grande dizionario della lingua italiana* (Battaglia 1988) finds no use of *pregno* to mean "saturated with moisture, swollen with rain" before *Purgatorio* 5, even though there are many subsequent examples of it. With this word, Dante's vulgarization of his scientific sources transforms the meteorological swelling that Guittone associated with the tumidity of pride into the promise of pregnancy. The thickening of the cooled air becomes an expectant *grossesse,* especially appropriate to the violent but fruitful pain of penitence which could be compared to that of a woman about to give birth. "But on the contrary there is what is said in Isaiah 26:17: 'as a woman about to give birth writhes and cries out in her pains, so we were,' that is, through repentance; which is to say, 'In fear of you, Lord, we have conceived, and have almost given birth and brought forth the spirit of salvation,' of the salvation of penitence, that is" (Aquinas 1854, 415).

It is the ancient poet Statius who, just released from his penance with an earthquake compared to the birth of gods (*Purg* 20.130–32), will give a Scholastic exposition on the mechanics of pregnancy later in the canticle. Statius's discourse on embryology in canto 25 is part of the explanation of the "fictitious" or aerial bodies of incorporeal souls that Dante has been encountering throughout Hell and Purgatory. Because these second, fictive bodies are formed in the surrounding air in a manner similar to rainbows, Statius's speech also depends upon meteorological science, a subject that has been dealt with recently by Simon Gilson (1997a).

The embryological discussion in *Purgatorio* 25 has been much more extensively studied as an example of Dante's adaptation of Scholastic science than has the meteorology of *Purgatorio* 5. Bruno Nardi (1949, 273) suggests that in *Purgatorio* 25 Dante is often "translating directly" from his medical sources. Yet, more recent critics have demonstrated that the scientific explanation about the facts of life is essentially a corollary for the production of poetry (see Freccero 1983; Mazzotta 1979; Martinez 1983; Shapiro 1998; and Ginsberg 1999). In *Purg* 24.52–54 Dante describes his poetic method as a method of "taking notes when Love inspires him." In *Purg* 25.70–72, Statius explains how the Prime Mover breathes into (or inspires) the embryo, prepared by nature's art, to form a new human soul. In both cases the inspiration of a divine source into a passive vessel (one is a poet holding a pen, the other is a womb gestating a fetus) produces language: the sweet new style in the case of poetry or a "speaking thing" in the case of human reproduction ("ma come d'animal divegna fante" [*Purg* 25.61]). The crucial node (*nodo / punto*) in both cases might be called, to use Marianne Shapiro's title, "the knot of body and soul."

Precisely because of this intersection of the elemental world with the divine, embryology was the part of medicine most closely tied to philosophy and, like meteorology, was the subject of intense study and commentary among Dante's contemporaries. For the moment I would just like to point out that this essential crux between body and soul appears as a problem of translation in Dante's first attempt to explain embryological development in the vernacular. In the *Convivio,* Dante described the production of a new human soul (*cotale produzione*) as something that cannot be manifested in language, in vernacular language, that is: "non è cosa da manifestare a lingua, lingua, dico veramente, volgare" (*Conv* 4.21.6 [Alighieri 1995]). This seems a standard excuse of the *volgarizzatori;* when the going gets tough, blame it on the insufficiency of the linguistic medium—that *je ne sais quoi* that, according to the translator, might be expressed perfectly in the language of origin but cannot be transferred to the idiom to which his audience is limited. Blame it on the insufficient vessel, the container that cannot hold all the meaning that pours out of the other one. Bruno Nardi (1949, 281) tried to remove from this statement ("lingua, dico veramente, volgare") any lament or disparagement of the vernacular tongue in particular, of which Dante is of course a champion in the *Convivio* and elsewhere, as Barański (1996), among others, has shown. According to Nardi (1949, 281), the origin of the human soul is just plain difficult for any human language to express—a secret of God, as Avicenna puts it.

Yet perhaps the vulgarity of the language that cannot manifest the union of body and soul is still to the point in the *Convivio,* marking it as a prose *volgarizzamento* of a certain kind in contrast to the vulgarization undertaken in the *Commedia.* In revisiting the question in the poetic context, Dante's Statius says that it is a difficult point and a stumbling block, but he also states it in the vulgar tongue and in vernacular verse—in fact, in terms that directly echo his manifesto of vernacular style in the previous canto. The only explicit reticence (!) of the account of human generation in canto 25 is in reference to the genitals, "ov' è più bello / tacer che dire"—an expression of the Latin *pudenda.* The crux of the matter becomes the transformation of an animal into a speaking thing, and has become cognate with the production of poetry in the vernacular.

The *Commedia,* like the *Convivio,* offers translations of contemporary science. Even more than in the earlier prose treatise, in the poem *volgarizzamento* has become an imperative, even at the risk of mistranslation. Statius himself is, of course, a notoriously unreliable translator of Latin, since Dante has him misrepresent a verse from the *Aeneid* in Italian while claiming its transformative effect on his life (*Purg* 22.40–41). Statius's role, as link between the ancient and the Christian worlds, may be to vernacularize, even if—and indeed this is stressed—the translation is unfaithful, especially if it leads—as it does in Statius's case—to the faith. In "vernacularizing" the *Aeneid,* Statius transforms the epic into "mamma" and nurse (*Purg* 21.97–98) which, in Dante's lexicon, as Gary Cestaro (1991) has shown, express the gender and role of the *volgare,* the mother-tongue. To Statius is also given the task of vulgarizing the science of embryology, together with its philosophical crux, into the vernacular rhymes of the sweet new style.

As readers of the *Purgatorio* know, Statius's reading of the *Aeneid* leads to the parturition of a newly saved soul out of the cornice of avarice, where the penitents call on "sweet Mary" like women about to give birth ("come fa donna che in parturir sia" [*Purg* 20:19–21]). Mary's own giving birth, we will recall, was said to be (by Virgil, of all people, back in *Purg* 3:38–39) that which alone can satisfy the innate human desire to know ("ché, se potuto aveste veder tutto, / mestier non era parturir Maria"). The goal of science is fulfilled only by the Incarnation, by parturition, by rendering knowledge into flesh. This is what vernacularization, not mere *translatio,* can accomplish—and it can accomplish it best not in faithful service translations but by full incorporation (and, by necessity, metamorphosis) of Latin learning into vernacular song.

11

The Body and the Flesh in the *Purgatorio*

Robert M. Durling

WHAT WE MAY CALL a distinction between the body and the flesh is vital to Dante's poetics in the *Purgatorio.* Somewhat simplifying our terminology,[1] we will call the flesh, or fleshliness, whatever hinders the soul in its ascent; it is the accumulation of mortal imperfection going back to Adam's sin, of sinful habits and the innate dispositions that such habits have intensified. The body, on the other hand, created "good in its own kind," with the bodily faculties of sense, motion, imagination, and memory, is the essential instrument of the soul, to such an extent that Dante's disembodied shades construct—organize—airy bodies, with which they operate, and there are many indications that these bodies are essential to the purgative process.[2] In this discussion I will focus primarily on the first terrace of Purgatory proper, that of pride (*Purg* 10–12).[3]

This first terrace sets forth Dante's conception of the purgative process more fully than any of the later ones. The reason is partly that much is to be set forth that will be assumed later, partly that pride, as the source and the fundamental motive of all sin (as in Augustine's *Confessions* 2.9–14 [Augustine 1955]), is the most serious disposition to be corrected in Purgatory, and its correction must be particularly elaborate. The target of the purgative process, on this terrace as on the others, is a disposition or tendency of the will: in the case of pride, the tendency to set oneself up above others, or, as Virgil explains in *Purg* 17:115–17, the desire to see others lowered so that one can be superior. This tendency or inclination is not itself an action; the wrong actions, sins, to which it led have all been forgiven.

The scene of the process of purgation is, with some variation, the same on each of the terraces of Purgatory proper: a narrow shelf circling the entire mountain, without any vegetation (there is one exception). The expanded paraphrase of the Lord's Prayer recited by the souls of the proud (11.1–24) calls it a "harsh desert" (11.14), and in the governing figural parallel with the Exodus, the terraces correspond to the Desert of Sinai, where, because of their stiff-necked disobedience, the children of Israel had to wander for forty years, until all those born in Egypt had died (commonly interpreted in the Middle Ages as referring to the penitential death of the "Old Man").

The process of purgation, as Dante represents it, is essentially that of redirecting love; it has two phases, destructive and constructive. In Aristotelian terminology, the old habit or form taken by the will must be broken down and the new habit or form imposed; gradual destruction of the old form may be simultaneous with the gradual imposition of the new form. On the terrace of pride, as well as on the others, this double process of learning and discipline involves a mode of suffering and a practice of meditation, including prayer and the contemplation of examples of the vice to be unlearned and the virtue to be learned. At the end of the process, in all cases but the last, one of the *P*s inscribed on the pilgrim's forehead by the angel at the gate is erased by the wing of the angel guarding the ascent, and the victory over vice is celebrated by the singing of one of the Beatitudes (Matt. 6:1–11); this moment obviously corresponds to that of priestly absolution in the sacrament of penance. As already said, the process is a reshaping and redirection of the will, and at the same time it is accompanied and made effective at each step of the way by God's help. Dante draws no sharp distinction between nature and grace, one of the many respects in which he is very un-Thomistic.

The terrace of pride gives special prominence to the Lord's Prayer, which Dante clearly considered a chief corrective to pride, since its sincere utterance requires an attitude of deep humility, which the penitent souls on the terrace practice and internalize as they recite their expanded paraphrase of the prayer (Matt. 6:9–13). The classic discussions of the Lord's Prayer are Augustine's *De sermone Domini in monte* and his *Epistle 130* (their importance can be gauged by the fact that they are the only authorities Aquinas cites in his own discussion of the Lord's Prayer in ST 2a.2ae.83.9). For Augustine the Lord's Prayer includes everything that prayer may rightly ask: "If you run through all the words of the [biblical] prayers, you will find nothing, I think, that is not contained and completed in the Lord's Prayer. Thus it is permitted to use these or other words, as long as we say the same things when we pray; but it must not be permitted to say different things" (*Ep. 130* 22 [Augustine 1895]). The exegetes follow Augustine in distinguishing seven petitions in the prayer, the first three valid eternally, the last four only in this life. He saw it as a particular remedy against pride (*De sermone Domini* 51 [Augustine 1967]): "Here rich men and those of noble birth in the eyes of the world are admonished, once they have become Christians, not to act proudly toward the poor and those of common birth; for all together address God as our Father: which they cannot truthfully and devoutly do unless they know each other to be brothers" (cf. *Ep. 130* 23 [Augustine 1895]).

Paraphrases were authorized by Augustine's "these or other words"; Dante's stresses the respects in which the Lord's Prayer enjoins humility, most of them identified by Augustine. As I have suggested elsewhere (Alighieri 2003, *Purg* 11.1–24*nn*), Dante seems to have studied Augustine's discussions of the Lord's Prayer with great attention; he may even have derived from them the suggestion of the mode of suffering of the proud. Commenting on the words "deliver us from evil," Augustine observes that in this life we cannot be entirely freed from it: "this cannot be hoped for in this life, as long as we carry about that mortality [*istam mortalitatem circumferimus*] into which we were drawn by the persuasion of the serpent" (*De sermoni Domini in Monte* 63 [Augustine 1967].)

This passage, written near the end of his life, involves a clear echo of one of the most striking passages in his *Confessions* (1.1 [Augustine 1990]), written much earlier: "And man, a certain portion of your creation, wishes to praise you; even man, carrying about his mortality, carrying about the testimony of his sin [*circumferens mortalitatem suam, circumferens testimonium peccati sui*] and carrying about testimony that you, God, resist the proud." The three "weights" man is said here to "carry about," his mortality, the testimony to his sin, and the testimony that God resists the proud, are identical in reference, since, first, man's mortality is the punishment for his sin (Gen. 2:17, 3:19); thus, second, his mortality testifies to his sin; and, third, since his sin resulted primarily from rebellious pride, man's mortality testifies to God's resisting the proud. It is but a small step from these correlations to seeing that the weight is also pride itself, since sin is always its own punishment.

In addition to its obvious connection with Augustine's metaphor, the logical structure of the circumambulatory penance done on the terrace of pride is also closely related to it: the penance is at the same time both punitive and expressive of the vice itself. Furthermore, the association between the weight of pride and that of mortality is obvious in Virgil's mention in *Purgatorio* 11 of the pilgrim's being weighed down by mortality (11.43–45, especially "lo 'ncarco" [the burden]), which calls attention to the analogy. However, Dante represents the weight also as a mode of practicing and thus acquiring the corrective virtue. When in *Purg* 11.53 Omberto Aldobrandini speaks of the weight "that masters my proud neck," he is using the terminology of retributive justice; he was proud and stiff-necked in life (among the many biblical occurrences of the idea, see especially Deut. 10:16, and cf. *Purg* 12:70–72), now he is forced to bend. He thus reveals that he has not yet understood the second aspect of his suffering: the weight that bends him down is that of his pride itself. We know from Omberto (*Purg* 11.52–57) that the weight of his stone prevents him from turning his head sufficiently to see the pilgrim: this is a commentary on pride's being essentially self-regarding. Souls at a later stage of purgation, like Oderisi da Gubbio, are able to turn their heads (*Purg* 11.73–78).

One implication of these passages is that those in the initial stages of the process are not able to see the examples of humility; they must gaze at the ground, able to contemplate only the examples of pride punished that are visible there (*Purg* 12:16–69): when the weight of their pride has lightened sufficiently, they can contemplate the examples of humility as they pass them, as well as see and identify others near them (as in *Purg* 11:109–26). (Thus, although on each terrace the examples of virtue are presented to the pilgrim before those of vice, that is not necessarily how the souls inhabiting the terraces experience them.) Practicing the virtue of humility, then, involves practicing the bodily postures and gestures that express it even though at first these may be merely imposed and not understood. Although Dante exploits this idea with great originality, it is by no means original with him. The medieval practice of adopting specific bodily positions for different kinds of prayer rested on such a recognition. As the *Modi orandi Sancti Dominici* put it: "the soul moves the members of the body that it may be the more swiftly lifted to God, that the soul that moves the body may be moved by the body . . . such a mode of prayer instills devotion alternately, from the soul into the body and from the body into the soul" (*Modi orandi* 1996, 1:52). The weight each of the proud must carry, then, is a version of the flesh; the body, bent beneath the load, is quite distinct from the load itself: it is the instrument by means of which each carries out his penance, and it is clear that the weight is not intrinsic to the body as such.

The examples of pride punished and humility exalted, clearly enough, present what is to be avoided and what imitated, respectively. They have an important rational function: it is critical to the acquisition of true virtue that the nature of the "right rule" be grasped by the mind. Not only do the examples of pride cast down instill fear; more important, they address the understanding, which must grasp the inherent absurdity of pride and identify the brevity and mortality of all human pretension. Hence, the anagram VOM is sculpted, as it were—like the mark of a tool, or a genetic characteristic—into the very material of the text (see Alighieri 2001, notes to 12.25–63; and cf. *OMO* in 23.32–33): if he does not rise above his mere human state, man is dust and returns to dust, a worm (cf. *Purg* 10.121–29). The association of these carvings with those on church floors covering tombs emphasizes that aspect of the lesson; it also suggests that the ultimate feeling they are to instill is that of humbled grief, whose bodily expression is the bowed head. The lesson in the absurdity and self-destructiveness of pride is essential preparation for what is to be learned from the examples of humility. The souls must be ready to see why, in order to see the examples, they must look up to them, spiritually as well as spatially. (It is made clear that the souls who appear at the end of canto 10 are coming from the pilgrim's left as he faces the carvings; thus, the examples of humility are to the penitent souls' left also—the side of the heart, as *Purg* 10.48 reminds us (see Alighieri 2003, *Purg* 10.100*n*).

One of the most interesting and subtle psychological insights set forth in Purgatory proper is that the mode of penance, especially on the three lowest levels, involves a separation of the self from its vice: the distinction between body and flesh we have traced involves the representation of pride, envy, and anger as distinct from the body and thus from true self. On the terrace of pride, the stones that closed around the damned (cf. *Inf* 10 and 31–33) have been escaped, and though they weigh the souls down, they can ultimately be trodden underfoot (as practiced in *Purgatorio* 12); the same principle separates the iron wires, the livid garments, and the livid rock from the souls / bodies of the envious and the smoke from the angry. This distinction between the tendency to be corrected and the essence of the body–soul complex is a theme of meditation for the penitents and a hallmark of Purgatory proper: in the Ante-Purgatory the programmatic separation has not taken place (Belacqua is the best example: his identification with his sloth is quite unreflecting). In the Ante-Purgatory a generic striving upward draws on the traditional parallel between the acquisition of virtue and the difficult ascent of a mountain; in Purgatory proper, however, the actual discipline takes place on the terraces, which are level, and its result *facilitates* the climb, which itself is no longer the locus of moral effort.

The process of re-education set forth by Dante on the terraces of Purgatory, and most fully on the terrace of pride, involves all the dimensions of the human being: physical, sensory, imaginative, emotional, intellectual. It expresses Dante's profound sense of the unity of the human body–soul complex, the central theme of the entire *Purgatorio.* In this process he gives art a major role. With their extended descriptions of the marble sculptures and of the reaction to them of the pilgrim and certain of the pentitents, cantos 10–12 are a major statement about the nature and function of the visual arts and, by implication, of poetry and of the *Comedy* itself.

As has often been observed, Dante attributes to the sculptures what had been recognized since antiquity as a chief virtue of art: mimetic vividness, lifelike representation, the holding of the mirror up to nature. The miraculous qualities he ascribes to the sculptures, such as the conveying of imagined dialogue, are intensifications of qualities he sees and values in the products of human art (see Alighieri 2003, *Purg* 10:28–99*nn*). As on all the terraces, the virtue is first exemplified by the Virgin Mary, and in *Purgatorio* 10, 13, 15, and 25—a majority of the cases—the words spoken by Mary in the Gospels are quoted. The very first example, in canto 10, is particularly interesting, since repeated emphasis is placed on the sculptures' actually being silent: they are so vivid that the viewer can imagine exactly what is said. "One would have sworn that he [the archangel Gabriel] was saying 'Ave!'" In the case of the Virgin, Dante's words are particularly significant (*Purg* 10.43–45):

> e avea in atto impressa esta favella:
> "Ecce ancilla Domini," propriamente
> come figura in cera si suggella

> and in her bearing was stamped this speech: "Ecce ancilla Domini," exactly as a figure is sealed in wax.

In other words, the Virgin's humility of soul so permeates her bodily gestures as to stamp them legibly with her utterance; her body is mere wax to the forming power of her soul, its word. We may note in passing that it is the Virgin's legibility that guarantees that of the archangel: note the *perché* (because) of verse 41. Perfection of virtue requires—is—the perfection of the relation of soul to body, and in this, as in all things, the Virgin is the model the souls must strive to follow. This conception of the permeating of the body with the "word" of the soul is close to what is said of the angel in *Purg* 2.44: "parea beato per iscritto" ("he seemed to have blessedness inscribed on him"): every detail of his appearance and bearing expressed his beatitude.

An important light is cast by these passages, incidentally, on Dante's conception of personification allegory: he connects it with the representation of bodily appearance and gesture, as in the pilgrim's description of Belacqua, "that fellow . . . appears more negligent than if Laziness were his sister" (*Purg* 4.110–11): it is as if there were a blood relation between Belacqua and the personification, his laziness so permeates his body (and in Dante's view such personality traits can indeed be inherited). Thus, there is a close relation between Dante's idea of personification and his treatment of the Virgin as the true exemplar of each virtue.[4]

The shining beauty attributed to the carvings in *Purgatorio* 10, perceived through the sense of sight, is also an integral part of their function; it draws the soul to love both the representation and what is represented. The delight felt by the pilgrim and his gratitude toward the Maker (*Purg* 10.97–99) are presumably shared by the penitent souls able to contemplate them. Although the point is not made explicit here, the Virgin, as the most virtuous and most beautiful human being (the two are virtuously synonymous for Dante), is supremely lovable. The example of the Virgin's humility is not only to instruct the souls in the nature of the virtue, but to arouse their love and through their love their ability as well as their desire to imitate her. Thus, the first appeal, made through the beautiful carving representing the Virgin's humility, is to the imagination and the soul's power of empathy. It is obviously Dante's conception that the images of virtue and vice remain in the penitents' imaginations and are to govern and inform their prayers and their meditations: they enable them to "think of what follows" (*Purg* 10.110).[5]

In order to see and speak with Oderisi, the pilgrim himself must bend equally low, and he preserves the posture throughout his dialogue with him. As he listens to Oderisi's account of the futility of artistic pride, his own pride is chastened (*Purg* 11.118–19). It is important that this occurs when he is bent over and to that extent shares in the penance. But, as throughout the *Comedy,* the pilgrim's relation to the penitent souls in Purgatory is primarily that of an observer who participates vicariously in what he witnesses. In this respect the figure of the pilgrim gazing intently upon the sculptures of the terrace of pride is a figure of the relation of the reader to the poem itself. Just as the pilgrim's vicarious participation includes a strong empathic element (see Alighieri 2003, *Purg* 10.130–35*n*), so too does the reader's, and through it the poet obviously hopes to involve the reader's body as well as his mind. Again, all this takes place through the bodily senses and through the bodily faculty of imagination, which receives the forms of outward things, stores them, recalls them, and presents them to the contemplation of the mind. It is through the combined functioning of sense, imagination, reason, and affect that the new form is to be "put on" by both soul and body.

NOTES

1. Traditional usage somewhat blurred the distinction, though it is fundamental. Saint Paul often uses the term "flesh" (Lat. *caro*) as synonymous with the natural or fallen body (e.g., Rom 7:21–25); at the same time, he maintains that the body is "the temple of the holy Spirit" (1 Cor. 6:16–19), and asserted a continuity of the "natural" body with the "glorious" or resurrected body; it will be absorbed, not abolished (2 Cor. 5:4, 1 Cor. 15:42–50). When Augustine attacks the classical view that the body is the source of evil (as in *Aen* 6.730–34 [see Courcelle 1955]), he characterizes the unfallen body and its flesh as "good in its own kind and degree" (*City of God,* 14.5); his point is that the source of evil is the will, a spiritual principle.

2. Dante represents a further development of Western optimism concerning human nature (see "Introduction" in Alighieri 2003). For the usefulness of the body in traversing Hell, see Alighieri 1996b, notes for *Inf* 23:1–33.

3. Most of this essay is adapted from the commentary that appears in the edition, with translation, that Ronald Martinez and I have prepared for Oxford University Press (Alighieri 2003).

4. On the close analogy between the relation of body and soul and the relation between the letter of a text and its inner meaning, see "Additional Note 13, The Body Analogy, 2: The Metaphorics of Fraud," in Alighieri 1996b.

5. The order of the examples from the life of the Virgin is discussed in an Additional Note (Alighieri 1996b).

12

From Plurality to (Near) Unicity of Forms: Embryology in *Purgatorio* 25

Manuele Gragnolati

In the thirteenth century, Christian eschatology with respect to body and soul undergoes a significant change of emphasis: the traditional focus on the Last Judgment and the resurrection of the body shifts toward a sense of "last things" which, if it does not erase the significance of bodily return at the end of time, concentrates nonetheless on the individual destiny of the separated soul and stresses its full experience right after physical death.[1] As we might expect from a fourteenth-century eschatological poem, the *Commedia* emphasizes that as soon as the soul leaves its earthly body, it undergoes a personal, individual judgment that immediately fixes the modality of its experience of pain or bliss in the afterlife. In a larger context, thirteenth-century theologians insisted that the fire of Hell and Purgatory is corporeal.

Dante confronts the issue of how a separated soul can experience physical pain in *Purgatorio* 25, where the pilgrim, upon seeing the distorted and emaciated features of the gluttonous, wonders how a soul can get thinner if it does not need food: "Come si può far magro / là dove l'uopo di nodrir non tocca" ("How can one grow lean there where the need of nourishment is not felt?" [*Purg* 25.20–21]).[2] As Virgil has no precise answer, it is Statius who gives a very long explanatory speech, which is divided in two parts: vv. 37–78 explore the origin of the human soul and its development from vegetative to sensitive to rational, while vv. 79–109 give a scientific account of what a shade is, describing the formation of the aerial body, which is able to experience pain, and which the human soul radiates in the otherworld.

The first part of Statius's speech generated a harsh debate in the 1920s between Giovanni Busnelli (1922, 97–297; and Alighieri 1964, 2:392–404) and Bruno Nardi (1920; 1960; 1966; 1967a; 1967b; 1990). Busnelli, who considered Dante a faithful disciple of Thomas Aquinas, wanted to show that the account of the generation of the soul is fully Thomistic. Nardi, on the other hand, showed Dante's freedom in following several doctrines and pointed out that Dante's account of the origin of the soul is much less close to Aquinas than Busnelli claimed. Étienne Gilson (1967 and 1974) restates Dante's full adherence to the Thomistic doctrine, while Kenelm Foster stresses Dante's ambivalence and is ambivalent himself. Foster agrees with Nardi but also says that it is not possible to reject completely the Thomistic sense that Busnelli claims: "E, tutto considerato, l'interpretazione di Nardi è forse quella che meglio risponde al senso del passo, senza tuttavia escludere del tutto che D. abbia voluto attribuirgli quel senso tomista che G. Busnelli vi scorge" (1976, 645).[3] In this essay, I propose again to discuss the passage on the formation of the soul. By inserting it in the controversy between plurality and unicity of forms, which started in Paris in the 1270s and continued until the first decades of the fourteenth century, I will show the reasons for and the implications of the ambivalence that the text indeed suggests and that is reflected by the scholarly debate. In particular, I will first discuss the ambivalent embryological doctrine in *Purgatorio* 25 and then connect it to two different understandings of the human being. Indeed, I will argue that this ambivalence informs the construction of the whole poem, particularly in the tension between the power of the separated soul and the significance of bodily return.

I will begin by considering the anthropological models implied by the philosophical doctrines of plurality and unicity of forms, according to which, respectively, in every being there are as many forms as different properties or there is one single substantial form.[4] I will show the implications that these doctrines had for the conception of the human being and the relation of body and soul primarily with the philosophy of Bonaventure (for plurality) and Thomas Aquinas (for unicity). The doctrine of plurality is the more traditional one and is assumed by Bonaventure, who follows the principles of universal hylomorphism—which conceives of any entity as composed of form and matter—and who, in the case of man, holds that soul and body are each composed of their own form and matter.[5] The advantage of this model was that it considered body as a concrete entity with its own existence, but its problem was that it threatened the unity of the human being, which risked becoming, rather than what we would today call a fully psychosomatic unity, a sort of partnership of two different entities, body and soul.[6] In order to connect body and soul, Bonaventure theorizes a mutual desire that one has for the other. The body is perfected and made alive by the soul but, at the same time, the soul also needs the body for completion; the soul longs for its body and is fully happy only when it can administer it: "When God created the body, He joined it to the soul; He united the two in a natural and mutual relationship. . . . Hence, the soul cannot be fully happy unless the body is returned to it, for the two have a natural ordination to each other" (*The Breviloquium* pt. 7, chap. 7, par. 4 [Bonaventure 1962]).[7] To support his argument, Bonaventure goes back to Augustine's concept of *desiderium*—the separated soul's desire for its body—and argues that the soul alone cannot enjoy full vision of God because it is distracted precisely by the desire for the body.[8]

The doctrine of unicity of form, already adumbrated by Albert the Great, is perfected by Thomas Aquinas. Aquinas rejects universal hylomorphism and asserts that man is composed of one substantial form, the soul, and the matter that it activates, its body. While Bonaventure conceived of body and soul as two different entities, Aquinas considers the soul as the only form of the body, and the body as the matter of the soul. The rational soul, which also has vegetative and sensitive powers, is the only substantial form of the human being, including its body: "In man there is no substantial form other than the rational soul, and it is due to the soul alone that a man is not only a human being, but also animal, living, body, substance, 'something'" (*De spiritualibus creaturis,* a. 1, resp.).[9] By giving absolute primacy to the soul as the only form of the person, the doctrine of unicity fully packs what self is, including what body is, into the soul. According to Aquinas's formulation, it is better to say that the soul contains the body and makes it one, rather than the opposite: "magis anima continet corpus et facit ipsum esse unum, quam e converso" (*Summa theologiae* 1a, q. 76, a.3, ad 1).[10] The fact that the soul was conceived of as the only form of the body gave rise to the idea of formal identity, which stressed that it is form that accounts for anything continuing to be that particular thing. Formal identity was stressed by theologians especially in discussions of resurrection, where they argued that the soul can express the nature of the body in any matter it activates. What self is, including what body is, is fully packed into the soul, which can make any matter it activates at resurrection be its body. Durand of St. Pourçain affirms explicitly that to make the resurrection body of Peter, God can use the dust that was once the body of Paul, because the soul of Peter will make whatever matter unites with it be its body (Bynum 1995, 259–60). As some scholars have pointed out, the primacy that the doctrine of unicity grants the soul came at a very high price; in fact, although it was spared in Paris, this doctrine was condemned at Oxford in 1277 and in 1284 (see Callus 1967, 1025–26; Zavalloni 1951, 219–21; Bynum 1995, 271–78). Some of the objections that were made to unicity of form stressed that it gave absolute primacy to the soul as the only form of the body so that body was at risk of being conceived as pure potency (Bazàn 1983; Tugwell 1990, 149–55; Bynum 1995, 271–78; and Quinn 1993). The doctrine of unicity sacrificed the commonsense notion of body as something material and concrete—a notion that, on the contrary, was well expressed by the principles of plurality, which, as we have seen, considered body as a separate entity from soul and granted it its own, concrete existence. The implications of unicity of form for both theology and cult practices were dangerous. If it is the rational soul that makes a human body be a body, in the case of relics for instance, what would be the point of venerating something that is not the body of the saint anymore (because it no longer contains the soul of the saint [i.e., it does not have the same form as before]) and that is not necessarily going to be resurrected (because what matters for identity is not matter but form)?[11] The doctrine of unicity of form disturbed a spirituality in which a concrete sense of the body was essential to self—a spirituality centered on the doctrine of the Incarnation, the veneration of relics and saints, and the careful burials of cadavers, which were considered an important part of the loved ones who had passed away. Moreover, the partisans of unicity are not always consistent in the use of this doctrine. They are, on the contrary, deeply ambivalent. On the one hand, they conceive of the soul as the single substantial form of the human being, which carries its whole structure and is able to subsist and experience the full vision of God without the body. On the other hand, they stress that the soul must be united with the body because of the ontological completeness of the person; soul alone is by definition incomplete and requires a body in order to express itself. This is why Thomas Aquinas, who stresses the separated soul's full power, can also say that without its body the soul is simply an imperfect fragment: "The soul that has separated from its body is therefore imperfect as long as it remains without its body. . . . The soul . . . is not the whole human being, and my soul is not me" ("Anima exuta corpore, quamdiu est sine corpore, est imperfecta. . . . . anima autem . . . non est totus homo, et anima mea non est ego" [*On 1 Cor.*, chap. 15, lectio 2; Aquinas 1876, 21:33–34; my translation]).[12]

I will now consider more specifically what the principles of plurality and unicity held about the formation of the soul in the human embryo—an issue that philosophers considered crucial. The two doctrines concentrated the debate upon three sets of alternatives: whether prime matter is absolutely passive potency or contains some actuality of its own; whether, in the process of becoming, matter is deprived of all precedent forms or not; and whether substantial form, including virtually all preceding forms, confers on prime matter its complete and specific determination or imparts one perfection only. If one takes as true the first hypothesis of each of these three sets, one advocates unicity of form; if one defends the second hypothesis, one advocates plurality of forms (Callus 1967, 1024–27).

With respect to embryology, the partisans of unicity of form, who believed that no substance can have two substantial forms at the same time, conceived of the evolution of the embryo as a discontinuous process in which a series of various generations and corruptions occur. Whenever something changes, its preceding substantial form must disappear and be replaced by a new form: "when a more perfect form supervenes this brings about the dissolution of the preceding one. However, it does so in such a way that the second form possesses whatever the first one does and something more into the bargain" (ST 1a, q. 118, a. 2, ad 2).[13] It is a discontinuous succession of forms in which each time a new and more perfect form appears, the old one corrupts itself. When the sensitive soul, which also contains the faculties of the vegetative soul, appears, the vegetative soul passes away, and when the rational soul is created by God, the sensitive soul disappears. What remains is the rational soul alone, which is created as already having both vegetative and sensitive faculties and is the only substantial form of man: "Therefore it must be said that the intellective soul is created by God at the completion of man's coming-into-being. This soul is at one and the same time both a sensitive and nutritive life-principle, the preceding forms having been dissolved" (ST 1a, q. 118, a.2, ad 2).[14] According to the principles of unicity of form, the soul is created by God as a "forma simplex," a simple, single form that contains all faculties, from the simplest to the intellectual, and is therefore fully immortal. This is why Aquinas can assume that, when the soul separates from its body, it keeps all its powers—the intellectual ones in act, and the sensitive and nutritive ones not in act but in potency; and these will be reactivated when the soul is reunited with its body at resurrection.[15]

Those who asserted plurality of forms stressed the empirical sense of change as a continuous process in which something evolves on the basis of the concept of act and potency. When the vegetative soul of an embryo is in an active state, the sensitive is in a state of potency, and when the sensitive is active, the rational is in potency (see Zavalloni 1951, 312–16). The human soul is one, but composed of different forms that have different properties and are added one onto the other: the vegetative soul transforms itself into a sensitive soul (that is, a soul that has vegetative and sensitive forms) and the sensitive soul transforms itself—through God's intervention—into a rational soul (that is, a soul that has vegetative, sensitive, and rational forms). All the forms preceding the intellectual one (which is the only one to be created directly by God) are educed from matter and are therefore supposed to pass away with the soul's separation from the body. The only form that has a divine origin and is, consequently, immortal is precisely the intellectual one.[16]

I will now consider Statius's account of the formation of the human soul. I will show that, on the one hand, Statius starts by following the more empirical theory of the continual evolution from one soul to the other, which is typical of the doctrine of plurality and is rejected by Thomas Aquinas. However, Statius ends up presenting a very powerful soul that possesses the same possibilities as the soul presented by the doctrine of unicity of form. Statius begins his speech with the explanation of the formation of the human seed in men (*Purg* 25.37–43). As Patrick Boyde has shown, Statius's explanation follows what Aristotle says in his *De generatione animalium* as commented on by thirteenth-century Christian philosophers using Galen and Avicenna (1981, 271–73). Perfect blood, which is the final result of food processed through three digestions (in the stomach, in the liver, and in a region of the heart), is imbued with a formative power that Statius calls "a tutte membra umane / virtute informativa" ("an informing power for all the bodily members" [*Purg* 25.40–41]). Most of this perfect blood goes to nourish the body through veins and arteries, while some of it remains in the heart and is transformed, through another digestion, into the sperm that goes to the genital organs (*Purg* 25.37–42). Statius continues to describe the generation and formation of the embryo, and, in the first part of his account, we find the idea of change as an evolution from potency to act so that the very formative power of the semen becomes a vegetative soul. This vegetative soul develops the sensitive faculties that it already had in potency:

> Anima fatta la virtute attiva
> qual d'una pianta, in tanto differente,
> che questa è in via e quella è già a riva,
> tanto ovra poi, che già si move e sente,
> come spungo marino; e indi imprende
> ad organar le posse ond' è semente.
> (*Purg* 25:52–57)

> The active virtue having become a soul, like that of a plant (but in so far different that this is on the way, and that has already arrived) so works then that now it moves and feels, like a sea-fungus; then it proceeds to develop organs for the powers of which it is the germ.

Statius's account presupposes continuity until the formation of the sensitive soul. In his polemics with Busnelli, Nardi is right when he says that Dante's account differs from Aquinas's, because the continuous process described in vv. 52–57 is different from Aquinas's principle of a discontinuous process in which the new form replaces the old one, which passes away.[17]

Having arrived at the sensitive soul, Statius has to explain how the embryo, gifted with vegetative and sensitive powers, becomes endowed with intellective faculties. Statius continues:

> Apri a la verità che viene il petto;
> e sappi che, sì tosto come al feto
> l'articular del cerebro è perfetto,
> lo motor primo a lui si volge lieto
> sovra tant' arte di natura, e spira
> spirito novo, di vertù repleto,

che ciò che trova attivo quivi, tira
in sua sustanzia, e fassi un'alma sola,
che vive e sente e sé in sé rigira.
(*Purg* 25:67–75)

Open your breast to the truth which is coming, and know that, so soon as in the foetus the articulation of the brain is perfect, the First Mover turns to it with joy over such art of nature, and breathes into it a new spirit replete with virtue, which absorbs that which is active there into its own substance, and makes one single soul which lives and feels and circles on itself.

When the brain has completely developed, the intellectual soul is created by God. God breathes forth the rational soul, which absorbs what it finds active in the fetus into its own substance, and becomes one single soul endowed with three different powers: vegetative, sensitive, and rational. It is here where the move from plurality to (near) unicity occurs. As we have already seen, Busnelli (1922, 248–74 and Alighieri 1964, 2:399) is wrong in referring only to Aquinas's doctrine. Aquinas states that the rational soul is created as already having vegetative / sensitive faculties and that the sensitive soul passes away with the creation of the rational soul; Statius, on the contrary, says that the rational soul absorbs the sensitive soul into its substance. At the same time, I want to argue against Nardi's anti-Thomistic interpretation of Statius's discourse, which is also different from the passages that Nardi considers as expressing the same conception as Dante's. According to these passages (quoted in note 17), the vegetative soul acquires first sensitive faculties, and then—with the direct intervention of God—rational powers. Statius's emphasis is different: he does not say that the sensitive soul becomes the rational soul because God irradiates the intellect into it; rather, he says that the rational soul, created by God, is the active and surviving agent, which absorbs into its substance the sensitive soul, thus acquiring vegetative and sensitive powers. Until he portrays the formation of the sensitive soul, Dante follows some tenets that differ from the principles of Thomism, but the move into the emphatically discontinuous process that is implied by the creation of the rational soul suggests a movement toward the Thomistic concept. When Étienne Gilson (1967, 128–29) says that Dante "has here taken sides with Thomas Aquinas in the . . . famous discussion on the unity of the substantial form in the composite, including man," he may be overstating the case.[18] At the same time, I would stress that the ambivalence is in the text, which indeed suggests the sort of Thomistic sense that Gilson perceives. At the moment of its creation, the rational soul does not have vegetative and sensitive powers and does not contain the structure of the body—as it would according to Aquinas. Only subsequently does the rational soul "pull into its substance," as Dante says, vegetative and sensitive powers. The difference with Aquinas is that the rational soul is not created as already possessing all its powers; rather, it absorbs the formative virtue and vegetative and sensitive powers from the embryo to which it unites. By absorbing all these other faculties, the rational soul makes them immortal so that they do not disappear with the soul's separation from the body.

Dante's "alma sola" is the result of a process different from the one described in Aquinas's doctrine, but the two resulting souls can "work" almost in the same way. After the account of the origin of the soul, Statius explains that the separated soul carries with it both what is human (the formative virtue and vegetative-sensitive powers) and what is divine (the intellectual ones created by God):

> Quando Làchesis non ha più del lino,
> solvesi da la carne, e in virtute
> ne porta seco e l'umano e 'l divino:
> l'altre potenze tutte quante mute;
> memoria, intelligenza e volontade
> in atto molto più che prima agute.
> (*Purg* 25:79–84)

> And when Lachesis has no more thread, the soul is loosed from the flesh and carries with it as faculties both the human and the divine; the other faculties all of them mute, but memory, intellect, and will far more acute in action thant before.[19]

Dante wants to grant to the separated soul the same "power" as Aquinas did and, like Aquinas, he imagines that the intellectual powers of the separated soul are in act ("in atto") while all the others are in potency ("mute"). But Dante goes further than Aquinas and does not wait for the resurrection in order to reactivate the "human" part of the person. In Dante's world the separated soul has the immediate chance of creating a body of air that allows it to express all its powers—not only the rational ones—in the eschatological time between physical death and the Last

Judgment. As soon as it has the opportunity, the formative virtue contained in the soul radiates forth in the very same way as it did with respect to the earthly living limbs: "Tosto che loco lì la circumscrive, / la virtù formativa raggia intorno / così e quanto ne le membra vive" ("As soon as space encompasses it there, the formative virtue radiates around, in form and quantity as in the living members" [*Purg* 25:88–90]). The air that surrounds the soul is shaped "virtualmente" (v. 96), that is, by virtue of the formative power which was in the semen and which the soul absorbed when it united to the embryo.[20] Because it is the air (not flesh) that makes it visible, the union of soul and aerial body is called a "shade" (not a "human being"). The soul furnishes every organ of sensation ("ciascun sentire"), from the simplest one to sight, thus allowing the shade to speak, laugh, weep, and sigh. The pilgrim's doubt which originated the whole explanation is finally answered:

> Però che quindi ha poscia sua paruta,
> è chiamata ombra; e quindi organa poi
> ciascun sentire infino a la veduta.
> Quindi parliamo e quindi ridiam noi;
> quindi facciam le lagrime e' sospiri
> che per lo monte aver sentiti puoi.
> Secondo che ci affliggono i disiri
> e li altri affetti, l'ombra si figura;
> e quest' è la cagion di che tu miri.
> (*Purg* 25.100–108)

> Inasmuch as therefrom it has its semblance, it is called a shade, and therefrom it forms the organs of every sense, even to the sight. By this we speak and by this we laugh, by this we make the tears and sighs which you may have heard about the mountain. According as the desires and the other affections prick us, the shade takes its form; and this is the cause of that at which you marvel.

In describing the function and the characteristics of the separated soul, Dante recognizes the advantages of the principles of unicity of form as they were expressed in the discussions about the resurrection body. Discussing whether all the limbs of the human body will resurrect, Aquinas says that the soul originally and implicitly contains everything that appears in the parts of the body, and that man cannot be perfect unless the body expresses externally what the soul contains implicitly.[21] The powers of the "alma sola" of Statius's account reflect the concept that the soul "contains" the structure of the body. The self, including physical characteristics and qualities, is fully packed into the souls of the *Commedia,* which radiate a body of air at the very moment when, theologically, they should have no body at all. Shades have not simply an exterior aspect, but also all the organs of the earthly body, including the ones that serve for excretion, as the description of Mohammed makes clear:

> Già veggia, per mezzul perdere o lulla,
> com'io vidi un, così non si pertugia,
> rotto dal mento infin dove si trulla.
> Tra le gambe pendevan le minugia;
> la corata pareva e 'l tristo sacco
> che merda fa di quel che si trangugia.
> (*Inf* 28.22–27)

> Truly a cask, through loss of mid-board or side-piece, gapes not so wide as one I saw, cleft from the chin to the part that breaks wind; his entrails were hanging between his legs, and the vitals could be seen and the foul sack that makes ordure of what is swallowed.

Aerial bodies are present not only in Hell and Purgatory but also in Heaven, where at a certain points the shades' features are hidden by the light that surrounds them and is a sign of the souls' intellectual joy. Nonetheless, the human features are there, carried in the individual souls as an expression of their unique individuality. And human features will be visible again with the resurrection of the body.

In constructing his poem, Dante has the soul account for the identity of the self, including physical identity. Recently, John Bruce-Jones (1995, 221) has affirmed that it is the doctrine of unicity of form which allows Dante to stage encounters with human souls that are substantial forms of real persons.[22] And Francesco Santi (1993, 288) has written that Dante's notion of the person in the *Commedia* is a "very clear example of Thomism," because the soul contains the substance of its body before resurrection. Both Bruce-Jones's and Santi's suggestions confirm my reading of the embryological doctrine explained in *Purgatorio* 25 and my emphasis on its significant move toward the principles of unicity that guarantee the soul's full power. At the same time, Dante's position is more complex and ambivalent than Bruce-Jones and Santi suggest, and Dante is not entirely a partisan of the

Thomistic conception of the soul as the only form of the person. If it is true that the "alma sola" described by Dante shares important characteristics with Aquinas's conception of the soul, it is also significant that he describes the process of evolution up to the occurrence of the sensitive soul according to the principles of plurality of forms.

In the last part of this essay, I want to suggest that the vacillation between the principles of plurality and unicity of form that characterizes the embryological doctrine of *Purgatorio* 25 is also reflected in the tensions of the *Commedia*'s eschatological panorama. Throughout the *Commedia,* Dante portrays both the strength of the separated soul and the necessity of bodily return as the ultimate moment of one's experience. On the one hand, he presents the soul as the guarantor of the self and the container of the structure of the body. The body of air that the soul radiates as soon as it leaves its earthly body symbolizes the full experience Dante grants the separated soul—and the stress on the soul's full experience is connected with the emphasis that contemporary eschatology placed on the period between physical death and resurrection. On the other hand, Dante stresses the provisional, temporary character of the shades and the important role that resurrection continues to play, showing that a soul without its real body is imperfect, that the shades are temporary surrogates of a wholeness that will be reconstituted at resurrection, and that ultimate, complete experience will be possible only after bodily return.[23] And, significantly, when the poem refers to the earthly body or the resurrection body, Dante employs the image of the body as clothing, an image that expresses the more traditional and concrete sense of body as something that is not contained by the soul, but as an entity that is distinct from soul and added to it as its completion (cf. *Inf* 13.103–104, 33.61–63; *Purg* 1.75, 11.44, 16.37–38, 30.13–15; *Par* 25.9 and 31.60).

In *Inf* 6.106–11, Virgil explained that with the resurrection of the body, the pain of the damned will increase. In *Paradiso* 14, the heavenly counterpart of this passage, the soul of Solomon explains that with the resurrection of the body the beatitude of the blessed will also increase:

> Come la carne gloriïosa e santa
> fia rivestita, la nostra persona
> piú grata fia per esser tutta quanta;
> per che s'accrescerà ciò che ne dona
> di gratüito lume il sommo bene,

lume ch'a lui veder ne condiziona;
onde la visïon crescer convene,
crescer l'ardor che di quella s'accende,
crescer lo raggio che da esso vene.
(*Par* 14.43–51)

When the flesh, glorious and sanctified, shall be clothed on us again, our persons will be more acceptable for being all complete; wherefore whatever of gratuitous light the Supreme Good gives us will be increased, light which fits us to see Him; so that our vision needs must increase, our ardor increase which by that is kindled, our radiance increase which comes from this.

Not only will the soul put on its flesh again, but the flesh will be "gloriosa e santa," that is, glorified with the gifts of *impassibilitas, agilitas, subtilitas,* and *claritas* that were usually referred to in thirteenth-century discussions of resurrection bodies (see Goering 1982). In particular, Solomon states that the appearance of the resurrection flesh will be brighter than the light that now surrounds the soul:

Ma sì come carbon che fiamma rende,
e per vivo candor quella soverchia,
sì che la sua parvenza si difende;
così questo folgór che già ne cerchia
fia vinto in apparenza da la carne
che tutto dì la terra ricoperchia.
(*Par* 14.52–57)

But even as a coal which gives forth flame, and with its white glow outshines it, so that its visibility is maintained, so shall this effulgence which already surrounds us be surpassed in brightness by the flesh which the earth still covers.

Here Dante refers to the principles of plurality and uses the image of the brand employed by Bonaventure when he describes the *claritas* of the resurrection body in his *Sentences* commentary (bk. 4, dist. 49, pt. 2, art. 2, sect. 2, q. 1). While Thomas Aquinas says that the clarity of the resurrection body will be produced by the "redundantia gloriae animae"—the overflowing of the soul's glory—into the body (bk. 4, dist. 44, q. 2, art. 4, solutio 1), it is significant that here Dante is closer to Bonaventure, suggesting that the resurrection body will itself have the "glow" that surpasses the "effulgence" provoked by the glory of the soul (see Chiavacci

Leonardi 1988, 261).[24] Solomon's praise of the splendor of the resurrection body is followed by the joyful response of all the souls, who show "disio d'i' corpi morti," desire for their dead bodies:

Tanto mi parver sùbiti e accorti
e l'uno e l'altro coro a dicer "Amme!,"
che ben mostrar disio d'i corpi morti:
forse non pur per lor, ma per le mamme,
per li padri e per li altri che fuor cari
anzi che fosser sempiterne fiamme.
(*Par* 14:62–66)

So sudden and eager both the one and the other chorus seemed to me in saying "Amen," that truly they showed desire for their dead bodies—perhaps not only for themselves, but also for their mothers, for their fathers, and for the others who were dear before they became eternal flames.

The idea of the sociability of the joys of Heaven is rare among theologians, who emphasized that the resurrection will entail the improvement of the individual's relation with God (see Bynum 1995, 303*n*92 and Harrison 1999). Dante might have found this idea in Bonaventure's *Sentences* commentary, where Bonaventure writes that at the resurrection the blessed will rejoice in others' happiness as much as in their own, and that Peter, in fact, will rejoice in Linus's happiness even more than Linus does (bk. 4, dist. 49, pt. 1, art. 1, q. 6). At the same time, Dante modifies Bonaventure's concept and makes it more intimate, because it is not Peter rejoicing in Linus's—or any other person's—glory, but everyone rejoicing in the idea of being reunited with their dearest loved ones. The rhyme words *amme / mamme / fiamme* express the certitude that with resumption of what now is a dead body, the spiritual flames will again become corporeal and, therefore, complete individuals.[25]

The ambivalence toward the principles of plurality and unicity of form that characterized embryology in *Purgatorio* 25 structures the eschatological conception of the whole *Commedia* and the relation between body and soul that it expresses. If, throughout the *Commedia,* Dante uses some principles of unicity to stress the soul's power and imagines that it can radiate a body of air that allows it to express itself before the resurrection, at the same time he stresses that the aerial body is not enough, and that soul without its real body is imperfect. Only when it reunites with the material, concrete body of resurrection (to which Dante refers, as we have seen, with images that echo the principles of plurality), will the soul stop being an incomplete fragment, no matter how bright and luminous, because it is finally reunited with its real body in the concrete, tangible, fleshly perfection of the whole person, "la persona tutta quanta."

Notes

1. On the complexity of this transition, see Bynum and Freedman 1999; see also Ariès 1974, 27–52; Morris 1972, 144–52; Le Goff 1984 and 1993; Bynum 1995, 279–317. I would like to thank Christoph Holzhey for his generous help in dealing with the complex matter discussed in this article.

2. For the materiality of the fire punishing the separated souls, see Klein 1960, 63; and Bynum 1995, 281. Citations of the *Commedia* are from Petrocchi's edition (Alighieri 1966–67); translations are from Singleton's (Alighieri 1970–75).

3. Both Bettoni 1970 and Maierù 1970 follow Nardi. For other readings of *Purg* 25 that follow Nardi, see Figurelli 1972; Padoan 1981; Toscano 1988; and Guagnini 1989. Cf. Boyde (1981, 271–80), who comments on *Purg* 25 with great knowledge and subtlety but does not refer to the debate between plurality and unicity of form, which I deem crucial for a thorough understanding of the passage. For a recent discussion of Statius's account, see Cogan 1999, 129–40.

4. For the controversy, I have used Callus 1960, 1961, and 1967; Michel 1915, 569–78; Zavalloni 1951; Gilson 1955, 416–20; Mazzarella 1978; Bazàn 1983; Santi 1987; Weber 1991, 74–198; Bynum 1995, 256–76; Dales 1995.

5. See Gilson 1949, 315–40; Vanni Rovighi 1974, 67–81; Mazzarella 1978, 63 and 277–87. In the following analysis on the anthropological conceptions that were implied in the doctrines of plurality and unicity, I am greatly indebted to Bynum 1995 (especially 229–78).

6. Aquinas, for instance, attacks plurality on the assumption that to assume several substantial forms in any compound—including the soul or the human being—would be irreconcilable with its unity (see Zavalloni 1951, 255, 269; Callus 1960, 583; Bazàn 1983, 395). For the attention that pluralists show toward bodiliness, see Santi 1987, 869–72; and D' Avray 1994.

7. As Dales (1995, 102) formulates Bonaventure's conception of body and soul, "each [i.e., soul and body] is composed of its own matter and form, but in neither case is the appetite of either one exhausted by its own matter and form; each has a remaining appetite to be joined to the other, the soul to perfect the body, the body to be perfected by the soul. It is in the composite that each one finds its highest development." See also Bynum 1995, 248–51.

8. Bonaventure implies as much when, defending Mary's bodily assumption into heaven, he argues that if Mary were not in heaven with her body, her soul would be hindered from enjoying God and could not be completely happy. See Bynum 1991, 257.

9. "In hoc homine non est alia forma substantialis quam anima rationalis, et per eam homo non solum est homo, sed animal et vivum et corpus et substantia et ens" (in Aquinas 1875, 14:19; my translation).

10. Citations from the *Summa theologiae* (which will be abbreviated ST) are from Aquinas 1964–81.

11. Santi (1987, 867) points out that, in his rejection of unicity of form, Henry of Ghent remarks that the people of London had protested against the partisans of unicity because this doctrine would have made vain the cult of Thomas Becket's head. For the heresies that followed from this interpretation of unicity of form, see Zavalloni 1951, 317–19; Michel 1915, 575–79; and Bynum 1995, 273–74.

12. Aquinas clarifies that "therefore, even if the soul attains salvation in the afterlife, this is not to say that I do or that the human being does" ("unde, licet anima consequatur salutem in alia vita, non tamen ego vel quilibet homo"). For the ambivalence of doctrine of unicity of form with respect to the significance of the body, see Bynum 1995, 266–71.

13. Aquinas conceives the process of human generation according to two principles that Zavalloni (1951, 253–55) and Bazàn (1983, 390–94) define as the principle of "la hiérarchie des formes" (according to which a more perfect principle can confer a less perfect determination, as well the determination proper to it) and the principle of "la succession des formes" (according to which each time one new form appears, any other preceding substantial form passes away).

14. "Sic igitur dicendum est quod anima intellectiva creatur a Deo in fine generationis humanae, quae simul est et sensitiva et nutritiva, corruptis formis praexistentibus."

15. In ST 1a, q.77 ("Whether all the powers of the soul remain in the soul when it is separated from the body"), art. 8, Aquinas writes that "all the soul's powers go back only to the soul as their source. But certain powers, namely understanding and will, are related to the soul taken on its own as their subject of inhesion, and powers of this kind have to remain in the soul after the death of the body. But some powers have the body–soul compound for subject; this is the case with all the powers of sensation and nutrition. Now when the subject goes, the accident cannot stay. Hence when the compound corrupts, such powers do not remain in actual existence. They survive in the soul in a virtual state only, as in their source or root." And in *Supplementum*, q. 70, art. 1, resp., we find the idea that the sensitive powers of the separated soul,

which remain only in a relative sense, will reactivate when the soul gets its body back: "Hence, others say that the sensitive and other like powers do not remain in the separated soul except in a restricted sense, namely radically, in the same way as a result is in its principle: because there remains in the separated soul the ability to produce these powers if it should be reunited to its body; nor is it necessary for this ability to be anything in addition to the essence of the soul, as stated above. This opinion appears to be the more reasonable." Quotations from the *Supplementum* (which was probably put together by Aquinas's disciple Reginald of Piperno with material from the *Sentence* commentary after his master's death) are from Aquinas 1947–48.

16. Michel (1937) explains that all the forms that are educed from matter (because they are potentally contained in primary matter) are liable to corruption and disappear at physical death: "Subordonnées à la forme proprement substantielle qu'est l'âme intellective, les formes inférieures, par exemple, la forme de la chair, la forme des éléments premiers et mixtes, sont sujettes à corruption. Ces formes inférieures se trouvent à l'état de puissance dans la matière et c'est avec une forme de corporéité particulière que l'âme humaine individuelle s'unit pour constituer la substance d'un corps humain. De même donc que cette substance, avant la génération, était en puissance dans la matière qui a été prise pour former le corps de l'individu, de même après la mort elle retombe par la corruption dans cette même matière, pour y rester cachée à l'état de puissance—de *raisons séminales,* dit plus expressément encore saint Bonaventure en reprenant le terme consacré par saint Augustin—jusqu'à ce qu'elle soit rappelée à l'existence par la voix du Dieu tout-puissant" (2560).

17. Nardi (1960, 22–33) shows that this initial, continuous process is close to the one described by Albert the Great in his *De natura et origine animae* (where, on the basis of the doctrine of *inchoatio formae,* which presupposes a sense of primary matter not as mere potentiality but as containing a sort of virtual or imperfect actuality, Albert describes the formation of the human soul and says that it is a substance that comes partly from the inside and partly from the outside) and argues that Statius's account is similar to a position that Aquinas himself had rejected several times: "Hence others say that the vegetative soul is potentially sensitive and that the sensitive soul is its act: so that the vegetative soul which at first is in the semen is raised to the perfection of the sensitive soul by the action of nature; and further that the rational soul is the act and perfection of the sensitive soul, so that the sensitive soul is brought to its perfection [*perducitur ad suum complementum*] consisting in the rational soul, not by the action of the generator but by that of the Creator" (*On the Power of God* 3.9.9 [Aquinas 1932, 1:157]). "Another theory, likewise inadmissible, is stated as follows. . . . [T]he aforsaid seminal power becomes a

vegetative soul; and later, the organs having been perfected and multiplied still more, the same power is raised to the level of a sensitive soul; and finally, with the perfecting of the organs' form, the same soul becomes rational [*eandem animam fieri rationalem*], not, indeed, by the action of that seminal power, but through the influx of an external agent" (*Summa contra Gentiles* 2.89 [in Aquinas 1955–57]). "Therefore others say that the same life-principle [*anima*] that was first merely vegetative, afterwards becomes sensitive through the activity of the seminal power, and finally the same life-principle becomes intellective [*et tandem ipsa eadem perducitur ad hoc ut ipsa eadem fiat intellectiva*], though not through the active seminal power but through the power of a higher agent, namely God, enlightening the soul from outside" (ST 1a, q. 118, a. 2, ad 2). For the continuity of the development in Statius's account up to the formation of the sensitive soul, see Boyde (1981, 275), who also stresses that Statius's "phraseology, syntax and deliberate repetition of key-words do present the embryo's development as one continuous process."

18. See also Gilson 1965, 80–81. Gilson's well-known passion for Aquinas might have misled him on some points and pushed him toward certain exaggerations. Nonetheless, he has the merit of restating the influence of Aquinas's philosophy in Dante's works after Bruno Nardi's fundamental, but sometimes too vigorous, attempt to distinguish Dante's positions from Aquinas's.

19. While Singleton translates "in virtute" (v. 80) as "in potency," I have changed the translation to "as faculties," because, as Chiavacci Leonardi explains in her commentary, "l'espressione *in virtute* non può significare 'in potenza,' cioè 'non in atto,' come molti spiegano, perché nella terzina seguente è detto chiaramente che le facoltà intellettive (*il divino*) restano *in atto* anche più acutamente di prima. Si dovrà dunque intendere *virtute* come 'virtù sostanziale,' nel senso che la parola ha anche a XVIII 51. Tutte le potenze, 'umane e divine,' sono infatti radicate ('in radice,' come si esprime Tommaso) nell'essenza stessa dell'anima" (Alighieri 1991–97, 2:746).

20. "E come l'aere, quand'è ben piorno, / per l'altrui raggio che 'n sé si reflette, / di diversi color diventa addorno; / così l'aere vicin quivi si mette / e in quella forma ch'è in lui suggella / virtüalmente l'alma che ristette" ("And as the air, when it is full of moisture, becomes adorned with various colors by another's rays which are reflected in it, so here the neighboring air shapes itself in that form which is virtually imprinted in it by the soul that stopped there" [*Purg* 25.91–96]).

21. "Whatever appears in the parts of the body is all contained originally and, in a way, implicitly in the soul. . . . neither could man be perfect, unless the whole that is contained enfolded in the soul be outwardly unfolded in the body, nor would the body correspond in full proportion to the soul. Since then at the resurrection it behooves man's body to correspond entirely to the soul,

for it will not rise again except according to the relation it bears to the rational soul, it follows that man must also rise again perfect, seeing that he is thereby repaired in order that he may obtain his ultimate perfection. Consequently all the members that are now in man's body must needs be restored at the resurrection" (*Supplementum,* q. 80, art. 1, resp. [in Aquinas 1964–81]).

22. "Non è forse neanche esagerato affermare che la posizione di Dante sulla materia prima (dalla parte dei tomisti se pure molto individuale) è una delle ragioni per cui si continua a leggere la *Divina Commedia.* . . . Il potere della *Commedia* è che in una serie di incontri con anime umane che sono le forme sostanziali di vere persone, il lettore deve affrontare dure e difficili verità sulla condizione umana. La cultura filosofica che rese possibile lo scrivere di questa *Commedia,* è una dove l'anima umana è l'unica forma sostanziale dell'uomo" (1995, 221).

23. I am currently researching Dante's ambivalence about the power of the (somatized) soul and its imperfection without its real body as part of a larger project on the significance of the body in medieval culture. For the same dialectics in Bonvesin da la Riva, another Italian eschatological writer, see Gragnolati 1999. For the importance that Dante grants the concept of resurrection in the *Commedia,* see Chiavacci Leonardi 1988; Lindheim 1990; and Kirkpatrick 1994, 243–45.

24. While Thomas Aquinas considers the qualities of the resurrection body as spillover from the soul into the body and, therefore, makes the four gifts of the resurrection body dependent on the soul, Bonaventure gives more importance to the body in itself, and makes a distinction between the four gifts' *dispositio* (which belongs to the body per se and derives from God) and *consummatio* (which depends on the soul that activates them). See also Wicki 1954, 287–88.

25. Within such theological language, the use of the word "mamme," typical of *sermo humilis,* is the sign of a move toward tenderness and intimacy. As Barolini (1992, 138) comments, "these souls are happily celebrating the future resurrection of their flesh, that most irreducible husk of selfhood, because only in the flesh will they fully experience their love for 'those who were dear to them *before* they were eternal flames.' In other words, their desire for their dead bodies is an expression of their desire to love fully in heaven what they loved in earth: their 'mamme,' their 'padri,' and the 'altri che fuor cari.' The rhyme of *mamme* with *fiamme,* the flesh with the spirit, is one of Dante's most poignant envisionings of a paradise where earthly ties are not renounced but enhanced."

13

Quando amor fa sentir de la sua pace

Giuliana Carugati

"AMOR mi mosse, che mi fa parlare" ("Love moved me, which compels me to speak"), Beatrice's words in *Inf* 2.72, resume and confirm the design that the *Vita Nuova* had already begun to configure, a design that De Robertis does not hesitate to label "poetic theology" (1961, 45). But what constitutes the basis for this theology? What place does it occupy in relation to the ecclesiastical theology that it both draws upon and reconfigures? Around these issues will circle the brief reflections that I propose here, reflections that retrace some of the most traveled inroads of Dante criticism.

One could begin by asking: what is the poet's point of departure—in terms of life and imagination, of thought and writing—when he starts out on his fictive voyage? The answer is simple: Dante's writing is born from the reflection on the nature of love:

> Allegro mi sembrava Amor tenendo
> meo core in mano, e ne le braccia avea
> madonna involta in un drappo dormendo.
> Poi la svegliava, e d'esto core ardendo
> Lei paventosa umilmente pascea:
> appresso gir lo ne vedea piangendo.
> (*A ciascun'alma presa e gentil core* [Alighieri 1967, 1:9–14])

Love seemed joyful, holding my heart in his hand, while in his arms he had my lady wrapped in a cloth, asleep. Then he awoke her and, though she was afraid, he humbly fed her with his heart which was burning. Then I saw him go away weeping.[1]

We are familiar with one response to this sonnet, a mocking and yet more fitting response than serious commentary may allow. But this is obvious. Less obvious, perhaps, is that the *donna di virtù,* the "lady of power," the divine hypostasis moved by love, of whom Dante speaks in *Inferno* 2, is born of an erotic conflict that the poet, notoriously the enemy of *varietade,* exorcises and resolves in his own distinctively poetic way, that is, by a mode of writing that gives way to *verace intendimento,* "true meaning" (*Vita Nuova* 25.10).

Without the woman first *pietosa* and then *gentile,* the reflection that begins initially *quasi come sognando,* "as in a dream" (*Conv* 2.12.4), gains momentum with the reinforcement of "the words of authors, sciences, and books" (2.12.5), and leads to the "Beatrice-as-idea"—the idea that gives substance to the *Vita Nuova,* the *Convivio,* and the *Commedia*—could not have taken form. The error that Dante so solemnly retracts before Beatrice in the *Purgatorio* is not so much a lack of adherence to the sixth or the ninth commandment (if this were the case, it would not be Beatrice whom Dante should petition for forgiveness) as a slowness to understand, an unjustified need to vary erotic experiences when one, and one only, the first thought-experience, should have sufficed. The poetry of praise, which had already originated in the *Vita Nuova,* had deemed it fit to situate itself around one "who was called by many Beatrice, who did not know how she was called." This name that coincided with the first, most vivid erotic emotion could not be abandoned, fitting as it was; it could not even be substituted with another, or with the non-name that sustains the composition of the *Convivio.* The emotion was the same, however—does not *Voi che 'ntendendo* say "e pensa di chiamarla donna, omai!" ("resolve to call her your lady hereafter")?—and for Dante it became fundamental to understand it. Only then, once it was understood, or at least stated, could the name of Beatrice return to fit it perfectly.

The feminine abstraction that appears in the *Convivio* is one with and the same as the dream-like abstraction of the *Vita Nuova,* or the fictive, loquacious abstraction of the *Commedia.* However, it surely corresponds more closely with those "words of authors, sciences, and books" that had sketched for Dante an answer to his first and foremost concern: what place does *eros* hold in the face of death? What theology, what discourse of god, and which god will reveal it? Or, better, of which god do we speak? What language may explain the self-transcendence that *eros* manifests in so powerful a manner? It is not enough merely to employ the symbolism of an institutional theology that, in its eschatological orientation, gives no space to *eros:* "Those who belong to this age marry and are given in marriage; but those who are considered worthy of a place in that age and in the resurrection from the dead neither marry nor are given in marriage. Indeed they cannot die anymore, because they are like angels and are children of God" (Luke 20:34–36). Instead, one must attempt to reclaim a different set of symbols, one that was more or less "in the air" for thousands of years: the Platonic *répertoire* of symbols found in Boethius and Albertus Magnus, in the *De causis* and in Alain de Lille (not to mention the *Roman de la rose*), and the only one that provides a space for that "thing" from which is born Dante's being as a man and as a writer.

Pietro Alighieri, commenting on the verses that introduce Beatrice in *Inferno* 2, writes:

> Truly a certain woman by the name of Beatrice, noted for her rectitude and beauty, happened to live in Florence at the time of the author: she belonged to a family of certain Florentines who were called Portinari. Our author, Dante, loved and courted this woman while she remained in life, and wrote then many poems in her praise. At her death, to give fame to her name, he desired to make a place for her in his poem principally as allegory and theological type. This is why here [*Inf* 2.51–102], the author, imagining that Virgil speaks of her, makes him describe her as, I quote, "O lady of power, through whom alone the human race lives above all the contents of that heaven whose circles are smallest," which is to say, that which extends from the moon to Empyrean. . . . In the same sense, Alainus in his poem, speaking also of the said theology as a woman, writes: "O regina poli, celi dea, filia summi / . . . cui superum sedes, celi via, limes olimpi, / extramundanus orbis, regioque Tonantis / tota patet, soliumque Dei, fatum quod ultra est" ["O queen of the pole, goddess of heaven, daughter of the highest . . . to whom lies open the abode of the superior beings, the way of the sky, the path of Olympus, the extraworldly universe, the entire region of the thunderer, the throne of God, that which is beyond fate"].[2]

Who is this queen of the celestial pole that Pietro invokes to explain Beatrice? There is at least one contemporary, Guillaume of Auxerre, who without hesitation recognizes in this figure the Neoplatonic *nous:* "hec puella est alma Noys que sapit que sursum sunt, cui patent cause et principia rerum" ("this maiden is the life-giving *nous,* who knows about beings above, to whom are manifest the causes and principles of things") (trans. Bossuat [Alain de Lille 1965, 44]). "Noys" is also the central figure of Bernardus Silvestris's *Cosmographia:*

> Porro Nois ego, dei ratio profundius exquisita, quam utique de se alteram se usia prima genuit—non in tempore sed ex eo quo consistit eterno—Nois ego, scientia et arbitraria divine voluntatis ad dispositionem rerum, quemadmodum de consensu ejus accipio, sic mee administrationis officia circumduco.
>
> (1.2)

> And I am Noys, the consummate and profound reason of God, whom his prime substance brought forth of itself, a second self, not in time, but out of that eternal state in which it abides unmoved. I, Noys, am the knowledge and judgment of the divine will in the disposition of things. I conduct the operations over which I preside accordingly as I am bidden by the harmonious action of that will.
>
> (trans. Wetherbee [Bernardus Silvestris 1973, 69])

Before either Alain or Bernardus Silvestris, and this time within the explicit vicinity of Dante, we find Boethius's *Philosophia:* eternal woman, ancient and coeval with the writer who evokes her, as great as the world but created in the measure of man, capable of touching and penetrating the celestial spheres and of escaping human perception and comprehension. The woman who consoles Boethius represents not merely a literary expedient, but rather the epistemological aspect, inseparable from its ontological counterpart, of the Platonic dyad or triad that constitutes the truth of ancient thought: the one, the father, the principle, who gives himself to be seen as *nous / psychè,* as the intelligible and intelligent world.

Plato's cosmos is contained inside the celestial sphere, which is the "appearing" of its soul, *psychè:* a divine intermediary being, suspended between the immutable and the mutable, between the same and the other, whose "insociable nature" (*Timaeus* 35a) (trans. Jowett [Plato, 1961]) it seeks to tame. Macrobius (*Commentarii in Somnium Scipionis* 1.14.8) merges *psychè* with *nous, anima mundi* with *intelligentia:*

> Anima ergo creans sibi condensque corpora—nam ideo ab anima natura incipit quam sapientes de deo et de mente noun nominant—ex illo mero et purissimo fonte mentis, quem nascendo de originis suae hauserat copia, corpora divina vel supera, caeli dico et siderum, quae prima condebat, animavit.

> Soul, creating and fashioning bodies for itself—on that account the creation, which men who really know about God and mind call *nous*, has its beginning in Soul—out of that pure and clearest fount of Mind from whose abundance it had drunk deep at birth, endowed those divine or ethereal bodies, meaning the celestial sphere and the stars which it was first creating, with mind.
>
> (trans. Stahl [Macrobius 1952, 143–44])

This notion infuses the whole of classical philosophy: to the One, identical to himself and unknowable, succeeds the cosmic soul, intelligent and intelligible, the appearing and becoming of *archè*. The primal place of its unveiling is the celestial sphere; it is the breath, *pneuma*, the fiery spirit, or (as Aristotle terms it) the ether of which the celestial bodies are made, which produces "becoming" and therefore generation. For Plato, the *psychè* itself is *sperma* (*Timaeus* 73b–d); it resides in the seed—or actually it is the same as the seed—and this seed is contained in the brain and in the marrow, even explicitly identified with the marrow: "And the seed, having life and becoming endowed with respiration, produces in that part in which it respires a lively desire of emission, and thus creates in us the love of procreation" (*Timaeus* 91a–b, trans. Jowett). Aristotle takes up and emphasizes the celestial, ethereal, pneumatic origin of sperm (*De generatione animalium* 736b 35): "For within the seed of everything there is present that which makes the seeds to be fertile, the so-called hot. This is not fire or that sort of capability, but *pneuma* enclosed within the seed and within the foamy part, and more precisely the nature in the *pneuma,* being analogous to the element of the stars" (trans. Balone [Aristotle 1992]). So, the cosmic soul, god of the heavenly bodies, literally penetrates into the marrow of man to become his generating force: it circulates in the male to confer upon him the power of life.

From the most ancient writers, the breath of the world, the cosmic soul, receives feminine names: "Kypris is not only Kypris"—writes Sophocles—"but she is called by many names. She is both Hades and immortal life, and a mad frenzy. . . . She sinks into the souls of all whose lungs have breath—who is not weaker than this god?" (Fragment 855, cited by Dronke 1965, 392). For Plotinus (whose formal distinction between *nous* and *psychè* is not maintained by everyone), the transcendent and universal soul is Aphrodite:

> Who then is Aphrodite . . . ? To us Aphrodite is twofold; there is the heavenly Aphrodite, daughter of Ouranos, and there is the other, the daughter of Zeus and Dione. . . . The Heavenly Aphrodite, daughter of Kronos—who is no other than the Intellectual principle—must be the Soul at its divinest: unmingled as the immediate emanation of the unmingled; remaining ever above, as neither desirous nor capable of descending to this sphere, never having developed the downward tendency . . . justly called not celestial spirit but God. . . . But following upon Kronos—or, if you will, upon Ouranos, the father of Kronos—the soul directs its act towards him and holds closely to him and in that love brings forth the eros through whom it continues to look towards him. . . . Love, thus, is ever intent upon that other loveliness, and exists to be the medium between desire and that object of desire.
>
> (trans. MacKenna [*Enneads* 3.5.2])

We are dealing with an "erotic" vision of being. But because death is ineluctably inscribed in being, Aphrodite divides herself, giving herself as "heavenly" and "earthly," the latter, the ephemeral, reabsorbed by the former, which is the eternal, immutable inflection of being.

What disturbs this erotic vision of the world? What happens to this catachretic construct that is the cosmic soul? When does it disappear or, rather, sink beneath orthodoxy, as the poetic and philosophical figure in feminine garb with which man represents for himself his own ontological insufficiency? Not even Saint Augustine dared to exclude the *anima mundi* from the new theological design that he himself with so much force was contributing to trace (see Bourke 1954, 436). For a long time, this figure, never altogether Christianized in an orthodox sense, survives confusedly in theological discourses, as evidenced by Manegold di Lautenbach's outraged list of the "dissonant and controverted opinions," according to which the ancients, "inflated with the reasonings of the flesh," more or less relinquished the truth, except perhaps Plato, "who appears to come close enough to the truth." Among the other "relinquishers of the truth" are some who hold the *anima mundi* to be "a self-moving number," while "some see it as *entelecheian,* which means 'form of the body,' some as the idea, some as the exercise of the five senses, some as a thin spirit, some as light, some as the spark of a star's essence, some as a spirit ingrown in the body, some as a spirit inserted into the atoms, some as made from the fifth essence, some as fire, some as air, some as blood, some as a mixture of earth and fire, or of earth and water, or of air and fire and spirit" (cited in Garin 1958, 28; my translation). It is the school of Chartres, with its cosmological and naturalistic reading of the *Timaeus,* that will finally distance the notion of the *anima mundi* from the theological sphere, a distancing the Council of Sens sanctioned by condemning Abelard's thesis that the Holy Spirit is the *anima mundi.* Thus, as we have seen, the cosmic and astral soul, intelligent and generating, *nous* and *psychè,* Aphrodite heavenly and earthly, reemerges at times "erotic" and at others institutional, according to the particular interests and social obligations of the author. From the narrow bounds of the concept in which it was, in reality, never confined, it gives itself freely in the body of poetry. Thus, Jean de Meun's *Reson* (but also *Nature*), thus Alain de Lille's "theologia," to which Pietro Aligheri, in what could at first seem an inexcusable incongruity, assimilates Beatrice without hesitation (a Beatrice who is already no longer the Portinari girl to whom his father Dante was "procus" and "amator").

Beatrice is born out of an idea of the world, out of a way of thinking about "being" that takes its origin from a reflection on the nature of *eros.* Now, thought is always a thought about *eros,* that is, about the transcendence of self to oneself, about being given to oneself by another, about the unreachable, transcendent unity that reveals itself only through the insatiate gesture that seeks it and, in tatters, fleetingly, *dimidia hora,* finds it. Might Dante's greatness be born from the tenacity and precision of thought with which the poet structures a theology of love? "I' mi son un che, quando / Amor mi spira, noto, e a quel modo / ch'e' ditta dentro vo significando" ("I am one who, when Love breathes in me, takes note; what he, within, dictates, I, in that way, without, would speak and shape" [*Purg* 24.52–54] [trans. Mandelbaum [Alighieri 1982)]).[3] We are in the grammatical present tense, one that detaches itself from its fictive purgatorial context, to extend to all of Dante's writing and its essential, inexhaustible source. And it seems that one could well see Dante as the first, outside of the protected discourse of the Song of Songs (protected, I mean, within the eschatologizing enclosure of the monastery), who dared to reintroduce an erotic thinking into the heart of a Christian *doxa* that was refractory, even reticent.

Beatrice, the poetic, the cosmic Beatrice, is born from the conflictual repetitions of the love-experience and the philosophical problem that results from them. The *Vita Nuova,* a thought that becomes a narrative, opens dramatically with the mythical moment of the birth of love: "lo spirito della vita, lo quale dimora nella secretissima camera del cuore, cominciò a tremare sì fortemente, che apparia ne li menimi polsi orribilmente; e tremando disse queste parole: *Ecce deus fortior me, qui veniens dominabitur michi*" ("the vital spirit, the one that dwells in the most secret chamber of the heart, began to tremble so violently that even the most minute veins of my body were strangely affected; and trembling it spoke these words" [2.4] [trans. Musa (Alighieri 1973)]).[4] Commentators send us back, rightly, to Albertus Magnus, but behind him lurks the inescapable outline of the erotic *pneuma* in Plato, Aristotle, and Galen, the *pneuma* that circles in the cosmos from the stars to the brain, the marrow, and the sperm: the breath, the spirit, the soul that are the "appearing," the incarnation of the god. The spirit "started to tremble" and "trembling, said"; the insistent trembling emphasizes the carnality of the phenomenon that Dante, like Plato and Saint Augustine before him, places at the center of his inquiry.[5] The tremor causes the ineffable unity of the first and last things to appear, to flash before us, or come to realization—"*Apparuit iam beatitudo vestra*"—as threatened blessedness, contingent on the unpredictability of fate and the fragility of the words that guard it. In the *Vita Nuova*'s "maravigliosa visione" (3.3.9), Love weeps because Bice dies. But what the death of Bice—the death out of which Beatrice is born—stages dramatically is that which is nevertheless inherent in erotic blessedness: the figure itself of the "freely given," that which is aleatory and ephemeral. The god weeps because in its incarnated divinity it confines itself eternally to the blindness of matter and finally to death. To place *eros* at the center of the circle (*Vita Nuova* 12.4) means to cause the *archè* to sink in the gesture in which the other appears—and which causes the other to appear. The god weeps because, at the center of the circle, it sees the eternal declining into death, which threatens the "circumference" made of *simulacra* perpetually *praetermittenda* and *praetermissa.*

One could say that Beatrice as "soul" is the giving and the enduring of love, the repetition of the erotic emotion: she is love itself: "e chi volesse sottilmente considerare, quella Beatrice chiamerebbe Amore per molta similitudine che ha meco" ("anyone of subtle discernment would call Beatrice Love, because she so greatly resembles me" [*Vita Nuova* 24.5]). Beatrice as "intelligence," on the other hand, is the word that the male-poet (but man is always, in some way, a poet) speaks: the words of god, the intelligibility of god: *nous, logos, theologia:*

> Vennemi volontade di volere dire anche in loda di questa gentilissima parole, per le quali io mostrasse come per lei si sveglia questo Amore, e non solamente si sveglia là dove dorme, ma là ove non è in potenzia, ella, mirabilmente operando, lo fa venire.
>
> (*Vita Nuova* 21.1)

> I felt a desire to write more, this time in praise of that most gracious lady, showing how, through her, this love is awakened, and how she not only awakens him there where he sleeps but also, how she, miraculously working, brings him into existence there where he does not potentially exist.

The *Convivio,* which, as we know, does not intend to derogate from the *libello,* might be seen as the attempt to systematize conceptually this interweaving of ancient theologies in which figures of thought overlap and penetrate each other, forsaking every logical reduction. It is an enterprise of the extreme difficulty of which the author is keenly aware: "E dico che 'move sovente cose che fanno disviare lo 'ntelletto.' E veramente dico; però che li miei pensieri, di costei ragionando, molte fiate voleano cose conchiudere di lei che io non le potea intendere, e smarrivami, sì che quasi parea di fuori alienato" ("And I say that it 'often stirs thoughts that bewilder the intellect.' I speak truly, for in speaking of her my thoughts many times desired to conclude things about her which I could not understand, and I was so bewildered that outwardly I seemed almost beside myself" [3.3.13; trans. Lansing here and elsewhere]).[6]

But the *canzoni* of the *Convivio* also represent the most successful synthesis of Dante's "erotic poetics," poetics that not even the *Commedia* will forsake. In fact, Beatrice will disturb the poem's theological-institutional equilibrium with her obstinate and incongruous presence even in the heights of the empyrean. Perhaps Dante criticism has been excessively occupied with the literal / allegorical opposition, as if the interpretative scheme that Dante proposes were to be taken, in its turn, by the letter, rather than valued as an integrated part of a poetic vision that transcends it. It is true that Dante himself misleads us; but this is Dante the exile, whose condition forces him to mount a stage different from the one of traditional love poetry, and to pursue a logical-conceptual "truth" with which his mythical-poetic vision is destined, ultimately, to collide. We find the authentic statement of his poetics, it seems to me, in chapter 12 of the second treatise of the *Convivio:* "Poi che la litterale sentenza è sufficientemente dimostrata, è da procedere a la esposizione allegorica e vera" ("Now that the literal meaning has been sufficiently explained, we must proceed to the allegorical and true exposition"). Now, we know that the "demonstration" of the literal meaning, besides being a "historical" introduction to the amorous conflict that the gentle lady brings about—"quella gentile donna, cui feci menzione ne la fine de la Vita Nuova" ("that gentle lady, of whom I made mention at the end of the *New Life*" [2.2.1])—is altogether other than an analysis of a sentimental episode, coming to resemble something between a compendium of astrotheology and an *explication de texte.* What about the "allegorical and true exposition"? The allegorical assumption prohibits the "historical" amorous conflict from being directly evoked here, but the loss of the "primo diletto de la mia anima," the first delight of his soul, is still recorded, as is the sweetness, transformed into the *virtù,* the power, of the second delight. But how could this sweetness and this power "dispel" and "destroy" "every other thought" (12.7), namely, the thought of the dead Bice? With the death of Bice and the birth of the new love, the "cosmic" thought takes form, the thought in which Dante expresses not something else, but love itself, catachretically, as thought: "quasi maravigliandomi apersi la bocca nel parlare de la proposta canzone, mostrando la mia condizione sotto figura di altre cose: però che la donna di cu'io m'innamorava non era degna rima di volgare alcuna palesemente poetare" ("almost in amazement I opened my mouth to speak the words of the canzone before us, revealing my condition beneath the figure of other things, because no rhyme in any vernacular was worthy to treat openly of the lady of whom I was enamored" [12.8]). What is the "condition" in which the poet finds himself? Is it love or the study of philosophy? Which is the woman he loves? What happened to the *gentile?* What is the true meaning—love for philosophy? What is the fictitious meaning—the allegorical image of the gentle woman? But had not the allegorical meaning been declared the true one? Dante's unease is evident, as is his desire to move in the direction of a Scholastic form of writing refractory to the power of metaphor.

Dante was born a poet of love, and a poet of love he remains. The audience to which the "new words"—the poetically and philosophically revolutionary "ragionare"—are addressed is the Intelligences of the third heaven, astral, pneumatic, and "gentle," as are the women who allow the amorous *pneuma* to pass through their eyes. These

Intelligences are the retinue and manifestation of the cosmic soul, of the ancient Aphrodite, or of Cyprian the fair, the *bella Ciprigna,* who sends down *il folle amore,* as we see in *Paradiso* 8. The heaven of Venus is not a palinode of the *canzone,* but rather an attempt to place in an eschatological perspective that *eros,* which is the first principle of life and of word: "e da costei ond'io principio piglio / pigliavano il vocabol della stella / che 'l sol vagheggia or da coppa, or da ciglio" ("and gave the name of her from whom I take my beginning, to the planet that is courted by the sun, at times behind her and at times in front" [*Par* 8.10–12; Mandelbaum translation modified]). Who is "costei ond'io principio piglio"? The divine *nous / psychè?* The mother of *eros* of which Plotinus speaks? Boethius's *Providentia / Philosophia?* The "donna mia chi'i' vidi far più bella" ("my lady whom I saw grow more beautiful" [*Par* 8.15])? The landscape is the same, and the correction that the mature poet is alleged to have made in the *Paradiso* is doubtful; witness these lines spoken by Cunizza: "e qui refulgo / perchè mi vinse il lume d'esta stella" ("I shine here because this planet's radiance conquered me" [*Par* 9.32–33]). *Eros* manifests itself differently, as is inevitable in each human life, and as is demonstrated by the exemplary lives of those loving spirits that the poet chooses to populate the sky of Venus: "Non però qui si pente, ma si ride, / non della colpa, ch'a mente non torna, / ma del valor ch'ordinò e provide" ("Yet one does not repent here; here one smiles—not for the fault, which we do not recall, but for the Power that fashioned and foresaw" [*Par* 9.103–105]). Therefore, the "valor ch'ordinò e provide" does not disappear: *eros,* the *eros* that cries over the ephemeral and over the muteness of the flesh, belongs to the sphere of the divine.

It is *eros, pneuma* proceeding from "intelligence" and manifesting itself in "soul," that imbues both the body and the mind with spirit, as stated in the opening verse of the *canzone Amor che ne la mente mi ragiona.* Dante writes in the *Convivio:*

> Amore, per lo quale si può conoscere quale è dentro l'anima, veggendo di fuori quelli che ama. Questo amore, cioè l'unimento de la mia anima con questa gentil donna, ne la quale de la divina luce assai mi si mostrava, è quello ragionatore del quale io dico; poi che da lui continui pensieri nasceano, miranti e esaminanti lo valore di questa donna che spiritualmente fatta era con la mia anima una cosa.
>
> (*Conv* 3.2.9)

> Love, whereby we are able to know the quality of the soul within by seeing outside it those things which it loves. This love (that is, the union of my mind with this gentle lady in whom so much of the divine light was revealed to me) is that speaker of whom I speak, for thoughts were continually being born of him that would gaze upon and ponder the worth of this lady who spiritually was made one with my soul.

Now, thought, born of love, which is where "l'anima più profondamente che altrove si ingegna" ("the soul invests, more than it does elsewhere, all its expressive resources [*Conv* 3.4.3; translation mine]), contemplates or configures, in "one mind" with it, that "self-giving" of the *archè* that appears to man in feminine figure:

> E se essa umana forma, essemplata e individuata, non è perfetta, non è manco del detto essemplo, ma de la materia la quale individua. Però quando dico: *Ogni Intelletto di là su la mira,* non voglio altro dire se non ch'ella è così fatta come l'essempio intenzionale che de la umana essenza è ne la divina mente.
>
> (*Conv* 3.6.6)

> And if the human form is not perfect when reproduced in individual beings, it is not the fault of the exemplar but of the material which furnishes individuality. Therefore when I say *Every Intelligence admires her from above,* I mean only that she is created as the intentional exemplar of the human essence which is in the divine mind.

From women, we move through the same *eros,* to the contemplation of Woman, *logos,* in which the *simplicissimum* of *archè* expands.

For man, for the male writer, to think of god is to think of woman: theology is erotically inflected (as the entirety of biblical prophetic and wisdom literature corroborates). He who falls in love, insofar as he thinks, thinks god in the only way in which god is thinkable, namely, in his intelligible hypostasis. When Dante says "quasi meravigliandomi" at the moment of consigning to us his philosophy, theology, and poetics, we know that he is well aware of the radical originality of his message, that is to say, of its profound antiquity. Dante's allegory here is none other than the investigation of an erotic emotion that he will never foreswear. We are indeed very far from an Augustinian Petrarch who prays (or does he?) to be an immovable stone ("immobile saxum") rather than be troubled by so many motions of the body ("tam multis corporis meis motibus turbari"), and who affirms that the use of

Venus takes away the vision of the deity ("usum Veneris conspectum divinitatis eripere" [*Secretum* 2]).

The great *canzone* around which we have been circling seems to move simultaneously within the two registers of theology (here of much more distinctly Proclian character, as confirmed through the citations of *De causis* that are found in the commentary) and of amorous poetry, providing ammunition for the supporters of both the literal and the allegorical. Love reasons in the mind and thinks of profound things, but desiringly, "disïosamente" (v. 2) and "Lo suo parlar sì dolcemente sona, / che l'anima ch'ascolta e che lo sente / dice: 'Oh me lassa, ch'io non son possente / di dir quel ch'odo de la donna mia!'" ("His speech sounds so sweetly that the soul, as she attends and hears, says: 'Alas that I am unable to express what I hear of my lady!'" [vv. 5–8]). This is not the rhetoric of a theologian; if anything it is that of a musician, and it certainly is not an oversight to have put the *canzone* in the mouth of the nostalgic, all too terrestrial, Casella in *Purgatorio* 2. Let us attend to *Amor che ne la mente:* "Li atti soavi ch'ella mostra altrui / vanno chiamando Amor ciascuno a prova / in quella voce che lo fa sentire" ("The gracious actions that she displays vie with each other in calling on Love with such a voice as must awaken him" [vv. 45–47]), and later "Cose appariscon ne lo suo aspetto, / che mostran de' piacer di Paradiso, / dico ne li occhi e nel suo dolce riso, / che le vi reca Amor com'a suo loco" ("In her aspect things appear that show the joys of Paradise—I mean in her eyes and her lovely smile; for it is there, as to the place which belongs to him, that Love leads them" [vv. 55–58]). Such carnality is even more evident in the intertextual reference in the *congedo* to the "fera e disdegnosa" ("the proud and disdainful woman" [v. 76]). We are, therefore, in the terrestrial range, the range of glances and smiles, of shudders of the body and of insatiate desire. And yet, behind the individuated form of the *donna gentile,* and precisely because the woman is *gentile,* the eternal "essemplo" emerges: "costei pensò chi mosse l'universo" ("she was in the mind of him who set the universe in motion" [v. 72]). If women are not perfect, "it is not the fault of the exemplar but of the material which furnishes individuality" (*Conv* 3.6.6). Women are introduced to the divine essence when they are noble, when they open themselves to love: "gentile è in donna ciò che in lei si trova, / e bello è tanto quanto lei simiglia" ("nobility in woman is what is found in her, and beauty is all that resembles her" [vv. 49–50]). The "individuated" woman, provides she "walks with her," the goddess, and "marks her gestures," enjoys, in the eyes of the poet, the privilege of touching the divine, which he may only name with his words.

But let us come to the "peace" of the verse that is my title, which appears in the second stanza of *Amor che ne la mente:*

> Non vede il sol, che tutto 'l mondo gira,
> cosa tanto gentil, quanto in quell'ora
> che luce ne la parte ove dimora
> la donna, di cui dire Amor mi face.
> Ogni Intelletto di là su la mira,
> e quella gente che qui s'innamora
> ne' lor pensieri la truovano ancora,
> quando Amor fa sentir de la sua pace.
> (vv. 19–26)

The sun that circles the whole world never sees anything so noble as when its light falls there where dwells the lady of whom Love makes me speak. All Intelligences on high gaze at her, and those who here below are in love still find her in their thoughts, when Love brings them to partake of his peace.

What is this peace? Let us turn to *Amor, che movi tua vertù da cielo,* a *canzone* that is even more unequivocally "terrestrial":

> Falle sentire, Amor, per tua dolcezza,
> il gran disio ch'i' ho di veder lei;
> non soffrir che costei
> per giovanezza mi conduca a morte:
> ché non s'accorge ancor com'ella piace,
> né quanto io l'amo forte,
> né che ne li occhi porta la mia pace.
> (vv. 54–60)

Make her feel with your sweetness, Love, the great longing I have to see her. Do not permit her to bring me to death by her youth; for she is not yet aware how fair she is, nor how intensely I love her, nor that in her eyes she bears my peace.

Or we could consider the other *canzone, E' m'incresce di me sì duramente,* that many authoritative critics believe refers to Bice herself, rather than to the *donna gentile,* where we find again "eyes" and "peace":

> Oïmè, quanto piani,
> soavi e dolci ver me si levaro,
> quand'elli incominciaro
> la morte mia, che tanto mi dispiace,
> dicendo: "nostro lume porta pace!"
> "Noi darem pace al core, a voi diletto,"
> diceano a li occhi miei
> quei della bella donna alcuna volta
> (vv. 10–17)

Alas, how soft, sweet and gentle they were as they lifted towards me, when they began to cause the death that so grieves me, saying; "Our light brings peace!" "Peace we'll bring to the heart and joy to you," they said—the eyes of the fair lady—to my eyes on several occasions.

Here the poet leaves no room for doubt regarding the erotic connotation of such peace, promised, however falsely, by the eyes of the "individuated" woman, whoever she may be. And, it seems to me, one might have at least some doubts about the meaning of the famous "peace" in the *canzone Così nel mio parlar voglio esser aspro:*[7]

> S'io avessi le belle trecce prese,
> che fatte son per me scudiscio e ferza,
> pigliandole anzi terza,
> con esse passerei vespero e squille:
> e non sarei pietoso né cortese,
> anzi farei com'orso quando scherza;
> e se Amor me ne sferza,
> io mi vendicherei di più di mille.
> Ancor ne li occhi, ond'escon le faville
> che m'infiammano il cor, ch'io porto anciso,
> guarderei presso e fiso,
> per vendicar lo fuggir che mi face;
> e poi le renderei con amor pace.
> (vv. 66–78)

Once I'd taken in my hand the fair locks which have become my whip and lash, seizing them before terce I'd pass through vespers with them and the evening bell: and I'd not show pity or courtesy, O no, I'd be like a bear at play. And though Love whips me with them now, I would take my revenge more than a thousandfold. Still more, I'd gaze into those eyes whence come the sparks that inflame my heart which is dead within me; I'd gaze into them close and fixedly, to revenge myself on her for fleeing from me as she does: and then with love I would make our peace.

Foster, who cannot be suspected of unorthodox tendencies, writes: "It is more than probable, in this welter of erotic violence, that Dante intended an allusion to the act of love" (Alighieri 1967, 2:280).

One could say that in "amorous" contexts the word "peace" retains not merely the allusive but also the connotative value that we find in the troubadours' *joi.* What is, then, the "peace" that, in the words of *Amor che ne la mente,* love causes to be felt in the thoughts of "people who fall in love"? Of the people who fall in love "here," not "up there," who overcome pride and disdain in order to become mediators of love? We have already answered this question, but our response is not yet complete. Because in "quando Amor fa sentir de la sua pace," as I read it, the two registers of the *canzone,* the amorous and the cosmotheological, come together, ingathered within the initial spark of thought, as thought of *eros.* This is where the *dimidia hora* of the mystic, the sinking of words in the "experience" of the absolute beginning coincides, in the words that speak about it, with the impenetrable instant of the peace of the flesh. *Quando Amor fa sentir de la sua pace:* this "partitive" construction—"de la *sua* pace"—has been widely commented upon. We will say that both words and the body know of only a partial peace. No totality is ever reached, *in via:* desire, and words, are reborn like the phoenix from their own ashes. God is only reached in death—real death. This is why Dante, for one, will keep speaking, "cantando il santo riso," without recanting anything, until his path will be cut off (cf. *Par* 23.59–63), and the poet will be enveloped by the silence of matter, and of god.

NOTES

1. The translations from Dante's lyrics, here and elsewhere, are Foster and Boyde's (Alighieri 1967).

2. Pietro is quoted from Dartmouth Dante Project (www.dartmouth. edu/ ~library/). Pietro refers, loosely, to *Anticlaudianus* 5.178–85. The translations from Pietro and Alainus are mine.

3. The translations from the *Divine Comedy,* here and elsewhere are Allen Mandelbaum's (Alighieri 1982 and 1984).

4. The translations from the *Vita Nuova,* here and elsewhere are from Mark Musa's (Alighieri 1973).

5. Other famous passages confirm the significance of *tremare,* from "chi avesse voluto conoscere Amore, fare lo potea mirando lo tremare de li occhi miei" (*Viva Nuova* 11.3) to "la bocca mi baciò tutto tremante" (*Inf* 5.136).

6. In the same vein, see also *Conv* 3.4.2–3: "a me conviene lasciare per povertà d'intelletto molto di quello che è vero di lei. . . . dico non pur a quello che lo mio intelletto non sostiene, ma eziandio a quello che io intendo sufficiente non sono, però che la mia lingua non è di tanta facundia che dire potesse ciò che nel pensiero mio se ne ragiona; per che è da vedere che, a rispetto de la veritade, poco fia quello che dirà" ("For because of the poverty of my intellect it is necessary to leave aside much that is true about her I assert that my inability extends not only to what my intellect does not grasp but even to what I do understand, because my tongue lacks the eloquence to be able to express what is spoken of her in my thought. Consequently it will be apparent that what I shall say concerning the truth will be quite little") and 3.4.9: "dico che nostro intelletto, per difetto de la virtù da la quale trae quello ch'el vede, che è virtù organica, cioè la fantasia, non puote a certe cose salire (però che la fantasia nol puote aiutare, che non ha lo di che), sì come sono sustanze partite da materia" ("I say that our intellect, by defect of that faculty from which it draws what it perceives, which is an organic power, namely the fantasy, cannot rise to certain things (because the fantasy cannot assist it, since it lacks the means), such as the substances separate from matter."

7. Contini's interpretation of this "pace" as "perdono" perhaps misses the mark out of an excess of philological preoccupation; see Alighieri (1946) 1970, 171.

PHILOSOPHIES: WORKS CITED

Aegidius Romanus 1556. *De regimine principum.* Rome: Antonius Bladus.

Alain de Lille. 1965. *Anticlaudianus.* Trans. Robert Bossuat. Paris: Vrin.

Albertus Magnus. 1890. *De meteoris.* Vol. 4 of *Opera Omnia.* Ed. August Borgnet. Paris: Vivès.

Alighieri, Dante. [1946] 1970. *Rime.* Ed. Gianfranco Contini. 2nd ed. Milan: Einaudi.

______. 1964. *Il Convivio ridotto a miglior lezione e commentato da G. Busnelli e G. Vandelli, con introduzione di Michele Barbi.* Ed. Antonio E. Quaglio. 2nd ed. 2 vols. Florence: Le Monnier.

______. 1966–67. *La Commedia secondo l'antica vulgata.* Ed. Giorgio Petrocchi. 4 vols. Milano: Mondadori.

______. 1967. *Dante's Lyric Poetry.* Ed. Kenelm Foster and Patrick Boyde. 2 vols. Oxford: Oxford University Press.

______. 1970–75. *The Divine Comedy.* Trans. and ed. Charles S. Singleton. 3 vols. in 6. Princeton, N.J.: Princeton University Press.

______. 1973. *The Vita Nuova: A Translation and an Essay.* Trans. Mark Musa. Bloomington: Indiana University Press.

______. 1982. *The Divine Comedy of Dante Alighieri: Purgatorio.* Trans. Allen Mandelbaum. Berkeley: University of California Press.

______. 1984. *The Divine Comedy of Dante Alighieri: Paradiso.* Trans. Allen Mandelbaum. Berkeley: University of California Press.

______. 1990. *Dante's Il Convivio: The Banquet.* Trans. Richard H. Lansing. New York and London: Garland.

______. 1991–97. *Commedia.* Ed. Anna Maria Chiavacci Leonardi. 3 vols. Milan: Mondadori.

______. 1994. *Purgatorio.* Vol. 3 of *La Commedia secondo l'antica vulgata.* Ed. Giorgio Petrocchi. Florence: Le Lettere.

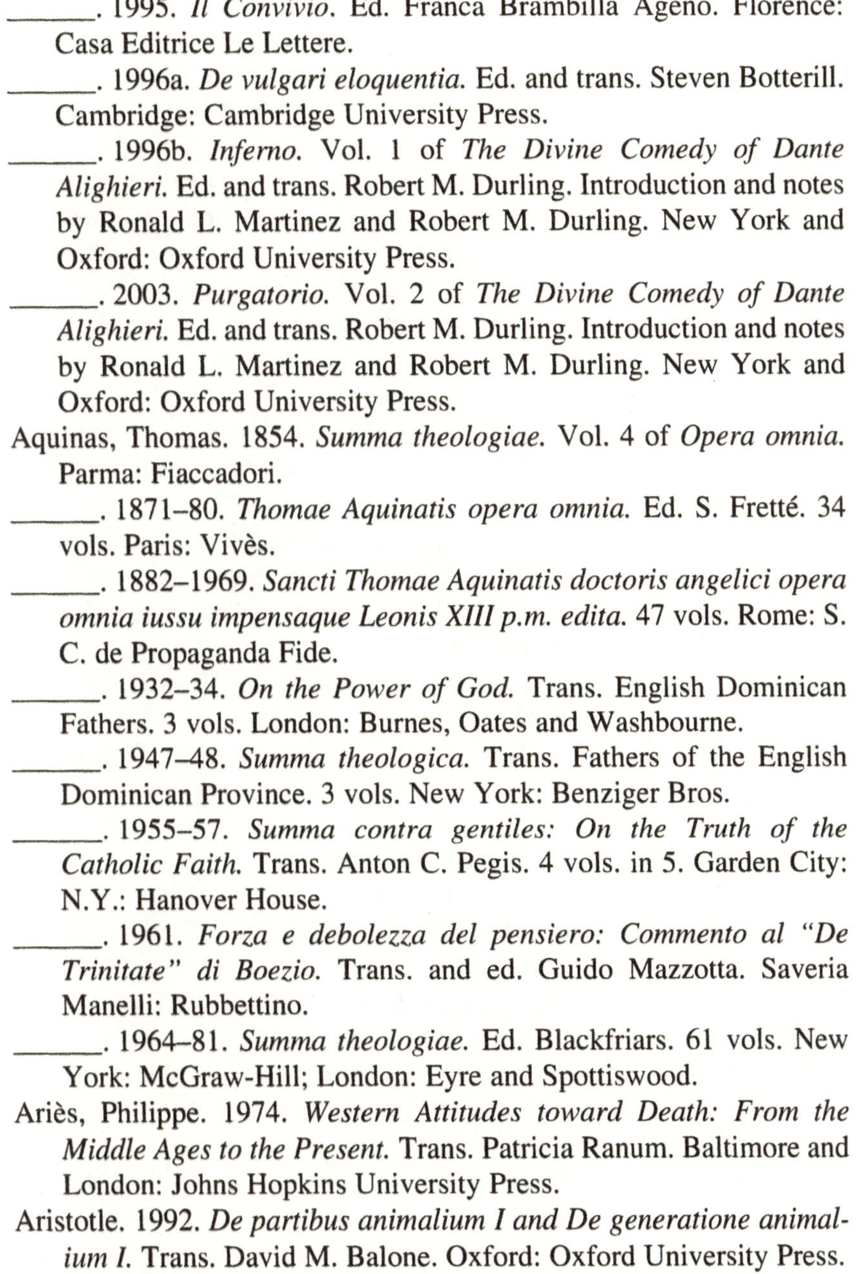

______. 1995. *Il Convivio*. Ed. Franca Brambilla Ageno. Florence: Casa Editrice Le Lettere.

______. 1996a. *De vulgari eloquentia*. Ed. and trans. Steven Botterill. Cambridge: Cambridge University Press.

______. 1996b. *Inferno*. Vol. 1 of *The Divine Comedy of Dante Alighieri*. Ed. and trans. Robert M. Durling. Introduction and notes by Ronald L. Martinez and Robert M. Durling. New York and Oxford: Oxford University Press.

______. 2003. *Purgatorio*. Vol. 2 of *The Divine Comedy of Dante Alighieri*. Ed. and trans. Robert M. Durling. Introduction and notes by Ronald L. Martinez and Robert M. Durling. New York and Oxford: Oxford University Press.

Aquinas, Thomas. 1854. *Summa theologiae*. Vol. 4 of *Opera omnia*. Parma: Fiaccadori.

______. 1871–80. *Thomae Aquinatis opera omnia*. Ed. S. Fretté. 34 vols. Paris: Vivès.

______. 1882–1969. *Sancti Thomae Aquinatis doctoris angelici opera omnia iussu impensaque Leonis XIII p.m. edita*. 47 vols. Rome: S. C. de Propaganda Fide.

______. 1932–34. *On the Power of God*. Trans. English Dominican Fathers. 3 vols. London: Burnes, Oates and Washbourne.

______. 1947–48. *Summa theologica*. Trans. Fathers of the English Dominican Province. 3 vols. New York: Benziger Bros.

______. 1955–57. *Summa contra gentiles: On the Truth of the Catholic Faith*. Trans. Anton C. Pegis. 4 vols. in 5. Garden City: N.Y.: Hanover House.

______. 1961. *Forza e debolezza del pensiero: Commento al "De Trinitate" di Boezio*. Trans. and ed. Guido Mazzotta. Saveria Manelli: Rubbettino.

______. 1964–81. *Summa theologiae*. Ed. Blackfriars. 61 vols. New York: McGraw-Hill; London: Eyre and Spottiswood.

Ariès, Philippe. 1974. *Western Attitudes toward Death: From the Middle Ages to the Present*. Trans. Patricia Ranum. Baltimore and London: Johns Hopkins University Press.

Aristotle. 1992. *De partibus animalium I and De generatione animalium I*. Trans. David M. Balone. Oxford: Oxford University Press.

______. 1995. *La Metaura d'Aristotile: Volgarizzamento fiorentino anonimo del XIV secolo*. Ed. Rita Librandi. Naples: Ligouri.

Augustine. 1895. *Sancti Aureli Augustini Hipponensis Episcopi Epistulae*. Ed. A. Grumbacher. CSEL 44. Leipzig: Freytag.

______. 1955. *Sancti Aureli Augustini De civitate Dei libri xxii.* Ed. Bernard Dombart and Alphonse Kalb. CCSL 47–48. Turnholt: Brepols.

______. 1967. *Sancti Aureli Augustini De sermone Domini in monte libri duo.* Ed. Almut Mutzenbecher. CCSL 35. Turnholt: Brepols.

______. 1990. *Sancti Aureli Augustini Confessionum libri xiii.* Ed. Lucas Verleijen, O.S.A. CCSL 27. Turnholt: Brepols.

Barański, Zygmunt G. 1996. "I trionfi del volgare: Dante e il plurilinguismo." In *"Sole nuovo, luce nuova": Saggi sul rinnovamento culturale in Dante.* Turin: Scriptorium. 42–77.

______. 1997. "Dante and Medieval Poetics." In *Dante: Contemporary Perspectives.* Ed. Amilcare A. Iannucci. Toronto: University of Toronto Press. 3–22.

Barolini, Teodolinda. 1992. *The Undivine "Comedy": Detheologizing Dante.* Princeton, N.J.: Princeton University Press.

Battaglia, Salvatore, ed. 1988. *Grande dizionario della lingua italiana.* Vol. 14. Turin: UTET. 133–36.

Bazàn, Bernardo C. 1983. "La corporalité selon saint Thomas." *Revue philosophique de Louvain* 4th ser., 51:369–400.

Bernardus Silvestris. 1973. *The "Cosmographia" of Bernardus Silvestris.* Trans. Winthrop Wetherbee. New York and London: Columbia University Press.

Berti, Enrico. 1984. "De Meteoris." In ED 2:364–65.

Bettoni, Efrem. 1970. "Anima." In ED 1:278–85.

Biffi, Vincenzo Cherubino. 1984. Introduction to *La Sapienza cristiana.* Milan: Jaca Book. 7–27.

Bonaventure. 1934. *Collationes in Hexaemeron* Vol. 5 of *Opera Omnia.* Quaracchi: College of Saint Bonaventure.

______. 1962. *The Breviloquium.* In *The Works of Bonaventure.* Trans. José de Vinck. 5 vols. Paterson, New Jersey: St. Anthony Guild.

Bono Giamboni. 1994. *Fiore di rettorica.* Ed. Giambattista Speroni. Pavia: Università di Pavia.

Botterill, Steven. 1994. *Dante and the Mystical Tradition: Bernard of Clairvaux in Dante's "Commedia."* Cambridge and New York: Cambridge University Press.

______. 1996. "Dante's Poetics of the Sacred Word." *Philosophy and Literature* 20:154–62.

______. 1997. "Dante and the Authority of Poetic Language." In *Dante: Contemporary Perspectives.* Ed. Amilcare A. Iannucci. Toronto: University of Toronto Press. 167–80.

Bougerol, Jacques Guy. 1961. *Introduction a l'étude de S. Bonaventure.* Tournai: Desclée.

Bourke, Vernon J. 1954. "St. Augustine and the Cosmic Soul." *Giornale di metafisica* 9:431–40.

Boyde, Patrick. 1981. *Dante, Philomythes and Philosopher: Man in the Cosmos.* Cambridge: Cambridge University Press.

______. 1993. *Perception and Passion in Dante's "Comedy."* Cambridge: Cambridge University Press.

Boyde, Patrick, and Vittorio Russo, eds. 1995. *Dante e la scienza.* Ravenna: Longo.

Bruce-Jones, John. 1995. "L'importanza della materia prima (Why Does Primary Matter Matter?): Aspetti della materia nella poesia e nel pensiero di Dante." In *Dante e la scienza.* Ed. Patrick Boyde and Vittorio Russo. Ravenna: Longo. 213–19.

Brunetto Latini. 1948. *Li livres dou tresor.* Ed. Francis J. Carmody. Berkeley: University of California Press.

Busnelli, Giovanni. 1922. *Cosmogonia e antropogenesi secondo Dante Alighieri e le sue fonti.* Rome: Civiltà cattolica.

Bynum, Caroline Walker. 1991. *Fragmentation and Redemption: Essays on Gender and the Human Body in Medieval Religion.* New York: Zone Books.

______. 1995. *The Resurrection of the Body in Western Christianity, 200–1336.* New York: Columbia University Press.

Bynum, Caroline Walker, and Paul Freedman. 1999. Introduction to *Last Things: Death and Apocalypse in the Middle Ages.* Ed. Caroline Walker Bynum and Paul Freedman. Philadelphia: University of Pennsylvania Press. 1–17.

Callus, Daniel A. 1960. "The Problem of the Plurality of Forms in the Thirteenth Century: The Thomist Innovation." In *L'homme et son destin d'après les penseurs du Moyen Âge: Actes du premier congrès international de philosophie médiévale (Louvain-Bruxelles, 28 août–4 septembre 1958).* Louvain and Paris: Nauwelaerts. 577–85.

______. 1961. "The Origins of the Problem of the Unity of Form." *The Thomist* 24:257–85.

______. 1967. "Forms, Unicity and Plurality of." In *New Catholic Encyclopedia.* New York: McGraw-Hill. 5:1024–27.

Carugati, Giuliana. 1991. *Dalla menzogna al silenzio: La scrittura mistica della "Commedia" di Dante.* Bologna: Il Mulino.

Cavalcanti, Guido. 1978. *Rime.* Ed. Marcello Ciccuto. Milan: Rizzoli.

Cestaro, Gary. 1991. "The Primal Scene of Suckling in Dante's '*De vulgari eloquentia.*'" DS 109:119–47.

Chiavacci Leonardi, Anna Maria. 1988. "'Le bianche stole': Il tema della resurrezione nel *Paradiso.*" In *Dante e la bibbia: Atti del Convegno Internazionale promosso da "Biblia" (Firenze, 26–27–28 settembre 1986).* Ed. Giovanni Barblan. Florence: Olschki. 249–71.

Cioffi, Caron Ann. 1992. "Fame, Prayer, and Politics: Virgil's Palinurus in *Purgatorio* V and VI." DS 110:179–200.

Cogan, Marc. 1999. *The Design in the Wax.* Notre Dame, Ind., and London: University of Notre Dame Press.

Colombo, Manuela. 1987. *Dai mistici a Dante: Il linguaggio dell'ineffabilità.* Florence: La Nuova Italia.

Cornish, Alison. 2000. *Reading Dante's Stars.* New Haven, Conn.: Yale University Press.

Courcelle, Pierre. 1955. "Les Peres de l'Église devant les enfers virgiliens." *Archives d'histoire doctrinale et litteraire du Moyen Âge* 30:5–74.

Cozzoli, Vittorio. 1993. *Il Dante anagogico: Dalla fenomenologia mistica alla poesia anagogica.* Chieti: Solfanelli.

Crespo, Roberto. 1986. "Volgarizzamenti." In *Dizionario critico della letteratura italiana.* Ed. V. Branca. Turin: UTET. 4:462.

Croce, Benedetto. 1921. *La poesia di Dante.* Bari: Laterza.

Cupitt, Don. 1998. *Mysticism after Modernity.* Malden, Mass.: Blackwell.

Dales, Richard C. 1995. *The Problem of the Rational Soul in the Thirteenth Century.* Leiden: Brill.

Davis, Charles T. 1980. "Poverty and Eschatology in the *Commedia.*" *Yearbook of Italian Studies* 4:59–86.

D'Avray, David L. 1994. "Some Franciscan Ideas about the Body." In *Modern Questions about Medieval Sermons: Essays on Marriage, Death, History, and Society.* Ed. Nicole Bérion and David L. d'Avray. Spoleto: Centro italiano di studi sull'alto Medioevo. 155–74.

Dembrowski, Peter F. 1986. "Learned Latin Treatises in French." *Viator* 17:255–69.

De Robertis, Domenico. 1961. *Il libro della "Vita Nuova."* Florence: Sansoni.

Dronke, Peter. 1965. "L'amor che move il sole e l'altre stelle." *Studi medievali* 6:389–422.

Ducos, Joëlle. 1998. *La météorologie en français au Moyen Âge (XIIIe–XIVe siècles).* Paris: Honoré Champion.

Durling, Robert, and Ronald Martinez. 1990. *Time and the Crystal: Studies in Dante's "Rime Petrose."* Berkeley: University of California Press.

Fahnestock, Jeanne. 1993. "Accommodating Science: The Rhetorical Life of Scientific Facts." In *The Literature of Science: Perspectives on Popular Scientific Writing.* Ed. Murdo W. McRae. Athens: University of Georgia Press.

Figurelli, Fernando. 1972. "Il canto XXV del *Purgatorio.*" In *Nuove letture dantesche.* Vol. 5. Florence: Le Monnier. 33–67.

Foster, Kenelm, O.P. 1972. "The Celebration of Order: *Paradiso* X." DS 90:109–24.

______. 1976. "Tommaso d'Aquino." In ED 5:626–49.

Freccero, John. 1968. "*Paradiso* X: The Dance of the Stars." DS 86:85–112.

______. 1983. "Manfred's Wounds and the Poetics of the *Purgatorio.*" In *Centre and Labyrinth: Essays in Honour of Northrop Frye.* Ed. Eleanor Cook et al. Toronto: University of Toronto Press. 69–82.

Garin, Eugenio. 1958. *Studi sul platonismo medievale.* Florence: Le Monnier.

Gilson, Étienne. 1949. *The Philosophy of St. Bonaventure.* Trans. Dom I. Trethowan. 2nd ed. London: Sheed and Ward.

______. 1955. *History of Christian Philosophy in the Middle Ages.* New York: Random House.

______. 1956. *The Christian Philosophy of St. Thomas Aquinas.* Trans. L. K. Shook. New York: Random House.

______. 1965. "Trois études dantesques pour le VIIe centenaire de la naissance de Dante." *Archives d'histoire doctrinale et littéraire du Moyen Âge* 40:72–93.

______. 1967. "Dante's Notion of a Shade: *Purgatorio* XXV." *Mediaeval Studies* 29:124–42.

______. 1974. "Qu'est-ce qu'une ombre? (Dante, *Purg*. XXV)." In *Dante et Béatrice: Études dantesques*. Paris: Vrin. 22–45.

Gilson, Simon A. 1997a. "Dante's Meteorological Optics: Refraction, Reflection, and the Rainbow." *Italian Studies* 52:51–62.

______. 1997b. "Dante and the Science of 'Perspective': A Reappraisal." DS 115:185–219.

______. 2000. *Medieval Optics and Theories of Light in the Works of Dante*. Lewiston, N.Y.: Edwin Mellen Press.

Ginsburg, Warren. 1999. *Dante's Aesthetics of Being*. Ann Arbor: University of Michigan Press.

Giordano da Pisa. 1974. *Quaresimale fiorentino, 1305–1306*. Ed. Carlo Delcorno. Florence: Sansoni.

Goering, Joseph. 1982. "The *De dotibus* of Robert Grosseteste." *Mediaeval Studies* 44:83–101.

Gragnolati, Manuele. 1999. "From Decay to Splendor: Body and Pain in Bonvesin da la Riva's *Book of the Three Scriptures*." In *Last Things: Death and Apocalypse in the Middle Ages*. Ed. Caroline Walker Bynum and Paul Freedman. Philadelphia: University of Pennsylvania Press. 83–97.

Guagnini, Elvio. 1989. "Canto XXV." In *Purgatorio*. Ed. Pompeo Giannantonio. Naples: Loffredo. 487–503.

Guardini, Romano. 1921. *Die Lehre des Heil. Bonaventura von der Erlösung: Ein Beitrag zur Geschichte und zum System der Erlösungslehre*. Dusseldorf: Schwann.

Guittone d'Arezzo. 1940. *Le rime*. Ed. Francesco Egidi. Bari: Laterza.

Harrison, Anna. 1999. "Community among the Saints in Heaven in Bernard of Clairvaux's *Sermons for the Feasts of All Saints*." In *Last Things: Death and Apocalypse in the Middle Ages*. Ed. Caroline Walker Bynum and Paul Freedman. Philadelphia: University of Pennsylvania Press. 191–204.

Jacopo Alighieri. 1952. *Il Dottrinale*. In *Poeti Minori del Trecento*. Ed. Natalino Sapegno. Milan: Ricciardi.

Jacopo Passavanti. 1925. *Specchio della vera penitenza*. Ed. Maria Lenardon. Città di Castello: Orfanelli Sacro Cuore.

Katainen, V. Louise. 1999. Review of *The Flowering of Mysticism: Men and Women in the New Mysticism, 1200–1350*, by Bernard McGinn. *Italica* 76:521–23.

Kirkpatrick, Robin. 1994. "Dante and the Body." In *Framing Medieval Bodies.* Ed. Sarah Kay and Miri Rubin. Manchester and New York: Manchester University Press. 235–53.

Klein, Robert. 1960. "L'enfer de Ficino." In *Unanesimo e esoterismo.* Ed. Enrico Castelli. Padua: Cedam. 47–84.

Kuhn, Thomas. 1977. *The Essential Tension: Selected Studies in Scientific Tradition and Change.* Chicago: University of Chicago Press.

Le Goff, Jacques. 1984. *The Birth of Purgatory.* Trans. Arthur Goldhammer. Chicago: The University of Chicago Press.

______. 1993. *L'immaginario medievale.* Milan: Mondadori.

Librandi, Rita. 1995. *La Metaura d'Aristotile: Volgarizzamento fiorentino anonimo del XIV secolo.* Naples. Ligouri.

Lindheim, Nancy. 1990. "Body, Soul, and Immortality: Some Readings in Dante's *Commedia.*" MLN 105:1–32.

Macrobius. 1952. *Commentarii in Somnium Scipionis.* Trans. William Harris Stahl. New York: Columbia University Press.

Maier, Annaliese. 1983. *Scienza e filosofia nel medioevo: Saggi sui secoli XIII e XIV.* Trans. Massimo Parodi and Achille Zoerle. Milan: Jaca Book.

Maierù, Alfredo. 1970. "Forma." In ED 2:969–75.

Martinez, Ronald L. 1983. "The Pilgrim's Answer to Bonagiunta and the Poetics of the Spirit." *Stanford Italian Review* 3:37–63.

Mazzarella, Pasquale. 1978. *Controversie medievali: Unità e pluralità delle forme.* Naples: Giannini.

Mazzotta, Giuseppe. 1979. "Literary History." In *Dante, Poet of the Desert: History and Allegory in the "Divina Commedia."* Princeton, N.J.: Princeton University Press. 193–218.

______. 1993. *Dante's Vision and the Circle of Knowledge.* Princeton, N.J.: Princeton University Press.

McGinn, Bernard. 1998. *The Flowering of Mysticism: Men and Women in the New Mysticism, 1200–1350.* Vol. 3 of *The Presence of God: A History of Western Mysticism.* New York: Crossroad.

Michel, A. 1915. "Forme du corps humain." In *Dictionnaire de théologie catholique.* Vol. 6. Paris: Letouzey et Ané. 546–88.

______. 1937. "Résurrection des morts." In *Dictionnaire de théologie catholique.* Vol. 13. Paris: Letouzey et Ané. 2501–71.

Modi orandi Sancti Dominici. 1996. *Modi orandi Sancti Dominici: Die Gebets- und Andachtsgesten des heiligen Dominikus—Eine Bilderhandschrift: Faksimile-Ausgabe.* 2 vols. Zurich: Belser.

Morris, Colin. 1972. *The Discovery of the Individual, 1050–1200.* New York: Harper & Row.

Nardi, Bruno. 1920. "Meditantur sua stercora scarabei." *Nuovo giornale dantesco* 4:56–62.

______. 1949. "Sull'origine dell'anima umana." In *Dante e la cultura medievale.* Bari: Laterza.

——. 1960. "L'origine dell'anima umana secondo Dante." In *Studi di filosofia medievale.* Rome: Edizioni di Storia e Letteratura. 9–68. (Originally published in *Giornale critico della filosofia italiana* 12 [1931]:433–56 and 13 [1932]:45–56 and 81–102.)

______. 1966. "Il canto XXV del *Purgatorio.*" In *Purgatorio.* Vol. 2 of *Letture dantesche.* Ed. Giovanni Getto. 2nd ed. Florence: Sansoni. 1173–91.

______. 1967a. "Raffronti fra alcuni luoghi di Alberto Magno e di Dante." In *Saggi di filosofia dantesca.* 2nd ed. Florence: La Nuova Italia. 63–72. (Originally published in GSLI 80 [1922]:295–303.)

______. 1967b. "Il tomismo di Dante e il padre Busnelli S.J." In *Saggi di filosofia dantesca.* 2nd ed. 341–80. (Rev. from GSLI 81 [1923]:307–34.)

______. 1990. "Sull'origine dell'anima umana." In *Dante e la cultura medievale.* Ed. Paolo Mazzantini. 2nd ed. Rome and Bari: Laterza. 207–24. (Originally published *Giornale dantesco* 39 [1938]:15–28.)

Padoan, Giorgio. 1981. "Il canto XXV del *Purgatorio.*" In *Purgatorio: Letture degli anni 1976–'79.* Rome: Bonacci. 577–600.

Pertile, Lino. 1996. "Bonconte e l'anafonesi (*Purg.* V. 109–18)." *Filologia e critica* 21:118–26.

Plato. 1961. *The Complete Dialogues.* Ed. Edith Hamilton and Huntington Cairns. Princeton, N.J.: Princeton University Press.

Plotinus. 1953. *The Enneads.* Trans. Stephen MacKenna. 6 vols. Boston: C. T. Branford.

Prandi, Stefano. 1994. *Il "diletto legno": Aridità e fioritura mistica nella "Commedia."* Florence: Olschki.

Pseudo-Augustine. 1865. *De vera et falsa poenitentia.* In PL 40:1113–30.

Pseudo-Dionysius. 1982. *The Devine Names*. Trans. Colm Luibheid. In *The Complete Works: The Classics of Western Spirituality*. New York: Paulist Press, 47–131.

Quinn, Patrick. 1993. "Aquinas's Concept of the Body and Out of Body Situations." *Heythrop Journal* 34:387–400.

Raichvarg, Daniel, and Jean Jacques. 1991. *Savants et ignorants: Une histoire de la vulgarization des sciences*. Paris: Éditions du Seuil.

Ratzinger, Joseph. 1971. *The Theology of St. Bonaventure*. Trans. Zachary Hayes. Chicago: Franciscan Herald Press.

Reeves, Marjorie. 1964. *The Influence of Prophecy in the Later Middle Ages: A Study in Joachimism*. Oxford: Oxford University Press.

Ristoro d'Arezzo. 1859. *La composizione del mondo*. Ed. Enrico Narducci. Rome: Tipografia delle scienze matematiche e fisiche.

______. 1997. *La composizione del mondo*. Ed. Alberto Morino. Parma: Guanda.

Salimbene da Parma. 1998. *Cronica*. Turnholt: Brepols.

Santi, Francesco. 1987. "Il cadavere e Bonifacio VIII, tra Stefano Tempier e Avicenna: Intorno a un saggio di Elisabeth Brown." *Studi medievali* ser. 3, 28:861–78.

______. 1993. "Un nome di persona al corpo e la massa dei corpi gloriosi." *Micrologus* 1:273–300.

Sarolli, Gian Roberto. 1971. *Prologomena alla "Divina Commedia."* Florence: Olschki.

Segre, Cesare. 1963. "I volgarizzamenti del Due e Trecento." In *Lingua, stile, e società*. Milan: Feltrinelli. 49–78.

Shapiro, Marianne. 1998. *Dante and the Knot of Body and Soul*. New York: St. Martin's Press.

Stabile, Giorgio. 1981. "Modelli naturali e analisi della vita emotive: Il Caso di Dante, *Rime* CXVI." In *Studi sul XIV secolo in memoria di Anneliese Maier*. Ed. A. Maierù and A. Paravicini Bagliani. Rome: Storia e Letteratura.

______. 1983. "Cosmologia e teologia nella *Commedia:* La caduta di Lucifero e il rovesciamento del mondo." *Letture classensi* 12:139–73.

Steenberghen, Fernand van. 1966. *La philosophie au XIII siecle*. Louvain: Publications Universitaires.

Stewart, Dana. 1993. "A Matter of Perspective: Optics and Poetics in the Early Italian Love Lyric." *Romance Languages Annual* 5:283–89.

Thomasset, Claude. 1998. "Dante et la météorologie." In *Le temps qu'il fait au Moyen Âge: Phénomènes atmosphériques dans la literature, la pensée scientifique et religieuse.* Ed. C. Thomasset and J. Ducos. Paris: Presses de l'Université de Paris–Sorbonne. 243–51.

Toscano, Tobia R. 1988. "Il canto XXV del *Purgatorio.*" In *La tragedia degli ipocriti e altre letture dantesche.* Naples: Liguori. 85–105.

Trexler, Richard C. 1987. *The Christian at Prayer: An Illustrated Prayer Manual Attributed to Peter the Chanter.* Binghamton, N.Y.: Medieval and Renaissance Texts and Studies.

Tugwell, Simon. 1990. *Human Immortality and the Redemption of Death.* London: Darton, Longman and Todd.

Ungaretti, Giuseppe. 1970. *Vita d'un uomo: Tutte le poesie.* Ed. Leone Piccioni. 3rd ed. Milan: Mondadori.

Vanni Rovighi, Sofia. 1974. *San Bonaventura.* Milan: Vita e Pensiero.

Weber, Edouard-Henri. 1991. *La personne humaine au XIIIe siècle: L'avènement chez les maîtres parisiens de l'acception moderne de l'homme.* Paris: J. Vrin.

Wicki, Nikolaus. 1954. *Die Lehre von der himmlischen Seligkeit in der mittelalterlichen Scholastik von Petrus Lombardus bis Thomas von Aquin.* Freiburg: Universitätsverlag.

Zavalloni, Roberto. 1951. *Richard de Mediavilla et la controverse sur la pluralité des formes.* Louvain: Éditions de l'Institut Supérieur de Philosophie.

RECEPTION

14

Virility, Nobility, and Banking: The Crossing of Discourses in the *Tenzone* with Forese

Susan Noakes

Introduction

In the last five years of the millennium, a lively debate about the authenticity of the *tenzone* of Dante with Forese has focused the attention of Dante scholars (Cursietti 1995; Alfie 1998) on a work otherwise not ranked high even among Dante's minor works.[1] The debate has turned above all on the *codicological* and *textual* history of this series of poems, although Cursietti has provocatively speculated about the poems' *contextual* history, alleging that much of its language draws on a hermetic homosexual code current in the early Quattrocento and that it is thus not authentically Dantean. Essentially standing with the majority of philologists and editors who have accepted the attribution made by the early manuscripts, Alfie has responded that the Quattrocento context posited by Cursietti is not necessary for an understanding of these poems. Alfie understands well how important the issue of this debate is, identifying Cursietti's hypothesis with an "attitude of mistrust towards the codices . . . [implying] that whenever extant material arouses disbelief, literary critics can simply discredit it" (Alfie 1998, 146–48). Alfie is, I think, quite right here; but, because he himself does not provide a literary critical analysis of the poems consonant with the codicological and philological analyses that he has presented, doubts about the authorship of the *tenzone* might still linger.

The reason for this lingering incredulity is that these sonnets seem "almost incomprehensible" in relation to the Dantean context as scholars have come to know it. To provide an interpretation of these poems which is satisfying—that is to say, consonant with both philological and codicological evidence and *also* comprehensible with respect to both Dante's work as a whole and its development and to Dante's time and place in history as the best evidence enables us to understand them—it is essential to add to the evidence of philology and codicology that of literary criticism, by which I mean here interpretation, carried out according to recognized canons of hermeneutics (see especially Betti 1955). Literary criticism, in turn, requires a demonstration of how these poems can be read within the context of what we know about the lives of Forese and Dante, the history of the linguistic and literary forms they and their audience recognized and used, and the characteristics of Dante's securely attributed works. What I propose to do here is to set forth just one or two of the elements of just such a context for what is surely Dante's *tenzone* with Forese, for I believe that, with the renewed exploration of all pertinent contextual elements, literary criticism can effect, in conjunction with philology and codicology, a reading of these poems as Dantean which is satisfying and will even help enrich interpretation of the *Commedia.*[2] If my presentation of these contextual elements is successful, it may at least begin to suggest to those familiar with the sonnets some features of the readings to come, in a venue that will permit sufficient space to develop them. (In lieu of these readings, I offer, at present, a new English translation of them, as an appendix to the present essay.)

Varieties of Context[3]

Cursietti's position is founded on a hypothesis that had been advanced much earlier, and that had been rejected by Barbi. Barbi's important contribution to the study of the context of the *tenzone* is summarized by Gianfranco Contini (in Alighieri 1965, 81–82):

> Gli argomenti con cui un certo numero di filologi, dal Witte e dal Fraticelli a Domenico Guerri, tentò d'invalidare l'attribuzione e di assegnare la tenzone a burchielleschi del primissimo quattrocento, sono deboli e arbitrari, e distrutti dalle sempre più numerose coincidenze documentarie, oltreché dalle allusioni, che in quella si fanno, al vizio della gola.
>
> The arguments used by certain philologists, from Witte and Fraticelli to Domenico Guerri, to try to discount the attribution [to Dante] and ascribe the *tenzone* to writers imitating [the obscure, bizarre style of] Burchiello in the very early Quattrocento are weak and capricious;

> [moreover, they are] vanquished by the still growing number of documentary convergences, as well as by the references made in the *tenzone* to the sin of gluttony.
>
> (my translation)

Barbi had pointed to the thematic correspondence between the *tenzone* and *Purgatorio* 23, relying in part upon this very correspondence between the *Commedia* and the *tenzone* to argue for the *tenzone*'s authenticity.[4] When Barbi (1924) first published a study of this *tenzone,* he had devoted forty-two pages to an explanation of Forese's remarks about Dante's father. The other issue Barbi treated at great length was the textual history of the poems, both individually and as a group of six poems ordered in a particular manner.[5]

Moving rather against the grain of the last fifty years of American literary criticism, the contextual exploration begun here will address above all the biographical considerations that appeared so important to Barbi. I hope to show that even forty-two pages were insufficient to explain, to twentieth-century ears, the complexity of what Dante's father, as invoked by Forese's tongue, meant to a late thirteenth-century Florentine audience. In so doing, however, I must discuss at least briefly the structure of the *tenzone,* also of great interest to Barbi. I will have to demonstrate elsewhere that this structure is best understood by reference to the biographical context, when more fully explored than previously, in terms of all its social, economic, and political dimensions. Simply put: biography is a study more resonant and dense today than it was for Barbi, or for the great figures who, from mid-century onward, banished it from the shores of American criticism.

I should begin by noting a point about the textual order of the poems: the symmetry between Dante's first sonnet and Forese's last. Both deal centrally with the body, in relation to either failed eros or failed retributive violence, and both employ centrally the terminology of money and commerce to elaborate on these failures in the bodily realm. Both poems, then, bring together discourses of corporality and economics. Moreover, both deal with a form of social and gender connection that was undergoing very rapid change in Dante's Florence: the lineage, the network of in-laws, step-siblings, friends, and so forth, which continued to be so frequently invoked in the discourses of Florentine society and government even as their economic importance faded.

My thesis is that this series of poems is integrally connected to the late thirteenth-century Florentine context, especially by its interweaving of three discursive themes: virility, nobility, and banking, or, to use less modern terms, moneylending or usury. I hope to show that, when considered in this context, the language of this *tenzone* is by no means an aberration of Florentine discourse in the 1290s. Thus, there is no need to seek the *tenzone*'s context elsewhere—for example, in the Quattrocento. I will argue that, as with Dante's other works, the *tenzone* with Forese is best read as an intervention in the major social, economic, literary, artistic, and political developments of his time, and that Dantists need to understand better all those contributing contexts in order to interpret this *tenzone* in all its cultural implications. Specialists, especially those in the United States, must venture outside their literary specialty to know and digest scholarship contributed by students of the broader Romance poetic tradition and of history in its many pertinent forms—social, anthropological, political cultural, economic, and art historical.[6]

The Dante handed down to us by much of, though fortunately not all, Dante commentary and criticism remains in surprising and important ways an ahistorical, decontextualized figure, read as if walled off from much of the material in contemporary historical records. Insofar as we have assumed that we understood the meaning of such concepts as "marriage," "nobility," and "family," students of Dante have contributed to this decontextualization. Specifically, Dante's implication in the competition among contending socioeconomic groups—as it is played out on the battlefield of gender and family relations with weapons both documentary and otherwise—has remained in several important domains largely unexplored.

Socioeconomic Context

To begin, let us review a few basic biographical facts about Dante, his interlocutor, and their relationship by marriage and lineage, as well as several important but often neglected historical details about wealth, society, and law in the late Florentine Duecento. Basic information about the Donati and Alighieri lineages has long been available, but details that have been interpreted and contextualized only quite recently, in part as the result of energetic archival labors focused on economic aspects of Florentine marriage practices, cast this familiar information—the "conventional wisdom" of Dante scholarship—in a new light.

Forese Donati was, of course, the brother of Corso Donati, who became during the 1290s the head of what would in the later years of that decade be known as the Black Guelph faction. Dante was related to the Donati by his marriage to Gemma di Manetto Donati, but this lineage relationship by marriage was of a different character than Dantists sometimes assume. Corso and Forese were sons of Simone Donati, not of Manetto. Sestan (1970, 560) calls the degree of family relationship "impossible to specify," and emphasizes that the Donati were never a united lineage (559). Noting that "the very numerous members of the house of Donati . . . had never been united (". . . il numerosissimo casato dei Donati . . . non era mai stato unito . . ."), Sestan recounts a notorious incident in late 1294, when Corso wounded one of his own cousins and the cousin's servant. Jenni (1970, 561) calls Dante's wife, Gemma, "perhaps Forese's cousin twice removed" ("di Forese doveva essere cugina in terzo grado"). What did it mean—in addition to the risks to limb and maybe life—to *become* a third cousin by marriage to Corso and Forese?

To help us address this question, we have several documents pertaining to Donati marriages in the thirteenth century, including some pertaining specifically to the Donati–Alighieri marriage. As a result of contextualized readings of these documents by social historians, we now know some facts about Donati marriage practices in the generation of Dante and Forese, especially because, to complement the famous poetic tradition (*Purg* 24.10, 13–15; *Par* 3.42–120 [especially vv. 43–108], glossed in *Par* 4.97–114) which has passed down to us the story of Simone's hapless daughter Piccarda, we have a number of legal documents relating to the two marriages and eventual retreat to a convent of Piccarda's sister Ravenna (Lansing 1991, 126–27 [especially note 7], 159).[7]

These documents depict the socioeconomic politics pursued by Simone and, later, Corso in marrying off the family women. Ravenna's first marriage was part of a peacemaking alliance between Guelphs and Ghibellines arranged after the Guelph-Angevin victory over Ghibelline-Imperial forces at the famous battle of Benevento (February 1266). This alliance, the result of Ghibelline catastrophe, led to several prominent marriages early in 1267, including that of Guido Cavalcanti (b. 1230) with a daughter of Farinata degli Uberti. For her part, Ravenna di Simone Donati was married to Farinata's son Azzolino. By Easter of that year, nonetheless, the Ghibellines, with the Uberti at their head, were exiled from Florence, and a mere three years later Azzolino was "captured . . . and decapitated in a public execution in Florence. . . ." Not only did Ravenna lose, in this horrifying manner, the husband her family had not long before given her; but she could not keep the two sons the brief marriage had produced, for they were by custom part of the husband's lineage. She was then to be married off by her family again to bring advantage to the Donati lineage. While still children, the family's boys were included in their paternal grandfather's penalty for heresy, a condemnation promoted by their mother Ravenna's family's party.

In the arrangements for Ravenna's second marriage, shortly after her first husband's decapitation, the Donati lineage seems to have had monetary advantage rather than political alliance or status as its primary goal. For Ravenna's second husband, Bello Ferrantini, was not an aristocrat, but rather "a newly rich banker and moneylender who traveled to the fairs in Champagne and had sums invested with [several leading banking firms]" (Lansing 1991, 126). When, after Bello's death in 1277, Ravenna tried to enter the convent at S. Iacopo a Ripoli with the three children left to her, Corso made such strenuous (and ultimately successful) efforts to gain control of Bello's property as to give "the impression that the Donati had originally contracted the marriage with an eye to Bello's wealth . . ." (Lansing 1991, 127).

It was in the very year of Bello's death that the marriage contract legally uniting the young adolescent Dante (at twelve or thirteen) to Manetto's daughter Gemma was registered. Aware of the fates of Ravenna and Piccarda, we may be tempted, from a social viewpoint, to count Gemma and her young husband fortunate that hers was a relatively distant connection to Simone Donati and his sons. In financial terms, certainly, the marriage was fortunate for Manetto's family: the contract's specification of the "meager" dowry of 200 *libre* (Lansing 1991, 129) is telling.[8] The Alighieri lineage's acceptance of this sum as dowry is indicative of their relationship to the Donati, as construed in 1277. First, this marital transaction suggests that, though less important than Simone's line, Manetto's branch of the Donati clan was successful in endowing a daughter with more prestige than capital: that is, Manetto married Gemma off respectably without significant diminution of the lineage's wealth.[9] The Alighieri presumably would have demanded a better dowry had they been in a position to do so.

Second, the implication of the marriage is not, as students of Dante have often assumed, merely a simple and univocal one: that the Donati and the Alighieri were on similar footing because their lines united in marriage. To be sure, a marriage represents an erasure of social boundaries between families, but, as Ravenna di Simone Donati's case shows, such erasure of boundaries was not always enduring. Marital "palimpsests" abounded, to such a degree that the social "text" that was Florentine society could become difficult to read on the "parchment" of marriage practices. Fundamental differences between the families supposedly united by marriage could, and frequently did, continue to inflect their relationships long after the marriage's consummation.[10]

The modest dowry conveys an implication contrary to that inferred by the "conventional wisdom" of much of Dante scholarship; it implies there was a considerable discrepancy in social level between Forese's family and Dante's.[11] When, following custom, a household was established, probably when Dante was about twenty (ca. 1285), the resources to support it likely came almost exclusively from the Alighieri side.

The jokes about wealth and poverty traded between Forese and Dante, probably in the period 1293–96 (the latter being the year of Forese's death), are rooted in the social ambivalence about boundaries among lineages embodied also in this marriage contract. To understand these two men as family equals trading barbs is to miss important elements in their relative positions and thus overlook nuances of texture in their presumed private relationships and, especially, in their presentations of their personae to the variously circumscribed audiences of late thirteenth-century Florence.

The character of the familial, social, and economic relationship between Dante and Forese is further suggested by details concerning social—or, better, anthropological—history and its relation to Florentine economics and politics at this turbulent period. The changes in the structure of Florentine society at this time cannot be adequately described with merely two stark labels: "Black" and "White." Used by contemporary historians, notably Dino Compagni, to paint a dramatic picture of thirteenth-century Florence, they preserve a self-serving explanation of violent historical change favored by those whose roots in Florence did not go as deep as those of the Donati or Cerchi or whose familial contributions to Florentine history were not as conspicuous. These now-familiar labels simplify a historical, legal, and anthropological process of great complexity, still not entirely understood.

Perhaps further attention by literary historians to the history of the rhetorical practices used to evoke the broad domains of sexuality, nobility, and banking will advance this analysis. The study of Dante's rhetorical practice in these domains would surely play an important part in such analysis. I submit that the *tenzone* with Forese is better understood when the nuances of the languages of power employed in Florence in the 1290s, nuances that the stark labels "Black" and "White" have tended to hide, are permitted to emerge in their various shades of (blood-stained) gray. But in order to perceive these shifting tonalities, students of Dante must take another look at legal and political documents remaining from this complex period.

Legal-Historical Context

The last decade of the thirteenth century marked the evolution and designation from within the Florentine "nobility"—a relatively large group loosely defined only from the eleventh century—of the smaller and more powerful group popularly and eventually legally defined as "magnates." The Alighieri had claims to being "noble," as Dante makes certain to tell his audiences by describing the knighting of his ancestor Cacciaguida, whom he comfortably positions in Paradise, in the realm of sanctified warriors (the Heaven of Mars). But even asserting that this ancestor had been knighted did not place the Alighieri anywhere near the feudal aristocracy in terms of status. To understand Dante's sense of his and his family's identity, students of the poet must examine carefully the term that is surely among those most crucial to Florentine political and social discourse in the 1290s: "magnate." The Alighieri were not legally magnates, while the Donati, like the Cavalcanti, were.

This legal discrimination points up a major difference between Dante and some of those with whom he sought most ardently to ally himself, and for that reason its role in his rhetorical practice must be examined with care. It is a detail that has long been known, for the young Salvemini, later a famous socialist journalist and scholar, published and discussed the evidence in 1899. It has, however, been swept to one side, above all in Anglo-American criticism, since Ottokar's argument (1926) that the Florentine oligarchy of Dante's time was essentially homogeneous, not pulled at by tensions one might associate with "class." Describing in 1929 Dante's socioeconomic position, Auerbach still struggled—as his language shows—with the ambiguity he saw in the evidence.[12] But, in the decades after 1929, this ambiguity was to a great extent covered over (for reasons, one might infer, that have more to do with twentieth-century politics than with the Duecento). Now, I submit, it is time for students of Dante to consider once again the definition of "magnate" as it evolved in Florence in the 1290s and its possible bearing on the context of the public relation of Dante to Forese.

The first Florentine statute that envisaged a group termed "magnates" was created in 1281, just a few years before Dante probably began family life with Forese's distant cousin Gemma. This statute, an attempt to regulate urban violence, restricted magnates in their practice of the vendetta.[13] The period of Dante's young manhood saw further and varied legal attempts to define the "magnati" as a group and to limit their power: such attempts, made throughout the 1280s and very early 1290s, culminated in the Ordinances of Justice in 1293 (see Cardini 1993 and Bonaini 1855), which means that their text is almost exactly contemporary with the *tenzone* with Forese, as dated by its editors. These Ordinances defined "magnate" by naming the magnate families and then imposed severe penalties on them, including the families' exclusion from almost all civic offices. In 1295, additional families were added to the list of magnates thus penalized and excluded (see Salvemini 1899, Appendix xii).

The importance of this legal designation to Dante emerges clearly from the narrative of his life after the Ordinances' passage. Precisely because the Alighieri were not named as magnates, Dante was able to affiliate himself with one of the *arti,* or guilds.[14] He therefore could and did participate in Florentine government, holding positions not open, for example, to members of the Donati or Cavalcanti lineages. Legally, Dante was not a magnate, but a member of the *popolo.* I would suggest that this legal fact is of considerable importance to any reader who would apprehend correctly, within the context of the Florentine 1290s, the tone of Dante's *tenzone* with Forese.

In stressing the heterogeneity, rather than the homogeneity, of the groups within which Dante lived and acted in this decade, and thus of the audiences for which he wrote at that time, I am offering a suggestion that might be misunderstood. I am not suggesting that Dante was *not* "noble" or was *not* a member of an "elite," just as I am not suggesting that he *was* a member of a "rising bourgeoisie" or "merchant class."[15] These clichéd terms seem to me too weighted to be used with any hope of accuracy. I am, rather, arguing that it is essential to bear in mind that Dante came into adult manhood in a period when the rules that created boundaries for behavior and social, political, and economic participation—written and unwritten rules which defined what are now called "identities"—were frequently challenged, tested, and reformed through many mechanisms. The most readily visible of these mechanisms of challenge and reformulation, after the passage of seven centuries, may well be statutory and contractual formulations, the language of law, especially the Ordinances of Justice. But we should not fail to ask whether some of Dante's works did not also contribute to the same set of challenges and reformulations, though perhaps less explicitly. The set of texts we need to read intertextually is not limited to Dante's own securely attributed works nor exclusively literary documents (to use what is, after all, a quite modern distinction).

Conclusion

Insofar as the only true conclusion to this essay must be a detailed reading of the poems, my conclusion here will, alas, disappoint, for such a reading must be deferred to another occasion. I hope, however, that the pertinence of the contextual material discussed and noted here will in any case be evident to careful readers of the poems. In this preliminary gathering together of elements from the socioeconomic and legal-historical contexts implicated in these poems, I have pursued a path that is interdisciplinary and oriented toward the discovery of close connections among various kinds of historical evidence—most conspicuously, a complementary relation between the evidence of manuscripts, and archives, and the evidence that is more broadly literary and historical. This is not the first occasion on which I have urged a return by Dantists to the study of primary sources in Florentine history (cf. Noakes 1968), nor will it be the last.

Yet, a return to primary sources, together with what—to paraphrase Alfie (1998)—might be termed a renewed trust in the codices, will not in itself be a sufficient ground for understanding the *tenzone* with Forese as part of a continuum of reflection on several contemporary issues, most conspicuously the debate on the nature of nobility, a continuum that also includes especially the *Convivio* and the *Commedia.* To locate the *tenzone* with Forese on such a literary historical continuum, we need to enlarge our sense of what Dante's writing *is.* The ways his writing was *used,* particularly in the first generations after the Risorgimento and then again under Fascism, as well as the ways it continues to be used today in a theological context, perhaps make today's Dante specialists reluctant to venture into such "extra-literary" conceptual terrains as social and economic hierarchies or corporal and political rhetoric. But this is a reluctance that must now be overcome if the *tenzone* and Dante's other works are to be read, in the fullest and most proper sense, intertextually, that is, in relation to other Florentine discourses of the late Duecento and early Trecento. As Dante's words travel across and then recross the various and complex discourses of Florentine society in that period of upheaval, they weave a rich series of texts. Specialists in the study of those texts must seek to understand *integrally,* as parts of a single whole, Dante's writing and contemporary "political culture," the "social logic" of this difficult text, to use the terms of the historians Muir and Spiegel. If we do not, someone is sure to come along again, to take this *tenzone* out of Dante's hands entirely and drop it into a context in the Quattrocento, for example. This is not the best way to honor Dante in the new millennium that we greet here.

APPENDIX
DANTE'S *TENZONE* WITH FORESE

1. *Dante to Forese*

Anyone who'd hear the ill-fated
wife of Bicci, called Forese, cough
could say she's perhaps wintered
where crystal is formed, in that country. 4
In the middle of August you find her with a cold:
so you can imagine what she's like in any other month . . . ;
and it does her no good to sleep with her socks on,
thanks to the blanket she has, from Shortsville. 8

The cough, the cold, and the other misfortune
Don't come to her because of the humors of age,
but because she feels something missing in her nest. 11
Her mother weeps, for several reasons,
crying: "Alas, and to think that for dried figs
I could have married her into the house of the counts Guidi." 14

2. *Forese to Dante*

The other night I had a bad cough,
because I had nothing to cover my back;
but as soon as it was daylight, I was moved
to go get something, wherever I could. 4
Listen where fortune put something on my shoulders:
I thought I'd find pearls in a tin cup
and lovely florins made of red gold;
and I found Alighieri in the ditches, 8
tied with a knot whose name I don't know,
whether it belonged to Solomon or some other wise man.
Then I crossed myself, looking to the east: 11
and he said to me: "For the love of Dante,
untie me." And I couldn't see how to do it:
I turned back, and finished my travels. 14

3. *Dante to Forese*

Sure, they'll tie you up with Solomon's knot,
little Bicci, these partridge breasts,
but the loin of gelded lamb will be worse,
because the skin will take revenge for the flesh; 4
so that you'll wind up closer to (the prison near) San Simone,
if you don't figure out how to stay away from there:
and understand, as to avoiding that nasty mouthful,
that at this point you're a little late to buy your way out of it. 8

But surely I've been told that you know a trick
that, if it's so, will put you back on your feet,
because it'll bring in a whole lot; 11
and, with time, it'll relieve you of all your fears
of papers, and you'll have to stop working;
but surely it put Stagno's boys in trouble. 14

4. *Forese to Dante*

Go take the stuff back to the San Gallo poorhouse before you
make smart remarks about anyone else's poverty,
because all of San Gallo's friends
need everything they can get this winter. 4
And another thing, if you think we're such beggars,
why do you come to us for charity?
From the Altafronte's soup kitchen you've taken away sacks
full so that I know very well that's how you feed yourself. 8

But surely it will be all right for you to work,
if God saves your siblings Tana and Francesco for you,
so you won't wind up in your uncle Belluzzo's gang. 11
One day they'll take you in at the old folks' home at Pinti;
and already I seem to see at the chow table,
with two buddies, Alighieri in his shirtsleeves. 14

5. *Dante to Forese*

Little Bicci, son of God knows who
(unless I ask Lady Tessa about that),
you've stuffed so much down your throat
that naturally it suits you to grab from others. 4
And already people are careful around him,
anyone who has a purse at his side, when he comes near,
saying: "This guy with the scarface,
we all know his sticky fingers." 8

And because of him someone's been laid in a sorry bed,
worrying if he's going to be nabbed for robbery,
someone tied to him the way Joseph was to Christ. 11
I can tell you, about Bicci and his brothers,
that, by their blood, with ill-got goods
they know how to treat their women as good brothers-in-law do. 14

6. *Forese to Dante*

Sure, I know you were Alighieri's son,
and I noticed how you avenged him,
so cleanly and prettily,
with the same dough he'd been trading in just the day
  before yesterday. 4
Even if you'd drawn and quartered one of them,
you shouldn't have been in such a rush to settle;
but your sack is so full
no two asses could carry it. 8

You've set a good example for us, I'll say that:
whoever beats you with a club
is one you'll pick as brother and friend. 11
I'll tell you the names of the ones who follow your lead;
but I'd better get myself some birdseed,
so I can count them up right. 14

NOTES

1. Especially helpful to me in my thinking for this essay has been Lansing 1991, located by its author in part as a response to Gabrielle Spiegel's call (1990) to attend to "the Social Logic of the Text in the Middle Ages." As Wallace (1993) pointed out in his review, Lansing's study provides significant material organized and interpreted in such a way that it should be a new point of departure for scholars considering Dante's political and social milieu. Important encouragement and feedback were also provided by colleagues and friends to whom I am most grateful, including Valeria Finucci, Ron Witt, Christopher Kleinhenz, Teodolinda Barolini, Kevin Brownlee, and Barbara Hanawalt. A study in which I discuss more fully the history of the debate over the authenticity of the *tenzone,* as well as contextual issues which space precludes treating here, is in preparation as "The Contexts of Dante's 'Tenzone with Forese': An Audience Divided."

2. When this paper was read in April 2000, partial explication of the first two sonnets (that is, first as ordered by Contini in Alighieri 1965) was provided; it has been necessary here to eliminate this explication to make room for a more complete presentation of contextual material. On the relation of the ideas presented here to the *Vita Nuova,* see Noakes 1990.

3. The complexities of Dante's relation to his multiple textual contexts are set forth most effectively in Mazzotta 1979 and Barolini 1984. On the importance of an interdisciplinary approach, see especially Geertz 1980 and Brownlee et al. 1991, where the introductory essay by Nichols explains why the "new medievalism" must be "resolutely eclectic" (1). For the concepts of context and discourse in the specific senses employed in this essay, see Bakhtin and Medvedev [1928] 1985. Within this conceptual framework, the social context—an integral feature of any verbal communication—cannot be separated from such communication; the meaning of any utterance includes three elements: (1) the speaker's position as social subject, refracted in the other, (2) the listener's horizon of understanding, and (3) the historical substance of the language the speaker and listener share, including the various meanings of the words as they are used in other discourses of the past and present for other ends.

4. The allusions to gluttony are taken to be indicators of authenticity because of Dante's placement of Forese Donati among the gluttons in *Purgatorio* 23.

5. Contini (Alighieri 1965) accepted the work as authentic based on correspondences between it and other of Dante's works, as well as on allusions to it in mid-Trecento works, including the *Decameron* and the *Corbaccio.* See also Barolini 1984, 47–56.

6. I intend the term "political culture" to embrace multiple energies and practices, as does "ritual" in Edward Muir's work (1997).

7. Earlier studies mention the documents relating to Ravenna's marriages, but do not read them as carefully as Lansing does.

8. In the same paragraph, Lansing also discusses several other (unedited) marriage contracts of the 1290s. The challenge of interpreting archival information about dowry magnitude is considerable. Cf. Lansing 1991, 131, for discussion of the unedited 1241 Florentine will of a member of the Adimari lineage which specifies dowries for as yet unmarried daughters in the event of the intestate death of a son without male heir. Lansing interprets the will to imply that any dowry smaller than 500 *libre* would have been "dishonorable" for an Adimari daughter in 1241. To be sure, a couple of generations can make an enormous difference in terms of value. Moreover, the Adimari stood far above the Alighieri, so that the benchmark for "honor" would also be located differently: the Adimari, in 1260, held much more urban and rural property than even the Donati, as may be inferred from Table 3.1 (51). In the mid-1290s, the Adimari were legally listed as *magnati* (a legal designation I will discuss below), residing—like their fellow magnates the Donati and the Cerchi—in the Por San Piero district of Florence (Lansing 1991, 239). Lansing (49–50) points out, though, that the Adimari's top position in her Table 3.1 may give a better indication of the degree to which they were hated than evidence of their real wealth, since the source of the Table is a Guelph survey of damage to Guelph property inflicted by the Ghibellines after the Battle of Montaperti.

9. See Lansing 1991, 129–30, especially Table 7.1, where the Donati-Alighieri contract is represented by the letter M standing farthest to the left.

10. The abundance of top-notch studies of Florentine social history proposes the best kind of interdisciplinary challenge to Dantists, who may welcome some orientation before plunging into this vast literature. To be sure, many studies of Florentine society (including Becker 1967; Brucker 1977; Herlihy 1985; Najemy 1982; and Trexler 1980) provide analyses which frame as a "prelude to the Renaissance," or transition, the later thirteenth and earlier fourteenth centuries. For the extensive literature on marriage, including dowries, see Klapisch-Zuber 1988, whose study focuses on the specific Trecento context that seems most applicable to Donati marriage practices. Klapisch-Zuber (1990) masterfully elaborates in archival and anthropological detail the broader social dance of alliance and contention within the evolution of which these practices are to be located. She formulates (142–43) most succinctly the social, economic, and political tension within which, I argue, Dantists should ground Dante and Forese's *tenzone*, with its first lines focused on the marriage bed: "Le mariage, l'alliance sont l'antidote de l'agressivité,

du conflit, de l'intérêt mal entendu." Unlike her work with D. Herlihy, based on an early Quattrocento *catasto* (census) and more widely read in the United States, Klapish-Zuber's 1990 study is based on *ricordanze*, the earliest of which—by Neri degli Strinati—is claimed by its author, writing during the period of composition of the *Commedia*, to have been begun toward the mid-Duecento, and to be based on conversations with members of the family already very old at that time, who were able to inform him about family history in the second half of the twelfth century (41). Duby (1981) provides necessary contexts for understanding Klapisch-Zuber's work, stressing the tenuousness of the sacramental character of high-medieval (feudal) marriage practice in France, and its evolution through economic and social negotiation. For a brief account of the debate between R. Goldthwaite and F. W. Kent about the relation between Florentine economics and family structure after the time of Boccaccio and its pertinence to earlier generations, see the preface to Lansing 1991. Molho (1994), who begins his study with the late fourteenth century, describes in vivid detail a "complex and precise calculus . . . [of] marriage [which] set up relations between families in command of capital of a material or symbolic kind." It is in the study of the problems in the relation of what Molho terms material and symbolic capital that the interpretation of Dante and Forese's *tenzone* offered here is to be located.

11. Another indication of the position of the Alighieri lineage is the marriage of Dante's half-sister Tana (Gaetana) to a moneychanger and Dante's half-brother Francesco's career in commerce. (To be sure, Forese flings the names of both these half-siblings at Dante in the *tenzone*'s fourth sonnet in a richly rhetorical gesture that envisions Dante's economic dependence on these relatives, certainly not aristocrats.)

12. Auerbach ([1929] 1961, 59–60) writes that Dante's "family had long been resident in Florence, but it cannot, when Dante was a young man, have been particularly wealthy or esteemed. . . . [C]ertain obscure allusions in the *tenson* between Dante and Forese Donati suggest that his father lived ingloriously and died unhappy. However, numerous passages in Dante's work and the reports of others show that he enjoyed an excellent and well-rounded education and that he had taken a part befitting his rank in the social, political, and military events of his youth. His marriage and the names of his friends confirm what we know from his early poems, namely, that he was at home in the leading circles of the nobility and upper bourgeoisie. Yet he probably owed that position more to his personal charm and talent than to his lineage and social standing, and that would account for its apparent ups and downs, for esteem due to personal accomplishments is far more dependent on caprice and fashion than is an inherited prestige. However, I do not believe that any very drastic conclusions should be drawn from the indications of his social

vicissitudes (contained, for example, in his sonnet renouncing Cavalcanti or in his poetic controversy with Forese), nor does it strike me as likely that Dante was ever seriously poor before his exile; the sum of his debts shortly before 1300 suggests rather that his credit was good, and the tone in which he laments the poverty and uncertainty of his existence in exile makes it seem quite certain that he had not previously known such straits."

13. Clearly, this has implications for the interpretation of the parts of our *tenzone* dealing with the lack of redress Dante's dead father has from his deficient son (see sonnet 6 and also, perhaps, sonnet 2): the successful carrying out of vendetta, in defiance of law imposed by the *popolo,* was a marker of magnate status, a status toward which Dante's father had reached out in the Donati marriage. For the context of vendetta, see Martines 1972 and, for its careful interpretation of the social meaning of vendetta, albeit in a slightly later period, and in Friuli, Muir 1993, especially chap. 6, "The Problem of Meaning."

14. Dante chose a guild that was to become very influential and may have showed signs of being especially important at the time. Dante scholars tend to know this guild as that of the *medici e speziali,* usually translated as "doctors and apothecaries," emphasizing the learned qualities of members of this guild. But *speziali* also included those engaged in one of the most lucrative forms of thirteenth-century commerce, the spice trade. Moreover, this guild was early expanded to include "mercers" (what Najemy [2000, 390] terms "dry-goods retailers"), in other words, merchandisers, retailers, shopkeepers. By 1308, this guild was considered one of the five major *arti* of Florence, together with that of Calimala, Cambio, Lana, and Por Santa Maria, and joined with them to form the "Mercanzia" ("an association of international merchants, bankers, and traders, . . . a formal corporation with jurisdiction over bankruptcies, reprisals, and commercial law, and soon thereafter with considerable political power over the guilds" [Najemy 2000, 395]).

15. Najemy (2000, 394) cautions usefully: "The Ordinances should not be seen as an assault by a rising merchant class against an older feudal nobility, but rather as the manifesto of the guild-based *popolo* against the *prepotenza* of the entire elite. But the *popolo*'s strategy was evidently to divide the elite and to allow some of its families to escape the punitive Ordinances and to retain their officeholding rights in the hopes that they would support the guild regime. Thus . . . many . . . families of great wealth, and in some cases of ancient lineage, were left off the magnate lists—although the *popolo* subsequently made clear that repeated episodes of disruptive behavior by any of them could result in their inclusion [in the magnate designation, and its consequent penalties and exclusions] at some later time."

15

Scatology and Obscenity in Dante

Zygmunt G. Barański

DANTE SCHOLARS, good bourgeois that they are, have normally taken considerable care to avoid the mix of sex and excrement that is *Inferno* 18. Indeed, as far as I have been able to ascertain, it is the only canto of the one hundred making up the *Commedia* that has never inspired an overarching critical reading independent of the demands of the cycles of *lecturae Dantis.*[1] When "obliged" by the conventions of the *lectura* to confront the sinful inhabitants of the first two *bolge,* Dantists have reacted with disdain, embarrassment, and discomfort, as if afraid of being tainted and overwhelmed by the *alito* ("exhalations" [v. 107]) emanating from the "sterco / che da li uman privadi parea mosso" ("excrement that seemed / as if it had been poured from human privies" [vv. 113–14]),[2] seemingly forgetful that they were confronting words on a page rather than an actual open sewer. The critics' squeamishness and sense of propriety, which, as regards Italian scholars, is exacerbated by the fact that, scandalously, it is Dante, *poeta nazionale e cattolico,* who is talking about shit and sex, have, in my view, led to bad criticism. Thus, Dantists have tended to concentrate on the panders and seducers, only summarily commenting on the flatterers, since the punishment of the former merely involves whips on bare flesh, and the sexual character of the *bolgia* is somewhat less explicit when compared to that of the second "pouch" of the *adulatores,* where prostitutes move provocatively in *merda* ("shit" [v. 116]). At the same time, however, considerable attention has been paid to Thais in order to explain the implications of her misquoting Terence's *Eunuchus*—a concentration of critical effort that has yielded some excellent historically and philologically sensitive results (see especially Barchiesi 1963).

The pity is that the same approach, which remembers *Inferno* 18's status as an early fourteenth-century literary text, has not been taken with the canto as a whole. Other parts of the *Commedia,* such as the descriptions of the naked soothsayers, of the mutilated Mohammed, and of the leader of the Malebranche who "avea del cul fatto trombetta" ("had made a trumpet of his ass" [*Inf* 21.139]), which also include overt scatological references, have equally been treated with little critical and historical sensitivity. Scholars have generally judged Dante's treatment of the flatterers to be "extreme," and have struggled to forge a critical framework and vocabulary able to accommodate, and hence explain and validate, the episode's presumed "extremism." To talk about *Inferno* 18's problematic subject matter and language, they have used terms such as "realistic," "objective," and "farcical," as well as definitions such as "avantgarde poetics of vulgarity," "infernal humour," and "stylistic-poetic process of degradation."[3] What is immediately striking about all these epithets and descriptions is their anachronism. Notions such as "realism," "farce," "humour," "vulgarity," "avantgarde" either were not current in the Middle Ages or had quite specific culturally determined meanings that may or may not be relevant to the context of *Inferno* 18 (for instance, given the deep ethical preoccupations with the dangers of laughter in much medieval moral writing, it is extremely unlikely that *risus* was something that Dante wanted to provoke with his evocation of the *adulatores*).

Dantists reveal somewhat greater historical sensibility when they assert that canto 18, like much of Malebolge, is an exercise in the "low style." Nevertheless, assertions of this kind, at least as they have been couched to date, are at best unnecessarily reductive. On the one hand, they assume that the *genus humilis* is a monolithic form of expression, when, in fact, it embraced a large variety of different literary types, only some of which are directly relevant to Dante's treatment of the panders, seducers, and flatterers—a point to which I shall return in due course. On the other hand, from a medieval rhetorical point of view, it is quite incorrect to characterize *Inferno* 18 as "low." It is undoubtedly the case that both the use of scatological language and the presence of a *meretrix* unambiguously indicate the *humilis* register. Indeed, by the fourteenth century, Thais had become a stock character of "comedy" and, like Davus, served as a metonymy for the *stilus* as a whole. At the same time, however, Dante's prostitute leaves the scene shedding her "low" associations. Virgil's presentation carefully translates her supposed exchange with Thraso into the vernacular, while maintaining the Latinate flavor of the original—a textbook instance of the "tragic," "high style": "Taïde è, la puttana che rispuose / al drudo suo quando disse 'Ho io grazie / grandi apo te?': 'Anzi maravigliose!'" ("That is Thaïs, the harlot who returned / her lover's question, 'Are you very grateful / to me?' by saying, 'Yes, enormously'" [*Inf* 18:133–35]). *Inferno* 18 stands as a classic example of Dante's syncretic plurilingual style, as many other elements in the canto clearly demonstrate, beginning with its opening line—"Luogo è in inferno detto Malebolge" ("There is a place in Hell called Malebolge")—which combines a Latin epic formula, *locus est,* with a "low" vernacular proper noun, *Malebolge,* that has its roots in the *Roman de la Rose* and in the *Fiore.* At the juncture in the *Commedia* when the poet has begun systematically to define and justify his new "comedy" (the term *comedía* makes its first appearance toward the end of *Inferno* 16), he is careful to underscore the differences between traditional forms of the *genus humilis* and his divinely inspired "comic" poem. This, not some conventional exercise in the "low" style, seems to have been Dante's primary aim in composing the cantos of Malebolge; and I shall have something further to say on this point too.[4]

Building on their belief regarding the canto's "low" status, interpreters of *Inferno* 18 also make the far from invalid claim that a close correlation exists between the sins depicted and Dante's formal and linguistic choices. Yet, the ways in which they have developed this insight reveal, once again, that lack of historical awareness which has dogged analyses of the canto. Thus, they frequently allude to the sinners' "extreme moral degradation," which they see "objectively" or "realistically" reflected in the poet's recourse to the language of the gutter. However attractive such an interpretation may appear at first sight, it signally fails to explain why Dante felt it necessary and appropriate to bring together the erotic, the excremental, and the two particular sins of fraud with which he opens Malebolge. Similarly, the idea that the panders, seducers, and flatterers represent an excessive form of moral debasement which has to be treated in an appropriately excessive manner goes against the logic of the ethical structure of Dante's Hell where much more grievous, and hence extreme, sins exist—sins that, nevertheless, are overwhelmingly depicted without the poet's having to resort to the language of the "human privies" (*Inf* 18.114). Somewhat naively, and revealing rather more of their own attitudes than Dante's, critics appear to assume that because the poet is presenting matters dealing with sex and deceit, he is inevitably dealing with a "degraded" and "degrading" subject matter that he would have felt obliged to present through an abject vocabulary and imagery. Yet, when proffering this view, they provide no evidence based on medieval sources to substantiate their conviction. Equally reductively, and driven by their desire to establish the "objectivity" of Dante's treatment, scholars equate the *genus humilis* both with what is generally deemed immoral and, more particularly, with matters relating to sex, thereby forgetting the scriptural pedigree of the *sermo humilis,* the poet's predominantly "tragic" treatment of the lustful in *Inferno* 5, and the fact that, if the "low" and immorality were as closely associated in the Middle Ages as they believe, then the whole of the first canticle should have been composed in this register.

What Dantists have failed to do when analyzing *Inferno* 18, as well as the other episodes to which I referred earlier, is explain the interaction between Dante's linguistic and ethical choices in terms of medieval culture, the only yardstick with which the "objectivity"—or "subjectivity"—of the poet's presentation can be measured. They have allowed the disgust they personally feel to control their reactions as exegetes, forgetful that their repugnance is an effect of Dante's verse, and that the poet, obviously through different rhetorical means, also wants us to feel disdain for the rest of Hell's inhabitants. Disgust, to put it plainly, is, ultimately, what we are always meant to feel when confronted by sin. It is not something peculiar to the *adulatores.* What is especially disconcerting, since such behavior goes against the critic's age-old duty to interpret texts, is that Dantists have not only distanced themselves, quite reasonably, from the sinners of canto 18, but also, quite unreasonably, from the words that Dante chose to evoke the two sets of defrauders. As a result, problems of style, of rhetoric, of literary tradition, and of intellectual history have been reduced to mere emotive effects at the service of generalizing moral ends—excrement as a sign of the "degradation" of the *adulatores* and of the need to shun their sin—a viewpoint that reveals almost nothing about flattery's specific characteristics. In addition, such emotive effects have been presented in absolute terms, as if, in every epoch and in every culture, "l'unghie merdose" ("[the] shit-filled nails" [v. 131]) of a "sozza e scapigliata fante" ("besmirched, bedraggled harridan"[5] [v. 130]) inevitably lead to the same psychological and ethical reactions. To put it a bit differently: Dantists have read and assessed *Inferno* 18 without ever posing the question of the role played in the Middle Ages by obscenity and scatology, elements that—whether one likes it or not—fundamentally delimit the canto; and hence they have failed to address the issue of the status and the impact on the poet of the texts in which such matters were discussed and presented. As far as I am concerned, the real "scandal" of *Inferno* 18 is to be found not in Dante's linguistic expressionism but in this critical failure.

Before offering what I hope is a historically warranted hypothesis for the interplay among language, ethics, and literature in *Inferno* 18, it is incumbent on me to say something, however fleetingly, about the highly complex problem of the position of obscenity and scatology in medieval culture. Let me begin by dealing with some questions of terminology, normally an illuminating point of departure. So far in this essay, I have been careful to distinguish between "obscenity" and "scatology," even though, in present-day usage, "obscenity" is often used as a blanket term that conflates the scatological with the sexual. For reasons that should become clear, I prefer to keep the two notions separate, although, as in *Inferno* 18, there is no doubt that the erotic and the excremental have long overlapped in Western culture. Put simply: I employ "obscenity" to designate base and / or explicit talk relating to sex, while I utilize "scatology" to mean base and / or explicit talk relating to excretory functions. Although the term *obscenitas* was current in both classical and medieval Latin, it was very rarely used to refer to the sphere of the lewd. Instead, the Middle Ages employed a whole series of other terms, all of which were negatively marked, and unambiguously defined *obscena verba* as sinful. First and foremost among these was *turpiloquium* (lewd talk) though this was flanked, *inter alia,* by designations such as *scurrilitas* (scurrilous joking) and *multiloquium* (loquacity). On the other hand, as far as I have been able to ascertain, no equivalent technical term to our "scatology" was current in medieval culture. This terminological discrepancy is highly suggestive. The proliferation of references to obscenity highlights a deep moral concern with and anxiety over matters relating to sex, or, better, with talking about sexual topics. A similar ethical preoccupation would appear not to have affected the use of scatological language, given the lack of a tag with which to describe this type of discourse. However, this fact, in itself, should immediately counsel caution when, as has regularly happened, we feel impelled to treat the erotic and the scatological elements of *Inferno* 18 as if they were somehow equivalent. Instead, it would seem rather more likely that, as far as the Middle Ages were concerned, the two spheres were viewed as distinct rather than as coterminous, even though they could both be present in the same text.[6]

Indeed, evidence for such a sense of their distinctiveness is apparent in *Inferno* 18. It has not been previously noted that, in the canto, Dante actually treats the excremental and the erotic in quite different ways. In very schematic terms, the poet is prepared to talk openly about the former but not about the latter, a diversifying approach that interestingly correlates with the suggestions coming from medieval terminological practice relating to scatology and obscenity. Thus, Dante graphically evokes the disgusting environment of the second *bolgia* of the eighth circle by drawing on strikingly explicit locutions, namely, "sterco" ("excrement" [v. 113]), "uman privadi" ("human privies" [v. 114]), "di merda lordo" ("smeared with shit" [v. 116]), "unghie merdose" ("shit-filled nails" [v. 131]), which he combines with plebeian terms with harsh rhyme sounds in rhyme position, such as: "si nicchia" ("whine" [v. 103]), "scuffa" ("snorted" [v. 104]), "stucca" ("sufficiency" [v. 126, from *stuccare,* meaning "to bore" or "to tire"]). All these elements are then effectively molded into highly vivid descriptions of the sinners and of their place of eternal punishment. In this respect, it is more than understandable why modern critics should have turned to a concept such as "realism" in order to define Dante's technique for presenting the *adulatores.* Conversely, the poet is coy when describing the sinners' libidinous conduct. The most explicit word he utilizes is "puttana" ("harlot" [v. 133]), though only after he has used the decidedly more neutral "fante" (see note 5). In any case, the term fixes Thais's profession rather than evoking the erotic activities in which she may have indulged. Elsewhere in the canto, he is carefully constrained and, in general, formally elegant, relying on concision, periphrasis, antonomasia, and allusion—textbook instances of *reticentia*—to indicate transgressive sexual behavior and attitudes. Thus, the sordid tale of a brother's prostituting his sister is reduced to the stark phrase "la sconcia novella" ("that filthy tale" [v. 57]) and to the characterization of the pander-sibling, Venedico Caccianemico, as "colui che la Ghisolabella / condusse a far la voglia del marchese" ("[he] who led Ghisolabella / to do as the Marquis would have her do" [vv. 55–56]); "femmine da conio" (v. 66), on the other hand, is an expression whose precise meaning ultimately cannot even be pinned down, and hence whose sexual force is dissipated, since it can designate either "women for sale" or "women to deceive," just as Thais's movements, "e or s'accoscia e ora è in piedi stante" ("and now she crouches, now she stands upright" [v. 132]), may possibly have sexual connotations or may simply describe the discomfort of her otherworldly condition; finally, Jason's shameful treatment of Hypsipyle is cloaked in Dante's own "ornate words": "con segni e con parole ornate / Isifile ingannò / . . . Lasciolla . . . gravida, soletta" ("with polished words and love signs he took in / Hypsipyle . . . / he abandoned her, alone and pregnant" [vv. 91–92, 94]). In formal terms, there is nothing here, as will be confirmed shortly, to cause either moral or stylistic offense.

It is clear that Dante deals with the scatological and the obscene as if the two belonged to different ethical, literary, and ideological traditions. In doing so, as my earlier discussion of the relevant terminology implies, the poet's practice accurately reflects medieval attitudes regarding the treatment of the erotic and the excremental. Ever since Paul's epistles, Christian moral writing had constantly warned against the dangers of *verba obscena,* of indulging in unbridled lewd speech. Basically, two major positions evolved on the question: a hardline viewpoint that had its origins in the Apostle's letters, and a more flexible approach that drew on the authority of Saint Augustine. Paul categorically forbids all reference to *immunditia:* "Fornicatio autem, et omnis immunditia, aut avaritia, nec nominetur in vobis, sicut decet sanctos: aut turpitudo, aut stultiloquium, aut scurrilitas, quae ad rem non pertinet" ("Fornication, however, and all uncleanliness, or greed, let it not be named among you, as befits saints, nor filthiness, nor foolish talk, nor scurrilous joking, which are not befitting" [Eph. 5:3–4]). The Bishop of Hippo, however, as he does elsewhere in his *oeuvre,* proposes a rather more pragmatic solution to the problem:

> Quisquis ergo ad has litteras inpudicus accedit, culpam refugiat, non naturam; facta denotet suae turpitudinis, non verba nostrae necessitatis; in quibus mihi facillime pudicus et religiosus lector vel auditor ignoscit. . . . Legit enim haec sine offensione . . . , sed in explicandis, quantum possumus, humanae generationis effectibus verba tamen, sicut ille [Paul, Rom 1:26], obscena vitamus.
>
> (*De civitate Dei* 14.23)

> Thus, if anyone approaches with impure thoughts what I am writing, he should shun his own guilt, not nature; he should stigmatize the actions of his own depravity, not the words imposed on us by necessity. The chaste and religious reader or listener will easily forgive my use of such words. . . . He will read these without taking offense . . . , yet, in explaining, as best I can, the process of human generation, I must try, like him, to avoid obscene words.

Augustine acknowledges the need to talk about erotic activity, not least because it is a fact of nature—the passage quoted refers to the thorny and much-debated problem regarding Eve and Adam's sexual relations before and after the Fall. At the same time, however, he stresses the obligation to shun salacious language, and places responsibility on the reader to avoid arousal when confronted by the author's carefully and modestly chosen words. Indeed, the rhetorical tradition supported the saint's standpoint by proscribing lewdly explicit language, while highlighting the usefulness of circumlocution when needing to address sexual matters.

Dante's practice in the *Commedia* conforms strictly to the Augustinian rhetorical position (though, if the poet is the author of both the *Fiore* and the sonnets to Forese, it is obvious that he was not consistent in this throughout his life). The passages already examined from *Inferno* 18 bear testimony to the fact of Dante's adherence to Augustine's precepts, as does the rest of the poem. For instance, Dante employs textbook periphrases to allude to the male and female reproductive organs: "lo membro che l'uom cela" ("the member that man hides" [*Inf* 25.116]) and "[sangue perfetto] scende ov' è piú bello / tacer che dire" ("[the perfect blood] descends / to what is best not named" [*Purg* 25.43–44]), while, when obliged to speak about human generation in *Purgatorio* 25, he uses a dryly scientific language, eliminating not just any reference to desire, but also to the human agents (vv. 37–60). After having criticized colleagues' work, it cheers me at this juncture to be able to correct my own earlier research—something that always gives me a perverse satisfaction since it reminds me how little I know and how provisional our discoveries inevitably are. I have often asserted that a key feature of the plurilingual *Commedia* is its all-embracing character. I should now like to refine my earlier statement and declare that Dante was careful to establish a limit to his poem's linguistic and thematic encyclopaedism. In keeping with contemporary ethical attitudes, Dante considered overt references to the sexual as sinfully transgressive, and hence unsuitable for his *sacrato poema.* At the same time, as I hope is becoming manifest, and as I shall soon document further, obscenity and scatology have an important role to play in the *Commedia*'s metaliterary infrastructure. Indeed, this is especially evident when we explore Dante's treatment of the excremental.

The reason why both the poet and Christian culture, unlike their response to the sexual, were quite sanguine about the scatological is straightforward. The Bible makes significant recourse to it. For instance, there are over twenty instances of *stercus* in the Vulgate.[7] These then inspired, especially through the commentary tradition, a massive use of the term in the writings of both the Fathers and the Doctors. Searching the Corpus Christianorum CD-Roms, I was overwhelmed by around a thousand references. Drawing on scatological language was part of religious writing, as a cursory glance at the works of Jacopone da Todi, for instance, immediately confirms. This fact is immensely important when considering the use Dante makes of excremental terminology in the *Commedia;* it constitutes yet another sign that he is doing God's work, that he is a *scriba Dei.* It also confirms how inadequate are those interpretations that banally trivialize Dante's "merda" as merely an expression of disgust. On the other hand, secular, classically grounded literary-critical opinion was rather more wary of scatology. For instance, it was accepted that authors writing in the "low style" could mention the breaking of wind, though it does not appear that they were granted license to refer to other excretory functions (Villa 1984, 89–90). In this context, Dante's farting devil cannot but take on metaliterary trappings. Malacoda appears in a group of cantos that, as I have already observed, define Dante's experimental *comedía* in opposition to established "comic" practices. Hence, the tension between Thais's "shit-filled nails" and the devil's trumpeting "ass" can be seen to indicate the poet's rejection of traditional Terentian "low" poetics in favor of the more flexible conventions of biblical *sermo humilis.* Indeed, as some of the fourteenth-century Dante commentators were quick to recognize (see especially Pietro Alighieri 1978, 290–91), it is precisely from Scripture that the poet took the idea of bringing together prostitution and excrement: "omnis mulier, quae est fornicaria, quasi stercus in via conculcabitur" ("every woman, who is promiscuous, will be trodden in the road as if she were excrement" [Eccles. 9:10]).

As ought to be apparent from the variety of texts already alluded to during the course of this short study, scatology and sex found space in a large number of different medieval works. The number and diversity of these is, in fact, astonishing. They include the Bible, scriptural commentary, religious verse, sermons, confessional manuals, treatises on sins, mystical literature, medical and scientific texts, encyclopaedias, legal tracts, works of rhetoric, poetics, and criticism, and a variety of "low" literary genres. Any half-thorough investigation of Dante's attitudes toward obscenity and scatology must engage with all of these—a task beyond the remit of this rudimentary sketch. But I should like to close by briefly considering the poet's relationship to a couple of these classes of texts, specifically the "low" literary forms and the treatises on sins.

There were several vernacular *humilis* subgenres—it is enough to think of the *fabliaux* and the *fatrasies*—that presented the sexual, often in association with the excremental, in an explicit manner. It is thus safe to assume that Dante was intent on ensuring that his "divine comedy" should not be confused with traditions that both he and the religious-cum-literary culture of his day deemed immoral and / or lacking in merit as literature. Confirmation of this orientation comes, once again, from the devils of barratry. As several scholars have demonstrated, most recently Michelangelo Picone (2000), the Malebranche can be interpreted as representing the medieval jongleurs, those *scurrae* whose activities were closely associated with *scurrilitas.* Though the majority of their largely orally performed works have not come down to us, we can arrive at a good sense of the nature of these from legal and religious texts describing the jongleurs' performances. Indecency, played for laughs and accompanied by obscene gesturing, appears to have been commonplace. Dante's condemnation of the devils' antics thus serves also to pass judgment on the *scurrae,* authors who talked openly about sex purely to amuse and for material gain. Their transgressive works were without moral *utilitas,* their sole aim was *delectatio,* entertainment based on laughter—a fact that underscores that *risus* could not have been one of *Inferno* 18's goals. On the other hand, the *Commedia,* too, is a text that transgresses established literary norms, but it does this for divinely inspired ethical ends and with a proper awareness, based, as we have seen, on the *sermo humilis,* of what should or should not be expressed. In defining his poem's plurilingual "comic" qualities, Dante ensured that the *Commedia* would not be confused either with conventional Terentian forms of the "low" or with the "style's" most extreme forms. He rejected both the constraints of the *genera dicendi* and the false freedom of *turpiloquium.*

The question of the proper and improper use of language lies at the heart of *Inferno* 18; and it is high time that I returned to my point of departure and said something about the medieval bases of Dante's treatment of the first two groups of the fraudulent. *Inferno* 18, as is the case with Malebolge as a whole, to which the canto, revealingly, stands as a *prooemium,* is heavily dependent on a branch of the treatises on sins, namely, that which dealt with the so-called "Sins of the Tongue" (Casagrande and Vecchio 1987), which, beginning in the twelfth century, had become increasingly popular and influential. Obviously, the linguistic and semiotic character of fraud has long been recognized by Dantists. Nevertheless, the "Sins of the Tongue" provide a historically appropriate framework within which to consider the poet's presentation of the eighth circle of Hell. Indeed, both the unambiguously linguistic character of the panders', seducers', and flatterers' wrongdoing and their association with sinful sexuality were almost certainly dictated by the widely recognized ties that connected such sinners and lasciviousness to the *peccata linguae.* Dante wanted to ensure that his cultural signals were clearly received. Starting with the canto's opening image of the fortified castle (vv. 7–18), many elements in *Inferno* 18 can also best be explained in terms of the conventions of the "Sins of the Tongue." It was a commonplace of the tradition that good people "guarded" their tongues: "Qui custodit os suum: custodit animam suam" ("Whoever guards his mouth, guards his soul" [Prov. 3:3]), and "hance bestiam [the tongue] inclusit deus in palato / uallauit muro dencium / clausit hostiis labiorum et obserauit seribus preceptorum ut bene teneretur et custodiretur" ("God shut this beast in the palate; he surrounded it with a wall of teeth; he closed it with the gates of lips; and he bolted it with the bars of precepts so that it should be well defended and guarded" [Étienne de Bourbon, c. 434v]). Dante's allusion to city walls, therefore, provides a first indication of the general *contrapasso* governing the otherworldly condition of the inhabitants of Malebolge. As an eternal reminder of their sinfulness, those who in life had failed to "guard" their tongues are punished by being "enclosed," not within city walls, since, metaphorically speaking, they had rejected their protection when alive, but, tellingly, within "fossi" ("ditches" [v. 17]) lying outside the "mura" ("walls" [v. 10]). More significant, the "Sins of the Tongue" provide the punishments for both *Inferno* 18's sets of sinners. The image of language as a whip is a memorable *topos* originating in Job (5:21), a book additionally important, as we shall see, in the context of *Inferno* 18, and which, together with the Psalms, the Sapiential Books, Paul's letters, and the Epistle of James, served as the key scriptural *auctoritates* in assessments of verbal sins. Equally, the *contrapasso* of the *adulatores* indelibly marks them in the treatise *Duplex est abstinentia, detestabilis et commendabilis* as archetypal linguistic sinners:

> Loquens debet attendere quid dicat, quomodo dicat, cui dicat et quando dicat. Quid debet homo loqui docetur 1 Pe. 4 [11], *Si quis loquitur quasi sermones dei,* et Eph. 4 [29], *Omnis sermo malus non procedat ex ore uestro: sed qui bonus est ad edificacionem fidei ut det gratiam audientibus.* Qui enim non timet coinquinare linguam suam plus quam alia membra pocius porcus uidetur quam homo. Porcus enim in cito ponit rostrum suum in luto sicut pedem. Item porcus semper habet os apertum ad stercora et non ad flores, sic mali ad stercora peccatorum non ad flores uirtutum. . . . De ore latrini et sepulcri non egreditur nisi fetor.
>
> (Oxford, Bodleian 185, c. 70v)

> A speaker should pay attention to what he ought to say, to how he should speak, to whom and when he should speak. What a person should say is taught in 1 Peter 4: *If anyone speaks let him do it as if with the words of God,* and Eph. 4: *Allow no evil speech to come forth from your mouth, but that which is beneficial for the edification of faith so that it may grant grace to those who hear it.* Whoever is not afraid of fouling his tongue more than his other members seems to be a pig rather than a human being. For a pig places its snout in dirt as readily as its foot. Equally a pig always has its mouth open to excrement and not to flowers, just like evil people keep their mouths open to the excrement of sins and not to the flowers of virtues. . . . Nothing comes out of the mouth of a toilet or a sepulchre except for stench.

The *contrapassi* of the panders, seducers, and flatterers are not the result, as Dantists have for too long maintained, of the poet's disgust for their sexual deceptions and practices, but are clear and rigorous—one might even be tempted to say "objective"—moral assertions of the ways in which their sinfulness had perverted the divine gift of speech.

Dante-pilgrim and -poet stand in direct opposition to such debasers of language. Discussions of the *peccata linguae* also dealt with those who employ their tongues virtuously, namely, the prudent and patient person: "prudens est qui futura prouidet, et premia et tormenta; et talis non murmurat de flagello. Libenter enim virgam tolerat qui a gladio pene eterne eum conseruat. Patienter eciam sustinet ab eo flagellari a quo celestem hereditatem expectat" ("the prudent person discerns future things, both rewards and sufferings; and such a person does not grumble about the whip. For he freely bears the rod who saves himself from the sword of eternal punishment. And furthermore he patiently endures being scourged by him from whom he expects the heavenly inheritance" [Peraldus 1479, G1r]). A key trait of the *prudens* is the way he uses language in a manner pleasing to God:

> Prudens est qui loquitur quando loquendum est. Unde ecclus xx [7], *Homo sapiens tacebit vsque ad tempus.* Prudentior est qui loquitur talia qualia debet loqui, vt qui loquitur verba pura a falsitate et a proximi nocumento et a contumelia dei. Unde prouerbiorum xv [26], *Sermo purus pulcerrimus est.* Prudentissimus vero est ille qui modum seruat in verbis qui scilicet dulciter loquitur absque clamore et asperitate quod non parum est vtile . . . non potest esse sermonis moderacio absque cordis moderacio.
>
> (Peraldus 1479, F1v)

> The prudent person speaks when he ought to speak. Thus Ecclus. 20: *The wise man will be silent until the time is right.* More prudent is the person who says those things which he ought to say, like him who speaks words pure from falsehood and from injury to others and from abuse of God. Thus Proverbs 15: *Pure speech is most beautiful.* Most prudent in fact is the person who maintains a measure in words, namely, who speaks sweetly and without noise and harshness what is rather useful . . . there can be no moderation in speech without moderation of the heart.

The similarities between the torments endured by the *prudens* and those suffered by the panders and seducers are self-evident, though the moral context is, naturally, completely different. The *adulatores,* too, are the negative anti-type of this prudent person, since Job, who was presented as the supreme example of prudence and patience, was traditionally depicted as *in stercore sedens.* As so often occurs elsewhere in Dante's Hell, the punishment of the sinners grotesquely parodies the ethically upright condition that they should have embraced in life. The complexity of the poet's vision in *Inferno* 18 is remarkable. Via the reference to the pilgrim's "chiara favella" (plain speech [v. 53]), the poet establishes a firm link between his own language and the *sermo purus* of the *prudens*, both of which stand in obvious contrast to Jason's lying "polished words" (v. 91). In the *Commedia*, in order effectively to communicate his divine message, Dante rejects the standard rhetorical conventions of the *genera dicendi*, not least because, as Jason reveals, "tragic" elegance is no guarantee of moral rectitude. Instead, like the other *scribae Dei*, he is prepared to approach language ethically and, hence, flexibly—a stance that permits him to have recourse, when appropriate, even to the language of the "human privies." By highlighting the poem's relationship to both scatology and obscenity, *Inferno* 18 and the other early cantos of Malebolge define its divinely ordained *humilis* parameters. Rather than being something marginal which needs to be dismissed swiftly to avoid embarrassment, the sexual and the excremental not only confirm the *Commedia*'s scriptural character, though they do this in conjunction with many other elements performing a similar function, but also, and in this respect quite uniquely, reveal its linguistic and thematic limits.

Notes

1. The main *lecturae* of *Inferno* 18 are: Fornaciari 1902; Gallarati Scotti 1968; Grana 1959; Barchiesi 1967; Caretti 1967; Sanguineti 1968; Accardo 1977; Martelli 1981; Storey 1990.

2. All quotations from the *Commedia* are taken from Petrocchi (Alighieri 1994), while translations are by Mandelbaum (Alighieri 1982–86). All translations from Latin texts are my own.

3. Though I take all the terms and phrases just quoted either from the *lecturae* cited in note 1 or from the standard commentaries to the *Commedia*, I purposely do not give references to specific studies. It is not my intention in this short paper to attack the writings of individual Dantists. My aim is simply to highlight what I deem to be a general flaw in Dante criticism. I take a similarly broad perspective when I go on to assess what critics have said about *Inferno* 18's stylistic register and its ethical character.

4. On the "low" register, comedy, and the *stili* in general, as well as their impact on Dante, see Barański 1995 and 1996, 15–182.

5. "Harridan" is, in fact, a mistranslation of the Italian *fante*. Singleton's "wench" (Alighieri 1970, 191, 327) comes closer to the mark. Chiavacci Leonardi (Alighieri 1991, 557) defines *fante* as a "woman of humble standing, low" and provides compelling proof against the term's having sexual connotations as many Dantists have claimed in Barbi's wake (1941, 321).

6. Though much has been written, especially in recent years, on sexuality in medieval culture, very little of this work takes a philological or historically informed approach to the question or considers this in relation to what I term "obscenity." The problem of scatology has been largely ignored. Considerable research in both areas still needs to be undertaken. In preparing this essay and developing my research on scatology and obscenity in medieval culture and in Dante, I have found the following studies particularly useful: Baldwin 1994; Bec 1984; Bloch 1986; Brundage 1987; Cadden 1995; Craun 1997; Elliott 1999; Lazzerini 1988; Payer 1993; Salisbury 1991; Ziolkowski 1998.

7. See Deut. 28: 27; Judg. 3:22; 1 Kings 2:8; 4 Kings 6:25; 9:37; 18:27; Tob. 2:11; Pss. 82:11; 112:7; Eccles. 9:10; 22:2; Isa. 5:25; 36:12; Jer. 9:22; Lam. 4:5; Joel 1:17; Soph. 1:17; Mal. 2:62; 1 Macc. 2:62; Luke 13:8; Phil. 3:8.

16

On Dante and the Visual Arts

Christopher Kleinhenz

THE EAGLE-LIKE FLIGHT of science and technology in the late twentieth century has had a salutary effect on the course of Dante studies, especially in terms of harnessing computer power to realize the cyber dreams of student and scholar alike. We must be prudent, however, in our flight in this dawning twenty-first century, for we do not wish our manmade Ulyssean wings to try to take us on a journey too perilous in the "mondo sanza gente" ("world that has no people" [*Inf* 26.117]).[1] Indeed, we should be cautious and judicious in our critical claims so that the monitory words of the eagle in *Par* 20.133–34 may not be directed at us: "E voi, mortali, tenetevi stretti / a giudicar" ("And you mortals, keep yourselves restrained in judging"). Toward the prudent study of the Middle Ages the concept of "interdisciplinarity," with the bigger picture—the cultural context—it promises to reveal, is crucial. This is the belief of scholars generally. Or, to be more accurate, we are confident in it as a desideratum; but as a credo, who will not properly confess his doubts about overleaping such chasms of altered circumstance and experience as lie between *us* and *them.* Is our whole interpretive enterprise based on the eagle-eye of the critic, then, reduced to mere feather-ruffling plausibility?

Luca Signorelli's fresco in the Chapel of San Brizio in the Duomo at Orvieto shows the Florentine poet engaged in what our latter-day argot calls "intertextuality": while composing his poem, Dante avidly consults another volume. This is comforting; this is what we like to see: it all but confirms the answers we proffer to critical questions of literary influence—particularly those demonstrated by direct textual citations and allusions. However, questions that will be raised in the course of this essay, concerning pictorial inspiration and influence on Dante, are much more uncertainly dealt with. Could Dante's shade attend the Dante2000 conference, we might well expect to hear heckling in the "grand style severe" (to use Matthew Arnold's mildly expressive phrase [1902, 266–67]). May he, may we, "restrain ourselves in judging" as the paradisiacal eagle advises. In the meanwhile, I will trust in the poet's higher preoccupations and in the sympathy of the reader for the riskier ingenuities of our business.

While it is a critical commonplace to compare the *Divine Comedy* to a Gothic cathedral because of its magnificent structure and subtle symmetries, I believe that Dante's poem might be better compared to a different sort of artistic work: for example, to the twelfth-century mosaic in the apse of the Church of Saint Clement in Rome. The mosaic attempts to comprehend in a harmonious view the entire cosmos: from the ordinary people—peasants, shepherds, women tending fowl—in the lower register, through the Fathers and Doctors of the Church (Saint Ambrose et al.), all the way to the angelic light of the Empyrean. This totalizing vision, like that of Dante, encloses the world within the ever-growing acanthus scrolls of the Living Cross. Here we may observe the same love of symmetry, of macrocosm and microcosm, of the perfect order that obtains in a Providential universe.

Just in the way this mosaic gave impulse to my foregoing comparison, so have various images from the figurative arts seemed to "suggest themselves" to Dante's mind during his composition of the *Comedy,* and been communicated to its design, whether at the level of a particular scene or episode, or of the poem as a structural whole. *Ut pictura poesis* ("a poem is like a picture" [Horace 1961, v. 361]). So far at least will we find Dante and Horace to agree. This association of image and text is propounded literally in *Purgatory* 11, where Oderisi da Gubbio describes the manuscripts illuminated by his hand and by Franco Bolognese as the "smiling . . . pages" ("ridon le carte" [*Purg* 11.82]). And in his dirge on the transience of earthly fame, Oderisi tellingly sets painters and poets in mutual relation:

Credette Cimabue ne la pittura
 tener lo campo, e ora ha Giotto il grido,
 sì che la fama di colui è scura.
Così ha tolto l'uno a l'altro Guido
 a gloria de la lingua; e forse è nato
 chi l'uno e l'altro caccerà del nido.
Non è il mondan romore altro ch'un fiato
 di vento, ch'or vien quinci e or vien quindi,
 e muta nome perché muta lato.
(*Purg* 11.94–102)

> Cimabue thought to hold the field in painting, and now Giotto has the cry, so that the other's fame is dim; so has the one Guido taken from the other the glory of our tongue—and he perchance is born that shall chase the one and the other from the nest. Earthly fame is naught but a breath of wind, which now comes hence and now comes thence, changing its name because it changes quarter.

Despite the realistic assessment of earthly fame given in the last tercet, art itself may be long in life and reach. That Dante thought so, we may gather by the didactic purpose he conceived for it, as well as by the lessons he accepted from it.

At least once in the *Comedy* Dante indicates a particular work of art. In the fifth ditch of the eighth circle of the *Inferno,* corrupt "soft money" politicians—the thirteenth-century "Boss Tweeds"—are immersed in boiling pitch and bedeviled with some very clever jabs indeed: "Qui non ha loco il Santo Volto! / qui si nuota altrimenti che nel Serchio!" ("Here's no place for the Holy Face! Here you'll swim otherwise than in the Serchio!"). The river Serchio runs through the Tuscan town of Lucca (which, we are given to know, supplies this part of Hell copiously), and the Santo Volto—the "Holy Face"—is an object of great veneration there. Here, in the *Inferno,* Dante plays on the fact that the Holy Face, the figure of Jesus on the Cross, was carved from black wood, and invests the entire episode with "black" humor, as it were. As the Lucchese barrator emerges from the boiling pitch, he appears to do the "dead man's float," thus presenting a black, cruciform figure—a mocking semblance of the Holy Face (Figure 1). Moreover, it is the sinner's true, spiritual face—his besmirched backside ("Quel . . . tornò sù convolto": "The sinner . . . rose again, rump up")—which the sarcastic devils identify with the Santo Volto.

We may speculate, likewise, on the closeness of Dante's depiction of Lucifer to the fallen angel in the mosaics in the cupola of the Florentine Baptistery, so beloved by the poet. With somewhat less assurance, we may attempt to discern certain artistic representations of the life of Saint Francis lying behind, indeed perhaps prompting, the words of Saint Thomas in *Paradiso* 11 (e.g., the early panel [1235] painted by Bonaventura Berlinghieri and found in the Church of Saint Francis in Pescia). Thomas's narration of certain key moments in the *poverello*'s life would suggest Dante's more-than-literary association with the legend. Are we expected to think of the glorious series of frescoes in the Upper Church of Saint Francis in Assisi? Should we see the fresco depicting the stigmata at La Verna as the visual stimulus for Dante's words:

nel crudo sasso intra Tevero e Arno
da Cristo prese l'ultimo sigillo,
che le sue membra due anni portarno.
(*Par* 11.106–108)

[O]n the harsh rock between Tiber and Arno he received from Christ the last seal, which his limbs bore for two years.

Or should we imagine that the allegorical scenes above the altar in the Lower Church in Assisi profoundly influenced the poet's presentation of the mystical marriage of Francis and Lady Poverty? Indeed, when Saint Thomas hastens to switch to a simpler mode of narration—"Ma perch' io non proceda troppo chiuso" ("But, lest I should proceed too darkly")—do we detect the poet's frustration in translating the fullness of impression he had gained from a visual medium into his own verbal one?

Dante will also allude generically to the figurative arts. On the first terrace of the mountain of Purgatory, the soul's penance for the sin of pride is to go about bent-over under large stone weights, a position that Dante describes as follows:

Come per sostentar solaio o tetto,
per mensola talvolta una figura
si vede giugner le ginocchia al petto,
la qual fa del non ver vera rancura
nascere 'n chi la vede; così fatti
vid' io color, quando puosi ben cura.
(*Purg* 10:130–35)

As for corbel to support a ceiling or a roof, sometimes a figure is seen to join the knees to the breast—which, unreal, begets real distress in one who sees it—so fashioned did I see these when I gave good heed.

Their burdened position suggests that of a caryatid or an Atlas figure, fitly reminiscent of the world-heavy spirit of paganism.[2] On this first terrace of Purgatory the pilgrim receives instruction in humility through the "visible speech" ("visibile parlare" [*Purg* 11.95]) of divinely sculpted reliefs, which relate, variously, the Annunciation to

Mary, David dancing before the Ark of the covenant, and the Emperor Trajan meting out mercy to the widow in her plight. Not for the sake of criticism, but for the sake of enchantment, we can only guess at the model Annunciation scene that intruded on Dante's imagination here: was it the richly colored mosaic by Pietro Cavallini in Santa Maria in Trastevere in Rome? Or was it Giotto's fresco in the Arena Chapel? Or, given the sculptural context, was it perhaps the wonderfully expressive relief by Giovanni Pisano for the pulpit of Sant'Andrea in Pistoia, executed in 1301? God, too, has set his hand to antithetical *exempla* of pride laid low—Lucifer, Nimrod, Arachne, et al. These, differently, are presented as being similar to pavement carvings, effigies, tomb covers embedded in church floors, on which our feet tread. The contrast between the form and the content of these two varieties of sculpture is both instructive and striking: on the one hand, we see the lifelike, vibrant examples of the virtue (humility) and, on the other, the dead, defeated examples of the vice (pride).

Since Dante conceived the other world partly in terms of cities (e.g., the City of Dis, or "that Rome whereof Christ is Roman" ["quella Roma onde Cristo è romano" (*Purg* 32.102)]), the architectural forms of urban spaces influenced his selection of images. Hell has its series of gated walls, like those that demarcated almost every medieval city (e.g., the Porta Romana in Florence). Perhaps, because of its inscriptions and free ingress, the great gate of Hell finds its right analogue in the classical triumphal arch (e.g., the Arch of Titus in the Roman Forum); especially if we would account the grim combination of ironies that the parallel owns: Death stands triumphant, proclaiming eternal victory, while the train of his captives—captives to lives of sin, deserters from Christ's hopeful army—passes through to damnation. The lesson of Divine Justice is read by all: "Lasciate ogne speranza, voi ch'intrate" ("Abandon every hope, you who enter" [*Inf* 3.9]). The lofty towers, too, of the medieval city—the fortress-homes of families no less prominent for their arrogance and brutality than for their wealth and rank—cue Dante's descriptions. Hence, in *Inferno* 31, the imposing towers of Monteriggioni and the Garisenda Tower of Bologna provide not exclusively visual terms of comparison to the giants who loom above the last circle, the pit of Hell, Lucifer's citadel.

Some critics have persuasively demonstrated how Dante borrows certain elements of Christian iconography (see, among others, Cassell

1984; Durling 1981; Herzman and Stephany 1978; Kleinhenz 1980, 1982, 1990, and 1999; Singleton 1965). In the *Inferno,* received iconic values are inverted. The Light of God, which blesses, becomes the light of fire, which burns. Punishment by fire is usually assigned to offenders against God: heretics, blasphemers, sodomites. The simonists, for example, are plunged headlong into the rock of Hell, their legs kicking the air and flames licking the soles of their feet. By appropriating and, at the same time, inverting the customary sign of Pentecost, when the Holy Spirit descended in tongues of fire on the heads of the Apostles, Dante tells us precisely what is the sin of simony: a sordid traffic in the things of grace.[3] Moreover, the composition of the scene, in which Dante and Virgil stand next to and converse with the upraised legs of Pope Nicholas III, matches up with the standard iconography developed from the apocryphal Acts of Peter, where Peter and Paul stand next to the fallen and inverted figure of Simon Magus—simony's eponym.[4] We cannot say for certain, of course, whether Dante's interpretation of the story was mediated by familiarity with the iconographers' work; or whether he drew, as they did, straight from the literary model (see Acts of Peter 1960, chaps. 6–32).

Other examples that we might cite in the same vein include the figure of Farinata as abject parody of the risen Christ, standing upright, but not triumphant in the fiery tomb in *Inferno* 10 (Cassell 1977 and 1984; Durling 1981); or the devilish mimicry of Christ the Good Shepherd in *Inferno* 21 (Kleinhenz 1982).[5] Here, instead of carrying the lost sheep back to the fold, which would figure the repentant sinner restored to salvation, the tender of souls—the "black devil" ("diavol nero" [*Inf* 21.29])—carries the lost reprobate to ever-renewed agony in boiling pitch.

Christian iconography serves Dante's positive purposes as well. Among the sights of the Empyrean and Celestial Rose, Beatrice shows the pilgrim, in particular, the throne prepared for Henry VII:

> E 'n quel gran seggio a che tu li occhi tieni
> per la corona che già v'è sù posta,
> prima che tu a queste nozze ceni,
> sederà l'alma, che fia giù agosta,
> de l'alto Arrigo, ch'a drizzare Italia
> verrà in prima ch'ella sia disposta.
> (*Par* 30.133–38)

> And in that great chair whereon you fix your eyes because of the crown that already is set above it, before you sup at these nuptials shall sit the soul, which on earth will be imperial, of the lofty Henry, who will come to set Italy straight before she is ready.

Dante might have meant this image to evoke the icon found in Byzantine art of the "empty throne" (the *Hetoimasia*), which derives in part from the description in the Apocalypse of the throne in heaven (see Kleinhenz 1999).[6] Although not common in Italy, this motif does appear in certain places that may be keyed to Dante's movements: in the sanctuary arch mosaic in Santa Maria Maggiore in Rome, in the Last Judgment mosaic in the cathedral at Torcello in the Venetian lagoon, and in cupola mosaics of both the Orthodox (Neonian) and the Arian Baptisteries in Ravenna. In this last instance the empty throne surmounted by the bejewelled cross signifies the throne prepared for the Second Coming of Christ; twelve processional figures—Peter, Paul, and ten apostles—wait with crowns. Not that Dante intended his own use of the motif to say as much; rather, drawing upon the same outward type, he was able to suggest that Henry VII possessed qualities that would have made him an excellent Christo-mimetic emperor. Dante's *Epistles* on the occasion of Henry's descent into Italy are replete with allusions to Christ, to the extent that Henry becomes, in fact, a messianic figure, the savior who will heal the wounds of Italy; one for whom the heavenly throne is prepared.[7]

Heretofore, I fear I have been too circumspect and slight—*too prudent,* perhaps—in my survey. I would like to conclude this essay by considering two points, one quite restricted and the other more general in scope, both of which concern the basic question of the way Dante may have been inspired by the visual tradition of the Middle Ages. In *Inferno* 31, as Dante and Virgil proceed through the gloomy dusk that surrounds the Great Pit, they hear a tremendous horn-blast, which is compared to the one sounded by Roland at Roncesvalles to notify Charlemagne of the defeat of the rear guard:

> Quiv' era men che notte e men che giorno,
> sì che 'l viso m'andava innanzi poco;
> ma io senti' sonare un alto corno,
> tanto ch'avrebbe ogne tuon fatto fioco,
> che, contra sé la sua via seguitando,
> dirizzò li occhi miei tutti ad un loco.

Dopo la dolorosa rotta, quando
Carlo Magno perdé la santa gesta,
non sonò sì terribilmente Orlando.
(*Inf* 31.10–18)

Here it was less than night and less than day, so that my sight went little ahead, but I heard a blast from a horn so loud that it would have made any thunderclap seem faint, and it directed my eyes, following back on its course, wholly to one place. After the dolorous rout when Charlemagne lost the holy gest, Roland did not sound a blast so terrible.

It is Nimrod, the "mighty hunter before the Lord" ("robustus venator coram Domino" [Gen. 10:9]) and the principal architect of the Tower of Babel, who blows the horn, cunningly condemned to inchoate unintelligibility, this and a garbled speech ("Raphèl maì amècche zabì almi") being the only articulation allowed him. The presence of the horn apparently follows from Nimrod's hunter character in the Bible; however, there does not appear to be an artistic convention or tradition specially endorsing this accessory detail. I would propose, nevertheless, a very subtle process by which the image of the horn makes its way from an artistic source into Dante's text. I refer to Giotto's fresco of the Betrayal by Judas in the Arena Chapel. As we see (Figure 2), the dramatic focus of the scene is on the kiss and on the intense gaze that joins Jesus and Judas; to make doubly sure, Giotto points our attention to it by means of the converging lances. Peter who lops off the guard's ear, the torches that flash in the early morning obscurity—these form subordinate actions and elements. I would have us remark, as I believe Dante did, the raised horn in the background: an oliphant that perhaps announces the arrest of Jesus, or perhaps a shofar that announces—with how much dire irony among unholy dealings—the Passover holy day. While receiving very little commentary in the critical literature, this horn of Giotto's, which signals the treachery of Judas, is, I would suggest, a striking visual correlative, if not ulterior impetus, to the explicit parallel Dante draws between Roland's horn and Ganelon's betrayal, as well as Nimrod's horn and the pilgrim's entrance to the circle of the traitors. Nimrod, to whom the horn attaches, is himself guilty of traducing the Will, by presuming to the Glory, of God. It is thus that Dante may have transmuted a single and minor component from the Arena Chapel into the very emblem of treachery.

My final, broader consideration concerns the possible influence of the visual arts on Dante's organization of the *Comedy.* We all are well aware of the symmetries that inform the poem; the verbal echoes, the glosses of different passages, one upon the other; the verbal descriptions—and hence the resulting visual similarities—that connect spatially disparate souls: Farinata with the giants and with Lucifer, or the simonists with Judas (see Kleinhenz 1974). We find something of the same in the visual practices of Giotto, who carefully positions episodes from the cycles of the life of the Virgin and of Jesus so as to disclose the mysterious typological relationships that exist among events in the Old and New Testaments, and thus to enhance the meaning and dynamic interaction of the entire artistic program. The most obvious parallelism may be found in the representations of the four cardinal and three theological virtues that are placed opposite their specific corresponding vice in the lowest register of the side walls in the Arena Chapel: Justice opposite Injustice; Hope across from Despair, and so on.[8]

However, there also exists in the *Comedy* a parallel structure, by which the poem may be read not only horizontally and linearly (that is, each canticle within itself), but also vertically (each canticle holding up foil-mirrors to the others). This, too, imitates certain designs found in the fresco and mosaic cycles of Dante's time. In terms of vertical readings of the *Comedy,* the sixth canto of each canticle deals with politics of increasingly larger scope: Florence in the *Inferno;* Italy in the *Purgatorio;* and Empire in the *Paradiso* (see, among others, Kay 1992). The pilgrim's encounter with Brunetto Latini in *Inferno* 15 is complemented—and corrected—by the meeting with Cacciaguida in *Paradiso* 15. These encounters are particularly characterized by their familial atmosphere and concern for the paternity of the spirit. But is there any doubt as to whose message Dante will ultimately heed? I would like to suggest that the idea for this kind of parallel structure came to Dante forcefully from his looking, since the time he was a small boy, and ever with love, upon the mosaics in the cupola of the Florentine Baptistery. Furthermore, I would suggest that this manner of "reading" was reinforced by his viewing of other visual narratives, especially those by Giotto in the Arena Chapel in Padua.

The great artistic program in the Baptistery was completed during the second half of the thirteenth century. In addition to the Last Judgment, the cupola shows stories of the Creation and the lives of

Joseph, Jesus, and John the Baptist (Figure 3). These narratives are presented in concentric bands, which begin to the right of the damned and move round to completion on the left of the saved. In the eight-sided Baptistery, three zones of the cupola are given over to the Last Judgment, with the great figure of Christ flanked on his right hand by the saved and on his left by the damned. The other five zones of the cupola contain the fifteen episodes in the four separate "storylines,"[9] and these are arranged so that they can be read both horizontally (that is, in their individual chronology), *and* vertically (in their typological and allegorical relations, whereby the meaning of one enhances and explicates that of another). But just as perfect correspondence between narrative bands does not obtain, so there is no mechanical scheme precisely linking all the hundred cantos of the *Comedy.*

It is a pity that we should trundle out the hackneyed observation that the church edifice in the Middle Ages was in itself a primary means of edification, only to pass on quickly to some other fact, because we are impatient to suffer the "edifying" ourselves and learn whether it is as we carelessly say it is. Let us examine some of the mosaics in the cupola.[10] In the first zone (Figure 4) we track down, in the first vertical segment, from the Creation in the top register to Joseph's dream of the sheaves and the sun, moon, and stars, to the Annunciation to Mary, and to the Annunciation to Zacharias. In the second vertical segment we see the Creation of Adam, Joseph relating the dream to his father and mother, the meeting of Mary and Elizabeth, and the Nativity of the Baptist. In the third vertical segment, we see the Creation of Eve, Joseph together with his brothers yet very much alone in the wilderness, the Nativity of Jesus, and John in the Wilderness. In this way the mosaics are made to "read" marvelously like the first chapter of the Gospel according to Saint John, whose text alludes richly and simultaneously to Creation, to the Old Testament prophetic past and to the relationship between Jesus and John the Baptist. So, too, in the third zone (Figure 5), we find the presentation in the temple aligned with the baptism of Christ; the lie of Potiphar's wife that succeeds in putting Joseph in prison is equivalent to Herodias's persuading Herod to imprison the Baptist. There is also the contrastive value of the slaying of Abel and the flight to safety in Egypt, as well as the comparative value of the imprisonments of Joseph and John the Baptist. In the fifth zone (Figure 6) we note the parallel scenes of Crucifixion and John's beheading. Yet, the embarking of Noah in the Deluge, like Christ's (temporary) deposition, reminds us that the great good soul is ever in God's care. And with the arrival of the dove and opening of the ark we discover, as the three Marys discover at the open tomb, the divine gift of new life. Thus, in the final vertical segment, we see the promise for renewal in the world after the cleansing flood; we witness the reunion of Joseph and his father; and, finally, we observe the open tomb as the sign of Christ's resurrection and the entombment of the Baptist, both of which exemplify the importance of sacrifice for faith. The four narrative bands—the history of the world, as Faith could once say—move forward together toward their inevitable, extraordinary consummation: the Last Judgment at the End of Time. Of these nine vertical segments, five show direct visual correspondences between at least two scenes, and three of the remaining four segments have scenes that are linked thematically. There are, in addition, other visual and verbal links between scenes in adjacent segments. The germs of great ideas that were planted by this spatial arrangement in the Baptistery grew and flourished with Giotto in the Arena Chapel and with Dante in the *Divine Comedy.* In both we see again the spectacle of Christian history in its double aspect of wonderful Providence and sublime Justice.

As a sensitive observer and keen admirer of the visual arts of his day, Dante learned much about their narrative and artistic techniques, and his great poem demonstrates their influence in many and diverse ways. As a literary work that reflects its historical and artistic context, that charges itself in living realities, and speaks them in powerful words and images the *Divine Comedy* has enduring human appeal. It is truly, as Dante himself said, "'l poema sacro / al quale ha posto mano e cielo e terra" ("the sacred poem to which heaven and earth have . . . set hand" [*Par* 25.1–2]).

Notes

1. All references to and translations from Dante's *Commedia* are from Alighieri 1970–75.

2. Other visual examples of this sort of figure may be seen in the mosaic in the Tribuna of the Florentine Baptistery, dating from 1225–28 (see Wilkins 1959).

3. For artistic representations of Pentecost, see Giotto's fresco in the Arena Chapel (Padua) and the panel from Duccio's *Maestà* in the Museo dell'Opera del Duomo (Siena).

4. For example, see the panel of Saint Peter with six scenes from his life (Siena, Pinacoteca Nazionale), executed by the so-called Master of the St. Peter Dossal, a follower of Guido da Siena. On the bottom left of the dossal is the scene depicting an inverted air-borne Simon Magus, supported by demons but apparently poised to plunge to earth, and the two figures of Peter and Paul standing on the ground. Other artistic examples (e.g., a twelfth-century capital of the cathedral of Autun, executed by Ghislebertus, and a twelfth-century sculpture on the archivolt of the portal of Ripoll Cathedral) are presented by Singleton 1965.

5. It should be noted that the baptismal font executed in the mid-twelfth century by Master Robert and located in the Church of San Frediano in Lucca has, in a prominent position, a Good Shepherd.

6. For a general discussion of this theme see Leclercq 1922, 671–73. For its presence in Italian art see Hall 1983, 94–95.

7. In his fifth letter ("Universis et singulis Italiae Regibus et Senatoribus almae Urbis" ["To all and singular Princes of Italy, and the Senatora of the Sacred City"]), Dante alludes to Henry as the "Sun of peace [that] shall appear on high" ("Titan exorietur pacificus" [5.1 in Alighieri 1966]) and continues: "Laetare iam nunc miseranda Italia etiam Saracenis, quae statim invidiosa per orbem videberis, quia sponsus tuus, mundi solatium et gloria plebis tuae, clementissimus Henricus, Divus et Augustus et Caesar, ad nuptias properat. Exsicca lacrymas, et moemoris vestigia dele, pulcerrima; nam prope est qui liberabit te de carcere impiorum, qui percutiens malignantes in ore gladii perdet eos, et vineam suam aliis locabit agricolis, qui fructum iustitiae reddant in tempore messis" (5.2 in Alighieri 1966 ["Rejoice, therefore, O Italy, thou that art now an object of pity even to the Saracens, for soon shalt thou be the envy of the whole world, seeing that thy bridegroom, the comfort of the nations, and the glory of thy people, even the most clement Henry, Elect of God and Augustus and Caesar, is hastening to the wedding. Dry thy tears, and wipe away the stains of thy weeping, most beauteous one; for he is at hand who shall bring thee forth from the prison of the ungodly, and shall smite the workers of iniquity with the edge of the sword, and shall destroy them. And his vineyard shall he let out to other husbandmen, who shall render the fruit of justice in the time of harvest"]).

In his seventh epistle addressed to Henry ("Gloriosissimo atque felicissimo Triumphatori et Domino singulari, Domino Henrico" ["To the most glorious and most fortunate Conqueror, and sole Lord, the Lord Henry"]), Dante compares the emperor's arrival in Italy to be like "the rising of the long-awaited

Sun" ("Titan, praeoptatus exoriens") for which "nova spes Latio saeculi melioris effulsit" (7.1 in Alighieri 1966 ["a new hope of a better age shone abroad upon Italy"]) and speaks of the Italians as those who, "going before their wishes in their joy, sang with Maro [Virgil] of the reign of Saturn, and of the return of the Virgin" ("Tunc plerique vota sua praevenientes in iubilo, tam Saturnia regna quam Virginem redeuntem cum Marone cantabant" [7.1]), an obvious reference to Virgil's Fourth Eclogue and its presumed prophecy of the coming of Christ. A few lines later in the same letter, Dante states his firm belief in and support for Henry: "in te credimus et speramus, asseverantes te Dei ministrum, et Ecclesiae filium, et Romanae gloriae promotorem. Nam et ego, qui scribo tam pro me quam pro aliis, velut decet imperatoriam maiestatem, benignissimum vidi et clementissimum te audivi, cum pedes tuos manus meae tractarunt, et labia mea debitum persolverunt. Tunc exultavit in me spiritus meus, quum tacitus dixi mecum: 'Ecce Agnus Dei, ecce qui tollit peccata mundi!'" (7.2 ["we believe and hope in thee, declaring thee to be the minister of God, the son of the Church, and the furtherer of the glory of Rome. For I too, who write as well for myself as for others, beheld thee most gracious, and heard thee most clement, as beseems Imperial Majesty, when my hands touched they feet, and my lips paid their tribute. Then my spirit rejoiced within me, when I said secretly within myself: 'Behold the Lamb of God, which taketh away the sins of the world'"]). Henry VII becomes in Dante's rich imagination a Christ figure.

8. For the symmetries and parallel structures of the Arena Chapel, see, among others, Alpatoff 1947, Bongiorno 1968, Cole 1996, Schlegel 1969, Settis 1994, and Stubblebine 1969.

9. There are fourteen in the first band, for the scene of the animals entering the ark occupies two segments.

10. See Wilkins 1959 for a pioneering study of the relationship of the mosaics in the Florentine Baptistery to the *Comedy.*

Figure 1: Woodcut, *Inferno* 21. Christophoro Landino, *Comento sopra la Comedia di Danthe Alighieri poeta fiorentino.* Venice: Iacob del Burgofranco, Pavese, 1529. By permission of the Department of Special Collections, Memorial Library, University of Wisconsin-Madison.

Figure 2: Giotto. Betrayal by Judas. Fresco. Arena Chapel (Padua, Italy). Reprinted by permission.

Figure 3: Mosaics, Cupola, Baptistery, Florence (Italy). Reprinted by permission.

Figure 4: Mosaics (detail), Cupola, Baptistery, Florence (Italy): first section. Reprinted by permission.

Figure 5: Mosaics (detail), Cupola, Baptistery, Florence (Italy): third section. Reprinted by permission.

Figure 6: Mosaics (detail), Cupola, Baptistery, Florence (Italy): fifth section. Reprinted by permission.

RECEPTION: WORKS CITED

Accardo, Salvatore. 1977. "Il canto XVIII dell'*Inferno*." In *Inferno: Letture degli anni 1973–'76*. Ed. Silvio Zennaro. Rome: Bonacci. 443–59.

Acts of Peter. 1960. In *The Apocryphal New Testament*. Trans. Montague Rhodes James. Oxford: Oxford University Press. 300–36.

Alfie, Fabian. 1998. "For Want of a Nail: The Guerri–Lanza–Cursietti Argument regarding the *Tenzone*." DS 116:141–59.

Alighieri, Dante. 1965. *Rime*. Ed. Gianfranco Contini. 2nd ed. Turin: Einaudi.

______. [1920] 1966. *Epistolae*. Ed. Paget Toynbee. 2nd ed. Ed. Colin Hardie. Oxford: Clarendon Press.

______. 1970–75. *The Divine Comedy*. Trans. and ed. Charles S. Singleton. 3 vols in 6. Princeton, N.J.: Princeton University Press.

______. 1991. *Inferno*. Ed. Anna Maria Chiavacci Leonardi. Milan: Mandadori.

______. 1994. *La Commedia secondo l'antica vulgata*. Ed. Giorgio Petrocchi. 4 vols. 2nd ed. Florence: Le Lettere.

Alpatoff, Michel. 1947. "The Parallelism of Giotto's Paduan Frescoes." *The Art Bulletin* 29:149–54.

Anonymous. ca. 1350. "Duplex est abstinentia, detestabilis et commendabilis." Bodleian Library MS. Bodl. 185, cc. 25v–114v.

Arnold, Matthew. 1902. "On Translating Homer." In *On the Study of Celtic Literature and On Translating Homer*. New York: Macmillan. 141–300.

Auerbach, Erich. [1929] 1961. *Dante, Poet of the Secular World*. Trans. Ralph Manheim. Chicago: The University of Chicago Press.

Bakhtin, M. M., and P. M. Medvedev. [1928] 1985. *The Formal Method in Literary Scholarship: A Critical Introduction to Sociological Poetics*. Trans. A. J. Wehrle. Cambridge, Mass.: Harvard University Press.

Baldwin, John W. 1994. *The Language of Sex: Five Voices from Northern France around 1200*. Chicago and London: The University of Chicago Press.

Barański, Zygmunt G. 1996. *"Sole nuovo, luce nuova." Saggi sul rinnovamento culturale in Dante*. Turin: Scriptorium.

______, ed. 1995. "Libri poetarum in quattuor species dividuntur." *Essays on Dante and "Genre."* Supplement 2 of The *Italianist* 15.

Barbi, Michele. 1924. "La tenzone di Dante con Forese." StD 9:5–149. 1941. Reprinted in *Problemi di critica dantesca*. Florence: 87–188.

______. 1932. "Ancora della Tenzone di Dante con Forese." StD 16:69–103. 1941. Reprinted in *Problemi di critica dantesca*. Florence: Sansoni. 190–214.

______. 1941. *Con Dante e i suoi interpreti*. Florence: Le Monnier.

Barchiesi, Marino. 1963. *Un tema classico e medievale: Gnatone e Taide*. Padua: Antenore.

______. 1967. "Arte del prologo e arte della transizione." StD 44:115–207.

Barolini, Teodolinda. 1984. *Dante's Poets: Textuality and Truth in the "Comedy."* Princeton, N.J.: Princeton University Press.

Bec, Pierre. 1984. *Burlesque et obscenité chez les troubadours*. Paris: Stock.

Becker, Marvin B. 1967. *Florence in Transition*. 2 vols. Baltimore: Johns Hopkins University Press.

Betti, Emilio. 1955. *Teoria generale della interpretazione*. 2 vols. Milan: Giuffrè.

______. Forthcoming. *A General Theory of Interpretation*. Trans. Susan Noakes. New York: Aldine / De Gruyter.

Bloch, R. Howard. 1986. *The Scandal of the Fabliaux*. Chicago and London: The University of Chicago Press.

Bonaini, Francesco. 1855. "Gli Ordinamenti di Giustizia del Comune e Popolo di Firenze compilati nel 1293." *Archivio storico italiano* N.S. 1:37–71.

Bongiorno, Laurine Mack. 1968. "The Theme of the Old and the New Law in the Arena Chapel." *The Art Bulletin* 50:11–20.

Brownlee, Marina S., Kevin Brownlee, and Stephen G. Nichols, eds. 1991. *The New Medievalism*. Baltimore: Johns Hopkins University Press.

Brucker, Gene. 1977. *The Civic World of Early Renaissance Florence*. Princeton, N.J.: Princeton University Press.

Brundage, James A. 1987. *Law, Sex, and Christian Society in Medieval Europe*. Chicago and London: The University of Chicago Press.

Cadden, Joan. 1995. *Meanings of Sex Difference in the Middle Ages.* Cambridge: Cambridge University Press.

Cardini, Franco. 1993. Introduction to *Ordinamenti di Giustizia, 1293–1993.* Florence: SP 44 Editore. vi–ix.

Caretti, Lanfranco. 1967. "Canto XVIII." In *Lectura Dantis Scaligera: Inferno.* Florence: Le Monnier. 583–616.

Casagrande, Carla, and Silvana Vecchio. 1987. *I peccati della lingua.* Rome: Istituto della Enciclopedia Italiana.

Cassell, Anthony K., 1977. "Dante's Farinata and the Image of the *Arca.*" *Yale Italian Studies* 1:335–70.

______. 1984. *Dante's Fearful Art of Justice.* Toronto: University of Toronto Press.

Chiavacci Leonardi, Anna Maria, ed. 1991. *Dante Alighieri: Commedia, Inferno.* Milan: Mondadori.

Cole, Bruce. 1996. "Virtues and Vices in Giotto's Arena Chapel Frescoes." In *Studies in the History of Italian Art, 1250–1550.* London: Pindar Press. 337–63.

Craun, Edwin D. 1997. *Lies, Slander, and Obscenity in Medieval English Literature.* Cambridge: Cambridge University Press.

Cursietti, Mauro. 1995. *La falsa tenzone di Dante con Forese Donati.* Anzio: De Rubeis.

Duby, Georges. 1981. *Le chevalier, la femme, et le prêtre: Le mariage dans la France féodale.* Paris: Hachette.

Durling, Robert M. 1981. "Farinata and the Body of Christ." *Stanford Italian Review* 2:5–35.

Elliott, Dyan. 1999. *Fallen Bodies: Pollution, Sexuality, and Demonology in the Middle Ages.* Philadelphia: University of Pennsylvania Press.

Étienne de Bourbon. n.d. *Tractatus de diversis materiis predicabilibus.* Oriel College Oxford MS. 68, cc. 15r–150v.

Fornaciari, Raffaello. 1902. *Il canto XVIII dell' "Inferno."* Florence: Sansoni.

Gallarati Scotti, Tommaso Fulco. 1968. "Il canto XVIII dell' "*Inferno.*" In *Letture dantesche: Inferno.* Ed. Giovanni Getto. 2nd ed. Florence: Sansoni. 333–44.

Geertz, Clifford. 1980. "Blurred Genres: The Refiguration of Social Thought." *The American Scholar* 49:165–79.

Goldthwaite, Richard A. 1968. *Private Wealth in Renaissance Florence: A Study of Four Families.* Princeton, N.J.: Princeton University Press.

Grana, Gianni. 1959. *Il canto XVIII dell' "Inferno."* Torino: SEI.

Hall, James. 1983. *A History of Ideas and Images in Italian Art.* New York: Harper & Row.

Herlihy, David. 1985. *Medieval Households.* Cambridge. Mass.: Harvard University Press.

Herzman, Ronald B., and William A. Stephany. 1978. "'O miseri seguaci': Sacramental Inversion in *Inferno* XIX." DS 96:39–65.

Horace. 1961. *De arte poetica.* In *Satires, Epistles and Ars Poetica.* Trans. H. Rushton Fairclough. Cambridge, Mass.: Harvard University Press. 450–89.

Jenni, Adolfo. 1970. "Forese Donati." In ED 2:560–63.

Kay, Richard. 1992. "Parallel Cantos in Dante's *Commedia.*" *Res Publica Litterarum* 15:109–13.

Kent, F. W. 1977. *Household and Lineage in Renaissance Florence.* Princeton, N.J.: Princeton University Press.

Klapisch-Zuber, Christiane. 1988. "Ruptures de parenté et changements d'identité chez les magnats florentins du XIVe siècle." *Annales E.S.C.* 43:1205–40.

______. 1990. *La maison et le nom: Stratégies et rituels dans l'Italie de la Renaissance.* Paris: Éditions de l'École des Hautes Études en Sciences Sociales.

Kleinhenz, Christopher. 1974. "Dante's Towering Giants: *Inferno* XXXI." RPh 27:269–85.

______. 1980. "Plutus, Fortune, and Michael: The Eternal Triangle." DS 98:35–52.

______. 1982. "Iconographic Parody in *Inferno* 21." *Res Publica Litterarum* 5:125–37.

______. 1990. "Dante and the Tradition of Visual Arts in the Middle Ages." *Thought* 256:17–26.

______. 1999. "Mito e verità biblica in Dante." In *Dante, mito e poesia: Atti del secondo Seminario dantesco internazionale (Monte Verità, Ascona, 23–27 giugno 1997).* Ed. Michelangelo Picone and Tatiana Crivelli. Florence: Franco Cesati. 367–89.

Lansing, Carol. 1991. *The Florentine Magnates: Lineage and Faction in a Medieval Commune.* Princeton, N.J.: Princeton University Press.

Lazzerini, Lucia. 1988. *Il testo trasgressivo.* Milan: Franco Angeli.

Leclercq, Henri. 1922. "Étimasie." In *Dictionnaire d'archéologie chrétienne et du liturgie.* Vol. 5, pt. 1. Ed. Fernand Cabrol and Henri Leclercq. Paris: Letouzey et Ané. 671–73.

Mandelbaum, Allen, trans. 1982–86. *The Divine Comedy of Dante Alighieri: A Verse Translation.* Toronto and New York: Bantam Books.

Martelli, Mario. 1981. *Canto XVIII dell' "Inferno."* Naples: Loffredo.

Martines, Lauro. 1972. *Violence and Civil Disorder in Italian Cities, 1200–1500.* Berkeley: University of California Press.

Mazzotta, Giuseppe. 1979. *Dante, Poet of the Desert: History and Allegory in the "Divina Commedia."* Princeton, N.J.: Princeton University Press.

Molho, Anthony. 1994. *Marriage Alliance in Late Medieval Florence.* Cambridge, Mass.: Harvard University Press.

Muir, Edward. 1993. *Mad Blood Stirring: Vendetta and Factions in Friuli during the Renaissance.* Baltimore: Johns Hopkins University Press.

______. 1997. *Ritual in Early Modern Europe.* Cambridge: Cambridge University Press.

Najemy, John M. 1982. *Corporatism and Consensus in Florentine Electoral Politics, 1280–1400.* Chapel Hill: University of North Carolina Press.

______. 2000. "Florence." In *The Dante Encyclopedia.* Ed. Richard Lansing. New York: Garland. 386–403.

Noakes, Susan. 1968. "Dino Compagni and the Vow in San Giovanni: *Inferno* XIX, 16–21." DS 86:41–63.

______. 1990. "Hermeneutics, Politics, and Civic Ideology in the *Vita Nuova:* Thoughts Preliminary to an Interpretation." *Texas Studies in Literature and Language* 32:40–59.

Ottokar, Nicola. 1926. *Il comune di Firenze alla fine del Dugento.* Florence: Vallecchi.

Payer, Pierre J. 1993. *The Bridling of Desire: Views of Sex in the Later Middle Ages.* Toronto: University of Toronto Press.

Peraldus. 1479. *Summa de vitiis.* Cologne: Quentell.

Picone, Michelangelo. 2000. "Canto XXI." In *Lectura Dantis Turicensis: Inferno.* Ed. Georges Güntert and Michelangelo Picone. Florence: Cesati. 291–304.

Pietro Alighieri. 1978. *Il "Commentarium" nelle redazioni ashburnhamiana e ottoboniana.* Eds. R. Della Vedova and M. T. Silvotti. Florence: Olschki.

Salisbury, Joyce E., ed. 1991. *Sex in the Middle Ages.* New York and London: Garland.

Salvemini, Gaetano. 1899. *Magnati e popolani in Firenze dal 1280 al 1295.* Florence: Carnesecchi.

Sanguineti, Edoardo. 1968. "Il canto XVIII dell'*Inferno.*" In *Nuove letture dantesche.* Florence: Le Monnier. 137–59.

Schlegel, Ursula. 1969. "On the Picture Program of the Arena Chapel." In *Giotto: The Arena Chapel Frescoes.* Ed. James H. Stubblebine. New York: Norton. 182–200.

Sestan, Ernesto. 1970. "Corso Donati." In ED 2:559–60.

Settis, Salvatore. 1994. "'Non tener pur ad un loco la mente.'" In *History of Italian Art.* Vol. 2. Trans. Claire Dorey. Cambridge: Cambridge University Press. 206–27, 256–58.

Singleton, Charles S. 1965. "*Inferno* XIX: O Simon Mago!" MLN 80:92–99.

Spiegel, Gabrielle M. 1990. "History, Historicism, and the Social Logic of the Text in the Middle Ages." *Speculum* 65:59–86. 1997. Reprinted in *The Past as Text: The Theory and Practice of Medieval Historiography.* Baltimore: Johns Hopkins University Press. 3–28.

Storey, H. Wayne. 1990. "XVIII." In *Inferno.* Vol. 1 of *Dante's "Divine Comedy": Introductory Readings.* Ed. Tibor Wlassics. Charlottesville: University of Virginia. 235–46.

Stubblebine, James H. 1969. "Giotto and the Arena Chapel Frescoes." In *Giotto: The Arena Chapel Frescoes.* Ed. James H. Stubblebine. New York: Norton. 71–100.

Trexler, Richard C. 1980. *Public Life in Renaissance Florence.* Ithaca, N.Y.: Cornell University Press.

Villa, Claudia. 1984. *La "Lectura Terentii."* Padua: Antenore.

Wallace, David. 1993. Review of *The Florentine Magnates,* by Carol Lansing. *Medium Aevum* 62:185.

Wilkins, Ernest Hatch. 1959. "Dante and the Mosaics in His Bel San Giovanni." In *The Invention of the Sonnet and Other Studies in Italian Literature.* Rome: Edizioni di Storia e Letteratura. 51–60.

Ziolkowski, Jan M., ed. 1998. *Obscenity: Social Control and Artistic Creation in the European Middle Ages.* Leiden: Brill.

HISTORIES

17

Dante's Jeremiads: The Fall of Jerusalem and the Burden of the New Pharisees, the Capetians, and Florence

Ronald L. Martinez

MY REMARKS in this study concern not "the promised end," but only "an image of that horror"; not the final apocalypse, but one of the devastating catastrophes offered by history, conceived and accomplished by human actors. My subject is Dante's representation in the *Commedia* of the destruction of Jerusalem and diaspora of the Jews, an event understood in medieval Christian historiography as divine vengeance for the crucifixion of Christ. As is known, this view, abandoned by Rome only after Vatican II, was in both medieval and modern times incalculably destructive of Jewish lives, property, and culture.[1] In a time when the Church's responsibility for the consequences of Christian antisemitism over the ages has invited fresh scrutiny, I will sketch in a very preliminary way to what extent the doctrine of the *vindicta Salvatoris,* the "vengeance of the Lord," explicitly mentioned in *Paradiso* 6–7, affects how the *Commedia* functions as poem, and how Dante adapts this doctrine to his invectives against Florence, the city that cast the poet into exile, as well as against other adversaries. My title is intended to recognize the close connection in medieval exegesis between a Gospel passage that looms large in my discussion, Christ's prediction of the Fall of Jerusalem upon his entrance into the city on Palm Sunday (Luke 19:36–46), and the prophecy of the conquest of Jerusalem by the Romans in 70 A.D., which Christian exegesis saw as implicit in the biblical book of Lamentations.[2] This same passage in Luke immediately precedes

Christ's expulsion of the moneychangers from the Temple, an episode that will also be significant for my study.

It is fair to say that the reflex comparing Florence to Jerusalem was both persistent and deep-seated in Dante's imagination. However, absent the name Florence in the *libello,* the use in the *Vita nova* of the incipit "Quomodo sedet sola civitas" to announce Beatrice's death forges a profound link between the poet's city deprived of Beatrice and the widowed Jerusalem of Lamentations (Vickers 1989, 99–103; Martinez 1998, 16–20, 26). At the other extreme of Dante's career as a writer, in his letter of 1312 warning the Florentines not to resist further Henry VII, Dante configures the conquered city in terms that recall the destruction of Jerusalem; not only those used by Christ in Luke 19, but those of the long tradition deriving from Christian adaptations of Josephus's *Jewish War* (for which see Schreckenberg 1972; Schreckenberg and Schubert 1992, Wright 1989, and Martinez 1997, 82–83). For example, the detail with which Dante concludes his visualization of the downfall of Florence, the scene of survivors bound and sent into exile (*Epistle 6* 16–17), exemplifies the epic topic of *ágein anágke,* which in this case could be translated as "forced march." The topic is typically found in Fall of Jerusalem narratives where it furnishes one of the bases for the Christian claim that the Jews were as a people bound over to perpetual servitude (Schreckenberg and Schubert 1992, 118–21).[3]

Political servitude is also the hard lot of Italy in *Purgatorio* 6, where the depictions of "serva Italia" ("slavish Italy") and Rome "vedova e sola" ("widowed and alone") draw on the text of Lamentations; and where Lam. 1.3 ("non invenit requiem") also furnishes the image of Florence as a woman who "finds no rest" on her bed.[4] Readers of the *Commedia* know well how the sixth canto of each canticle (*cantica*) treats secular politics, and thus entails allusion to Florence. The juxtaposition of Florence and Jerusalem is especially subtle in the *Paradiso* where—although Florence remains unnamed—Justinian's disapproval of resistance to the Empire (*Par* 6.97–111) cannot but recall the Florentine kind Dante discourages in his letter (*Epistle 6* 5–14).[5] Of course, *Paradiso* 5 and 6 also contain Dante's incorporation of the Fall of Jerusalem as just vengeance for the crucifixion ("come giusta vendetta / poscia vendicata fu da giusta corte" ["how just vengeance was avenged by a just court"; *Par* 7:50–51]).[6] Given that the riddling formula of vengeance avenged is thrice repeated in cantos 6 and 7 (*Par* 6.92–93, 7.20–21, 7:50–51), that the event itself is underscored by Justinian as the most remarkable in his catalogue of Roman history (*Par* 6.82–90), and that *Paradiso* 6 and 7 juxtapose God's historical vengeance to the salvific intervention of the Incarnation, it seems difficult to overestimate the import of the Lord's vengeance in Dante's poem, at least in principle.

The pairing of Florence and Jerusalem as cities reserved for divine vengeance is widespread in Dante's work. I will limit myself here to discussing four cantos of the *Commedia, Inferno* 19 and 23 and *Purgatorio* 20 and 23. These cantos are interrelated in manifold ways, which I will first sketch out by way of introducing a somewhat fuller discussion of the pairing of two cantos: both the 23rd cantos, and *Purgatorio* 20 in relation to *Inferno* 19. All these cantos allude to the supremely violent, foundational event of the Christian era which occasioned the Fall of Jerusalem. Both *Inferno* 19 and *Inferno* 23 represent crucifixions either indirectly (the inverted placement of the damned popes, imitating Peter's inverted crucifixion) or directly (Caiaphas), while *Inf* 21.112–14 remembers the seismic Good Friday event to which the broken bridges over the *bolge* testify. *Purgatorio* 20 includes Boniface seen as "crucified" and concludes with another earthquake that heralds Statius's release from purgation, while *Purgatorio* 23 includes reference to Christ's cry of dereliction from the cross.[7]

All four cantos also display maxims of rhetorical ferocity and intensity, set off by Dante's favorite targets of avarice and hypocrisy: thus, the initial apostrophe to Simon Mago in *Inferno* 19 heralds the pilgrim's lengthy attack on Pope Nicholas III and his brethren, during which he throws the words of Christ himself in Nicholas's face—indeed toward his feet. This is followed in canto 23 by the beginning of an attack on the *frati godenti.*[8] Like his attack on the *godenti,* the pilgrim's attacking Nicholas is authorized by the ferocity of Christ's attacks on the hypocrisy of chief priests, scribes, and pharisees in the Gospel. After all, the popes of canto 19 are for Dante linear descendants of the *pontifices et pharisei* who make up the *concilium* or Sanhedrin of John 11:47—first among them, Boniface VIII, "prince of the new Pharisees" (*Inf* 27.85). Dante balances this attack on corrupt spiritual guides of Christendom with Hugh Capet's recital of Capetian avarice and deceit in *Purgatorio* 20, while the laceration (*strazio* [*Inf*

19:57]) of the Church by papal simony—including that of Boniface—is ironically answered in the second *cantica* by the torment inflicted on Boniface himself by Philip the Fair. Forese's prophecy of Florence's imminent disaster rounds out the tally of jeremiads (*Purg* 23.97–111).

These are also pairings of cantos that equate Florence with Jerusalem. The breaking of the font of the Florentine baptistery in *Inferno* 19, damage done in the good cause of saving a life, contrasts with the papal savaging of the Church. Dante draws Jerusalem into his comparison of the corrupt alliance of Clement V with Philip the Fair to that of Antiochus Epiphanes and the High Priest Jason (2 Macc. 4:7–9): as Clement's association with Philip corrupts the Church, the collaboration of Jason and Antiochus had defiled the Jerusalem Temple with pagan practices.[9] In *Inferno* 23 the doom prepared for Jerusalem by the Sanhedrin for their condemnation of Christ is juxtaposed to the *frati godenti*'s disastrous governance of Florence. The text of *Purgatorio* 20 places Florence, burst open by the lance of Charles of Valois, next to the Templar order, the emblem and defender of crusader Jerusalem, as both are attacked at the behest of Philip the Fair. Finally, in *Purgatorio* 23, a grim future is predicted for Florence soon after the narrator's comparison of the dieting gluttons with the inhabitants of Jerusalem starved by the six-month Roman siege of 70 A.D., a precise act of the "vengeance of the Lord."

As the Incarnation and crucifixion and the Fall of Jerusalem are theologically and linguistically imbricated in *Paradiso* 6–7, cantos 23 of the *Inferno* and the *Purgatorio* are linked by cause and effect, or, rather, by crime and its punishment. Given the logic of the *vindicta Salvatoris,* the representation in *Inferno* 23 of Caiaphas crucified on the floor of the sixth bolgia for having advised the Sanhedrin to sacrifice Christ prepares the reference to the inhabitants of Jerusalem in the simile of *Purg* 23.25–30. Dante announces this preparation by identifying that council of the Sanhedrin as "per li Giudei mala sementa" ("the council that sowed so ill for the Jews" [*Inf* 23.123]). But the forecasting of the Fall of Jerusalem is also deeply implicit in Dante's fashioning of the whole episode, beginning with the form of the *contrapasso* itself.

Crucified in supine position, Caiaphas bears the weight of the lead-clad hypocrites who repeatedly tread on him and so avenge the crucifixion of Christ. By the logic of *contrapasso* Caiaphas suffers the way

Christ, in mounting the cross, "bore our sorrows" ("dolores nostros ipse portavit" [Is. 53:4]).[10] But Loderingo suggests that Caiaphas's crucifixion directly punishes the words of advice Caiaphas had offered the Sanhedrin in his role as chief priest: "that it was expedient to put one man to death for the people" (*Inf* 23.116–17). The scriptural text to which Loderingo refers (John 11:50) concludes with a short, but important, clause that Loderingo does not paraphrase: "it is expedient for you that one man should die for the people, *and that the whole nation perish not*" (emphasis added). Readers point out that Caiaphas's advice is hypocritical because the statement is motivated by the expediency of killing Christ to protect the Sanhedrin, given that, if the people rallied to Christ "the Romans will come, and take away our place and nation" (John 11:48).

In light of the historical results of Caiaphas's counsel, it is clear that the advice of the chief priest proves disastrously ill-advised. The same can be said of the Sanhedrin's fear of losing their place, which Caiaphas's advice was intended to assuage, for the Roman siege destroyed the Temple, abrogated the cult, and leveled the city; the inhabitants were killed or relegated to captivity.[11] Caiaphas's words not only prepare the Christomimetic *contrapasso* imposed on members of the Sanhedrin, they also adumbrate the loss of Jerusalem mentioned in *Purgatorio* 23. This latter event emerges precisely as the act of divine vengeance, indeed the historical *contrapasso* for the crucifixion, as Dante states it in *Paradiso* 6–7. More than simply establishing that Dante saw the Fall of Jerusalem as implicit in the decision of the Sanhedrin, the text of *Inferno* 23 shapes the emergence of its implication through the system of parallel cantos, thus through the structure of the poem itself.

We can now also apply this scheme to the pairing in *Inferno* 23 of Jerusalem ruled by the chief priests to Florence adminstered by the *frati godenti,* who were sent to pacify Florence after the Ghibelline defeat at Benevento in 1266 and hypocritically sided with the Florentine Guelphs, at least according to the testimony of contemporaries (Giovanni Villani 1990, 430–31; Salimbene 1942, 2:671–72).[12] That the *godenti* closely participate in the crucifixion of the Pharisees is suggested in the comparison of their leaden capes to squeaking "scales," recalling the *statera Christi,* the cross as a balance or scale, so that they too must endure being "on the cross" or indeed "bearing the cross," as

Christ was said to "bear his cross" ("baiulans sibi crucem" [John 19:17]).[13] The fateful and unwitting enunciation of the logic of atonement in Caiaphas's disastrous advice is matched by Loderingo's equally unwitting allusion to the doctrine when he describes the Florentine office of *podestà* as consisting in the choice of a single man to pacify the city ("un uom solingo, per conservar sua pace").[14] Like the historical ironies of Caiaphas's advice, the last few words of Loderingo's statement stand in ironic rebuke of the Friars' misgovernment. If Caiaphas and the Sanhedrin prepare the destruction of Jerusalem, of which Christ predicted that not "a stone upon a stone" would be left (Luke 19:44), in Dante's poem the *godenti* prepare not the pacification but the physical destruction of Florence, which Loderingo identifies with mention of the razing of the Uberti houses in the vicinity of the Gardingo, leaving ruins apparently still visible in 1300.[15]

Thus implicated in the burdens traditionally attributed to Jerusalem, Forese's prophecy of retribution awaiting Florence (*Purg* 23.98–111) follows with rigorous logic. Exactly what catastrophic event Dante intends with Forese's prophecy remains disputed. Recently Anna Maria Chiavacci-Leonardi (Alighieri 1994, 686) has returned to the view that Dante anticipates the coming of Henry VII in 1312–13, bringing the passage into conformity with Dante's letter foreseeing the reduction of Florence by Henry VII.[16] But that both prophecies recall the destruction of Jerusalem, though in quite different ways, has perhaps not been sufficiently emphasized (cf. Martinez 1997, 76*n*29).[17]

Forese's attack on fashionable Florentine women as barbarians and Saracens may itself involve allusion to contemporary Jerusalem, which had been in Saracen control since 1187. As John Pecham (1895, 625) reminds his readers in his commentary on Lamentations, its Temple was "still profaned by the Saracens." But it is upon the striking and terrifying images Forese fashions for his prophecy that we should focus our attention: that is, on the Florentine women with mouths open to howl ("per urlare . . . le bocche aperte" [*Purg* 23.108]) and the infant now consoled by a lullaby ("che mo si consola con nanna" [*Purg* 23.111]) who will grow up only to face the day of God's wrath. Of course, wailing and ululation are mentioned in dozens of biblical prophecies of doom (e.g., Jer. 25:34), but Dante's inclusion of women and children here may be taken as a version of the narrative topic describing capture and exile that is most devastating when it strikes the innocent.[18] Thus, I think it is warranted, in reading Forese's prophecy, to keep in mind Christ's own use of this topic in his prophecies in Luke 19–23 and Matthew 23 of the coming destruction of Jerusalem. With grim irony, in Luke 23:29 and 21:23, Christ blesses those who are sterile ("beatae steriles"), who do not give birth ("ventres qui non genuerunt"), and who do not nurse offspring ("ubera quae non lactaverunt"); woe to those who are with child ("vae praegnantibus").[19] In this context, the menacing lines of Forese's prophecy require fuller citation:

Ma se le svergognate fosser certe
di quel che'l ciel veloce loro ammanna
Già per urlare avrian le bocche aperte.
(*Purg* 23.106–108)

But if those shameless ones knew what the swift heavens are preparing for them, they would already have opened their mouths to howl.

On the terrace of the gluttons, whose jaws gnaw vainly on nonexistent food (*Purg* 24.28), we can perhaps infer a punning subtext that depends on the verb *Ammanna,* which means "prepare," but which also inevitably suggests the *manna* of the Exodus (*Purg* 11.13). With a violent transumption of meaning, one can imagine the women open-mouthed, expecting to be fed. Not for them, however, awaits (replace with: the hope of) an Exodus fueled with miracle food and leading to the Promised Land. Rather than opening their mouths in praise of the Lord ("*Labia mea Domine,* [aperies]" [*Purg* 23.11]), the diet Forese foretells will goad them to howling and, like the Jews some lines back who "lost Jerusalem" (v. 29), the Florentine women will be excluded from the inheritance reserved for the "true Israel." If my proposed reading seems too bold, consider the conditional syntax of *Purg* 23.106–108: "se fosser certe . . . / Già per urlare avrien le bocche aperte" ("but if those shameless ones knew . . . they would already have opened their mouths to howl"). The construction transforms the words of Christ's tearful apostrophe to Jerusalem (Luke 19), where Christ suggests that if the city knew its approaching doom, it too would weep. In Christ's words the protasis of the conditional clause is stated but the apodosis elided: "quia si cognovisses, et tu . . ." ("for if thou also hadst known, you too . . ."); we are to take as understood "*fleres,*" "you would weep." Commentaries and homilies on the passage pieced out the elliptical syntax: the most well known of these was Gregory the

Great's *Homily 39,* read everywhere in Europe on the tenth Sunday after Pentecost (also known as "Destruction of Jerusalem Sunday" [see Wright 1989, 23–27]).[20] The homily expands Christ's words regarding Jerusalem as follows: "si damnationem suam quae eis imminet agnovissent, semetipsos cum lacrymos [electorum] plangerent" (PL 76.1293–1301). That is, if they had been cognizant of the damnation threatening them, they would have wept for themselves along with those elect souls who routinely weep for their sins, like the penitent souls of Purgatory itself.[21]

I turn now to *Purgatorio* 20, with its antecedents in *Inferno* 19. As I noted earlier, Hugh Capet's vision of Capetian mayhem occurs in the midst of a recapitulation of crucifixion events. Participating in this recapitulation are the three "triumphal" entries Hugh foresees at the climax of his invective. The first is the piercing of Florence with the lance of Charles of Valois in 1302 ("a Fiorenza fa scoppiar la pancia" [20.75]). The second is the entrance of the lilies of France into Anagni in 1303 ("in Alagna entrar lo fiordaliso" [20.88]). The third is the reenactment of the crucifixion with Boniface as Christ and the bearing of Philip's greedy sails against the Templars ("porta nel Tempio le cupide vele" [20.93]), begun in 1307 and concluded in 1312 with the suppression of the order. In casting his prophecies in the form of violent "entries" by the French crown, Hugh Capet ironically invokes the universal precedent for medieval triumphal entries: Christ's entry into Jerusalem in Luke 19. How this precedent affects the meaning of the passage will emerge in a moment (see Kantorowicz 1944, 209–11).

I shall begin with the last of the entries. The image of Philip the Fair bearing his "greedy sails" has stirred discussion of late, but much about this complex metaphor remains obscure (see Scott 1996, 173–76 [esp. 173*n*37]). Philip's aggression against the Temple is, I think, usefully seen in juxtaposition to a characteristic project of Capetian monarchs, the outfitting and deployment of crusades to the Holy Land. Indeed, the Council of Vienne of 1311–12 (Barber 1978, 221–22; Schein 1991, 239–57) gave Philip the chance both to take the cross and to finalize action against the Templars. It is on this basis that Dante conceives of Philip's move against the Templars as a nautical expedition, as crusades normally began with passage by ship to what was for good reason called *outremer.* The context of crusading facilitates the rich ironies Dante constructs around Philip's action. For in destroying the Templars, Philip dismantled and despoiled the force that, however suspect because of its wealth, had been founded to defend pilgrims from robbery. In his *De laude novae militiae* Saint Bernard of Clairvaux (1983, 510–12) hailed the order as the divinely appointed defender of Jerusalem and of the Temple itself.

The Templars had their headquarters in the Al-Aqsa mosque, thought to be the *Templum Solomonis,* while their seals represented the Dome of the Rock, assumed to be on the site of the *Templum Domini* itself (Barber 1994, 180, 369; Rosenau 1979, 65, 70). In relation to Dante's text, these versions of the Temple deserve scrutiny.[22] In one sense the Temple that Philip attacks in Dante's text is the Paris Temple, long a treasury of the French crown and the occasional depository of the tithes paid by the French church to the papacy and to the king. Philip's attack is also on the Jerusalem Temple, not only as an icon of the Templar order but as the emblem of the Church that Dante saw Philip leading into corruption. From this perspective, when Philip bears his greedy sails into the Temple he echoes and perverts Christ's one recorded act of physical violence, the scourging of the money-changers from the Temple (Luke 19). Given the close narrative and exegetical association of the entry into Jerusalem and the cleansing of the Temple, such an implication follows directly from Hugh Capet's account of the three entries ordered by Philip.

Some elaboration may be helpful. In the text of St. Bernard's mentioned above, the order's zeal to defend the Temple is praised with the psalm text (68:10) of Christ's cleansing of the Temple: "zelus domus tua comedit me" ("zeal for your house hath eaten me up"), a text Dante himself uses (*Epistle* 11.10) to declare his own zeal for cleansing the Church. Given their fervor for the purity of the Temple, Bernard (1983, 512) calls Templars the new Maccabees, appealing to the conventional association of crusaders with the second-century B.C. Jewish rebels who recovered Jerusalem and purified the Temple after it was defiled by the Hellenizing King Antiochus (cf. John of Salisbury 1909, 2:193). In the context of *Purgatorio* 20, considering Templars as Maccabees resonates strongly with Hugh Capet's fifth exemplum against avarice, in which he recalls the angelic repulsion of Heliodorus's attempt to despoil the treasure of the Jerusalem Temple on behalf of King Seleucus (*Purg* 20.113). Heliodorus's failure contrasts sharply with Philip's successful raid on Templar wealth, recalled a few lines earlier—especially as both Paris and Jerusalem Temples were in effect banks (Barber 1978, 39–40)—the latter of money for the support of women and orphans (2 Macc. 3:10).[23] Moreover, in Macc. II, the expulsion of Heliodorus immediately precedes the account of Jason, whose buying of the High Priesthood from Antiochus Epiphanes furnished an early archetype of simony and resulted in the defilement of the Temple. This is the text on which, as we saw, Dante draws in *Inf* 19.85–86 to characterize the relation of Philip to Pope Clement V.[24] The apocryphal account that probably informed Dante's text explains Philip's action in *Purgatorio* 20, narrating his extraction from Bertrand le Got, the unelected Clement V, of a promise that he would turn over to Philip five years' tithes paid to the papacy by the French clergy (see Guido of Pisa 1974, 362–64).[25] This was a diplomatic anticipation of Philip's raid on the Temple, long the depository of such tithes, thus a despoliation of the Church and subversion of the crusades, traditionally financed out of the tithes (see Barber 1978, 35).[26]

Thus, Philip's rapacious bearing of his "cupide vele" into the Temple renews the violence of Seleucus and the abominations of Antiochus. His parodic "crusade" into the figurative Temple of Jerusalem results not in the expulsion of profaning Saracens, the putative object of crusade, but in the defilement of the Temple itself, so that it becomes "not a house of prayer, but a den of thieves (*spelunca latronum* [Christ's words in Luke 19]).[27] Parallels both with Luke 19 and with the crusades are central to Dante's critique of Philip's behavior: for if Trecento exegesis saw Jesus' attack on the moneychangers as fulfilling the Maccabean repulsion of Heliodorus (Henry 1987, 78, 138; Wilson and Wilson 1984, 171), the scene of Christ's entry to Jerusalem was seen by contemporaries as having been reiterated by the triumphant entry of the crusaders into Jerusalem in 1099.[28]

If Philip's attack on the Templars is a perverted crusade, the expedition of Charles of Valois to Florence to favor the Black Guelphs is compared to a joust with the spear of Judas striking and bursting the swollen belly of the city (Scott 1996, 17; and Alighieri 1994, 596–97). This mirroring of Judas's suicide by hanging and its consequences is widely acknowledged, and we can also readily see how the image of a joust exploits the context of chivalric exploit and crusading.[29] Although Charles's mission against Florence, touted as a mission of peacemaking, could not be a crusade, the expedition to southern Italy to recover the kingdom of Sicily for Boniface did have the official status of a crusade, even though the adversaries were Christian antagonists of papal ambitions (cf. *Inf* 27.88).[30] Finally, in the context of Capetian crusading, which had reached an apex of publicity and expenditure with the crusades of Louis IX in the mid-thirteenth century and which heavily emphasized the acquisition of relics of the Passion, the spear Charles wields to pierce Florence's belly must parody the story of the spear of Longinus (told by Fulcher of Chartres [1989, 228–30]), said to have opened Christ's side to release the sacraments, and claimed to have been recovered by crusaders at Antioch during the first crusade (Ligato 1996; Derbes 1991, 575). After the reign of Louis IX, it would be unlikely that Dante did not know the extent to which the cult of relics was implicated in the crusading policy of the French crown (see Weiss 1998), and the parody of the relic in Charles's jousting against bloated Florence may well be, by metonymy, an attack on Capetian crusading policy more generally.

The close interrelation of the three entries noted above—Charles's coup d'état in Florence, the entry into Anagni in pursuit of Boniface, and Philip's attack on the Templars and on the Temple, the Church—begins to emerge. Driven by pride, treachery, and avarice, Philip and his agents penetrate, possess, and defile the spaces that are their objectives. All three entries allude to the agency of chief priests, and each entails perverse commerce. Judas is the *mercator pessimus* ("evil merchant") who traffics with the Pharisees for the life of Christ; Philip, in entering the "Temple" to despoil it, becomes like the *mercatores et nummulari* (merchants and moneychangers) whom Christ expels from the Temple, and who Gospel commentators insist were encouraged in their activity by the chief priests.[31] To Philip's role as "the new Pilate" (20.91) the only role corresponding to a chief priest is that of Boniface himself, at once vicar and surrogate of Christ as he suffers his passion at the hands of the "living thieves" Sciarra Colonna and Guillaume de Nogaret. But it is important to remember that this "crucifixion" of Boniface is the fulfillment in *Purgatorio* 20 of the expected arrival in *Inferno* 19 of the chief priests Boniface and Clement V, whose complaisance before the ambitions of the French crown had made possible the depredations of Philip regretted by Hugh Capet. Finally, in a more complex nexus, the bursting open of Florence with Judas's lance, which since Benvenuto many readers have seen as a reference to the diaspora of Florentine White Guelphs (including Dante), may also be taken as echoing the diaspora of the inhabitants of Jerusalem after the Fall of the city to the Romans, the event Christ predicts just prior to scourging the moneychangers in the Temple.[32] Moreover, given the presence of Dante in the Florentine diaspora, the figure of the Church defiled by avarice, betrayal, and doubtful transactions resonates powerfully with Cacciaguida's subsequent prophecy of the pilgrim's exile, which, in the words of the old crusader, is being planned even as he speaks, "là dove Cristo tutto dí si merca" ("there where Christ is sold every day" [*Par* 17.51]), a verse which fuses the unique historical betrayal by Judas with the everyday buying and selling within the Temple, figurally the Church, as countenanced by the simonist Boniface VIII.

The image of Florence pierced by Charles's lance, evoking at once the body of Christ pierced on the cross and the body of Judas bursting on the gibbet, contains within itself allusion to the entire chain of events beginning with Judas's treachery and concluding with the vengance for the crucifixion, the diaspora after the fall of Jerusalem. Given that Hugh Capet's utterance both reiterates the spectacle of the crucifixion and calls out to God to avenge the outrages of Philip (20.94–96), it is with a certain structural logic that the Fall of Jerusalem, the historical penalty for the crucifixion of Christ, finds mention in the following canto, during Statius's account of his arrival in Rome at the time when "the good Titus . . . avenged the wounds / whence the blood that Judas sold came forth" [21.83–84]). In mentioning the selling of Christ's blood, this passage almost inevitably alludes to one of the infamous acts attributed to Titus in the accounts of the *vindicta Salvatoris:* the selling of the surviving Jews thirty to a piece of silver, in retaliation for Judas's sale of Christ, a disconcerting example of how deeply embedded in Dante's text is the theological prejudice that sees in the Fall of Jerusalem the vengeance of the Lord.[33]

Dante's acceptance of the historiographical principle of the *vindicta Salvatoris* explicit in *Paradiso* 6–7 may not therefore be discounted as merely conventional and pro forma. Rather, it is woven into the poetic structure of the *Commedia,* prepared in *Inferno* 23 and fulfilled in *Purgatorio* 23, alluded to in the violent entries promulgated by Philip the Fair, and appearing again in *Purgatorio* 21 as a structural "fulfillment" of Hugh Capet's prophetic utterances.[34] Although in excoriating the *pontifices et pharisei* Dante appears to de-emphasize the guilt of the whole people, the *minores,* as the moderating Augustinian tradition had long maintained (see Hood 1995, 1–12 and Cohen 1983), his acceptance of the *vindicta Salvatoris* seems to require extending culpability to the whole Jewish people, both at the crucifixion and in perpetuity, not just to the chief priests or *maiores.* In the case of the hypocrites, Dante's treatment is consistent with that of Aquinas (Hood 1995, 77–105), for whom the chief priests were arguably blind to Christ's divine nature but still fully culpable, for they willfully resisted knowing him and killed him maliciously, out of envy and hate, while the people, if genuinely ignorant at the crucifixion, were no longer exonerable after the evidence of the resurrection. Still, it is remarkable that with the exception of the Gospel-dictated conspirators of the Sanhedrin and Judas, Dante places no Jews in Hell, instead filling up places that thirteenth-century antisemitism might have assigned to them—among the proud, envious, sullen, avaricious, heretical, murderous, usurious, and thieving—exclusively with Christians, and in notable cases with Florentines or figures closely related to Florence.

This shift of the burden of the Jews to Florence, ecclesiastics, and Capetians is one of the more interesting and potentially complex aspects of Dante's treatment of the Fall of Jerusalem. It appears sufficiently systematic. For example, when the *frati godenti* identify their band as the "collegio / de l'ipocriti tristi" [*Inf* 23.91–92] they draw to themselves Christ's condemnation of the Pharisees as *hypocritae tristes* (Matt. 6:16). Their hoods hang down over their eyes ("davanti agli occhi" [*Inf* 23.62]) like those of Cluniac monks, but also like the oversized phylacteries, hoods, and blindfolds that Christian illustrators placed on Jews and on the personified Synagogue.[35] In *Epistle* 6 Dante will describe Florence's calamity as servitude in punishment for perfidy, echoing the language of *servitus* and *perfidia iudeorum* applied to the Jews for centuries, language that, in the wake of the struggles against heresy and Islam, became in the twelfth and thirteenth centuries progressively more virulent (see Cohen 1982 and Abulafia 1995). I have argued elsewhere that the *inveterata durities* and blindness to the Christian message that appears in dozens of Christian *adversus Iudaeos* texts (Williams 1935; Ruether 1979; Schreckenberg 1988; Abulafia 1995) seems to inform Dante's representation of a stony-hearted Ugolino (Martinez 1997, 63–68), whose confrontation with the choice of Abraham was the occasion some years ago of a suggestive study by John Freccero (1986, 152–66). As perhaps a defining case, if we trust Leonardo Bruni's testimony (1928, 51–63), the newly exiled Dante addressed a letter to the Florentines with the refrain of Christ's Good Friday reproaches from the cross: "My people, what have I done to you?" This address places the Florentines in the position attributed to the Jews who, having presumably failed to heed the time of their visitation, had been denied the inheritance and ceased to be "the true Israel."[36]

If Dante has indeed shifted accusations traditionally leveled against Jews to Christian adversaries, his procedure is of course not unprecedented, especially in the context of the Fall of Jerusalem narrative. As Amnon Linder (1996) and others remind us, until the advent of the crusades reignited interest in the historical city, the dominant understanding of the Fall of Jerusalem among Christian exegetes was the tropological one offered by Gregory the Great in his notorious *Homily 39.* In this view Jerusalem besieged is the soul of the Christian assailed by demons, temptations, and heresies, and the Fall of the city the soul overthrown by Satan.[37] Such a tropological view is appropriate to Dante's comparison, for example, of the gluttons to the "people who lost Jerusalem" (*Purg* 23.29) especially as they can and do look forward to reaching the promised land of Eden. Such a view might also apply to Ugolino, who fails the test of hunger in the tower when, turning away from the eucharistic offer his sons act out before him, he cleaves to his obsession with vengeance. The Florentines addressed in *Epistle* 6 are also on notice by Dante Alighieri that unless they receive, rather than resist, the emperor, their reckoning is fast approaching (*Epistle* 6 15–18). Stephen Wright has argued that, although Gregory was not especially tolerant of Jews, the tropological reading of the Fall of Jerusalem narrative has the effect of imaginatively placing the Christian soul in the place of the Jewish sufferer in the Holy City, even though, as Wright (1989, 23–26) acknowledges, in a dehistoricized and depoliticized context. But it is probable that such a tropology must in the last analysis implicitly ratify the antisemitic premises of its discourse, despite its apparent redirection of them. These difficult issues await extended treatment not possible here.

An example of how such tropological displacement can powerfully inform Dante's verse is the poet's digression in *Purgatorio* 6, mentioned at the outset. In successive personifications of Italy, Rome, and Florence, Dante deploys imagery drawn from the abjection of Jerusalem as described in Lamentations. The second of these is Rome "widowed and alone" (6.113), which takes up again the narrator's reproaches of neglectful emperors-elect by addressing the emperor directly at *Purg* 6.114: "My Caesar, why do you not accompany me?" Speaking from within the narrator's own apostrophe, this is a voice of female gender that expresses both dispossession and erotic longing, for medieval exegesis of Lamentations attributed the sorrow and abjection of the widowed Jerusalem to her loss, through sin or apostasy, of the bridegroom, Christ; her longing is for his return and her redemption in the nuptial embrace ([Pecham] 1895 and Martinez 1997, 51–52, 75–76). Given the rhetorical intensity of its production, I therefore take the prosopopeic voice of Rome to be the voice of Dante's most intimate, unfulfilled desire, the intensity of which we can gauge by its echo of the starving Gaddo's appeal to Ugolino ("padre mio che non m'aiuti") and from the original of Gaddo's cry in the lament of dereliction from the cross (Matt. 27:46): "Eli, eli, lamma sabacthani" ("My God, my God, why hast thou forsaken me?").[38]

The poet's participation in Rome's voice of dispossession also emerges from his uses, in the digression, of the possessive pronoun. This series begins with the occasion of the digression itself, the vision of civic harmony that has Sordello speak to Virgil of Mantua as "tua terra" (*Purg* 6.75). But just as it is the embrace of Virgil and Sordello that sets off the poet's deploration of violence in Italy, so the possessive phrases "Cesare mio" (6.114) and "Fiorenza mia" (6.127) a few verses later become, paradoxically, possessives of dispossession. Indeed "Fiorenza mia," spoken in a tone of ironic disdain, is a plausible adaptation of the first words attributed to Christ in his reproaches from the cross: Popule meus. Such a dispossession is the more complete if the sense of desolation in the digression might constitute an implicit planctus for Henry VII, as Maurizio Perugi (1983, 104–5) has proposed: that Caesar would never more be Rome's, any more than Florence would ever again be Dante's. Dante's troping of himself as one of the dispersed citizens of an ideal Rome or Jerusalem has thus come to resemble—more correctly, to appropriate—the historical experience of the Jews after the Fall of Jerusalem.

NOTES

1. That the doctrine led to the shedding of blood is a matter of record; in medieval Jewish reports of the massacres during the first crusade the crusaders claimed they were carrying out Jesus' prediction of future vengeance (Parkes 1976, 65).

2. The typological association of Jeremiah, supposed author of Lamentations (or Threni, as the book was known in the Middle Ages), with Christ's prophecy in Luke 19 was well established in the thirteenth century; Durand (1859, 501) held it to be implicit in the Palm Sunday liturgy.

3. For the legal servitude of early thirteenth-century Jews, see Cohen 1996, 30–51. But the concept of the *servitus Judeorum* was an ancient one, based on the guilt of the crucifixion and the enslavement of Jews at the capture of Jerusalem in 70 A.D.; cf. Innocent III in Grayzel (1933, 115, 127).

4. Originally noted by Scartazzini and Roncaglia (see Martinez 1997, 76).

5. Justinian's mention of Guelph-Angevin lilies (*Par* 6.100–108) has been taken also as a reference to Florence (Alighieri 1975, 2:125).

6. Dante's phrasing here has been traced to Orosius's *Historia adversus paganos* 7.3.8 (Alighieri 1975, 124). All texts and translations of Dante's *Commedia* are taken from Alighieri 1996a and 2003.

7. For the import of the crucifixion and of Christ's life in these parts of the poem, see Fergusson 1953, 111–14 and especially Scott 1996, 175–76.

8. *Inf* 23.109 ("O friars, your evil . . ."). Commentators refer to the *praecisio* ("Quos ego . . .") in Neptune's chastisement of the unruly winds at *Aeneid* 1.135 (Raimondi 1972, 56); but an indirect allusion to the Benedictine *Rule* may also be possible: "causa sunt ruinae populi sacerdotes mali" ("evil priests cause the ruin of peoples") *Regula* 11.46; in Ullmann 1955, 41.

9. It is significant that the defilement and despoliation of the Temple by Antiochus and the ensuing Maccabean revolt are the subject of the first chapter of Josephus's *Jewish War* (Flavius Josephus 1968, 639–40).

10. Marrow (1979, 82–84) shows how late medieval images of Christ "trod upon," his blood "pressed out" by the "yoke" of the cross, were fashioned by exegetes from Augustine to Saint Bernard, who drew upon passages traditionally associated with the Passion, such as Ps. 55:3 ("my enemies have trodden on me all the day long"). Matt. 23:3, one of Christ's attacks on the Pharisees, also must figure here: "they bind heavy and insupportable burdens, and lay them on men's shoulders." All translations of the Vulgate are from Douay-Rheims 1899.

11. Guido da Pisa (1974, 446) captures the logic precisely: "the damnation of the Jews followed upon this advice. Because of this advice they were destroyed to the foundations" (my translation). He closely follows Augustine on

John 11:43, as reported in Aquinas's *Catena aurea* (1860, 384): "for after the passion and glorification of the Lord the Romans took from them their place and their people, expunging the one and transferring the other" (my translation).

12. For studies of the Gaudenti, see De Stefano 1938 and Raimondi 1972, 52–61.

13. Wormald (1938) studies the cross as *statera* (the term appears in v. 6 of the *Vexilla regis,* the hymn whose incipit Dante quotes in *Inf* 34.1). Derbes (1996, 11–37) examines Christ bearing the cross in thirteenth-century Italian painting. The image of cross as balance is implicit of Christ's atonement at *Par* 13.41–42.

14. An ironic reference to Macc 1:8, 16, praising the Roman constitution, is also possible here. Readers have noted the apparent allusion here to Virgil's reference to Palinurus's sacrifice, *Aen.* 5.815, which medieval readers sometimes took as referring to the sacrifice of Christ.

15. Views of the two friars as hypocrites are qualified by Salvemini (1960, 205–8) and de Stefano (1938, 250–57). Guido da Pisa (1974, 445) notes that because of Loderingo and Catalano Ghibelline dwellings "were razed to the foundations," recalling his phrasing for Jerusalem in note 13 above. Villani (1990, 61) observes that the Gardingo marked the place where the city had been destroyed by Totila.

16. Cassell 1978 documents clerical attacks on violations of sumptuary laws by Florentine women, but offers no compelling alternative to the hypothesis that Henry is the avenger.

17. Omitting reference to passages that pertain to the Fall of the city in Lamentations. (e.g., 1:18–22), Baruch (e.g., 4.19–29) and the Josephus-Hegesippus tradition (not to mention Luke 19), Di Patre (1989) misses the rhetorical emphases of Dante's *Epistle 6* 15–18.

18. For this *topos* of pathos in descriptions of innocent victims in the conquered city, see Schreckenberg 1992, 117–21 and Guittone d'Arezzo 1990, 161 and 175–76. Guittone relies on accounts of the Fall of Jerusalem, although Margueron annotates only the echo of Threni 1:1 at period 11 (Guittone d'Arezzo 1990, 168).

19. The inclusion of women and children in Christ's prophecies in Luke 19–23 has been seen as influencing late Duecento representations of the Passion, especially the scenes on the *Via Crucis* (Derbes 1996, 113–38).

20. Linder (1996) describes the liturgy and development of the tenth Sunday after Pentecost, commemorating the destruction of Jerusalem.

21. Cf. as well Giordano da Pisa's Palm Sunday sermon (Moreni 1831, 2: 271–72). For the mourning of the souls in Purgatory in compliance with the scriptural exhortation to mourn in this life, see Martinez 1997, 45–50 and 73–75.

22. Medieval views of the Temple mount are summarized in Krinsky 1970 and Rosenau 1979, 33–90. Whether the round Templar churches of Europe were intended to recall the *Templum domini* or the Holy Sepulchre is disputed (see Barber 1994, 369).

23. During Philip's reign, the royal treasury was shifted from the Temple to the Louvre; but the Templars occasionally furnished financial services.

24. In *Histoire ancienne des juifs* (12.6–7 [Flavius Josephus 1968, 377]), Josephus reports that Antiochus looted the temple.

25. Clement did turn over three years' tithes for Philip's Flemish wars (Barber 1978, 24, and Dupré-Theseider 1939, 3–8).

26. By Philip's time the tenths were devoted to the king's military needs, but the pope's consent was technically required for their disbursement.

27. Given the narrative link between Christ's prophecy of the destruction of Jerusalem and the cleansing of the Temple in Luke 19, the designation of Jerusalem itself as "den of thieves" appears in Hegesippus's narrative (PL 15.2237: "eras mortis habitaculum, diversorium scelerum, *latronum spelaeum*" [emphasis added]). Bruno of Asti accuses simoniacs within the Church in exactly these terms (Rough 1973, 75).

28. The gloss is found in Rabanus Maurus's *Comentaria in libros Machabeorum* (PL 109.1227). For Christ's entry as the prototype of the crusaders' entry into Jerusalem, see Derbes 1991, 573–74. The crusader Baldwin, brother of Godfrey of Boulogne, was also a second "Judas Maccabee" (Theoderich 1986, 18).

29. Before Dante, the troubadour Peirol compares his knight's lance to the boom of a ship ("per lansa l'antenna fort e dura" in "Ren no val joves," [Peirol 1953, 138–39]).

30. Boniface sent Charles to attempt the recovery of Sicily, lost in 1282 to the Aragonese (Housley 1982, 23).

31. This identification of Judas's betrayal with commerce, possibly antisemitic in intention, was widespread in devotional treatises (see Bonaventure 1961, 325), where one finds a reliance on the phrase "wicked merchant" (Derbes 1996, 90–91). For the chief priests' involvement in the commercial activities of the Temple, again with antisemitic overtones, in thirteenth- and fourteenth-century Italian painting, see Bongiorno 1968, 17–19 and Schreckenberg 1996, 147–48.

32. Benvenuto's view (in Alighieri 1973, 2:485) that understood the city's bursting as the expulsion of its chief citizens ("intestina vitalia, praecipuos cives") is rejected by Chiavacci Leonardi (Alighieri 1994, 596–97). See Rough 1973, 17–36 and 1980, 27–28 for the exegetical tradition on the expulsion of the moneychangers, which in the twelfth and thirteenth centuries channeled attacks on simony and usury.

33. Schreckenberg (Schreckenberg and Schubert 1992, 117–21) discusses this event in Josephus and Hegesippus. The twelfth-century French Chanson de geste *La Venjeance nostre seigneur* (Gryting 1952) makes the counter-selling of the Jews the centerpiece of Titus's vengeance (see *laisses* 20, 30, 36, 42, 54, 62, 94, 95). Orosius (note 8 above) does not mention that Christ's blood had been sold.

34. Antonetti (1979, 237–41) concludes that Dante's attitudes to contemporary *Giudei* are bland and conventional.

35. Raimondi (1972, 53) quotes John of Salisbury's Gospel-inspired attack on hypocrites of the well-gowned monastic orders, "dilatantes phylacteria, et magnificantes fimbrias" ["broadening their phylacteries, enlarging their fringes"]. Schreckenberg (1996, 154) and Blumenkrantz (1966, 55) consider large phylacteries found in antisemitic images.

36. In the same vein, Dante's letter to the Italians warns that whoever resists the emperor will be like the wicked vinedressers whose vine will be let out to others (*Epistle* 5 6, quoting Matt. 21:41); the identification of the wicked vinedressers with the Jews was widespread in the late Duecento; see Bonaventure 1961, 290–91.

37. Linder (1996, 118) notes the return of Christian interest in the historical Jerusalem after the conquest of 1099; for the tropology in Gregory's sermon (see note 8; Wright 1989, 24–27).

38. Longfellow (Alighieri 1892, 1:170) translated Gaddo's cry as "father, why do you not help me," but gave the cry of Rome to Caesar the more Christomimetic phrasing: "Caesar, why have you forsaken me" (2:37).

18

From Francis to Solomon: Eschatology in the Sun

Ronald Herzman

TOWARD THE BEGINNING of *Paradiso* 11 (vv. 22–27), Thomas Aquinas tells the pilgrim Dante that the source of his current perplexity lies in two questions that have emerged in the course of the description of the circle of sages who are also Thomas's companions within the sun.[1]

> Tu dubbi, e hai voler che si ricerna
> in sì aperta e 'n si distesa lingua
> lo dicer mio, ch'al tuo sentir si sterna,
> ove dinanzi dissi: "U'ben s'impingua,"
> e là u' dissi: "Non nacque il secondo;"
> e qui è uopo che ben si distingua.[2]

> You are perplexed and would fain have my words made clearer, in plain and explicit language leveled to your understanding, where I said just now "where there is good fattening" and again where I said "there never arose a second"; and here is need that one distinguish well.

Thomas will answer Dante's questions, but in his own way and in his own time. His answers to these questions, whose meaning is a puzzle to the reader no less than to the pilgrim at this point, will be woven in and out of the complex narrative of the Circle of the Sun. Indeed, it could be argued that much of the remaining discourse of the Circle of the Sun never moves too far away from these questions. The answer to the "where there is good fattening" question begins with the figure of Francis of Assisi, as Thomas's lead into a more general discussion of church corruption and church reform. The answer to the "never arose a second" question begins and ends with the figure of Solomon. This essay is a meditation on the fact that Saint Francis of Assisi and King Solomon find themselves joined together in a curious way within the Circle of the

Sun. The punch line is that this joining is not without eschatological significance, that these two unlikely partners share an eschatological importance in the complicated criss-crossings of that sphere.

Francis in the Sun

I have previously made the claim that the Francis of Assisi whom the pilgrim encounters in the Circle of the Sun in *Paradiso* 11 is the apocalyptic Francis of Bonaventure—the forerunner of the last times, the figure of *renovatio* within the Church, the angel of the sixth seal (Herzman 1992). Bonaventure (1978, 181) quotes both Apoc. 6:9 and 7:2 in describing Francis:

> And not without reason
> is he considered to be symbolized by the image of the Angel
> who ascends from the sunrise
> bearing the seal of the living God,
> in the true prophecy
> of that other Friend of the Bridegroom,
> John the Apostle and Evangelist.
> For "when the sixth seal was opened,"
> John says in the Apocalypse,
> "I saw another Angel
> ascending from the rising of the sun,
> having the seal of the living God."

Dante appropriates this apocalyptic energy in his portrait of Francis. The description begins with solar imagery taken from the apocalyptically charged prologue to the *Legenda Maior* (itself a reference to Apoc. 7:2), which is present as well in the identification of Beatrice surrounded by a crown of twelve stars (the twelve luminaries who form a circle of light above Dante and Beatrice) with the woman clothed with the sun of Apocalypse 12 (Beale 1985). The episode reaches a climax in Dante's description of the stigmatization of Francis, which among other things provides for both Bonaventure and Dante striking visual proof that Francis is the angel of the sixth seal.

The wounds of the stigmata are the seal on Francis's body authenticating him as a document to be read, since he has incorporated into his body the apocalyptic seal of the living God (Herzman 1992, 407).

What I had failed to notice is another now seemingly obvious and clear significance to this sealing: the visual pun that connects the red wax seals of a document (in this case the rules for the Franciscan order) with the blood-red wounds of the stigmata on his body (the order's ultimate rule and document) also visually re-creates the sun itself, the rising sun of Apoc. 7:2 and the rising sun of *Par* 11.49ff. By incorporating into himself the wounds of the son, Francis has become the sun in a way that energizes the opening characterization of him in the *Paradiso*. This meaning may well be present in Bonaventure too, but it would seem to be of even greater significance in Dante's appropriation than in Bonaventure precisely because this narrative is taking place within the Circle of the Sun. The *Timaeus* (47c) tells us that we become what we contemplate and urges us to contemplate the Divine (Cornford 1959, 45). Dante's Christianized Timaean cosmology in the beginning of the Circle of the Sun tells us that the cosmos is a manifestation of the Trinity, and thus our contemplation of the cosmos will lead us back to the Trinity. In the story of Francis we are also given an example of this kind of contemplation, but within an incarnational / Franciscan / affective framework, an effective complement to the more rational mode of contemplation outlined at the beginning: Francis is one model success story for the kind of contemplation urged on the readers at the beginning of *Paradiso* 10.

Despite his overwhelming presence in the Circle of the Sun, Francis is not really "there," not even in the way that the other figures in the *Paradiso* are "not really there"—he is there only to the extent that his story is being told by Thomas. He is there because he is the key to the first question that Dante has: "Where there is good fattening" (*Par* 11.14). The answer to the question, an extended discourse on the subject of church reform, begins with the life of Francis. He is also "there" as a part of the mind-boggling set of intersections that characterize the Circle of the Sun: the relation of parts to the whole in the construction of the Circle of the Sun reflects the relationship of parts to the whole in the cosmos itself, which in turn is a reflection of the Trinity, the ultimate exemplar of parts related to the whole. As the twin wheels of the universe, equator and ecliptic, criss-cross in tension, so do the lives of the twin reformers, Francis and Dominic, whose stories are told chiastically by the great theologians of the other's order, the Dominican Thomas for Francis, the Franciscan Bonaventure for Dominic. The way of love is narrated by the greatest exemplar of the way of knowledge, as the way of knowledge is narrated by the greatest theologian of the way of love.

Third, Francis is there because of what he has to teach Dante. He is a powerful model for the pilgrim. The virtues so uniquely embodied in Francis, the virtues of poverty and humility, are precisely the virtues that Dante must appropriate for his own journey. Humility is the virtue that speaks to Dante's character; poverty, the virtue that speaks to his circumstances, the circumstances of exile. He must learn humility, because the pride of the artist remains his besetting sin (see especially Hawkins 1999). He must learn poverty, because he must learn how to do without, so that exile can teach him the lessons of powerlessness. Without these Franciscan virtues he will be unable to turn exile into vision (Herzman 1992, 405).

Francis is a model for Dante in other ways as well. Dante's prophetic calling, his insistence on church reform, would have him, a layman, step into the breach brought about by the corruption of the clerical–ecclesiastical system. Francis himself (as opposed to what happened later within the Franciscan order) conspicuously refused ordination. Like Francis, Dante is not a priest, but is called to priestly functions. Further, Francis's fraternalization and vernacularization of piety correspond to Dante's vernacularization (and fraternalization) of poetry. As Francis is given an honorary place in the sun, so is Dante the pilgrim.[3] He thus becomes part of that company without being there in much the same way as Francis becomes part of that company without being there. It is difficult to avoid the conclusion that just as Francis's body has been sealed with the seal of the living God, Dante's poem is being similarly sealed.

Dante's martyrdom through exile is also the spiritual martyrdom of writing the poem. In this, he has the model of both Francis and John the Revelator, the great apocalyptic writer-in-exile. In the *Golden Legend*'s account, for example, John's exile to Patmos comes after a failed attempt at martyrdom and before a successful one (Jacobus de Voragine 1993, 1:51). John is the model for Francis, and both John and Francis are models for Dante. In *Paradiso* 11, Francis's reception of the stigmata on La Verna (carefully re-configured by Dante to look like Patmos—an island surrounded by water) comes after the failed martyrdom of his preaching before the sultan (Herzman 1992, 406).

In any list of Francis's greatest hits, is this story of Francis and the sultan likely to appear? The account of Francis in *Paradiso* 11 is necessarily extremely selective, describing in eighty verses what Bonaventure has the leisure to do in several hundred pages. Why this scene? (It is interesting to note what Dante does not draw upon: the far more popular sermon to the birds, for one example.) Francis's meeting with the sultan is included by Dante in part because it introduces the theme of martyrdom in a direct and explicit way. Francis was looking for martyrdom, and this was a good way to find it. But he failed to find it at the hands of the sultan because God had something more interesting in mind for him, a unique kind of spiritual martyrdom which sealed him as a unique figure for his time and for all times.[4] Francis's attempt failed. God's attempt succeeded.

In *Purgatorio* 32, the seven-part history of the tribulations of the Church suffered during its various *tempora* is also based on the opening of the seven seals of Apoc. 6:8. One of these tribulations is generally interpreted to be the coming of Islam. My suggestion is that the congruence of these two incidents shows that Dante is likewise working out the ages of church history in Francis's life in the Circle of the Sun: the events in Francis's life which are chosen by Dante are chosen in part because they are the apocalyptic events of *Purgatorio* 32 rewritten *in bono*. Francis's meeting with the sultan helps place his life within an apocalyptic scheme of history already outlined in the poem. But paradox comes very close to contradiction in this episode, since early Franciscan exegesis also looked at Francis's meeting with the sultan as a gesture of reconciliation as well as a desire for martyrdom, a desire to undo the spirit of the crusades. Francis's preaching to the sultan is a sign of the peaceable kingdom. From this perspective, the episode also helps explain Mohammed's placement in Hell as a sower of discord. Francis is attempting to overcome that very discord—to be an instrument of peace—by reconciling the body that Mohammad had sundered.[5]

Interwoven with the narrative of Francis's life taken from Bonaventure is the allegory of Francis's marriage to Lady Poverty. Auerbach pointed out over fifty years ago that this image comes from another set of sources (Auerbach 1985, 229–30). The story of Francis and Lady Poverty is narrated most extensively in an early Franciscan document called the *Sacrum Commercium*. The marriage itself is depicted most famously in a fresco on the ceiling of the lower church of the basilica at Assisi. Weaving these two sources into the text allows Dante to make a set of associations not present in Bonaventure. Most interestingly, Dante takes the famous episode from Bonaventure where Francis strips himself naked before the bishop of Assisi and returns his worldly possessions to his father, and fixes that to be the very marriage ceremony of Francis and his Lady.[6]

ché per tal donna, giovinetto, in guerra
dal padre corse, a cui, come a la morte,
la porta del piacer nessun dissera;
e dinanzi alla sua spirital corte
et *coram patre* le si fece unito;
poscia di dì in dì l'amò più forte.
(*Par* 11.58–63)

for, while still a youth, he rushed into strife against his father for such a lady, to whom, as to death, none willingly locks the door; and before his spiritual court *et coram patre* he was joined to her, and thereafter, from day to day, he loved her ever more ardently.

Dante's astonishing instinct for synthesis thus merges the language of marriage into the episode of Francis's stripping himself naked. This in turn suggests that the marriage of Francis / stripping of Francis is a rewriting *in bono* of the apocalyptically charged Donation of Constantine, generally interpreted to be the third *status ecclesiae* in Dante's purgatorial unfolding of church history. The comments of Robert Kaske (1983), whose work has provided a kind of *glossa ordinaria* to this purgatorial history, are instructive here. On the one hand, his hard-core exegetical labors have led him to the conclusion that the third *status ecclesiae* must in fact refer to the Donation. On the other, he is somewhat reluctant to make this identification because outside of Dante he "can find no example of the *status ecclesiae* which includes or mentions the Donation, and no account of the Donation which hints at the *status ecclesiae*" (97). So Kaske is "force[d] to the tentative conclusion that it is an original adaptation by Dante—added presumably because from a medieval perspective the Donation is one of the critical points of Christian history, and also because it provides a necessary basis for the powerful later image of the car completely overgrown with feathers" (98). A gloss on the *glossa* would point out that of all the *status* present in Dante's narrative, identification of the third *status* with the Donation comes closest to being intuitively obvious, given the pervasive importance of the Donation and its consequences within the poem itself. Such a gloss might also point out that given Dante's daring in so many other aspects of the poem, his "original" reading of the dynamics of eschatological history should come as absolutely no surprise, especially given the fact that, as Kaske himself points out (1983, 93), "the identity of the various status differs greatly . . . according to the time and historical outlook of the exegetes." The figural connection between the two events, the Donation of Constantine and the Marriage of Francis to Lady Poverty, is implied in the most important reference to the Donation within the poem, the pilgrim's invective against ecclesiastical corruption in *Inf* 19.115–17:

> Ahi, Costantin, di quanto mal fu matre,
> Non la tua conversion, ma quella dote
> Che da te prese il primo ricco patre!

> Ah, Constantine, of how much ill was mother, not your conversion, but that dowry which the first rich Father took from you!

The marriage imagery here is complex and suggestive. If the Donation is a dowry, the pope is married to the Church, a marriage that from this time on will bring about evil and illegitimate offspring. But the passage also implies that the papacy is now simultaneously also married to another bride, wealth, and that this union will likewise bring about evil offspring—the dowry has in a sense replaced the Church as the bride of the vicars of Christ. The marriage of Francis and Lady Poverty repairs the damage done by this ill-fated marriage of the papacy and wealth: Francis, the rich merchant's son, returns everything to his father and in the process acknowledges, as Bonaventure puts it, that henceforth he will have no father but "our Father who art in heaven" (1978, 194). Or, in the language of Dante, Francis's marriage to Lady Poverty frees him henceforth to live a life of poverty by allowing him to return a "dowry" to his "first rich father."

Solomon in the Son

Auerbach (1985, 230) has pointed out that Francis's marriage to Lady Poverty gets its multivalent energy from a larger tradition of mystical marriage whose most important spokesperson is Bernard of Clairvaux.[7] Among Solomon's many accomplishments, he is the author of the Song of Songs.[8] He thus becomes an eschatological figure here not only because of the eschatological importance of that text, but also because his presence here looks forward to the figure of Bernard at the end of the poem, the author of the Song of Songs pointing toward the most important commentator on the Song of Songs, who in turn enables Dante to achieve the goal of his journey, the eschatologically charged final vision of God.[9]

The closing simile of the clock tower at the end of *Paradiso* 10 (vv. 139–48) inescapably brings the Song of Songs into play in the Circle of the Sun:

> Indi, come orologio che ne chiami
>   ne l'ora che la sposa di Dio surge
>   a mattinar lo sposo perché l'ami,
> che l'una parte e l'altra tira e urge,
>   tin tin sonando con sì dolce nota,
>   che 'l ben disposto spirto d'amor turge;
> così vid' ïo la gloriosa rota
>   muoversi e render voce a voce in tempra
>   e in dolcezza ch'esser non pò nota
>   se non colà dove gioir s'insempra.

> Then, like a clock which calls us at the hour when the Bride of God rises to sing her matins to her Bridegroom, that he may love her, in which the one part draws or drives the other, sounding *ting! ting!* with notes so sweet that the well-disposed spirit swells with love, so did I see the glorious wheel move and render voice to voice with harmony and sweetness that cannot be known except there where joy is everlasting.

Coming immediately after the introduction of Siger of Brabant, the last of the twelve sages in Thomas's wheel, this simile, complex even by Dante's standards, suggests among other things the interconnecting harmonies in the relationship of the parts to the whole in the placement of the sages. It suggests as well how the complex relationships between parts and the whole on earth are a re-creation of similar relationships in the cosmos. The circles of the spheres are re-created on earth, the tower clock itself being a set of interrelationships between interconnected circles. Moreover, such a clock would also help order human life on earth by keeping track of equinoxes and seasons. The description of the clock foregrounds the purpose of the clock: that the Church, the Bride of Christ, be able to woo Christ the Bridegroom. The mystical marriage of Solomon's Song of Songs as definitively interpreted by Bernard is re-created both in the description of the mystical marriage between Christ and his Church and in the description of the very working of the clock itself: like the marriage between Francis and Lady Poverty in *Paradiso* 11, the simile is charged with sexual energy: thrusting, pulling, swelling. The love that moves the sun and the other stars, as it is adumbrated here, is erotic love.

Thomas the teacher gives answers when Dante the pupil is capable of understanding them. Solomon has been given a privileged place in the Sun, the wisest of the wise. The second question Dante has at the end of canto 10 is, "Why?" From so many candidates on display here, what privileges Solomon? What does it mean to say that Solomon did not have an equal with respect to wisdom? Thomas gives no answer until after the biography of Francis has been narrated, until the biography of Saint Dominic has likewise been narrated by Saint Bonaventure, and until Bonaventure has also introduced a second complementary group of twelve sages. Only then, as the master of ceremonies for the Circle of the Sun, does he return to the question, answering it, in good Scholastic fashion, by making a set of distinctions. First, he excludes from consideration those who were created directly by an act of God, outside of the regular order of human generation, which is to say that he excludes Adam and Christ, special cases that, once properly understood, do not contradict what he has said about Solomon. Second, in *Par* 13.94–96, he says that Solomon excelled in a particular kind of wisdom.

> Non ho parlato sì, che tu non posse
> ben veder ch'el fu re, che chiese senno
> acciò che re sufficiente fosse[.]

> I have not so spoken that you cannot plainly see that he was a king, who asked for wisdom, in order that he might be a worthy king.

Solomon excelled in the prudence of a good ruler.

Thomas, self-deprecatingly contrasting this prudential knowledge with the more abstract and theoretical knowledge of the theologian, the philosopher, and the mathematician—indeed with the kind of knowledge that he excelled in back on earth—makes a second distinction:

Solomon possessed the maximum amount of wisdom of a particular kind (Herzman and Towsley 1994, 105). But the question remains: what privileges Solomon and this particular kind of wisdom? Dante's description of Solomon is often taken to be a loose paraphrase of 1 Kings 3:5–13, where Solomon asks for an understanding heart, "to judge thy people and discern between good and evil." And so it is. But Solomon reveals "wisdom to suffice a worthy king" in other texts as well. If we examine texts such as 1 Kings 4:7 (where Solomon governs according to the rule of time as it is set up in the cosmos in the signs of the zodiac), 1 Kings 6:7 and 1 Kings 6:31 (where both Solomon's house and Solomon's Temple are built according to principles of sacred architecture which re-create the mathematical ratios and harmonies of the heavens), and 1 Kings 7:23–25 (which suggest that Solomon's entire building project can be seen as a microcosm of the universe), Solomon's wisdom in ruling his kingdom comes to look suspiciously like the wisdom of God in the disposition of the universe, which is the keynote sounded at the beginning of the Circle of the Sun.[10] These examples taken together suggest why Solomon was thought to be the most important exemplar of Plato's ideal of the philosopher-king (Pelikan 1997, 119).

In one of the most cosmologically charged verses in the Solomonic canon, God creates according to measure and number (Wis. 11:20). Solomon, who conducts his business in imitation of God's way of creation, seems to have learned his craft from observing God's way of creation, thereby giving witness to what it means to be made in the image and likeness of God. He carries forth the imperatives of Genesis 1, his own work on earth attempting to re-create the harmony of God's creation. This connection suggests some of the eschatological implications of the Book of Wisdom as it informs the Circle of the Sun. The Book of Wisdom is the Pseudo-Dionysius of the scriptural canon. Written after the Jewish encounter with the Hellenistic world, and especially the world of the *Timaeus* and its cosmology, it was considered to have been written much earlier by Solomon. The Judaized Hellenistic cosmology of Wisdom was Christianized Hellenistic cosmology in the hands of the Church Fathers, most especially (in the West) Augustine. As possibly the most important text mediating the Timaean cosmology of the Circle of the Sun, the Book of Wisdom is responsible for Dante's Christian cosmological explication of the universe. Indeed, this was precisely the function that it had among the Church Fathers. The Book of Wisdom was the book that brought together the *Timaeus* and Genesis on the beginning of the world (Pelikan 1997, 3). In the hands of Augustine, interpretation of the Book of Wisdom engaged the most fundamental doctrines of Christianity, helping him to articulate his understanding of the nature of creation, of the Incarnation, and of the Trinity (Pelikan 1997, 111–32). Thus, all the Trinitarian energies of the Circle of the Sun, energies which themselves are the formal cause and the final cause of most of what is encountered there, have as their silent subtext the enormous energy of Solomon's cosmological treatise. And as it happens, in these Augustinian explorations, Christian mysteries were seen to have significant eschatological implications. Specifically, creation and the creation of humans in the image and likeness of God are doctrines with eschatological implications. That humans are made in the image and likeness of God can be looked at as a way of seeing our distinctiveness as creatures, but also as a kind of promissory note that is not fully redeemed until the end of time—in what Eastern Christianity calls the doctrine of salvation by theosis. A Western articulation of that idea can be found in the writings of one of Solomon's fellow sages in the Sun, Boethius, who in the *Consolation of Philosophy* states: "Therefore, every happy man is a god, though by nature God is one only; but nothing prevents there being as many as you like by participation" (1973, 3:23–25; see also Pelikan 1997, 128). This participatory divinization is the universal goal of the journey of humankind, but also the specific goal of the pilgrim, whose absorption into the mystery of the Trinity at the end of the poem marks the final cause of his journey and the efficient cause of his poem.

The poem's eschatological ending is mirrored in the cosmology of the sun. In his explanation of why Solomon must be considered to be the greatest of the sages in the Sun, Thomas warns Dante of the necessity of making proper distinctions. He cites by way of example thinkers who failed to make such distinctions, including the Trinitarian heretics Sabellius and Arius. Sabellius sees no essential difference in the Father, Son, and Holy Spirit. Arius, believing that the Father and the Son were not of one substance, and that Jesus was the instrument created by God for creating the world, sees no sameness among the persons of the Trinity. Fortunately, the universe created by a Trinitarian God is constructed out of the proper balance of sameness and difference:

Vedi come da indi si dirama
  l'oblico cerchio che i pianeti porta,
  per sodisfare al mondo che li chiama.
Che se la strada lor non fosse torta,
  molta virtù nel ciel sarebbe in vano,
  e quasi ogne potenza qua giù morta;
e se dal dritto più o men lontano
  fosse 'l partire assai sarebbe manco
  e giù e sù de l'ordine mondano.
(*Par* 10.13–21)

See how from there the oblique circle which bears the planets branches off, to satisfy the world which calls on them; and were their pathway not aslant, much virtue in the heavens would be vain, and well-nigh every potency dead here below; and if it parted farther or less far from the straight course, much of the order of the world, both above and below, would be defective.

In a Sabellian universe, there would be no change of seasons, the angle of the ecliptic and the equator being either too close together or non-existent. In an Arian universe, winters would be too cold and summers too hot to sustain life, the ecliptic and the equator joining each other at too great an angle. The universe created by a Trinitarian god reflects a Trinitarian god, achieving exactly the right balance between sameness and difference. Or, to put it another way: only because the proper balance between sameness and difference exists within the Trinity can "all that moves in mind and space" be fashioned in such "sublime proportions" as we are shown at the beginning of *Paradiso* 10. Thus, when Dante takes the universe into himself in the final canto of the poem, that universe is to be understood as a trace of the Trinity. The Circle of the Sun is an eschatological preview of the pilgrim's divinization by participation in the final canto.

Solomon himself gives a kind of eschatological preview in *Paradiso* 14. After the hymn to the Trinity sung by the entire constellation of souls, Solomon gets to provide a formal ending to the Circle of the Sun, the last word before the pilgrim's ascent to Mars. Only by reflecting on the degree to which Solomon is an eschatological figure in the totality of his appearances in the Circle of the Sun can we see how it is appropriate that when he finally does get to speak in his own voice he talks of the resurrection of the body and of the desire of the souls to be united with their resurrected body—which is to say he points toward the eschatological completeness of the end of time. What cosmology does as a way of showing how space—the created cosmos—is nothing less than a reflection of the Trinity, eschatology does by showing how time moves us closer to participating in that same Trinity. Creation anticipates consummation, and the Circle of the Sun, about consummation as much as it is about creation, provides a way to link these two realities together.

Francis, the eschatological herald of the Incarnation, and Solomon, the eschatological harbinger of the Trinity, point Dante to the end of his journey, and point the readers toward understanding what happens when they gets there.

Notes

1. I thank Greg Ahlquist, Kimberly Ednie, Richard Emmerson, Weston Kennison, William Stephany, Laura Sythes, and Gary Towsley for their help on this project.

2. The text and translation for all quotations from the *Commedia* are from Alighieri 1970–75.

3. Rebecca Beale (1996) has called attention to the apocalyptic iconography of Dante's placement within the sun.

4. This is a theme present as early as the first life by Thomas of Celano, which was begun only two years after Francis's death in 1226. See Thomas of Celano 1999, 231.

5. Like any episode in the story of Francis, the interpretive history of Francis before the sultan is very complex. When told in both Celano and Bonaventure, the emphasis is clearly on the issue of martyrdom (though Bonaventure's version itself is very complex and nuanced). Strong evidence for the counter interpretation—for the meeting with the sultan as a gesture of reconciliation—emerges from a careful, contextualized study of the earlier rule for the order, *Regula non bullata* 16: "Those Going Among the Saracens and Other Nonbelievers": "As for the brothers who go, they can live spiritually among the Saracens and nonbelievers in two ways. One way is not to engage in arguments or disputes but to be subject to every human creature for God's sake and to acknowledge that they are Christians" (Francis of Assisi 1999, 74). Also important is James of Vitry's description of Francis before the sultan (Jacques De Vitry 1999, 584). See Hoeberichts 1997 for an extended and learned (though somewhat polemical) discussion of these issues, which includes an attempt to reconcile the two tendencies.

6. Both images are present, though at different levels, in the basilica in Assisi—the marriage in the lower church, the stripping as part of the upper church cycle based on Bonaventure. Did Dante know the church in Assisi (cf. Auerbach 1985, 229)?

7. Botterill (1994a) presents on a larger canvas the Cistercian origins of Franciscan spirituality.

8. Given the extraordinarily large number of roles that Solomon plays in Scripture as both author and character, it is interesting to look at the commentary tradition to see what gets emphasized there. Many early commentaries focus on the issue of Solomon's salvation, regularly debated in early Christian history. In the process, the wide range of texts that Solomon was believed to have authored are mentioned in passing, so that the tradition gives some sense of his importance as both author and "character" in Scripture. But much more needs to be said about Solomon in the *Commedia.* On Solomon and Wisdom, see Cornish 2000, 93–197. My reading in the commentary tradition relies on the Dartmouth Dante project.

9. On the Song of Songs as an eschatologial text, see Matter 1990. Bernard's first sermon on the Song of Songs provides an extraordinarily suggestive gloss to many of the issues raised here.

10. For these references I am indebted to my colleague Gary Towsley, and the course we teach together: "Medieval Poetry and Cosmology."

19

Already and Not Yet: Dante's Existential Eschatology[1]

Amilcare A. Iannucci

MILLENNIAL ANXIETY, that disquieting feeling that things are at their end and that a better and everlasting age is about to dawn, gripped Dante's time with the same forceful intensity as it gripped our own on the eve of the year 2000 (see Pullan 1972). To be sure, there were good reasons for this anxiety (Procacci 1973, 13–43). Both the empire and the papacy, the bulwarks of medieval security, were on the verge of collapse. The ambitious plans of Frederick I and Frederick II to restore the empire and its universal power lay in ruins, and the defeat and death of Manfred in the battle of Benevento in 1266 ended the last hopes of imperial world hegemony. Worse still, the Chair of Saint Peter was battered and bent. Gone was the glorious era of Innocent III (1198–1216), whose pontificate marked the climax of the medieval papacy. In its stead were the machinations of Boniface VIII (1294–1303), whom many regarded as the Antichrist. His infamous and earth-shattering humiliation at Anagni in 1303 was surpassed, in terms of public horror, only by Clement V's (1305–14) decision in 1309 to transfer the papal court from Rome to Avignon, where it remained for the next seventy years. Without emperor, without pope, the Italian city-states floundered. Instead of political unity there developed ferocious internecine warfare, especially in Florence where Guelphs and Ghibellines were locked in endless deadly disputes. It is this overall societal malaise that Dante excoriates in his great invective against Italy and Florence in *Purg* 6.76–151, in which he describes Italy as "a ship without a helmsman," Rome as "widowed and alone," and "all the towns as full of tyrants."

Signs of this millennial anxiety were everywhere to be seen. Dante's age was especially neurotic about the future. Astrology, that starry chartering of one's destiny, had re-entered the West, prior to Dante's time, through Jewish and Arabic scholars who had for centuries studied in the East. Now it took off, and standard texts such as Ptolemy's *Tetrabiblos* became the astrological bibles of the Middle Ages. Moreover, as Bruno Nardi points out (1985, 283ff.), Dante's world was one of dreams, visions, and divinations. People were intent on discerning the signs of the future, and, as a result, the "prophetic" so infused Dante's cultural milieu that it was discussed by theologians and philosophers alike. Even Scholastic thinkers of the ilk of Albert the Great, who devoted a commentary to Aristotle's *De somno et vigilia,* shared in this common interest. More important, doomsday cults abounded and were fed by millennial and apocalyptic prophets. The most important of these seers was Joachim of Flora (1130–1201). The basis of his belief was a Trinitarian conception of the whole of history.[2] Accordingly, in his major works, such as the *Liber de concordia novi ac veteris testamenti,* the *Expositio Apocalypsim,* and the *Psalterium decem chordarum,* he presented a cyclical view of history, in which the age of the Father, the Old Testament era, characterized by fear and servile obedience, and that of the Son, the New Testament era, characterized by faith and filial obedience, would give way to the age of the Holy Spirit, which would be characterized by love and liberty. Using references such as Apoc. 7:2, 14:6, and, especially, 20:1–10, Joachim argued that this age of the Spirit would begin in 1260 and would represent an *evangelium aeternum* in which the visible Church would become absorbed by the spiritual, Jews would be converted, Greeks and Latins would reconcile, wars would cease, and universal love would reign supreme. Although Joachim's views were condemned by the Church in 1215, he attracted scores of followers who continued his apocalyptic bent. In 1254, for example, the Franciscan Gerard of Borgo San Donnino claimed to complete Joachim of Flora's pattern of the three ages of history by proclaiming the *Eternal Gospel,* which superseded both the Old and the New Testaments. Still later, Ubertino of Casale (1259–1330), the leader of the Spiritual Franciscans, authored a work, *Arbor vitae crucifixae Jesu Christi,* a collection of apocalyptic ideas on the Church and society. The influence of these prophets was enormous and spawned a host of religious cults at whose heart beat the reforming urgency and millennial gloom of the present moment. Not only did this anxiety affect the conventional religious orders, such as the early Dominicans and Franciscans, but it also gave rise to many disparate splinter groups such as the Joachites, the Spiritual Franciscans, their radical offshoot, the Fraticelli, and the Beguines. Outside these religious groups, but sharing in their anxiety, stood the general masses. Subjected to all these worrisome tendencies, devoid of political and religious security, the long-standing butt of frequent incursions, feuds, struggles, plagues, and a generally difficult life, these people represented anxiety at its fullest and resembled, as Dante puts it referring to Florence, "a sick woman / who finds no rest upon her feather-bed, / but, turning, tossing, tries to ease her pain" ("quella inferma / che non può trovar posa in su le piume, / ma con dar volta suo dolore scherma" [*Purg* 6.149–51]).[3]

Dante himself shows signs that he participated in the trademarks of this anxiety. Astrological references abound in the *Commedia,* which is framed as an elaborate dream / vision, fictional or not. More important is his attitude toward the millennial spirit of his times. First, he places Joachim of Flora among the blessed in the secondary crown of the twelve illuminated spirits within the fourth Heaven, the sphere of the Sun. His placement here of an individual whose views had been condemned by the Church reflects not only "his desire for the renewal of the Church that Joachim had preached" (Alighieri 1924, 3:815) but even perhaps his espousal of the millennial belief of the Calabrian monk, whom he describes as having "the gift of the prophetic spirit" ("di spirito profetico dotato" [*Par* 12.141]). Furthermore, at key moments in the *Commedia,* especially in the first canto of the *Inferno* as the pilgrim begins to undertake his journey, and in the closing canto of the *Purgatorio* as the pilgrim is about to ascend through the various spheres of Heaven, Dante delivers enigmatic apocalyptic prophecies about the imminent future. Much ink has been spilled over the meaning of both the *veltro* of *Inf* 1.101 and the Five / Hundred and Ten and Five ("un cinquecento diece e cinque") of *Purg* 33.43–45. It is not my intention here to rehash these heated debates. Rather, I simply suggest that both prophecies may be millennial predictions, the *veltro* being an allusion to Christ as the redeemer "who will restore low-lying Italy" ("di quella umile Italia fia salute" [*Inf* 1.106]) and the transposed Latin letters for 500, 10 and 5, namely DUX, being a reference to Christ as the judge who will come at the end of time. Finally, both these prophecies have to be related to Dante's experience of the *candida rosa* in the Empyrean, a rose from which Dante views history from the perspective of its *telos,* or end, and thus sees the harvest of time. Beatrice is the pilgrim's guide to this experience. As she comments on the rose's great area she notes that its tiers are "now so full / that little room is left for any more" ("li nostri scanni si ripieni, / che poca gente più ci si disira" [*Par* 30.131–32]). Quite clearly, this can mean only one of two things: either the number of the elect is very small, or Dante believed that the course of history was coming to an end. Given the apocalyptic nature of the scene atop the Mountain of Purgatory (*Purg* 28–33), a scene that brings the poem's historical metaphor to its close, it is more than likely that Dante thought that history was approaching its last days, a fact, underscored by his remark in the *Convivio* (2.14.13): "We are already in the last age of the world, and we are truly awaiting the consummation of the movement of the heavens" ("e noi siamo già ne l'ultima etade del secolo, e attendemo veracemente la consumazione del celestiale movimento").[4] But although Dante participated in the millennial anxiety of his time, he did not embrace it. That he did not do so can only be explained by his view of eschatology. This view Dante slowly and gradually developed, taking his cue from an attentive biblical reading of salvation and salvation history and an existentially biased Scholastic ethic.

Dante's eschatology may be summed up in one phrase, "already and not yet," that is, "already accomplished and not yet completed." This theological formula (Cullman 1951, 141) refers to eschatology seen from a communal perspective and to two distinct moments in time, namely, Christ's first coming and his return at the end of time. Both sides of this formula are elaborated in the richly allegorical scene atop the Mountain of Purgatory. There the pilgrim enters the Earthly Paradise, encounters Matelda, witnesses an extraordinary procession, is judged by Beatrice and led by Matelda to drink the waters of Eunoe, the final step in his ritual act of purification before the ascent through Heaven. In all this Dante first states what has already been accomplished. This is figured by the new, redeemed Eden and its original life of innocence before the Fall, which Christ's redemptive deeds have made it possible for humankind to regain. Dante prepares the ground for this "already" in the dream in *Purg* 27.94–108, a dream that is the Old Testament promise of a new Eden, and a dream that in the very next canto is fulfilled and materializes before Dante's eyes (*Purg* 28.1–21). Moreover, the "already" is reinforced by Matelda and Beatrice, who are the embodiments of the two women of Dante's dream, Leah and Rachel. In terms of pagan myth, Matelda is a figure of the virgin Astraea, who incarnated Justice in the poets' dream of a golden age. But in terms of Christian history and what has already been accomplished, Matelda is a figure of a redeemed Adam and Eve, restored to the place from which the first parents were originally banished (*Purg* 28.91–96). Beatrice, on the other hand, is a figure of Christ, the symbol of the second Adam, who brought about the reconciliation between God and humankind. Finally, in the allegorical procession (*Purg* 29.43–154), Dante reviews the whole of universal history from this same perspective of that same "already." At its center stands the griffin, Christ as both God and human, who pulls the chariot that is the Church. In short, the Incarnation has established the Kingdom of God on earth and has made possible the reconciliation of God and humankind.

On the other hand, all is not perfect in the present time, which is suspended delicately between what has been accomplished and what is not yet complete. Therefore, Dante also calls attention to this second moment of the "not yet" in the drama of the Earthly Paradise. For the comic event of the "already" past does not rule out the tragedy of the "not yet" present during which time sin continues to exist, a fact reinforced by Dante in his review of the calamities that have befallen the Church from its foundation to his own day (*Purg* 32.106–60). These and sin will end only when the "not yet" ends, when Christ comes in final judgment and the just are separated from the damned. Dante draws attention to this "not yet" moment twice in the Earthly Paradise. First is the descent of Beatrice, a figure of Christ at the *parousia* (Iannucci 1979, 23–24), into the chariot (*Purg* 30.22–33). Moreover, Beatrice comes to judge not only Dante, but, insofar as he is a figure of every human being, all humankind as well. Thus, we as readers and sinners stand like Dante before her in her capacity as Judge. Second is the vision of the rapt Beatrice in the final canto of the *Purgatorio.* There, she envisions in the not-too-distant future the approach of a favorable constellation, under which a Five / Hundred and Ten and Five "dispatched by God will slay the whore / together with that giant who sins with her" ("nel quale un cinquecento diece e cinque, / messo di Dio, ciderà la fuia / con quel gigante che con lei delinque" [*Purg* 33.43–45]). The giant and the whore, who had materialized in the preceding canto, are usually interpreted to represent papal corruption and imperial interference. However, given the overall apocalyptic nature of the closing cantos of the *Purgatorio* in general and of Beatrice's prophecy in particular, it is also possible, I believe, to see them as emblematic of the Antichrist. In this case, the identity of the enigmatic Five Hundred and Ten and Five becomes clearer. It is Christ, who in all apocalyptic imagery is pictured as locked in a great cosmic battle from which he emerges victorious at the *parousia.*

Therefore, in the drama of the Earthly Paradise, Dante lays bare his eschatological belief. This belief is stated from a communal perspective. Christ by his death and resurrection has conquered sin and death and ushered in for humanity as a whole that "already" which is pregnant with the illumination of grace and the possibility of salvation. At the same time, sin continues to exist and will not be eradicated until Christ comes again in glory. This is the "not yet" future toward which humankind is advancing and for which it is waiting hopefully. These two moments of "already" and "not yet" root salvation history in the cosmic Jesus, who is truly the Alpha and the Omega, the beginning and the end, and, so constituted, they establish eschatology at the center of the Christian message. Just as important, they carry with them an urgent ethic that is underlined by the individual existential present. As John the Baptist makes clear, with Jesus "the kingdom of heaven is at hand" (Matt. 3:2), and this "already" moment must be acknowledged and accepted with true repentance by each individual if humankind is to prepare for the "not yet" future coming of the Lord. Thus, Dante's eschatology is not only communal but also individual, and carries with it the connotation that all human beings have an ethical choice in this eschatological moment of "already" and "not yet" to use free will to embrace Jesus or to misuse free will to satisfy their own desires. In other words, what determines the eternal fate of all human beings is their openness to God in Christ. Accordingly, past, future, and present collapse in an eschatological vision that sees the present as the *kairos,* the decisive moment in which "already" and "not yet" are intimately joined. Thus, the individual fate of all the souls whom the pilgrim encounters in the afterlife is determined by their response to the *kairos.* They exist beyond the grave, to use Alan Charity's elegant phrase (cf. 1966, 197ff.), as post-figurations of their earthly selves, or, as I would prefer to describe them, as eschatological responses to the *kairos.*

The many episodes of the *Commedia* abound with these eschatological responses. I limit myself to three examples, one from each *cantica.* In the fifth canto of the *Inferno,* the second circle of Hell, the pilgrim encounters among the souls of the lustful that of Francesca da Rimini, who had gone to her grave fresh from an act of illegitimate love with her husband's brother Paolo (*Inf* 5.82–142). As I have argued elsewhere (1990), this canto deals with "[coloro] che la ragion sommettono al talento" (*Inf* 5:39), those whose unchecked passion leads to their own destruction and that of others. The emotional and social upheaval caused by their illicit passion is reflected in their punishment: they are buffeted by an infernal storm (*Inf* 5.31–33). At first sight Francesca appears to have been an unwitting victim of love. Dante summons her, as Virgil instructs him, in the name of love, and her response is couched in the rhetoric of courtly love, one response, in particular, echoing one of Dante's own poems (*Inf* 5.100). But underlying the allure and seduction of her words describing the quality of her love is the reality that she and Paolo are damned precisely because of it. In life, Francesca chose not to be open to the God who is the Christ, but idolized another god, Cupid, instead. Thus, both she and Paolo chose to love each other more than they loved God, chose to replace the laws of charity with those of courtly love, and chose to undermine the Christian notion of free will by taking refuge in blind love. As a result of their decisive decision both in and to the *kairos,* their decision to abandon the Kingdom of God, already and yet to come, they end in both physical and spiritual death, a death that both blunts and completes the triple anaphora of Francesca's triumphant proclamation of the laws of love: "Amor . . . Amor . . . Amor . . . morte" (*Inf* 5.100–106). Thus, beyond the grave, Francesca and Paolo exist as fulfillments of their earthly selves, still joined in a single illicit embrace, still defending their illegitimate passion, and still blind to the consequences of their acts. Thus, they are condemned as failed eschatological responses to the *kairos,* and their single tomb opens into Hell.

In the first canto of the *Purgatorio* the pilgrim reaches the island of Purgatory and there meets a solitary patriarch ("un veglio solo") who is its custodian (*Purg* 1:31ff.). This individual is none other than Cato of Utica, famed among Romans for his moral independence and resolute character. He, of course, had opposed Julius Caesar in the civil war and, having failed, committed suicide so as not to yield his liberty to Caesar.

Dante greatly admired Cato, expressing his reverence for him both in the *De Monarchia* (2.5.15) and the *Convivio* (4.5.16; 4.6.9–10; 4.27.3). But his placement of Cato here as the custodian of Purgatory is extraordinary, a position that Cato enjoys "in spite of [his] being a pagan, the enemy of Julius Caesar, and a suicide—characteristics which are normally apt to land people in Dante's Hell" (Alighieri 1954, 41). Dante, however, ignores these negative characteristics and instead portrays Cato as having been delivered, during Christ's Harrowing of Hell, from Limbo where he, as a pagan, had gone at death, and conveyed to Purgatory. Cato is an extreme example who, like other extreme examples, such as Virgil (*Inf* 4.31ff.), Buonconte da Montefeltro (*Purg* 5.64–136), Statius (*Purg* 21 and 22), and Trajan and Ripheus (*Par* 20.100–26), is chosen by Dante to underscore a particular point. The point with respect to Cato is precisely his salvation, the mechanics of which are not discussed, but the certainty of which is assured. In elaborating this point, Dante focuses on Cato as a prefiguration of the proper eschatological response to the *kairos*. For Cato prized freedom above all else, regarding it as so precious that he sacrificed his very life for it (*Purg* 1.71–72). Accordingly, his suicide is regarded by Dante "not as a sinful revolt against God's law, but as a divinely bidden assertion of liberty" (Alighieri 1972, 318). Thus, before the coming of Christ, Cato espied the importance of freedom for ridding oneself of evil impulses and thereby represents *in germine* that Christian freedom which is a prerequisite for embracing the Kingdom of God here and now. For this reason, Cato, like the Hebrew patriarchs, glimpsed the eternal freedom of the children of God, and his voluntary choice of death over political servitude in the service of freedom seals his eschatological fate. Now in the afterlife he is the guardian of Christian freedom, encouraging all the souls entrusted to him to despise all earthly things and so liberate themselves from the servitude of sin. Dante, as Auerbach points out, saw Cato as a *figura futuorum* (1959, 64ff.), but Cato's decision to place liberty above death also anchors him as an existential and eschatological embracing of the true freedom of the impending Kingdom of God, an embracing that rescues Cato from the damned and spirits him on his way to Paradise.

Chief among the souls of the crown of illuminated spirits within the Sphere of the Sun is Saint Thomas Aquinas (*Par* 10.82ff.). His leading position among these souls, emphasized by his being accorded a speaking role, reflects the enormous respect Dante had for Saint Thomas, who was first among Dante's many Scholastic theological sources. Moreover, Dante's placement of the Angelic Doctor here among the souls of the blessed in Heaven underscores his sacramental value as a positive eschatological response. For Thomas is the very antithesis of Francesca. Rather than submit to blind passion he spent his life subjugating that passion to the light of reason and devoted himself, in everything that he did, to the service of God. There can be no doubt as Étienne Gilson notes (1939, 118) that Dante "a profondement admiré et aimé saint Thomas." This admiration and this love are due, as Kenelm Foster painstakingly points out (1977, 63–65), to two basic motives on Dante's part. The first is intellectual and connotes Dante's "gratitude to the Aristotelian scholar, the author of the commentaries" (63). For Thomas represented a proper use of intelligence, which is "intelligere componendo et dividendo . . . quod est ratiocinari" (ST, 1a. q. 85. a. 5) and, as such, became for Dante a special figure of *discrimination,* charged with *discerning* the relations among things. The second is moral and takes us to the heart of Thomas's eschatological fate as delineated by Dante. Intelligence is only one side of the coin. The reverse is Thomas's extraordinary goodness, a goodness that found expression in the saintliness of his monastic calling and a goodness that earned for him the moniker "il buono frate Tommaso." Thus, Thomas was throughout his life open to the Kingdom of God and saw no contradiction between his stance as a faithful follower of Jesus Christ and his pursuit of human reasoning. Theology was for him "fides quaerens intellectum," and it is Thomas's extraordinary faith that not only made it possible for him to acknowledge the reality of God in Christ, but also guaranteed his eschatological destiny as one of the elect in Heaven. In fact, as Thomas is a graced creature of love, so does he discern the same quality in the pilgrim, for whom he prophesies a similar fate after death (*Par* 10.83–87).

In short, these three souls, Francesca, Cato, and Thomas, are otherworldly embodiments of eschatological responses to the Kingdom of God. Through them Dante brings into focus the decisive importance of the *kairos,* or present time, to both the "already" and the "not yet." Thus, it is the existential present that keeps both moments in tension and relates the individual eschatological destiny to the communal aspect of providential history. Acceptance of the Christ-event which has already taken place, and a guarded vigilance for Christ's final coming, demands that the individual now decide either to live free from sin and so be an instrument of betterment in the unfolding Kingdom of God here on earth, or to forget the Kingdom entirely and pursue one's own selfish desires. It is this decision that seals the ultimate eschatological fate of us all. The present is thus the door to the beyond. Although the otherworldly fate of all the *Commedia*'s souls bears this out, Dante, at the end of the *Inferno,* uses another extreme example, the souls of Fra Alberigo and Branca Doria, in order to bring alive their status as eschatological responses. Both are among the damned, placed in the lowest circle of Hell for the heinous crimes of murder of their guests (*Inf* 33.118–57). But in 1300, the year of the pilgrim's journey, both are still alive. To remove this contradiction Dante resorts to a startling device whereby the sinners' souls, once the crime is perpetrated, descend to Hell while their bodies remain alive, occupied by a demon during the course of their earthly existence (*Inf* 33.142ff.). In this manner, both Fra Alberigo and Branca Doria represent, allegorically, and in a very extreme way, the eschatological belief of Dante, who establishes an intimate connection between the individual decision of the *kairos* and the eternal reality of salvation or damnation, between the present and the future life, between imminent and realized eschatology.

What are Dante's sources for his eschatology, with its communal unfolding of "already" and "not yet" and its emphasis on the decisiveness of the *kairos* for individual salvation? The communal aspect of Dante's eschatology is rooted in Saint Paul's teaching on cosmic soteriology. Paul's eschatology is explicitly Christ-centered. The pivotal turning point in salvation history is Christ, "the fullness of time" (Gal. 4:4; Eph. 1:10), "the first born among many" (Rom. 8:29; Col. 1:18) and "the first fruits of those who have fallen asleep" (1 Cor. 15:20). Paul sees the Incarnation and, especially, the Resurrection of Christ as having established a new age in which death is abolished and life and immortality become certainties (2 Tim. 1:10). Thus, Paul sees himself and all other believers as living in a new age which has already been realized historically by Christ's first coming. At the same time Paul relates this new age, which he refers to as the Kingdom of God (1 Thess. 2:12), to the future return of the Lord in glory. For Christ not only has already come, but will come again, when "he shall descend from Heaven with a shout . . . and when the dead in Christ shall rise first" (1 Thess. 4:16). There is, therefore, a contrast between "things already present" and "things yet to come" (Rom. 8:38; 1 Cor. 3:22) and a concomitant realization that the present is eschatologically related to both past and future as a period of possible grace and salvation, effected through the outpouring of God's Spirit (1 Cor. 2:12). But in order to achieve both grace and salvation we have to believe in the Christ who has and is yet to come. It is for this reason that Paul encourages believers "to put away the old man [symbolized by Adam and death] and put on the new man" who is the Christ (Eph. 4:22; Col. 3:9). The general framework of Paul's eschatology is, therefore, that of the difference between the first and second coming of Christ. Between these two moments stands the present, which exists in permanent tension between what has already taken place in Christ and that which is not yet fully realized.[5]

The individual aspect of Dante's eschatology is indebted to Aquinas's existentially dynamic treatment of human acts and their eschatological relationship to what lies beyond this life.[6] Human acts allow us to win or not to win the supreme happiness or good, that is, God, for which we were created. In these acts the will is of paramount importance. For only the human, in its freedom, is capable of making decisions ("dicendum quod homo est liberi arbitrii" [ST, 1a, q. 83. a. 8]). The will, as an appetitive power in the human, inclines the human toward, or away from, the universal aspect of things, seen by the intellect as appealing or repulsive. Accordingly, the will is the source of all voluntary behavior, whether good or bad ("voluntas . . . est principium actum voluntariorum, sive bonorum sive malorum" [ST, 1a.2ae, q. 74. a.1]). Thus, the will is the source of sin ("principium peccatorum" [ST, 1a.2ae, q. 74. a.1]). Moreover, when a soul is so disordered that it turns from its last end, God, who is love, there arises mortal sin, and Saint Thomas likens mortal sin to death, in which the principle of life is lost ("unde quando anima deordinatur per peccatum usque ad aversionem ab ultimo fine, scilicet Deo. . . . tunc est peccatum morale. . . . sicut enim in corporalibus deordinatio mortis, quae est per remotionem principii vitae, est irreparabilis secundum naturam" [ST, 1a2ae, q. 72. a. 5]). If this lost condition is not reversed through repentance in this life, then it leads to eternal damnation ("Et ideo quae cumque peccata avertunt a Deo caritatem auferentia, quantum est de se, inducunt rectum aeternae poenae" [ST, 1a2ae, q. 87. a. 3]). There is thus an intimate connection between willing for, or against, God in this life and the state of the soul in the afterlife, as countless passages of the *Supplement* bear witness.[7] For at death, the moment of separation of soul from body, souls are conveyed immediately either to Heaven or to Hell, unless the soul is in need of purgation first (*Suppl.* 69.2). Moreover, souls assigned to Heaven or Hell, can never leave there (*Suppl.* 69.3). In fact, their blessedness or damnation is eternal and is only intensified after the final judgment (*Suppl.* 93.1 and 98.7), when the soul is reunited with the body to produce an identical human (*Suppl.* 79.2). Thus, for St. Thomas, as for Dante, there is an intimate eschatological connection between the decisions of this present life and future happiness or damnation. It is often remarked that Dante owes his principle of *contrapasso* to Saint Thomas, but he also owes a good deal more. For Dante's overreaching concept of the souls in the afterlife as post-figurations of their earthly existence or as embodiments of decisions which they had taken to the *kairos* while on earth, can be traced in all its elaborate detail to the thought of the Angelic Doctor.

Eschatology has had a meager history in comparison with the other branches of theology and has usually been reserved as an appendix or add-on to standard theological texts. This situation has radically changed in the twentieth century, which has seen "a renaissance of eschatological thinking . . . unparalleled in the history of Christian thought" (Braaten 1985, 328). This renaissance, in turn, has reestablished eschatology as the center piece of Christianity (see Komonchak 1990) and as a catalytic agent exercising an important critical function on the whole of theology.[8] As Jürgen Moltmann notes (1967, 16): "The eschatological is not one element of christianity, but is the medium of the Christian faith. . . . Hence eschatology can not really be only a part of christian doctrine. Rather, the eschatological outlook is characteristic of all christian proclamation, of every christian existence and of the whole Church." At the center of this eschatological movement is a profound sensitivity for the human as an existential present looking to the future and, as Karl Rahner notes (1985, 150), what must drive theological reflection on this eschatology is not:

> an anticipatory reporting of events that are to happen "late" but the prospective view—necessary for man with his spiritual freedom of decision—from his present situation in saving history, governed by the event of Jesus Christ, to the final fulfillment of this his own existential

> situation, which is already eschatologically determined. The purpose of this prospective view is that man should understand the present as his definitive future hidden in the present and already offering him salvation now if it is accepted as the deed of God, the only ruler, the time and manner of which remain incalculable.

Dante would have agreed. In the *Commedia* he has fashioned an elaborate eschatological reflection that is governed by Rahner's prospective view. Dante understands all too well that the future lies hidden in the present and that the time of decision is now, that urgent moment of the *kairos* which is delicately poised between the already reality of the coming of Christ and the yet to be reality of his return.[9] In this, as in most other matters, Dante is resolutely modern. Moreover, his eschatological thinking provides the key to his perennial fascination for all readers of his poem. What is important for Dante, and for us, is the individual being trying to make sense of this life and trying to effect the best decisions possible. These decisions determine the future, not only ours individually, but the collective future of all our fellow human beings and of the whole world. Thus, we appreciate that our acts are not ours alone but have wide-reaching consequences. As we enter upon a new millennium, a millennium that carries with it the memories of repeated wars, the horrors of the holocaust, the possibility of nuclear destruction, and the ecological depletion of the planet, we read Dante precisely because he is a vibrant reminder that each one of us is ultimately called to responsibility for the future. Thus, for Dante, the present and future are intimately linked, and the *Commedia* presents an ever-gripping tale at whose heart beats eschatology, "[the extrapolation] from the present into the future" (Rahner 1966, 337).

Notes

1. Eschatology is the study of τα ἐσχατα, the last things. Seen from a theologically dogmatic position, eschatology is, as Karl Rahner notes (1968, 328), "a forward look which is necessary to man for his spiritual decision in freedom, and is made from the standpoint of his situation in saving history as this is determined by the Christ-event." Apocalyptic, on the other hand, is a genre of revelatory literature which descended from that popular in second-century Judaism and which, by extension, has come to mean any otherworldly or mysterious vision that includes a foreknowledge of the condition of the

last things. To be sure, apocalyptic is an important strand in the unfolding of medieval literature and played a decisive role in the formation of Dante's *Commedia.* The primary focus of this essay, however, is eschatology. For an overview of apocalyptic, see Russell 1978. For a discussion of the influence of apocalyptic on medieval literature in general and on Dante in particular, see the studies in Emmerson and Herzman 1992.

2. An overview of Joachim of Flora, including sources and influence, is provided by Bloomfield 1957. For biographies of Joachim, see Bett 1931 and Buonaiuti 1984. For his historical thought and its influence, see De Leo 1988, Heft 1971, Lerner 1995, McGinn 1985, Reeves 1969 and 1976; and West 1975 and 1983. For the association between Joachim and Dante, see Ciccia 1997 and Piromalli 1966.

3. Citations from Dante's *Comedy* are taken from Alighieri 1966–67; translations are Mandelbaum's (1980–82).

4. All citations from Dante's *Convivio* are taken from Alighieri 1966.

5. It is significant that a major study of Paul's eschatological thought, by Andrew Lincoln (1981), is entitled *Paradise Now and Not Yet.*

6. The following remarks are not intended to be an exhaustive analysis of Thomas's detailed and nuanced study of the human act in the *prima secundae* of the *Summa.* Rather, they focus on the will as the source of our turning toward or against God, and the relationship of those key decisions to one's eschatological fate, both at the time of death, when the soul is separated from the body, and at the final coming, when the soul is reunited with the body.

7. The *Supplementum,* of course, is not of direct Thomistic authorship. But it reflects Thomistic doctrine, being gathered from Saint Thomas's commentary on the Fourth Book of the *Sentences* of Peter Lombard. Thus, although some contradictions exist between the *Supplementum* and the *Summa,* the work on the whole represents Thomistic thought.

8. The thinker who triggered the renaissance of eschatology was Johannes Weiss, especially his *Jesus' Proclamation of the Kingdom of God* (1971). Weiss argued that eschatology was the life-blood of primitive Christianity and that it is impossible to understand the Gospel of Jesus Christ without understanding its eschatological framework. Weiss's work was continued by Albert Schweitzer (1923, 1950, 1968), and especially, Karl Barth (1933), who established an eschatological basis to biblical Christology. Barth points out that "Christianity that is not entirely and altogether eschatology has entirely nothing to do with Christ" (314). This biblical renewal then led to the pioneering and ecumenically driven efforts of Jürgen Moltmann, who, in countless works devoted to the theology of hope, the future of creation, and the possibility of life after death (1967, 1970, 1979, 1998), sought to establish eschatology as the center of the Christian message. Moltmann essentially sees the future as

something that breaks in upon the present from above. The future, therefore, is about advent (*adventus*) and represents something radically different from the present. Of equal importance to twentieth-century eschatological thought has been the work of Karl Rahner (1964, 1966, 1972). In contrast to Moltmann's primary emphasis on the "not yet" Rahner stresses the "already" brought about by the coming of Jesus and the outpouring of his Spirit. Rahner, therefore, grounds eschatology in the existential experience of the present and sees the future as that which brings to fruition the dynamism of present experience as transcendental revelation. In addition to these ground-breaking theologians who have sought to place eschatology at the center of Christian proclamation, there are a number of thinkers who have endeavored to establish eschatology's critical function on the other theological branches. Chief among these has been Bernhard Häring, who established the moral dimension of eschatology and the ethical imperative of the *kairos* as a moment of salvific opportunity (1961–66 and 1966), and Henri de Lubac (1950) and Johannes Baptist Metz (1965, 1967, 1969, 1991), who elaborated the social imperative of eschatology with its summons to build a better world.

9. Alan Charity (1966) and, more recently, William Franke (1996) have drawn attention, albeit in different ways, to this aspect of Dante's thought.

20

Dante after Dante

Albert Russell Ascoli

WHAT MY RATHER SLIPPERY TITLE seems to suggest is a meditation on the *Fortuna* of Dante's name and the *oeuvre* it designates after the author's death: perhaps a foray into the thickets of early Dante commentary (e.g., Sandkühler 1967; Jenaro-MacLennan 1974; Palmieri and Paolazzi 1991; Parker 1993), or a study of Dante's impact on later authors (e.g., McDougal 1985; Menocal 1991; Pite 1994; Pike 1997; Havely 1998), or, for that matter, a look at the different uses of Dante that have been made at different times and different places by later critics (e.g., Vallone 1981; Mazzotta 1986; Barański 1992). In the end, however, I will not be exclusively concerned with any of these. Rather than a case study, I will offer a theoretical and methodological discourse around the problem of conceiving Dante's relationship to his readers as it unfolds both textually and historically. I will offer some examples—rather predictable examples once you see where I am headed—but the main point is to ask some questions about the way we understand what it means to read Dante and his works, and to assert the desirability of reconsidering both our and Dante's own discourses on reading, as they have intertwined over the centuries.

Let me begin by going back to that pesky title. Its first and primary meaning is the obvious one: what happens to Dante when, to recall Auden on Yeats, "he becomes his admirers"? What is the history of reading Dante, the story of Dante's readers? The same three words can, however, be read in two further ways that suggest opposing answers to that primary question. First is the iterative, multiplicative implication: Dante after Dante after Dante after Dante, to the last syllable of recorded time, or at least until the millennium: Dante times two thousand. Here the idea would be that there are potentially as many interpretations of Dante's texts as there are readers to appropriate them, and that we should understand the destiny of Dante's writings as one of endless historically, geographically, ideologically and / or idiosyncratically driven reconfigurations.

At the antipodes from this approach we could claim to read Dante "after Dante," in the sense that "after" has in the expression "after a fashion," that is, "in the manner of" or "in accordance with." In other words, we could read Dante's texts as we suppose Dante would have us read them, following his intention, in other words. In fact, Dante gives us an unusually high degree of support in pursuit of those intentions.[1] Most significant, he continually models the process of reading:[2] he reads his own works—in fact, turns those readings *into* his works, teaching us how to read him (though perhaps not how to read him reading himself).[3] Here, texts caught in the historical drift, their meaning changing as they change times and places, and as the responses of their readers dictate. There, a notion of a text that embodies and enacts an author's intentions, that imposes its meanings across time and space on its readers,[4] shaping their responses to accord with the original will (and testament) of Dante Alighieri, "Florentine by birth but not by customs."

I will come back to the way in which the text where this last phrase appears—the so-called *Epistle to Cangrande*—can be seen as pointing up serious problems with both versions of reading "Dante after Dante." Now, instead, let us consider a well-known Dantean passage that openly poses the dilemma just described—namely, how to construe the respective roles of reader and author in the process of constructing textual significance. The words are Statius's in *Purgatorio* 22, and they recount the effect of his reading of Virgil's fourth *Eclogue*: "Facesti come quei che va di notte, / che porta il lume dietro e se non giova / ma dopo sé fa le persone dotte" ("You did as one who walks at night, who carries the light behind him and does not help himself, but instructs the persons coming after" [67–69]).[5] The image is mimetically preposterous: how can a person guide someone else when he cannot see where he himself is going? The very difficulty of the image points to a conflict between two referents systematically conflated in the name "Virgilio": (1) the human person, the author in the modern sense of a book; and (2) the book itself as *auctoritas* in the medieval sense. As book, "Virgilio" lights the way to Christianity for readers; as person, as unredeemed human soul, he stumbles hopelessly about in the half-light of Limbo. In other words, Virgil's text expresses a meaning unknown to its author, which he did not intend, and which must be found, even invented, by allegorizing readers (Mazzotta 1979, 220–22; see also Martinez 1995, 158–61).

What, then, of Dante? Is the figuration of Virgil's authorial plight applicable to him and his book as well? The answer partly depends, paradoxically, on whether we, the readers, want to respect Dante's authorial intention or not (and, long before that, on how well we are able to identify the nature of that intention). The episode in question clearly distinguishes Dante's authorship and resulting text from Virgil's: where Virgil's text means Christianity against its author's intention, and where Statius's text hides its author's true intentions, Dante, it would seem, writes what he means, and means what he writes: "I' mi son un che, quando / Amor mi spira, noto, e a quel modo / ch'e' ditta dentro vo' significando" ("I in myself am one who, when Love breathes within me, take note, and to that measure which he dictates within, I go signifying" [*Purg* 24.52–54]). This does not mean, however, that we find Dante's account entirely persuasive, much less empirically substantiated, given the many different meanings that have been assigned to his texts over the centuries, including the passages just quoted. Perhaps the fate of Virgil's text in some sense forecasts the historical destiny of Dante's, whether Dante intended it or no.

Let me now pass to a series of three more examples that should give conceptual and historical definition to the problem being posed, though they will necessarily be brief, heuristic, inconclusive. The first of these texts is the *Vita Nova*, which explicitly gives a series of lessons in how Dante wishes to be read, by way of illustrative readings—both structural and biographically genetic—that he makes of his own poetry. The second is a piece of writing that stands at a crossroads between the two types of readings defined earlier. The *Epistle to Cangrande* is either yet another example of Dante reading Dante, or an instance of a reader imitating, even to the assumption of the author's name, the way in which Dante glosses himself. The last example—which I will treat, though of necessity as Dante might say, with shameful brevity—is not a single piece of writing at all, but rather a "social text," a debate over who the reader of Dante in the *Epistle* really is—Dante or another—that spirals continually around the question of what the correct reading of Dante might be, multiplying Dantes as it goes: Dante after Dante after Dante.

The *Vita Nova* is the book of a reader—a reader who is discovering himself as a writer or, rather, as an "author." Before going on to describe what I mean, I need to rehearse two current postulates about the activity of reading in the Middle Ages through which Dante shapes a discourse of reading and writing. The first point is that, from a normative late-medieval perspective, the activity of reading (*lectio*) is sharply distinguished from that of authoritative writing (*auctoritas*).[6] "Authors" are classical poets, or Doctors of the Church, or biblical scribes, or, come to that, God.[7] Readers are those who, now, here, gloss the works of those authorities, defining their intentions for them.[8] The second point is that textual meaning in the Middle Ages is largely produced by readers rather than predetermined by authors. Literature is understood to be a branch of ethics, and its meaning thus lies in its effects on the moral life of the reader.[9] Moreover, medieval readers, through highly developed techniques of allegoresis, are free to reshape texts to suit their own purposes.

Dante presents a particularly resistant test case for both these assertions. Over the course of his career he strives to put himself among the *auctores*, and his works among the *auctoritates*.[10] At the same time, he is constantly giving direct and indirect evidence of a desire to shape the reader's understanding of a significance—ethical and spiritual, to be sure—of which he feels himself to be in control. Moreover, as early as the *Vita Nova* he does these things in full awareness of the medieval models of readership against which his own practice must define itself:[11] in the process he both mirrors them, and transforms them (cf. Noakes 1988).

From the outset, the *Vita Nova* presents itself as a reader's book:

> In quella parte del *libro* della mia memoria dinanzi a la quale poco si potrebbe *leggere*, si trova una *rubrica* la quale dice 'Incipit *Vita nova.*' Sotto la quale rubrica io trovo *scritte le parole* le quali è mio *intendimento d'assemplare* in questo libello; e se non tutte, almeno la loro *sentenzia.* (emphasis added)

> In that part of the book of my memory before which there is little to read is a chapter heading that says "Incipit *Vita Nova.*" Under that heading I find written the words that it is my intention to copy out in this little volume; and if not all of them, at least their basic meaning.[12]

Much has been written about these lines.[13] With no special claim to innovation, I note: (1) that the *Vita Nova* presents itself as a scribe's or compiler's transcription of another book of the same name; (2) that in choosing this figure to describe his book, the "io" who writes has tacitly turned himself into a text to be glossed and studied, effecting the conflation of person and book which, as in the case of Dante's Virgil, is the structure of *auctoritas*; (3) that the separation between Dante as authoritative text to be glossed and Dante as transcriber, compiler, and commentator on that text is the separation between past and present (again echoing the traditional structure of *auctoritas*).

A further complication is introduced almost immediately to this model, when, in rapid succession, Dante records a dream vision, describes the composition of a poem recounting that dream, and makes a formal division of the poem into its parts (chapter 3). He then tells of sending the poem out to readers—specifically to the poets he calls the "fedeli d'amore" including his "primo amico," Guido Cavalcanti—and then points up their failure to decipher its meaning accurately.[14] Dante's *libello* is a book that records the contents of his memory figured as a book. And within that book of memory there are biographical events, but also poetic texts produced by and recording those events: texts within the text now transcribed in yet another text.

And the focus, again, is reading, interpreting. Take the sending of the poem to the "fedeli d'amore." With this gesture Dante asserts his own credentials as a writer by showing that he has a readership concerned with understanding the meaning of his poem; he is a poet not only because he writes in verse, but also because others treat him as one by reading him both "passively and actively."[15] That readership, in turn, is composed of the community of writers into which he hopes to be assimilated. Thus, the poetic debut in which the newest writer submits himself humbly to the judgment of his betters also turns the tables, and submits them to him as their superior by converting them from writers into readers. Crucially, he also insists that as readers they are unsuccessful: no one, not even Guido, ultimately decodes the poem correctly, even though its meaning is now clear even to "li più semplici." What remains unclear, however, is whether Dante himself was any better at interpreting either the vision or the poem than the others were (cf. Stone 1994, 135–36). Sending the poem around, in fact, may also be construed as an attempt on Dante's part to learn the meaning of the vision and the words he wrote about it, though his stress falls on his readers' failures rather than on his own.

But even if the question of Dante's understanding of his own work at the time of its writing remains open, his dual role as author of poems and as reader of them is firmly established by this point. Having already divided himself into glossed text and transcriber-compiler-commentator, he now further divides the scene of the transcription (the *Vita Nova* as we read it) into poems (artifacts of the past that are being transcribed), and prose, which he further divides into "ragioni" (present, selective narration of the past in which the poems were composed) and "divisioni" (products of the present which analyze the poems synchronically, as timeless objects).[16] As is now well established, the act of surrounding it textually by "ragioni" and "divisioni" also plays on the medieval separation of humble modern *lector* from the *auctor*, whose texts are "worthy of faith and obedience" and, above all, of readerly commentary. The purpose is to put Dante as writer into the position of an *auctoritas*.[17]

At the very same time, however, the traditional distinction between reader and author is being collapsed. Dante chooses the "fedeli d'amore" to be his readers because they are, in fact, poets, if not *auctores*, and their interpretive responses come back in the form of poems. And even as Dante divides and subdivides himself textually, he is taking no pains to conceal the fact that the author of the poems and the reader of them are one person, though they remain separated in time (cf. Moleta 1978, 369–78). Even that last separation will disappear, however, in the final chapter of the *libello*, when "Dante reader" reveals that the upshot of his recording of a textualized past and his glossing of the texts he produced in that past, is that he—Dante reader—hopes in the future to "dicer di lei quello che non fue mai detto d'alcuna" ("say of her that which has never been said of any woman" [Alighieri 1984, chap. 42, par. 2]). In other words, that "the past is prologue" and that the reader will soon turn "author" again, as the temporal gap between them vanishes.[18] I leave aside the additional thorny but germane questions of whether Dante revised any of the poems in the "present" time of writing the *libello*,[19] or whether, once written out, the book—especially its conclusion—was subsequently revised (Pietrobono 1932; Nardi 1944; cf. Marti 1965; Corti 1983, 146–55; Harrison 1988, 144–51).

What the first poem and the last chapter have in common is that neither one admits that Dante reader is *now* in full control of the meaning of the writer's work. Dante seems as perplexed by the meaning of the first vision as the other poets. And in the final chapter he expressly claims to be unable to put the "mirabile visione" into words. Between the first vision and the last, however, comes a pivotal moment that theorizes an ideal relationship connecting the writing of a poetic text and the definitive gloss upon it by the one who writes. I mean the chapter traditionally numbered 25, where the Dante-reader who writes the *libello* sets out to justify his use of the figure of prosopopoeia, that is, the figuration of Love as a "substance" (a person), when in fact it is an "accident in a substance" (i.e., an emotional experience). As has been observed, this and the preceding chapter occupy a privileged narrative and thematic place vis-à-vis the first vision of Love, designating an illuminating shift in Dante's perspective from traditional erotic Love to Love as transcendent principle—similar to Beatrice—perhaps equivalent to the Christian God (Singleton 1949, 55–77, 90–92, 112–14; Durling and Martinez 1990, 392–93*n*50; cf. Harrison 1988, 10–11, 50–55). What I will now argue is that it operates a parallel, upward shift of conversion or internal palinode[20] in Dante's conception of the relation between reading and writing which both trades on the traditional *auctor / lector* dichotomy and points the way beyond it to a more modern concept of the author who is simultaneously a reader and whose understanding of his own text (*intendimento*) is thus identical to his original intention (*intendimento*) in composing it (cf. Durling and Martinez 1990, 64–65).

As is well known, Dante defends his use of apparently deceptive poetic figures by arguing that although modern poets (implicitly including the ones to whom he sent that first sonnet) are restricted in subject matter to love between men and women, their basic enterprise is identical to that of the classical poets, who make continual use of the trope of personification. This is the first step down a road that will make Dante equal with the classical literary *auctores*, signally as "sixth among so much wisdom" (*Inf* 4.102), in the gathering of the great poets in Limbo (Barolini 1984, 188–89; Brownlee 1984, 602–605; Iannucci 1993b; Picone 1997a). What concerns me here, however, is a qualification, twice repeated, which he puts on his extension of poetic license from the classics to his own time and his own writings. This is the second:

> E acciò che non ne pigli alcuna baldanza persona grossa, dico che né li poete parlavano così sanza ragione, né quelli che rimano deono parlare così non avendo alcuno ragionamento in loro di quello che dicono; però che grande vergogna sarebbe a colui che rimasse cose sotto vesta

> di figura o di colore rettorico, e poscia, domandato, non sapesse denudare le sue parole da cotale vesta, in guisa che avessero verace intendimento (par. 10).[21]

> And so that no vulgar person may become overbold because of this, I say that the classical poets did not speak in this way without reason, and that the vernacular rhymers should not speak thus if they cannot give a rational account of what they say. For it would be a great shame to one who, rhyming of matters under the cloak of figurative language or rhetorical colors, did not when asked know how to strip his words of said cloak so that they could be truly understood.

In his excellent notes De Robertis points out that the imperative for a poet to unpack his poetic tropes in "reasonable," "readerly" prose constitutes a justification of the *prosimetrum* structure of the *Vita Nova*,[22] as it also does in *Convivio.*[23] For my purposes, this amounts to saying that a modern poet worthy of the name must be able to demonstrate control over the informing intention of that work (cf. Harrison 1988, 64–65). In this he differs, implicitly at least, from the classical poets, who are not required to give any such demonstration since their authority guarantees that they are "worthy" (and since, short of returning from the grave, they could not do so!). In other words, this chapter first assimilates the writing of modern poets to that of the classics, but then transforms the medieval notion of the *auctor*, whose meanings are revealed by the commentary of modern *lectores*, to a proto-modern idea of the *author*, whose explicit intentions govern the meaning of his own work, quite apart from the readings of others. In short, Dante here previews authorial intention in a modern acceptation.

However, there is one further point to be made. This account of Dante's intentions in personifying Love can be taken as a delayed exegesis of the first dream vision, which he was unable or unwilling to expound when he first presented it. Just as in the prose immediately preceding the excursus on personification Dante had established a hierarchy between himself and Guido Cavalcanti, as between Beatrice and "Primavera," so this retrospective interpretation of that first dream sets him apart from all the "fedeli d'amore" and, in fact, from all his other readers, as the privileged interpreter of his own text(s). At the same time, however, his reading of the significance of Love is at best problematically applicable in relation to the presentation of "Amore" in chapter 24. At that point, as already seen, Love no longer is just an "accident in a substance," but rather is identical with a substance, namely, Beatrice or Christ. If this is so, then Dante's claim that modern "dicitori in rima" are restricted to emotional love between men and women is a red herring, at least in his own case (cf. Singleton 1949, 58, 75–76; Durling and Martinez 1990, 393*n*50). He has clearly violated his own imperative for full self-exegesis by failing to account for the dramatic turn that his representations of Love have taken. In other words, here Dante is not a completely candid or accurate reader of his own text.

To summarize: we can see in the *Vita Nova* a tendency that will be even more fully realized in the *Convivio*, *De vulgari eloquentia*, and, indeed, in the *Commedia* itself: namely, the poet's desire, bound up with his quest for poetic legitimacy and *auctoritas*, to assert his intentional control over the significance of his texts by providing anticipatory / internal readings of them. At the same time, from the point of view of our original dichotomy between reading Dante "after Dante," as Dante would wish us to read him, on the one hand, and reading Dante according to our own readerly lights, on the other, important complications have been introduced. Notably, we could argue that there are readings of the *Vita Nova* more faithful to its textual realities than Dante's own, that Dante-*lector* is only one among other readers of these works. And this is true in at least two senses. First, Dante's readings are often either tactically motivated (as in this specific case) or transformative in a larger sense (as in the very project of collecting and recontextualizing the "scattered rhymes" of youth that constitutes the *Vita Nova* to start with). Second, we can read "Dante as reader" in a way not available to him: while he writes poems and reads those poems, we can read not only the poems, but also his transformative and / or deceptive readings of them.

Let us now turn, more briefly, to a text that, perhaps better than any other, dramatizes the theoretical problem of reading "Dante after Dante," the *Epistle to Cangrande*. The *Epistle* claims as its first-person-singular author "Dantes Alagherii florentinus natione non moribus"; as its recipient the Lord of Verona, Cangrande della Scala; and as its mission to accompany a gift of the first ten cantos of the *Paradiso* with a general introduction (in the mode of the academic prologue or *accessus*) and the beginnings of a textual commentary. What concerns me here is the claim that prefaces the generic turn after paragraph 4 when, "formula consumata epistole" (having exhausted the epistolary mode),[24] the authorial voice declares that the balance of the document will provide a prologue and commentary on the *Paradiso* cantos it accompanies, and that he will now speak "sub lectoris officio," in the role of a reader of the poem he ostensibly authored. As in the *Vita Nova,* the division of the textual figure of Dante into author and reader has a double and paradoxical effect.[25] On the one hand, as just noted, the *Epistle* reproduces the traditional *lector* / *auctor* dialectic around a very new kind of writing, conferring *auctoritas* on it. On the other hand, having one figure play both roles radically alters the relationship between them. This "Dante," like the author of the *Vita Nova* and *Convivio* before him, usurps the place of his readers, usurps the *de facto* control that the "ethical poetics" and the commentary tradition assigned them over his text, and imposes his own meanings in place of theirs.

A tacit figure for this process is given in paragraph 28 of the *Epistle*, where the commentator calling himself "Dante" defends the author, or "agens" Dante, from possible accusations of presumption by comparing him to Nebuchadnezzar:

> Si vero in dispositionem elevationis tante propter peccatum loquentis oblatrarent, legant Danielem, ubi et Nabuchodonosor invenient contra peccatores aliqua vidisse divinitus, oblivionique mandasse.
>
> But if critics should attack the writer violently because, notwithstanding his subjection to sin, he thought to raise himself up to such a height, let them read the book of Daniel, where they will find that even to Nebuchadnezzar it was divinely given to see certain things against the sinners, and then to lose them in forgetfulness.

This biblical text has a special place in the historical Dante's writings. For example, there is the description of Beatrice who "[f]é sí . . . qual fé Daniello, / Nabuccodonosor levando d'ira / che l'avea fatto ingiustamente fello" ("did as Daniel did, soothing the anger that had made Nebuchadnezzar unjustly cruel" [*Par* 4.13–14]), in which Dante is also clearly compared to the Babylonian dreamer. Even more appositely, the Dante of the *Monarchia* is not afraid to speak with the voice of Daniel in his dual roles as prophet (author?) and judge (interpreter?): "Conclusit ora leonum, et non nocuerunt michi: quia coram eo iustitia inventa est in me" (3.1.1: "He [God] shut the lions' mouths, and they did not harm me, for in his sight righteousness was found in me" [cited from Dan. 6:22]; cf. Pézard 1973; Hawkins 1999, 20–23).[26]

These images from the *Commedia* and the *Monarchia* together suggest a potent analogy that clearly underlies the passage in paragraph 28 and that, if not created by Dante himself, has its origins in Dantean texts. Daniel is the interpreter, the successful "reader," of Nebuchadnezzar's dream. (We remember the Dante who interprets, or fails to interpret, his own visions in *Vita Nova*.) But he is also, at least titularly, the author of the biblical book in which are represented both the "text" of Nebuchadnezzar's dream and the gloss of Daniel on it. By figuring "Dante agens" as Nebuchadnezzar, "Dante-*lector*" (or pseudo-Dante-reader) clearly puts himself in the place of Daniel. And by referring to the Book of Daniel as the source of the story, he assumes both of Daniel's roles, and thereby dramatizes the interrelationship of reading and writing. Or, rather, he simultaneously occupies all *three* of the roles available in the biblical text. "Dante" / Daniel glosses "Dante" / Nebuchadnezzar, and they both are characters in the writing of "Dante" / Daniel: this Dante who conflates Daniel and Nebuchadnezzar occupies simultaneously the positions of prophetic-author, exegetical-reader, and textual character.[27]

To this point, despite obvious linguistic, stylistic, and formal differences, we are not so very far from the *Vita Nova* as described earlier. What makes the *Epistle* particularly relevant to the topic at hand, however, is that it straddles not only the boundary between Dante-author and Dante-reader, but also the boundary separating Dante's reading of his own works from the interpretations of readers "after Dante." Is the *Epistle* Dante's own reading of the *Commedia*? Or is it the reading-as-writing of an exceptionally able forger, whose purpose is to create the fiction that his reading of the *Commedia* is identical with Dante's, and whose deceptions are most convincing precisely because he mimics Dante's drive to self-exegesis?[28]

Here what interests me is not at all which of these alternatives is true. One of them certainly is, but, just as certainly, we do not know which one with any certainty. In a recent essay, I argued at length that it is not so easy to keep the "authentic" and "inauthentic" Dantes as separate as one might hope (Ascoli 1997). There, I make in detail two complementary arguments that here can be summarized only in general terms: first, that even if the document was not written by Dante, it *is* written very much by someone who knew Dante's texts very well and understood his auto-exegetical impulse profoundly (as the example of Daniel and Nebuchadnezzar above suggests); and, second, that even if it was written by Dante, that does not mean that it is an accurate, much less a complete, guide to reading the *Commedia* (cf. Battaglia Ricci 1983, 11). What concerns me here is how this text can figure—philologically (in the indeterminate standing of the textual tradition), historically (in the accumulation of conflicted readings around it), analogically (in its problematic posing of the role of authorial intention in determining a work's meaning, in ways that can be applied to later critical attempts to either reproduce or enact such an intention), in sum, heuristically—the problem of separating the two notions of reading "after Dante" with which I began this essay.

If the *Epistle* is authentic, it reflects the author's impulse to preempt the way his readers interpret him. If the *Epistle* is *not* Dante's, it reflects the ways in which Dante's readers have time and again sought to justify *their* interpretations of the poem by claiming—often deceptively—that they are reading "after Dante," according to the protocols the author himself has given them for reading. Together these two possibilities, empirically and ideally exclusive of each other—but imaginatively and historically co-present in the critical tradition—represent a relentless dialectic in which the author attempts to curtail the reader's freedom, while readers set out to usurp the author's control over meaning.

In either case, the result is the production not of faithful reflections of the *Commedia*, but rather of *rewritings* for specific purposes that may differ significantly from those of the text being read. One might speculate that it is the knowledge that this is the way reading takes place that partially motivates Dante's compulsion to anticipate and preempt his readers' responses. In fact, he says as much at one point in the process of justifying his vernacular self-commentary in the first book of the *Convivio* (though the subject is translation rather than commentary *per se*, the relevance is clear):

> Onde pensando che *lo desiderio d'intendere queste canzoni*, a alcuno illiterato avrebbe fatto lo comento latino transmutare in volgare, e temendo che 'l volgare non fosse stato posto per alcuno che l'avesse laido fatto parere . . . providi a ponere lui, *fidandomi di me più che d'un altro.*[29]
>
> (1.10.10 [emphasis added])

> Whence, thinking that the desire to understand these *canzoni* would have led some unlettered person to have the Latin commentary translated into the vernacular, and fearing that the vernacular version would be done by someone who would make it appear unattractive . . . I had the foresight to do so, trusting in myself more than in anyone else.

The force of the passage only increases if we recall that the "fede" Dante invests in himself here ("fidandomi di me") is the characteristic mark of the true author, "degno di fede e d'obedienza" (worthy of faith and obedience), in the well-known definition adduced later in *Convivio* 4.6.5 (see Stabile 1970 and Ascoli 1989 and 2000a).

If in closing we now turn to our third example, the readings of the *Epistle* by Dante critics, we can see the flip side of the problem of reading Dante "after Dante." Debate about the authenticity of the *Epistle* begins only with the writings of Filippo Scolari in the first half of the nineteenth century. Scolari's two interventions, in 1819 and again in 1844, adduce some philological evidence that puts Dantean authorship in doubt without disproving it, and lay the groundwork for the major lines of "objective" attack that have been carried on up through the present.[30] Nonetheless, the arguments as such emerge fully only in the second intervention, as rationalized replies to attempted refutations, while the initial attack is transparently grounded in Scolari's sense that the "Dante" of the *Epistle* is incompatible with the way that he, Scolari, believes that the *real* Dante thinks and writes. Scolari's Dante is a political, and especially an anti-ecclesiastical Dante, a Dante particularly well suited to the climate of the Mazzinian pre-Risorgimento, and almost wholly incompatible with the eminently theological, eschatological Dante of the *Epistola.* Scolari himself in his first essay describes perfectly a mechanism by which a commentator might appropriate Dante's voice in order to mask his own very different purposes, a description that we today are likely to think fits Scolari himself and many of those caught up in the debate (at least the ones who do not agree with us): the *Epistola* "sarà senz'altro [lo scritto] di qualche antico commentatore, il quale per acquistare più fede al suo detto tentò di far credere scrittura di Dante quello ch'egli [stesso] ha pensato . . . intorno alla *Divina commedia*" (21): ([the Epistle] is doubtless the work of some ancient commentator, who, in order to gain *faith* in what he says, tried to make us believe the writing of Dante what he himself thought about the *Divine Comedy* [trans. and emphasis mine]).

Today, the arguments have evolved, but the basic structure remains the same, and is shared—surprisingly—by exponents of both views. Whatever their differences, participants on both sides ground their arguments in the claim that they are reading "in the manner of Dante," and that the authenticity of the *Epistle to Cangrande* is to be judged ultimately on whether it matches the Dante whose intentions they believe they have understood clearly, whose guidelines for reading they believe they have mastered.[31] This is true of the Singleton-Holländer line that finds confirmation of a primarily theological reading in the *Paradiso* commentary, and, above all, in the apparent analogy drawn between the four senses of Scripture and the signifying process of the *Commedia* as a whole (Singleton 1954; Hollander 1969, 1993, 1994). This is true of the positions of those who find the definition of "comedia" in paragraph 10 of the *Epistle* inconsistent both with Dante's explicit discussions of the term elsewhere and, especially, of his linguistic practice in the *Commedia* itself (especially Kelly 1989, 1994; Barański 1991a, 1991b).

In the end, the lesson (the *sententia* produced by a *lectio*) of the *Epistle* and its readers is that the quest to read as Dante would have us read him, as Dante insistently tells us he wanted us to read him, gives rise, empirically and ironically, to Dante after Dante after Dante. It may be that among these many Dantes, as among the many King Henry IV's that walk the field of battle in the first Shakespearean play of that title,[32] as among the three rings of Boccaccio's fable (*Decameron* 1.3), there is one that it is true, authentic, worthy, as it were, "of faith and obedience." (But for now we await in vain for that millennial eschaton, that last critical judgment, which will tell us, once, and for all, whether we are reading Dante "after Dante," or not.)

Notes

1. The point becomes especially clear if one compares Dante to Chaucer, or even the authors of the *Roman de la Rose*. For related discussions of authorship and readership in Chaucer and the *Roman*, see, respectively, Lerer 1993 and Hult 1986.

2. I will not here attempt to reproduce the vast critical literature that surrounds particular Dantean episodes in which the reading process is foregrounded, perhaps most famously the scene of Francesca and Paolo's reading in *Inf* 5. The endlessly vexed question of Dantean allegory sometimes confronts, but more often elides, the fact that this slippery term designates both a mode of writing and a practice of interpretation (Scott 1990; cf. Whitman 1987; Copeland and Melville 1991). A critic who has focused particularly useful attention on the larger question of reading in Dante is Noakes

1988, especially chaps. 2 and 3. See also the classic essays of Auerbach 1954 and Spitzer 1959 on Dante's addresses to his readers in the *Commedia.*

3. The literature on Dantean self-exegesis is extensive, particularly if one gives a reasonably broad definition to the term. The phenomenon is economically defined by Contini [1939] 1970c, whose influence continues to be felt in contemporary criticism: "un costante della personalità dantesca [è] questo perpetuo sopraggiungere della riflessione tecnica accanto alla poesia, quest'associazione di concreto poetare e d'intelligenza stilistica" (4). In general, see Sarolli 1971; Mazzotta 1979; Iannucci 1981; Battaglia Ricci 1983; Barolini 1984. On the specific phenomenon of Dante's writing of formal commentaries on his own works (in *Vita Nova, Convivio,* and, perhaps, *Epistle to Cangrande)* see Jenaro-MacLennan 1960; Battaglia Ricci 1983; Minnis et al. 1988, 373–87, 439–45; Noakes 1988, 68–80; Picone 1987 and 1995; Ascoli 1989 and 1997; Stillinger 1992; Barański 1996a and 1996b. For the related phenomenon of an allusive and "palinodic" rereading / rewriting of earlier works in later ones see the discussion and bibliography in Ascoli 1995.

4. Harrison eloquently describes this tendency along with his own (in my view only partially successful) attempt to avoid it by focusing on "the text itself": "In what follows I try to confront the *Vita Nuova* on its own terms and at the same time to avoid the hermeneutic trap of Dantology. The trap is one that Dante himself set up by embedding within his own works the hermeneutic guidelines for interpreting them. The history of Dantology has for the most part followed these guidelines in a persistent effort to expose the authorial intent and genius that governs his artifacts" (1988, ix; cf. 64–65). In a related vein Menocal 1991 offers a sustained meditation on how "Dante's Cult of Truth" elicited writerly responses that reflect and resist Dante's shaping vision of how his works should be read. A more extreme critique of the pursuit of "meaning" in Dante is in Stone 1994.

5. Citations and translations of the *Commedia* are from the Durling edition (Alighieri 1996a and 2003).

6. On the *auctor* and medieval authorship see esp. Chenu 1927; Nardi [1961] 1966; Hult 1986; Minnis 1988; Minnis et al. 1988; Stillinger 1992; Ascoli 2000a; on the medieval reader, see Allen 1982; Noakes 1988; Dagenais 1994. For an important account of some of the ways in which late-medieval readers negotiated a space for themselves as authors, see Copeland 1991. On Dante's negotiations between his "natural" status as reader and his aspiration to authorship, see Contini [1965] 1970b, 76–77: "Dante è un produttore di *auctoritates.* Culturalmente egli è un uomo del medio evo per il quale . . . la sentenza . . . è fonte di conoscenza non meno . . . che il ragionamento e l'esperienza diretta; salvo che, invece di limitarsi a incastonare e glossare detti memorabili . . . egli ne produce dei suoi, e conferisce lo stesso piglio legislativo a tutti i suoi

enunciati," as well as Ascoli 1989, 1991 and 1997. Given my focus on the "future" of Dante's *oeuvre,* one aspect of the question of reading and writing that remains bracketed for purposes of this essay is that of the materiality of medieval texts and the exploration of reading and writing from that perspective. On these issues see Petrucci 1995; for recent and important contributions to Dante studies in this area see Ahern 1982, 1990, 1992; Storey 1993; Steinberg 1999; Holmes 2000.

7. For a strictly temporalized account of the hierarchies of ecclesiastical authority, which places the belated interpretations of the "decretalists" in a distinctly inferior position with respect to Scripture and the early Fathers of the Church, see *Monarchia* 3.3.11–16: "est advertendum quod quedam scriptura est ante Ecclesiam, quedam cum Ecclesia, quedam post Ecclesiam. Ante quidem Ecclesiam sunt vetus et novum Testamentum, quod 'in eternum mandatum est' ut ait Propheta. . . . Cum Ecclesia vero sunt veneranda illa concilia principalia quibus Cristum interfuisse nemo fidelis dubitat, cum habeamus ipsum dixisse discipulis ascensurum in celum: 'Ecce ego vobiscum sum in omnibus diebus usque ad consummationem seculi,' ut Matheus testatur. Sunt etiam scripture doctorum, Augustini et aliorum, quos a Spiritu Sancto adiutos qui dubitat, fructus eorum vel omnino non vidit vel, si vidit, minime degustavit. Post Ecclesiam vero sunt traditiones quas 'decretales' dicunt: que quidem etsi auctoritate apostolica sunt venerande, fundamentali tamen Scripture postponendas esse dubitandum non est, cum Cristus sacerdotes obiurgaverit de contrario. . . . Quod si traditiones Ecclesie post Ecclesiam sunt . . . necesse est ut non Ecclesie a traditionibus, sed ab Ecclesia traditionibus accedat auctoritas . . ." (Alighieri 1979c [translation in Alighieri 1996c: "It must be borne in mind that some scriptures preceded the church, others coincided with the founding of the church, and others followed it. Before the church are the Old and New Testaments, which 'he hath commanded forever,' as the Prophet says. . . . Contemporaneous with the church are those venerated principal councils at which Christ was present, as no believer doubts, since we know that he said to the disciples as he was about to ascend to heaven: 'Lo, I am with you always, even to the end of the world,' as Matthew bears witness. There are also the writings of the doctors of the church, of Augustine and others; anyone who doubts that they were helped by the Holy Spirit has either entirely failed to see their fruits or, if he has seen them, has not tasted them. Then after the church come the traditions called 'decretals,' which, while certainly to be revered on account of their apostolic authority, yet must take second place to the fundamental scriptures, given that Christ reproached the priests for doing the opposite. . . . Now if the traditions of the church come after the church, as has been shown, it must be the case that the church does not derive its authority from the traditions, but that the traditions derive their authority from the church"]).

8. The situation is in fact more complicated, as can be seen from Saint Bonaventure's often-cited distinction among four categories of textual production: *scriptor* (copyist), *compilator* (compiler of the sayings of others), *commentator* (the reader who explains and clarifies the writings of others), and the *auctor* proper (commentary on the *Sentences* of Peter Lombard; from Stillinger 1992, 1).

9. Among the leading proponents of this view are Allen 1982 and Dagenais 1994.

10. Much of the discussion of Dantean authority has focused on his definition of a relation to the classical poets, above all, Virgil and Ovid, on the one hand, and to "God's way of writing" on the other. Singleton 1954 makes the claim that Dante is imitating Scripture in the *Commedia.* Holländer 1968 (144–45) showed clearly how the "sacrato poema" situates Dante between Virgil as "maestro e autore" and God as "verace Autore." Representative studies on various aspects of these intertwined questions are Mazzotta 1979; Barolini 1984; Jacoff and Schnapp 1991; Iannucci 1993a; Martinez 1995; Picone 1997; Hawkins 1999. For my perspective on Dante's evolving struggle with the categories of medieval authorship and authority, see Ascoli 1989, 1991, 1997, 2000a. See also Minnis et al. 1988 and Botterill 1997.

11. On various explicit and implicit readers addressed by the *Vita Nova,* see Ahern 1990 and 1992; Noakes 1990.

12. All citations are from the De Robertis edition (Alighieri 1984); translations are my own. I accept both the retitling of the work by Gorni (Alighieri 1996b) and the critique of Barbi's division of the work into forty-two chapters by Gorni (1995 and Alighieri 1996b) and by Cervigni and Vasta (Alighieri 1995, 19–28). I continue to use Barbi's chapter numbers for reference, but not for interpretive purposes.

13. My focus on the *Vita Nova* as a book whose form and content echo and transform medieval discourses on the interactions of authorship and readership develops issues raised by a number of previous critics, most notably: Singleton 1949; De Robertis 1970; Picone 1977a, 1977b, and 1987; Mazzotta 1983; Harrison 1988; Noakes 1988; Stillinger 1992; Ahern 1992. I have also benefited in many ways from ongoing conversations on this subject with Ronald Martinez.

14. Readings of chapter 3 tend to focus on the remarkable dream vision and its poetic interpretations (see Singleton 1949, 13–14; Harrison 1988, 17–28; Noakes 1990, 49–52; Stillinger 1992, 46–51; Stone 1994), but rarely probe the significance of sending the poem around for interpretation to the "fedeli d'amore."

15. The reference is to *De vulgari eloquentia* 2.8.3, "lectio passio vel actus legendi" (Alighieri 1979a), where Dante elaborates a crucial distinction

between active and passive poetic "singing" on analogy with the traditional Scholastic distinction between active and passive *lectio.* This dense passage is clearly relevant to our discussion of the conceptual interpenetration of the roles of author (singer) and reader, a point that I will take up in forthcoming work. See also Ascoli 1991, 215–16, and note 43.

16. On the complex *prosimetrum* structure of the *Vita Nova,* especially the prose "ragioni" and "divisioni," see Rajna 1902; Singleton 1949, 29–54; Vallone 1963; De Robertis 1970; Picone 1977a, 1977b, 1987; Moleta 1978; Mazzaro 1981, chap. 4; D'Andrea 1982; Noakes 1988, chap. 3; Harrison 1988, 62–66; Durling and Martinez 1990, 55–69; Stillinger 1992, chaps. 2–3; Barolini 1994; Botterill 1994b.

17. De Robertis (Alighieri 1984, 3) notes: "È tra i caratteri più significativi [della *Vita Nova*], ed elemento costitutivo di essa, la prepotente forza di autoaffermazione che la percorre da capo a fondo, la vocazione, per così dire, di autorità, in cui è compresa e riassunta la stessa vocazione poetica." The relation of the form of the *Vita Nova* to the larger project of the constitution of Dantean poetic authority is explored in depth by Picone 1987; Menocal 1991, chap. 1; Stillinger 1992, chaps. 2–3; Harrison 1988, 54–65.

18. For a suggestive reading of the narrative temporality of the last chapter, see Harrison 1988, 128–57. On the temporality of the *libello* as a whole, see Singleton 1949, 25–35, 114–15; De Robertis 1970, 11; Noakes 1988, 77–80; Stillinger 1992, 81–84, 114–15; Barolini 1994; Cervigni and Vasta in Alighieri 1995, 28–44. My own understanding of the Dante-author to Dante-reader transition in the chapter has been considerably sharpened by Stanley (Toby) Levers, a Berkeley student whose seminar paper on this topic won the Dante Society undergraduate essay prize for 2000.

19. See, for instance, De Robertis 1970, 13–14 et passim, and his note on "Era venuta ne la mente mia" (Alighieri 1984, 213–14*nn*).

20. On the *Vita Nova* as palinodic text (as against the more usual focus on its place in later Dantean palinodes—cf. Barański 1995) see Ascoli 1995, 179*n*8.

21. The first passage reads as follows: "Dunque, se noi vedemo che a li poete hanno parlato a le cose inanimate, sì come avessero senso e ragione . . . e non solo cose vere, ma cose non vere . . . degno è lo dicitore per rima di fare lo somigliante, ma non sanza ragione alcuna, ma con ragione la quale poi sia possibile d'aprire per prosa" ("Hence, if we see that the classical poets have spoken to inanimate things as if they had feeling and intelligence . . . and not only to real things but to fictive ones . . . the vernacular speaker in rhyme is worthy of doing something similar, but not without any good reason—rather with a reason that can be expounded in prose" [par. 8]). For glosses on chapter 25, see Singleton 1949, esp. 29–30, 48–50, 57–58, 74–76; Grayson 1972, 16–17, 42–46, 64–66; Picone 1979, 18–26; Harrison 1988, 54–68.

22. "[Q]ui Dante si referisce alla particolare funzione che la prosa ha nella *Vita nuova,* di 'aprire' appunto la 'ragione' delle rime. Per cui il capitolo vale non solo come interpretazione del parlar poetico, ma come 'poetica' dello stesso libro" (Alighieri 1984, 176*n,* repeated from De Robertis 1970, 231–32). See also Grayson 1972, 42–43; Harrison 1988, 57, 62, who sees this "theoretical" moment as being at odds with Dante's practice throughout the *libello.*

23. For example, *Conv* 1.2.17: "Intendo anche mostrare la vera sentenza di quelle [le canzoni che saranno commentate nel *Convivio*] che alcuno vedere non si può s'io non la conto, perché è nascosa sotto figura d'allegoria: e questo non solamente darà diletto buono a udire, ma sottile ammaestramento e a così parlare e a così intendere l'altrui scritture." From the general perspective of this essay it is important that Dante claims that his glosses will teach his readers both to be writers themselves ("a così parlare") and to be interpreters of the writings of others.

24. All references to the *Epistle* are from Alighieri 1979b; translations are my own.

25. I obviously do not agree that the "agens" of the *Epistle* (par. 6 and 14) refers to the protagonist of the *Commedia* rather than to its author (cf. Mazzoni 1955, 177; Contini [1957] 1970a, 39–40), but rather support Nardi's view ([1961] 1966, 297–300) that it designates the author (see also Ascoli 1997, 336–38, 352*n*89).

26. See Hawkins 1999, 21–22, for a related discussion of the *Monarchia,* which I have also treated in an unpublished lecture: "No Judgment among Equals: Authority and Division in the *Monarchia.*"

27. This simultaneity of roles partially corroborates Mazzoni's position concerning the *agens* (see note 26 above), in the sense that it suggests that "Dante-*agens*" is *both* author and character, not to mention reader.

28. See Ascoli 1997 and 2000b. Important contributions to the controversy include: Scolari 1819 and 1844; D'Ovidio 1901; Torracca [1902] 1912; Moore 1903; Pietrobono [1937] 1954; Mancini 1943; Mazzoni 1955 and 1959; Hardie 1960; Nardi 1960 and [1961] 1966; Padoan 1965; Paolazzi [1986] 1990; Minnis et al. 1988; Barolini 1990; Barański 1991a; Holländer 1994; Brugnoli 1997. Two works that retrace the debate for differing purposes are Hollander 1993 and Ahern 1997, the latter of which is particularly noteworthy as one of the only serious attempts to deduce who might have attempted such forgery and what his (or her) purposes might have been.

29. All citations from the *Convivio* are taken from Alighieri 1988; translations are my own.

30. These include: the inadequacy of the *titulus* heading (par. 10); the lack of an early and trustworthy manuscript; the question of dating the document in relation to Dante's association with Cangrande della Scala; the

problem of presumed stylistic and conceptual incompatibility with the authentic works; the possibility that the "echoes" of it in Boccaccio and other Trecento Dante commentators are actually the source material on which a forger might have worked.

31. My argument here is eloquently anticipated by Barolini 1990, 140: "by revealing one's position with regard to the paternity of the Epistle, one potentially reveals a host of other vested interests and beliefs." Barolini argues that the *Epistle* is not a necessary interpretative guide to the *Commedia*, which reveals its own meanings plainly enough (143: "the answers that I seek regarding the poem are to be found in the poem itself"; cf. Harrison cited in note 4 above). On this latter point I remain a hopeful agnostic.

32. *Henry IV, Part 1* 5.3.1–28, especially line 25: "The king hath many marching in his coats."

HISTORIES: WORKS CITED

Abulafia, Anna Sapir. 1995. *Christians and Jews in the Twelfth-Century Renaissance*. London: Routledge.

Ahern, John. 1982. "Binding the Book: Hermeneutics and Manuscript Production in *Paradiso* 33." PMLA 97:800–809.

______. 1990. "The Reader on the Piazza: Verbal Duels in Dante's *Vita Nuova*." *Texas Studies in Language and Literature* 32:18–39.

______. 1992. "The New Life of the Book: The Implied Reader of the *Vita Nuova*." DS 110:1–16.

______. 1997. "Can the *Epistle to Cangrande* be Read as a Forgery?" In *Seminario Dantesco Internazionale / International Dante Seminar* I. Ed. Zygmunt Barański. Florence: Le Lettere. 281–307.

Alighieri, Dante. 1892. *The Divine Comedy of Dante Alighieri*. Trans. Henry Wadsworth Longfellow. 3 vols. Boston and New York: Houghton Mifflin.

______. 1924. *La Divina Commedia di Dante Alighieri con il commento di Tommaso Casini*. 6th ed. Rev. S. A. Barbi. 3 vols. Florence: Sansoni.

______. 1954. *Monarchy and Three Political Letters*. Ed. Donald Nicholl. London: Weidenfeld and Nicolson.

______. 1966. *Convivio*. Ed. Maria Picchio Simonelli. Bologna: Pàtron.

______. 1966–67. *La Commedia secondo l'antica vulgata*. Ed. Giorgio Petrocchi. 4 vols. Milan: Mondadori.

______. 1970–75. *The Divine Comedy*. Trans. and ed. Charles Singleton. 3 vols in 6. Princeton, N.J.: Princeton University Press.

______. 1970. *Il libro della "Vita Nuova."* Ed. Domenico De Robertis. 2nd ed. rev. Florence: Sansoni.

______. 1972. *La Divina Commedia*. Ed. C. H. Grandgent. Cambridge, Mass.: Harvard University Press.

______. 1972–73. *La Divina Commedia*. Ed. Tommaso Casini and Silvio Adrasto Barbi. 3 vols. Florence: Sansoni.

______. 1979a. *De vulgari eloquentia*. In vol. 2 of *Opere minori*. Ed. Pier Vincenzo Mengaldo et al. Milan and Naples: Ricciardi.

______. 1979b. *Epistole*. Ed. Arsenio Frugoni and Giorgio Brugnoli. In vol. 2 of *Opere minori*. Ed. Pier Vincenzo Mengaldo et al. Milan and Naples: Ricciardi.

______. 1979c. *Monarchia*. Ed. Bruno Nardi. In vol. 2 of *Opere minori*. Ed. Pier Vincenzo Mengaldo et al. Milan and Naples: Ricciardi.

______. 1984. *Vita Nuova*. In vol. 1, pt. 1 of *Opere minori*. Ed. Domenico De Robertis and Gianfranco Contini. Milan and Naples: Ricciardi.

______. 1988. *Convivio*. In vol. 1, pt. 2 of *Opere minori*. Ed. Cesare Vasoli and Domenico De Robertis. Milan and Naples: Ricciardi.

______. 1991. *Inferno*. Ed. Anna Maria Chiavacci Leonardi. Milan: Mondadori.

______. 1994. *Purgatorio*. Ed. Anna Maria Chiavacci Leonardi. Milan: Mondadori.

______. 1995. *Vita Nuova*. Ed. and trans. Dino S. Cervigni and Edward Vasta. Notre Dame, Ind.: University of Notre Dame Press.

______. 1996a. *Inferno*. Vol. 1 of *The Divine Comedy of Dante Alighieri*. Ed. and trans. Robert M. Durling. Introduction and notes by Ronald L. Martinez and Robert M. Durling. New York and Oxford: Oxford University Press.

______. 1996b. *Vita Nova*. Ed. Guglielmo Gorni. Turin: Einaudi.

______. 1996c. *Monarchy*. Trans. Prue Shaw. Cambridge: Cambridge University Press.

______. 2003. *Purgatorio*. Vol. 2 of *The Divine Comedy of Dante Alighieri*. Ed. and trans. Robert M. Durling. Introduction and notes by Ronald L. Martinez and Robert M. Durling. New York and Oxford: Oxford University Press.

Allen, Judson. 1982. *The Ethical Poetic of the Later Middle Ages*. Toronto: University of Toronto Press.

Antonetti, Pierre. 1979. *La vita quotidiana a Firenze ai tempi di Dante*. Milan: Rizzoli.

Aquinas, Thomas. 1852–1873. *Catena aurea in quatuor evangelia*. In *Opera omnia*. Parma: Fiaccadori.

Ascoli, Albert Russell. 1989. "The Vowels of Authority (Dante's *Convivio* IV.vi.3–4)." In *Discourses of Authority in Medieval and Renaissance Literature*. Ed. Kevin Brownlee and Walter Stephens. Hanover, N.H.: University Press of New England. 23–46.

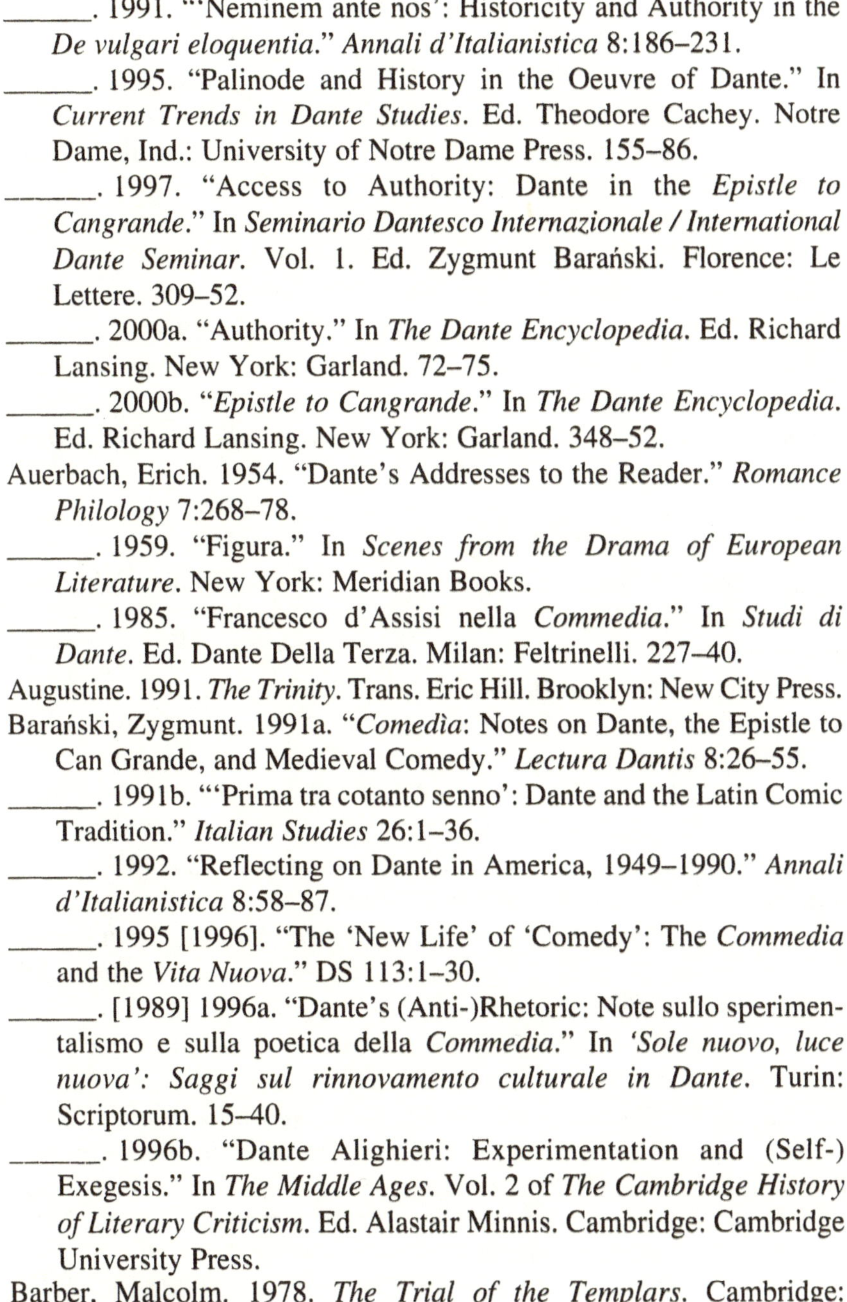

______. 1991. "'Neminem ante nos': Historicity and Authority in the *De vulgari eloquentia*." *Annali d'Italianistica* 8:186–231.

______. 1995. "Palinode and History in the Oeuvre of Dante." In *Current Trends in Dante Studies*. Ed. Theodore Cachey. Notre Dame, Ind.: University of Notre Dame Press. 155–86.

______. 1997. "Access to Authority: Dante in the *Epistle to Cangrande*." In *Seminario Dantesco Internazionale / International Dante Seminar*. Vol. 1. Ed. Zygmunt Barański. Florence: Le Lettere. 309–52.

______. 2000a. "Authority." In *The Dante Encyclopedia*. Ed. Richard Lansing. New York: Garland. 72–75.

______. 2000b. "*Epistle to Cangrande*." In *The Dante Encyclopedia*. Ed. Richard Lansing. New York: Garland. 348–52.

Auerbach, Erich. 1954. "Dante's Addresses to the Reader." *Romance Philology* 7:268–78.

______. 1959. "Figura." In *Scenes from the Drama of European Literature*. New York: Meridian Books.

______. 1985. "Francesco d'Assisi nella *Commedia*." In *Studi di Dante*. Ed. Dante Della Terza. Milan: Feltrinelli. 227–40.

Augustine. 1991. *The Trinity*. Trans. Eric Hill. Brooklyn: New City Press.

Barański, Zygmunt. 1991a. "*Comedìa*: Notes on Dante, the Epistle to Can Grande, and Medieval Comedy." *Lectura Dantis* 8:26–55.

______. 1991b. "'Prima tra cotanto senno': Dante and the Latin Comic Tradition." *Italian Studies* 26:1–36.

______. 1992. "Reflecting on Dante in America, 1949–1990." *Annali d'Italianistica* 8:58–87.

______. 1995 [1996]. "The 'New Life' of 'Comedy': The *Commedia* and the *Vita Nuova*." DS 113:1–30.

______. [1989] 1996a. "Dante's (Anti-)Rhetoric: Note sullo sperimentalismo e sulla poetica della *Commedia*." In *'Sole nuovo, luce nuova': Saggi sul rinnovamento culturale in Dante*. Turin: Scriptorum. 15–40.

______. 1996b. "Dante Alighieri: Experimentation and (Self-) Exegesis." In *The Middle Ages*. Vol. 2 of *The Cambridge History of Literary Criticism*. Ed. Alastair Minnis. Cambridge: Cambridge University Press.

Barber, Malcolm. 1978. *The Trial of the Templars*. Cambridge: Cambridge University Press.

______. 1994. *The New Knighthood: A History of the Order of the Temple*. Cambridge: Cambridge University Press.

Barolini, Teodolinda. 1984. *Dante's Poets: Textuality and Truth in the "Comedy."* Princeton, N.J.: Princeton University Press.

______. 1990. "For the Record: The *Epistle to Cangrande* and Various American Dantisti." *Lectura Dantis* 6:140–43.

______. 1994. "'Cominciandomi dal principio infino a la fine' (*Vita Nuova* XXIII.15): Forging Anti-Narrative in the *Vita Nuova*." In *La gloriosa donna de la mente: A Commentary on the "Vita Nuova."* Ed. Vincent Moleta. Florence: Olschki. 119–40.

Barth, Karl. 1933. *The Epistle to the Romans*. London: Oxford University Press.

Battaglia Ricci, Lucia. 1983. *Dante e la tradizione letteraria medievale*. Pisa: Giardini.

Beale, Rebecca S. 1985. "Beatrice in the Sun: A Vision from Apocalypse." DS 103:57–78.

______. 1996. "Bonaventure, Dante, and the Woman Clothed With the Sun." DS 114:209–28.

Benvenuto da Imola. 1991. *Lettore degli antichi e dei moderni*. Ed. Pantaleo Palmieri and Carlo Paolazzi. Ravenna: Longo.

Bernard of Clarivaux. 1971. *On the Song of Songs* I. Trans. Kilian Walsh. Spencer, Mass.: Cistercian Publications.

______. 1983. *Liber ad milites templi de laude novae militiae*. In Vol. 1 of *Obras comopletas de San Bernardo*. Ed. Cistercian Monks of Spain. Madrid: Biblioteca de autores cristianos. 495–543.

Bett, Henry. 1931. *Joachim of Flora*. London: Methuen.

Bloomfield, Morton. 1957. "Joachim of Flora: A Critical Survey of His Canon, Teachings, Sources, Biography, and Influence." *Traditio* 13:249–311.

Blumenkrantz, Bernhard. 1966. *Le juif mediéval au miroir de l'art chrétien*. Paris: Études Augustiniennes.

Boethius. 1973. *Tractates and De Consolatione Philosophiae*. Trans. H. F. Stewart et al. Cambridge, Mass.: Harvard University Press.

Bonaventure. 1961. *Meditations on the Life of Christ*. Trans. Isa Ragusa. Ed. Isa Ragusa and Rosalie B. Green. Princeton, N.J.: Princeton University Press.

______. 1978. *The Soul's Journey into God, The Tree of Life, the Life of Francis*. Trans. and ed. Ewert Cousins. New York: Paulist Press.

Bongiorno, Laurine Mack. 1968. "The Theme of the Old and the New Law in the Arena Chapel." *The Art Bulletin* 50:11–20.

Botterill, Steven. 1994a. *Dante and the Mystical Tradition: St. Bernard of Clairvaux in the "Commedia."* Cambridge: Cambridge University Press.

______. 1994b. "'Però che la divisione non si fa se non per aprire la sentenzia de la cosa divisa.' (*Vita Nuova* 14, 13): The *Vita Nuova* as Commentary." In *La gloriosa donna de la mente: A Commentary on the "Vita Nuova."* Ed. Vincent Moleta. Florence: Olschki. 61–76.

______. 1997. "Dante and the Authority of Poetic Language." In *Dante: Contemporary Perspectives.* Ed. Amilcare A. Iannucci. Toronto: University Toronto Press. 167–80.

Braaten, C. 1985. "The Kingdom of God and Life Everlasting." In *Christian Theology: Introduction to Its Traditions and Tasks.* Ed. P. Hodgson and R. King. Philadelphia: Fortress Press. 328–52.

Brownlee, Kevin. 1984. "Why the Angels Speak Italian." *Poetics Today* 5:597–610.

Brugnoli, Giorgio. 1997. "Il punto sull'*Epistola a Cangrande.*" In Seminario *Dantesco Internazionale / International Dante Seminar.* Vol. 1. Ed. Zygmunt Barański. Florence: Le Lettere. 353–71.

Bruni Aretino, Leonardo. 1928. *Humanistisch-Philosophische Schriften.* Ed. Hans Baron, 50–63. Leipzig and Berlin: Teubner.

Buonaiuti, Ernesto. 1984. *Gioacchino da Fiore: I tempi, la vita, il messaggio.* Cosenza: L. Giordano.

Cassell, Anthony K. 1978. "'Mostrando con le poppe il petto' (*Purg.* XXIII, 102)." DS 96:73–81.

Charity, Alan. 1966. *Events and Their Afterlife: The Dialectics of Christian Typology in the Bible and Dante.* Cambridge: Cambridge University Press.

Chenu, M. D. 1927. "Auctor, Actor, Autor." *Bulletin du Cange: Archivium Latinitatis Medii Aevi* 3:81–86.

Ciccia, Carmelo. 1997. *Dante e Gioacchino da Fiore.* Cosenza: L. Pellegrini.

Cohen, Jeremy. 1982. *The Friars and the Jews: The Evolution of Medieval Anti-Judaism.* Ithaca, N.Y.: Cornell University Press.

______. 1983. "The Jews as Killers of Christ in the Latin Tradition, from Augustine to the Friars." *Traditio* 39:1–27.

———, ed. 1996. *From Witness to Witchcraft: Jews and Judaism in Medieval Christian Thought*. Wiesbaden: Harrassowitz.

Contini, Gianfranco. [1957] 1970a. "Dante come personaggio-poeta della *Commedia*." In *Un'idea di Dante: Saggi danteschi*. Turin: Einaudi. 33–62.

______. [1965] 1970b. "Un'interpretazione di Dante." In *Un'idea di Dante: Saggi danteschi*. Turin: Einaudi. 69–111.

______. [1939] 1970c. "Introduzione alle *Rime* di Dante." In *Un'idea di Dante: Saggi danteschi*. Turin: Einaudi. 3–20.

Copeland, Rita. 1991. *Rhetoric, Hermeneutics, and Translation in the Middle Ages*. Cambridge: Cambridge University Press.

Copeland, Rita, and Stephen Melville. 1991. "Allegory and Allegoresis, Rhetoric and Hermeneutics." *Exemplaria* 3.1:157–87.

Cornford, Francis M. 1959. *Plato's Timaeus*. Indianapolis: Bobbs Merrill.

Cornish, Alison. 2000. *Reading Dante's Stars*. New Haven, Conn.: Yale University Press.

Corti, Maria. 1983. *La felicità mentale: Nuove prospettive per Cavalcanti e Dante*. Turin: Einaudi.

Cullman, Oscar. 1951. *Christ and Time: The Primitive Christian Conception of Time and History*. London: S.C.M. Press.

Dagenais, John. 1994. *The Ethics of Reading in Manuscript Culture: Glossing the "Libro de buen amor."* Princeton, N.J.: Princeton University Press.

D'Andrea, Antonio. 1982. "La struttura della *Vita Nuova*: Le divisioni delle rime." In *Il nome della storia: Studi e ricerche di storia e letteratura*. Naples: Liguori. 25-58.

Dartmouth Dante Project. http://dciswww.dartmouth.edu:50080/v3?db=7&conn=89017443&page=d: Jacopo della Lana (1324–28); L'Ottimo (1333); Pietro di Dante (1340–41); Cassinese (1350–75) Benvenuto da Imola (1380); Anonimo Fiorentino (1400); Serravalle (1416–17).

De Leo, Pietro. 1988. *Gioacchino da Fiore, aspetti inediti della vita e delle opere*. Soveria Mannelli: Rubbettino.

Derbes, Ann. 1991. "A Crusading Fresco Cycle at the Cathedral of Le Puy." *The Art Bulletin* 73:561–76.

______. 1996. *Picturing the Passion in Late Medieval Italy*. Cambridge: Cambridge University Press.

De Robertis, Domenico. 1970. *Il libro della "Vita Nuova."* 2nd ed. Florence: Sansoni.

De Stefano, Antonino. 1938. "Le origini dei Frati Gaudenti." In *Riformatori ed eretici del medioevo*. Palermo: Ciuni. 211–69.

Di Patre, Patrizia. 1989. "I modi dell'intertestualità dantesca: Tradizione classica e biblica in un frammento di prosa (*Ep*. VI. 12-24)." StD 61:289–306.

Douay–Rheims. 1899. *Holy Bible*. Baltimore: John Murphy Company.

D'Ovidio, Francesco. 1901. "L'*Epistola a Cangrande*." In *Studi sulla "Divina Commedia."* Milan and Palermo: Sandron. 448–85.

Dupré-Theseider, Eugenio. 1939. *I papi di Avignone e la questione romana*. Florence: Le Monnier.

Durand, Guillaume. 1859. *Rationale divinorum officiorum*. Naples: Dura.

Durling, Robert M., and Ronald L. Martinez. 1990. *Time and the Crystal: Studies in Dante's "Rime Petrose."* Berkeley: University of California Press.

Emmerson, Richard K., and Ronald B. Herzman. 1992. *The Apocalyptic Imagination in Medieval Literature*. Philadelphia: University of Pennsylvania Press.

Fergusson, Francis. 1953. *Dante's Drama of the Mind*. Princeton, N.J.: Princeton University Press.

Flavius Josephus. 1968. *Histoire ancienne des juifs et La guerre des Juifs contre les romains*. Trans. Arnauld d'Andilly and J. A. C. Buchon. Paris: Lidis.

Foster, Kenelm. 1977. *The Two Dantes and Other Studies*. London: Darton, Longman and Todd.

Francis of Assisi. 1999. "Earlier Rule (The Rule of 1221)." In *The Saint*. Vol. 1 of *Francis of Assisi: Early Documents*. Ed. Regis Armstrong, Wayne Hellmann, and William Short. New York: New City Press. 63–86.

Franke, William. 1996. *Dante's Interpretive Journey*. Chicago: The University of Chicago Press.

Freccero, John. 1986. "Bestial Sign and Bread of Angels." In *The Poetics of Conversion*. Ed. Rachel Jacoff. Cambridge: Harvard University Press. 160–70.

Fulcher of Chartres. 1989. *A History of the Expedition to Jerusalem*. Trans. Frances Rita Ryan. Knoxville: University of Tennessee Press.

Gilson, Étienne. 1939. *Dante et la philosophie*. Paris: J. Vrin.

Giovanni Villani. 1990. *Nuova cronica*. Ed. Giuseppe Porta. Parma: Guanda.

Gorni, Guglielmo. 1995. "'Paragrafi' e titolo della *Vita Nova*." SFI 53:203–22.

Grayson, Cecil. 1972. *Cinque saggi su Dante*. Bologna: Pàtron.

Grayzel, Solomon. 1933. *The Church and the Jews in the Thirteenth Century*. Philadelphia: Dropsie College.

Gryting, Loyal A. T. 1952. *The Oldest Versions of the Twelfth-Century Poem "La Venjeance nostre seigneur."* Ann Arbor: University of Michigan Press.

Guido da Pisa. 1974. *Expositione et glose super Comoediam Dantis*. Ed. Vincenzo Cioffari. Albany: State University of New York Press.

Guittone d'Arezzo. 1990. *Lettere*. Ed. Claude Margueron. Bologna: Commissione per i testi di lingua.

Hardie, Colin G. 1960. "The *Epistle to Cangrande* Again." *Deutsches Dantes Jahrbuch* 38:51–74.

Häring, Bernhard. 1961–66. *The Law of Christ: Moral Theology for Priests and Laity*. Trans. Edwin G. Kaiser. 3 vols. Westminster, Md.: Newman Press.

______. 1966. *This Time of Salvation*. New York: Herder and Herder.

Harrison, Robert. 1988. *The Body of Beatrice*. Baltimore and London: Johns Hopkins University Press.

Havely, Nick. 1998. *Dante's Modern Afterlife: Reception and Response from Blake to Heaney*. New York: St. Martin's Press.

Hawkins, Peter. 1999. *Dante's Testaments*. Stanford, Calif.: Stanford University Press.

Heft, James. 1971. "Joachim of Flora's Theology of History." Diss. University of St. Michael's College, University of Toronto.

Henry, Avril. 1987. *Biblia pauperum: A Facsimile and Edition*. Ithaca, N.Y.: Cornell University Press.

Herzman, Ronald B. 1992. "Dante and the Apocalypse." In *The Apocalypse in the Middle Ages*. Ed. Richard K. Emmerson and Bernard McGinn. Ithaca, N.Y.: Cornell University Press. 398–413.

Herzman, Ronald B., and Gary W. Towsley. 1994. "Squaring the Circle: *Paradiso* 33 and the Poetics of Geometry." *Traditio* 98:95–125.

Hoeberichts, J. 1997. *Francis and Islam.* Quincy, Ill.: Franciscan Press.

Hollander, Robert. 1968. "Dante's Use of *Aeneid* I in *Inferno* I and II." *Comparative Literature* 20:142–56. 1963. Reprinted in *Il Virgilio dantesco: tragedia nella "Commedia."* Florence: Olschki.

______. 1969. *Allegory in Dante's "Commedia."* Princeton, N.J.: Princeton University Press.

______. 1993. *Dante's "Epistle to Cangrande."* Ann Arbor: University of Michigan Press.

______. 1994. "Response to Henry Ansgar Kelly." *Lectura Dantis* 14–15:96–111.

Holmes, Olivia. 2000. *Assembling the Lyric Self: Authorship from Troubadour Song to Italian Poetry Book.* Minneapolis and London: University of Minnesota Press.

Hood, John Y. B. 1995. *Aquinas and the Jews.* Philadelphia: University of Pennsylvania Press.

Housley, Norman. 1982. *The Italian Crusades.* Oxford: Oxford University Press.

Hult, David. 1986. *Self-Fulfilling Prophecies: Readership and Authority in the First "Roman de la Rose."* Cambridge: Cambridge University Press.

Iannucci, Amilcare A. 1979. "Beatrice in Limbo: A Metaphoric Harrowing of Hell." DS 97:23–45.

______. 1981. "Autoesegesi dantesca: La tecnica dell' 'episodio parallelo' (*Inferno* 15–*Purgatorio* 11)." *Lettere italiane* 33:305–28. (Originally published as "Autoesegesi dantesca: La tecnica dell' 'episodio parallelo' nella *Commedia.*") 1984. Reprinted in *Forma ed evento nella "Divina Commedia."* Rome: Bulzoni. 83–114.

______. 1990. "Forbidden Love: Metaphor and History." *Annali della facoltà di lettere e filosofia* 11:341–58.

______, ed. 1993a. *Dante e la 'bella scola' della poesia: Autorità e sfida poetica.* Ravenna: Longo.

______. 1993b. "Dante e la 'bella scola' della poesia (*Inferno* 4.64-105)." In *Dante e la 'bella scola' della poesia: Autorità e sfida poetica*. Ed. Amilcare A. Iannucci. Ravenna: Longo. 19–37.

Jacobus de Voragine. 1993. *The Golden Legend.* Trans. William Granger Ryan. 2 vols. Princeton, N.J.: Princeton University Press.

Jacoff, Rachel, and Jeffrey Schnapp, eds. 1991. *The Poetry of Allusion: Dante and Virgil in Dante's "Commedia."* Stanford, Calif.: Stanford University Press.

Jacques De Vitry. 1999. *Historia Occidentalis.* In *The Saint.* Vol. 1 of *Francis of Assisi: Early Documents.* Ed. Regis Armstrong, Wayne Hellmann, and William Short. New York: New City Press. 581–85.

Jenaro-MacLennan, Luis. 1960. "Autocomentario in Dante y comentarismo latino." *Romanica* 19:82–123.

______. 1974. *The Trecento Commentaries on the "Divina Commedia" and the "Epistle to Cangrande."* Oxford: Clarendon Press.

John of Salisbury. 1909. *Ionnis Saresberiensis episcopi carnotesis Policraticus sive De nugis curialium et vestigiis philosophorum libri VIII.* 2 vols. Ed. D. I. Webb. Oxford: Clarendon Press.

Kantorowicz, Ernst H. 1944. "The 'King's Advent' and the Enigmatic Panel in the Doors of Santa Sabina." *The Art Bulletin* 26:207–31.

Kaske, Robert E. 1983. "The Seven *Status Ecclesiae* in *Purgatorio* XXXII and XXXIII: A Survey of Christian History." In *Dante, Petrarch, and Boccaccio: Studies in the Italian Trecento in Honor of Charles S. Singleton.* Ed. Aldo S. Bernardo and Anthony L. Pellegrini. Binghamton: State University of New York Press. 89–113.

Kelly, Henry Ansgar. 1989. *Tragedy and Comedy from Dante to Pseudo-Dante.* Berkeley: University of California Press.

______. 1994. "Cangrande and the Ortho-Dantists" and "Reply to Robert Hollander." *Lectura Dantis* 14–15:61–96, 111–15.

Komonchak, Joseph A., et al., eds. 1990. *The New Dictionary of Theology.* Collegeville, Minn.: Liturgical Press.

Krinsky, Catherine. 1970. "Representations of the Temple of Jerusalem before 1500." *Journal of the Warburg and Courtauld Institutes* 33:1–19.

Lerer, Seth. 1993. *Chaucer and His Readers: Imagining the Author in Late-Medieval England.* Princeton, N.J.: Princeton University Press.

Lerner, Robert E. 1995. *Refrigerio dei santi: Gioacchino da Fiore e l'escatologia medievale.* Rome: Viella.

Ligato, Giuseppe. 1996. "The Political Meanings of the Relic of the Holy Cross." In *Autour de la première croisade: Actes du Colloque de la Society for the Study of the Crusades and the Latin East (Clermont-Ferrand, 22–25 juin 1995)*. Ed. Michel Balard. Paris: Sorbonne.

Lincoln, Andrew T. 1981. *Paradise Now and Not Yet: Studies in the Role of the Heavenly Dimension in Paul's Thought, with Special Reference to His Eschatology*. Cambridge: Cambridge University Press.

Linder, Amnon. 1996. "Jews and Judaism in the Eyes of Christian Thinkers of the Middle Ages: The Destruction of Jerusalem in Medieval Christian Liturgy." In *From Witness to Witchraft: Jews and Judaism in Medieval Christian Thought*. Ed. Jeremy Cohen. Wiesbaden: Harrassowitz.

Lubac, Henri de. 1950. *Catholicism: A Study of Dogma in Relation to the Corporate Destiny of Mankind*. London: Burns, Oates & Washburne.

Mancini, Augusto. 1943. "Nuovi dubbi ed ipotesi sulla *Epistola a Cangrande*." *Atti del Reale Accademia d'Italia: Rendiconti, Classe di Scienze morali, storiche e filologiche*, ser. 7, 4:227–42.

Mandelbaum, Allen, trans. 1980–82. *The Divine Comedy of Dante Alighieri*. 3 vols. Berkeley: University of California Press.

Marrow, John. 1979. *Passion Iconography in Northern European Art of the Late Middle Ages and the Early Renaissance: A Study of the Transformation of Sacred Metaphor into Descriptive Narrative*. Kontrijk, Belgium: Van Ghemmert.

Marti, Mario. 1965. "Vita e morte della presunta doppia redazione della *Vita Nuova*." In Vol. 1 of *Studi in onore di Alfredo Schiaffini*. Rome: Edizione dell'Ateneo. 657–69.

Martinez, Ronald. 1995. "Dante and the Two Canons: Statius in Virgil's Footsteps (*Purgatorio* 21–30)." *Comparative Literature Studies* 32:151–75.

______. 1997. "Lament and Lamentation in *Purgatorio* and the Case of Dante's Statius." DS 117:45–88.

______. 1998. "The Rhetoric of Threnody in the *Vita Nuova*." MLN 113:1–29.

Matter, F. Ann. 1990. *The Voice of My Beloved: The Song of Songs in Medieval Western Christianity*. Philadelphia: University of Pennsylvania Press.

Mazzaro, Jerome. 1981. *The Figure of Dante: An Essay on the "Vita Nuova."* Princeton, N.J.: Princeton University Press.

Mazzoni, Francesco. 1955. "L'*Epistola a Cangrande.*" *Rendiconti della Accademia Nazionale dei Lincei: Classe di Scienze morali, storiche e filologiche,* ser. 8, 10:157–98.

______. [1959] 1966. "Per l'*Epistola a Cangrande.*" In *Contributi di filologia dantesca.* Florence: Sansoni. 7–37.

Mazzotta, Giuseppe. 1979. *Dante, Poet of the Desert: History and Allegory in the "Divine Comedy."* Princeton, N.J.: Princeton University Press.

______. 1983. "The Language of Poetry in the *Vita Nuova.*" *Rivista di studi italiani* 1:3–14.

______. 1986. "The American Criticism of Charles Singleton." DS 104:27–44.

McDougal, Stuart Y., ed. 1985. *Dante among the Moderns.* Chapel Hill: University of North Carolina Press.

McGinn, Bernard. 1985. *The Calabrian Abbot Joachim of Fiore in the History of Western Thought.* New York: Macmillan.

Menocal, Maria Rosa. 1991. *Writing in Dante's Cult of Truth from Borges to Boccaccio.* Durham, N.C., and London: Duke University Press.

Metz, Johannes Baptist. 1965. *The Church and the World.* New York: Paulist Press.

______. 1967. *The Evolving World and Theology.* New York: Paulist Press.

______. 1969. *Theology of the World.* New York: Herder and Herder.

______. 1991. *No Heaven without Earth.* London: S.C.M. Press.

Minnis, Alastair J. 1988. *Medieval Theory of Authorship: Scholastic Literary Attitudes in the Later Middle Ages.* 2nd ed. Philadelphia: University of Pennsylvania Press.

Minnis, Alastair J., and A. B. Scott, with David Wallace, eds. 1988. *Medieval Literary Theory and Criticism, c. 1100–c. 1375: The Commentary Tradition.* Oxford: Clarendon Press.

Moleta, Vincent. 1978. "The *Vita Nuova* as Lyric Narrative." *Forum Italicum* 12:369–90.

Moltmann, Jürgen. 1967. *Theology of Hope on the Ground and the Implications of a Christian Eschatology.* London: S.C.M. Press.

______. 1970. *The Future of Hope: Theology as Eschatology*. New York: Herder and Herder.

______. 1979. *The Future of Creation*. London: S.C.M. Press.

______. 1998. *Is There Life after Death?* Milwaukee, Wis.: Marquette University Press.

Moore, Edward. 1903. "The Genuineness of the Dedicatory *Epistle to Can Grande*." In *Studies in Dante, Third Series*. Oxford: Clarendon Press. 284–369.

Moreni, Domenico. 1831. *Prediche del B. Fra Giordano da Rivalto recitate in Firenze dal MCCCIII al MCCCVI*. 2 vols. Florence: Margheri.

Nardi, Bruno. 1944. "Dalla prima alla seconda *Vita Nuova*." *Nel mondo di Dante*. Rome: Edizioni di Storia e Letteratura. 1–20.

______. 1960. *Il punto sull'Epistola*. Florence: Le Monnier.

______. [1961] 1966. "Osservazioni sul medievale 'accessus ad auctores' in rapporto all' *Epistola a Can Grande*." In *Saggi e note di critica dantesca*. Milan and Naples: Ricciardi. 268–305.

______. 1985. *Dante e la cultura medievale*. Bari: Laterza.

Noakes, Susan. 1988. *Timely Reading: Between Exegesis and Interpretation*. Ithaca, N.Y.: Cornell University Press.

______. 1990. "Hermeneutics, Politics, and Civic Ideology in the *Vita Nuova*: Thoughts Preliminary to an Interpretation." *Texas Studies in Language and Literature* 32:18–39.

Padoan, Giorgio. [1965] 1977. "La mirabile visione di Dante e l'*Epistola a Cangrande*." In *Il pio Enea, l'empio Ulisse*. Ravenna: Longo. 30–63.

Paolazzi, Carlo. [1986] 1990. "Nozione di 'Comedìa' e tradizione retorica nella dantesca '*Epistola a Cangrande*.'" StD 58: 87–186.

Parker, Deborah. 1993. *Commentary and Ideology: Dante in the Renaissance*. Durham, N.C.: Duke University Press.

Parkes, James. 1976. *The Jew in the Medieval Community*, 2nd ed. New York: Hermon Press.

[Pecham, John]. 1895. *Expositio threnorum Ieremiae propheta*. In Vol. 7 of *Sancti Bonaventurae opera omnia*. Quaracchi: College of St. Bonaventure. 607–51.

Peirol. 1953. *Peirol, Troubadour of Auvergne*. Ed. S. C. Aston. Cambridge: Cambridge University Press.

Pelikan, Jaroslav. 1997. *What Has Athens to Do with Jerusalem? Timaeus and Genesis in Counterpoint.* Ann Arbor: University of Michigan Press.

Perugi, Maurizio. 1983. "Il Sordello di Dante e la tradizione mediolatina dell'invettiva." StD 55:23–135.

Petrucci, Armando. 1995. *Writers and Readers in Medieval Italy: Studies in the History of Written Culture.* Trans. Charles Radding. New Haven: Yale University Press.

Pézard, André. 1973. "Daniel et Dante ou les vengeances de Dieu." StD 50:1–96.

Picone, Michelangelo. 1977a. "Strutture poetiche e strutture prosastiche nella *Vita Nuova.*" MLN 92: 117–29.

______. 1977b. "Modelli e struttura nella *Vita Nuova.*" *Studi e problemi di critica testuale* 15:50–61.

______. 1979. *"Vita Nuova" e tradizione romanza.* Padua: Liviana.

______. 1987. "La *Vita Nuova* fra autobiografia e tipologia." In *Dante e le forme dell'allegoresi.* Ed. Michelangelo Picone. Ravenna: Longo. 59–69.

______. 1995. "Songbook and Lyric Genres in the *Vita Nuova.*" In *"Libri poetarum in quattuor species dividuntur": Essays on Dante and "Genre."* Ed. Zygmunt G. Barański. Supplement to *The Italianist* 15:158–70.

______. 1997. "Dante and the Classics." In *Dante.* Ed. Amilcare A. Iannucci. Toronto: University of Toronto Press. 51–73.

Pietrobono, Luigi. 1932. "Il rifacimento della *Vita Nuova* e le due fasi del pensiero dantesco." In *Saggi danteschi.* Torino: Nuova Biblioteca Italiana. 25–98.

______. [1937] 1954. "L'*Epistola a Cangrande.*" In *Nuovi studi danteschi.* Turin: Società Editrice Internazionale. 199–244.

Pike, David L. 1997. *Passage through Hell: Modernist Descents, Medieval Underworlds.* Ithaca, N.Y.: Cornell University Press.

Piromalli, Antonio. 1966. *Gioacchino da Fiore e Dante.* Ravenna: Longo.

Pite, Ralph. 1994. *The Circle of Our Vision: Dante's Presence in English Romantic Poetry.* Oxford: Clarendon Press.

Procacci, Giuliano. 1973. *History of the Italian People.* Harmondsworth: Penguin.

Pullan, Brian. 1972. *A History of Early Renaissance Italy: From the Mid-Thirteenth to the Mid-Fifteenth Century.* New York: St. Martin's Press.

Rahner, Karl. 1964. *Inquiries*. New York: Herder and Herder.

______. 1966. *More Recent Writings*. Vol. 4 of *Theological Investigations*. London: Darton, Longman, and Todd.

______. 1972. *On the Theology of Death.* New York: Herder and Herder.

______. 1985. "Eschatology." *Dictionary of Theology*. Ed. Karl Rahner and Herbert Vorgrimler. New York: Crossroads.

———, ed. 1968. *Sacramentum Mundi.* New York: Herder and Herder.

Raimondi, Ezio. 1972. "Una città nell'inferno dantesco." *Metafora e storia*. Turin: Einaudi. 49–65.

Rajna, Pio. 1902. "Per le divisioni della *Vita Nuova*." *Strenna dantesca* 1:111–14.

Reeves, Marjorie. 1969. *The Influence of Prophecy in the Later Middle Ages: A Study in Joachimism.* Oxford: Clarendon Press.

______. 1976. *Joachim of Fiore and the Prophetic Future*. London: S.P.C.K.

Rosenau, Helen. 1979. *Vision of the Temple*. London: Oresko.

Rough, Robert. 1973. *The Reformist Illuminations of the Gospels of Matilda, Countess of Tuscany*. The Hague: Nijhoff.

______. 1980. "Enrico Scrovegni, the Cavalieri Gaudenti, and the Arena Chapel in Padua." *The Art Bulletin* 62:24–35.

Ruether, Rosemary Radford. 1979. "The *Adversus Judaeos* Tradition in the Church Fathers: The Exegesis of Christian Anti-Judaism." In *Aspects of Jewish Culture in the Middle Ages*. Ed. Paul. Szarmach. Albany: State University of New York Press. 27–50.

Russell, D. S. 1978. *Apocalyptic: Ancient and Modern.* Philadelphia: Fortress Press.

Salimbene de Adam. 1942. *Cronica*. Ed. Ferdinando Bernini. 2 vols. Bari: Laterza.

Salvemini, Gaetano. 1960. *Magnati e popolani in Firenze dal 1280 al 1295*. Ed. Ernesto Sestan. Milan: Feltrinelli.

Sandkühler, Bruno. 1967. *Die frühen Dantekommentare und ihr Verhältnis zur mitteralterlichen Kommentartradition*. Munich: Münchner romanistiche Arbeiten.

Sarolli, Gian Roberto. 1971. "Autoesegesi dantesca e tradizione esegetica medievale." In *Prolegomena alla "Divina Commedia."* Florence: Olschki. 1–39.

Schein, Sylvia. 1991. *Fideles cruci*. Oxford: Clarendon Press.

Schreckenberg, Heinz. 1972. *Die Flavius-Josephus-Tradition in Antike und Mittelalter*. Leiden: Brill.

______. 1988. *Die christlichen Adversus-Judaeos-Texte (11.–13. Jh.)*. Frankfurt am Main: Peter Lang.

______. 1996. *The Jews in Christian Art: An Illustrated History*. New York: Continuum.

Schreckenberg, Heinz, and Kurt Schubert. 1992. *Jewish Historiography and Iconography in Early and Medieval Christianity*. Minneapolis: Fortress Press.

Schweitzer, Albert. 1923. *Christianity and the Religions of the World*. Trans. Johanna Powers. New York: George H. Doran Company.

______. 1950. *The Mystery of the Kingdom of God: The Secret of Jesus' Messiahship and Passion*. Trans. Walter Lowrie. London A. & C. Black.

______. 1968. *The Kingdom of God and Primitive Christianity*. Trans. L. A. Garrard. London: A. & C. Black.

Scolari, Filippo. 1819. "Note ad alcuni luoghi delli primi cinque canti della *Divina Commedia*." Venice: Tipografia Picatti.

______. 1844. "Lettera critica intorno alle epistole latine di Dante Alighieri." Venice: Tipografia all'Ancora.

Scott, John A. 1990. "Dante's Allegory of the Theologians." In *The Shared Horizon*. Ed. Tom O'Neill. Dublin: Irish Academic Press. 27–40.

______. 1996. *Dante's Political Purgatory*. Philadelphia: University of Pennsylvania Press.

Singleton, Charles. 1949. *An Essay on the "Vita Nuova."* Baltimore and London: The Johns Hopkins University Press.

______. 1954. *Elements of Structure*. Vol. 1 of *Dante Studies*. Cambridge, Mass.: Harvard University Press.

Spitzer, Leo. 1959. "The Addresses to the Reader in the *Commedia*." *Romanische Literaturstudien, 1936–56*. Tübingen: Niemeyer. 574–95.

Stabile, Giorgio. 1970. "Autore"; "Autorità." In ED 1:454–60.

Steinberg, Henry Justin. 1999. "The Magnates, the Popolo, and the Lyric: Anthologies of Poetry in Italy from the *Memoriali Bolognesi* to Dante." Diss. University of Minnesota, Twin Cities.

Stillinger, Thomas. 1992. *The Song of Troilus: Lyric Authority in the Medieval Book.* Philadelphia: University of Pennsylvania Press.

Stone, Gregory. 1994. "Dante's Averroistic Hermeneutics (On 'Meaning' in the *Vita Nuova*)." DS 112:133–59.

Storey, H. Wayne. 1993. *Transcription and Visual Poetics in the Early Italian Lyric.* New York: Garland.

Theoderich of Würzburg. 1986. *Guide to the Holy Land.* Trans. Aubrey Stewart. 2nd ed. New York: Italica Press.

Thomas of Celano. 1999. *The Life of Saint Francis by Thomas of Celano (1228–1229).* In *The Saint.* Vol. 1 of *Francis of Assisi: Early Documents.* Ed. Regis Armstrong, Wayne Hellman, and William Short. New York: New City Press. 171–308.

Torracca, Francesco. [1902] 1912. "L'*Epistola a Cangrande.*" In *Studi danteschi.* Naples: Perrella. 248–304.

Ullmann, Walter. 1955. *The Growth of Papal Government in the Middle Ages.* London: Methuen.

Vallone, Aldo. 1963. *La prosa della "Vita Nuova."* Florence: Le Monnier.

______. 1981. *Storia della critica dantesca dal XIV al XX secolo.* 2 vols. Padua: Vallardi.

Vickers, Nancy J. 1989. "Widowed Words: Dante, Petrarch, and the Metaphors of Mourning." In *Discourses of Authority in Medieval and Renaissance Literature.* Ed. Kevin Brownlee and Walter Stephens. Hanover, N.H.: University Press of New England. 97–108, 270.

Villani, Giovanni. 1990. *Nuova Cronica.* Ed. Giuseppe Porta. Parma: Guanda.

Weiss, Daniel H. 1998. *Art and Crusade in the Age of Saint Louis.* Cambridge: Cambridge University Press.

Weiss, Johannes. 1971. *Jesus' Proclamation of the Kingdom of God.* Trans. Richard Hyde Hiers and David Larrimore Holland. Philadelphia: Fortress Press.

West, Delno C. 1975. *Joachim of Fiore in Christian Thought: Essays on the Influence of the Calabrian Prophet.* New York: B. Franklin.

______. 1983. *Joachim of Fiore: A Study in Spiritual Perception and History*. Bloomington: Indiana University Press.

Whitman, Jon. 1987. *Allegory: The Dynamics of an Ancient and Medieval Technique*. Oxford: Clarendon Press.

Williams, A. Lukyn. 1935. *Adversus Judaeos*. Cambridge: Cambridge University Press.

Wilson, Adrian, and Joyce Lancaster Wilson. 1984. *A Medieval Mirror: Speculum Humanae Salvationis, 1324–1500*. Berkeley: University of California Press.

Wormald, Frances. 1938. "The Crucifix and the Balance." *Journal of the Warburg and Courtauld Institutes* 1:276–80.

Wright, Stephen K. 1989. *The Vengeance of Our Lord: Medieval Dramatizations of the Destruction of Jerusalem*. Toronto: Pontifical Institute of Mediaeval Studies.

REWRITINGS

21

Ovid and the *Exul Inmeritus*

Michelangelo Picone

Ab Ovidio principium. Our Western literary tradition has continually had to reckon with Ovid, the classical author who not only mediated between Greek and Latin culture, but was also perfectly in tune with Christian culture. This general observation regarding Ovid's profound literary influence will be examined in an especially enlightening case. What follows will thus be a careful consideration of the thematic treatment of exile in Ovid and in Dante's *Divine Comedy.*

Ovid projects a triple image on medieval civilization in general and on Dante in particular. First, he is seen as a love poet: his *corpus eroticum* (which includes the *Heroides* and the elegies contained in the *Amores* as well as the *Ars amatoria* and the *Remedia amoris*) will become part of the medieval academic curriculum and will constitute the "founding text" of the Romance lyrical tradition, from the poetry of the troubadours to Dante's *Vita Nova.*[1] Second, Ovid is viewed as a mythological poet: his *Metamorphoses* represents the obligatory point of reference for any medieval discourse with myth and constitutes the ultimate model for subsequent literary invention. Indeed, we may define Dante's *Commedia* as the book of Christian metamorphoses (see Jacoff and Schnapp 1991; Sowell 1991; and Picone 1993; 1994, 173; 1997; and 1999). Lastly, and most important for our present purpose, Ovid is seen as a poet of exile. The elegies composed during his exile in Tomis (the five books the *Tristia* comprises and the four the *Epistulae ex Ponto* comprises) place him in an emblematic position, one with which the medieval reader could closely, perhaps even most closely, identify. To the Christian mind, the image of a man deprived of his homeland and of the affections of his family, forced to live in a hostile geographical and social climate, was poignant and readily assimilable. If in classical times many poets had sung of love and most had treated mythological themes, not one had developed the theme of exile to the extent or in the manner that Ovid did, allowing the painful reality of his own remote existence to suffuse his pages.

Ovid, therefore, became the uncontested classical model for a theme that is central in medieval literature from the Carolingian era to Dante: the theme of exile (see Hexter 1986, 83–107; but especially Smolak 1978 and Viarre 1982). The basis for this *imitatio* is not only the author's work, but his very life. Ovid's biography was in part recounted in his poetry and in part reconstructed according to hagiographical canons developed during the Middle Ages. A perfect example of this is the apocryphal poem *De vetula,* which is composed of some two thousand hexametric lines. The *De vetula* is a pseudo-autobiography of Ovid that dates back to the first half of the thirteenth century; a prose *accessus* informs us that it was found in the poet's tomb in Colchis. The poem itself narrates the *mutatio vitae* of its purported author, including the conversion to Christianity that occurred in the last years of his life, when he had lost all hope of returning to his beloved Rome ("certus ab exilio se iam non posse reverti" [see Klopsch's edition (1967) of the Middle-Latin text]). Literary criticism has recognized the enormous impact that both the real Ovid and the pseudo-Ovid had on medieval exilic poetry. It has shown how, for the medieval reader, his elegies represented the bitter reality of exile on an individual and historical level, while the *De vetula* represented the drama of exile on a universal, meta-historical level, as a necessary, albeit painful, step in man's journey toward spiritual salvation. On the other hand, literary criticism has not taken into account the profound influence Ovid's life and literary output while in exile had on the author of the *Divine Comedy,* undoubtedly the greatest of all medieval exile poems.[2] I have already revealed traces of the *De vetula* in *Purgatory* 19 and 22 (see, respectively, Picone 2001 and 1992); what I would like to do here is closely examine the extensive intertextual echoes of Ovid's poetry, especially his *Tristia,* in Dante's *Commedia.*

One of the merits of American Dante scholarship has been to introduce the figure of the "Everyman" to the interpretation of the *Commedia.* This fundamental medieval figure serves as a useful interpretative tool in that it allows us to discern the underlying communicative structure of the sacred poem (see Singleton 1957). The first-person protagonist is, according to this view, Everyman: all humanity participates in the pilgrim's otherworldly adventure, in his journey toward the city of God. In fact, the salvation achieved by the protagonist on the literal level corresponds to the salvation desired by humanity on the allegorical level. This is the way in which the problem of the *énonciation* is solved in Dante's *Commedia:* the concept of Everyman relates the authorial "I" to his audience, quite simply to all humanity. In order to resolve the problem posed by the *énoncé,* by the poem's narrative structure, we need to resort to another medieval dramatic figure, one that has not yet received the attention it deserves: the Wanderer.[3] Though exiled from the world in which he lives, this figure is actually in the best position to begin his journey homeward toward God. The term "wanderer" translates the biblical expression "advena . . . et peregrinus" that Abraham uses (Gen. 23:3–4) to refer to himself. He is both a foreigner in the land where he lives and a traveler on his way to his remote homeland. As we know, in his letter to the Hebrews (11:13–14), Saint Paul applies this term to all Christians, who live on this earth as "*peregrini et hospites,*" since their true homeland is in heaven. The same condition applies to the protagonist of the *Commedia;* he is also a man who has been exiled from his native land. However, he is different in that he is able to transform his historico-social rejection into an act of spiritual elevation by substituting the attainment of celestial citizenship for the loss of his worldly citizenship.[4]

In the *Commedia* Dante combines the Christian view of exile just outlined with the elaborate conception of exile presented by Ovid in his *Tristia.* Better said: Dante projects Ovid's *fictio*—which is actually full of historical and psychological truth—onto the perspective of religious truth presented in the biblical text and commented on by the Fathers of the Church. In so doing, Dante not only surpasses the old *auctor* Ovid, but proves he has reached the absolute summit of poetic writing. In reality, his writing is no more than a *rewriting* of the biblico-classical thematics of exile; in it, he clarifies the structural similarities and, more important, the ideological divergencies between his models.

Let us now consider how these two models, the classical and the biblical, relate to each other. The narrative scheme underlying Ovid's *Tristia* is similar to that found in Genesis or in Saint Paul's Epistles. An initial CRIME is followed by a PUNISHMENT, which consists of the banishment from the original homeland; the punishment takes the form of LIFE in the place of exile; finally, life in exile is preceded and/or followed by a JOURNEY away from the place of exile and toward the original homeland (that is, by the real or hoped-for RETURN). While these basic structural elements are identical in Ovid and the biblical texts, their functional roles and their semantic values are drastically different. The analogue of Ovid's factual and personal crime takes on an allegorical and universal meaning in the Bible. Ovid's "carmen et error"—the literary work and the act judged harmful to common morality and to the majesty of Augustus—corresponds to the sin of pride committed in Eden by Adam and Eve but attributed to all mankind. In order to achieve redemption, divine intervention—not only royal clemency—will be necessary. In the same way, while Ovid's punishment is historical (he was relegated to Tomis, a city at the farthest reaches of the empire), the punishment given our forebears is historical as well as meta-historical (their banishment from Eden entails the loss of man's image and likeness to God). For Ovid, exile was a temporary state (since he hoped to persuade Augustus to rescind his punishment); in the Bible, exile is man's everlasting and immutable condition. The Christian knows that, as long as he lives on this earth, he lives in exile; his punishment can be erased only in the hereafter.

We have just touched on a fundamental point of difference between the ancient world and the Christian one: a Christian does not demonize the experience of exile as Ovid did; on the contrary, he exalts it by recognizing the positive value it conceals behind its overtly negative appearance. Viewed in this manner, exile is transformed from an act of social alienation into a potent means of spiritual identification. The Christian, who realizes that he no longer belongs to the world in which he lives, prepares himself to become a citizen of the place where he will live forever. This view of exile has substantial repercussions on the elements of our narrative scheme. Let us consider first the effects on the element of the JOURNEY. Ovid described his sea voyage to Tomis in absolutely negative terms; constant storms were said to have placed his life at risk. For the exiled Christian, however, the voyage takes on an essentially positive value: in fact, the *peregrinatio* and the *navigatio* become metaphors for the recovery of the lost divine image. A similar antithesis holds for the treatment of the next element, the RETURN home, in the two ideological systems. Ovid's painful longing for Rome is replaced by the Christian's equally fervid desire to regain the place of his original happiness, namely, Paradise. In other words, the medieval counterpart to the classical *nostros* is none other than the *quête.* The concept of *nostros* is represented emblematically by Homer's Ulysses (with whom, it is no accident, Ovid continually compares himself in his *Tristia* [see especially Rahn 1958 for Ovid and Smarr 1991 for the *Commedia*]). The concept of the quest is symbolized negatively by Dante's Ulysses in *Inferno* 26 and positively by the pilgrim in *Paradiso* 33, who is finally able to see God *facie ad faciem.*

In the *Tristia,* Ovid gives us a moment-by-moment report of his exile.[5] The *Tristia*'s five books cover the various stages of its author's difficult life in Tomis: the enforced departure from his beloved Rome, the journey by sea to Tomis, the endless sojourn in a bleak and inhospitable land. The first book is dedicated to the perilous journey by ship across the Black Sea; the second comprises a lengthy elegy, a kind of memorial that contains Ovid's spiritual testament. The third, fourth, and fifth describe his life in Tomis, where he had two major concerns. First of all, he was preoccupied with his day-to-day survival in a climate that was harsh both atmospherically and socially. Secondly, he busied himself with his literary endeavors—more precisely, with the composition of his elegies. In the usual paratextual places (the initial and often the final elegies of each book), Ovid took the opportunity to speak not only *about* his work, but directly *to* his work. In fact, the *Tristia*'s five books are personified alongside the first-person narrator; they were intended to plead Ovid's cause before the supreme judge, Augustus. Moreover, they were meant to make the journey to Rome that was denied the man who authored them. If in the last two books the dialogue established between the exiled author and his Roman readers is especially intense, in the *Epistulae ex Ponto* it becomes the sole focus. The conative function of Ovid's exilic poetry thus dominates over its poetic and meta-literary functions; the attempt to persuade his audience, to win the Romans over to his side, becomes paramount.

In the *Divine Comedy* Dante also tells us about the different stages of his exile, from the historical causes that brought it about, to the dramatic moment of enforcement, to the bitter reality of the experience itself (see especially Iannucci 1984 and Mazzotta 1993). We must observe, however, a fundamental change of perspective: Dante does not insert his narrative in the temporal dimension of the present, as Ovid does; instead, he places it in the future. Whereas exile is represented as testimony in the *Tristia,* it is represented as prophecy in the

Commedia. The various phases of his exile are announced in sequence, and at regular intervals, to the protagonist of the *Commedia* in his encounters with the souls in Hell, Purgatory, and Paradise. From Ciacco in *Inferno* 6 to Cacciaguida in *Paradiso* 17, the pilgrim will be presented with the various pieces that make up the puzzle of his life as an exile. Only in the last encounter with Cacciaguida will the puzzle appear before him in its historical completeness; only then will its meta-historical significance become clear. While there are several structural and semiotic implications of this change in temporal perspective from the Ovidian intertext to the Dantean text, I will limit myself here to the most salient.

How is exile regarded in the two texts? In the *Tristia,* Ovid the author and Ovid the character are in close contact; that is, the experience of events and the poetic recording of those events run parallel. In contrast, in the *Commedia* there is a major temporal delay between the pilgrim's journey in the hereafter (imagined to have taken place during Holy Week of the year 1300) and the writing of the poem, which takes place many years later, from 1307 to the death of the poet in 1321. Dante the author writes the *Divine Comedy* during the period of his exile (to be more precise, from the moment in which his expulsion from Florence appears final); Dante the pilgrim carries out his eternal journey a few years before he is expelled from the city where he was born. While the author of the *Divine Comedy* knows of his exile (in fact, this knowledge is precisely what spurs him to compose the work), the pilgrim does not know of his exile. The souls he meets inform him of his fate. The "prophetic" dimension of the work (recall here that we are dealing with *post factum* prophecies) thus becomes less important than its poetic dimension, in accordance with the author's intention to attain a higher rhetorical and stylistic level. In other words, the temporal and mental "distance" that Dante places between himself and the event allows him to comprehend it more fully, and hence describe it to us more effectively. For Dante, prophecy is a literary strategy that allows him not only to avoid elegy, but also to raise himself to the level of an authentic and epic vision of reality. Furthermore, the poet's exile, as seen from the otherworldly vantage point of the *Commedia,* does not engender the self-pitying reactions typical of Ovid in his *Tristia.* It leads to the revelation of the deeper meaning of exile, the same meaning given by Saint

Paul: exile is the normal condition of man *in itinere,* of man on his way toward his true, celestial homeland.

We have just seen how Dante's change in perspective results in a different appraisal of the state of exile; in essence, exile is viewed as an ennobling experience, not a degrading one. A second implication of this change in perspective concerns the way in which the place of exile is viewed. In the *Divine Comedy* the axiological system of the *Tristia* is overturned: Dante's unattainable Florence becomes the very negation of the concept of city, just as its historical and semantic analogue (Tomis, NOT Rome) did for Ovid. The poet-pilgrim's itinerary is one that leads him "away from Florence to a people just and sane" (*Par* 31.39); from the false homeland of this world, which has become a *civitas diaboli,* toward the authentic homeland of the hereafter, the *civitas Dei.*[6] While Ovid wanted desperately to return to (even get close to) Rome, Dante wanted to get as far away from Florence as possible. He therefore undertakes his journey to the hereafter. Recall that Ovid, prohibited from visiting Rome himself, sends his elegies to Rome in his stead; in his *Tristia* 1.1 and 3.1 he personifies the book, presenting it as a kind of "country bumpkin" that sees the big city for the first time. Not surprisingly, Dante exploits the same comparison to describe the pilgrim's amazement at the sight of the "candida rosa" (*Par* 31.31–39).

Despite these patently negative value judgments, Dante's attitude toward Florence is at best ambivalent, as many critics have noted (Iannucci 2001). Described by the poet-pilgrim as a terrestrial offshoot of Hell, the city is compared to a "wicked stepmother" in *Paradiso* 17. Yet it is also capable of evoking in him displays of affection, as we see clearly in *Inferno* 19, where he fondly recalls "my beautiful San Giovanni," or in *Inferno* 23, where he reminisces about "the fair stream Arno" and "the great town." Should we consider this as a sentimental lapse? As a resurfacing of the Ovidian model? In all probability it is neither. What underlies this apparently ambivalent attitude is the stark contrast between the former Florence, virtuous and hence loved and longed for by the pilgrim, and the current Florence, corrupt and hence scorned and condemned by him. Dante's nostalgia is for the original Florence, the city enclosed "within the ancient circle," the one that Cacciaguida remembers in *Paradiso* 15, while his invectives are directed at the modern Florence, the city whose "name is spread through Hell" (*Inf* 26.3). This contrast can help us explain how Dante, in his *Epistles* 3, 5, and 6 (written in the same years as the beginning of the sacred poem) is able to use the double title *florentinus* and *exul* as his signature.[7] Although he is an exile, Dante still considers himself to be a citizen of Florence, both because he has been unjustly condemned (hence the *inmeritus*) and because he has stayed true to the city's authentic spirit. This cannot be said of the Florentines who continue to live there, the "florentini intrinseci," who in his view have betrayed that spirit.

Dante thus defines himself as *exul inmeritus* in the *Epistles.* This same protest of innocence surfaces repeatedly in the sacred poem, starting with the first episode in which exile is raised, the encounter with Ciacco in *Inferno* 6. Ciacco's claim in v. 73—that in Florence only two honest men can be found ("Giusti son due")—represents a not so thinly veiled allusion to Dante himself. More important, however, we need to consider the claim as an act of vindication: Dante is a potential *salvator patriae,* if only his fellow citizens would listen to him. Clearly, the relevant intertext here is Genesis 18, where it is said that God would save Sodom from destruction only if he could find ten honest men. Perhaps less obvious is the dialogue with the Ovidian text that is operating here. While Ovid in the *Tristia* admits both his literary and factual guilt (his *carmen* and *error,* respectively), Dante in the *Commedia* recognizes only the first, categorically rejecting the second. The fact that he moved away from Beatrice and the "dolce stile" in his youth certainly engendered a moral decline and "traviamento" (going astray). However, this moral decline was limited to the personal sphere, leaving the political sphere untouched. Politically, then, Dante sees himself as pure; he has proven himself loyal to the ideal of a just society, not to the interest of a political party. Poetically, however, Dante has not remained faithful to Beatrice, and in order to purge himself he resorts to a palinodic mode of discourse. Ideologically, the use of palinode stems from his rejection of the works that were not inspired by Beatrice (the *rime petrose,* the *rime dottrinali,* and the *Convivio*) on the one hand, implying a return to the work produced under the influence of the "gentilissima" (the *Vita Nova*) on the other. While Ovid's *reprobatio* affects his entire *corpus eroticum,* Dante condemns only his lyrics inspired by carnal love and chooses to extol those inspired by spiritual love.

Clearly, the relationship between Tomis, city of exile, and Rome, city of origin, is overturned in Dante's *Commedia,* where the city of exile is precisely Dante's city of origin, Florence. The true place of

Christian exile, Hell, thus takes on the characteristics both of the historical Florence of Dante's time and of the literary Tomis as it is described in Ovid's *Tristia.* Hell, the place farthest away from God, the eternal abode of the damned souls, is also the realm from which there is no return—just as Tomis was for Ovid, who was never to set foot again in his beloved Rome, and who died in that desolate and faraway place.

Tomis is depicted in the *Tristia* as the non-city, the absolute antithesis of Rome, a place full of horror and squalor. Previous authors had only imagined, not experienced, such a dire reality. The description of Tomis presented in the *Tristia* (especially Book 3) is deliberately cast in the most dismal of tones. What seems to be a nightmare is tragically real. The region is apparently devoid of plant life, and what little the land does yield is inedible. How can we not think of *Inf* 13.4–6, where the souls of those who committed suicide dwell in a land where there are "no green leaves . . . / no smooth boughs . . . / no fruits . . . but thorns with poison"? The people who live in Tomis, a similarly barren place at the very edge of civilization, bear little resemblance to humans. They are barbarians who live like animals, and they speak a language no one understands.

One of the *Tristia*'s most striking images is that of the intense, endless cold. In the only elegy contained in Book 2, Ovid describes the Roman province where Tomis is located, Istria, as being situated at the mouth of the Danube, beneath the sign of Ursa Major, the most prominent northern constellation. Ovid, sacrificial victim, must therefore suffer alone in the place where the "Parrhasian virgin" (Callisto, loved by Jupiter and changed into a bear by the jealous Juno) reigns. Relegated to this most remote and hostile of regions and exposed to the polar cold and enemy attacks perpetrated by the barbaric tribes that lived beyond the Danube, Ovid becomes the quintessential figure of the *exul.* The passage closes emblematically with a vision of the Black Sea transformed into an endless expanse of ice (vv. 188–96 [Ovid 1988]):

solus ad egressus missus septemplicis Histri
   Parrhasiae gelido virginis axe premor

. . . .

Cumque alii causa tibi sint graviore fugati,
   ulterior nulli, quam mihi, terra data est.
Longius hac nihi est, nisi tantum frigus et hostes,
   et maris adstricto quae coit unda gelu.

> I alone have been sent to the mouths of the seven-streamed Hister, I am crushed beneath the Parrhasian virgin's icy pole. . . . Though others have been exiled for weightier cause, a more remote land has been assigned to no one; nothing is farther away than this land except only the cold and the enemy and the sea whose waters congeal with the frost.

The literary invention of the frozen sea (validated by Ovid's real-life experience) is further developed in the tenth elegy of Book 3. Winter causes everything in Tomis to freeze: the ground is "marble-white with frost." The very inhabitants are ice-statues; their hair "tinkles with hanging ice," and their beards "glisten white with the mantle of frost" that covers them. Finally, the Danube and the Black Sea freeze over (3.10.27–34):

> ipse, papyrifero qui non angustior amne
>   miscetur vasto multa per ora freto,
> caeruleos ventis latices durantibus, Hister
>   congelat et tectis in mare serpit aquis;
> quaque rates ierant, pedibus nunc itur, et undas
>   frigore concretas ungula pulsat equi;
> perque novos pontes, subter labentibus undis,
>   ducunt Sarmatici barbara plaustra boves.

> The very Hister, not narrower than the papyrus-bearing river, mingling with the vast deep through many mouths, freezes as the winds stiffen his dark flood, and winds its way into the sea with covered waters. Where ships had gone before now men go on foot and the waters congealed with cold feel the hoof-beat of the horse. Across the new bridge, above the gliding current, are drawn by Sarmatian oxen the carts of the barbarians.

Frigid winds cause the blue waters of the Danube (Hister) to harden as they thrust themselves into the sea and become indistinguishable underneath the rock-hard surface of ice. Across this natural bridge of ice, Sarmatian oxen pull the carts of their masters, barbarians who carry with them death and destruction.

Such an appalling description of the winter landscape along the Danube must have seemed incredible to the Roman reader; hence the author's sorrow-laden words of warning (3.10.35–40):

> Vix equidem credar, sed, cum sint praemia falsi
>   nulla, ratam debet testis habere fidem:
> vidimus ingentem glacie consistere pontum,

lubricaque inmotas testa premebat aquas.
Nec vidisse sat est, durum calcavimus aequor,
undaque non udo sub pede summa fuit.

I may scarce hope for credence, but since there is no reward for a falsehood, the witness ought to be believed—I have seen the vast sea stiff with ice, a slippery shell holding the water motionless. And seeing is not enough; I have trodden the frozen sea, and the surface lay beneath an unwetted foot.

Mind you, reader (Ovid seems to be saying), that what you are reading is not literature but life, not poetic invention but historical truth, a reality that I myself have endured. I not only have looked upon that frozen surface, I have walked across it, my footsteps visible on those solidified waters.

Twelve centuries later, another poet lived through the same unbelievable adventure as Ovid had (or so he would have us believe). He also trod upon a frozen lake, though this one was inhabited by the souls of traitors. Of course, I am referring to Dante, who, relying on Ovid alone, "invented" the place of Christian exile: the frozen lake of Cocito, the point in the universe farthest from God. Immobilized within or outstretched atop the surface of this immense "ice" that is the last of Hell's four rivers (see *Inf* 14.115–20) are to be found those who betrayed their homeland and society's highest values.

Dante's description of this spiritual "last land" calls to mind its Ovidian intertext. After Virgil warns the pilgrim to watch where he puts his feet for fear he might trample upon the heads of the damned who are "fixed in ice," we are presented with the last circle of Hell (*Inf* 32.22–24 [Alighieri 1970]):

Per ch'io mi volsi, e vidimi davante
e sotto i piedi un lago, che per gelo
avea di vetro e non d'acqua sembiante.

At this I turned and saw before me, and under my feet, a lake which through frost had the semblance of glass and not water.

Lucifer's wind has caused the water to harden to the point that it attains the solidity of glass. This metamorphosis has reminded some scholars of the *rime petrose;* however, I believe that Dante could never have imagined such a transformation had he not read the *Tristia.* Especially important for Dante are vv. 29–30 and 31–32 of the elegy we just discussed. If we look closely at the *comparatio* that follows, we realize that the historical equivalent chosen by Dante to render the idea of the river in Hell he visited is the same one so frequently evoked in Ovid's poem, the Danube (though Dante refers to the river at its source in Austria rather than at the end of its run near the estuary, as Ovid did). Furthermore, the allusion to the river Don (the "Tanai") is also taken from the *Tristia* 3.4.49.

Non fece al corso suo sì grosso velo
di verno la Danoia in Osterlicchi
né Tanaì là sotto il freddo cielo
com'era quivi; che se Tambernicchi
vi fosse su caduto, o Pietrapiana,
non avria pur da l'orlo fatto cricchi

Never did the Danube in Austria, nor the far-off Don under its cold sky, make in winter so thick a veil for their current as there was here; for had Tambernic fallen on it, or Pietrapiana, it would not have given a creak, even at the edge.

The claim implicit in these verses—that the otherworldly reality described surpasses by far any earthly reality—reveals the superiority of Dante's poetry over the poetry of Ovid, who was only able to describe an extreme geographical reality. In other words, the *comparatio* points to a clear case of literary *Überbietung* (see especially Curtius 1953, 162–65). Dante, creator of the infernal Cocito, surpasses Ovid, describer of the frozen Danube and Black Sea. Thus, the theme of the poetic challenge developed in *Inferno* 24 and 25 ("Let Ovid be silent" [*Inf* 25.97]) resurfaces here, though the challenge is no longer between Dante and Ovid, author of the *Metamorphoses;* it is between Dante and Ovid, author of the *Tristia.* The ideological foundation of the challenge, however, remains the same. The merely immanent truth of exile expressed by the classical poet Ovid is completed and fulfilled by the transcendental truth of exile discovered by the Christian poet Dante.

The theme of Dante's exile finds its definitive ideological and poetic realization in *Paradiso* 17. After a series of prophecies delivered, from Farinata to Brunetto, from Currado Malaspina to Forese, the pilgrim receives the final revelation concerning his exile from his illustrious ancestor, Cacciaguida. In order to dispel the cloud of mystery surrounding all previous revelations, which had been couched in the deliberately vague and ambiguous language of ancient oracles, Cacciaguida uses the clear, explicit language of Christian truth (vv. 31–35):

Né per ambage, in che la gente folle
già s'inviscava pria che fosse anciso
l'Agnel di Dio che le peccata tolle,
ma per chiare parole e con preciso
latin rispuose quello amor paterno.

In no dark sayings, such as those in which the foolish folk of old once ensnared themselves, before the Lamb of God who takes away sins was slain, but in clear words and with precise discourse that paternal love replied.

Cacciaguida's prophecy reveals both the historical and the spiritual significance of Dante's exile. First, the *sensus litteralis* of the pilgrim's oft-heralded exile—the series of events that characterize it as he wanders from court to court—is made clear. More important, its *sensus allegoricus*—the understanding that, as a man living exiled from his celestial homeland, he must find the way back to God—is powerfully conveyed. The power of this hermeneutical perspective lies in part in the book metaphor (Curtius 1953, 326–32; but also Battistini 1986), for Cacciaguida reads about the events of the exile's life directly from the divine book. The "contingency which does not extend beyond the volume of your material world" (vv. 37–39) can be understood only in the light of divine vision, as vv. 16–18 also demonstrate:

così vedi le cose contingenti
anzi che sieno in sé, mirando il punto
a cui tutti li tempi son presenti.

so you, gazing upon the Point to which all times are present, do see contingent things before they exist in themselves.

It is precisely in this manner that Cacciaguida frames his remarks to the pilgrim in canto 17. Though he recounts each event of Dante's exile (the false accusations launched against him, his painful departure, the hardships confronted, his "first refuge"), he does so in the light of the final triumph of justice and truth found in God's presence. While the restoration of peace and justice on earth is entrusted to Cangrande della Scala, whose military and political prowess is praised by Cacciaguida (vv. 76–93), the task of imparting the truth revealed by Cacciaguida is entrusted only to the author of the *Comedy* himself. In the last part of the canto (vv. 100–42) the poet's prophetic mission is described and confirmed. Verses 97–99 are especially significant in that they "seal" Cacciaguida's prophecy:

Non vo' però ch'a' tuoi vicini invidie,
poscia che s'infutura la tua vita
via più là che 'l punir di lor perfidie.

Yet I would not have you envious of your neighbors, since your life shall be prolonged far beyond the punishment of their perfidies.

The exiled Dante need not envy his fellow citizens still living in Florence; on the contrary, it is his own destiny that is extraordinarily enviable. The decadent citizens of Florence will receive an exemplary punishment, while Dante will obtain the laurel crown, symbol of poetic glory, and eternal salvation.

The pilgrim's encounter with Cacciaguida is framed by two Ovidian myths: the myth of Phaethon at the beginning of the canto, and the myth of Hippolytus toward the middle of the canto.[8] These myths—whose function is to indicate the true meaning of the pilgrim's journey—are, of course, similar in several important respects. First, each of the two heroes dies in the same manner, by falling from his chariot. Second (and more important for our discussion), both their deaths occur while they are in exile, far from their respective homelands. Phaethon, son of Helius by one of his mistresses, Clymene, had wanted to drive the sun's chariot in order to confirm his divine parentage. Unable to control the winged horses, he is struck by Jupiter's thunderbolt and falls into the river Eridanus, where he dies *procul a patria,* "far from his native land, in a distant part of the world" (*Metamorphoses* 2.323). Clymene, who had "roved the whole world" ("peregrina condita riva" [2.337]) in search of her son's remains, found them "buried on the foreign river bank." She broods over the spot, weeping desperately. Here is how Dante synthetizes this myth in *Par* 17.1–4:

Qual venne a Climenè, per accertarsi
di ciò ch'avëa incontro a sé udito
quei ch'ancor fa li padri ai figli scarsi;
tal era io.

As he who still makes fathers chary toward their sons came to Clymene to be reassured about that which he had heard against himself, such was I.

The allusion to Phaethon's tragic story of human *hybris* is followed later on in the canto by the story of Hippolytus. We recall that the young Hippolytus, a devoted follower of Artemis, dared to spurn the great Aphrodite. To make him pay for his *hybris,* Aphrodite impels Phaedra, wife of Theseus and stepmother of Hippolytus, to fall desperately in love with her stepson. Rejected, she falsely accuses Hippolytus of attempting to seduce her. The youth is consequently banished from Athens by his enraged father. As he is riding away from the city in a chariot, the sudden appearance of a sea monster so frightens the horses that they upset the chariot. Hippolytus, violently thrown out, dies. But once Hippolytus is in the Underworld, Asclepius's miraculous herbs bring him back to life. He is thus able to live a second life in a place (*Latium*) far from his homeland. Furthermore, he has assumed a new identity, and has a new name: *Virbius,* or "bis vir," meaning "twice a man" or "the man who lived twice." Let us look more closely at Dante's version of the myth (*Par* 17.46–48):

Qual si partio Ipolito d'Atene
per la spietata e perfida noverca,
tal di Fiorenza partir ti convene.

As Hippolytus departed from Athens, by reason of his pitiless and perfidious stepmother, so from Florence must you depart.

In both cases, Dante recounts only the beginning of the myth: Phaethon's demand for an explanation on the part of his mother in the case of the first, and Hippolytus's departure from his homeland for his place of exile (*exiliis suis,* "my own exile" [*Metamorphoses* 15.515]) in the case of the second. Nevertheless, Dante expects his readers to remember each story in its entirety. In effect, the pilgrim's otherworldly journey can be fully understood only in the light of the complete underlying myths. Insofar as the pilgrim achieves his goal where Phaethon failed miserably, his journey transforms the ultimate meaning of the first myth from tragic to comic. Moreover, the pilgrim's journey imbues the myth of Hippolytus with Christian truth. Simply put: the pilgrim has become a modern *Virbius.* He too is unjustly banished and, close to spiritual death, finds himself at the gates of Hell, achieving salvation thanks to the miraculous intervention of "three blessed ladies" (*Inf* 2.124). Finally, once his journey in the otherworld has ended, he can lead a new, more meaningful life: as an exile who fully accepts his status as such, and as a poet who has found his true identity.

As we have just seen—and as scholars have long noted—the presence of Ovid's *Metamorphoses* is a significant one in *Paradiso* 17.

What scholars of the *Comedy* have not thus far realized is the importance of Ovid's *Tristia* to the structure and thematics of this canto. I will now show that the textual echoes of Ovid's exilic work are continuous and systematic in this canto as well as in the others I have already discussed. To begin with, the scene in which the pilgrim leaves Florence, which I have just compared to Hippolytus's departure from Athens, is patterned after the episode in which Ovid spends his last night in Rome (*Tristia* 1.3). Here are the relevant verses in *Paradiso* 17 (55–57):

Tu lascerai ogne cosa diletta
più caramente; e questo è quello strale
che l'arco de lo essilio pria saetta.

You shall leave everything beloved most dearly; and this is the arrow which the bow of exile shoots first.

Remembering his own final farewell to wife and family, Ovid expresses his emotions using virtually the same words: "cum repeto noctem, qua tot mihi cara reliqui" ("the night I abandoned so much I dearly treasured" [v. 3]). Dante translates the simple quantifier *tot* ("many") as the more forceful "ogni cosa," and renders the ethical dative *mihi* even more striking by using the subject pronoun "tu," placing it at the beginning of the verse. Similarly, the adjective *cara* becomes the adverb "caramente," which is intensified by the adjective "diletta" ("ogne cosa diletta / più caramente" ["everything beloved / most dearly"]). Finally, the verb *reliqui* becomes "lascerai" ("you shall leave"), signaling in effect a shift from narrative time to discursive time, from Ovid's testimonial regarding the past to Dante's prophecy regarding the future (though it is *post factum*). Dante's addition to the Ovidian intertext is especially noteworthy: he compares the act of leaving home to the first arrow shot from the "bow of exile" ("l'arco de lo essilio" [v. 57]). Exile is thus seen metaphorically as a bow whose arrows are the successive and inevitable hardships associated with this painful experience, and bidding farewell to loved ones is the first of these hardships. Of course, this is true in a general chronological sense; more significant, however, it is true in a stricter literary sense. Indeed, the moment in which Ovid bids farewell to Rome is the very first scene of his *Tristia.* The melancholy atmosphere so characteristic of the *Tristia* is already present in the previous tercet, to which we now turn (vv. 52–54):

La colpa seguirà la parte offensa
in grido, come suol, ma la vendetta
fia testimonio al ver che la dispensa.

The blame, as always, will follow the injured party, in outcry, but vengeance shall bear witness to the truth which dispenses it.

The essential theme of blame and punishment thus arises again. While Ovid admitted he was to blame (albeit with some reservations and clarifications), Dante categorically refuses to do the same. Dante's exile represents an act of malfeasance perpetrated by the victorious Black faction over the defeated White Guelphs, the party to which Dante belonged. As a consequence, true punishment (that is, divine punishment) will be applied to the members of the Black Guelphs who are to blame for having fabricated false accusations against the innocent members of the White faction, including Dante. Only God can restore order and justice to humanity by allowing the truth ("il ver") to triumph over a false outcry ("il grido"). Furthermore, where Ovid recognizes the source of blame as himself, Dante attributes blame to those who accused him falsely. While Ovid considers exile an excessive punishment for his crime, Dante considers divine retribution a just punishment for his political adversaries (according to *Par* 17.96–99, his enemies will be annihilated).

Our final consideration regards the closest point of dialogical contact between Ovid's *Tristia* and Dante's *Comedy,* one that concerns the fundamental question: what is the ultimate value of exilic poetry? Or, to put it another way: what is the nature of the task entrusted to the exiled poet? Our two poets are diametrically opposed in the responses they offer. Whereas Ovid believes that the poetry of his *Tristia* is clearly inferior to the poetry he produced before his exile (particularly in the *Metamorphoses* and the *Fasti*), Dante is convinced that his *Comedy* represents the culmination not only of his own literary corpus, but of the entire literary tradition that preceded it. Of course, these radically opposing views of the nature of exilic poetry are direct corollaries of the poets' appraisals of the experience of exile itself. What for Ovid was a degrading experience was a quintessentially ennobling one for Dante. We have further proof of this in *Par* 17.106–11. After hearing his illustrious forefather's prediction of exile, the pilgrim declares that he is ready to accept his destiny on the one hand, yet states that he is perplexed about his duty as poet of the *Comedy* on the other. Should he tell the whole truth as it is manifested to him over the course of his journey, or should he act more cautiously, so as not to incur the wrath of his powerful protectors? After all, if a false political accusation caused his banishment to begin with, the proclamation of an uncomfortable poetic truth could make his life as an exile even more difficult (vv. 106–11):

> Ben veggio, padre mio, sì come sprona
> lo tempo verso me, per colpo darmi
> tal, ch'è più grave a chi più s'abbandona;
> per che di provedenza è buon ch'io m'armi,
> sì che, se loco m'è tolto più caro,
> io non perdessi li altri per miei carmi.

> I see well, my father, how time spurs toward me to give me such a blow as is heaviest to whosoever is most heedless; wherefore it is good that I arm myself with foresight, so that if the dearest place be taken from me, I lose not all the rest by reason of my songs.

Florence, affectionately referred to as the "dearest place" ("loco . . . più caro"), is strictly opposed to "all the rest" ("li altri"), clearly the places of exile. Having already lost the former, Dante does not want to risk losing the latter on account of his poetry. This is certainly an echo of what may be the most famous lines of the *Tristia* (2.207–208):

> Perdiderint cum me duo crimina, carmen et error,
> alterius facti culpa silenda mihi.

> It was two offences undid me, a poem and an error: on the second. My lips are sealed.

Dante "lifts" two key words from his Ovidian intertext. *Perdiderint* becomes "perdessi," and *carmen* is transliterated as "carmi"; in both cases, however, he has radically transformed the word's semantic value. While the object of the verb used by Ovid is the personal pronoun *me,* allowing these lines to be interpreted as "they made me lose that which was most dear to me, my family and my homeland," the object of the verb used by Dante is "the others," that is, the places where he will be sent in exile. Ovid "lost" Rome because of his erotic poetry, but Dante does not want to lose his places of refuge because of his epic poetry. Ultimately, though Dante never "lost" his native Florence, at least not in the same sense as Ovid "lost" Rome, for his native city was unjustly taken away from him ("se loco m'è *tolto* più caro"), he does run the risk of "losing" the hospitality bestowed upon him by generous benefactors such as Cangrande della Scala. No trace is left in Dante's text, therefore, of Ovid's *culpa,* since Dante does not admit any political guilt (the equivalent of Ovid's *error*), and his literary sin is cleared when he bathes in the waters of the Lethe. At this point, then, the pilgrim is confronted with the task of composing the definitive *carmen,* his *Divine Comedy.* This sacred poem—as Cacciaguida himself says in vv. 124–42—will proclaim eternal truth. In so doing, it will guarantee the exiled poet access to a place infinitely superior to any on earth.

Notes

1. As I have tried to demonstrate in Picone 2000, the *prosimetrum* of the *Vita Nova* is modeled on the poetic text of Ovid's *Remedia* accompanied by the prosastic medieval commentary. For the tradition of Ovid's *corpus eroticum* see Hexter 1986, 15–82.

2. An exception is represented by Smarr 1991, who argues for the presence of the *Tristia* (4.10) in the episode of Dante's Ulysses.

3. For the presence of this figure in medieval English literature see Smithers 1957–59 and Leslie 1985.

4. The best treatment of the theme of *peregrinatio* is found in Ladner 1967 and Ferguson 1975; for its presence in Dante, see Basile 1990.

5. For my analysis of Ovid's exilic poetry I rely on Dickinson 1973; Stroh 1981; Ehlers 1988; and Claasen 1988.

6. Text and translation from the *Commedia* are cited from Alighieri 1970–75. For the *Tristia* I have utilized the text and translation of Arthur L. Wheeler (Ovid 1988).

7. I note as example the title of the *Epistle 6:* "Dantes Alagherii *florentinus* and *exul inmeritus* scelestissimis Florentinis intrinsecis."

8. For the presence of the myth of Phaeton, see Brownlee 1986 and Picone 1994, 176–82; for the myth of Hippolytus, see Chiarenza 1983 and Schnapp 1991.

22

The Re-Formation of Marsyas in *Paradiso* 1

Jessica Levenstein

NEAR THE OPENING of the *Paradiso* Dante appeals for aid to Apollo:

> O buono Appollo, a l'ultimo lavoro
> fammi del tuo valor sì fatto vaso,
> come dimandi a dar l'amato alloro.
> Infino a qui l'un giogo di Parnaso
> assai mi fu; ma or con amendue
> m'è uopo intrar ne l'aringo rimaso.
> Entra nel petto mio, e spira tue
> sì come quando Marsïa traesti
> de la vagina de le membra sue.
> (*Par* 1.13–21)

> O good Apollo, for this last labor make me such a vessel of your worth as you require for granting your beloved laurel. Thus far the one peak of Parnassus has sufficed me, but now I have need of both, as I enter the arena that remains. Enter into my breast and breathe there as when you drew Marsyas from the sheath of his limbs.[1]

At first glance, the intention of the invocation seems clear enough: the poet enlists the god's help to meet the special challenge of describing Paradise. Upon further examination, however, it seems that the last *terzina* of the appeal resists interpretation. What does Dante mean when he writes, "Entra nel petto mio, e spira tue / sì come quando Marsïa traesti / de la vagina de le membra sue"? On a literal level, Dante prays to Apollo to breathe into his breast as the god did when he separated Marsyas from his body. Yet, we have no indication of how Apollo might have breathed while punishing his challenger. We may then conclude that Dante has collapsed the events of the Marsyas episode; he asks Apollo to breathe into him with the same breath as vanquished the satyr in the contest that preceded the events referred to in this *terzina.* Even so, the request is difficult to comprehend: Apollo did not win the music competition with Marsyas with his breath. As Dante surely knows, Apollo is traditionally associated with the lyre and would not have played a wind instrument in the contest. How, then, can we understand this puzzling part of the invocation? The easiest solution is to interpret it loosely, as the poet's request that Apollo allow him to exercise his art as well as the god did when he conquered Marsyas (Bosco 1985, 299–300; Padoan 1971).[2] Even with this interpretative latitude, however, we are left with the uncomfortable feeling that we have not adequately accounted for Dante's truncation of the myth. The question remains: why does Dante focus on Marsyas's punishment rather than the contest, which seems more immediately relevant? What, moreover, is the effect of his choice?

Dante's presentation of the punishment poses still another problem: he has taken considerable liberties with his source material, the sixth book of Ovid's *Metamorphoses.*[3] While Ovid's Marsyas is flayed to death, Dante's Apollo pulls an unharmed satyr from his skin. What is behind the poet's radical reimagination of Ovid's myth? Certainly, Dante did not misread the Roman poet: he proves himself elsewhere an exceptionally astute reader of Ovid. Nor can he have altered his version of the Marsyas story solely to point out a gap between pagan and Christian ethics: this might have been achieved with fewer distortions to the original story. This essay will argue, instead, that the *Commedia* revisits and revises the Marsyas tale in order to announce the centrality of the themes of inspiration, identity, and rebirth to Dante's poetic arrival in Paradise. I hope to show that, through his adjustment of the Ovidian text, the poet entreats the pagan god to deliver him from a limiting poetic identity. That is, through the figure of Marsyas, Dante petitions the god for a metamorphosis of his own.

Ovid's Marsyas

According to Greek mythology, Athena invented the flute, realized that playing it distended her cheeks, and threw it away. A satyr, Marsyas, discovered the instrument, and with it challenged Apollo to a music contest. The god easily vanquished the satyr and punished him by flaying him alive. Marsyas died in agony, and the tears of his mourners formed a river that took his name.[4] The *Metamorphoses* presents a partial version of this story, laying particular emphasis on the satyr's punishment. Ovid's story begins in medias res; the narrator only gestures toward the events leading up to the punishment. The contest itself is not described, and it is unclear whether or in what ways Apollo's song is superior to his mortal challenger's.

Instead, Ovid's narrator in the *Metamorphoses* recounts the flaying in graphic detail: "cruor undique manat, / detectique patent nervi, trepidaeque sine ulla / pelle micant venae; salientia viscera possis / et perlucentes numerare in pectore fibras" ("Blood flows down on every side, the sinews lie bare, his veins throb and quiver with no skin to cover them: you could count the entrails as they palpitate, and the vitals showing clearly in his breast" [6.388–91]).[5] He then relates Marsyas's anguished response to his pain: "'quid me mihi detrahis? . . . / a! piget, a! non est . . . tibia tanti'" ("'Why do you tear me from myself? . . . Oh, I repent! Oh, a flute is not worth such a price!'" [6.385–86]). With this brief question ("quid me mihi detrahis?") Ovid reveals a pivotal element of Marsyas's self-conception: the Marsyas of the *Metamorphoses* appears to locate his identity both in the skin that is being removed and in the soul that remains. He presumes that his *me* and his *mihi* together constitute his *ego*. His self is torn from his self, in an act of self-fragmentation that he helplessly observes. Like so many characters in the *Metamorphoses,* Marsyas is witness to the dissipation of his own sense of wholeness; with full consciousness, he experiences the splintering of his sense of self. The satyr's poignant entreaty thus gives literal expression to the kind of profound struggle with identity and self-alienation that the emotional core of Ovid's poem comprises (Fränkel 1945, 99; Barkan 1986, 14–15). At the same time, as I will demonstrate, Marsyas's revelation of his fragmented sense of self provides Dante with an articulation of the very problem he confronts at the outset of the *Paradiso.*[6]

While the satyr's sense of self-sundering emblematizes the experience of many characters in the *Metamorphoses,* it also marks the crucial difference between their fates and his. Other individuals in Ovid's poem may face a confusing redefinition of the self, in which they are conscious of being simultaneously themselves and something other than themselves, but their ensuing transformations tend either to crystallize an aspect of their identities or to allow them to give vent to their sorrows (Barkan 1986, 66, 71). Marsyas, on the other hand, fragments until he no longer exists. He must confront the very end of the self, the cessation of his consciousness. Tortured until he dies, the satyr experiences no consolatory metamorphosis.[7] Rather, he participates in his own literal disintegration, splintering into non-existence. Without his skin, Marsyas is no more: "nec quicquam nisi vulnus erat" ("he was nothing but a wound" [6.388]). Just as Marsyas's "quid me mihi detrahis?" locates at least part of his identity in corporality, the narrator too seems to situate the satyr's selfhood in his physical integrity. Once he is torn apart, his physical injury supplants his identity. As the satyr disintegrates, his existence is reduced to corporeal suffering, to a wound caused by the removal of his skin. He has been nullified. Marsyas's story ends here, but the tale concludes with a metamorphosis that pays him tribute: the tears of his friends are transmuted into a river, known by the satyr's name.

Book 6 of Ovid's *Fasti* fills in some of the gaps left by the *Metamorphoses*'s account, narrating the events that precede the torture described in the *Metamorphoses*. The speaker, Athena, explains the origin of the flute and the effect it wrought on her appearance. She then recounts that a satyr discovered the discarded instrument, learned to produce sounds with it, and grew proud of his musical skill: "iamque inter nymphas arte superbus erat: / provocat et Phoebum" ("And now he bragged of his skill among the nymphs and challenged Phoebus" [6.706–707]). Athena recalls that the nameless challenger was defeated by the god and flayed alive. Without devoting any attention to the details of the satyr's death, or alluding to his mourners, Athena communicates the outline of the story: Marsyas arrogantly entered into a contest with Apollo that cost him his life.[8]

DANTE'S MARSYAS

Readers of Dante's revision of the Marsyas tale traditionally focus on this arrogance, on the pridefulness of the satyr's challenge, arguing that Dante appears to distance his undertaking from the presumption that marks the song of the mortal challenger by aligning himself with the triumphant Apollo in *Paradiso* 1. Dante thus draws attention to the contrast between Marsyas's prideful audacity and his own humble stance before divinity. In this reading, Dante names Marsyas in order to disclaim him (Holländer 1969, 215–16). The strategic benefit to Dante's disavowal is evident: the poet wants to be on the winning team.

Other readers of this passage propose that the poet's need to disavow Marsyas points instead to his awareness of the lingering similarity between himself and the prideful satyr. Dante's reference to Marsyas's defeat as he prepares to deliver his account of the pilgrim's heavenly journey, then, expresses his personal anxiety about artistic overreaching. As he nears the divine vision, exalting his subject matter and upping the poetic ante, Dante uses the figure of Marsyas as a penetrating reminder to himself of the consequences of poetic arrogance. Dante alludes to Marsyas in order to exorcise his presence from the *Commedia,* to guarantee against the pride he exemplifies. Marsyas stands at the threshold of the *Paradiso* as a talisman, to ward off artistic immodesty, and as a caveat to prod the poet to seek guidance from God (Bosco 1985, 300–302; Parodi 1957, 381; but for a different view see Pasquazi [1966] 1985, 278*n*1).

Such readings may be consistent with other passages in the *Commedia* and may ring true psychologically, but Dante's invocation to Apollo lends them little textual support. While the central role of pride in both the pilgrim's and the poet's struggle to reach the heavenly heights is indisputable, the poet's allusion to Marsyas does not address the sin at all; he makes no reference to Marsyas's challenge, or to the temerity that prompted it. Rather, following the example of the *Metamorphoses,* he elides the events leading up to the flaying and focuses instead on Apollo's punishment of the satyr (Padoan 1971, 842; Chiarenza 1975, 133). Indeed, the poet refers to the episode not through the mortal's arrogance, nor through the song competition, but through the separation of Marsyas from his skin. It seems only fitting, then, that an examination of the passage should start from Dante's description of Marsyas's excoriation.

In the *Metamorphoses,* Apollo strips Marsyas's skin from his body as the satyr cries out, "quid me mihi detrahis?" In the *Commedia,* Dante begs Apollo to enter him and breathe there as he did when he detached Marsyas from the sheath of his limbs: "Entra nel petto mio e spira tue / sì come quando Marsïa traesti / de la vagina de le membra sue." The poet's invocation clearly revisits the Ovidian passage: Dante's "traesti" patently translates Ovid's "detrahis." Yet, while Ovid portrays the god's removal of the skin from the satyr, Dante describes the god's removal of the satyr from the skin. He redirects Apollo's motion: the god no longer draws skin away from man, but man away from skin. In reorienting the perspective of the flaying, Dante amends Ovid's depiction of it: he presents a scene of deliverance rather than a scene of torture. In Dante's revision of the scene, Marsyas is released, through divine intervention, from the casing of his body (Chiarenza 1975, 136; Brownlee 1991, 209–10). Moreover, entreating the god "Entra nel petto mio," Dante transforms Marsyas's literal disembodiment into the poet's spiritual embodiment. Ovid's portrayal of death through corporeal absence is thus replaced by Dante's request for supernatural presence.

Dante's expurgated version of Ovid's gruesome delineation of torment implies that Apollo neither acts against Marsyas's wishes nor causes the satyr suffering of any kind. The *Commedia*'s edited representation of Marsyas's persecution, in fact, suggests nothing more threatening than a scene of Christian martyrdom, effected by a benign divinity, *buono* and beneficent.[9] Indeed, the poet's petition to Apollo to reenact the scene of Marsyas's flaying appears to appeal to the god for martyrdom (Brownlee 1991, 207; Schnapp 1986, 215). Moreover, the assertion with which Dante opens the canto, "vidi cose" ("I have seen things" [*Par* 1.5]), confirms his function as martyr—the origin of the word "martyr" being the Greek word for "witness" (Ferguson 1990, 575; Frend 1967, 65–68).[10] Finally, Dante's entreaty to Apollo to enter his chest and breathe, "Entra nel petto mio, e spira tue," implies in another way as well that the poet invokes Apollo in order to welcome an inspired martyrdom: martyrs are legendarily filled with the Holy Spirit before they die (Ferguson 1990, 578).[11] Throughout the *Paradiso,* the pilgrim thus fills the role of martyr: he acts as eyewitness to God's glory while, with God's aid, the poet testifies to that glory.

The poet's request for inspired martyrdom also gestures toward Dante's self-alignment with the divine word. When he evokes Marsyas, Dante asks Apollo to enter into him and lend him his breath. Similarly, as he opens the invocation, Dante beseeches the god, "a l'ultimo lavoro / fammi del tuo valor sì fatto vaso, / come dimandi a dar l'amato alloro." The poet wishes to be a vessel for divine expression; he wants his words to have been literally in-spired by divinity (Brownlee 1991, 207). Dante positions himself as God's mouthpiece; he is the divinely inspired *vaso,* the instrument through which God's word is made known.[12]

In order to represent God, however, Dante needs to be made godlike in his skill. As is clear from his expression of poetic inadequacy before the invocation to Apollo, "vidi cose che ridire / né sa né può chi di là sú discende" ("I have seen things which whoever descends from up there has neither the knowledge nor the power to relate" [*Par* 1.5–6]), the poet requires heavenly assistance to accomplish the task. He requires divine ability to match the divine vision. The poet thus asks God to enter him, "entra nel petto mio," in order to help his verse follow the pilgrim to God's level (Chiarenza 1975, 135; Brownlee 1991, 210, 213). Dante's request that Apollo enter his breast is meant to achieve his own successful poetic elevation. He hopes that, through God's inspiration, he can make divine use of his poetic instrument, language. His implicit self-identification with Marsyas, then, suggests his effort to rise to the level of divinity. Yet, while the Ovidian satyr thinks artistic skill alone can bring him to the level of the god, Dante acknowledges that divinity cannot be approached without the help of God himself.

Dante's amended reenactment of the conflict between Marsyas and Apollo, moreover, serves as an opportunity for him to correct Ovid's notions of identity, by replacing the satyr's panicked "quid me mihi detrahis?" with the less urgent "sì come quando Marsïa traesti / de la vagina de le membra sue." In Ovid's version of the tale, when Marsyas is flayed by the god, he feels his identity split into the *me* of his skin and the *mihi* of his soul. In Dante's account of the episode, however, *Marsïa* is withdrawn in one piece, leaving the unnecessary "vagina de le membra sue" behind. The body is figured as a meaningless wrapper, irrelevant to identity. In Dante's revision of the story, *Marsïa* continues to exist even separated from his *membra*, while in Ovid's version of the tale, Marsyas fractures into two separate pieces and then disintegrates altogether. The Ovidian Marsyas appears to imagine a fundamentally decentralized identity, located in both his inner and his outer selves, in both his body and his soul. Dante's modification of the episode, on the other hand, implies that identity outlasts corporeal presence. Indeed, by rewriting the violent fracture of Marsyas's selfhood as a benevolent release from an insignificant container, Dante seems to situate identity with the soul; identity endures long after the body has perished (cf. *Conv* 2.8.8; *Inf* 10.15; *Par* 7.67–69; and see Gilson 1949, 123–27 and Nardi 1949).

As decisively as Dante repairs the fissure in Marsyas's sense of selfhood, however, he seems afflicted by similar misgivings in the face of heavenly *raptus*. Dante's belief in his own individual psychosomatic integrity is cast severely in doubt when he attempts later in the canto to delineate the voyage to the divine vision, using terms that recall Paul's own ambiguous account of his rapture in 2 Corinthians: "S'i' era sol di me quel che creasti / novellamente, amor che 'l ciel governi, / tu 'l sai, che col tuo lume mi levasti" ("whether I was but that part of me which Thou didst create last, O Love that rulest the heavens, Thou knowest, who with Thy light didst lift me" [*Par* 1.73–75]). That is, while the poet's revision of the Ovidian episode in vv. 19–21 locates Marsyas's identity in his soul alone, Dante's own sense of the relationship between body and soul appears to grow less clear as the canto progresses and the pilgrim begins to face the glory of the divine. His uncertain account of the *raptus* begs the questions: does the pilgrim's paradisal self include his body? Does the soul constitute the entire self, or does it merely stand as a part of the self, the part created last?[13]

The stability of identity is thus a particular concern both for the pilgrim as he prepares to enter Paradise, with or without his physical being, and for the poet as he begins to compose the final canticle of the *Commedia.* Indeed, identity is primary among Dante's concerns from the final cantos of the *Purgatorio* onward; in the Earthly Paradise not only is he forced to examine his past and account for his behavior but, for the first and only time in the poem, he is called by name. At the conclusion of his interview with Beatrice on Mount Purgatory, moreover, Dante's sense of his own identity is remade: the pilgrim emerges from the river Lethe with no memory of earlier transgressions, and he rises from Eunoe "rifatto" (*Purg* 33.143), a new man. When this new Dante ascends to Paradise, he continues to feel himself change, but, unable to communicate his metamorphosis, the poet explains, "Trasumanar significar *per verba* / non si poria" ("the passing beyond humanity may not be set in words" [*Par* 1.70–71]). The pilgrim moves beyond humanity, to a state that the poet is incapable of verbalizing.[14] As the opening verses of the canticle make clear, the poet's skill cannot match the pilgrim's vision, "vidi cose. . . ."[15] The identities of both pilgrim and poet are thus severely destabilized at the entry to Paradise; the pilgrim no longer exists in a human realm, the poet no longer believes himself capable of adequate verbal expression, and the pilgrim's experience and the poet's ability dramatically diverge.

In the *Metamorphoses,* the mortal artist who dares to rise to the level of the god is punished with a fragmentation of self that results in non-existence. In the *Commedia,* Dante attempts to manage an identity that threatens to splinter into two separate entities—the pilgrim who journeys to God's glory and the poet who fails to follow him there completely. At the same time, the "remade pilgrim" faces a crisis of selfhood as he observes himself pass beyond any familiar realm, beyond humanity itself. Dante's employment of the Marsyas story, at the beginning of the *Paradiso,* therefore, effectively confronts the dominant problem of the divided self in this canto. By deploying the Marsyas episode, Dante allows the Ovidian tale to speak to his own teetering sense of identity and to express his anxiety over this new identity's intersection with his artistic goals. By revising the Marsyas episode, moreover, Dante communicates his hopeful resolution of his identity's upheaval: through God's intervention, he will emerge from this challenge whole, unscathed, and ready to face the divine vision.[16]

Dante registers his longing for such an outcome by identifying himself with a re-formed version of Marsyas. At the same time, he indicates just how radical such a metamorphosis will have to be by describing the satyr's flaying in language that recalls a scene of childbirth. According to Dante, Apollo pulls Marsyas from "la vagina de le membra sue." While "vagina" does not take on any documented gynecological meaning in Italian until the eighteenth century, the image of Marsyas being drawn from a "vagina" suggests nativity both visually and thematically.[17] Dante's satyr is pulled from a sheath in one piece; he is reborn through the intervention of the god. Likewise, Dante himself requires rebirth. The poet's reference to the parturition of Apollo's gladness ten verses later: "parturir letizia in su la lieta / delfica deïtà dovria la fronda / peneia" ("the Peneian frond ought to beget gladness in the glad Delphic deity" [*Par* 1.31–33]), moreover, reinforces the sense that at the outset of the third canticle we are witnesses to a delivery.

It is not surprising to find that Dante uses parturition as an analogue to spiritual reformation: a link between the transmutation achieved by penitence and the pain of childbirth has been well established in the *Purgatorio.* We recall that as the avaricious repent on the fifth terrace, they cry out for the Virgin Mary, "come fa donna che in parturir sia" ("even as a woman does who is in labor" [*Purg* 20.21]), and when the mountain quakes as a sign of the completion of Statius's purgation, Dante asserts "certo non si scoteo sì forte Delo, / pria che Latona in lei facesse 'l nido / a parturir li due occhi del cielo" ("assuredly Delos was not shaken so violently before Latona made her nest therein to give birth to the two eyes of Heaven" [*Purg* 20.130–32]). As Dante surely recognized, the metaphor is particularly useful to describe the two-part process of repentance, one in which anguish is rewarded with delight. Just as the penitents endure first the pain of purgation and then the bliss of the ascent to Paradise, so does a parturient woman experience first the suffering of childbirth and then the joy of a newborn child.[18]

Like the penitents, then, Dante endures a painful transformation that ultimately gives rise to gladness. In his case, however, the two-part process takes place twice, first for the pilgrim and then for the poet. The pilgrim is reborn at the end of the *Purgatorio:* "Io ritornai da la santissima onda / rifatto sì come piante novelle / rinovellate di novella fronda / puro e disposto a salire a le stelle" ("I came forth from the most holy waves, remade even as new trees renewed with new foliage, pure and ready to rise to the stars" [*Purg* 33.142–45]). As the poet begins to relate what the remade pilgrim sees, however, it becomes clear that he too requires rebirth. If we understand that Dante implicitly identifies himself with the satyr in his reference to Marsyas at the beginning of the canticle, we see that his entreaty to Apollo, like other verses in the canto, addresses the discrepancy between the pilgrim's and the poet's capacities. The pilgrim may have been remade at the top of Mount Purgatory; he may be pure and ready to mount to the stars, but the poet is not. Both pilgrim and poet need to "trasumanar" in order to produce the *Paradiso.* Thus, through his re-formation of the fractured figure of Marsyas, the poet asks to be delivered into the same state of transhuman understanding as the pilgrim (cf. Pasquazi 1985, 278*n*1).[19]

To find a precedent for his interest in poetic "trasumanar," Dante need look no further than his source material for the Marsyas story, the *Metamorphoses.* Ovid famously concludes his poem with a confident prediction of artistic apotheosis:

> cum volet, illa dies, quae nil nisi corporis huius
> ius habet, incerti spatium mihi finiat aevi:
> parte tamen meliore mei super alta perennis
> astra ferar, nomenque erit indelibile nostrum,
> quaque patet domitis Romana potentia terris,
> ore legar populi, perque omnia saecula fama,
> siquid habent veri vatum praesagia, vivam.
> (*Metamorphoses* 15.871–79)

> When it will, let that day come which has no power save over this mortal frame, and end the span of my uncertain years. Still in my better part I shall be carried immortal far beyond the lofty stars and I shall have an undying name. Wherever Rome's power extends over the conquered world, I shall have mention on men's lips, and, if the prophecies of bards have any truth, through all the ages I shall live in fame.

Ovid claims that his "pars melior," his poem, will survive his death. Through the *Metamorphoses,* he will live forever beyond the stars, "super alta . . . astra" (vv. 873–74). Dante the poet, in the verses examined here, asks Apollo to help him achieve a similar poetic ascension. While in the Earthly Paradise it was the pilgrim's rebirth that allowed him to "salire a le stelle," at the opening of the *Paradiso* it is now the poet who awaits transformation. The poet needs to be reborn to gain parity with the pilgrim, to travel with him to the stars, to dwell, like Ovid, "super alta . . . astra." Dante asks for a metamorphosis of his own, a poetic transformation that can deliver him to a state beyond humanity. Only then can he too declare "vivam."

When Ovid's Apollo punishes Marsyas for his artistic impudence, he puts an end to his being. When Dante's Apollo, on the other hand, handles the satyr, he merely removes him from his former, bodily existence. The transformation that was denied Marsyas in Ovid's account of the story is provided by Dante's treatment of the tale in the *Commedia.* The metamorphosis experienced by so many of Marsyas's Ovidian counterparts is finally offered the satyr by Dante's divinity. In the *Paradiso,* Dante's God transfigures Marsyas, changing him from a corporeal being to an immaterial soul. Rather than eradicate the satyr, Dante's God transforms him and, along with him, the poet who retells his story. At the opening of the *Paradiso,* both Marsyas and Dante are reborn: incorporeal artists privileged by divine grace with eternal life, they have been granted a *vita nuova.*

Notes

1. I cite from Petrocchi's edition of the *Commedia* (Alighieri 1966–67) and from Singleton's translation (Alighieri 1970–75), which I have occasionally modified. I am grateful to Kevin Brownlee and Alison Cornish, whose suggestions brought me closer to an understanding of Marsyas's complex role at the beginning of the *Paradiso.*

2. For a reading of this passage that offers the unlikely claim that Dante supposed the god played the flute in the contest with the satyr, see Brewer 1941, 44. Brewer's argument is plausible only insofar as Ovid does not specify Apollo's instrument in his account of the god's contest with Marsyas. Apollo's association with the lyre is altogether too firm for Dante to have been unaware of it.

3. While the *Metamorphoses* is most often named as Dante's source for this passage, Mazzoni (1964, 1357) has argued for the additional influence of the *Fasti,* and Renucci (1949, 24*n*) has suggested the presence of John of Salisbury's *Policraticus* as well.

4. Marsyas is mentioned by many Greek authors, primarily in connection with the etiology of the river bearing his name (Herodotus, *Historiae* 7.26; Xenophon, *Anabasis* 1.2.8; Pausanias, *Descriptio Graecae* 10.30.9) and the events leading up to Marsyas's challenge (Aristotle, *Politics* 8.6.8; Apollodorus, *Biblioteca* 1.4.2; Hyginus, *Fabulae* 165). In Plato's *Symposium* (221e–222a), Alcibiades likens Socrates to Marsyas, claiming that Socrates' arguments, which conceal an essential core within an outer coating, resemble Marsyas's body.

5. For the texts and translations of Ovid's works, I use the Loeb editions (Ovid 1984 and 1989) whose English translations I have occasionally modified.

6. Bömer (Ovid 1976, 109) points to two other lines in Ovid's poem which similarly literalize self-alienation: the earth's retreat into herself when she is scorched by Phaethon's veering chariot ("rettulit os in se" [2.303]) and the description of Ascalaphus's loss of self as he is transformed into an owl ("ille sibi ablatus" [5.546]).

7. My understanding of Marsyas's "quid me mihi detrahis?" as a poignant expression of loss notably diverges from interpretations offered by several other readers of the episode who view the line as an indication of Ovid's delight in cruelty (cf. Galinsky 1975, 195 and Anderson 1972, 202).

8. Ovid's more immediate successors also refer to the story (Lucan, *De bello civile* 3.205–208 and Statius, *Thebaid* 4.184–86). The patent imprudence of Marsyas's challenge becomes the focal point of the tale for several of its subsequent allegorizers. Fulgentius (1898, 73–77), John of Garland (1933, 58), and Arnulf of Orléans (1932, 217) all interpret Marsyas as a symbol of foolishness and Apollo as a symbol of wisdom. Giovanni del Virgilio (1931, 73), on the other hand, refigures Marsyas's arrogant challenge to Apollo as an academic dispute: Marsyas is a foolish sophist, espousing fallacious ideas before Apollo, who stands for reason.

9. The *Commedia*'s reconstruction of Marsyas's excoriation recalls the legend, widely known at Dante's time, that it was the flaying of Bartholomew, a first-century saint, that earned him martyrdom (Jacobus de Voragine 1993, 109–16).

10. Biblical attestations of the link between martyr and eyewitness include Luke 24:48 and Acts 1:22. The connection is enacted explicitly in Acts 7:55,

where, just before he is stoned to death, Stephen gazes into heaven and sees the glory of God. Dante evokes Stephen's vision in *Purg* 15.111–12.

11. For example, as he regards the divine vision before he is stoned to death, Stephen is filled with the Holy Spirit (Acts 7:55). For a study of the "poetics of martyrdom" in the *Paradiso,* see Schnapp 1986, 170–238. Ronconi (1964, 42) points out biblical models for Dante's entreaty "Entra nel petto mio" (for example: 2 Sam. 6:9 and Prov. 2:10).

12. Dante establishes his poetics of inspiration well before his voyage to Paradise, as we can see in his exchange with Bonagiunta da Lucca on the terrace of gluttony (*Purg* 24.52–54). Padoan (1971, 843) proposes an imaginative link between Dante's desire for inspired truth and Apollo's flaying of Marsyas.

13. In his invocation to Apollo, Dante presents Marsyas's body neutrally: it is a "vagina," which is neither boon nor burden. For readings of Dante's invocation to Apollo that see the presentation less neutrally, arguing for the poet's elevation of the body in *Paradiso* 1, see Renucci 1949, 28 and Bosco 1985, 308. Several passages in the *Commedia,* however, explicitly figure the body as an onus from which the soul desires to free itself (*Par* 1.140 and *Par* 31.88–90). For a provocative challenge to the traditional view of the body / soul divide in medieval thought, see Bynum 1991, 245–56 and Bynum 1995, 291–305.

14. Because he cannot describe his internal transformation in words, Dante employs another Ovidian episode to help characterize his altered state of being: "Nel suo aspetto tal dentro mi fei, / qual si fé Glauco nel gustar de l'erba / che 'l fé consorto in mar de li altri dèi. / Trasumanar significar *per verba* / non si poria; però l'essemplo basti / a cui esperïenza grazia serba" (*Par* 1:67–72). For the density of Ovidian imagery in *Paradiso* 1, see Holländer 1969, 202–20. For the allegorical significance of the Glaucus episode, see also Singleton 1958, 27–31 and Brownlee 1991, 210–12.

15. The sense that Dante undergoes a struggle as he arrives in Paradise is also supported by the way he describes the third realm while he invokes Apollo: "ma or con amendue / m'è uopo intrar ne l'aringo rimaso" (vv. 17–18). Heaven is figured as an "aringo," an "arena." By calling Paradise an "aringo," the poet signals the difficulty of the challenge confronting his identity as he rises toward God and again implies that in order to make the journey he must undergo a type of difficult martyrdom.

16. The idea that the *Commedia*'s revision of the Marsyas episode draws attention to Dante's tenuous sense of identity gains further support from the consideration of an additional Ovidian figure who bears a suggestive similarity to Dante's Marsyas: Hercules, the semi-divine son of Jupiter. Poisoned by a toxic tunic, in Book 9 of the *Metamorphoses,* Hercules attempts to ease his suffering by removing the garment but the cloth adheres to his skin and the hero must tear them both off in agony. The description of this self-inflicted

excoriation naturally shares several features with Ovid's tale of Marsyas's flaying—in both cases, Ovid lingers on the details of the lacerated skin and the muscles left bare. For Hercules, however, this torture does not spell an end to his existence. Jupiter decrees that the immortal part of his son will remain beyond the power of death and that, once his perishable body has expired, Hercules will be received in heaven. The hero is then transformed, emerging as a god from his mortal frame, like a snake sloughing off old skin, "utque novus serpens posita cum pelle senecta" (*Metamorphoses* 9.266). Thus, while Marsyas's flaying results in death in the *Metamorphoses,* Hercules's flaying brings him eternal life. In this respect, Dante's Marsyas, whose selfhood outlives his transformation, seems to bear a closer resemblance to the god, whose flaying leads to apotheosis, than to his namesake, whose torture results in annihilation. Moreover, the Marsyas of the *Paradiso* visually recalls Hercules as well: just as Hercules emerges from his mortal frame like a snake sloughing off old skin, so Dante's Marsyas emerges from the "vagina" of his body. The story of Hercules is mentioned several times in the *Commedia: Inf* 9.98–99, 12.68, 25.32, 26.108, 31.132; and *Par* 9:102–103. In *Conv* 3.3.7, Dante makes it clear that his source for the story of Hercules is Ovid's *Metamorphoses.*

17. During Dante's time, the word is understood primarily as "sheath" in both Latin and Italian. However, there is at least one attestation of an anatomical understanding of the word in ancient Rome. Plautus punningly employs the word in a double entendre referring to sexual intercourse in *Pseudolus* 4.7.85.

18. In *Purg* 3.37–39 the poet makes clear that Mary's labor was a necessary response to man's sinfulness. The biblical precedents for the use of parturition as a metaphor for struggle have been well attested by Dante's commentators and include: Jer. 4:31; Is. 13:8, 26:17, 42:14; Ps. 47:7; John 16:21. The passage in John, in particular, makes use of the image of childbirth to depict a bipartite experience, a period of grief occasioned by Christ's death, followed by a period of joy occasioned by his resurrection. Among the commentators, several have pointed out that the parallel between the penitents and a woman in labor as especially apt because in both cases suffering is compensated by future joy. See Venturi 1874, 175.

19. The Christological associations of the word *vagina* (see Augustine [PL 36.105], Alain de Lille [PL 210.991], and Peter Lombard [PL 191.117], for Christ's appropriation of the *vagina humanitatis*) lend further support to the notion that at stake in Dante's plea to Apollo, in his description of a Marsyas delivered from the "vagina de le membra sue," is the poet's transcendence of human limits. Dante must reverse Christ's actions in order to imitate him. While Christ took on a new form, a *vagina humanitatis,* for the sake of man's salvation, to achieve his own salvation Dante must remove himself from the "vagina de le membra sue."

23

Dante in England

David Wallace

MY TOPIC here is not Dante in English, but rather Dante in England, a notion that still, perhaps, resonates strangely. The business of Englishing suggests Dantean conceits, tropes, and figures being exchanged for their nearest native equivalents. But the notion of Dante in England suggests a different degree of *translatio* in which the Italian poet retains a kernel of ineluctable foreignness, a quality that, on closer scrutiny, mysteriously renders English constructions of religion, art, and culture foreign to themselves. Some of the English embarrassments I allude to here might be associated with those of Spenser's *Faerie Queen*, Book 1: an attempt to imagine an authentically English form of state-sponsored religion that repeatedly finds it cannot do without those foreign, Catholic trappings that would give such a religion historical depth and pedigree. We might then surmise that the topic of "Dante in England" will lead us rapidly back to a deep history of bookburning, peopleburning, and cultivated xenophobia. But my contention is that the history of imagining Dante and his *Commedia* in England has been (by and large, and to my own surprise) benign, often comical. I may be stacking the deck of this argument by beginning with a Max Beerbohm cartoon, but there are elements of Beerbohm that usefully (indeed, brilliantly) summarize long-term attitudes.[1]

Beerbohm's vision of "Dante in Oxford" (Figure 1) reminds us that Dante has indeed been alive and well in Oxford for the last century or so, thanks to the Oxford Dante Society. The cartoon's title picks up on the sense of something faintly comical, out of alignment, in the notion of "Dante in Oxford." The rubicund, Anglican proctor, flanked by his bulldogs, interrogates the outlandish visitor, complacent in the assumption that he (the proctor) is on native ground. But this is clearly a two-way interrogation: Dante—distracted perhaps from contemplation of the moon, stars, and heavens adorning Beerbohm's sky—looks down upon the proctor and his minions as upon very earthbound figures; and we cannot help but notice how the strong verticalities of Dante's profile align with the perpendicular gothic tower that looms above the proctor.[2] Dante, of course, wears the cap and long robe authentic to his age; the proctor wears academic regalia inherited from that earlier time. Here, as so often is the case, Dante's "showing up" shows up what might otherwise be regarded as most essentially English. Beerbohm, we might note, had been an undergraduate at Merton College, Oxford, the most distinguished of English medieval colleges, founded (just one year too early) in 1264.[3]

This comic theme of the English encountering the foreignness of Dante (who then in turn discovers the foreignness of the native scene) is beautifully realized in a 1952 novel by Barbara Pym, acclaimed by Philip Larkin (another Oxford poet) as "the most underrated writer of the century."[4] The novel, *Excellent Women*, concerns the blameless lives of certain middle-class ladies of the Church of England. Toward the end of the novel, two neighbors of the first-person protagonist—Miss Lathbury—move out from the downstairs flat. In leaving, they feel obscurely moved to memorialize themselves by scratching verse on a window with a diamond ring. "A line of Dante" seems appropriate for the graffito, Rocky, the male neighbor says, "if I could remember one" (236).

> "I only know 'abandon hope all ye who enter here,'" I [Miss Lathbury] said, "which doesn't seem very suitable, and that bit about there being no greater sorrow than to remember happiness in a time of misery."
>
> "Ah, yes," Rocky clapped his hands together, "that's it!
>
> 'Nessun maggiore dolore,
> Che ricordarsi del tempo felice
> Nella miseria.'"
>
> "It seems an unkind way to greet new arrivals," I said doubtfully.
>
> "Oh, don't you believe it—people love to recall happiness in a time of misery. And anyway, they won't know what it means."
>
> (237)

A few pages later, the new tenants move in, and they do know what it means. "I think we shall be happy here," Miss Edgar says:

> "We have found an *omen*," she lowered her voice almost to a whisper and pointed to the direction of the window.

I saw Rocky's lines from Dante scratched on the glass.

"What is it?" I asked.

"Our Beloved Dante," said Miss Boniface reverently. "Could anything be happier? Those wonderful lines." And she quoted them with a rather better accent than Rocky had managed.

"Whoever engraved them has made a small mistake," said Miss Edgar. "It should of course be *Nessun maggior dolore*, without the final 'e,' you see. Still, perhaps this person was thinking of Lago di Maggiore, no doubt it was the memory of a happy time spent there."
(243)

Miss Lathbury interrogates her new neighbors and learns that they "had lived in Italy for many years and were now eking out their small private incomes by teaching Italian and doing translations"; she soon decides that

Miss Boniface and Miss Edgar were going to be very pleasant and cooperative, a real asset to the parish, in fact.

"And where is the nearest Catholic Church?" asked Miss Edgar.

"Oh very near, not two minutes' walk away," I said, "Father Malory and his sister are friends of mine. He was engaged to be married, but it was broken off," I added chattily.

I thought that they looked a little surprised at this, and then it suddenly dawned on me that perhaps they meant *Roman* Catholic, so I hurried to explain myself.

"Oh, well, mistakes will happen," said Miss Edgar pleasantly. "Of course we know about Westminster Cathedral, but there must surely be a church nearer than that."

"Oh, yes, there is—St Aloysius, and Father Bogart is the priest there. I believe he is a very nice man." "A lovely man," was how Mrs Ryan had described him at the jumble sale and I had often seen him on his bicycle, a fresh-faced young Irishman, waving to a parishioner or calling out "Bye-bye now!" as he left one after a conversation.

I gathered that they had "gone over" in Italy, which seemed a suitable place to do it in, if one had to do it at all.
(244)

The English narrator here finds herself suddenly descended into a dark wood of foreign names: Bogart, Ryan, Aloysius. The last, it so happens, is also an Oxford name: the Oxford church dedicated to the Jesuit saint Aloysius Gonzaga (d. 1591) also lends its name to Sebastian Flyte's teddybear in *Brideshead Rivisited.* Father Malory, at least, seems reassuringly insular in recalling the name of the great late-medieval English romancer: except that the *Morte d'Arthur*, of course, is very substantially translated—or, as Caxton has it, "reduced" ("led back": *reducere*)—from the French (Malory 1977, xv). Bogart and Ryan, however, are irreducibly un-English; and yet, of course, their cathection to Dante, as Irish Catholic names, is more authentic and immediate than anything Anglicans might dream of. Seamus Heaney has much fun with this in tracing the migration of T. S. Eliot—the most celebrated of twentieth-century Dante worshipers—from "the intellectual mysteryman from Missouri" to "the English vestryman" (Heaney 1985a, 7). High Church Anglicanism, which often seems more full of smells and bells than anything found in Rome, is still—for Heaney—a Catholicism with its underpants on. Heaney, Joyce, and other Irish writers, I would suggest, exult in the common religious axis connecting Dublin (or Ulster) to Rome by deploying Dante with an unmediated directness unavailable to English writers in England (Wallace 1993; O'Donoghue 1998). T. S. Eliot may find a wraith-like relative of Dante's Brunetto in his London *Wasteland*, but Heaney's equivalent figures, encountered at Lough Beg or Lough Derg, seem more securely grounded.

Heaney's humorous recognition of the residual embarrassment attending Eliot's Anglican deployment of the Catholic Dante is isomorphic with his recent, egregious, and wholly successful plot to leave his Celtic footprints all over the Anglo-Saxon Ur-text (and perennial fixture of the Oxford English tripos), *Beowulf* (Heaney 2000). Seamus in Heorot has something of the same resonance as Dante in England.

The last part of our Barbara Pym citation—the embarrassed talk of "going over" to Rome—suggests Victorian scares and scandals featuring Oxford figures such as John Henry Newman and Gerard Manley Hopkins while opening a crack or crevice to deeper levels of historical anxiety. The deepest level here, of course, is the Reformation itself; we might thus expect anxieties attending Dante and his Catholicism to be at their highest pitch in sixteenth-century England. But this is not the case: the overwhelming majority of references from this period adduce

Dante positively (as an antipapal writer, a sort of Italian Lollard) or in humorously appreciative vein. What proved crucial here, I would suggest, was the presence in 1559 of John Foxe at the printing office of Oporinus in the Lutheran stronghold of Basle as the first edition of Dante's *Monarchia* rolled off the press. In the 1570 edition of the *Actes and Monuments*, printed after Foxe's return to England, Dante appears as "an hereticke": a heretic, that is, in the eyes of *Catholic* authorities, for his writing "wherein he proveth the pope not to be above the Emperour," for his preaching against "the vayne fables of Monkes and Friers," for his critique of those who would feed Christ's flock "not with the foode of the Gospel, but with winde," for comparing popes with wolves, and so on (Foxe 1570, 485b; Caesar 1989, 29–31). It may well be that such positive press for Dante in Foxe's "Book of Martyrs"—the most influential book of religion, next to the Bible and prayerbooks, in Protestant England—rendered the *Commedia* a safer text to own or at least read than we have hitherto assumed. Indeed, in his recent survey of Dante citations in British books up to 1640, J. C. Boswell (1999, xiii) has expanded the Dante database inherited from Toynbee by a remarkable 120 percent. In John Bishop's *Beautifull blossomes, gathered* of 1577, for example, we discover an account of Ugolino clearly suggesting familiarity with the Dantean text and / or its commentaries (Boswell 1999, 54–55; STC 3091). From 1590 we have *Tarltons newes out of purgatorie*—characterized by its subtitle as "a jest" and a "jigge"—telling of the place "all our great grandmothers haue talkt of, that Dant hath so learnedly writ of"; the following year Robert Greene, in a similar jesting vein, claims Dante as his fellow "countriman" and "Englishes" a snippet of Italian as a long, pseudo-Dantean passage of his own invention (Boswell 1999, 84–85, STC 23685; 87–88, STC 12241). The year 1599 sees Dante adduced to the cause of Matthew Sutcliffe's *De turcopapismo, hoc est, de Turcarum & papistarum adversùs Christi ecclesiam*; the year following sees tercets from the *Inferno* and the *Purgatorio* popping up in another text of wonderful title, Tomasso Garzoni's *The first hospitall of incurable fooles: erected in English, as neer the first Italian modell as [an] unskilfull hand could devise* (Boswell 1999, 110–11, STC 23460; 112–13, STC 7196). The first dissident note is not heard until 1603, when Robert Parsons expresses his sheer incredulity at what Foxe (1570) has set in train. "Mark what men Fox doth coople togeather as of one faith," Parsons exclaims in his shoulder note; Foxe speaks, Parsons says, of "*Dantes & Petrarca* (Italian poets) that neuer held any iote of protestant religion in the world. And yet are brought inhere by Iohn Fox, as men of his Church and beleefe, with the greatest falshood and foolery in the world. And this forsooth, for that in some place of their works, they reprehend the manners of Rome, or liues of some Popes in those daies" (in Boswell 1999, 122–23, STC 19416). This spirited, "just a doggone minute!" objection is swept aside the very next year by the prevailing tide of pro-Dantean citation that sees the reprint of Sutcliffe's *De turcopapismo* and a new anti-papal treatise by George Abbot, archbishop of Canterbury.

We might expect that things will finally change after 1707 when, following the Act of Union, the need to cohere a newly united United Kingdom against foreign threats—real and imagined—leads to a sharpening of anti-Catholic discourse. This does indeed happen: but perhaps more slowly than one might expect.[5] The emphasis now is that Dante is *alien* to English understanding: "though I formerly knew Italian extremely well," says Lord Chesterfield in 1750, "I could never understand him; for which reason I had done with him" (Toynbee 1909, 1:255). This attitude hardens as the century wears on. In 1780, for example, Martin Sherlock, chaplain to the bishop of Derry, characterizes Dante's poem as "the worst that there is in any language," consisting chiefly of "a tissue of barbarisms, absurdities, and horrors" (Toynbee 1909, 1:376). Two years later, Horace Walpole launches the most magnificent English Protestant wrecking-ball at Dante, deeming him "extravagant, absurd, disgusting, in short a Methodist parson in Bedlam" (Toynbee 1909, 1:340). Walpole's one-liner makes no effort to comprehend the edifice it would destroy: Catholicism, which comes before the establishment of the true Church of England, and Methodism, which comes after, meet and embrace in lunatic unintelligibility. Studied incomprehension of foreigners and aliens is, of course, one of the most salient features of eighteenth-century English insularism as (even as) it extends its military and mercantile reach across the globe. The visual master of this mode is Hogarth: his 1749 painting (and subsequent etching) *The Gate of Calais*, for example, features three ecstatic women or nutty nuns (bottom left in Figure 2) discovering the face of Christ on a fish; a starving Jacobite (bottom right), escaped from Culloden; the Holy Spirit flying above a Catholic eucharist (center, through the gate), but only as painted on a pub sign. And observing all this (center left), the head of Hogarth himself: the heroic English artist / artisan, recording the follies of this foreign, Catholic, yet once-English world (note the English coats-of-arms above the gate) for native English consumption. This Hogarth's head—which began to circulate as an image in its own right—is clearly echoed in the figure of Beerbohm's scribbling proctor. Beerbohm is clearly emerging here as a commentator of genius: for he precisely captures the moment at which Dante will be encountered, first and foremost, as a stranger in Oxford and England.

The crucial determinant here of this alien-making process, *Entfremdung*, is not religion, but the exigencies of nationalism. Since, after 1945 and 1989, European nationalism is hopefully in abeyance, it may well be that attitudes to Dante in England before 1558 (the loss of Calais, in English hands since 1347) prove prophetic of any future England might have as a European nation. And I would like to conclude by briefly considering two moments that situate Dante in England and as part of England in this earlier period. The first begins with John Leland's discovery of Dante in Somerset in the 1530s—that is, of a Latin translation of the *Commedia* in Wells Cathedral Library (see Wallace 1999). This text was brought to Wells by Nicholas Bubwith, bishop of Bath and Wells, on his return from the Council of Constance in 1418. This remarkable church council, which ran for three-and-a-half years, became in effect an international postgraduate institute, drawing scholars and proto-humanists from all over Europe. Bubwith, along with his neighboring bishop of Salisbury, joined a Dante study circle supervised by Giovanni de Bertoldi de Serravalle, bishop of Firmano. In January 1416, Bertoldi was inspired to begin translating the *Commedia* into Latin; the following month he began an accompanying commentary. It was this translation (with or without its commentary) that Leland was to discover at Wells more than a century later. It now seems rather comical (at least to English ears) to speak of "Dante in Somerset," since Wells is now a quiet town in a county affectionately derided for its rural idiocy. But before the depredations of the Reformation, Somerset—between Glastonbury and Wells—was an intellectual center of European stature. The library that housed the Dante at Wells, built from Bubwith's legacy, was at its time of construction the largest in England (easily outstripping comparable sites in

Durham, Canterbury, and New and Merton Colleges, Oxford). The scholarly culture surrounding Bubwith's library at Wells was extremely distinguished: there was a choir school and a grammar school (generating the earliest-surviving English example of academic drama); there was an intensive culture of Latinity, featuring numerous noted humanists and contacts with Erasmus; and there was Polydore Vergil, royal historiographer, appointed archdeacon of Wells in 1508 (a title he retained even after his return to Urbino in 1553). And there is nothing in this milieu that would flag the "Dantes translatus in carmen Latinum" discovered by Leland as alien or foreign. Indeed, this Dante integrates perfectly with the academic culture, at once English and European, of which it forms part. Bertoldi's translation has the character of a parallel text, keeping tenaciously abreast of the Italian original, verse by verse (Wallace 1999, 15). We will need to revise our assumption, then, that there was no linear translation of the *Commedia* available in England until the nineteenth century; there was such a translation, located at the heart of one of the most powerful intellectual milieus on English ground.

My last port of call in this backward and forward itinerary is, of course, Chaucer. Following trips to Italy in the 1370s, the English poet staged a sort of nervous breakdown in verse called *The House of Fame* in which, within the tight restraints of French-derived octosyllabics, he registers the magnitude of Dante's achievement. By the end of his *Troilus*, having expanded his line, Chaucer actually risks comparisons with Dante by situating himself as "sesto tra cotanto senno" (*Inf* 4.102 [Chaucer 1987, 5:1792]) and by essaying imitation of *Par* 14.28–30 in his very next stanza: "Thow oon, and two, and thre, eterne on lyve, That regnest ay in thre, and two, and oon, Uncircumscript, and al maist circumscrive" (5:1863–65). The lines to be read immediately after this last stanza—the opening of *The Legend of Good Women*—josh Dante in time-honored fashion: men say, Chaucer says, "That ther ys joy in hevene and peyne in helle"; and yet, Chaucer continues, "there nis noon dwelling in this contree / That eyther hath in hevene or helle ybe" (F3.5–6). Such humorous sparring in no way detracts from the pervasive debt Chaucer owes Dante as a poet of modernity and antiquity fashioning an illustrious vernacular from the imperfect resources of his mother tongue. Such commitment to the vernacular passed out of fashion in Italy shortly after Dante's death; even Pietro Alighieri preferred *latinitas* as the medium for expounding his father's poem. But, given the retarded state of his own native tradition, Chaucer was more than eager to absorb every lesson on the *vulgaris illustris* that Dante had to teach. Specifically, Chaucer grasps that the study of Latinity should strengthen vernacular eloquence from within. After Chaucer's death, English poets sought to apply Latinity from without: that is, by finding aureate terms to apply or slap onto their poetic surfaces. It may not be altogether gratuitous, then, to consider Chaucer as Dante's most authentic Trecento continuator as a vernacular poet; their dates are different, but (in certain delimited but vital respects) their times are the same. It is a happy coincidence indeed that they should share centennial years.

In 1782, Joseph Ritson attacked Thomas Warton, professor of poetry at Oxford, for including Dante in his *History of English Poetry*. "To what purpose," Ritson asks, "is all this long dissertation upon *Dante*? What possible connection is there between the *Divina Comedia*, and the History of English Poetry?" (Toynbee 1909, 1:386–87). I have tried to suggest that such connections are indeed extensive, not just in matters of poetic borrowing but in all manner of movement across a European culture extending from London to Florence, from Wells to Urbino (rather than ending with Calais Gate). And since the resumption of such movement represents the best hope of revival for English culture—following four hundred years of global colonial distraction—I would like to end with some words of reassurance for the literary culture of Oxford, the university that has played the leading role in this account of Dante in England. Until very recently (the end was announced in May 2000) all undergraduates studying the English tripos at Oxford were required to study Anglo-Saxon. This was indeed a remarkable achievement of disciplinary enforcement; one is genuinely hesitant to criticize any curriculum that saw undergraduates grappling with philological complexities (rather than concentrating on the reading of twentieth-century novels). And yet there is something disquieting in the notion of an English curriculum overseeing a triumphal march from Old to Middle to modern English, since such notions of linguistic continuity mesh with ideas of racial essentialism best left in the nineteenth century with the likes of Hippolite Taine.[6] My hope, then, is that Oxford undergraduates, now relieved of compulsory Anglo-Saxon, be offered a range of texts from the greater European milieu from which English culture developed (and to which, hopefully, it will return: a return to be negotiated within the expanded and diversified parameters of postcolonial European space). One such text might be the *Song of Roland*, edited from its best and earliest manuscript: Bodleian Library, Oxford, MS Digby 23, written some seventy-five years after the Battle of Hastings (Crane 1999, 40). Another would certainly be *Beowulf*, newly glamorized and defamiliarized by its Heaneyian translation. And another would certainly be Dante: for in the twenty-first century, as in the fourteenth through seventeenth, there need be nothing alarming or incongruous about the notion of Dante in England. One hopes, however, that the ghost of earlier incongruity and alarm will remain: for the history of Dante in England has been (all things considered) surprisingly benign; a *commedia* with a small "c."

Notes

1. "Dante in Oxford" is one of the twenty drawings that *The Poet's Corner* (1904) comprises; drawings for this collection formed part of Beerbohm's second exhibition at the Carfax Gallery, London.

2. Robert Viscusi (1986, 77) sees in this quadrangle landscape "a little of Magdalen, a little of Merton."

3. Beerbohm entered Merton College, Oxford, in 1890, and left in 1894 without taking a degree; in 1945 he became an honorary Fellow. Alison Milbank (1998, 47) suggests that Beerbohm might have been inspired to caricature by "the scholarly Dantist Paget Toynbee, [who] sought to trace the poet's errant steps to fourteenth-century Oxford." After mature consideration, Toynbee (1910, 93) considered the notion of Dante's studying in Oxford "extremely doubtful"; a more likely source of inspiration for Beerbohm was William Ewart Gladstone's "Did Dante Study in Oxford?" Gladstone, building upon "corroborative evidence" supplied by Sir James Lacaita and Dean Plumptre (Gladstone 1982, 1041) triumphantly avers that in imagining Dante at Oxford, we stand "upon the firm ground of history." His penultimate sentence might be read as a challenge that Beerbohm, as celebrated dandyish saunterer through life, could hardly resist: "He [Dante] did not go [to Oxford] to saunter by the Isis, or to scale the height of Shotover: he went to haunts already made illustrious (to cite no other names) by Roger Bacon, by Grossetête, and by Bradwardine" (1042). Beerbohm had a lifelong fascination with Gladstone; as a boy, he sought out cabinet ministers to caricature and frequented the Strangers' Gallery in the House of Commons in order to get a good view of Gladstone in particular (McElderry 1972, 19). In "Dante in England" John W. Hales (1882, 38a) traces Dante to Paris and argues that "there is some ground for believing that he passed on into England."

4. Thus the blurb on the back cover of the paperback Plume / Penguin edition.

5. Voltaire's celebrated critical essay of 1740 does get translated, in 1758, but even then the Englishing is far from harsh: where Voltaire characterizes the *Commedia* as "poëme bizarre," Thomas Nugent speaks of Dante's "whimsical poem" (in Toynbee 1909, 1:205, 247).

6. See, for example, Taine 1871 and 1885; and Appiah 1995, who writes: "It is the conception of the binding core of the English nation as the Anglo-Saxon race that accounts for Taine's decision to identify the origins of English literature not in its antecedents in the Greek and Roman classics that provided the models and themes of so many of the best-known works of English 'poesy,' not in the Italian models that influenced the drama of Marlowe and Shakespeare, but in *Beowulf,* a poem in the Anglo-Saxon tongue, a poem that was unknown to Chaucer and Spenser and Shakespeare" (285).

Figure 1: *Source*: Sir Max Beerbohm. *The Poets' Corner*. London: Heinemann, 1904. Reprinted by permission of the Syndics of Cambridge University Library.

Figure 2: *Source*: William Hogarth. *The Complete Works of William Hogarth: In a series of one hundred and fifty superb engravings on steel from the original pictures*. London: London Printing & Publishing Co. [1890?]. Reprinted by permission of the Syndics of Cambridge University Library.

Moby-Dante?

Piero Boitani

A FEW MONTHS after the publication of my *Ombra di Ulisse* (1992), it was announced that the famous Italian actor Vittorio Gassman would stage in Genoa on October 12, 1992, for the five-hundredth anniversary of Columbus's "discovery" of America, a play he had written entitled *Ulisse e la balena bianca* (Ulysses and the White Whale [Gassman 1992]).[1] I jumped from the armchair where I was lying in post-publishing, self-satisfied torpor, and asked myself what might prompt a respectable seventy-year-old theater man to embark on such a "folle volo" and what exactly he was after. For in my book I had devoted a couple of pages (111–12) to the relationship between Dante's Ulysses and Melville's *Moby-Dick* in the context of all the "shadows" that mythical character projects from the later Middle Ages on to the Renaissance and Romanticism, and particularly on the *imaginaire* of European "discoverers" such as Columbus and Vespucci and their interpretation by American literary figures (see Boitani 1994, 89–92, exp. from Boitani 1992, 111–12).

Gassman's was virtually a one-man show. Basing himself on Pavese's translation of *Moby-Dick,* he dramatized the novel (this was not difficult, of course, given the Shakespearean inspiration and the actual theatrical structures of some central scenes), played the role of Ahab with his usual stentorean bravado, filled the text with passages from Ferenczi, Tennyson, Hölderlin, Jimenez, Nietzsche, Pessoa, Whitman, Alberti, and Lucretius—some of the quotations were the same I had used—and, after the *Pequod*'s wreck and Ishmael's survival, had Ahab recite Ulysses's account of his last voyage from *Inferno* 26. The play ended with darkness falling on the words "infin che 'l mar fu sovra noi richiuso."

It was clear from Renaissance interpreters, poets, and navigators such as Daniello, Tasso, Vespucci, and Pedro Sarmiento de Gamboa, that Dante's Ulysses had "discovered" America. It was equally obvious that the way in which the *Pequod* founders, with the vortex that gulps it down, was an echo of the shipwreck of *Inferno* 26, on which Melville superimposed the fall of Milton's Satan and the time of the Flood.

What had authorized my intertextual reading and Gassman's bombastic performance? What, aside from their obsession with Dante's Ulysses, makes Italians so absolutely convinced of the relationship? Critics have never been able to pinpoint Dante's influence on *Moby-Dick.* Some, including Glauco Cambon and, above all, Howard Schless, have indeed tried bravely, but nothing more than hints and guesses have been proved.[2] There are, I believe, at least two reasons: a suggestion and a fact. The suggestion comes from one of the greatest readers of the twentieth century, Jorge Luis Borges. He concluded his short essay on "El último viaje de Ulises" in *Nueve ensayos dantescos* (1983, 18) with the following paragraph:

> To my knowledge, a deeper affinity has not yet been indicated: that of the infernal Ulysses with another misfortuned captain, *Moby-Dick*'s Ahab. The latter, like the former, weaves his own perdition by dint of wakes and courage; the general theme is the same, the end is identical, the last words are almost the same. Schopenhauer has written that in our lives nothing is involuntary; both fictions, in the light of this prodigious pronouncement, are the process of a hidden [*oculto*] and intricate suicide.
>
> (my translation)

Who was I—and who was Vittorio Gassman—to contradict Borges, the blind modern Homer who has pursued the ancient one in a famous story (1981), written a sonnet on "Odyssey, Book XXIII" (1964), and devoted a poem to Herman Melville (1999)?

Siempre lo cercó el mar de sus mayores,
Los sajones, que al mar dieron el nombre
Ruta de la ballena, en que se aúnan
Las dos enormes cosas, la ballena
Y los mares que largamente surca.
Siempre fue suyo el mar. Cuando sus ojos
Vieron en alta mar las grandes aguas
Ya lo habia anhelado y poseido
En aquel otro mar, que es la Escritura,
O en el dintorno de los arquetipos.
Hombre, se dio a los mares del planeta

Y a las agotadoras singladuras
Y conoció el arpón enrojecido
Por Leviathán y la rayada arena
Y el olor de las noches y del alba
Y el horizonte en que el azar acecha
Y la felicidad de ser valiente
Y el gusto, al fin, de divisar a Itaca.
Debelador del mar, pisó la tierra
Firme que es la raíz de las montañas
Y en la que marca un vago derrotero,
Quieta en el tiempo, una dormida brújula.
A la heredada sombra de los huertos,
Melville cruza las tardes de New England
Pero lo habita el mar. Es el oprobio
Del mutilado capitán del *Pequod,*
El mar indescifrable y las borrascas
Y la abominación de la blancura.
Es el gran libro. Es el azul Proteo.

He was always surrounded by the sea of his elders, / The Saxons, who named the ocean / *The Whale-Road,* thereby uniting / The two immense things, the whale / And the sea it endlessly ploughs. / The sea was always his. By the time his eyes / First took in the great waters of the high seas / He had already longed for and possessed it / On that other ocean, which is Writing, / And in the outline of the archetypes. / A man, he gave himself to the earth's oceans / And to the exhausting days at sea / And he came to know the harpoon reddened / By Leviathan and the rippled sand / And the smells of nights and mornings / And chance on the horizon waiting in ambush / And the happiness of being brave / And the pleasure, at last, of spying Ithaca. / The ocean's conqueror, he strode the solid / Earth out of which mountains grow / And on which he charts an imprecise course / As with a sleeping compass, motionless in time. / In the inherited shadows of the gardens / Melville moves through the New England evenings, / But the sea possesses him. It is the shame / Of the *Pequod*'s mutilated captain, / The unreadable ocean with its furious squalls / And the abomination of the whiteness. / It is the great book. It is blue Proteus.

(trans. Kessler [in Borges 1999])

No intelligent, sensitive reader can resist this. Borges sees Melville as the Saxon descendant of Ulysses as well as the "shadow" of Ahab and the biblical rewriter, possessed by the "contours of archetypes," of the "great book," the "azure Proteus"—in short, the new *Odyssey.* As mythical and poetic discourse, Borges's is impeccable. And, when we discuss *Moby-Dick,* we are talking about myth and *poiesis,* are we not?

But, I would insist, we are not speaking of mere fantasy. There is a fact as well as the suggestion. Herman Melville bought a copy of Cary's Dante, *The Vision,* on June 22, 1848. This book exists, is in New Haven, Connecticut, and can be consulted.[3] Using it, Lea Bertani Newman (1993) has—I think—proved beyond a doubt that Melville employed the *Divine Comedy* while composing *Mardi* (1849).[4] Critics had already shown the reasonably strong Dantean influence on *Pierre* (1852) (see Giovannini 1949; Schless 1960; Wright 1960; and Gollin 1968). *Moby-Dick* (1851) falls in between these two, after *Redburn* (1849) and *White Jacket* (1850). In *White Jacket,* the tar Jack Chase continually talks of, and even quotes, Homer and Ulysses, calling the first a "tar" and the second "a sailor and a shipwright." He associates both with Columbus and Camões, whom he particularly loves and who, of course, often sings of Homer's and Dante's Ulysses. But it is the narrator himself who, centering the whole first half of his book on Cape Horn, finds no better way of celebrating it than by evoking the very same cluster of myths: "Who has not heard of it?" he writes, "Cape Horn, Cape Horn—a *horn* indeed, that has tossed many a good ship. Was the descent of Orpheus, Ulysses, or Dante into Hell, one whit more hardy and sublime than the first navigator's weathering of that terrible Cape?"[5]

A descent into Hell; of course, Melville is talking of three different *nekyiai:* those of Orpheus, of Homer's Odysseus, and of Dante. But the proximity of the two names, Ulysses and Dante, points, I suspect, to an almost inevitable mental association between their respective descents into Hell in Dante's own *Inferno.* Cary's final note (1847) to *Inferno* 26, in which he links the prophecy of Tiresias to Homer's Ulysses and "the fate which there was reason to suppose had befallen some adventurous explorers of the Atlantic ocean," may have encouraged Melville to think in such mythic fashion. And, indeed, the final chapter of *Mardi* shows clearly how well Melville "had been reading about one 'unreturning wanderer' who 'steered his bark' through untracked seas and ultimately did 'wreck'" (Newman 1993, 331).

Does this, to put it bluntly, represent the genesis of Ahab? It is pretty maddening to note that not the slightest marginal mark accompanies *Inferno* 26 in Melville's Dante. The American novelist, we must acknowledge, seems to have been totally unimpressed, or left mute and speechless, by that canto. The latter hypothesis is more likely. In his reading of the *Comedy,* Melville was in fact as wily as Ulysses. On the whole, his attention to the *Inferno* and the *Purgatorio* looks like that of someone who already knew them, whereas he now concentrates on the *Paradiso,* particularly the latter's final cantos. For instance, the margins of *Paradiso* 33 in his copy of Cary (1847) are filled by his almost constant pencil line, sometimes doubled (as in the case of "and, in that depth, / Saw in one volume clasp'd of love, whate'er / The universe unfolds," with the *terzina*s that precede and follow it), sometimes on both sides of the text ("Thus in the winds on flitting leaves was lost / The Sibyl's leaves" and "In that abyss / Of radiance, clear and lofty, seem'd, methought, / Three orbs of triple hue, clipt in one bound"), once by the word "Dance" when Bernard, at the end of his prayer to the Virgin, points to Beatrice: "vedi Beatrice con quanti beati / per li miei prieghi ti chiudon le mani!"

Melville also notes the famous Argo simile—what T. S. Eliot (1965, 50) was to call "the real right thing, the power of establishing relations between beauty of the most diverse sorts; . . . the utmost power of the poet." "One moment," Cary (1847) nobly translates, "seems a longer lethargy, / Than five-and-twenty ages had appear'd / To that emprize, that first made Neptune wonder / At Argo's shadow darkening on his flood." Melville ignores Cary's first two footnotes, which attempt an explanation of the passage and quote Catullus, but underlines the third, where a couplet from Spenser's *Faerie Queene* (2.12.44) is given in full by Cary: "The wondred Argo, which in wondrous piece / First through the Euxine seas bore all the flower of Greece" (1847, 526).

The Argo and the Argonauts must have enthralled Melville. Another passage he marked in his Cary (1847, 363) was the opening of *Par* 2.1–18, which ends with an allusion to Jason and "those, glorious, who pass'd o'er / To Colchos":

> All ye, who in small bark have following sail'd,
> Eager to listen, on the adventurous track
> Of my proud keel, that singing cuts her way,
> Backward return with speed, and your own shores
> Revisit; nor put out to open sea,
> Where losing me, perchance ye may remain
> Bewilder'd in deep maze. The way I pass,
> Ne'er yet was run: Minerva breathes the gale;

Apollo guides me; and another Nine,
To my rapt sight, the arctic beams reveal.
Ye other few who have outstretch'd the neck
Timely for food of angels, on which here
They live, yet never know satiety;
Through the deep brine ye fearless may put out
Your vessel; marking well the furrow broad
Before you in the wave, that on both sides
Equal returns. Those, glorious, who pass'd o'er
To Colchos, wonder'd not as ye will do,
When they saw Jason following the plough.

Was Melville aware of the echoes and counterpoints these six tercets play on *Inferno* 26? We have no way of knowing. But we do know that he must have read that canto very carefully indeed, for when he comes to *Paradiso* 27 he traces a continuous pencil line along the two tercets that describe Dante's view of the earth from the threshold of the ninth Heaven:

From the hour
When I before had cast my view beneath,
All the first region overpast I saw,
Which from the midmost to the boundary winds;
That onward, thence, from Gades, I beheld
The unwise passage of Laërtes' son;
And hitherward the shore, where thou, Europa,
Madest thee a joyful burden.
(Cary 1847, 496–97)

In case Melville had lost his memory at this point, Cary's footnote on Gades would reawaken it: "See Hell, Canto xxvi, 106," it goes. Yes, Melville knew the canto of Ulysses fairly well.

The question is: how, if at all, did it affect *Moby-Dick?* Things are more complex here. Dante is mentioned twice in the novel within a few pages. The first time, Melville celebrates the Sperm Whale's "fountain" and ends up exalting its head in somewhat ironical, ambiguous fashion. "He [the Sperm Whale] is," he writes, "both ponderous and profound. And I am convinced that from the heads of all ponderous profound beings, such as Plato, Pyrrho, the Devil, Jupiter, Dante, and so on, there always goes up a certain semi-visible steam, while in the act of thinking deep thoughts" (Melville 1972, 482). In the next line, Ishmael jokingly places himself "sesto tra cotanto senno" (*Inf* 4.102), seeing reflected in a mirror before him "a curious involved worming and undulation of the atmosphere over [his] head." Only a couple of pages later, Dante is evoked again, now in connection with the Sperm Whale's tail:

> Out of the bottomless profundities the gigantic tail seems spasmodically snatching at the highest heaven. So in dreams, have I seen majestic Satan thrusting forth his tormented colossal claw from the flame Baltic of Hell. But in gazing at such scenes, it is all in all what mood you are in; if in the Dantean, the devils will occur to you; if in that of Isaiah, the archangels.[6]
> (Melville 1972, 486)

The light, half-ironical ambiguity of "The Fountain" is gone. What we have instead is the ineradicable ambiguity of the Whale when apprehended by a human subject. The Whale looks like Dante's Lucifer and Milton's Satan: a devil, if the percipient is in a Dantean mood; an archangel, if he is in Isaiah's. Ahab's perception of Moby-Dick is, in this context, Dantean. Earlier on, in the famous theatrical, Shakespeare-inspired chapter entitled "The Quarter-Deck," Ahab talks to Starbuck, who reproaches him for wanting "vengeance on a dumb brute." The captain replies that he sees Moby-Dick as the "wall" keeping humanity prisoner, the "mask" behind which "some unknown but still reasoning thing puts forth the mouldings of its features." "Sometimes I think," Ahab confides to Starbuck, "there's naught beyond. But 'tis enough. He tasks me, he heaps me; I see in him outrageous strength, with an inscrutable malice sinewing it" (262). Dante's Lucifer appears in *Inferno* 34 as an enormous giant. The giants of *Inferno* 31 look like the towers around the walls of Monteriggioni, and to make sure the reader understands the proportions as well as the nature of these partly unnatural creatures, Dante devises three explanatory *terzine,* or tercets. "Nature," he writes in Cary's translation, "when her plastic hand / Left framing of these monsters, did display / Past doubt her wisdom, taking from mad War / Such slaves to do his bidding; and if she / Repent her not of the elephant and whale, / Who ponders well confesses her therein / Wiser and more discreet; for when brute force / and evil will are back'd with subtlety, / Resistance none avails."

In his "Footnote for a Sub-Sub-Librarian," Howard Schless (1961, 311–12) had already caught the point. But we should go further. Dante mentions "balene" and adds, to the giants' detriment, "l'argomento de la mente," the "mal volere," and the "possa." Outrageous strength, with an inscrutable malice sinewing it: Ahab sees the White Whale—and this is quite a central point—as a Dantean giant, the prefiguration of Dante's own Satan.

Shortly afterward, in the following chapter ("Sunset"), he presents himself—we thus move from the object to the subject of perception—as "damned, most subtly and most malignantly! damned in the midst of Paradise" (266)—in short, as Milton's Satan: "What I've dared, I've willed; and what I've willed, I'll do! They think me mad—Starbuck does; but I'm demoniac, I am madness maddened!" The echo of Milton's "unconquerable will, / And study of revenge, immortal hate, / And courage never to submit or yield" (*Paradise Lost* 1.106–108) is unmistakable (see Melville 1972, 764). Did Melville know that Milton's lines had been put into the mouth of Ulysses himself by Tennyson (1969, 145), who closed his poem "Ulysses" (70) on the Homeric–Dantean hero with "strong in will / To strive, to seek, to find, and not to yield"? We cannot be sure, although we can say it is likely.[7]

All the same the Ulyssean *imaginaire* is deeply embedded in *Moby-Dick*'s fabric. Several of the "shadows of Ulysses" recur in the novel: within history, for instance, Columbus, who, Melville informs us, comparing his voyages to whaling expeditions, "sailed over numberless unknown worlds to discover his one superficial western one"; or Magellan, whose circumnavigation of the globe the *Pequod* imitates, but which Ishmael considers aimless wandering toward "barren mazes" or inevitable shipwreck (Melville 1972, 379; cf. 340). In myth and literature, Ahab is preceded by the Prometheus who so obsessed the Romantic imagination (Ishmael compares them explicitly); by Faust, whom he obliquely but most clearly embodies; and above all by the Ancient Mariner—as the evocation of the albatross and the skeleton, ghost-like whaler *Albatross* prove. But even Perth the blacksmith, who forges Ahab's harpoon, is a Ulyssean character. He embarks on his first, and last, voyage as an old man, like Dante's Ulysses, when he reaches Gibraltar. The impulse that prompts him—death-longing which manifests itself as desire for the Unknown—looks like a perfectly Romantic reincarnation of Ulysses' "ardore," and to top it all Melville conjures up the Sirens (1972, 596–97):

> Death seems the only desirable sequel for a career like this; but Death is only a launching into the region of the strange Untried; it is but the first salutation to the possibilities of the immense Remote, the Wild, the

> Watery, the Unshored; therefore, to the death-longing eyes of such men, who still have left in them some interior compunctions against suicide, does the all-contributed and all-receptive ocean alluringly spread forth his whole plain of unimaginable, taking terrors, and wonderful, new-life adventures; and from the hearts of infinite Pacifics, the thousand mermaids sing to them—"Come hither, broken-hearted; here is another life without the guilt of intermediate death; here are wonders supernatural, without dying for them. Come hither! bury thyself in a life which, to your now equally abhorred and abhorring, landed world, is more oblivious than death. Come hither! Put up thy grave-stone, too, within the churchyard, and come hither, till we marry thee!"[8]

Ahab himself is, of course, an ultra-Ulyssean Ulysses. An old man who abandons his wife and child, he persuades his men to follow him in his desperate undertaking, in an "oration" that quickly turns into an initiation ceremony and act of diabolic communion. Dante's Ulysses wishes to experience the otherworld and reaches the threshold of the new one, the mountain of Earthly Paradise forbidden to humanity after the Fall: hence his sinking by the Christian God. Ulysses' audacious final journey is undertaken out of a desire for exclusively human knowledge: without, but not against, a God whom in any case he does not know. Ahab, a "grand, ungodly, god-like" (176) old man, is in obsessed pursuit of a White Whale that he has turned into a satanic God. Ulysses' "ardore" becomes Ahab's fire.[9] Increasingly resembling a timelessly old Adam (the first trespasser), in this key chapter Ahab nurtures limitless anger, a radical, ontological rage that is "the sum of all . . . hate felt by his whole race from Adam down" (283) toward fate and all the evils that flesh has forever been an heir to.[10]

Ulysses trespasses beyond the Pillars of Hercules because he wants to attain what he considers man's "semenza," his primeval aim—envisaged as it were by Genesis and Aristotle's *Metaphysics*—to pursue virtue and knowledge.[11] He is, therefore, killed by the highest Other, which his tongue of fire then challenges, sotto voce, from the depths of Hell. Ahab goes further: passing his own Pillars of Hercules,[12] he wants to kill the Other. Driven by an irresistible, "nameless, inscrutable, unearthly" power, he is a living tongue of fire, a "darkness leaping out of light" who calls to the bar the supreme Fire, the "unbegotten," "unborn," "omnipotent" Spirit himself. What can a reader think when she or he stumbles, in that moment when Ahab descries Moby-Dick's spout again on the third day of the chase, onto "three shrieks" that go up from the three mast-heads "as if the tongues of fire had voiced it" (675)?[13] Ahab, she or he (and Dante) will opine, "fulfills" Ulysses by trying to take the ultimate rebellion of his prefiguration to its extreme conclusion, actively contesting the Other who "willed" Ulysses' shipwreck.

For better or for worse, this is quite a big part of Western history, the line that ends up with Nietzsche's murder of God. Given Dante's Ulysses and his successors in our history and literature, Ahab seems inevitable (see Boitani 1999, 6).[14] "Ambas ficciones," we should reflect with Borges, "son el proceso de un oculto e intricado suicidio" (Borges 1983, 118). Both terminate with the "turbo," the whirlpool that sinks captain, men and ship "infin che 'l mar fu sovra noi richiuso" (*Inf* 26.142).

In fact, *Moby-Dick* does not end there; Ishmael survives. He, too, is drawn toward the "closing vortex" and revolves, "like another Ixion," "round and round" "that slowly wheeling circle" until the black bubble at its center bursts upward and he is thrown back up together with Queequeg's coffin. He hangs on to this until he is rescued by the *Rachel*, thus escaping "alone" "to tell" us the news like Job's servant (687) (cf. Job 1:19).

Ishmael's tale and Melville's own writing of it are different from Ahab's Inferno. Not only does he emerge from the abyss after three days like Dante from Hell to Purgatory (Schless 1961, 303–10), he also sees his story as an enterprise somewhat akin to Dante's *Paradiso*. In the "Brit" chapter he warns us against the sea, inviting us to consider its infinite dangers, alienness, malignant subtleness, and cannibalism. Like Dante in his address to the readers at the beginning of *Paradiso* 2 (a passage we have seen marked by Melville in his Cary), Ishmael concludes his peroration by openly trying to persuade us not to "push off" from land:

> Consider all this; and then turn to this green, gentle, and most docile earth; consider them both, the sea and the land; and do you not find a strange analogy to something in yourself? For as this appalling ocean surrounds the verdant land, so in the soul of man there lies one insular Tahiti, full of peace and joy, but encompassed by all the horrors of the half known life. God keep thee! Push not off from that isle, thou canst never return!
>
> (381)

Melville's writing of *Moby-Dick* is, on the other hand, presented as water never sailed. Dante invoked the nine Muses which, he says in Cary's translation, "the arctic beams reveal." He ended that passage (378) with an allusion to the Argonauts and the *Paradiso* itself with the shadow of the *Argo.* Here is Melville celebrating his subject, whales:

> Nor when expandingly lifted by your subject, can you fail to trace out great whales in the starry heavens, and boats in pursuit of them; as when long filled with thoughts of war the Eastern nations saw armies locked in battle among the clouds. Thus at the North have I chased Leviathan round and round the Pole with the revolutions of the bright points that first defined him to me. And beneath the effulgent Antarctic skies I have boarded the Argo-Navis, and joined the starry Cetus far beyond the utmost stretch of Hydrus and the Flying Fish.

Ishmael, we are told, is "above all things appalled" by the whiteness of the whale. But Ishmael himself, though one of Ahab's crew and indeed possessed by "a wild, mystical, sympathetical feeling" toward his captain, also receives, by squeezing whale sperm, a kind of second baptism which seems to cleanse his former sins and makes him closer than ever to his fellow sailors. He understands, then, that unlike Dante's Ulysses and Guido da Montefeltro, man should "calare le sarte" and return like Homer's Odysseus to his wife, bed, and country. At precisely this point, ready now "to squeeze case eternally," he becomes a new Jacob and indeed a new Dante,[15] seeing, "in thoughts of the visions of the night," "long rows of angels in paradise, each with his hands in a jar of spermaceti":

> Would that I could keep squeezing that sperm for ever! For now, since by many prolonged, repeated experiences, I have perceived that in all cases man must eventually lower, or at least shift, his conceit of attainable felicity; not placing it anywhere in the intellect or the fancy; but in the wife, the heart, the bed, the table, the saddle, the fire-side, the country; now that I have perceived all this, I am ready to squeeze case eternally. In thoughts of the visions of the night, I saw long rows of angels in paradise, each with his hands in a jar of spermaceti.
>
> (527)

Above all, Ishmael looks capable of an enchantment, which comes close to Dante's "stupore" in the *Paradiso.* When, for instance, the *Pequod* sights a "grand armada" of whales, some "amour[ing] in the deep" in spite of the dreadful massacre the men are carrying out in their midst, Ishmael seems bent on contemplating a heavenly dance—the kind of dance that attracts Melville in his reading of *Paradiso* 25 and 33:

> And thus, though surrounded by circle upon circle of consternations and affrights, did these inscrutable creatures at the centre freely and fearlessly indulge in all peaceful concernments; yea, serenely revelled in dalliance and delight. But even so, amid the tornadoed Atlantic of my being, do I myself still for ever centrally disport in mute calm; and while ponderous planets of unwaning woe revolve round me, deep down and deep inland there I still bathe me in eternal mildness of joy.
>
> (498)

A reader of the *Comedy* might compare the second part of this paragraph with the "equal ecstasy," the "joy past compare," the "gladness unutterable," the "one universal smile . . . of all things" which Dante describes, and Melville marks, at the beginning of *Paradiso* 27, or with "the sense of sweet" that springs from Dante's vision of God and "still trickles in [his] heart" while he composes *Paradiso* 33: "Thus in the sun-thaw is the snow unseal'd"—Melville underscores in his copy—"Thus in the winds on flitting leaves was lost / The Sibyl's sentence."

It might not be by mere chance that when Moby-Dick, "the grand god," finally "reveal[s] himself" on the first day of the chase, Ishmael should extol his appearance by means of an image that Dante had used upon ascending to the Primum Mobile. Dante—and we saw Melville pay particular attention to the passage in his Cary—had evoked both the "varco / folle d'Ulisse" and "the shore, where thou, Europa, / Madest thee a joyful burden." Ishmael recounts that:

> A gentle joyousness—a mighty mildness of repose in swiftness, invested the gliding whale. Not the white bull Jupiter swimming away with ravished Europa clinging to his graceful horns; his lovely, leering eyes sideways intent upon the maid; with smooth bewitching fleetness, rippling straight for the nuptial bower in Crete; not Jove, not that great majesty Supreme! did surpass the glorified White Whale as he so divinely swam.
>
> (656)

In short, Melville approaches the beatific vision. He now seems to read Dante with Isaiah's eyes. The Whale's whiteness looks like the "radiance" of Cary's *Paradiso* 33.[16]

Immediately afterward, however, Moby-Dick attacks Ahab's boat, revealing "malicious intelligence" and a "revolvingly appalling . . . aspect," his "mighty mildness of repose in swiftness" turned suddenly into "planetarily swift . . . ever-contracting circles" (658, 660). *Inferno* will not be separated from *Paradiso,* and only Ishmael survives into the *Purgatorio* and the contemplative life of *Rachel* (Schless 1961, 310–11). On the second day of the chase, the *Pequod* at first resembles Dante's own poetic vessel, which, upon entering the unbound ocean of Heaven and of God, leaves "the furrow broad . . . in the wave" and will make readers wonder more than "those, glorious, who pass'd o'er / To Colchos" "when they saw Jason following the plough." "The ship," Melville (1972, 665) writes, "tore on; leaving such furrow in the sea as when a cannon-ball, missent, becomes a plough-share and turns up the level field."

But Melville knew only too well that even in *Paradiso* 2 that wave, echoing contrapuntally the final line of *Inferno* 26, "on both sides / Equal returns." His own simile goes in that direction. Hence, the circles that haunt the final part of *Moby-Dick*—a series of eleven whirlpools of which we have just seen the ninth and which take up and tragically transform the "Descartian vortices" (cf. Melville 1972, 765 [for 257] and 952–64 [for 684]) beheld much earlier from "The Mast-Head"—culminate, after Ahab's metamorphosis into Macbeth, Othello, and Antichrist, with the twelfth, truly Dantean and Ulyssean turbo. "Hell at last," Milton would expand, talking of Satan the archangel's and his companions' fall, "Yawning received them whole, *and on them closed,* / Hell their fit habitation fraught with fire / Unquenchable."[17]

> And now, concentric circles seized the lone boat itself, and all its crew, and each floating oar, and every lance-pole, and spinning, animate and inanimate, all round and round in one vortex, carried the smallest chip of the *Pequod* out of sight.
>
> . . . and so the bird of heaven, with archangelic shrieks, and his imperial beak thrust upwards, and his whole captive form folded in the flag of Ahab, went down with his ship, which, like Satan, would not sink to hell till she had dragged a living part of heaven along with her, and helmeted herself with it.[18]
>
> Now small fowls flew screaming over the yet yawning gulf; a sullen white surf beat against its steep sides; then all collapsed, and the great shroud of the sea rolled on as it rolled five thousand years ago.
>
> (684–85)

The "grand god," Moby-Dick, kills his "grand, ungodly, god-like" would-be murderer: it is a pretty good, devilish comment on the fate of Dante's Ulysses. So, Borges was right, Gassman was right, maybe even I have been partly right. A long time ago, in fact in the last millennium, I wrote that "Melville so perfectly understood the tragic message of Dante's Ulysses that he [had Ishmael recount] a *nekyia,* another circular *mythos.* The myth is a Genesis narrating the entry of the New World into History with the shadow of a transgression and the 'great shroud' of death. Now, through Whitman's poetry, America is celebrating itself and Christopher Columbus. With Melville that same America is paying for its original sin by repeating, as if in ritual sacrifice, the shipwreck of the Ulysses who had discovered it" (1994, 92). I might not wish to change this statement, almost as bombastic as Gassman's performance, but if I did I would formulate it—today, in 2000, and on the seven hundredth anniversary of the Easter Eve when Dante met Ulysses in Hell—as follows. When he came upon the *Comedy,* Melville must have thought it was a kind of gigantic whale, a sort of Moby-Dick. Did he not evoke Dante à propos of both head and tail—that is, *beginning and end*—of the Sperm Whale? When he wrote his own "undivine Comedy," *Moby-Dick,* he perhaps (hence the question mark in my title) imagined himself not only as a rewriter of the Bible, Marlowe, Shakespeare, Milton, and Goethe, but also as a "Moby-Dante."

Notes

1. I am indebted to Guido Almansi for his preface to Gassman 1992.

2. Though bibliography on the Melville–Dante relationship is scant, see Cambon 1969; Giovannini 1949; Mathews 1958; Schless 1960 and 1961; Avallone 1976; and Young 1991.

3. Page references are to this edition (Cary 1847). The volume is the property of William Reese of New Haven, Connecticut. Without his unfailing courtesy, generosity, and efficiency in supplying me with photocopies and allowing me to inspect the book I would have been unable to write this essay.

4. Newman's study (1993) contains additional critical bibliography on the Melville–Dante relationship. I wish to thank Lea Bertani Newman for helping me with great kindness throughout the preparation of this essay.

5. See Melville 1990, 274 and 98; as well as 13, 217 (for quote from *Odyssey* 5.393–94), 275, 313 (for Camões), 367 (Chaucer's Shipman), and 402 (Camões).

6. See Beaver's comments ad loc. in Melville 1972, 854–55, 858–59.

7. The poem, written in 1833, was published in 1842. Melville could have known of, or read, it from the copy of Tennyson's *Poems* (1842) owned by his sister Augusta since 1844 (see Newman 1993, 338). Sealts (1988) does not include any works by Tennyson, but how likely is it that Melville ignored the most famous of all living English poets?

8. Perth is a "humanized" Ahab. I have already pointed out the death-impulse of Dante's Ulysses (1992, 43–46).

9. Note Ahab's luciferine invocation to the "clear spirit of clear fire" in "The Candles" chapter (616).

10. Adam, who in *Paradiso* 26, echoing *Inferno* 26, calls his original sin (in Cary's translation) the "transgressing of the mark," is again evoked by Ahab toward the end: "I feel deadly faint, bowed, and humped, as though I were Adam, staggering beneath the piled centuries since Paradise" ("The Symphony" [651–52]).

11. "Semenza" and "fatti non foste" (*Inf* 26.118–19) allude to Gen. 1; "ma per seguir virtute e conoscenza" (*Inf* 26.120) is an echo of the very first sentence of Aristotle's *Metaphysics* (already used by Dante at the opening of the *Convivio*) as well as of concepts derived from the *Nicomachean Ethics.*

12. The Pillars of Hercules are mentioned in *Moby-Dick* (251–52). Later, they are evoked again in "The Grand Armada" chapter, when the *Pequod* goes through the Straits of Sunda (488).

13. Beaver (Melville 1972) recalls Acts 2:2–3. Melville's "tongues of fire" would, of course, be an inversion of the Pentecostal ones, precisely like the fraudulents' in *Inferno* 26–27. One should also note the proximity of the tongues of fire to the shipwreck in *Moby-Dick.*

14. Ahab's famous retort to Starbuck on the second day of the chase (672) seems sinisterly post-Satanic, post-Faustian, and pre-Hitlerian: "Ahab is for ever Ahab, man. This whole act's immutably decreed. 'Twas rehearsed by thee and me a billion years before this ocean rolled. Fool! I am the Fates' lieutenant; I act under orders. Look thou, underling! That thou obeyest mine." A re-creative version of the sinister quality of the novel and of the encounter between Ahab and Moby-Dick is found in Ferrucci 1996, 232–35.

15. In *Par* 22.61–72, Dante is promised by Saint Benedict full view of Heaven, like Jacob's of the "scala."

16. Cary 1847, 527: "In that abyss / Of radiance, clear and lofty, seem'd, methought, / Three orbs of triple hue, clipt in one bound" (*Par* 33.115–17). Melville marked the passage as well as Cary's relevant footnote: "This passage

may be compared to what Plato, in his second Epistle, enigmatically says of a first, second, and third, and of the impossibility that the human soul should attain to what it desires to know of them, by means of any thing akin to itself." Plato would be of importance to *Moby-Dick* (cf. "Plato, Pyrrho, the Devil, Jupiter, Dante" [482]).

17. Cf. *Paradise Lost* 6.874–77, which rewrites Is. 5:14, with possible Dantean reminiscence I have italicized in the text.

18. On which Beaver (Melville 1972, 964) comments "like Satan 'thrusting forth his tormented colossal claw'" and recalls (965) *Paradise Lost* 6.840–41.

25

Still Here: Dante after Modernism

Peter S. Hawkins and Rachel Jacoff

GIVEN THAT A NEW CENTURY typically turns against the tastes of its predecessor, there was every reason to expect that the Dante rediscovered in nineteenth-century Britain and America would fall out of favor with writers intent on "making it new." Yet, on the contrary, it was in the English-speaking world of the 1900s that Dante became the great Poet Interlocutor, the master of *poetare.* The list of those in the twentieth century who have been in sustained dialogue with him is both diverse and long; it is also strikingly full of Americans, whether by birth or residence. Pound and Eliot come first, and after them Auden, Lowell, and Merrill. At our own turn of the century there are Charles Wright and Gjertrud Schnackenberg, Nobel Prize winners Seamus Heaney and Derek Walcott, our recent poet laureate, Robert Pinsky, and any number of others.

The connections made with Dante are extremely varied, as if his celebrated universality has made it possible for poets to engage his work on many different levels, and often on utterly divergent terms. He was venerated by Pound and Eliot (in Seamus Heaney's phrase) as the "aquiline patron of international Modernism" (1985a, 16); but during the same period was treated quite playfully by Beckett, Joyce, and Stevens. Dante's intense interest in the relationship of poets to one another—and thus in questions of origin and descent, poetic paternity and filiation—proved particularly attractive to twentieth-century writers looking to position themselves both within and against literary tradition. As the *Comedy* demonstrates, conversations with dead masters can enable the living to find their own distinctive voices.

The great case in point is Eliot's adaptation of the Brunetto Latini encounter in *Inferno* 15 in order to place himself in Dante's lineage. In the second section of the poem *Little Gidding,* and in a justly celebrated English attempt at *terza rima,* Eliot conjures a "familiar compound ghost" who appears to the narrator in the aftermath of a London blitz (see especially Charity 1974; Leland 1992; and McDougal 1988). The passage is a brilliant modernist update of the *Inferno*'s burning plain, a fleeting afterlife encounter in the "Unreal City" of World War II. Eliot's sustained imitation of Dante has rightly been taken as tribute to a mentor whose influence extends from *Prufrock* through the *Quartets*—an acknowledgment of Dante as "maestro e autore." Yet, like the ghost itself, Eliot's homage is at once "intimate and unidentifiable," that is, both a tribute to the exemplar poet and an evasion of his authority. In a series of moves perhaps learned from Dante's own handling of Virgil, Eliot establishes his ability to rewrite the text he imitates, to alter what he loves, and to exert power over the "master" he venerates.

The results, however, are mixed. To begin, Eliot offers us only "*some* dead master" rather than anyone in particular. This was a clear choice: Eliot is on record as not wanting his ghost to represent a single historical figure (McDougal 1988, 78). Instead, his paternal shade is a composite of Pound, Yeats, Swift, Mallarmé, and, of course, Homer, Virgil, and the author of the *Comedy*. While Dante did not fear to take on Brunetto directly, Eliot chose to be more oblique with his master. As a result, the encounter lacks the emotional charge of *Inferno* 15, for unlike Dante's pilgrim, the narrator of *Little Gidding* does not meet someone with whom he has a history, who can speak to him about his past and future—someone to whom he is indebted. Instead, a personal mentor becomes merely an "exasperated spirit," and the figure likened by Dante to the loser of a famous race in Verona, merely "some" generic dancer in a dance:

From wrong to wrong the exasperated spirit
Proceeds, unless restored by that refining fire
Where you must move in measure, like a dancer.
(1962, 142)

Because Eliot wanted his encounter with the dead to be more purgatorial than infernal, he grafted *Purgatorio* 26 onto *Inferno* 15, "compounding" his Brunetto figure with Guido Guinizzelli and Arnaut Daniel. Furthermore, Dante's proto-humanist lover of literature, besotted with the possibility of making himself eternal through the books in which he lives on, becomes in *Little Gidding* a figure with virtually no interest in poetry. Eliot's "brown baked" ghost is concerned with human folly and the need to repent and forgive. Echoing Oderisi's austere injunctions against fame in *Purgatorio* 11, he represents the turn toward prayer and repentance enjoined by Guinizzelli and Arnaut. As a result, the *Little Gidding* encounter warns against the futility of "a lifetime's efforts" without giving any sense (as Dante always does) of the exuberant pleasures a poet might legitimately take in purifying "the dialect of the tribe." The creative tension between virtue and virtuosity that electrifies the entire *Comedy*—and the exquisite irony of admiration and critique simultaneously on display in *Inferno* 15—collapse under the ghost's withering negations. Eliot may well have set out to lessen his anxiety before Dante by "compounding" him with other writers and, in effect, by demonstrating (to quote the poem *East Coker*) that "The poetry does not matter" (1962, 125). He may also have wanted to distance himself from the lure of poetry in what was to be his poetic swan song. In any event, Eliot's refusal to compete on the same terms as his avowed precursor suggests that the problem lies with modernity, not with the limitations of his individual talent.

As is no doubt true of many in our generation, Derek Walcott first got his Dante through Eliot, who by the 1940s had established the literary canon with which any ambitious poet would have to contend. For Walcott, in *Epitaph for the Young*—published in 1949 when he was only nineteen—this meant writing a parody of *Little Gidding* in which Eliot himself (though very much alive in 1949) plays the "noble shade" who comes from another shore to scold and admonish the ephebe of St. Lucia.

> At which harsh words my heavy soul tears flooded,
> Nor had I near a handkerchief, but that noble shade
> Perceiving that my nose run, with natural artifice
> Lent me a corner of his gown and I blew gustily
>
> . . . .
>
> And as the geese go clanking across an autumn moon
> So that noise they make seems like a fallen chain
> So did my nose vibrate through the fiery shades[.]
> (in Balfour 1998, 225–26)

The iconoclast Caribbean poet eager to claim his connection to the Greats takes liberties with his sources. He defiles his master's flowing sleeve, pokes fun both at Dante's epic rhetoric and at Eliot's pomposity, "gustily" blowing his nose at all "the fiery shades" of European tradition.

This prankish levity becomes serious business in Walcott's later work, where conversation with the dead is a recurrent trope in the poet's bid to connect with the past and make room for his own present. In this effort, Walcott bypasses Eliot's mediation and goes back directly to Dante and Homer; like the revenants in their works, his ghosts are intimate *and* identifiable. In the 1990 *Omeros,* for instance, there is a brief encounter with James Joyce, an extended meeting with the protean (and in that way "compound") Homer / Omeros himself, and, most poignant, a conversation with Walcott's own father, Warwick, who died when the poet was only a year old. Walcott has often spoken about his childhood discovery of a notebook containing his father's transcribed poetry, and of his early sense that he was called to take up the literary work his father began but never achieved. To meet the ghost of Warwick, therefore, is to encounter his poetic vocation not through some "cara e buona imagine paterna" (*Inf* 15.83) but in the person of his actual father.

The meeting with the father had occurred as early as *Epitaph for the Young,* when the poet discerned among a crowd of moving shadows someone "whose face I sought through life": "I said / Bending my face to his / 'Are you here, Ser Brunetto?'" (Balfour 1998, 226). Walcott follows Eliot by making the effect of the scene purgatorial rather than infernal; he also removes the undercurrent of irony that characterizes *Inferno* 15. And so, Warwick's admonition to his son, despite its unmistakable echoes of Dante, is meant to be taken straight: "If Thou observe the Star that guides the mariner / Beyond the dubious haven of the promontory, you will please our Father."

Walcott replays this encounter twice in *Omeros.* The most significant of these moments occurs at the end of Book 1, when the poet wanders in memory to his childhood home on St. Lucia. Suddenly Warrick Walcott appears to tell his own story, and to claim his proper role in his son's vocation:

> "In this pale blue notebook where you found my verses"
> —my father smiled—"I appeared to make your life's choice,
> and the calling that you practice both reverses
>
> and honours mine from the moment it blent with yours."
>
> (1.xii.1)

In a departure from Dante in *Inferno* 15, Eliot in *Little Gidding,* and the smoky obscurity of Walcott's own *Epitaph for the Young,* here ghost and mortal walk through the town in broad sunlight, looking at the scene before them, and reminiscing about the city's past. It is in that explicitly social setting that father gives son his commission as a poet:

> "Measure the days you have left. Do just that labour
> which marries your heart to your right hand: simplify
> your life to one emblem, a sail leaving harbour,
>
> and a sail coming in."
>
> (1.xiii.2)

These words resonate with Brunetto's nautical imagery in *Inferno* 15 (already echoed in *Epitaph for the Young*); they also serve as an emblem of the poem we are in the process of reading, which on many levels is a voyage of exploration and return. Yet, as the conversation between father and son unfolds, it is clear that here the motive for metaphor is meant to be much larger than the acquisition of individual fame—a value that does not fare well in *Omeros.* Indeed, as Warwick makes clear about his own amateur efforts (and by extension, the more successful efforts of his son), true poetry is always to be preferred to mere acclaim. The poet must speak for others, especially for those who have neither scribe nor audience. Therefore, Walcott is to speak about the people of the island and their untold history. Looking at "the hills of infernal anthracite" visible from the town of Castries, Warwick urges his son to pay attention to the walking rhythms of the native women who carry baskets of coal down the mountainside, moving "like ants or angels." "They walk, you write," says Warwick: "give those feet a voice" in the "slow, ancestral beat" of verse:

> "Kneel to your load, then balance your staggering feet
> and walk up that coal ladder as they do in time,
> one bare foot after the next in ancestral rhyme.
>
> Because Rhyme remains the parenthesis of palms
> shielding a candle's tongue, it is the language's
> desire to enclose the loved world in its arms."
>
> (1.xiii.3)

Correcting Brunetto's glorification of literature as the way to make the individual self eternal, Warwick speaks instead about poetry's social mission; in effect, he picks up the mantle of Dante's Cacciaguida as he commissions the author of *Omeros* to tell the whole story. But instead of recording "those souls that unto fame are known" (*Par* 17.138), Walcott must attend on the contrary to those who are "unknown, raw, insignificant." This encounter ends with a deliberately comic reversal of epic tradition. Instead of the failed embrace we expect from one who is writing in the line of Homer, Virgil, and Dante, father and son now actually exchange a kiss, as if to seal the covenant of their "one voice." The shade of Warwick then disappears within the "alternating shades" of the street, reabsorbed into the magical realism of *Omeros*—a mythic phantasmagoria that requires no afterlife setting for conversations between the living and the dead.

Seamus Heaney's engagement with Dante is most evident in three books of his poetry: *Field Work* (1979), *Station Island* (1985), and *Seeing Things* (1991). His translation of the Ugolino episode at the end of *Field Work* draws an implicit connection between the tragic political landscape of Northern Ireland and the implacable hatred of Guelph and Ghibelline, Bianchi and Neri, in thirteenth-century Tuscany. Whereas the specifically political dimensions of Dante's work play no significant role in either Eliot or Walcott, they engage Heaney as fully as they did Osip Mandelstam and Anna Akhmatova. Reading Dante in translation in the 1970s, he said in a recent interview, meant recognizing "some of the conditions of Medieval Florence—the intensities, the factions, the personalities—as analogous to the Belfast situation. Farinata rising out of the tomb could be [Ian] Paisley." *Field Work* also contains the lyric "The Strand at Lough Beg," Heaney's elegy for Colum McCartney, a second-cousin who was murdered in the course of sectarian violence. With its epigraph a description of *Purgatory*'s "isoletta" (1.100–103), the elegy reworks Virgil's washing away of the infernal smudge that darkens the pilgrim's face. Heaney offers his own kinsman a similar gesture of cleansing and renewal:

> I turn because the sweeping of your feet
> Has stopped behind me, to find you on your knees
> With blood and roadside muck in your hair and eyes.
> Then kneel in front of you in brimming grass
> And gather up cold handfuls of the dew
> To wash you, cousin. I dab you clean with moss
> Fine as the drizzle out of a low cloud.

I lift you under the arms and lay you flat.
With rushes that shoot green again, I plait
Green scapulars to wear over your shroud.
(1979, 17–18)

The volume *Station Island* takes its title from the sequence of twelve poems at its center. Heaney describes this collection as "a sequence of dream encounters with familiar ghosts, set on Station Island on Lough Derg in Co. Donegal" (1985b, 18). His engagement with this traditional site of a penitential three-day vigil of fasting and prayer constitutes both a *rite de passage* and an occasion for self-confrontation, self-criticism, and, finally, liberation. The "familiar ghosts" the poet meets represent significant elements of his past, both familial and intellectual; they are also a series of alter egos—versions of what the poet himself might have become under different circumstances. Once again, Dante offered him a model for what he was trying to bring together: "the combination of personality, political fury, psychological realism. All the voices speaking, and the accusations flying, the rage and the intimacy. . . ."

Two of Heaney's old teachers appear, greeted with rueful affection, in an episode that recalls the meeting with Brunetto Latini. There are also encounters with William Carleton and Patrick Kavanaugh, poets who themselves made the Lough Derg pilgrimage the subject of their verse. Heaney notes in his essay "Envies and Identifications" (1985a) that Lough Derg was an overdetermined site, given the number of Irish writers who had already written about it. Somehow, however, Dante's *Purgatorio* allowed this landscape of pilgrimage to become fresh territory. Nonetheless, Heaney's ambivalence toward the traditional piety of Lough Derg, not to mention his whole Irish Catholic upbringing, is dramatized in several Station Island encounters, including the first and the last. Simon Sweeney, an "old Sabbath-breaker who has been dead for years" and a "mystery man" from the poet's youth admonishes him as he is about to begin the pilgrimage, "Stay clear of all processions." A priest he had known when a young man asks him, "what are you doing here?," mindful that Heaney had long ago "gotten over" Catholic piety: "all this you were clear of you walked into / over again." At the end of this extended sojourn with the dead, none other than James Joyce appears to cast aspersions on this "peasant pilgrimage" and to warn him off "any common rite."

Heaney is especially taken with violent, untimely deaths such as Dante assembles in Ante-Purgatory, at the bottom of the mountain. In Heaney's case, the ghosts are all victims of Protestant–Catholic violence who force him to confront his own complicity and cowardice. Colum McCartney, the cousin for whom he had written an elegy in *Field Work,* shows up now to indict the redemptive transformation of his murder that Heaney attempted in "The Strand at Lough Beg":

> You confused evasion and artistic tact.
> The Protestant who shot me through the head
> I accuse directly, but indirectly, you
> Who now atone perhaps upon this bed
> For the way you whitewashed ugliness and drew
> The lovely blinds of the Purgatorio
> And saccharined my death with morning dew.
> (Section viii)

Still another figure in this group is Francis Hughes, an IRA hunger striker who died in prison. After hearing Hughes's "voice from blight / and hunger," the poet slips into a surreal dream that figures his own "softly awash and blanching self-disgust": he cries out, "I repent / My unweaned life that kept me competent / To sleepwalk with connivance and mistrust." The dream seems at first to absolve the poet; nonetheless, he wakes with a sense of remorse that occasions yet another confession:

> I hate how quick I was to know my place
> I hate where I was born, hate everything
> That made me biddable and unforthcoming.
> (Section ix)

For all this self-conscious regret, *Station Island* does not end in a spirit of remorse but rather with poems that suggest the possibility of retrieval and return, the "need and chance to salvage / everything." In the final section of the poem, Heaney presents himself as a convalescent standing on the threshold of a new life. The sequence concludes with James Joyce boldly urging him to move on, to liberate himself from the political, religious, and even linguistic entanglements of his Irish past. Given the way Eliot's "familiar compound ghost" demeans the value of artistic achievement in favor of spiritual matters, it is significant that Heaney's ghost-ridden poem moves in the opposite direction, as Joyce charges him to swim out on his own, to "Let go, let fly, forget" (Section xii). The work concludes with a cleansing cloudburst that in effect brings the relief Heaney has been seeking all along. He is meant to give himself over, says Joyce, to "work lust."

Throughout *Station Island* the oppositions between life and art, politics and literature, historical responsibility and private fulfillment are presented through a multiplicity of ghostly encounters. Heaney himself identifies the core of the poem as a tension between two often contradictory commands. The claims of history, of the public and private past, of religion, are all given their due; yet, in the end, the poem grants Heaney permission to move beyond these terms and oppositions. The ghosts eloquently rehearse the claims of the past with force, but then fade into silence. The poet's own work begins afresh (see especially Oldcorn 1989 and O'Donoghue 1998).

The dead come to speak to these poets in a variety of ways: in Eliot's reconstruction of a wartime air raid; in Walcott's fluid dreamscape; in Heaney's Irish purgatory. For Charles Wright, however, the porous boundary between the dead and the living is none other than the poet's daytime landscape. Looked at hard enough, home territory opens up to the imagination, becomes the meeting place of the living and the dead. In contrast to James Merrill's conjuring of ghosts in "The Changing Light at Sandover," Wright knows that landscape serves as his "Ouija board": "When I write to myself, I'm writing to the landscape, and the landscape is a personification of the people on the other side. That would be my ideal audience. One writes for approval, in a strange way. And I'm trying to tell them that I understand and that I'm doing the best I can" (1988, 112). Many of his poems take as their theme a desire to reach the "other side," to recover the dead and to engage with them.

In the course of collecting and reissuing his work, Wright has understood himself to be writing a "trilogy of trilogies." "Sky Diving," the final poem in *Negative Blue,* the final trilogy, alludes to the *Comedy*'s last line at its very center when Wright speaks of his "subject" as "the form that moves the sun and the other stars." But it is in the second of these trilogies, *The World of the Ten Thousand Things,* that Dante is most frequently conjured through subtle allusion or outright reference. As Wright has said in an interview, Dante for him is the poet par excellence, "the great Buddhistic center of absolute attention and regard, the true magnetic field of seriousness toward which all real poems gravitate"

(1988, 178). Wright has especially been drawn to the luminosity of the *Paradiso:* "[t]he great poet of light is Dante. Everyone else is shadow" (1988, 22). Even to imagine an afterlife is to reckon with the *Comedy,* as we are explicitly told in "The Southern Cross."

> Thinking of Dante, I start to feel
> What I think are wings beginning to push out from my shoulder blades,
>
> And the firm pull of water under my feet.
> Thinking of Dante, I think of La Pia,
>   and Charles Martel
> And Cacciaguida inside the great flower of Paradise,
> And the thin stem of Purgatory
>   rooted in Hell.
>
> Thinking of Dante is thinking about the other side,
> And the other side of the other side.
> It's thinking about the noon noise and the daily light.
>
> (1990, 45)

There are many allusions to Dante in these poems: a bumblebee becomes Geryon in "Yard Journal," the first poem of the *Zone Journals* (1988); and "Laguna Dantesca" and "Hawaii Dantesca" from *The Southern Cross* offer brief riffs on moments in the *Comedy.* However, Wright's only direct confrontation with the poet takes place in *A Journal of the Year of the Ox.* The longest of his journal poems, it is a sequence of thirty-two entries; each one is dated, beginning with January 1985 and concluding on Christmas day of the same year. 1985 also marks the poet's own fiftieth year, and thus is the occasion for a series of memories and reappraisals. As in many of Wright's poems, we move among totemic landscapes: Eastern Tennessee (where he grew up), Italy (where he discovered poetry and art), and Virginia (where he now lives in the shadow of the Blue Ridge).

Visits and visitations are key events in the poem's "undernarrative," Wright's term for the disguised structural girding of the sequence (1995, 117). He recalls sites associated with what he calls America's "medieval" writers: Poe's room and Emily Dickinson's Amherst home; later he visits Petrarch's house at Arqua. But Wright himself also receives a visit. In the central poems of the sequence, all set in northern Italy, he experiences the possibility of a transcendence that he at once craves and avoids. Suddenly, his reveries are interrupted by the presence of a stranger:

Who is it here in the night garden,
  gown a transparent rose
Down to his ankles, great sleeves
Spreading the darkness around him wherever he steps,
Laurel corona encircling his red transparent headcap,
Pointing toward the Madonna?
Who else could it be,
  voice like a slow rip through silk cloth
In disapproval? *Brother,* he says, pointing insistently,
A sound of voices starting to turn in the wind and then disappear as though
Orbiting us, *Brother, remember the way it was*
In my time: nothing has changed:
Penitents terrace the mountainside, the stars hang in their bright courses
And darkness is still the dark:
  concentrate, listen hard,
Look to the nature of all things
And vanished into the oncoming, disappearing
Circle of voices, slipstreaming through the oiled evening.

Hmmm . . . Not exactly transplendent:
  Look to the nature of all things[.]

(1990, 168–69)

Wright's colloquial "Hmmm . . ." may register the reader's reaction as well: the encounter, and especially the mantra ("*Look to the nature of things*"), are, in fact, "Not exactly transplendent." Given the Buddhistic enlightened one spoken of in his prose, and the master of radiance reflected in his poetry, this ghostly Dante comes as a surprise and perhaps even a disappointment. His blessing seems strangely Lucretian—a word of advice more befitting the author of *De rerum natura* than the visionary of the *Paradiso.* Nonetheless, the encounter and its benediction are recalled toward the poem's end:

  there is a word, one word,
For each of us, circling and holding fast
In all that cascade and light.
Said once, or said twice,
  it gathers and waits its time to come back
To its true work:
  concentrate, listen hard.

(1990, 176)

Wright's Dantesque ghost is Brunetto and Cacciaguida compounded with the spirit of a Zen master. Recalling the *Paradiso*'s "cascade and light," the poet discovers how to "consider the nature of all things" as they present themselves in the here and now of familiar landscapes and quotidian reality—in the world of Wright's own ten thousand things.

Dante is a major presence in Gjertrud Schnackenberg's *A Gilded Lapse of Time*, a sequence of twenty poems set in the same Ravenna where Dante died and is entombed. It is a poem about lapses, glimpses, and breakage; about links and gaps between this world and the next. Dante does not appear personally, as he does to Wright; instead, he is intermittently addressed by Schnackenberg as she reflects on the ruins of Byzantium, on the interface between this world and the next, and on the possibilities of her own poetry. She ponders the effect of Dante's speech on her silences:

> I would lay open those years that I could not
> Speak. Years I could only thumb the page
> Into featureless velvet, unraveling the bleary gilt
> Where the kingdom had glinted but guttered out,
> Where I copied out your verses by hand
> In a foreign language, and as I wrote I could see
> Those rhymes throb down the length of the page
> And that sound—a glimpse of that sound,
> After which everything I had scribbled
> In my own hand came to a weightless bubble[.]
>
> (Section 15)

Throughout the sequence, there are beautiful and knowing invocations of Dante, as in the following lines:

> Where the night creation glittered—
> I looked, to try to fix it in my sight,
> I raised my eyes to the high wheels,
> I tried to turn with you to see
> That point at which the fixed stars
> Twinkle in translations,
> Where one motion and another cross,
> Where east and west mingle
> With unfamiliar orbits and constellations
> Before which we could grow
> Forgetful, as if our lives and deeds

No longer mattered—were it not that
We still hear that weeping there below.
(Section 19)

This last line returns to one of Schnackenberg's preoccupations, the relationship between poetry and pain. In this context she several times recalls *Inferno* 13: Dante's inadvertent rending of the thorn bush becomes her emblem of "the bubbling injury at the root of speech" (Section 14). We find a broken branch at the very outset of *A Gilded Lapse of Time;* so too at the poem's end, when she discovers that she can wound as well as be wounded. In a dream, Schnackenberg finds that she has inadvertently struck a honeycomb that figures sacred speech in general and Dante's poem in particular. At the dream's end, the poet in quick succession is struck by an angel, finds her mouth bloodied, and sees Dante's death mask; this mask then turns into a honeycomb whose words "were a stream of bees floating toward me in sunlight." Earlier in the sequence she had spoken matter of factly of the honeycombs that "a poet touches to his lips, / Seeking to cross the threshold, to signify a sacred conversation." Now, however, she speaks from experience, and her own initiation is marked by fear and pain.

When I opened your book I thought you spoke,

Or else it was Gabriel lifting to my lips
A tablespoon of golden, boiling smoke
So wounding to my mouth I turned my back

On the source of poetry, and then I woke.
(Section 20)

The burning honey in this final image recalls a previous mention of Isaiah's "mortifying coal, the supernatural ember / [that] had scorched his lips" (Section 8). Language and pain are connected for both prophet and poet; pain, in fact, is the price of speech. Seeking both revelation and power, Schnackenberg's densely packed lyrics enfold epic ambitions profoundly associated with Dante's accomplishment. His voice becomes her own—at least until she wakes.

Looking back at the various unexpected roles Dante has played in twentieth-century poetry, we now look forward to the unpredictable continuation of this story. Near the beginning of the nineteenth-century Dante revival, Shelley characterized the *Comedy* and its author as a fire long buried but now ready to burst into flame: "his very words are instinct with spirit; each is a spark, a burning atom of inextinguishable thought; and many yet lie covered in the ashes of their birth, and pregnant with a lightning which has yet found no conductor" (1891, 32–33). Over a hundred years later, in the 1930s, Mandelstam employed a futurist lexicon to claim that this medieval poem was in fact a rocket about to be launched: "It is unthinkable to read the cantos of Dante without aiming them in the direction of the present day. They were made for that. They are missiles for capturing the future" (1979, 420). Given Dante's preoccupation with precursors and peers, he would not have been surprised to learn that, among "la futura gente," it would be *poets* who most forcibly recognized him as their contemporary. Could even he, however, have guessed that his Florentine vernacular would have so fired the imagination of the Western world or enjoyed so long a poetic afterlife in English?

REWRITINGS: WORKS CITED

Alain de Lille. 1844–64. *Liber in distinctionibus dictionum theologicium.* In PL 210:686–1011.

Alighieri, Dante. 1966–67. *La Commedia secondo l'antica vulgata,* ed. Giorgio Petrocchi. 4 vols. Milan: Mondadori.

______. 1970–75. *The Divine Comedy.* Trans. and ed. Charles S. Singleton. 3 vols. in 6. Princeton, N.J.: Princeton University Press.

Anderson, William. 1972. *Ovid's "Metamorphoses"—Books 6–10.* Norman: University of Oklahoma Press.

Appiah, Kwame Anthony. 1995. "Race." In *Critical Terms for Literary Study.* Ed. Frank Lentricchia and Thomas McLaughlin. 2nd ed. Chicago: The University of Chicago Press. 274–87.

Arnulf of Orléans. 1932. *Allegoriae super Ovidii Metamorphosin.* In Fausto Ghisalberti, "Arnolfo D'Orléans: Un cultore di Ovidio nel secolo XII." *Memorie del reale istituto lombardo di scienze e lettere: Classe di lettere, scienze morali e storiche* 24, 2:157–234.

Augustine. 1844–64. *Enarrationes in psalmos.* In PL 36:67–1027.

Avallone, C. 1976. "Melville's 'Piazza.'" *ESQ: A Journal of the American Renaissance* 22:221–33.

Balfour, Mark. 1998. "The Place of the Poet: Dante in Walcott's Narrative Poetry." In *Dante's Modern Afterlife: Reception and Response from Blake to Heaney.* Ed. N. R. Havely. New York: St. Martin's Press. 223–41.

Barkan, Leonard. 1986. *The Gods Made Flesh: Metamorphosis and the Pursuit of Paganism.* New Haven, Conn.: Yale University Press.

Basile, Bruno. 1990. "Dante e l'idea di *peregrinatio.*" In *Il tempo e le forme: Studi letterari da Dante a Gadda.* Modena: Mucchi. 9–36.

Battistini, Andrea. 1986. "L'universo che si squaderna: Cosmo e simbologia del libro." *Letture classensi* 15:61–78.

Boitani, Piero. 1992. *L'ombra di Ulisse: Figure di un mito.* Bologna: Il Mulino.

______. 1994. *The Shadow of Ulysses: Figures of a Myth.* Trans. A. Weston. Oxford: Oxford University Press.

______. 1999. "The Shadow of Ulysses beyond 2001." *Comparative Criticism* 21:3–19.

Borges, Jorge Luis. 1964. "Odisea, Libro Vigésimo Tercero." In *El otro, lo mismo.* Buenos Aires: Emecé.

______. 1981. "El inmortal." In *El Aleph.* Madrid: Alianza. 7–28.

______. 1983. *Nueve ensayos dantescos.* Madrid: Espasa-Calpe.

______. 1999. "Herman Melville." *Selected Poems.* Ed. Alexander Coleman. New York, Viking. 376–77.

Bosco, Umberto. 1985. *Dante vicino.* Caltanissetta and Rome: Sciascia.

Boswell, Jackson Campbell. 1999. *Dante's Fame in England: References in Printed British Books, 1477–1640.* Newark: University of Delaware Press.

Brewer, Wilmon. 1941. *Ovid's "Metamorphoses" in European Culture.* Vol. 2. Francestown, N.H.: Marshal Jones.

Brownlee, Kevin. 1986. "Ovid's Semele and Dante's Metmorphosis: *Paradiso* XXI–XXII." MLN 101:147–56.

______. 1991. "Pauline Vision and Ovidian Speech in *Paradiso* 1." In *The Poetry of Allusion: Virgil and Ovid in Dante's "Commedia."* Ed. Rachel Jacoff and Jeffrey Schnapp. Stanford, Calif.: Stanford University Press. 202–13.

Bynum, Caroline Walker. 1991. "Material Continuity, Personal Survival, and the Resurrection of the Body: A Scholastic Discussion in Its Medieval and Modern Contexts." In *Fragmentation and Redemption: Essays on Gender and the Human Body in Medieval Religion.* New York: Zone Books. 245–56.

______. 1995. *The Resurrection of the Body in Western Christianity, 200–1336.* New York: Columbia University Press.

Caesar, Michael, ed. 1989. *Dante: The Critical Heritage 1314 (?)–1870.* London: Routledge.

Cambon, Glauco. 1969. "Dante's Presence in American Literature." *Dante's Craft: Studies in Language and Style.* Minneapolis: University of Minnesota Press. 119–45.

Cary, Rev. Henry Francis. 1847. *The Vision; or Hell, Purgatory, and Paradise of Dante Alighieri, Translated by the Rev. Henry Francis Cary, M.A., A New Edition, Corrected.* London: Henry G. Bohn.

Charity, A. C. 1974. "T. S. Eliot: The Dantean Recognitions." In *"The Waste Land" in Different Voices.* Ed. A. D. Moody. London: Edward Arnold. 117–62.

Chaucer, Geoffrey. 1987. *The Riverside Chaucer.* Ed. Larry D. Benson. Boston: Houghton Mifflin.

Chiarenza, Marguerite. 1975. "Pagan Images in the Prologue of the *Paradiso.*" *Proceedings of the Pacific Northwest Council on Foreign Languages* 26:133–36.

______. 1983. "Time and Eternity in the Myths of *Paradiso* XVII." In *Dante, Petrarch, Boccaccio: Studies in the Italian Trecento in Honor of Charles S. Singleton.* Ed. Anthony L. Pellegrini and Aldo S. Bernardo. Binghamton, N.Y.: Medieval and Renaissance Texts and Studies. 135–55.

Claasen, J. M. 1988. "Ovid's Poems of Exile. The Creation of a Myth and the Triumph of Poetry." *Antike und Abendland* 34:158–69.

Crane, Susan. 1999. "Anglo-Norman Cultures in England, 1066–1460." In *The Cambridge History of English Literature.* Ed. David Wallace. Cambridge: Cambridge University Press.

Curtius, Ernst Robert. 1953. *European Literature and the Latin Middle Ages.* Trans. Willard R. Trask. Princeton, N.J.: Princeton University Press.

Dickinson, Robert J. 1973. "The *Tristia:* Poetry of Exile." In *Ovid.* Ed. J. W. Binns. London: Routledge and Kegan-Paul. 154–90.

Ehlers, Wilhelm. 1988. "Poet und Exil. Zum Verständnis der Exildichtung Ovids." *Antike und Abendland* 34:144–57.

Eliot, T. S. [1929] 1965. *Dante.* London: Faber.

______. 1962. *The Complete Poems and Plays: 1909–50.* New York: Harcourt, Brace and World.

Ferguson, Everett. 1990. "Martyr, Martyrdom." In *The Encyclopedia of Early Christianity.* Ed. Everett Ferguson. New York and London: Garland. 575–79.

Ferguson, Margaret W. 1975. "Saint Augustine's Region of Unlikeness: The Crossing of Exile and Language." *The Georgia Review* 29:842–64.

Ferrucci, Franco. 1996. *The Life of God (as Told by Himself).* Chicago and London: The University of Chicago Press.

Foxe, John. 1570. *Actes and Monuments.* London: John Daye.

Fränkel, Hermann. 1945. *Ovid: A Poet between Two Worlds.* Berkeley: University of California Press.

Frend, W. H. C. 1967. *Martyrdom and Persecution in the Early Church.* New York: New York University Press.

Fulgentius. 1898. *Mitologiarum.* In *Fabii Planciadis Fulgentii V. C. Opera.* Ed. Rudolph Helm. Leipzig: Teubner. 1–80.

Galinsky, G. Karl. 1975. *Ovid's "Metamorphoses": An Introduction to the Basic Aspects.* Berkeley: University of California Press.

Gassman, Vittorio. 1992. *Ulisse e la balena bianca.* Milan: Longanesi.

Gilson, Étienne. 1949. *Dante the Philosopher.* Trans. David Moore. London: Sheed & Ward.

Giovanni del Virgilio. 1931. *Allegorie Librorum Ovidii Metamorphoseos.* In Fausto Ghisalberti. "Giovanni del Virgilio: Espositore delle *Metamorfosi.*" *Giornale dantesco* 34:1–110.

Giovannini, G. 1949. "Melville's *Pierre* and Dante's *Inferno.*" PMLA 64:70–78.

Gladstone, William Ewart. 1982. "Did Dante Study in Oxford?" *The Nineteeth Century* 8:1032–42.

Gollin, R. 1968. "*Pierre*'s Metamorphosis of Dante's *Inferno.*" *American Literature* 39:542–45.

Hales, John W. 1882 [January 1]. "Dante in England." *The Bibliographer: A Journal of Book-Lore* 2:37a–39b.

Heaney, Seamus. 1979. *Field Work.* London: Faber and Faber.

______. 1985a. "Envies and Identifications: Dante and the Modern Poet." *Irish University Review* 15.1:5–19.

______. 1985b. *Station Island.* New York: Farrar, Straus and Giroux.

______. 1991. *Seeing Things.* London: Faber and Faber.

———, trans. 2000. *Beowulf.* New York: Farrar, Straus and Giroux.

Hexter, Ralph J. 1986. *Ovid and Medieval Schooling.* Munich: Arbeo Gesellschaft.

Hollander, Robert. 1969. *Allegory in Dante's "Commedia."* Princeton, N.J.: Princeton University Press.

Iannucci, Amilcare A. 1984. "Fortuna, tempo, e l'esilio di Dante." In *Forma ed evento nella "Divina Commedia."* Rome: Bulzoni. 117–43.

______. 2001. "Firenze, città infernale." In *Dante: Da Firenze all'aldilà.* Ed. Michelangelo Picone. Florence: Franco Cesati. 217–32.

Jacobus de Voragine. 1993. *The Golden Legend.* Trans. William Granger Ryan. 2 vols. Princeton, N.J.: Princeton University Press.

Jacoff, Rachel, and Jeffrey T. Schnapp, eds. 1991. *The Poetry of Allusion: Virgil and Ovid in Dante's "Commedia."* Stanford, Calif.: Stanford University Press.

John of Garland [Giovanni di Garlandia]. 1933. *Integumenta Ovidii: Poemetto inedito del secolo XIII.* Ed. Fausto Ghisalberti. Messina and Milan: Principato.

John of Salisbury. [1909] 1965. *Ioannis Saresberiensis episcopi Carnotensis Policratici.* Ed. Clement C. J. Webb. 2 vols. Frankfurt: Minerva.

Klopsch, Paul. 1967. *Pseudo-Ovidius De Vetula.* Leiden: Brill.

Ladner, Gerhart B. 1967. "*Homo Viator:* Medieval Ideas on Alienation and Order." *Speculum* 42:233–59.

Leland, Blake. 1992. "'Siete voi qui, Ser Brunetto?' Dante's *Inferno* 15 as a Modernist Topic Place." *ELH* 59:965–86.

Leslie, Roy F., ed. 1985. *The Wanderer.* Exeter: University of Exeter Press.

Malory, Sir Thomas. 1977. *Works.* Ed. Eugène Vinaver. 2nd ed. Oxford: Oxford University Press.

Mandelstam, Osip. 1979. "Conversation about Dante." In *The Complete Critical Prose and Letters.* Trans. Jane Gary Harris and Constance Link. Ann Arbor, Mich.: Ardis. 397–442.

Mathews, J. C. 1958. "Melville's Reading of Dante." *Furman Studies* N.S. 6:1–8.

______. 1965. "The Interest in Dante Shown by Nineteenth-Century American Men of Letters." *Studi americani* 11:77–104.

Mazzoni, Guido. 1964. "Il canto 1 del *Paradiso.*" In *Letture dantesche.* Ed. Giovanni Getto. Florence: Sansoni. 1351–64.

Mazzotta, Giuseppe. 1993. "Theology and Exile." *Dante's Vision and the Circle of Knowledge.* Princeton, N.J.: Princeton University Press. 174–96.

McDougal, Stuart Y. 1988. "T. S. Eliot's Metaphysical Dante." In *Dante among the Moderns.* Ed. Stuart Y. McDougal. Chapel Hill: University of North Carolina Press. 57–81.

McElderry, Bruce. 1972. *Max Beerbohm.* New York: Twayne.

Melville, Herman. 1972. *Moby-Dick.* Ed. Harold Beaver. Harmondsworth: Penguin.

______. 1990. *White Jacket, or, the World in a Man-of-War.* Oxford and New York: Oxford University Press.

Milbank, Alison. 1998. *Dante and the Victorians.* Manchester: Manchester University Press.

Nardi, Bruno. 1949. "L'immortalità dell'anima." *Dante e la cultura medievale.* Bari: Laterza. 284–308.

Newman, Lea Bertani Vozar. 1993. "Melville's Copy of Dante: Evidence of New Connections between the *Commedia* and *Mardi.*" In *Studies in the American Renaissance.* Ed. J. Myerson. Charlottesville: University Press of Virginia. 305–338.

O'Donoghue, Bernard. 1998. "Dante's Versatility and Seamus Heaney's Modernism." In *Dante's Modern Afterlife: Reception and Response from Blake to Heaney.* Ed. Nick Havely. Houndmills: Macmillan. 242–57.

Oldcorn, Anthony. 1989. "Approssimazioni e incontri: Il dantismo di Seamus Heaney." *Letture classensi* 18:261–84.

Ovid. 1976. *"Metamorphosen": Kommentar, Buch VI–VII.* Ed. Franz Bömer. Heidelberg: Universitätsverlag.

______. 1984. *Metamorphoses.* Trans. Frank Justus Miller. Rev. G. P. Goold. 3rd ed. Cambridge, Mass.: Harvard University Press.

______. 1988. *Tristia and Ex Ponto.* Trans. Arthur L. Wheeler. Rev. G. P. Goold. 2nd ed. Cambridge, Mass.: Harvard University Press.

______. 1989. *Fasti.* Trans. James George Frazer. Rev. G. P. Goold. 2nd ed. Cambridge, Mass.: Harvard University Press.

Padoan, Giorgio. 1971. "Marsia." In ED 3:842–43.

Parodi, E. G. 1957. *Lingua e letteratura.* Ed. Gianfranco Folena. Venice: Neri Pozza.

Pasquazi, Silvio. [1966] 1985. *All'eterno dal tempo: Studi danteschi.* 3rd ed. Rome: Bulzoni.

Peter Lombard. 1844–64. *Commentarium in Psalmos.* In PL 191:31–1296.

Picone, Michelangelo. 1992. "*Auctoritas* classica e salvezza cristiana: Una lettura tipologica di *Purgatorio* XXII." *Italianistica* 21:379–95.

______. 1993. "L'Ovidio di Dante." In *Dante e la "bella scola" di poesia: Autorità e sfida poetica.* Ed. Amilcare A. Iannucci. Ravenna: Longo. 107–44.

______. 1994. "Dante argonauta: La ricerca di miti ovidiani nella *Commedia.*" In *Ovidius redivivus: Von Ovid zu Dante.* Ed. Michelangelo Picone and Bernhard Zimmermann. Stuttgart: Metzler & Poeschel.

______. 1997. "Dante and the Classics." In *Dante: Contemporary Perspectives.* Ed. Amilcare A. Iannucci. Toronto: University of Toronto Press. 51–73.

______. 1999. "Dante e i miti." In *Dante: Mito e poesia.* Ed. Michelangelo Picone and Tatiana Crivelli. Florence: Franco Cesati. 21–32.

______. 2000. "Il *prosimetrum* della *Vita Nova.*" *Letteratura italiana antica* 2:17–26.

______. 2001. "Canto XIX." In *Lectura Dantis Turicensis: Purgatorio.* Ed. Georges Güntert and Michelangelo Picone. Florence: Franco Cesati. 287–306.

Pseudo-Ovidius. 1967. *De vetula.* Ed. Paul Klopsch. Leiden and Cologne: Brill.

Pym, Barbara. 1978. *Excellent Women.* New York: Plume / Penguin.

Rahn, Helmut. 1958. "Ovids elegische Epistel." *Antike und Abendland* 7:105–20.

Renucci, Paul. 1949. "Dante et le mythe de Marsyas." *Bulletin de la société d'études dantesques* 1:21–33.

Ronconi, Alessandro. 1964. "Per Dante interprète dei poeti latini." StD 41:5–44.

Schless, H. H. 1960. "Flaxman, Dante, and Melville's *Pierre.*" *Bulletin of the New York Public Library* 64:65–82.

______. 1961. "*Moby-Dick* and Dante. A Critique and Time Scheme." *Bulletin of the New York Public Library* 65:289–312.

Schnackenberg, Gjertrud. 1992. *A Gilded Lapse of Time.* New York: Farrar, Straus and Giroux.

Schnapp, Jeffrey T. 1986. *The Transfiguration of History at the Center of Dante's "Paradise."* Princeton, N.J.: Princeton University Press.

______. 1991. "Dante's Ovidian Self-Correction in *Paradiso* XVII." In *The Poetry of Allusion: Vergil and Ovid in Dante's "Commedia."* Eds. Rachel Jacoff and Jeffrey T. Schnapp. Stanford, Calif.: Stanford University Press.

Sealts, M. 1988. *Melville's Reading: A Check-List of Books Owned and Borrowed.* Rev. ed. Columbia: University of South Carolina Press.

Shelley, Percy Bysse. 1891. *A Defense of Poetry*. Ed. Albert S. Cook. Boston: Ginn and Co.

Singleton, Charles S. 1957. *Commedia: Elements of Structure*. Cambridge, Mass.: Harvard University Press.

______. 1958. *Journey to Beatrice*. Cambridge, Mass.: Harvard University Press.

Smarr, Janet L. 1991. "Poets of Love and Exile." In *Dante and Ovid: Essays in Intertextuality*. Ed. Madison U. Sowell. Binghamton, N.Y.: Medieval and Renaissance Texts and Studies. 139–51.

Smithers, G. V. 1957–59. "The Meaning of the *Seafarer* and the *Wanderer*." *Medium Aevum* 26:137–53; 28:1–22.

Smolak, Kurt. 1978. "Der verbannte Dichter (Identifizierung mit Ovid im Mittelalter und Neuzeit)." *Wiener Studien* 91:158–91.

Sowell, Madison U., ed. 1991. *Dante and Ovid: Essays in Intertextuality*. Binghamton, N.Y.: Medieval and Renaissance Texts and Studies.

Stroh, Wilfried. 1981. "Tröstende Musen: Zur literaturhistorischen Stellung und Bedeutung von Ovids Exilgedichten." *Aufstieg und Niedergang der römischen Welt* 31:2638–84.

Taine, H. A. 1871. *History of English Literature*. Trans. H. Van Laun. 2 vols. New York: Holt and Williams.

______. 1885. *Notes sur l'Angleterre*. 8th ed. Paris: Hachette.

Tennyson, Alfred. 1969. *Tennyson: A Selected Edition*. Ed. C. Ricks. London: Longman.

Toynbee, Paget. 1909. *Dante in English Literature from Chaucer to Cary (c. 1380–1844)*. 2 vols. London: Methuen.

______. 1910. *Dante Alighieri: His Life and Works*. 4th ed. London: Methuen.

Venturi, Luigi. 1874. *Le similitudini dantesche: Ordinate, illustrate, e confrontate*. Florence: Sansoni.

Viarre, Simone. 1982. "Exil ovidien, exil médiéval." In *Présence d'Ovide*. Ed. Roger Chavallier. Paris: Les Belles Lettres. 261–71.

Viscusi, Robert. 1986. *Max Beerbohm, or The Dandy Dante*. Baltimore: John Hopkins University Press.

Walcott, Derek. 1990. *Omeros*. New York: Farrar, Straus and Giroux.

Wallace, David. 1993. "Dante in English." In *The Cambridge Companion to Dante*. Ed. Rachel Jacoff. Cambridge: Cambridge University Press. 237–58.

______. 1999. "Dante in Somerset: Ghosts, Historiography, Periodization." *New Medieval Literatures* 3:9–38.

Wright, Charles. 1988. *Halflife: Improvisations and Interviews, 1977–87.* Ann Arbor: University of Michigan Press.

______. 1990. *The World of the Ten Thousand Things: Poems, 1980–1990.* New York: Farrar, Straus and Giroux.

______. 1995. *Quarter Notes: Improvisations and Interviews.* Ann Arbor: University of Michigan Press.

Wright, N. 1960. "*Pierre:* Herman Melville's *Inferno.*" *American Literature* 32:167–81.

Young, P. 1991. "The Machine in Tartarus: Melville's *Inferno.*" *American Literature* 63:208–24.

NOTES ON CONTRIBUTORS

JOHN AHERN's numerous articles on Dante have appeared in PMLA, *Romanic Review, Dante Studies, Parnassus,* and *American Poetry Review.* He holds the Dante Antolini chair of Italian Letters at Vassar College and is currently vice president of the Dante Society of America.

ALBERT RUSSELL ASCOLI is Gladys Arata Terrill Distinguished Professor in the Department of Italian Studies of the University of California, Berkeley. He is the author of *Ariosto's Bitter Harmony: Crisis and Evasion in the Italian Renaissance* (Princeton University Press, 1987), and of numerous essays. With Victoria Kahn, he edited *Machiavelli and the Discourse of Literature* (Cornell University Press, 1993). He is completing work on a study of the career of Dante Alighieri, entitled *Authority in Person: Dante and the Emergence of Modern Authorship.*

ZYGMUNT G. BARAŃSKI is Serena Professor of Italian at the University of Cambridge and a Fellow of New Hall. He has written extensively on Dante, on medieval Italian literature, and on modern Italian culture. He is the editor of *The Italianist.*

TEODOLINDA BAROLINI is Lorenzo Da Ponte Professor of Italian and Chair of the Department of Italian at Columbia University. She is the fifteenth President of the Dante Society of America (1997–2003), and the author of *Dante's Poets: Textuality and Truth in the "Comedy"* (Princeton University Press, 1984; Italian trans. Bollati Boringhieri, 1993) and *The Undivine "Comedy": Detheologizing Dante* (Princeton University Press, 1992; Italian trans. Feltrinelli, 2003). She is working on issues of gender in medieval Italian literature and a commentary to Dante's lyrics for the Biblioteca Universale Rizzoli.

PIERO BOITANI is Chair of Comparative Literature at the University of Rome "La Sapienza." He is a fellow of the British Academy and the

Accademia Europea, and in 2002 received the Feltrinelli Prize for Literary Criticism. His recent publications include *The Shadow of Ulysses: Figures of a Myth* (Oxford University Press, 1994) and *The Bible and Its Rewritings* (Oxford University Press, 1999).

STEVEN BOTTERILL is Associate Professor of Italian Studies and Associate Dean of the Undergraduate Division at the University of California, Berkeley. His publications on Dante include *Dante and the Mystical Tradition: Bernard of Clairvaux in the "Commedia"* (Cambridge University Press, 1994), an edition and translation of the *De vulgari eloquentia* (Cambridge University Press, 1996), and numerous articles.

GIULIANA CARUGATI is Assistant Professor of Italian and Comparative Literature at Emory University. Her publications on Dante include *Dalla menzogna al silenzio* (Il Mulino, 1991), and she is currently working on a book on Dante's Beatrice, *Il ragionare della carne.*

GARY P. CESTARO is Associate Professor of Italian and Comparative Literature at DePaul University. He has published several articles on Dante and grammar and is the author of the forthcoming *Dante and the Grammar of the Nursing Body* (University of Notre Dame Press). He is currently editing a collection of essays, *Queer Italia: Same-Sex Desire in Italian Literature and Film* (forthcoming, Palgrave / St. Martin's).

ALISON CORNISH is Associate Professor of Italian in the Department of Romance Languages and Literatures at the University of Michigan. She is the author of *Reading Dante's Stars* (Yale University Press, 2000), and articles on Dante. Her current research is in the area of the culture of translation in the thirteenth and fourteenth centuries.

ROBERT M. DURLING was educated at Harvard and has taught at Haverford, Cornell, and the University of California at Santa Cruz, from which he retired in 1993. He recently translated Dante's *Purgatorio* (with introductions and notes by Ronald L. Martinez and Robert M. Durling, Oxford University Press, 2003).

GUGLIELMO GORNI teaches Italian philology at the University of Rome "La Sapienza." His research interests include meter, Leon Battista

Alberti, and literature of the sixteenth century. His publications on Dante include *Il Dante perduto: Storia vera di un falso* (Einaudi, 1994), *Dante nella selva* (Pratiche, 1995 and 2002), *Dante prima della "Commedia"* (2001), and a new edition, with commentary, of the *Vita Nova* (Einaudi, 1996).

MANUELE GRAGNOLATI is Lecturer in Italian Literature at the University of Oxford. He has written articles on Dante, Bonvesin da la Riva, Matteo Maria Boiardo, Giovanni Pascoli, and Filippo Tommaso Marinetti. He is currently completing a book manuscript entitled *Experiencing the Afterlife: Body and Soul in Dante, Bonvesin da la Riva, and Medieval Culture.*

PETER S. HAWKINS is Professor of Religion at Boston University and directs the Luce Program in Scripture and Literary Arts. He is author of *Dante's Testaments: Essays in Scriptural Imagination* (Stanford University Press, 1999) and co-editor with Rachel Jacoff of *The Poets' Dante: Twentieth-Century Reflections* (Farrar, Straus and Giroux, 2001).

RONALD HERZMAN is State University of New York Distinguished Teaching Professor of English at the College at Geneseo. He is the author, with William Cook, of *The Medieval Worldview* (Oxford University Press, 1983) and, with Richard Emmerson, of *The Apocalyptic Imagination in Medieval Literature* (University of Pennsylvania Press, 1992). His recent work on Dante includes "Dante and the Apocalypse" (in *The Apocalypse in the Middle Ages*), *Visibile Parlare:* Dante's *Purgatory* and Luca Signorelli's San Brizio Frescoes" (in *Studies in Iconography*), and, with Gary Townsley, "Squaring the Circle: *Paradiso* 33 and the Poetics of Geometry" (in *Traditio*).

AMILCARE A. IANNUCCI is Professor of Comparative Literature and Director of the Humanities Centre at the University of Toronto. He is the author of numerous books and articles on various topics, focusing especially on issues of literary and cultural appropriation and reception. In particular, he has written extensively on Dante, including *Forma ed evento nella "Divina Commedia"* (Bulzoni, 1984), *Dante e la "bella scola" della poesia* (Longo, 1993), and the forthcoming *Dante, Cinema, and Television.*

RACHEL JACOFF is Margaret Deffenbaugh and LeRoy Carlson Chair of Comparative Literature and Professor of Italian Studies at Wellesley College. She is the editor of *The Cambridge Companion to Dante* (Cambridge University Press, 1993) and, with Peter S. Hawkins, *The Poets' Dante: Twentieth-Century Reflections* (Farrar, Straus and Giroux, 2001).

CHRISTOPHER KLEINHENZ is the Carol Mason Kirk Professor of Italian Literature at the University of Wisconsin–Madison. His books and edited volumes include *The Early Italian Sonnet* (Milella, 1986), *Medieval Studies in North America* (Medieval Institute Publications, 1982), *Saint Augustine, the Bishop* (Garland, 1994), and *Fearful Hope* (University of Wisconsin Press, 1999). He is also the co-translator of *Il Fiore and il Detto d'Amore, Attributable to Dante.* He serves as Editor of *Dante Studies.*

JESSICA LEVENSTEIN has published work on Dante and Ovid, the classical tradition in the Italian Middle Ages, and Boccaccio. She teaches at the Horace Mann School in New York City.

RONALD L. MARTINEZ is Professor of Italian Studies at Brown University. Among other publication projects, he is collaborating with Robert M. Durling on an edition, with translation and commentary, of Dante's *Divine Comedy* for Oxford University Press (*Inferno,* 1996; *Purgatorio,* 2003; *Paradiso* in preparation).

GIUSEPPE MAZZOTTA is Sterling Professor of Italian at Yale University and Chair of the Department of Italian. He is the author of *Dante, Poet of the Desert: History and Allegory in the Divine Comedy* (Princeton University Press, 1979) and *Dante's Vision and the Circle of Knowledge* (Princeton University Press, 1993), as well as a number of essays. He has also edited *Critical Essays on Dante* (Hall, 1991). He is at present finishing a biography of Dante.

SUSAN NOAKES is Professor of French and Italian at the University of Minnesota, Twin Cities, where she serves as director of the Center for Medieval Studies. She works on the relations between literature and political, economic, and social history in the late Middle Ages and early Renaissance. She has long been interested in the character and history of interpretive practices.

Lino Pertile is Professor of Italian Literature at Harvard University. He is the author of *La puttana e il gigante: Dal cantico dei cantici al Paradiso terrestre di Dante* (Longo, 1998), and the co-editor of *The Cambridge History of Italian Literature* (Cambridge University Press, 1999).

Michelangelo Picone is Professor of Italian Literature at the University of Zurich. He has published extensively in the field of the lyric and narrative traditions of the Middle Ages, from the troubadours to Dante and Petrarch, and from the Fabliaux to Boccaccio's *Decameron.* He has recently edited the *Lectura Dantis Turicensis,* a complete reading of the one hundred cantos of Dante's *Divine Comedy* (Cesati, 2000 / 2002).

F. Regina Psaki is the Giustina Family Professor of Italian Language and Literature at the University of Oregon. She has published on Dante, Boccaccio, chivalric romance in Old French and Old Italian, and feminist medieval studies. Her work in progress includes a project on Dante's Beatrice in the *Commedia,* and another on medieval misogynist writing, both serious and parodic.

H. Wayne Storey is Professor of Italian and Medieval Studies, and Director of Medieval Studies at Indiana University. He has published issues in textual editing, pre-Dantesque poetry, manuscript studies, and Trecento literary history. His recent work focuses on thirteenth-and fourteenth-century manuscript traditions and editorial features of medieval codices. He is currently collaborating on the commentary and facsimile-interpretive editions of the *Rerum vulgarium fragmenta* for the seventh centenary of Petrarch's birth (2004).

David Wallace is Judith Rodin Professor of English at the University of Pennsylvania. He is editor of *The Cambridge History of Medieval English Literature* and, with Carolyn Dinshaw, of *The Cambridge Companion to Medieval Women's Writing.* His most recent book was *Chaucerian Polity* (Stanford University Press, 1997), and his next is provisionally entitled *Placing Premodernism.*

INDEX

Adam; creation of, 283, 290*f;* and Eve, 266, 338, 392, 443, 449*n*10
Adultatores, 259, 262, 264, 270, 271
Aeneid (Aen) (Virgil), 3, 5, 45, 173–74, 182
aerial bodies, xiv, 125–26, 192, 202, 205
Ahern, John, x, xi, 1–15
air, 173, 175, 216–17
Akhmatova, Anna, 456
Alan of Lille (Alain de Lille), 91, 93, 213–14, 217
Albert the Great, 97, 154, 194, 208*n*17, 335
Albertus Magnus, 49, 172, 173, 177, 213, 218
Alexander IV, Pope, 156
Alfie, Fabian, 251
Alighieri, Dante; developing beyond courtly poet, xii, 66–89; in England, xvii, 422–31, 431*nn*1–3, 432*nn*4–6, 433*f*–434*f;* family lineage of, 244, 246–50, 256*nn*8–10, 257*nn*11–12, 258*n*13; father of, xiv–xv, 243, 257*n*12, 258*n*12; guild chosen by, 249, 258*n*14; handwritten manuscripts of, 1; marriage of, 244–47, 256*nn*9–10, 257*n12*, 258*n*13; as medieval Christian, 126; mystical qualifications of, 146, 148, 151*n*5, 151*n*8; Ovid, and, x, xvi, 389–407, 407*nn*1–8; as poet of love, 211, 220; *poeta* v. *personaggio,* 147, 150, 213; poetry on death of, 2–3; as reader/author, 274, 349–62, 362*nn*1–2, 363*nn*3–6, 364*n*7, 365*nn*8–15, 366*nn*16–21, 367*nn*22–30, 368nn31–32; readers of, xvi, 7, 8, 349–62, 362*nn*1–2, 363*nn*3–6, 364*n*7, 365*nn*8–15, 366*nn*16–21, 367*nn*22–30, 368nn31–32, 403; self-exegesis of, 350, 357, 359, 363*n*3; visual arts and, 274–84, 284*nn*1–2, 285*nn*3–7, 286*nn*8–10, 287*f*–92*f,* 287f–292f
Alighieri, Iacopo, 6, 170
Alighieri, Pietro, 5, 213, 217, 226*n*2, 267, 429–30
amatory language, 119
Amor, che movi tua vertù da cielo, 224
Amor che ne la mente, 224
amore, use of term, 104
Andrea de' Mozzi (bishop), 98, 101
anima mundi, 216–17
Antichrist, 334, 339, 447
Antiochus, collaboration with Jason (High Priest), 304
Aphrodite, 215–16, 217, 221, 403
apocalyptic tradition, xvi, 301, 321–22; eschatology v., 346*n*1; in literature, 346*n*1; in Middle Ages, 335–36; in *Purg,* xvi, 336–42; Saint Francis in the portrayal of Bonaventure, and, 321–22, 324–26, 332*n*5, 333*n*6; Trinity as basis for, 335
Apollo, 408–10, 411–14, 416, 419*n*1, 419*n*8, 420*n*15, 420*nn*12–13
Apostle's letters, 265
Aquinas, Thomas, xiii, xiv, 49, 85; in Circle/Heaven of Sun, 152–55, 162, 164–68, 320, 322, 328–29, 341–42; Dante's eschatology indebted to, 347*nn*6–7, 344–45; Kenelm Foster on, 342; Jews and, 313, 316*n*11; plurality v. unicity of forms and, 193–94, 196–200, 203–4, 206*n*6, 207*n*9, 207*nn*12–13, 207*n*15, 208*n*17, 210*n*24; on pregnancy, 180; on Saint Francis, in *Par* 11, 276–77; on sodomy, 91, 102*n*1; on vapor, 177–78
Arab scholars, 335
Argonauts, 439–40, 445

Aristotle, 49, 78, 85, 87*n*7, 156; *Convivio* and, 49; *De generatione animalum* by, 197; *De somno et vigilia* by, 335; erotic *pneuma* in, 218; four elements of, 172–73; *Metaphysics* by, 49, 443, 449*n*11; *Meteorologica* by, 173, 177, 178, 180; on nature, 97; neo-Aristotelian debates and, 167; v. Neoplatonism, 67; Parisian neo-Aristotelians and, 156; *Physics* by, 167
arithmetic, 154, 156, 157
Arius, 158, 165, 330–31
Ark of the covenant, 278
Arnaut Daniel, 452–53
Ars poetica, Comedy as, 144–45, 151*n*3
arts, visual, Dante and, 274–84, 284*nn*1–2, 285*nn*3–7, 286*nn*8–10, 287*f*–292*f*
Ascoli, Albert Russell, xvi, 349–68
astrology, 46, 334–35
astronomy, 172
Auden, W. H., 451
audience. *See* reader(s)
Auerbach, Erich, 249, 257*n*12, 326–27
Augustine, Saint, 218; *anima mundi* and, 216; on body/flesh, 190*n*1; Book of Wisdom and, 330; *Confessions* by, 185; on erotic activity, 265–66; on Lord's Prayer, 184–85
Augustus, 393
avarice, sin of, 65, 182
Averroës, 156–57, 164, 167
Avicenna, 167, 197

Balduino, Armando, 22
Ballata, 27, 28–30, 37*n*20, 37*n*25
banking, Florentine, 244, 246, 248, 257*n*11
Baptistery; Florentine, mosaics in, 276, 282–84, 284*n*2, 286*nn*9–10, 289*f*–292*f;* Orthodox/Arian, mosaics in, 280
Barański, Zygmunt, xv, 181, 259–73
Barbi, Michele; Dante's lyrics and, 86*n*1; editing of *Vita Nova* by, 16, 18–19, 21, 28, 29, 30, 33, 34*n*1, 35*n*6, 36*nn*15–17, 36*n*19, 47–48, 53–54, 55*n*1, 365*n*12; *Non mi poriano giammai fare ammenda* and, 18–20; *tenzone* by, xiv–xv; on *tenzone* of Dante with Forese, 242–43
Barilli, Rossi, 90
Barolini, Teodolinda, ix–xviii, 65–89, 114*n*3, 210*n*25, 368*n*31
Barth, Karl, 347*n*8
battlefield, death on, 171, 173
beatitude, intellectual/philosophical, 157, 446
Beatrice; Cacciaguida's replacement of, 113; cosmic, 217; Dante's mind and, 74, 87*n*5; death of, 109–11, 302; v. *Donna petra,* 86; eschatology and, 337–38; idea of, 212; interview with, 415; introduced in *Inf* 2, 213; love and, xiii, 109, 111–13, 115–30, 217–18, 356–57, 396; Nebuchadnezzar, and, 358; nobilizing effects of, 24–25; pilgrim in love with, 104, 110; "poetic theology" and, 211; reassignment of prophetic encounter from, 13; showing throne prepared for Henry VII, 279–80, 285*n*7; silent v. talkative, 66, 82, 87*n*2, 109; as soul/love/intelligence, 217–18
beauty, 79, 83, 86, 88*n*10
Beck, Friedrich, 48–49
Beckett, Samuel, 451
Bede, 154
Bédier, Joseph, 52
Beerbohm, Max, 422–23, 431*n*1, 431*n*3, 433*f*–434*f*
Belacqua, 189
Belfast, compared to Florence, 456
Bello Ferrantini, 246
Benevento, Battle of, 245, 305, 334
Benvenuto da Imola, 179, 311–12, 318*n*32
Beowulf, 431, 432*n*6
Bernard of Clairvaux, 150, 327–28, 333*n*9
Bernard, Saint, 110–13, 309
Bertrand le Got, 310
Bessarion, Cardinal, 49
Bible, xv, 426, 448
Bice, 218, 220, 224
binary opposition, gender based on, 95, 102*n*8
Bishop, John, 426

Black Guelph faction, 245, 310, 405
Black Sea, 397–98, 400
blood, 216
boat, analogy of autonomous, 122
Boccaccio, Giovanni, 3–4, 5, 6, 13; *Comedy* and, 3–4, 6, 13, 98; *Corbaccio* by, 78; on Dante's poetic development, 21; *Decameron* by, 69–70, 81–82, 87*n*2, 94, 102*n*4, 362, 367*n*30; male freedom and, 69–70; proto-feminism and, 67; *Trattatello in laude di Dante* by, 3–4; *Vita Nova* and, 31, 32
Bodmer Foundation, 51, 55*n*5
body(ies); aerial v. earthly, xiv, 125–26, 192, 202, 205; *anima mundi* as form of, 216–17; Augustine on, 190*n*1; critical "turn toward," 115, 130*n*1; Dante and, x, xii, xiv; Dante Studies (DS) on, 116–17; female, 116; v. flesh, in *Purg*, 183–90, 190*n*1, 191*n*2, 191*n*4; position during prayer, 186–87; posthumous fate of, 171; recent scholarship on, 115–16; relationship to soul, 67, 414–15, 420*n*13; resurrection of, 157, 203, 204; sharing of one space by two, 120–21; usefulness of, in traversing Hell, 191*n*2
Boethius, 49, 154; *Consolation of Philosophy* by, 100, 330; *De Trinitate* by, 160, 168*n*4; on eternal woman, 214; *Philosophia* of, 66; on nature, 97; Platonic repertoire of symbols in, 213; *Providentia/Philosophia* of, 214, 221
Boitani, Piero, xvii, 435–50
Bologna, Camera Actorum collection in, 20, 38*f*–39*f*
Bonaccorsio di Rombolini, 19
Bonaventura Berlinghieri, 276
Bonaventure, Saint, xiii, xiv, 319*n*36; in Circle/Heaven of Sun, 152–54, 156–57, 160, 162–65, 168*n*2, 168*n*7, 321–22, 324–26, 332*n*5, 333*n*6; *Collationes in Hexaemeron* by, 154–57, 160, 163, 168*n*2; plurality v. unicity of forms and, 193–94, 204, 206*n*7, 207*n*8; on textural production, 365*n*8
Bonconte da Montefeltro, 171–76, 178–79
Boniface VIII, Pope, 111, 303–4, 311–12, 318*n*30, 334
Bono Giamboni, 170
Book of Wisdom (Solomon), 156, 329–30
Borges, Jorge Luis, 436–37
Boswell, Jackson Campbell, 426
Boswell, John, 96–97
Botterill, Steven, xiii, 143–51
Boyde, Patrick, 80, 86*n*1, 87*n*7, 88*n*10, 179, 197, 208*n*17
Branca, Vittore, 1
Brewer, Wilmon, 419*n*2
Brideshead Revisited (Waugh), 425
Brownlee, Kevin, ix, 418*n*1
Bruce-Jones, John, 202
Brugnolo, Furio, 22, 35*n*8
Brunetto Latini, 94, 103*n*10, 170, 425, 451–52, 455, 457
Bruni, Leonardo, 314
Bubwith, Nicholas, 428–29
Buddhism, 459, 461, 462
Busnelli, Giovanni, xiv, 193, 198–99
Bynum, Caroline Walker, 67, 195, 206*nn*1–2, 206*n*5, 207*nn*11–12

Caccia da Castello, 27
Cacciaguida, 107, 395; Beatrice, replacement by, 113; boat analogy of, 122; knighting of, 248; pilgrim's last encounter with, 394, 400–402; prophecy of pilgrim's exile by, 312; Warwick, speaking like, 455
Caesar, Julius, 93, 285*n*7, 315, 319*n*38, 340–41
Caiaphas, 304–6
Cambon, Glauco, 436
Cancelleresca (notarile script), 12
Cangrande della Scala, 4; Dante's *Epistle to*, 3, 350–51, 357, 359–62, 363*n*3, 367*nn*24–25, 367*nn*27–28, 367*n*30, 368*n*31
Canzoni, 27, 30–34, 37*n*21, 37*n*23, 37*n*25; *Amor, che movi tua vertù da cielo*, as "terrestrial," 224; *Amor, da che convein pur ch'io mi doglia*, 106; *Così nel mio parlar voglio esser*

aspro, 225–26, 227*n*7; courtly, 80; *Da poi che la Natura ha fine posto* (Cino da Pistoia), 1; *Doglia mi reca ne lo core ardire* (Dante), xii, 67–70, 73–74, 77–86, 87*n*8, 88*n*13, 89*n*14, 106, 114*n*3; *Donna pietosa e di novella etate* (Dante), 30–31; *Donne ch'avete intelletto d'amore* (Dante), 30–32, 37*n*22, 42*f,* 77; *E' m'incresce di me sí duramente,* 224–25; *Poscia ch'Amor del tutto m'ha lasciato* (Dante), xii, 68, 73–78, 81, 87*n*9, 88*nn*10–11; *Su per la costa, Amor, de l'alto monte* (Cino da Pistoia), 2
Capelli, Robert, 35*n*10
Carleton, William, 457
Carugati, Giuliana, xiii, 211–27
Cary, Rev. Henry Francis, 438–41, 444–46, 448*n*3, 449*n*10, 449*n*16
Casagrande, Carla, 269–70
Casella *(Purg),* 223
Cassell, Anthony, 317*n*16
Cassiodorus, 163
Cathars (of Provence), 164
Catholicism, 425; of Dante in England, xvii, 422, 425–28; Irish, 425, 457
Cato of Utica, 340, 342
Cavalcanti, Guido, 2, 20–21, 38*f,* 162, 248; *Biltà di donna e di saccente core* by, 72; *Guido, i' vorrei che tu e Lapo ed io* (Dante) addressed to, 72–73; on love, 109; marriage of, 246; "philosophizing" of, 170; *Vita Nova* and, 21, 22–23, 27–28, 31, 33, 35*n*11, 37*n*37
Cestaro, Gary, xii, 90–103, 182
Chalcidius, 154
chance, principle of, 167
Charles Martel, 105
Charles of Valois, 310–11, 312, 318*n*30
Charon, Virgil's rebuke to, 4–5
Chartres, school of, 217
chastity, 88*n*10, 88*n*11, 107
Chaucer, Geoffrey, 362*n*1, 429–30, 432*n*6
Chesterfield, Lord, 427
Chi è questa che ven (Cavalcanti), 22
Chiavacci Leonardi, Anna Maria, 209*n*19, 306
childbirth, 182, 416–17, 421*n*18
Chiose (Iacopo Alighieri), 6–7
chivalry, 65, 164
Christ; as center of Cosmos, 156; Dante's eschatology and, 335–46, 346*n*1, 347*n*8; fall of Jerusalem and, 301–15, 316*nn*1–11, 317*nn*12–21, 318*nn*22–32, 319*nn*33–38; imitation/mimicry of, 163, 279, 421*n*19, 456; throne imagery and, 280; visual arts portrayal of, 276, 278, 280–84, 287*f*–292*f*
Christianity. *See also* Catholicism; church corruption/reform and, 320, 322, 338; circle of wisdom of, 152; doctrine of, 118, 122; Donation of Constantine as critical to, 325–26; ethics, 409; exile and, 389, 391–92, 394, 396–97, 399–401; faith conveyed in poetry of, 120; fall of Jerusalem and, 301–15, 316*nn*1–11, 317*nn*12–21, 318*nn*22–32, 319*nn*33–38; history of, 324–26, 338; iconography of, 278–81; medieval, 116, 126; moral writing of, 265; Muslims and, 164; mysticism in, 148; nature and, 97; new *mathesis* of, 153–54; paganism and, 173, 284*n*2, 304, 338, 409; reconciliation of concepts of, 120; response to scatology by, 267; on sexuality, 94, 267; Vatican II and, 301
Chrysostom, 154
Church of England, 423, 425, 427
Church of Saint Clement (Rome), mosaic in, 275
Church of Saint Francis (Pescia), 276
Church of Saint Francis in Assisi (Upper/Lower), 277
Ciacco *(Inf),* 394, 396
Cino da Pistoia, 8, 9, 21–23, 35*n*9; *Da poi che la Natura ha fine posto* by, 1; Dante's sonnet to, 106; *Sta nel piacer della mia donna Amore* by, 20–22, 35*n*8, 38*f; Su per la costa, Amor, de l'alto monte* by, 2; writing of, influenced by *Comedy,* 1–2

Circle/Heaven of Sun, 107–9. *See also* Sun; arithmetic and, 154; conceptual-metaphorical patterns in, 153; eschatology and, 320–32, 332*nn*1–5, 333*nn*6–10; love in, 107–9; pilgrim ascending to, 158, 161, 167, 320–21, 323, 326, 331; Saint Francis of Assisi in, 320–26, 332, 332*n*5; Saint Bonaventure in, 152–54, 156–57, 160, 162–65, 168*n*2, 168*n*7, 321–22, 324–26, 332*n*5, 333*n*6; Solomon in, 320–21, 326–32, 333*nn*8–9; Thomas in, 152–55, 162, 164–68, 320, 322, 328–29, 341–42; Trinity and, 322, 330–32

cities, gated walls of, 269, 278

citizenship, celestial v. worldly, 391, 407*n*4

Clareno, Angelo, 156

classical tradition v. biblical (poetry), 391–92

Clement IV, Pope, 171

Clement V, Pope, 111, 304, 310, 311, 334

Codex Escorial e.III.23, 22–24, 35*n*8, 35*n*9

Collationes in Hexaemeron (Bonaventure), 154–57, 160, 163, 168*n*2

Columbus, Christopher, 448

Comedy (Commedia) (Dante), xii–xiii, xiv–xv, xix. *See also Inferno (Inf); Paradiso (Par); Purgatorio (Purg);* as *Ars poetica,* 144–45, 151*n*3; Bologna and, 4–7; commentaries/glosses of, 6, 9–10, 13–14, 51; compared to Gothic cathedral, 275; copies distributed by Dante, 1, 2–3, 4, 12, 13–14; courtly values in, 73–74; critical/diverse editions of, xix–xx, xxii, 46–47, 47; desexualization of love in, 118; early responses to, 5–6, 7–14; as "epic" poem, 146, 149; eschatology and, 203–6, 334–46, 346*n*1, 347*nn*2–8, 348*n*9; exile and, 389–97, 399–407; female figures in, 106; first copies of, x, xi, 1–15, 51; as gift, 4–7, 168; Ilaro (monk), given copy of, 10–13; installments of, 2–6, 12–13, 14–15; Jerusalem paired with Florence in, 301–15, 316*nn*1–11, 317*nn*12–21, 318*nn*22–32, 319*nn*33–38; Latin v. Italian and, 9, 14; *Moby-Dick* and, 435–36, 438–48, 448*nn*3–4, 449*n*8, 449*nn*10–11, 449*n*13, 449*nn*15–16, 450*n*17; multiple dedications in, 3–4; *Ottimo Commento* on, 51; philologists and, 46–48; plurilingual style of, 261, 266–67, 268–69; portrayal of love in, 104–14; prophecy in, 393–94, 400–401; reading and, 357, 359, 360, 361–62, 368*n*31; science and, xiv; scriptural character of, 267–72, 362, 365*n*10; sexuality in, 116, 118–19; *stilnovo* of, 111–14, 114*n*1; textual integrity of, 10–13; vertical readings of, 282; visual arts and, 276, 282–84

"Commiato" (Ungaretti), 143–45, 147, 151*n*2, 151*n*4

Compagni, Dino, 247–48

Confessions (Augustine), 185

context; Dante, and, 242–51, 255*nn*1–5, 256*nn*6–10, 257*nn*11–12, 258*nn*13–15; Dante Studies (DS) and, 244; legal-historical, of Florence, 248–51, 255*n*3, 257*n*12, 258*nn*13–15; of scatology/obscenity in *Inf* 18, 260–62, 263–64, 273*n*6; socioeconomic, of Florence, 244–48, 250–51, 255*n*3, 256*nn*8–10, 257*nn*11–12

Contini, Gianfranco, xvii, 1, 50, 55*n*7, 227*n*7, 363*n*3; Dante's lyrics and, 86*n*1, 87*n*9; on *tenzone* of Dante with Forese, 242–43, 255*n*5

Convivio (Dante), 51; Ageno and, 49; Aristotle and, 49; feminine abstraction in, 212–13; gender based on binary opposition in, 102*n*8; liberal arts/planet analogies in, 101, 103*n*11; love in, 221–22; Milky Way in, 178; *philosophus* (ideal reader) evoked in, 7, 8; production of human soul described in, 181; reading and, 356–58, 360–61, 367*n*23

copyists/compilers. *See* Notaries; Scribes
Cornish, Alison, xiv, 169–82, 418*n*1
Corso Donati, 245, 246
Così nel mio parlar voglio esser aspro, 225–26, 227*n*7
courtly dualism, 66, 67, 71, 77–79, 82, 85–86, 87*n*7
courtly lyrics, 66–89
courtly poet, Dante's development beyond, xii, 66–89
courtly values, in *Comedy,* 73–74
Creation, 153, 161, 330, 332
Croce, Benedetto, 171
Crusades, 310–11, 314
Cultural Studies, x, xiv
Cunizza, in Heaven of Venus, 105
Cupid, 340
Cupitt, Don, 146–49
Cursietti, Mauro, 241–42

Da poi che la Natura ha fine posto (Cino da Pistoia), 1
Dales, Richard, 206*n*7
Damian, Saint Peter, 91
Daniel, Book of, 359
D'Anjou, Charles, 105
Dante. *See* Alighieri, Dante
Dante Society of America, ix, xviii, xx, xxiii; Dante2000 conference of, ix–x, xx, xxiii, 151*n*7, 274
Dante studies, field of; aerial bodies debate in, xiv; body and, 116–17; critical readings of sex/excrement avoided by, 259–60, 262–63, 272, 272*n*1, 272*n*3, 273*n*6; decontextualization of, 244; effect of science/technology on, 274; "Everyman" idea of, 390–91; setting agenda for, ix; textual consciousness of, xix
Dantismo, 65
Danube river, 397–98, 400
Davis, Charles T., 152
De Robertis, Domenico, 21, 35*n*7, 36*n*16, 211, 356, 365*n*12, 366*n*17
De vulgari eloquentia (Dante), xii, 98, 101, 365*n*15; reading and, 357, 365*n*15; on reason, 145–46
Decameron (Boccaccio), 69–70, 81–82, 87*n*2, 94, 102*n*4, 362, 367*n*30
deeds, aligned with men, 69, 87*n*4
Del Virgilio, Giovanni, 5
desire, xii, 65; anatomy of, 88*n*13; continuum of, 85–86; Dante's language of, 114*n*1; God and, 123–25; male, 78–79, 87*n*8; meditation on, 77; sexual, 118; for wealth, 65
Detto, 50
Devil, 440. *See also* Lucifer; Satin; deprived of Bonconte's soul, 171–72, 174; farting, 267, 268
Diana, example of chastity, 107
Dickinson, Emily, 460
Dino Compagni, xxi
Dionysius, 154, 161
Divine Comedy. See Comedy (Commedia)
divinity, approaching, 413–14, 415–16, 418
Documenti d'Amore (Francesco da Barberino), 2
Doglia mi reca ne lo core ardire (Dante), xii; gender in, 67–70, 73–74, 77–86, 87*n*8, 88*n*13, 89*n*14; love in, 106, 114*n*3
Dominic, Saint, 67, 118, 124, 130*n*5, 152, 163–67
Dominicans, 174–75, 322, 335
Donati (family) lineage, 244–49, 256*nn*7–10
Donation of Constantine, 325–26
Donatus, 154
Donna gentile, 223, 224
Donna me prega (Cavalcanti), 20–21, 38*f*
Donna petra, Beatrice v., 86
Donna pietosa e di novella etate (Dante), 30–31, 37*n*22
Donne ch'avete intelleto d'amore (Dante), 30–32, 37*n*22, 42*f,* 77
Donneare, verb, 73–74, 87*n*9
Doomsday cults, 335
dualism, courtly, 67, 71, 77–79, 82, 85–86, 87*n*7
Durand of Saint Pourçain, 195
Durante, mystery of poet, 50
Durliat, Marcel, 128
Durling, Robert, ix, xiv, 183–91

E' m'incresce di me sí duramente, 224–25
Eagle *(Par),* 123, 274–75
earth, 123, 175, 216
Economou, George, 96
Eden, 337, 392
education, medieval models of, 153
Eleatics, 165
Eliot, T. S., xvii, 439, 451, 458, 459; *Little Gidding* by, 451–54; *Wasteland* by, 425
Embryology; in *Purgatorio* 25, xiv, 192–206, 206*nn*1–7, 207*nn*8–15, 208*nn*16–17, 209*nn*18–21, 210*nn*22–25; Statius's discourse on, 180–82; vulgarization of, 171, 182
England; Church of, 423, 425, 427; Dante in, xvii, 422–31, 431*nn*1–3, 432*nn*4–6, 433*f*–434*f*
Enrichetto delle Querce, 18–20
Epistle to Cangrande della Scala, 3, 350–51, 357, 363*n*3, 367*nn*24–25; as possible forgery, 359–62, 367*nn*27–28, 367*n*30, 368*n*31
Epistles (Dante), 280, 285*n*7; on Florence, 313–14, 319*n*36, 395–96, 407*n*7
Epistles, of Saint Paul, 265, 270, 391
Epitaph for the Young (Walcott), 454–56
Eros, x, 212–13, 217–18, 221–22, 226
eroticism; Augustine, on, 265–66; courtly lady/love and, 65, 75; erotic *pneuma* and, 218, 220, 221; inflecting theology, 222; language/love and, 118–19; love and, 117, 118–19, 328, 355; in Malebolge, 261; in Middle ages, 265; Ovid's *corpus eroticum* and, 389, 406, 407*n*1; "peace" and, 225–26, 227*n*7; poetry and, 219; redemptive, 118; sublimated, 104, 111; world vision and, 216
eschatology, xvi; v. apocalyptic tradition, 346*n*1; Beatrice and, 337–38; Christ and Dante's, 335–46, 346*n*1, 347*n*8; Christian, 192; in Circle/Heaven of Sun, 320–32, 332*nn*1–5, 333*nn*6–10; *Comedy* and, 203–6, 334–46, 346*n*1, 347*nn*2–8, 348*n*9; Dante's existential, 203–6, 334–46, 346*n*1, 347*nn*2–8, 348*n*9; Hell and Dante's, 343; in *Inf* 5, 340; Jews and, 335; Last Judgment and, 200–201; panorama in *Comedy,* 203–6; in *Purg* 1, 340–41; Saint Paul and, 343, 347*n*5
ethics; Christian, 409; of freedom, 166, 168; literature as branch of, 352; structure of Hell and, 261, 271
Eve, 266, 338, 392
"Everyman" figure, 390–91
Excellent Women (Pym), 423–25, 432*n*4
excrement, in Dante, 259, 261–65, 267, 272
exile; Christianity and, 389, 391–92, 394, 396–97, 399–401; *Comedy* and, 389–97, 399–407; Dante's, 113, 219, 257*n*12, 323, 391–97, 399–407; during Middle Ages, 389–90; guilt in context of, Dante v. Ovid's admission of, 405–7; Ovid in, 389–407, 392–93, 395–98, 407*nn*1–8; of pilgrim, 312, 394–95, 401, 405–7; poetry, xvi, 405–7; Saint Paul on, 394–95; White Guelphs in, 5, 312, 405
Expositio virgilianae continentiae (Fulgentius), 45
Expositione de songni, in Umbrian Martelli, 27, 36*nn*16–18
eye (observing), analogy of, 122

Faerie Queen (Spenser), 422, 439
Fahnestock, Jeanne, 169
Faith, marriage to Dominic, 118, 164
false knights, 75–76
"Fante," 264, 273*n*5
Farinata degli Uberti, 246, 279, 282, 456
Fascism, 251
father, Dante's; life of, 257*n*12, 258*n*12; remarks on, by Forese Donati, xiv–xv, 243
female. *See* women
feminism, proto, 67
Feruto sono isvariatamente (Giacomo da Lentini), 20, 39*f*
Field Work (Heaney), 456–57, 458
Filologia dantesca, 51

fire, 173, 175, 216–17, 279, 443, 449*n*9, 449*n*12, 464
Five/Hundred and Ten and Five (*Purg* 33.43–45), 336, 338–39
flatterers, 259, 260, 261, 269
Fledermaus, 9
flesh, body v., 183–90, 190*n*1, 191*n*2, 191*n*4
Florence/Florentine society, 316*n*5; changes in, 243–44, 247–48; compared to Belfast, 456; Dante's attitude toward, 334, 336, 395–96, 402, 406, 407*n*7; guilds, 249, 258*n*14; internecine warfare in, 334; as Jerusalem, xv–xvi, 301–15, 316*nn*1–11, 317*nn*12–21, 318*nn*22–32, 319*nn*33–38; legal-historical context of, 248–51, 255*n*3, 257*n*12, 258*nn*13–15; "magnates," 248–49, 258*n*15; nobility in, 65, 244, 248–50, 257*n*12; Ordinances of Justice in, 249, 258*n*15; *Popolo,* 249, 258*n*15; social/gender connection in Dante's, 243–44; socioeconomic context of, 244–48, 250–51, 255*n*3, 256*nn*8–10, 257*nn*11–12; sodomitic culture of, 92–94; vendetta practice in, 249, 258*n*13; in *Vita Nova,* 302
Florentine Baptistery, mosaics in, 276, 282–84, 284*n*2, 286*nn*9–10, 289*f*–292*f*
Folgore da San Gimignano, 71–72
Folquet, in Heaven of Venus, 105
foreknowledge, divine, 122
Forese Donati, xiv–xv, 109. *See also* Donati (family) lineage; on Dante's father, xiv–xv, 243; Florence prophecy of, 304, 306–7; *tenzone* of Dante with, xiv–xv, 241–54, 255*nn*1–5, 256*nn*6–10, 257*nn*11–12, 258*nn*13–15
form, v. content, 67
Fortuna, 97
Foster, Kenelm, 80, 86*n*1, 87*n*7, 88*n*10, 159, 193, 225, 342
Foucault, Michel, 92–94
Foxe, John, 426–27
Fradenburg, Louise, 93–94, 102*n*3
Francesca da Rimini; historical reconstruction of, 67–68, 79, 84; love and, 104, 106, 114*n*3, 342; pilgrim's encountering of, 340; reading in *Inf* by, 362*n*2
Francesco da Barberino, 2
Francis of Assisi, Saint, 67, 151*n*8, 152, 162–64, 166, 167–68; artistic representations of life of, 276; in Circle/Heaven of Sun, 320–26, 332, 332*n*5; v. Dominic, 67, 124, 130*n*5, 322; marriage of Lady Poverty and, 108, 118, 163, 277, 324–26, 333*n*6; meeting sultan, 324, 332*n*5
Franciscans, 156, 158, 162, 322; Friar Anastasio as, 2; Cistercian origins of, 333*n*7; v. Dominicans, 130*n*5, 152–53, 168*n*1; Santa Croce monastery of, 2; Spiritual, 335–36
Franco Bolognese, 275
Frati godenti, 303, 304, 306, 313
Freccero, Carla, 93–94, 102*n*3
Freccero, John, 314
Frederick III (king of Sicily), 3–4
freedom, ethics of, 166, 168
fresco(es); depicting betrayal by Judas, 280, 288*f;* depicting marriage of Francis and Lady Poverty, 324–25, 333*n*6; depicting stigmata at La Verna, 277; despoiled, 129–30; by Giotto, in Arena Chapel, 278, 281, 282–83, 284, 285*n*3, 286*n*8, 288*f;* by Signorelli, in Chapel of San Brizio, 274
Fulgentius, 45
future, v. present, 393–94

Gaddo, 315, 319*n*38
Gagliardi, Antonio, 85–86
Galen, 218
Garisenda tower, 19–20
Gassman, Vittorio, 435, 448*n*1
Gates of Calais (Hogarth), 427–28, 434*f*
Gemma di Manetto Donati, 245, 246–47, 249
gender. *See also* Men; Women; based on binary opposition, 95, 102*n*8; Dante, and, x, xii; in Dante's lyric poetry, 65–89; in *Doglia mi reca* (Dante),

67–70, 73–74, 77–86, 87*n*8, 88*n*13, 89*n*14; dramas of Ovid, 95, 103*n*9; in Florentine society, 243–44; grammatical model of, 95, 101; *Inf* 5 and, 68, 79, 84, 88*n*13, 114*n*3; sodomy and, 92, 93, 95
Genesis, Book of, 391, 443; 10:9, 281; 18, 396
Genus humilis, 260, 261, 262
Gerard of Borgo San Donnino, 152, 335
Ghibellines, Guelphs v., 245–46, 256nn8, 305, 317*n*15, 334, 456
ghosts, 457–59
Giacomo da Lentini, 20, 21, 39*f*
Gianciotto Malatesta, 67–68
giants, 338, 441–42
Giardini, Piero, 6
gift; *Comedy* as, 168; economy of, 153
Giles of Rome, 170
Gilson, Étienne, 161, 193, 199–200, 209*n*18, 342
Gilson, Simon, 180
Giordano da Pisa, 174–76
Giotto, 282; Arena Chapel frescoes by, 278, 281, 282–83, 284, 285*n*3, 286*n*8, 288*f*
Giovanni d'Antonio, 5
Giovanni Pisano; relief by, 278
Giraut de Borneil, 78, 87*n*9
Giuseppe Martini di Lugano, 55*n*1
Gluttony/gluttons, 243, 255*n*4, 307, 314, 420*n*12
God; Dante, as mouthpiece of, 413–14; desire and, 123–25; eyewitness to, 413; generosity of, 160; harmonized, 161; help from, 413–14; just/merciful, 122; knowledge and, 123–25; love of, v. rational love, 113–14; meditation between Dante, and, 112; playfulness of, 166–67
godhead, inner, 158–59
Goethe, 448
Gorni, Guglielmo, xi, xv, 1; editing of *Vita Nova* by, 16, 18, 35*n*6, 44–55, 365*n*12
Gragnolati, Manuele, xiv, 192–210
grammatical models; of gender/sexuality, 95, 101; of nature, 101
Gratian, 154
Greene, Robert, 426
Gregory the Great, 307–8, 314, 319*n*37
Guelphs; Black, 245, 310, 405; exiled White, 5, 312, 405; Ghibellines v., 245–46, 256nn8, 305, 317*n*15, 334, 456; Guelph-Angevin victory and, 245, 316*n*5; notaries, 5, 7
Guido da Polenta, 6
Guido Guinizelli, 2, 170, 452–53
Guido, i' vorrei (Dante), 72–73
guilds (Florentine), 249, 258*n*14
Guillaume de Nogaret, 311
Guillaume de Saint Amour, 152
Guillaume of Auxerre, 213
Guittone d'Arezzo, 2, 22, 75, 88*n*10, 88*n*12, 89*n*14, 176–78, 189

Hadewijch, 148
Häring, Bernhard, 347*n*8
Harrison, Robert, 363*n*4
Hawkins, Peter S., x, xvii, 451–64
Heaney, Seamus, xvii, 425, 451, 456–59
Heaven; of love, Dante's, 106; Virgin Mary's assumption into, 207*n*8
Heaven of Sun. *See* Circle/Heaven of Sun
Heaven of Venus, 104–7, 109, 221
Heliodorus, 309–10
Hell; Dante's eschatology and, 343; disdain for inhabitants of, 262; ethical structure of Dante's, 261, 271; fire of, 175; as Florence/Tomis, 397–400; Lucifer's citadel in, 278; Malebolge *(Inf)* in, 260, 261, 269–70, 272; *Moby-Dick* and, 438, 440, 443–44, 447; no Jews in, 313; traversing, 191*n*2
Henry IV, Part I (Shakespeare), 362, 368*n*32
Henry VII, 1, 315; Dante's letter of 1312 on, 302, 306, 317*n*17; throne prepared for, 279–80, 285*n*7
Hercules, 420*n*16, 443, 449*n*12
Hermaphroditus (Ovid's), 95, 103*n*9
Herzman, Ronald, xvi, 320–33
Hippo, Bishop of, 265–66
Hippolytus, myth of, 402–4, 407*n*8
Hogarth, William, 427–28, 434*f*
Holy Face (Santo Volto), 276, 287*f*

Homer, 452, 454, 456; Ulysses/Odysseus, of, 393, 437–38, 445
homosexuality, xii; *Natura* and, 92, 95–97, 100, 103*n*10; nature and, 90–92, 95, 96–97, 100–101; queer, use of word and, 91–92; sodomy v., 91–92, 93–94, 102*n*3
Horace, 275
horn, image of, 280–81
Hugh Capet, 308–9, 311, 312
Hugh of Saint Victor, 154
Hughes, Francis, 458
humility, virtue of, 186, 187, 323

Iacopone da Todi, 148, 151*n*8, 162, 267
Iannucci, Amilcare, xvi, 334–48
"ideal copies," concept of, 17
"ideal reader," Dante's, 7
Il Fiore, 50, 152
Ilaro, Brother (monk), 13–14, 14–15
Incarnation, 332, 343
Inferno (Inf), 2, 3, 5, 7; 1.69, as indication of early copies circulating, 2; 1.101, *veltro* of, 336; 2, Beatrice introduced in, 213; 3.94–96, Virgil's rebuke to Charon, 4–5; 5, Dante's eschatology and, 340; 5, gender and, 68, 79, 84, 88*n*13, 114*n*3; 10.80, Cino da Pistoia, canzone contains allusions to, 1; 11, Virgil, on sodomy in, 91, 95–96, 102*n*2; 13, letters of Pier della Vigna, and, 20; 13.22–29, notary copying, 7; 15.72, scatology/obscenity in, xv, 259–72, 272*nn*1–4, 273*nn*5–7; 18.114, "human privies" language in, 261, 264, 272; 19; 23, pairing of Florence and Jerusalem in, xv–xvi, 303–4, 308, 311–13, 316*n*8; 19.97–99, reprimand to Nicholas V, in, 5; 21, mimicry of Christ, in, 279; 28.22–27, description of Mohammed, in, 202, 260; 31, towers in, 20, 278; 31.10–18, horn-blast heard by Dante and Virgil, in, 280–81; Brunetto Latini, on sodomy in, 98, 99; Ciacco in, 394, 396; dedication of, 3; Francesca da Rimini reading in, 362*n*2; Malebolge in, 260, 261, 269–70, 272; sodomy in, 91–92, 94–101, 102*n*2, 102*n*6, 103*n*11; Ulysses canto of, 49–50
Infra gli altri difetti del libello (Cino da Pistoia), 2
intelligence, v. theology, 342
Io mi sono tucto dato a trager oro (anonymous), 20, 38*f*
Isadore of Seville, 154
Isaiah, Book of, 180
Isfacciato di Montecatini, 20–21
Islam, coming of, 324
Italian Jews, *Comedy* read by, 8
Italy, Dante's invective against, 334, 336

Jacoff, Rachel, x, xvii, 125, 130*n*4, 451–64
Jacopo Passavanti, 174
James, Epistle of, 270
Jason (High Priest); collaboration with Antiochus, 304; treatment of Hypsipyle by, 265
Jean de Meun, 152, 217
Jerome, Saint, 174
Jerusalem; fall of, paired with Florence, xv–xvi, 301–15, 316*nn*1–11, 317*nn*12–21, 318*nn*22–32, 319*nn*33–38; *Inferno* and, xv–xvi, 303–4, 308, 311–13, 316*n*8; *Paradiso* and, 301, 302, 305; *Purgatorio* and, xv–xvi, 303–12, 314
Jesus. *See* Christ
Jews; apocalyptic literature and, 346*n*1; Aquinas and, 313, 316*n*11; eschatology and, 335; Hell and, 313; Hellenistic world and, 329; as scholars, 335
Joachim of Flora, 152, 153, 155–56, 157, 335, 347*n*2
Joachistic views, 152, 156, 157
Job, Book of, 270, 271
John of Parma, 156
John of the Cross, 147, 149
John the Baptist, 283, 289*f*–292*f*, 339
John the Revelator, 323
jongleurs, 268
Jordan, Mark, 90–91

Joseph, portrayed in mosaics, 283, 290*f*
Joyce, James, 425, 451, 457, 458–59
Judas; betrayal by (fresco), 280, 288*f;* as evil merchant, 311, 318*n*31; lance of, 311–12
justice; divine, 122, 278; Florentine Ordinances of, 249, 258*n*15; retributive, 186
Justinian, 44–45, 302–3, 316*n*5

Kairos, 339, 340, 341, 342–43, 346
Kaske, Robert, 325
Katainen, V. Louise, 148, 151*n*8
Kavanaugh, Patrick, 457
Klapisch-Zuber, Christiane, 256nn10
Kleinhenz, Christopher, xv, 274–86
knowledge; classical model of, 153; as dance of wisdom, 154, 157–58; disowning of, 162; divine foreknowledge as, 122; God and, 123–25; as love, 160; man's scope of, 168; perfect, 147; separate spheres of, 157
Kypris (cosmic soul), 215

La Verna, fresco depicting stigmata at, 277
Lachmannian stemmatics, 16–17; neo, 34*n*1
Lamentations, book of, 301, 302, 316*n*2, 317*n*17
lance, image of, 311–12, 318*n*29
Lancia, Andrea, 3, 51
language; amatory, 119; debasers of, 270–71; of desire, 114*n*1; eroticism and, 118–19; of poetry, 120, 125, 127; proper v. improper, 269
Lansing, Carol, 245–46, 255*n*1, 256*nn*7–10
Lansing, Robert, ix
Lanza, Antonio, 47
Last Judgment, 282–83, 284, 289*f,* 292*f;* mosaic, in cathedral at Torcello, 280
Latin works, translated into Italian, 169, 170, 179, 182, 428
Leah (Dante's), 338
Lecturae Dantis, 259, 272*n*1, 272*n*3
legal-historical context, of Florentine society, 248–51, 255*n*3, 257*n*12, 258*nn*13–15
Leggiadria, 70–71, 73–76, 87*n*6, 88*n*11
Leland, John, 428
Levenstein, Jessica, xvi–xvii, 408–21
Levers, Stanley (Toby), 366*n*18
Libello (Vita Nova), 17, 18, 28–31, 33, 36*n*19, 48, 219, 302, 353–55, 366*n18*
Libellus (booklet), 8, 15
Libro-registro v. libro da banco, 13
Linder, Amnon, 314
Linus, 205
literature; apocalyptic, 346*n*1; as branch of ethics, 352
Little Gidding (Eliot), 451–54
Living Cross, 275
Loderingo, 305–6, 317*n*15
Lombard, Peter, 154
Longinus, spear of, 311
Lord's Prayer, 127, 184–85
Lough Derg pilgrimage, 457–58
Louis IX, 311
love, xii; "amorose fronde" metaphor for, 83, 86; anatomy of, 88*n*13; appetite and, 85–86; as basis for Dante's writing, 211, 220; Beatrice and, xiii, 109, 111–13, 115–30, 217–18, 356–57, 396; birth of, in *Vita Nova,* 217–18; Cavalcanti on, 109; chivalric, 164; in Circle/Heaven of Sun, 107–9; *Comedy's* desexualization of, 118; *Comedy's* portrayal of, 104–14; in *Convivio,* 221–22; courtly, 65, 75; Dante/Ovid, as poets of, 389; desexualization of love, in V*ita Nova,* 118; *in Doglia mi reca* (Dante), 106, 114*n*3; earthly, 116; erotic, 117, 118–19, 328, 355; Francesca and, 104, 106, 114*n*3, 342; of God v. rational love, 113–14; heaven of, 106; human sexual v. divine, 117; "il folle amore" (frenzied love) as, 106; v. intellect, 67, 85; knowledge as, 160; makes two into one, 82; men and, 69–70, 87*n*4; in *Par* 10, 107–8, 109; perfect, 147; physical v. spiritual, 104, 108–9; of pilgrim for Beatrice, 104, 110; *Purgatorio* on, 107, 223; Virgil on, 18, 106, 112, 113–14, 340; Virgin Mary and, 111–12, 124; women and, 79, 82–84

"low style" poetics, 260–61, 267, 272*n*4
Lowell, Robert, 451
Lucifer, 276, 278, 282, 441. *See also* Devil; Satan
Lucy, Saint, 111–13
Luke; 19, cleansing of Temple in, 310, 318*n*27; 19–23, 307–8, 317*n*19; 19:36–46, 301–2, 316*n*2; 20:34–36, 213
lyre, playing of, 409, 419*n*2
lyric poems/poetry; courtly, 66–89; early editorial forms of Dante's, 16–37, 34*n*1, 34*n*5, 35*nn*6–13, 36*nn*14–19, 37*nn*20–26, 38*f*–43*f;* gender in, 65–89; Lachmannian stemmatics applied to, 17

Macabees, 309, 310, 316*n*9
MacKenzie, Lynn Erin, xviii
Maestà (Simone Martini), 2
Mahieu de Vilain, 173
male narcissism, 77
Malebolge *(Inf)*, 260, 261, 269–70, 272
Malebranche, 260, 268
Mallarmé, Stéphane, 452
Malpaghini, Giovanni, xi
"Mamme," use of word, 205, 210*n*25
Mandelstam, Osip, xvii, 456
Manegold di Lautenbach, 216
Manetto Donati, 245, 246–47
Manichaeism, moral, 85
Marlowe, Christopher, 432*n*6, 448
marriage; of Cavalcanti, 246; of Dante, 244–47, 256*nn*9–10, 257*n12*, 258*n*13; Dante's view of, 106, 107, 108–9, 118; of Faith and Dominic, 118, 164; in Florentine society, 245–47, 256*nn*7–10, 257*nn*11–12; of Lady Poverty and Francis, 108, 118, 163, 277, 324–26, 333*n*6
Mars, pilgrim's ascent to, 331
Martelli 12 *(Vita Nova)*, 27–29, 31–32, 37*n*24, 37*n*26, 42
Martinez, Ronald, xv–xvi, 191*n*3, 301–19
martyrdom, 323–24, 332*nn*4–5, 413, 419*nn*9–10, 420*n*15, 426
Mary. *See* Virgin Mary
Matelda *(Purg)*, 337–38
Mathesis, new Christian, 153–54
Matthew, Book of; 6:1–11, 184; 6.9–13, 184; 23, 307
Maurus, Rabanus, 154
Mazzotta, Giuseppe, xiii–xiv, xx, 152–68
McCartney, Colum, 456, 458
McGinn, Bernard, 148, 151*n*7
Mechthild of Magdeburg, 148
medieval culture. *See also* Middle Ages; Christianity and, 116; dualism in, 67; "Everyman"/Wanderer figure in, 390–91, 407*n*3; modernity's limiting of, 117–18, 126–30; question of artist signature in, 128–29; sexuality in, 273*n*6
Melville, Herman, xvii, 435–48, 448*nn*2–3, 449*nn*5–10, 449*nn*12–14, 449*n*16, 450*n*18
Memoriali bolognesi, 7; *Non mi poriano giammai fare ammenda,* 18–20; legal filler in, 19
men; deeds aligned with, 69, 87*n*4; love and, 69–70, 87*n*4; virtue assigned to, 79, 83, 88*n*10
Meretrix, 260
Merrill, James, 451, 459
Metamorphoses (Ovid), xvi–xvii, 103*n*9, 389, 400, 402–4, 409–12, 417, 419*n*3, 420*n*16
Metaphysics (Aristotle), 49, 443, 449*n*11
Meteorologica (Aristotle), 173, 177, 178, 180
meteorology, science of, 171–73, 176, 180. *See also* weather
Michel, A., 208*n*16
Middle Ages. *See also* Medieval culture; apocalyptic tradition in, 335–36; astrology in, 46, 334–35; church edifice of, 283; context of scatology/obscenity in *Inferno* 18, 260–62, 263–64, 273*n*6; Dante inspired by visual tradition of, 274–84, 284*nn*1–2, 285*nn*3–7, 286*nn*8–10, 287*f*–292*f;* eroticism in, 265; exile during, 389–90; "interdisciplinarity" in study of, 274; reading/readers in, 352, 363*n*6, 365*n*8, 365*n*10, 365*n*13

Milbank, Alison, 431*n*3
millennial anxiety, 334–35, 337
Milton, John, 436, 442, 447, 450*nn*17–18
misogynistic writing, 78
Moby-Dick (Melville), xvii, 435–48, 448*nn*2–3, 449*nn*5–10, 449*nn*12–14, 449*n*16, 450*n*18
modernism, Dante after, xvii, 451–64
modernity; dualist orientation of, 115, 130*n*2; limiting of medieval culture by, 117–18, 126–30
Mohammed, description of, in *Inf* 28.22–27, 202, 260
Moltmann, Jürgen, 345, 347*n*8
Monarchia, 358–59, 364*n*7, 367*n*26, 426
moneychangers, Christ's expulsion of, 302, 310, 318*n*32
Monte, 25
moon; pilgrim's arrival in sphere of, 120–22; waxing/waning of, 101, 103*n*11
Moravia, Alberto, 90–91
Morte villana, di pietà nemica (Dante), 20–21, 25–26
Moruello Malaspina, 3
mosaic(s); arch, Santa Maria Maggiore (Rome), 280; in Church of Saint Clement (Rome), 275; in Florentine Baptistery, 276, 282–84, 284*n*2, 286*nn*9–10, 289*f*–292*f;* Joseph, portrayed in, 283, 290*f;* Last Judgment, in cathedral at Torcello, 280; in Orthodox/Arian Baptisteries, 280
Mountain of Purgatory, 337, 415
Muir, Edward, 251
Muslims, 164
Muzerelle, Denis, xxi
mysticism, x, xiii; in Christianity, 148; Dante's qualifications for, 146, 148, 151*n*5, 151*n*8; in *Paradiso,* 144–51, 151*nn*7–8; supernatural experiences and, 147, 149

Najemy, John, 258*n*15
names; foreign, 425; given v. family, xxi, 50
Nardi, Bruno, xiv, 180–81, 193, 198–99, 206*n*3, 208*n*17, 335
Nathan (prophet), 154
nationalism, European, 428
Natura (Dante), homosexuality and, 92, 95–97, 100, 103*n*10
natural philosophy, vernacular translation of, 169–82
nature; Aristotle, on, 97; Boethius, on, 97; Christianity and, 97; grammatical model of, 101; holding mirror to, 188; homosexuality and, 90–92, 95, 96–97, 100–101; Thomas, on Nature, in *Par* 13.76–78, 97
Ne li occhi porta (Dante), 20–30, 35*n*12, 38*f*
Nebuchadnezzar, 358–59
Nella Donati, 109
Neo-Aristotelian; debates, 167; Parisians as, 156
Neoplatonic thought, xiii, 67, 147
New Testament, 282, 335, 364*n*7. *See also* Bible; Scripture; Book of Matthew in, 184, 307
Newman, Lea Bertani, 438, 448*n*4
Nicholas III, Pope, 279, 303
Nicholas V, Pope, 5
Nichols, Stephen, 17
Nietzsche, Friedrich, 435, 444
Nimrod (hunter), 281
nineteenth-century, Dante rediscovered in, 451
Noah, 284, 292*f*
Noakes, Susan, xiv–xv, 241–58, 362*n*2
nobility, 65, 244, 248–50, 257*n*12
Non mi poriano giammai fare ammenda (Dante), 16, 18–19
Northern Ireland, 456
notaries. *See also* Scribes; Bolognese, 6–7, 19–20; *Comedy* and, 2, 4, 5, 6, 7; Tuscan, 20–21
"Noys," 213–14
numbers; wisdom hidden in, 158

obscenity, 268, 273*n*6; v. scatology, 263, 265
Oderisi da Gubbio, 186, 190, 275–76, 452
Odysseus. *See* Ulysses
Odyssey, 155

Old Testament, 282, 283, 335, 337, 364*n*7. *See also* Bible; Scripture; Book of Daniel in, 359; Book of Genesis in, 281, 391, 396, 443; Book of Isaiah in, 180; Book of Job in, 270, 271; Book of Lamentations in, 301, 302, 316*n*2, 317*n*17; Book of Proverbs in, 269
Oldcorn, Tony, 114*n*1
Omberto Aldobrandini, 186
Omeros (Walcott), 454–56
One, the, 160, 161, 215
opposites, reconciliation of, 67, 82–83, 85–86, 117, 120, 122, 125, 130*n*4
Ordinances of Justice, Florentine, 249, 258*n*15
Ornato, Ezio, xxi
Orosius, 154, 316*n*6
Ottimo Commento (Lancia), 51
Ottokar, Nicola, 249
Ovid; admission of guilt by, 405–7; *corpus eroticum* of, 389, 406, 407*n*1; Dante and, x, xvi, 389–407, 407*nn*1–8; *De vetula* as pseudo-autobiography of, 390; in exile, 389–407, 392–93, 395–98, 407*nn*1–8; *Fasti* by, 411; as author of founding texts of Romance lyrical tradition, 389; gender dramas of, 95, 103*n*9; Hermaphroditus and, 95, 103*n*9; to his readers, 399; as love poet, 389; Marsyas and, 409–11, 412–14, 418, 419*n*7; *Metamorphoses* by, xvi–xvii, 103*n*9, 389, 400, 402–4, 409–12, 417, 419*n*3, 420*n*16; Phaethon/Hippolytus myths and, 402–4, 407*n*8; poet Dante, v., 400; Rome longed for by, 392–93, 395–97, 404, 406; Tiresias, and, 95, 103*n*9; Tomis and, 389, 392–93, 395–98; *Tristia* by, 391–400, 404–7, 407*n*2, 407*n*6; *Vita Nova* modeled on *Remedia* by, 389, 407*n*1
Oxford, Dante and, 422–23, 425, 428, 430, 431*n*1, 431*n*3, 433*f*

paganism, 173, 284*n*2, 304, 338, 409
Paisley, Ian, 456
Palinodes, Dantean, 363*n*3, 366*n*20, 396
Palma di Cesnola, Maurizio, 50
Panders, 260, 261, 269, 270, 271
Paolo Malatesta, 67–68, 340, 362*n*2
Paradise, 443; Dante's arrival in, 409, 420*n*12; as home, 392; pilgrim's arrival in, 415–16, 417–18
Paradise Lost (Milton), 436, 442, 447, 450*nn*17–18
Paradiso (Par), 3, 5, 13; 1, re-formation of Marsyas, in, xvi–xvii, 408–18, 418*n*1, 419*nn*2–10, 420*nn*11–16, 421*nn*17–19; 2.37–45, pilgrim's arrival in sphere of moon in, 120–21; 4.19–21; 3.79–81, pilgrim's meeting of Piccarda, in, 121–22; 6.3–18, nature of Christ in, 45; 8.55–57, Charles Martel in, 105; 9, patron's early knowledge of, 3; 10, Dante's eschatology and, 341–42; 10, love in, 107–8, 109; 11, life of Francis, in, xvi; 11, narration by Thomas, in, 276–77; 13.76–78, Thomas, on Nature in, 97; 13.112–42, Thomas, on human reason in, 98; 14.43–51; 14.52–57, Solomon, on resurrection of body in, 203–4; 17, Ovid's *Metamorphoses* in, 403–4; 20.62, sonnet on Dante's death echoing, 3; 23.132;28.97, *canzone* on Dante's death alluding to, 2; 26.13–14, aerial v. earthly bodies in, 125–26; 30, Beatrice, showing throne prepared for Henry VII, in, 279–80, 285*n*7; 30.40, intellectual light of, 104; Bernard of Clairvaux, in, 150, 327–28, 333*n*9; as cinematic experience, 150; dedication of, 3–4; eagle in, 123, 274–75; fall of Jerusalem and, 301, 302, 305; final episode of, 147, 149–50; Jerusalem and, 301, 302, 305; journey metaphor in, 13.130–38, 165–66; Charles Martel in, 105; mysticism in, 144–51, 151*nn*7–8; Neoplatonist vocabulary of, 147; Thomas on Saint Francis, in *Par* 11, 276–77; transcending contradiction in, 115–30; transliterations into Hebrew of 5.73–84, 13.52–53, 20.49–54, 2; Trinitarian motif in, 158–61, 168
Parsons, Robert, 426–27

Pasquale, Papa, 36*n*16
patrons; *Comedy* given to, 1, 2, 3, 6; Dante's dedicating individual *cantiche* to, 3
Paul, Saint, 280, 343; account of rapture by, 415; epistles of, 265, 270, 391; eschatological thought of, 343, 347*n*5; on exile, 394–95; Peter and, standing by Simon Magus, 279, 285*n*4
peace, 224–25; erotic connotations of, 225–26, 227*n*7
penitence, 174–75, 178
Pentecost, 270, 285*n*3, 308, 317*n*20
Peraldus, 271
personification, 189
Pertile, Lino, xii, 104–14, 178–79
Perugi, Maurizo, 315
Peter of Spain, 154
Peter, Saint, 205, 279, 280, 285*n*4, 334
Petrarca, Francesco, xxiii, 36*n*14, 37*n*21, 460–61; "Augustinian," 222–23; *Comedy* and, 5–6, 9, 14
Petrocchi, Giorgio, 46–47
Phaethon, myth of, 402–3, 407*n*8
Pharisees, 303, 316*n*10
Philip the Fair, 304, 308–12, 318*n*23, 318*nn*25–26
philology(ies), x, xi, xv, 1; absolute/without adjectives, 51–53; changing science of, xi–xii, xv, 3–54, 55*n*7; *Comedy* and, 46–48; conjectural, 50; critical text and, 52–53, 54; first copies of *Comedy* and, x, xi, 1–15; material, 17, 18
philosophical-theological debates, 153, 155–56
philosophy, x, xiii, 153–54, 155
Physics (Aristotle), 167
Pia *(Comedy),* 106
Piccarda Donati, 79, 106, 121, 245, 246
Picone, Michelangelo, xvi, 268, 389–407
Pier della Vigna, 51, 55*n*1
Pietro Cavallini, 278
Pilgrim; arrival in Paradise by, 415–16, 417–18; arrival in sphere of moon by, 120–22; ascending to Circle/Heaven of Sun, 158, 161, 167, 320–21, 323, 326, 331; ascent to Mars by, 331; bliss of, 117, 119; Cacciaguida and, 312, 394, 400–402; description of Belacqua by, *Purg* 4.110–11, 189; divinization by participation and, 331; eagle on doubt of, 123; error in *Purg* 10.136–39, by, 127–28; as "Everyman," 390–91; exile of, 312, 394–95, 401, 405–7; Francesca da Rimini encountered by, 340; instruction in humility for, in *Purg,* 277; in love with Beatrice, 104, 110; as martyr, 413; meeting of Charles Martel by, 105; as modern *Virbius,* 403; *Ps* on forehead of, 184; speaking to Oderisi da Gubbio, 190; upward progress of, 122–25; weighed down by mortality in *Purg* 11, 186
Pinsky, Robert, 451
Plato, 97, 147, 216, 419*n*4; Boetius and, 213; cosmos of, 214; erotic *pneuma* in, 218; influence on *Moby-Dick,* 440, 449*n*16; Neoplatonic thought and, xiii, 67, 147; philosopher-king ideal of, 329; on *sperma,* 215
Plotinus, 156–57, 170, 221
plurality v. unicity of forms, souls and, 192–206, 206*nn*1–7, 207*nn*8–15, 208*nn*16–17, 209*nn*18–21, 210*nn*22–25
plurilingual style, of *Comedy,* 261, 266–67, 268–69
Pneuma, erotic, 218, 220, 221
Poe, Edgar Allan, 460
poetry. *See also* Lyric poems/poetry; biblical v. classical tradition in, 391–92; Christian faith conveyed in, 120; on Dante's death, 2–3; definitions, 144, 145, 150; ecstatic nature of, 144; erotic, 219; exile, xvi, 405–7; facts of life as corollary for, 180–81; language of, 120, 125, 127; "low style," 260–61, 267, 272*n*4; "Poetic theology" and, 211; of praise, 212; twentieth-century, 451–63
poets; classical v. modern, 355–56, 366*n*21; courtly, Dante's development beyond, xii, 66–89; Dante v.

Ovid, as, 400; Dante/Ovid as love, 389; Durante, mystery of, 50; *poeta* v. *personaggio* and, 147, 150, 213
political loyalty, 65
Pollack, Tamara, 54
Popolo (Florentine), 249, 258n15
Poscia ch'Amor del tutto m'ha lasciato (Dante), xii, 68, 73–78, 81, 87*n*9, 88*nn*10–11
Pound, Ezra, 451, 452
Poverty, Lady, 108, 118, 163, 277; marriage of Francis and, 108, 118, 163, 277, 324–26, 333*n*6
poverty, virtue of, 153, 157, 323
prayer, body position during, 186–87
predestination, 122
pregnancy, 180
present v. future, in narrative structure, 393–94
pride, sin of, 180, 183, 184, 185–88, 190, 277, 392, 412
prophecy; Beatrice and, 13; in *Comedy*, 393–94, 400–401; by Forese, on Florence, 304, 306–7; of pilgrim's exile by Cacciaguida, 312
prostitute, 259; Thais as, 260–61, 264–65, 267; whore as, 338–39
Protestant-Catholic violence, 458
Protestantism, English, 423, 425–27
Proverbs, Book of, 269
Psaki, F. Regina, xii–xiii, 115–30
Psalms, 270
Psuedo-Dionysius, 160–61, 329
punishment; sin and, 264, 269–70, 271; theme of, 391–92, 405, 409, 410, 412
purgative process, 183–84, 186–88, 191*n*2
Purgatorio (Purg), 2, 5, 13; 1, Dante's eschatology and, 340–41; 2.81, Italian summary of *Aen* citing, 3; 5, cadaver of Bonconte da Montefeltro in, 171–76, 178–79; 5, rainstorm in, 172–78, 180; 5, science and, xiv; 6, personification of Rome in, 315, 319*n*38; 9, Saint Lucy in, 112, 113; 10–12, body and, xiv; 10.130–35, burdened position in, 277, 284*n*2; 10.136–39, pilgrim's error in, 127–28; 11, Oderisi da Gubbio in, 275–76; 11, pilgrim weighed down by mortality in, 186; 16.73–75, transliterations into Hebrew of, 8; 17.115–117, Virgil, on pride in, 183; 18, Virgil, on love in, 106, 112, 113–14; 20;23, pairing of Florence and Jerusalem in, xv–xvi, 303–12, 314; 25, embryology in, xiv, 192–206, 206*nn*1–7, 207*nn*8–15, 208*nn*16–17, 209*nn*18–21, 210*nn*22–25; 31.52–60, death of Beatrice in, 109–11; 33.43–45, Five/Hundred and Ten and Five in, 336, 338–39; apocalyptic nature of, xvi, 336–42; body v. flesh in, 183–90, 190*n*1, 191*n*2, 191*n*4; Casella in, 223; central theme of, 188; dedication of, 3; fire of, 175; on love, 107, 223; marble sculptures/carvings in, 187–89; Matelda in, 337–38; notaries copying, 6–7; pilgrim's instruction in humility in, 277
Pym, Barbara, 423–25, 432*n*4
Pythagoras, 154

Qual hom ripende altru,' 20, 39*f*
queer, use of word, 91–92
Quellenforschung (source-study), xv
Quirini, Giovanni, sonnet on Dante's death by, 3, 5

Rachel, 338
Rahab, 105
Rahner, Karl, 345–46, 346*n*1, 347*n*8
Ravenna Donati, 245–46, 256*n*7, 462
reader(s); Cavalcanti as, 353, 356; Dante's female, 80–81, 82; Dante's ideal (*philosophus*), 7; Dante's mercantile, 65; Dante's relationship to, xvi, 7, 8, 349–62, 362*nn*1–2, 363*nn*3–6, 364*n*7, 365*nn*8–15, 366*nn*16–21, 367*nn*22–30, 368nn31–32, 403; Ovid addressing, 399
reader/author, Dante as, 274, 349–62, 362*nn*1–2, 363*nn*3–6, 364*n*7, 365*nn*8–15, 366*nn*16–21, 367*nn*22–30, 368nn31–32

reading; *Comedy* and, 282, 357, 359, 360, 361–62, 368*n*31; *De vulgari eloquentia* and, 357, 365*n*15; by Francesca da Rimini, in *Inf,* 362*n*2 in Middle Ages, 352, 363*n*6, 365*n*8, 365*n*10, 365*n*13; process of, 350, 362*n*2; of Virgil, 2, 350–51, 353, 365*n*10, 452; *Vita Nova* and, 351–59, 363*n*4, 365*nn*11–14, 366*nn*16–21, 367*n*22
reconciliation; mathematical medium of, 157; of opposites, 67, 82–83, 85–86,117, 120, 122, 125, 130*n*4
Reformation, 426
relics, cult of, 311
repentance, 417
Rerum vulgarium fragmenta, 18
Resurrection, 157, 203, 204, 205, 210*nn*23–24
Richard of Saint Victor, 154
Risorgimento, 251
Ristoro d'Arezzo, 177
Ritson, Joseph, 430
Rocke, Michael, 92–94
Rome; mosaic in Church of Saint Clement in, 275; mosaic in Santa Maria Maggiore in, 280; Ovid's longing for, 392–93, 395–97, 404, 406; personification of, in *Purg* 6, 315, 319*n*38

Sabellius, 158, 165, 330–31
Salimbene de Parma, 156
Salisbury, Bishop of, 428
salvation, attaining, 171, 343
Salvemini, Gaetano, 249
Sanguineti, Federico, 47
Sanhedrin, council of, 304–5
Santa Maria Maggiore, mosaic in, 280
Santi, Francesco, 202, 207*n*11
Santo Volto (Holy Face), 276, 287*f*
Sapiential Books, 270
Satan, 314, 441, 447, 450*n*18. *See also* Devil; Lucifer
scatology, 260, 263–64, 267–68, 272, 273*n*6; obscenity v., 263, 265
Schnackenberg, Gjertrud, xvii, 451, 462–64
Scholastic thought, 88n12, 328, 335, 342, 365*n*15; on form/metaphor, 220; on pregnancy, 180; on sodomy, 91, 95, 97; on weather analysis, 178
Sciarra Colonna, 311
science; *Comedy* and, xiv; effect on Dante studies, 274; of meteorology, 171–73, 176, 180; *Purg* 5 and, xiv; secular, 156; vulgarizing, 169–82
Scolari, Filippo, 361
Scribes, xi, 18–34, 36*n*18
Scripture. *See also* Bible; New Testament; Old Testament; *Comedy* and, 267–72, 362, 365*n*10; hierarchies of ecclesiastical authority and, 364*n*7; sex and, 272; Solomon's role in, 333*n*8
seal, image of, 321–22, 323
seducers, 75–76, 89*n*14, 260, 261, 269, 270, 271
Seleucus, King, 309–10
self, sense of, 410–11, 414–15, 416, 419*n*6
Sergi, Giuseppe, 126–27
Serra, Ettore, 144, 145
Sestan, Ernesto, 245
sex, xii; between Adam and Eve, 266, 392, 443, 449*n*10; deceit and, 262, 270; desire and, 118; and excrement, critical readings avoided on, 259–60, 262–63, 272, 272*n*1, 272*n*3, 273*n*6; open talk about, 268; *reticentia* and, 264; scatology and, 263; scripture and, 272; sinful, 268
sexuality; in *Comedy,* 116, 118–19; grammatical model of, 95, 101; historical constructions of, 116; in medieval culture, 273*n*6
Shakespeare, William, 362, 368*n*32, 432*n*6, 441, 448
Shapiro, Marianne, 181
Shelley, Percy Bysse, 464
Sherlock, Martin, 427
shipwrecks, images of, 165–66, 173–74, 444, 448, 449*n*12
Sì lungiamente, 32–33, 37*n*26
Siger of Brabant, 154–55, 157, 167, 327
signature question, of medieval artists, 128–29

Signorelli, Luca, 274
Silvestris, Bernardus, 214
Simon Magus, 279, 285*n*4
Simone Donati, 245, 246
Simone Martini, 2
sin, 183, 185; of avarice, 65, 182; disgust when confronted by, 262, 270; of pride, 180, 183, 184, 185–88, 190, 277, 392, 412; punishment and, 264, 269–70, 271; "Sins of the Tongue" and, 269–70
Singleton, Charles, 362, 418*n*1, 420*n*14
socioeconomic context, of Florentine society, 244–48, 250–51, 255*n*3, 256*nn*8–10, 257*nn*11–12
Socrates, 156, 419*n*4
sodomy, xii; Aquinas on, 91; Dante and, 90–103; gender and, 92, 93, 95; v. homosexuality, 91–92, 93–94, 102*n*3; in *Inf,* 91–92, 94–101, 95–96, 98, 99, 102*n*2, 102*n*6, 103*n*11; practice of, in Florence, 92–94; Scholastics on, 91; Virgil on, 91, 95–96, 102*n*2; water images and, 95, 98, 99–100, 101, 103*n*11
solar. *See* Sun
Solomon, King, 154, 156, 165; Book of Wisdom of, 156, 329–30; in Circle/Heaven of Sun, 320–21, 326–32, 333*nn*8–9; as emblem of wisdom, 165, 168*n*7; on resurrection of body, *Par* 14.43–51; 14.52–57, 203–4; role in scripture, 333*n*8; Song of Songs by, 327–28, 333*n*9
Sonar bracchetti (Dante), xii, 68–73
sonnet(s); *Biltà di donna e di saccente core* (Cavalcanti), 72; to Cino da Pistoia, 106; critical of *Comedy,* 2; cycle of Folgore da San Gimignano, 71–72; on Dante's death, by Cangrande della Scala, 3; double, 21–22; *Guido, i' vorrei* (Dante), 72–73; of Guittone d'Arezzo, meteorological metaphor in, 176–77; *Infra gli altri difetti del libello* (Cino da Pistoia), 2; *Non mi poriano giammai fare ammenda* (Dante), 16, 18–20; *Sonar bracchetti* (Dante), xii, 68–73; structural features/formats of, 18–19, 20–21, 23, 35*n*10, 37*n*20
soothsayers, naked, 260
Sordello, 315
soul(s); Beatrice, and, 217–18; burial and, 173–74; Devil deprived of Bonconte's, 171–72, 174; humility of, in Virgin Mary, 188–89; immortality of, 157; Kypris as cosmic, 215; origin of human, 181; plurality v. unicity of forms and, 192–206, 206*nn*1–7, 207*nn*8–15, 208*nn*16–17, 209*nn*18–21, 210*nn*22–25; production described in *Conv,* 181; relationship to body, 67, 414–115, 420*n*13; universal, as feminine, 215–16
spear, of Longinus, 311
speech, divine gift of, 270–71
Spenser, Edmund, 422, 432*n*6, 439
sperm *(sperma),* 215
sphere of moon, pilgrim's arrival in, 120–22
Spiegel, Gabrielle, 251, 255*n*1
spirituals (Franciscan), 153, 156
Sta nel piacer della mia donna Amore (Cino da Pistoia), 20–22, 35*n*8, 38*f*
Station Island (Heaney), 456, 457–59
Statius, 180–82; Embryology discourse of, 180–82; as extreme example, 341; plurality v. unicity of forms and, 192, 197–202, 206*n*3, 208*n*17; purgation of, 416; on reader/author role, 350–51; on Titus, 312
Stephen, 419*n*10, 420*n*11
Stevens, Wallace, 451
Stigmata, 277, 321–22, 323
Stilnovo, of *Comedy,* 111–14, 114*n*1
Storey, H. Wayne, x, xi, xviii, xix–xxiii, 16–37
Strauss, Johann, II, 49
Sultan, 324, 332*n*5
Summa theologiae (ST) 1a, q. 77, 207*n*15; 1a, q. 118, a. 2, ad 2, 196–97
sun, 160–61. *See also* Circle/Heaven of Sun; solar imagery and, 321–22, 332*n*3; solar theology and, 161–62
Supplement (Suppl), 345, 347*n*7
Sutcliffe, Matthew, 426
Swift, Jonathan, 452
symmetries, 275, 282–84, 286*nn*8–9

Tedaldi, Pieraccio, 2
Templars, 308–11, 318*nn*22–23
Tennyson, Alfred, 435, 442, 449*n*7
Tenzone; by Michele Barbi, xiv–xv; of Dante, with Forese Donati, xiv–xv, 241–54, 255*nn*1–5, 256*nn*6–10, 257*nn*11–12, 258*nn*13–15; Sicilian, 21, 34*n*5
Terza rima; Comedy summaries *(capitoli)* in, 9–10; Dante's invention of, 11; Eliot's attempt at, 451–52; inscriptions for *Maestà,* 2
Terzina, 23, 25, 26, 35*n*10, 36*n*14
Thais, 264–65, 267; misquoting of *Eunuchus* by, 259; as stock comic character, 260–61
theology; epistemological value of, 153–54; erotically inflected, 222; of history, 157; intelligence v., 342; philosophical debates and, 153, 155–56; poetic, 211; solar, 161–62; Trinity and, 153, 155, 156, 157–58, 160–61, 165, 168
throne imagery, 280–81
Tieri degli Useppi da San Gimignano, 4–5
Timaeus, 215, 217, 322, 329–30
Tiresias (Ovid's), 95, 103*n*9
Titus, 312, 319*n*33
Tomis, Ovid's exile in, 389, 392–93, 395–98
towers, 19–20, 278
Towsley, Gary, 333*n*10
Toynbee, Paget, 426, 427, 431*n*3
Trajan, Emperor, 278, 341
translation; issue of, xxii–xxiii; of Latin works into Italian, 169, 170, 179, 182, 428
Trattatello in laude di Dante (Boccaccio), 3–4
Trinity, 124; as basis for apocalyptic view, 335; Circle/Heaven of Sun and, 322, 330–32; theological discussion of, 153, 155, 156, 157–58, 160–61, 165, 168
Tristia (Ovid), 391–400, 404–7, 407*n*2, 407*n*6
Tundale's Vision, 107
twentieth-century, Dante rediscovered in, 451
Ubertino of Casale, 335
Ugolino, 314, 315
Uguccione della Faggiuola, 3, 13–14
Ulysses; canto (*Inf* 26.132), 49–50; Dante's, xvii, 393, 407*n*2, 435–36, 439–40, 442–43, 444, 445, 448, 449*n*8; Homer's (Odysseus), 393, 437–38, 445; *Moby-Dick* and, 435, 437–38, 440, 442–43, 445, 447–48, 449*n*7; sea journey of, 155; Tennyson's poem on, 442, 449*n*7
Ungaretti, Giuseppe, 143–45, 147, 151*n*2, 151*n*4
universal hylomorphism, 193, 194
universal soul, as feminine, 215–16
universe, Christian explanation of, 329–30

vagina, meaning associated with, 412, 416, 420*n*16, 421*n*19, 421*nn*18
Vatican Barberiniano Latino 4036, 25–26, 32–33, 35*n*13, 37*n*26, 40*f,* 43*f*
Vatican Chigiano L.VIII.305, 25–26, 28–29, 30–32, 41*f,* 55*n*7
Vatican II, 301
Vecchio, Silvana, 269–70
vendetta, practice of (Florentine), 249, 258*n*13
Vergil, Polydore, 429
Vindicta Salvatoris, 304, 312–13
Virgil, 44–46, 452, 456; *Aeneid* by, 3, 5, 45, 173–74, 182; Ambrosian, commissioned by Petrarch, 5; reading of, 2, 350–51, 353, 365*n*10, 452
Virgil (Dante's); and Dante, with Nicholas III, 279; horn-blast heard by, *Inf* 31.10–18, 280–81; on love, 18, 106, 112, 113–14, 340; on pride in *Purg* 17.115–117, 183; rebuke to Charon, by, 4–5; remains of, 171; on sodomy, in Inf 11, 91, 95–96, 102*n*2
Virgin Mary, 191*n*5, 282; Annunciation to, 277–78, 283, 290*f;* assumption into heaven by, 207*n*8; chastity example of, 107; giving birth by, 182, 416–17, 421*n*18; humility of soul in, 188–89; love and, 111–12, 124

virility, 244
virtue; assigned to men, 79, 83, 88*n*10; of humility, 186, 187, 323; "mischiata" (mixed), 74, 76; perfection of, 188–89; of poverty, 153, 157, 323
visual arts, Dante and, 274–84, 284*nn*1–2, 285*nn*3–7, 286*nn*8–10, 287*f*–292*f*
Vita Nova (Dante), 2, 16–34, 34*n*1, 35*nn*6–13, 36*nn*14–19, 37*nn*20–26, 38*f*–43*f*, 48–49; birth of love in, 217–18; Boccaccio and, 31, 32; Cavalcanti and, 21, 22–23, 27–28, 31, 33, 35*n*11, 37*n*37; courtly paradigm of, 77; desexualization of love in, 118; earlier versions of, 17, 23–34, 35*nn*11–12, 36*nn*16–17, 51; editing of, by Michele Barbi, 16, 18–19, 21, 28, 29, 30, 33, 34*n*1, 35*n*6, 36*nn*15–17, 36*n*19, 47–48, 53–54, 55*n*1, 365*n*12; editing of, by Gorni, 16, 18, 35*n*6, 365*n*12; Florence in, 302; *libello*, 17, 18, 28–31, 33, 36*n*19, 48, 219, 302, 353–55, 366*n18*; Magliabechiano Cl. VI 143 copy of, 29–33, 37*nn*20–21, 37*n*26; Martelli 12 and, 27–29, 31–32, 37*n*24, 37*n*26, 42i; modeled on Ovid's *Remedia*, 389, 407*n*1; reading and, 351–59, 363*n*4, 365*nn*11–14, 366*nn*16–21, 367*n*22; scribes and, 18–34; *stemma*, 47–48, 54; Vatican Barberiniano Latino 4036 and, 25–26, 32–33, 35*n*13, 37*n*26, 40*f*, 43*f;* Vatican Chigiano L.VIII.305 and, 25–26, 28–29, 30–32, 41*f*, 55*n*7
Volgarizzamento, 169, 181, 182
Volgarizzatori, 170, 174, 181

Walcott, Derek, xvii, 451, 453–56, 459
Wallace, David, xvii, 255*n*1, 422–34
Walpole, Horace, 427
Wanderer, figure, 390–91, 407*n*3
Warton, Thomas, 430
Wasteland (Eliot), 425
water, 172–77; sodomy and, 95, 98, 99–100, 101, 103i11; into vapor, 173, 177–79
wealth, desire for, 65
weather, 171, 172, 175, 178. *See also* meteorology, science of
Weiss, Johannes, 347*n*8
Wells Cathedral Library, 428–29
Whitman, Walt, 448
will; absolute v. contingent, 121; divine, 121–22; freedom of, 122; perfect alignment of, 147; purgation process and, 183–84
wisdom; Christian circle of, 152; knowledge and, 154, 157–58; quest for, 165; Solomon and, 156, 165, 168*n*7, 329–30
women. *See also* Gender; animal comparisons of, 75–76, 81, 86; attack on Florentine, 306–7, 317*n*16; beauty rather than virtue assigned to, 79, 83, 86, 88*n*10; bodies of, 116; chastity of, 88*n*10, 88*n*11, 107; contemplation of, 222–24; as courtly ladies, 65, 75; Dante's invectives against, 109; in Dante's lyrics, 65–89; eternal, 214; memorable, in *Comedy*, 106; misogynistic writing and, 78; moral critique of, 77; as readers of Dante, 80–81, 82; role of, 65; universal soul of, 215–16
Wright, Charles, xvii, 459–62
Wright, Stephen, 314

Yeats, William Butler, 452

www.ingramcontent.com/pod-product-compliance
Lightning Source LLC
Chambersburg PA
CBHW051549100726
47898CB00001B/27

* 9 7 8 0 8 2 3 2 2 2 7 2 8 *